THE TURKISH - AMERICAN RELATIONSHIP BETWEEN 1947 AND 2003: THE HISTORY OF A DISTINCTIVE ALLIANCE

THE TURKISH - AMERICAN RELATIONSHIP BETWEEN 1947 AND 2003: THE HISTORY OF A DISTINCTIVE ALLIANCE

NASUH USLU

Nova Science Publishers, Inc.
New York

Senior Editors: Susan Boriotti and Donna Dennis
Coordinating Editor: Tatiana Shohov
Office Manager: Annette Hellinger
Graphics: Wanda Serrano
Editorial Production: Marius Andronie, Maya Columbus, Vladimir Klestov,
Matthew Kozlowski and Tom Moceri
Circulation: Ave Maria Gonzalez, Vera Popovich, Raymond Davis, Melissa Diaz,
Magdalena Nuñez, Marlene Nuñez and Jeannie Pappas
Communications and Acquisitions: Serge P. Shohov

Library of Congress Cataloging-in-Publication Data

Uslu, Nasuh, 1966-
   The Turkish - American relationship between 1947 and 2003: the history of a distinctive
alliance / Nasuh Uslu.
        p. cm.
      Includes bibliographical references and index.
      ISBN 1-59033-832-4.
        1. United States—Foreign relations—Turkey. 2. Turkey—Foreign relations—United States.
     3. United States—Foreign relations—1945-1989. 4. United States—Foreign relations—1989-
     I. Title.

E183.8.T8 U85 2003
327.561073'09'045—dc22   20030162218

Copyright © 2003 by Nova Science Publishers, Inc.
                    400 Oser Ave, Suite 1600
                    Hauppauge, New York 11788-3619
                    Tele. 631-231-7269   Fax 631-231-8175
                    e-mail: Novascience@earthlink.net
                    Web Site: http://www.novapublishers.com

Printed in the United States of America

CONTENTS

ABBREVIATIONS

AID	Agency for International Development
BNDD	Bureau of Narcotics and Dangerous Drugs
CENTO	Central Treaty Organization
CIA	Central Intelligence Agency
CSTD	Cumhuriyet Senatosu Tutanak Dergisi
DBB	Dışişleri Bakanlığı Belleteni
JP	Justice Party
JUSMMAT	Joint United States Military Mission for Aid to Turkey
MMTD	Millet Meclisi Tutanak Dergisi
MLF	Multilateral Force
NATO	North Atlantic Treaty Organization
NSC	National Security Council
NSP	National Salvation Party
RPP	Republican People's Party
TUSLOG	The United States Logistics Group
UNFICYP	United Nations Force in Cyprus

TURKISH PRONUNCIATION

C c is pronounced as j in "jar"
Ç ç is pronounced as ch in "charm"
G g has always a hard pronunciation as g in "get"
Ğ ğ is not pronounced but lengthens the preceding vowel.
I ı is pronounced approximately as u in "measure"
İ i is pronounced as i in "is"
J j is pronounced as s in "measure"
Ö ö is pronounced as eu in French "deux"
Ş ş is pronounced as sh in "shop"
Ü ü is pronounced as u in French "une"

PREFACE

The year 1964, in which Turkey received the famous Johnson letter, is rightly considered by many scholars as a turning point in Turkish foreign policy. Until that time foreign policy discussion among Turkish politicians and public opinion was very rare, if not absent totally, and was far from criticizing the official line. In spite of strong disagreements over other matters, Turkish political parties and groups had formed an undeclared consensus on the state's foreign policy decisions and actions, seeing this attitude as a national duty. The new constitution in 1960 prepared the ground for public discussions by providing all political groups with means to voice their ideas. But one had to wait until 1964 to see widespread criticism of foreign policy.

Starting in the last ten days of December 1963, Greek Cypriot atrocities against the Turkish Cypriots attracted the close attention of Turkish people and led them to pressurize their government to intervene in Cyprus militarily. The failure of the Turkish government to intervene in Cyprus apparently because of U.S. pressures, including the Johnson letter with its serious threats, caused widespread criticisms and demonstrations against the United States in Turkey. Subsequently, in the second half of the 1960s, all aspects of U.S.-Turkish relations and Turkish foreign policy became the main subjects of public discussion, overshadowing disputes over internal matters. Turkey's alliance with NATO and its military relations with the USA were particularly questioned by leftist circles and the press and some went so far to suggest withdrawal from NATO. In this atmosphere Turkish rulers, too, felt the need to make some changes in foreign policy by improving relations with the Eastern bloc and the Third World and by being more careful in dealings with the United States. As a part of their new approach, they took some actions in the military field, which could displease the Americans.

The importance of these developments, which are still frequently cited by Turkish politicians and scholars, for Turkey's foreign policy inspired me to study them in detail. I particularly wanted to analyze views of different political groups including ruling elite on Turkey's relations with the United States to see the effect of public discussions on Turkey's official foreign policy line and to question the real character of changes in Turkish foreign policy. In the meantime, to study U.S.-Turkish relations in this period from the point of small-big state relationships in the light of theoretical considerations emerged as an attractive option. This necessitated the inclusion of Turkey's involvement in the 1962 Cuban missile crisis in the research in order to see the state of the U.S.-Turkish alliance prior to the uneasy 1964-1975 period. The subject did not attract public discussion at that time and has not been studied by Turkish scholars but it was at least as important as the Cyprus question and the

Johnson letter was for Turkey's security and its relations with the USA. I thought it would be an important contribution to the understanding of Turkish foreign policy and U.S.-Turkish relations to study all aspects of this event in the light of recent revelations.

The cooperation in the military field, of course, constitutes the basis of the U.S.-Turkish relationship. I wanted to study it in a wider perspective by giving the reasons for its establishment and continuity, noting how it was like in the 1950s and by mentioning recent developments to complete the picture. Apart from analyzing the events of the U.S.-Turkish military alliance in 1960-75, including important actions of the Turkish government to gain more initiative in this area and the U.S. arms embargo against Turkey in 1975, I also aimed to give the evaluation of the alliance by both sides by analyzing the NATO discussion in Turkish politics in the 1960s, by giving figures on military and economic transactions and by explaining Turkey's strategic importance for the USA.

The Cyprus question is the factor that has the most important impact on relations between Turkey and the United States. In spite of the existence of many studies on various aspects of the issue, it would be a new contribution to comprehend the implications of the Cyprus problem for the U.S.-Turkish alliance. However, to do this within the limits of two chapters posed a problem. The original study of this matter was itself of the length of a whole thesis. To conform to the length limitations of a book, the treatment of this subject therefore had to concentrate on the Cyprus policies of the United States and Turkey and the effect of these policies on their relationship.

The opium issue in the 1960s and in the first half of the 1970s is generally considered a side issue in the Turkish-American relationship. The only aspects, which are normally mentioned on the subject, are the U.S. dislike for the Demirel government because of its failure to ban opium cultivation, the prohibition of opium by the Erim government as an act to please the Americans and the resumption of opium production by the Ecevit government as act of independence. However, in the course of the study, I realized that the issue was very complicated, had many aspects concerning internal and foreign policies and public opinions of both states and became a serious matter at certain times even threatening the alliance between the two countries. I aimed to give a detailed analysis of the matter from the point of view of both sides, which had not been done before.

I should also note that I studied all events of the 1960-75 U.S.-Turkish relationship to see how far Turkey was influenced by the United States and how far the United States was able to affect Turkish actions on these incidents. A seminar, which I prepared for this purpose, proved useful in the detailed study of these subjects.

The above points were my original concerns when I started my study in January 1990. After receiving my Ph.D. degree on Turkish-American relations in the 1960-1975 period, I focused on the latter periods to complete the picture. Thus, this book is the product of a comprehensive study, which lasted more than ten years. All its deficiencies belong to me. I thank all my colleagues, who inspired, guided, criticized and helped me during my study.

Chapter 1

INTRODUCTION

1. THE SIGNIFICANCE OF THE SUBJECT

When the United States and Turkey established alliance relations immediately after the Second World War, foreign policies of both countries were experiencing a radical change. As the most powerful state in the world, the United States had decided to give up its traditional isolationist policy and to undertake global responsibilities. The main aim of U.S. policy after that moment was to confront and contain the Soviet Union and its bloc. The alliance with Turkey was a part of this new U.S. approach. By aligning with the USA, Turkey, too, abandoned its traditional neutralist policy, which had prevented it from establishing alliances, especially with big powers. Its main concern was to be a part of the Western world. Today, in the aftermath of the cold-war period, the alliance between the United States and Turkey still constitutes an important aspect of their foreign policies. This alliance is significant in today's world politics because it influences events in important regions such as the Middle East, the eastern Mediterranean, the Balkans, and Central Asia, including Russia and former Soviet republics.

This study attempts to explain the basis of this important relationship and the factors affecting it. In order to gain a thorough understanding of the relationship between Turkey and the United States today, it is necessary to know why the two countries chose to establish their alliance and to maintain it in spite of internal and international changes that adversely affected their relationship. This relationship has been studied within the context of Turkey's westernization policy, its need for foreign aid to develop its economy and for military assistance to ensure its security, its sensitivity to foreign influences and interventions, its insistence on its national causes, its importance for U.S. global and regional interests and strategies, the character of the international regime, and alliance perceptions and special internal conditions of both states. Foreign policy-making structure and factors and determinants of foreign policies in both the United States and Turkey have also been examined.

The 1960-1975 period has a particular importance. After experiencing a perfect honeymoon period in the 1950s, the durability, strength and cohesion of the U.S.-Turkish alliance were tested by the severe problems between 1960 and 1975. Looking at these problems will provide insights into the current relationship.

In 1960 the Turkish Republic experienced its first military coup and saw a radical change in its political system. Encouraged by military officers removing a rightist government and by the more pluralist and pro-freedom constitution of 1960, leftist groups launched an all-out campaign to increase their influence in domestic politics and to this end from 1964 they attacked Turkey's relations with the USA and NATO. The bargaining over Turkey's Jupiter missiles by the United States with the Soviet Union during the Cuban crisis of October 1962 occurred without any serious public criticism and damage to the U.S.-Turkish relationship largely because of public ignorance of the incident. However, when the U.S. response to the Cyprus question, which emerged in December 1963 as a serious matter, was perceived by Turkish rulers and people as anti-Turkish, the domestic politics of Turkey after that time were dominated by criticism of the United States and Turkey's contacts with the Americans. Military relations were particularly targeted to the extent that the Turkish government had to force the U.S. administration to review bilateral agreements signed since 1947 and that Turkey had to take some actions in the military field that would not please the Americans. Such developments can be seen in relations between the two states at any time. Studying these past experiences will help academics and politicians assess current problems in perspective and enable them to suggest solutions with a clearer awareness of the likely consequences.

In the 1960s the most important accusation made by Turkish leftists and believed by many others was that U.S.-Turkish contacts acquired the character of a patron-client relationship. It was widely propagated that Turkey was dependent on the USA in almost every field and was under the heavy influence of the United States in its decisions and actions. Similar claims can be heard frequently in big-small state relations. For instance, in the late 1980s and the early 1990s, Islamists have voiced almost the same kinds of opinion. Our study questions whether or not leftists' claims in the 1960s reflected the truth and hopes to give clues for the understanding of current and future events.

In this context, one important thing which this study tries to explain is the characteristics and different aspects of a big-small state relationship. Turkish-American relations in the 1960-1975 period present a good case to analyze how an alliance between a relatively small state and a superpower works. The transactions between the USA and Turkey and the features of both states appear to reflect many aspects of the patron-client relationship. The Turkish position during the Cuban missile crisis; U.S. president Johnson's letter to the Turkish prime minister, which included heavy threats to force Turkey not to intervene in Cyprus; considerable U.S. economic and military aid to Turkey; the armament of the Turkish army with U.S. weapons; U.S. pressures on Turkey to force her to ban opium production; and the U.S. arms embargo against Turkey, aiming to change its Cyprus policy can all lead one to the conclusion that, as a small state, Turkey fell victim to U.S. influence in this period. However, one can easily show evidence for the opposite claim: Turkey's improving relations with Eastern bloc and Third World countries; Turkish support for the Arabs in the Arab-Israeli conflict; some Turkish actions in the military arena such as not allowing U-2 flights from Turkish territory, reviewing bilateral agreements with the USA, not allowing the use of U.S. bases for non-NATO purposes, and changing the duty status formula applied to U.S. personnel in Turkey; not banning opium production and later resuming it after it was banned by a non-party government; and Turkish intervention in Cyprus all point in the other direction.

By studying individual examples in this context, this study tries to provide answers to the following important questions:

In a small-big state relationship which side gets more benefits? To what extent can a big state influence and change foreign policies, decisions and actions of its small ally and force her to act in a certain way? To what extent can a big state influence national causes and internal policies of its small ally? How does a big state get involved in matters concerning its small ally and how does it react when actions of this ally seem to damage its global and national interests? To what extent can a big state punish its small ally in these cases? What are the difficulties faced by a small state in its relations with its bigger ally? For instance, how can its survival be put under threat because of its alliance relations with a big partner and how can its interests be bargained by its big ally with other powers? How does a small state act when it faces threats and pressures from its big ally? To what extent does heavy dependence on a big power restrict the freedom of decision and action of a small state? How could a small state be influenced or threatened by a big power if it did not have alliance relations with this state? How does a small state's determination on one national issue make her reject influences and threats of its big ally? How do public consensus and pressures in one issue affect the attitude of the small state's rulers in their dealings with a big power in this issue?

The related questions are also important. What is the effect upon the views, decisions and actions of the rulers of a small state who are proud of its independence when they suspect it is being treated as a satellite? How does a small state's regime affect its relations with its big ally? How and why does a small state follow the lead of its big ally in international events even without considering its own interests? What are the alternatives for a small state when it is cornered or deserted by its big ally? For example, can it opt for neutrality or change sides? To what extent can a small state have a flexible foreign policy and improve its relations with enemy and other powers while having alliance relations with a big power at the same time? To what extent can a small state take a major action in spite of opposition from its big ally? How does the overall international climate (bipolarity, multipolarity, tense confrontation, détente, etc.) affect relations between a small and big state? Which factors restrict decisions and actions of both sides of a big-small state relationship? For example, how do mutual interests and the need each felt for the other affect one side's decision to influence the other or reject the influence of the other?

In addition to the answers to these questions, analysis of changes in Turkey's foreign policy in the period of our study will contribute to an understanding of Turkish foreign policy past, present and future, and will also give clues that will help an assessment of the characteristics and prospects of small states' foreign policies in general. In the 1965-1975 period, it appeared that Turkish rulers tried to pursue a more independent foreign policy, remaining outside the influence of the United States and the NATO alliance. A study of the reasons for these efforts and the extent of their success will contribute to the current knowledge of the subject.

This study will also try to show how important internal conditions of a state are in determining its foreign policy decisions and its relations with other states. In the context of our study the following examples can be cited:

(a) The role of Turkish leftists and the press in initiating foreign policy discussion in Turkey for the first time and in forcing rulers to reconsider foreign policy.

(b) The effect of Turkish public opinion on Turkey's Cyprus policy and its dealings with the USA on this issue.

(c) The role of electoral concerns in the Turkish government's rejection of the U.S. demand to prohibit opium cultivation.

(d) The effect of public opinion on Turkish rulers' efforts to make changes in military relations with the United States.

(e) The impact of Turkey's traditional westernisation policy on its relations with the USA.

(f) The extent to which having a military regime influenced Turkey's receptiveness to U.S. demands.

(g) The effect of the U.S. Congress and the power competition between the Congress and the administration on U.S. policies toward the Cyprus question, Turkey's opium production and U.S.-Turkish military relations.

(h) The impact of Greek-American lobby groups in the United States on the Johnson letter and the U.S. arms embargo against Turkey.

(i) The role of the U.S. public's preoccupation with the drug abuse problem in getting the U.S. government to put pressure on Turkey to prohibit opium production.

This study aims to provide a uniquely comprehensive analysis of U.S.-Turkish relations from 1947 up to the present. Turkey's involvement in the Cuban missile crisis of October 1962 has been studied in the light of most recent revelations in great detail. The fact that Turkey's survival was put under great threat during the crisis because of her alliance relations with the United States and that U.S. rulers bargained the missiles belonging to Turkey without informing her cannot be forgotten by Turkish authorities as a serious lesson which will guide their future dealings with the Americans.

Military contacts are still the basis of the U.S.-Turkish relationship and the conditioning and amount of U.S. military assistance to Turkey continue to be a problem between the two countries. The signing of a general military co-operation agreement arises as a serious matter in relations at regular intervals. This thesis examines different aspects of U.S.-Turkish military contacts and by also noting both the previous and more recent developments it clarifies the nature of today's U.S.-Turkish alliance. Its exposition of the ideas of defenders and critics of Turkey's alliance with the USA and NATO in the 1960s is of relevance to the current evaluation of this alliance.

The Cyprus problem, too, is a continuing problem of both Turkish foreign policy and U.S.-Turkish relations. It is still a national cause for Turkey considerably influenced by public opinion and the United States still tries to find ways to affect Turkey's Cyprus policies. Looking at the roots of the problem and analyzing U.S. and Turkish attitudes and interactions on the matter in a historical perspective will certainly help an understanding of the present situation, its future prospects and its impact on the U.S.-Turkish alliance. Any proposed solutions to the problem need to be made in the light of this knowledge. U.S. President Johnson's letter in 1964 is a good example of a diplomatic mistake, which alienated the recipient state considerably and caused changes in its foreign policy. It is still frequently cited by Turkish politicians and scholars in the course of discussing foreign policy and Turkish-American relations. The U.S. arms embargo against Turkey in 1975, which was aimed at forcing Turkish rulers to make concessions in Cyprus, is also fresh in Turkish minds, reminding them how the United States can try to punish their country and how the U.S. Congress can affect relations between the two states.

The opium question was short-lived and ceased to be a problem after 1974. However, its implications are still alive. It demonstrates how internal public pressures can lead the U.S. administration to pressurize its close ally and how easily Turkey can attract the antagonism of American people and Congress. It also shows how open pressures on Turkey, forcing her to act in a certain way, can provoke a severe response.

2. THE PURPOSE OF THE STUDY

The aims of the study are implicit in the preceding section. The chief aim is to examine the nature, characteristics and general trends of the U.S.-Turkish alliance between 1950 and 2003. It particularly tries to find out whether Turkey was a satellite of the United States and whether U.S.-Turkish relations fitted the pattern of a small-big or a patron-client relationship in the 1950-1975 period. It examines individual examples in this context.

Secondly, the study analyses events of the U.S.-Turkish relations in the 1960-1975 period in order to reflect their true character and reveal unknown aspects. It aims to give comprehensive knowledge of these events with their causes and consequences and their impact upon the U.S.-Turkish alliance.

Another intention is to explain changes in the direction of Turkish foreign policy. It explores the character of these changes, why they occurred, and questions how successful they were. To this end, the study analyses the ideas of anti-American critics and the attempts of the Turkish government to implement a more independent policy staying outside U.S. influence.

The study seeks to explain factors affecting U.S.-Turkish relations and reasons for the continuity of the U.S.-Turkish alliance. To achieve this, it includes a discussion of determinants and formal policy-making structure of foreign policies in Turkey and the USA.

A further important objective of this research is to discover the true reasons, motives and aims behind U.S. attitudes toward Turkey in different incidents. In other words, to examine whether U.S. rulers had biased opinions about Turkey while pressuring her or whether their attitude was more or less objective. Similarly, an attempt is made to find out true intention of Turkish rulers in their apparently anti-American actions related to changes in Turkish foreign policy.

3. THE SCOPE AND FOCUS OF THE STUDY

The study covers all political and military contacts between the United States and Turkey in the 1960-1975 period. It also mentions events before 1960 and after 1975 to explain the roots of problems and subsequent developments. The economic aspect is briefly touched upon when it is thought to be useful in understanding relations, though the fact that the two nations' trading patterns reveal their economies to be more complementary than competitive means that economic factors were less important than military and political considerations in shaping their relationship. Between 1960 and 1975 Turkey generally exported agricultural products and imported manufactured industrial materials. Turkey's major exports included cotton, tobacco, hazelnuts, raisins, minerals (including chromium), textiles, food beverages and industrial products, while her major imports were non-electric machinery, iron and steel products, means of transport (including motor vehicles), crude oil and petroleum products, electrical machinery, rubber and plastics products, agriculture-based processed products, cereal (including wheat) and textiles. On the other hand, the United States was one of the leading powers in the export of manufactured goods though manufactures also occupied the most important place in her imports. Major U.S. exports were machinery, automobiles and parts, aircraft and parts, iron and steel products, chemicals, electrical, construction and agricultural machinery, fuels, wheat, etc. The USA imported mainly machinery, transport equipment, petroleum products, forest products, iron and steel products, chemicals, coffee, etc. Trade relations between the USA and Turkey in the 1960-75 period fit these trade patterns and demonstrate that the US-Turkish trade was complementary rather than competitive. While Turkey exported to the USA mainly agricultural products (tobacco, fruits, vegetables, nuts, some raw minerals and metals, animal products, textile and cereals), U.S. exports to Turkey included mainly manufactured goods (non-electric and electrical machinery, road vehicles and other transport equipment, wheat, chemicals, petroleum and products, metal manufactures, iron and steel, textiles and rubber products). Although in this period both Turkey and the USA exported wheat and textiles, Turkey's exports of these products were not large enough to pose any problems to their relationship.[1]

In Chapter II, which discusses the relevant theories, arguments on the patron-client relationship, dependency and influence are mostly related to actual issues in Turkish-American relations between 1960 and 1975. The arguments in this chapter determine the treatment of topics dealt with in detail in later chapters. The theoretical framework established in this chapter can be used in the analysis of present relationships as well.

Similarly, the consideration in Chapter III of factors influencing foreign policies of Turkey and the USA assists understanding of the current as well as the 1960-1975 situation.

In the discussion of U.S.-Turkish military relations, a detailed picture is given of the relationship from its establishment up to the 1980s and where necessary to complete the picture brief reference is made to the current situation. The general basis of the relationship and the factors that influence it are also considered.

Turkey's role in Western-led defense projects in the Middle East and its initiatives in the context of the Baghdad Pact of 1955 were prices, which it had to pay for its alliance initiatives with the USA. The subject was studied in Chapter V in these lines.

Turkey's involvement in the Cuban missile crisis is studied in great detail to reach correct conclusions. Daily and even hourly developments are given where necessary, though to keep the account within bounds summaries are provided of certain stages, and to present a clear picture the history from 1959 to 1963 of the Jupiter missiles, which caused Turkey's involvement in the crisis, is explained briefly.

The Cyprus issue, which placed enormous strains on the alliance, is covered in chapters VII and VIII. Incidents of the Cyprus problem in the 1960-1975 period which have direct implications for the U.S.-Turkish relationship are summarized and more attention is directed to the Cyprus policies of the two countries and the impact of the matter on dealings between them and their foreign policies.

---

[1] For more detailed information on Turkish-US trade see Appendix D.

The chapter on the opium problem provides a brief background from the beginning of the century, describes developments between 1969 and 1974 in great detail and summarizes its aftermath until the 1980s in order to present the matter in perspective. The need to give both sides' opinions objectively determined the length of this chapter.

The chapter on the 1980s analyses the one of the most critical periods of Turkish-American in the aftermath of the embargo practice, which poisoned the relationship. The following chapter focuses on radical changes in Turkish-American relations and in Turkish foreign policy in the post-Cold War period with projections on their future.

The focus of the study is of course the examination of ideas mentioned in the theoretical chapter and their application to the events in the U.S.-Turkish relationship in the concerned period. The examination of alleged U.S. influences on Turkey in these events can be given as the main focus of the thesis.

4. Methodology

As a first step to begin the study, I reviewed the literature, acquired a detailed knowledge of historical events which are related to the study directly or indirectly, and became familiar with important personalities who were involved in the concerned events and with foreign policy-making processes both in the United States and Turkey. In these early stages of the research, I also gained familiarity with the theoretical considerations. In order to find the answer to the main question of the first part of the study, that is whether Turkey was a satellite of the United States in the 1950-1975 period, Turkish newspapers, magazines and parliamentary records were searched and some Turkish statesmen were interviewed. Subsequently a seminar study, titled *Was Turkey a Tool of the U.S. Policy*, was prepared in the light of the data and this paper became the guide of the research in its later stages. Other sources, including the American ones, were obtained and used during the detailed study of each chapter's subjects. In this stage, the problems were reconsidered and the relevance or otherwise of the theories to what had actually happened was examined. Finally, conclusions were drawn and the aspects that deserve future study when documents become available were noted.

Since the period of our study covers very recent events many of the relevant documents, particularly the official records, are still classified by both sides and consequently not available for inspection. Nevertheless, every effort has been made to consult all primary sources that are available, to gain further insights by interviews and correspondence with influential people who were personally involved in the events concerned and to supplement this with recourse to extensive secondary sources and the considered views of scholars and commentators who have reflected at length upon various aspects of this subject.

First of all, almost all published and declassified primary documents concerning U.S.-Turkish relations in the 1960-1975 period were used during the course of the research. These primary sources include public statements of governments, foreign ministries and other interested ministries; agreements between Turkey and the United States; joint communiqués announced at the end of official talks between the two states; statements of officials of both sides; memoirs of statesmen; parliamentary discussions in Turkey and congressional hearings in the United States; bulletins of foreign ministries; interviews with former Turkish foreign ministers, etc.

The author's interviews with former Turkish foreign ministers Osman Olcay and Ü. Haluk Bayülken, former Turkish MP and diplomat Kamran İnan, Turkish academic Seyfi Taşhan and retired Turkish academic and columnist Fahir Armaoğlu were helpful in clarifying some events of Turkish-American relations and understanding characteristics of Turkish foreign policy.

In order to get the whole picture of the Turkish side on U.S.-Turkish relations the author spent great amount of time going through all issues of major Turkish newspapers and magazines and records of Turkish parliamentary discussions in the period of 1960-1975. The Durham University Library and the Turkish Grand National Assembly Library provided means for this effort. Duygu Sezer's book, *Kamuoyu ve Dış Politika*, too, was useful in pointing to other articles in numerous Turkish newspapers. Newspapers and magazines had the additional merit of giving the general atmosphere of Turkish domestic politics at that time and providing official statements and news of U.S.-Turkish contacts. Articles by Turkish statesmen, academics, politicians and columnists in these papers reflected the opinion of the Turkish government, opposition and public. Records of parliamentary discussion undoubtedly provide a good contemporary evaluation by the government and opposition of the U.S.-Turkish alliance and its associated events.

The Turkish Foreign Ministry's bulletin, the semi-official Turkish magazine, *Foreign Policy*, and official books on the visits of Turkish Presidents and Prime Minister to the USA and on the opium question provided for the thesis official documents, records of events, and statements and articles by Turkish officials. The book by Nihat Erim, who was the Turkish representative in the Geneva talks of July-August 1964, provided a first-hand account of Cyprus events. Series of articles and books by Metin Toker, the son-in-law of Turkish Prime Minister İsmet İnönü, too, were useful in conveying information on different topics, including the Cuban missile crisis and the Cyprus question. Haluk Ulman, who joined the Geneva conferences in July and August 1974 as a member of the Turkish delegation, gave the account of these conferences from the Turkish point of view. Books and articles by other Turkish and Turkish Cypriot officials including Turkish Cypriot leader Rauf Denktash supplied official documents and the viewpoint of the Turkish side on the Cyprus question. The author made a detailed use of books of Turkish political leaders and party and government programs in preparing the section on foreign policy-making structure of Turkey. Metin Tamkoç's book, *The Warrior Diplomats*, and the thesis of J. E. Sowerwine, too, were helpful in this subject. Turkish Prime Minister Demirel's long press conference in February 1970 greatly assisted the study of U.S.-Turkish bilateral military agreements. The author also benefited from books by retired Turkish admiral Sezai Orkunt and Senator Haydar Tunçkanat as these included opinions of Turkish military officers and official documents of U.S.-Turkish military relations. The Turkish Finance Ministry's book was used in preparing the tables of U.S. economic assistance to Turkey.

On the American side, hearings in the U.S. Congress provided a detailed account of views of U.S. congressmen and officials on the opium question, U.S.-Turkish military relations, the arms embargo and the Cyprus problem. Reports prepared by the Library of Congress servicemen for committees of the U.S. Congress clarified the U.S. position and gave detailed information in various subjects including U.S. bases and facilities in Turkey, Turkey's strategic importance for the USA, the Cyprus question, and the arms embargo. Memoirs by some U.S. statesmen supplied first-hand accounts of some events: Truman's memoirs on the Truman doctrine, George Ball's memoirs on the Cuban missile crisis and on the Cyprus question in 1964, Henry Kissinger's memoirs on the Cyprus crisis in 1974 and Jimmy Carter's memoirs on the foreign policy-making structure of the United States. The memoirs of Robert Kennedy, the U.S. Attorney-General in 1962 and the brother of President Kennedy, were used in the chapter studying the Cuban missile crisis and due attention was paid to the memoirs attributed to Soviet Premier Khrushchev. Books and articles by former U.S. ambassadors, James W. Spain, George McGhee and Monteagle Stearns, too, contributed to the study. Documents provided by U.S. and British sources before 1960 were used in the explanation of military relations in the 1950s. The author also made the use of U.S. public laws concerning Turkish-American relations. Figures of assistance to Turkey were obtained from the book published by the U.S. Agency for International Development. On the Cuban missile crisis, the author benefited from books of former U.S. officials who were actively involved in the crisis as close aides of the President and saw the classified documents. Some declassified documents, White House Tapes, were also obtained by the author. U.S. official Harvey R. Wellman's article was particularly useful in presenting the U.S. government's position on the opium question. Books and articles of former U.S. officials and U.S. experts on Turkey such as George Harris, Ferenc A. Vali, Dankwart A. Rustow, Richard C. Campany, etc., too, helped the author in analyzing U.S.-Turkish relations.

Some third-party sources were also used for our research. *Middle East Record* provided summaries of events and voting patterns in the United Nations. *Keesing's Contemporary Archives* were helpful in tracking down international incidents concerning U.S.-Turkish relations. *International Organisation* was used for the record of UN discussions on the Cyprus question. *The Journal of Defense and Diplomacy*, Jane's books on weapons and SIPRI's book supplied figures for Turkey's military equipment supplied by the United States. The correspondence between the Turkish and Soviet premiers, Khrushchev and Gürsel, and between U.S. President Johnson and Turkish Prime Minister İnönü were obtained from *Middle Eastern Affairs* and *Middle East Journal*. Memoirs of Greek statesmen, Andreas Papandreou and Dimitri S. Bitsios, cast useful light on the Cyprus question from the point of U.S.-Turkish relations. The author also benefited from the thesis of M. Allan Turner on the opium problem between the USA and Turkey. Finally, he also consulted numerous secondary sources.

5. THE OUTLINE OF THE STUDY

Chapter II examines the U.S.-Turkish alliance in the light of alliance theories by pointing to reasons for the establishment and continuity of this alliance and factors affecting its general situation and its cohesion. U.S. and Turkish perceptions of their alliance are also considered in this section. By using theoretical studies on these subjects the chapter then questions whether U.S.-Turkish contacts gained the character of a patron-client relationship and whether Turkey was dependent on the USA in different areas. Finally, the chapter examines the U.S. influence on Turkey and mentions some minor events of U.S.-Turkish relations between 1960 and 1975 in this context.

Chapter III provides the framework and background of subjects examined in the following chapters by explaining determinants, factors and policy-making structure of U.S. and Turkish foreign policies in the light of historical incidents.

Chapter IV analyses all events and problems of U.S.-Turkish military relations from the establishment of the U.S.-Turkish alliance in 1947 to the end of the arms embargo in 1978 and mentions some important developments after 1978. It explains how and why this alliance was formed and then developed in the 1950s. After shortly mentioning developments of the Turkish junta period, the chapter examines the importance of the Johnson letter in 1964 for the U.S.-Turkish military alliance. Then, the Turkish government's initiatives to make some changes in military relations with the USA, influenced by widespread public criticism, are considered at length. Views of Turkish critics who defended and those who criticized Turkey's alliance with the USA and NATO are analyzed in the following section and then military relations of the 1970s including the arms embargo are briefly described. Finally, the chapter gives figures on military and economic assistance and military equipment which Turkey received from the USA and analyses Turkey's strategic importance for Washington, including U.S. bases and facilities on its territory and its position vis-a-vis the Middle East.

Chapter V tries to explain why Turkey, which was reluctant to become involved in Middle East politics, was involved in Western-led defense projects in the Middle East in the 1950s. It discusses the origins, establishment and end of the Baghdad Pact and focuses on the Turkish role in defense plans for the Middle East. It also concentrates on Turkish attempts to draw the Arab world into an alliance with the West in facing international communism and to explain the consequences of the Turkish initiatives for Turkish foreign policy.

Chapter VI constitutes a detailed examination of Turkey's involvement in the Cuban missile crisis because of the U.S.-supplied Jupiter missiles on her territory. First, it explains why and how the Jupiters were stationed in Turkey over a long period of time and became the subject of U.S. attempts to remove them. Then, it mentions the role of these missiles in the Soviet move to deploy nuclear missiles to Cuba. After giving a detailed account of discussions among U.S. officials during the crisis on the possibility of trading the Jupiters with Soviet missiles in Cuba and citing the Soviet proposal on this, the chapter describes how Turkey came to a be a first target of a nuclear war whose outbreak became highly possible. Then, it explains how the United States made a secret deal with the Soviets on the Jupiters to end the crisis. In the final section, the chapter gives Turkey's attitude during the crisis and analyses implications of the Cuban crisis and the removal of the Jupiters for Turkey.

Chapter VII, which describes developments of the Cyprus question between 1960 and 1965, starts with explaining how the USA was involved in the matter and worked to station NATO soldiers on Cyprus. In this context, it gives the account of George Ball's visit to Greece, Turkey and Cyprus and U.S. pressures on Turkey to prevent its intervention in Cyprus. After mentioning the U.S. attitude during the UN Security Council discussions on the Cyprus question in March 1964, the Chapter explains how President Johnson tried to prevent a Turkish intervention in Cyprus by sending his famous letter to the Turkish prime minister in June 1964 and later tried to mediate between Greece and Turkey on the matter by talking to the Turkish and Greek prime ministers in Washington. The following sections provide information on the Geneva talks between Turkish and Greek delegation in July-August 1964, mediated by Johnson's special envoy Acheson, the August 1964 Cyprus crisis and U.S. and Turkish policies and interests on the Cyprus question.

Chapter VIII focuses on the Turkish intervention in Cyprus in July and August 1974 from the point of U.S.-Turkish relations and the subsequent U.S. arms embargo against Turkey. It starts with explaining the U.S. role in Greek-Turkish secret talks on the Cyprus question between 1965 and 1974 and in ending the November 1967 Cyprus crisis and then mentions

Cyprus policies of the USA and Turkey in the 1967-1974 period. Subsequently, the chapter analyses the Cyprus coup and the Turkish military intervention in Cyprus by focusing on U.S. role in and U.S. attitude toward these events. U.S. reactions to Turkish actions during this critical period are particularly emphasized in this context. Finally, the chapter analyses the arms embargo imposed by the U.S. Congress on Turkey in detail with its causes, consequences and implications.

Chapter IX is a detailed account of U.S.-Turkish controversy over the opium production of Turkey mainly between 1969 and 1974. Firstly, it summarizes the history of the problem until 1969 and then explains views of U.S. officials on Turkey's opium production and their efforts and pressures on Turkish rulers to achieve the prohibition of opium cultivation in Turkey. After describing Turkish rulers' views on the problem, their efforts to prevent illegal opium production and trafficking and the reasons of their failure to ban it completely, the chapter analyses the Turkish opium ban in 1971 with its reasons and implementation. Finally, the chapter examines the U.S.-Turkish controversy surrounding the resumption of Turkish poppy production in 1974 by mentioning the views of Turkish authorities and the reaction of the U.S. administration and Congress and summarizes the aftermath of the problem.

The main issues studied in Chapter X are the military, strategic and economic aspects and the problems of Turkish-American relations the 1980s. Chapter XI analyses the process of Turkey's participating in the new world system as a more active world power with its repercussions on its relations with the USA. Its focuses on the meaning and value of the Turkish-American alliance from the Turkish perspective in gaining an effective position in the new world order and also mentions its main problems.

The final chapter of the book contains a general evaluation of U.S.-Turkish relations between 1950 and 2003 and a summary of the findings of the research including validity of the theories mentioned in Chapter II, explains its own contribution to scholarly understanding of the subjects and points to aspects that would repay further study.

Chapter 2

THEORETICAL STUDY OF
U.S.-TURKISH RELATIONS

The aim of this chapter is to examine theoretical explanations of Turkish-American relations between 1960 and 1975. It first gives the reasons for the establishment of the U.S.-Turkish alliance, which came to the existence with the Truman doctrine in 1947 and which was formalized with Turkey's entry into NATO in 1952. Secondly, the chapter illuminates factors affecting the alliance in general and its cohesion specifically, and then gives the U.S. and Turkish perceptions of their alliance. Thirdly, it tries to answer the three questions, which constitute the core of the study itself: 1- Was the U.S.-Turkish relationship an example of patron-client relationship? 2- Was Turkey heavily dependent on the USA? 3- Was Turkey influenced by the USA in its decisions and actions? Finally, the chapter studies the examples of U.S. influence on Turkey (U.S. influence on the Turkish economy, U.S. intervention in Turkish internal politics, the Turkish recognition of China, and the appointment of Komer as U.S. ambassador to Turkey), leaving the analysis of other examples to the other chapters (Turkish military dependence on the USA, implications of the Cuban missile crisis for U.S. influence on Turkish security and U.S. influence on Turkey's Cyprus and opium policies).

1. REASONS FOR ALLIANCE FORMATION

Turkey decided to establish an alliance with the United States for the three main reasons: to protect its security, to obtain military and economic aid and to strengthen its Western-style state structure. The reason, which made U.S. rulers enter into alliance relations with Turkey, was Turkey's strategic importance for U.S. interests in the Middle East and for its global policy of containing the Soviet Union.

a) Security

In the opinion of many scholars, a common external threat to the security of countries is the primary source of alliances. Two states, A and B, form a military alliance since they have a similar perception of a common threat and they want to deter that threat by combining their military resources in the event of an external military aggression. In a more particular case, if power A fears that power C harbors aggressive designs against her and if she feels herself weaker than power C, she seeks an alliance with a more powerful state B who will help her maintain her security and strengthen her power. Weaker members of the international system who confront a major security threat often rely on the guarantee of a powerful alliance and external aid of a powerful allied state because they cannot obtain security by use of their own capabilities.[1] By making an alliance with a lesser state, a strong power aims to prevent its adversary from gaining resources of the lesser state[2] and advancing its influence towards strategic places.

The main factor, which brought the United States and Turkey together within an alliance, was the Soviet threat to the security of Turkey. The Russians have always been a potential threat and enemy for the Turks since the rivalry and fighting began between the empires of the Ottomans and the Russians. The traditional Russian desire to reach warm waters through the Black Sea and the Turkish Straits and the possibility of Russian invasion of eastern Anatolia have constituted a nightmare for the Turks for centuries. In the post-war period, when the Soviet Union abolished the Treaty of Friendship of 1925 between the two countries, wanted the revision of the Montreaux Convention of 1936 on the Turkish Straits to the advantage of the Black Sea countries and made some territorial demands in eastern Anatolia, Turkey immediately began to seek the military and diplomatic support of the United States and became willing to pay any price to secure its involvement in the Western alliance which emerged as a counter force against the Soviet Union.[3] Although the immediate Russian military threat seemed to have disappeared after October 1947 and the new leadership of the Soviet Union launched some peace initiatives towards Turkey after 1953, Turkish policy-makers continued to see the Soviet Union as the major potential threat to Turkey and therefore insisted on preserving close ties with NATO and the United States.[4]

In the post-World War II period, American rulers came to see Turkey as an important part of their global policy of containing Soviet expansion and decided to extend military and economic aid to her to block "the Soviet aggression." They believed that without strong U.S. support Turkey might be transferred by the Soviet Union to a springboard for political and military expansion into the Near and Middle East where the United States had important interests.[5]

One important problem for weak states is the ambiguity of outside support in the event of facing an external aggression. History shows that outside support for weak states does not come or arrives late or is given only in expectation of future benefits.[6] Lesser powers also fear that great powers may reach an agreement at their expense.[7] In the 1960s, there was a great deal of discussion among Turkish politicians regarding the genuineness of the U.S. and

---

[1] Robert L. Rothstein, *Alliances and Small Powers*, New York: Columbia University Press, 1968, pp. 24, 25, 29, 49, 50, 118, George Liska, *Alliances and the Third World*, Baltimore: The John Hopkins Press, 1968, pp. 26, 27, Michael Handel, *Weak States in the International System*, London: Frank Cass, 1981, p. 121, Robert L. Rothstein, "On the Problems of Being Small and Poor" in William C. Olson et al. (eds.), *The Theory and Practice of International Relations*, Englewood Cliffs, N. J.: Prentice Hall, 1983, p. 36.
[2] Ole R. Holsti, P. Terrence Hoppman and John D. Sullivan, *Unity and Disintegration in International Alliances*, New York: Wiley and Sons Inc., 1973, p. 97.
[3] Kemal H. Karpat (ed.), *Turkey's Foreign Policy in Transition*, Leiden: E. J. Brill, 1975, pp. 1-2.
[4] Mehmet Gönlübol, "NATO, USA and Turkey" in Karpat (ed.), *Turkey's Foreign Policy in Transition*, pp. 47, 49.
[5] George S. Harris, *Troubled Alliance*, Washington D. C.: American Enterprise Institute, 1972, p. 21.
[6] Rothstein, *Alliances and Small Powers*, p. 24.
[7] Handel, *Weak States in the International System*, p. 179.

NATO guarantee for Turkish security.[8] The Turks also suspected that U.S.-Soviet agreements on some issues would increase the Soviet threat to Turkey.[9]

b) Assistance Need

Economic and military needs force a lesser power to seek an alliance with a greater power.[10] To strengthen their developing economy and to fulfil their plans of economic construction and development, lesser powers need economic aid from developed countries and in many cases to secure economic aid of these powers they join military alliances established by them. A state that lacks sufficient capacity to build her own sophisticated weaponry and defense system necessary to deter external threats may choose to join in an alliance to get weapons easily.

Turkey's need for military and economic assistance and America's response to it played an important part in the Turkish-American alliance. Although Turkey did not join the Second World War until the last minute and did not suffer war damage, her economy in the post-war period was very weak. After the Democrat Party came to power, which promised more wealth for the people by pursuing an economic policy giving more weight to the private sector, Turkey's economic aid needs increased considerably. The new government had based its ambitious economic plans and projects on the availability of vast foreign economic aid and investment.[11] During the war Turkey's military expenditures were very high because she had kept her troops deployed throughout the war. In the post-war period, Turkey's security worries derived from the Soviet pressure impelled her to keep her army at its existing size and to modernize it. Turks' desire to join NATO and the Western world and their exaggeration of the Soviet threat were considerably motivated by their desire for economic and military aid from the United States. In the 1947-1974 period, the United States was the main source of Turkey's military and economic aid,[12] but U.S. aid fell short of meeting Turkish expectations and this cast a shadow on relations.

c) Strategic Reasons

When a lesser state needs an alliance with a great power, she often prefers a geographically remoter one.[13] However, an alliance with a distant great power could prove less reliable because it might be more difficult to agree on a common response to local conflicts and distance might mean a less certain military commitment in case of attack; the weak state might be overwhelmed in the interval between an attack and the arrival of aid.[14] To overcome these disadvantages, the weak state sometimes urges the great power to station

---

[8] See the section on the NATO discussion in Turkish politics in Chapter IV.

[9] See the section on détente in Chapter IV.

[10] Holsti et al., *Unity and Disintegration in International Alliances,* p. 13, George Liska, *Nations in Alliance,* Baltimore: John Hopkins Press, 1968, p. 14.

[11] Leo Tansky, *U.S. and USSR Aid to Developing Countries: A Comparative Study of India, Turkey, and the U.A.R.,* New York: Frederick A. Praeger Publishers, 1967, pp. 39, 46.

[12] See the tables of U. S. aid to Turkey and military equipment of the Turkish army in Chapter IV.

[13] Olson et al. (eds.), *The Theory and Practice of International Relations,* p. 220, Holsti et al., *Unity and Disintegration in International Alliances,* p. 13.

[14] Rothstein, *Alliances and Small Powers,* p. 118, Handel, *Weak States in the International System,* p. 128.

troops and maintains bases on its territory and thus it tries to obtain automatic intervention of the great power.[15] A lesser state's closeness to a threatening great power and her geographic location and strategic importance also affect the decision of that state in making an alliance with a different great power. If a smaller state is very close to a great power and if it is in the way of natural expansion of that power, she seeks the alliance of a more powerful state to balance the regional great power.[16] The important strategic location of a small power vis-a-vis the powerful enemy state is an important reason for a great power to extend her alliance to that small state.

Turkey had a very long frontier with the Soviet Union, the leader of the Warsaw Pact, and she was within the zone of Soviet natural influence and expansion. Turkey, therefore, felt it necessary to continue its alliance with the United States not because the USA was remote from Turkey but because it was the only country that could balance the Soviet Union's power.[17] Thus, the remoteness of the United States to Turkey had no major influence on the decision of the Turks to choose the USA as an ally. Turks were happy with the presence of U.S. troops and facilities in their territories, thinking that it would secure automatic U.S. help in the event of an aggression. When the U.S. Congress imposed an arms embargo on Turkey in February 1975, the Turkish government did not stop the U.S. bases from functioning immediately because it believed that their presence was to Turkey's advantage. Turkish rulers always claimed that because of her strategic importance to major great powers Turkey could not afford to stay outside the Western alliance.[18] Turkey's geographical location was an important factor in the minds of US decision-makers: Turkey adjoined the Soviet Union and also the Middle East region; it constituted a natural barrier between the two regions; its straits and relatively large army and base facilities on its territory were valuable assets for the West; so it was particularly important to keep Turkey in the Western camp.[19]

d) Ideology

Many scholars consider a common or similar ideology of secondary importance in making an alliance after security needs.[20] Ideology plays relatively less part in making or breaking an alliance. However, alliances established by powers which have identical or similar ideological and cultural values are more durable and effective. They bring about more co-operation and fewer problems.[21] States are likely to prefer making alliances with partners with whom they share common institutions, social and political values.[22]

Turkish leadership has always claimed that Turkey is a democratic and secular country sharing common values with the Western world.[23] The Turks clearly assigned more

---

[15] Handel, *Weak States in the International System*, p. 126.

[16] Rothstein, *Alliances and Small Powers*, p. 121.

[17] Gönlübol, "NATO, USA and Turkey", p. 47.

[18] President Cevdet Sunay's speech in the White House in 1967, *Amerika'da Onbir Gün*, Ankara: Yarın Yayınları, 1967, p. 26.

[19] See the section on Turkey's strategic importance in Chapter IV.

[20] Olson et al. (eds.), *The Theory and Practice of International Relations*, p. 220, Holsti et al., *Unity and Disintegration in International Alliances*, p. 30.

[21] Holsti et al., *Unity and Disintegration in International Alliances*, pp. 54, 265, 268, Liska, *Nations in Alliance*, p. 90.

[22] Holsti et al., *Unity and Disintegration in International Alliances*, p. 12.

[23] President Sunay's speech in the White House, *Amerika'da Onbir Gün*, p. 18.

importance to the ideological dimension and expected their alliance with the USA and NATO would help them maintain better relations with the West and pursue westernization policies at home whereas American rulers were more interested in U.S. national interests.[24] In the aftermath of World War II, ruling elite in Turkey held almost the same views as the American administration with regard to political and economic systems and shared their political and ideological perceptions. In general, however, Turkish and American nations differed in many aspects such as culture, religion and democratic experience.[25] Nevertheless, this did not affect the general direction of Turkish-American relations though ideological differences caused some resentment against the United States among the Turkish nation.

e) Internal Reasons

States also enter into alliances in order to ensure domestic stability[26] and to cover failures in domestic politics. Obtaining political, economic and military support of a powerful and internationally respected alliance strengthens the government's position vis-a-vis its potential and actual enemies and increases its prestige in the eyes of the people. One motive of a small state in aligning with a great power might be to achieve an increase in its status internally and internationally by enjoying the great power's reputation.[27] Sometimes for a weak state to find a patron is to find a scapegoat that can be blamed for domestic failures.[28]

Turkish rulers saw their alliance with the West as an insurance of Turkey's political and democratic process and as a proof of Turkey's greatness as a "civilized" Western country. Economic and military aid of the West was one of their main sources of strength. When they faced economic and political crises at home, Turkish ruling elite looked at the West as their savior, expecting aid and statements supporting their regime. Economic failures and foreign policy failures, especially on the Cyprus question, were attributed to the West's negative attitude. Allegedly, in June 1964, Turkish Prime Minister İnönü sought U.S. disapproval for Turkish intervention in Cyprus in order to save his government's prestige by blaming the USA for non-intervention.[29]

f) Neutrality Option

Generally small states are advised not to enter into an alliance with a more powerful state because of possible grave dangers. Machiavelli wrote: "a prince ought never to make common cause with one more powerful than himself, unless necessity forces him to it." Egyptian leader Nasser rephrased the idea as follows: "an alliance between a big and small power is an alliance between the wolf and the sheep, and it is bound to end with the wolf

---

[24] See the section on U. S. and Turkish perceptions of the alliance in this chapter.

[25] In the words of former U.S. Ambassador to Greece, M. Stearns, "we shared [with Turkey] a security threat more than we shared political values, economic interests, or a common historical experience." Monteagle Stearns, *Entangled Allies: U.S. Policy Toward Greece, Turkey and Cyprus*, New York: Council on Foreign Relations Press, 1992, p. 21.

[26] Liska, *Alliances and the Third World*, p. 28.

[27] Ibid., p. 29, Handel, *Weak States in the International System*, p. 148.

[28] Handel, *Weak States in the International System*, p. 148.

[29] See the section on the Johnson letter in Chapter VI.

devouring the sheep."[30] However, to pursue neutrality and non-alignment a small state must meet certain criteria: it "must not be so potentially powerful as to threaten to shift the balance if incorporated by one side; the citizens of the small state must be willing to withdraw from world affairs...[;] the small state must be strategically irrelevant and politically non-provocative";[31] and it must not be under the threat of a great power.[32] Turkish politicians did not see non-alignment as a viable alternative because of the Soviet threat, Turkey's strategic importance and shortage of national resources.

2. FACTORS AFFECTING ALLIANCES

a) Costs-Benefits

An alliance relationship brings some costs and problems as well as benefits. States have to consider advantages and disadvantages of making an alliance with a state or a group of states before deciding to join it and subsequently they should from time to time reconsider their positions within this alliance in the light of recent developments. Haas defines an alliance as "a relationship in which a formal agreement specifies the rights and obligations of the members of alliance."[33] States aim to maximize their rights and to minimize their obligations when they join an alliance or, at least, they try to balance rights and obligations. If a state feels that the balance of costs and benefits within the alliance favors the other side, it seeks means to keep the balance or, as the last resort, it leaves the alliance.

The US-Turkish alliance was criticized by some Turkish politicians and scholars since they saw it as a one-sided alliance. The major Turkish opposition party and leftist radicals claimed that the USA benefited from the alliance much more than Turkey did. By the end of the 1960s, even leaders of the governmental party had been affected by this opinion. Public discussion on the costs and dangers of Turkey's alliance with the USA forced Turkish leaders to reconsider it and to take some initiatives to change the state of relations between the two countries.[34]

Some costs and dangers of an alliance, which were also mentioned by the Turkish critics of Turkey's alliance with the USA and NATO, are as follows:[35] The alliance may expose the state to the retaliation of a neighboring or remote great power by provoking her.[36] The small state, as the weakest link in the alliance, may become the preliminary target of an enemy attack.[37] It may face new and unexpected threats by small allies of the enemy power[38] and may become involved in the conflicts of the great power, for which it is unprepared, or which it might disapprove.[39] If there are bases of a great power on its territory, the small state might

---

[30] Rothstein, *Alliances and Small Powers*, p. 117.

[31] Ibid., p. 32.

[32] Ibid., p. 247, Handel, *Weak States in the International System*, p. 121.

[33] E. B. Haas, *Beyond the Nation-State*, Stanford: Stanford University Press, 1964, p. 13.

[34] See the section on Turkish efforts to gain more independence in its military relations with the USA in Chapter IV.

[35] For views of the Turks in this regard see the section on the NATO discussion in Turkish politics in Chapter IV.

[36] Rothstein, "On the Problems of Being Small and Poor", pp. 44, 48.

[37] Ibid., pp. 61-62, 120-121, 123.

[38] *Liska, Alliances and the Third World*, p. 28.

[39] Handel, *Weak States in the International System*, p. 129, Rothstein, "On the Problems of Being Small and Poor", p. 44.

find itself on the target list of another power.[40] The alliance might weaken the state's integrity by forcing it to dissipate its strength[41] and bring for it high defense budgets, increased costs of communications, and bigger military bureaucracy.[42] Finally, the alliance also might cause the state some loss of independence, status, prestige and influence.[43]

The reasons for alliance formation, which were mentioned above, constitute benefits of the alliance. Additionally, the alliance might help a state influence policies of its allies in a favorable direction and prevent allies from following adventurist policies.[44] A multilateral alliance seems to offer more benefits: it provides more deterrence and defense, a precise commitment, political and material support of more states, more bargaining, more compromise and thus more opportunity for the small state to advance its own views. The possibility that the alliance will become a tool of one great power is diminished. It may cost less in terms of external pressure and domestic discontent.[45] Although Turkey's military arrangements were mainly with the United States, Turkish rulers emphasized the multilateral character of NATO and made comparisons with the position of other members while defending Turkey's alliance with NATO. They argued that being a member of NATO provided the opportunity to influence U.S. policies and decreased the possibility of an U.S. armed action or intervention against Turkey.[46]

b) Goals of Members

Goals and interests of states in making an alliance affect their relations with their allies. Some scholars regard parallel interests, not necessarily common or identical ones, as one of the foundations of an alliance.[47] States with considerably different expectations from an alliance are less likely to be compatible alliance partners.[48] If the members of an alliance have limited clear and unambiguous purposes, their alliance becomes more durable and stable.[49]

Although, at the start, the United States and Turkey had a common interest, to block the expansion of Soviet influence, each tended to use the alliance for its own interests. The Turks believed that they were helping American national interests and therefore they had the right to expect from the Americans support for Turkish national interests even when those interests were outside the US-Turkish alliance.[50] The Turkish leadership considered the American actions, particularly in the Cyprus question, primarily in terms of Turkey's own interests, ignoring the American interests such as keeping good relations with Greece. On the other hand, the United States seemed not to accept that Turkey could have national interests outside

---

[40] Handel, *Weak States in the International System*, p. 129.
[41] Rothstein, "On the Problems of Being Small and Poor", p. 44.
[42] E. N. Botsas, "the U.S. Cyprus Turkey Greece Tetragon: the Economics of an Alliance", *Journal of Political and Military Sociology*, vol. 16, No. 2, Fall 1988, p. 252.
[43] Rothstein, "On the Problems of Being Small and Poor", pp. 47, 259.
[44] Ibid., pp. 49-50.
[45] Ibid., pp. 124-126, 260.
[46] The author's interview with former Turkish foreign ministers Ü. Haluk Bayülken and Osman Olcay, who drew attention to U.S. actions against certain other nations at various times.
[47] Olson et al. (eds.), *The Theory and Practice of International Relations*, pp. 220, 221, Rothstein, "On the Problems of Being Small and Poor", p. 56.
[48] Holsti et al., *Unity and Disintegration in International Alliances,* p. 23.
[49] Ibid., pp. 57, 263.
[50] Richard C. Campany, *Turkey and the United States*, New York: Praeger, 1986, pp. 80, 82.

the NATO alliance, which were not compatible with the U.S. global strategy[51] and that she could have another enemy apart from the Soviet Union.

c) Strength and Size of Members

In an alliance between a small state and a big power, differences are more likely to arise.[52] If the strength and size of two powers are markedly unequal, these powers usually face many problems in their alliance since their perception of world events and their purposes in the international arena are very different.[53] The weaker state naturally fears that its physical, political and cultural identity will be violated by its more powerful ally.[54] It is always suspicious that its big ally will use various means to increase its influence over it or that the larger state will try to intervene in its internal affairs and to penetrate its domestic politics. There is a general belief that big powers use alliance partnership to increase their influence on the members of the alliance since its allies are linked to the alliance in so many ways.[55] When the big power helps its smaller ally with a considerable amount of economic and military aid, the suspicion is always there that the smaller country becomes the client or satellite of the big power.[56] Some scholars, however, argue that in an alliance the bigger power does not necessarily gain all the advantages, but sometimes the lesser power has more influence on the bigger one in fulfilling its desires.[57] The stronger state may feel itself obliged to transfer wealth or other resources to the weaker and to prevent the weaker from collapse to maintain its prestige in the eyes of the enemy camp.[58]

The United States and Turkey are unequal powers in strength and size. The USA is the most powerful state in the world, whereas Turkey is a developing country, which needs external aid for its security and economy. At the same time, the Turks are very proud of their history, identity and potential capacity. They claim equal status with developed powers, including NATO members, and refuse to accept any foreign domination in their country.[59] Foreign influence and interference are always an important concern for the Turks, since they do not forget the memories of the old capitulations and Western influence on the Ottoman Empire. In the 1960s, the propaganda of the Turkish leftist radicals portrayed Turkey as a puppet of the United States and put this view across repeatedly to Turkish public opinion, particularly when the USA seemed to take a negative action in the Cyprus dispute. As a fact,

---

[51] Stearns, *Entangled Allies*, p. 16.

[52] In the theoretical analysis of relationships between powers, 'size' is often used as a synonym for strength, strong powers being described as 'big' and weak ones as 'small'.

[53] Henry A. Kissinger, *The Troubled Partnership*, New York: McGraw Hill, 1965, p. 226, Rothstein, *Alliances and Small Powers*, p. 57.

[54] Liska, *Nations in Alliance*, p. 13.

[55] Campany, *Turkey and the United States*, p. 7, Olson et al. (eds.), *The Theory and Practice of International Relations*, pp. 28, 222, Raymond Aron, "The Quest for a Philosophy of Foreign Affairs" in Stanley Hoffmann (ed.), *Contemporary Theory in International Relations*, Englewood Cliffs, N. J.: Prentice Hall Inc. 1960, p. 87, Rothstein, "On the Problems of Being Small and Poor", pp. 121-124.

[56] Harris, *Troubled Alliance*, p. 204.

[57] Ibid., p. 205, Campany, *Turkey and the United States*, p. 6, S. Hoffmann, "The Diplomatic-Strategic Chessboard" in Olson et al. (eds.), *The Theory and Practice of International Relations*, pp. 32-33, Handel, *Weak States in the International System*, pp. 129, 131.

[58] Rothstein, "On the Problems of Being Small and Poor", p. 120.

[59] Campany, *Turkey and the United States*, p. 81.

Turkish ability to influence the USA for its own interests stayed very weak, while the USA had a relatively free hand to affect Turkey in regional and international events.

It should also be noted that alliances are affected by domestic political structure and events of member countries. Domestic support for the alliance strengthens it considerably. The U.S.-Turkish alliance came under the influence of domestic political situations in both countries, especially on the Cyprus and opium questions.

d) Cohesion of Alliance

Partners of an alliance try to maintain the cohesion of the alliance as long as they benefit from it. The cohesion of the alliance is strengthened by the continuing external common threat and it is weakened by the reduction of the common threat.[60] Consultation, compromise and strong commitment are important factors in keeping cohesion of an alliance. In the case of an uncertain commitment, the great power might assume that the small has agreed to do whatever is in the interest of the strong whereas the small power's domestic politics may be consumed by a heated debate over the nature of its commitment to the great power, the latter's intention to help and the possibility of withdrawing the commitment.[61] Extensive consultations between two allies are likely to increase their solidarity and cohesion.[62] Big powers tend to wish to be consulted by their smaller allies if any important internal, regional or international events seem to have importance for the alliance.[63]

The cohesion of the Turkish-American alliance partly depended on the seriousness of the Soviet threat to Turkey and the Western camp. When the Soviet threat seemed reduced, Turkey and the USA pursued more independent policies outside their alliance. Lack of consultation between the two allies caused some problems. The Turkish authorities complained that the USA did not inform them about some American activities related to the American bases in Turkey, they also resented the unilateral withdrawal of American Jupiter missiles from Turkey. The United States criticized the Turkish leadership for their intention of landing in Cyprus without the knowledge of the USA.

Alliance cohesion also depends on the character of the international system. It declines as tension, conflict and potential threat are reduced in the international arena.[64] In a bipolar system, "the greater the inter-alliance conflict, the greater the intra-alliance cohesion; conversely, the greater the inter-alliance détente, the less the intra-alliance cohesion."[65] In the period of détente, smaller powers within alliances feel freer to improve their relations with states from the enemy camp.[66] Moreover, if the polarity of the international system is very tight, the cohesion of alliances in the two camps is stronger. When the polarity is reduced, cohesion decreases.[67] As long as more great powers emerge in the international arena, cohesion is reduced in favor of smaller powers.

---

[60] Ibid., pp. 5-6, Holsti et al., *Unity and Disintegration in International Alliances,* pp. 17, 88.
[61] Rothstein, "On the Problems of Being Small and Poor", p. 119.
[62] Campany, *Turkey and the United States,* p. 5, Holsti et al., *Unity and Disintegration in International Alliances,* p. 16.
[63] Liska, *Nations in Alliance,* p. 74.
[64] Holsti et al., *Unity and Disintegration in International Alliances,* p. 58.
[65] Ibid., p. 92.
[66] Ibid., p. 97.
[67] Ibid., p. 93.

The United States and Turkey had more cordial and close relations in the 1950s, when the East-West conflict was tenser. In the second half of the 1960s and at the beginning of the 1970s when détente was a more dominant tendency in the international system, Turkey felt that she could improve her relations with the Eastern bloc and Third World countries despite her alliance with the USA and NATO. The emergence of China and France as dissidents in the main power blocs emboldened Turkish authorities to pursue a more independent policy. At the same time, Turkey's importance seemed diminished in the eyes of Americans in the détente period, and the American administration became less anxious to continue aid to Turkey.

The Turkish-American alliance between 1959 and 1975 is a typical example of the bipolar world alliances. In the cold war period, in which the world was divided into two enemy camps, the state of the relationship between the superpowers affected the condition of the US-Turkish alliance. The model of the position of a smaller state within one of the ideological camps and management of intra-bloc problems by its super power is relevant. It is, however, necessary to look at the special internal and international conditions of the two countries such as geographical location, historical heritage, cultural and political identity, foreign policy making process, traditional state policy, effect of public opinion, etc.

3. THE U.S. AND TURKISH PERCEPTIONS OF THEIR ALLIANCE

a) The Turkish Perception

The Turks viewed their alliance with the United States in the light of their long-pursued efforts of Westernization, attributing a great importance to it in the way of becoming an integral part of the Western world. In their opinion, Turkey had to continue its alliance with America because this policy not only helped to fulfil her national interests, but more importantly it represented a relationship between two states which shared the same ideology and moral principles.[68] In his visit to Washington in June 1964 immediately after receiving President Johnson's disappointing letter, Turkish Prime Minister İnönü said, "we, the Turks, believe that friendship between states relies not on temporary interests but on common moral principles."[69] Turkish President Cevdet Sunay expressed his belief that close friendship and alliance between Turkey and the USA was a consequence of their shared moral principles and aims such as the love of freedom and democracy.[70] As an example of how far ideological thinking affected the minds of Turkish politicians, the speech of Turkish MP Gökhan Evliyaoğlu may be cited. In an atmosphere of great public criticism directed toward the Western states because of their attitudes on the Cyprus question, Evliyaoğlu claimed that

---

[68] It is ironic that as late as the spring of 1974, Turkey still had not joined the European bureau of the U.S. State Department but she remained the responsibility of State's Bureau of Near Eastern and South Asian Affairs. Stearns, *Entangled Allies*, p. 8.

[69] *Cumhuriyet*, 23 June 1964, p. 7.

[70] *Dışişleri Bakanlığı Belleteni*, April 1967, pp. 48, 49.

Turkey did not have the right to criticize the West because she failed to become a part of this world and to reach its level of democracy.[71]

This approach of Turkish politicians to the alliance with America led them to be too anxious to fulfil requirements of this alliance without any hesitation. At almost every opportunity, they proudly expressed their loyalty to the alliance.[72] But they felt badly let down when this loyalty did not appear to be reciprocated. In their eyes, for instance, Turkey was right in her policy toward the Cyprus question; therefore, she should have been supported by the Western states. The feeling of not getting enough in return for fulfilling alliance responsibilities really made the Turks angry.

b) The U.S. Perception

For the Americans, the Turkish-American relationship meant the protection of mutual economic and military interests rather than ideological closeness. In their eyes, both sides had to give something in order to get some gains, meaning that the alliance was a classic alliance relationship between two states, which aimed at maximizing their gains by establishing an alliance. This also meant restriction of independence of the two states to a reasonable extent. As former U.S. official Harris expressed it: "the virtually complete independence in terms of military and economic self-sufficiency that is often urged by Turkish critics of the United States is clearly impossible."[73] The American perception of the alliance did not include a romantic relationship forcing the two sides to support each other in every event regardless their practical national interests.

In their dealings with the Turks, the Americans expressed the importance of having the same ideological principles. As President Johnson said in his speech of welcome to Turkish President Sunay on 3 April 1967: "there is special close friendship between Turkey and the United States, which can be understood only by free people believing in a strong brotherhood relationship."[74] However, it was America's strategic interests in that part of the world that were of prime concern to the Americans.[75] The Americans did not oppose the undemocratic military regime in Turkey, which came to power on 27 May 1960; they extended recognition to it three days after the military coup and promised more economic and military aid. The most important thing for the Americans was Turkey's continuing membership in NATO and CENTO, helping the protection of Western interests in the Near and Middle East.

---

[71] *Millet Meclisi Tutanak Dergisi* (*MMTD*), term 1, sess. 3, vol. 30, p. 295.
[72] Prime Minister İ. İnönü, *MMTD*, term 1, sess. 2, vol. 16, pp. 570-571, İ. İnönü, ibid., term 3, sess. 1, vol. 2, p. 290, Foreign Minister F. C. Erkin, Cumhuriyet Senatosu Tutanak Dergisi (CSTD), term 1, sess. 4, vol. 24-3, p. 1017, the Turkish junta's announcement of loyalty to NATO and CENTO, *Cumhuriyet*, 27 May 1960, p. 1.
[73] Harris, *Troubled Alliance*, pp. 204-205.
[74] *Dışişleri Bakanlığı Belleteni*, April 1967, p. 47, *Amerika'da Onbir Gün*, pp. 15-16.
[75] Stearns, *Entangled Allies*, p. 21.

4. PATRON-CLIENT STATE RELATIONSHIP, DEPENDENCY AND INFLUENCE

a) Patron-Client State Relationship

To determine whether a patron-client relationship is the appropriate model for Turkish-American relations, it is first necessary to examine whether Turkey is a weak (small) state, which can easily be made a client. Characteristics of weak states are summarized by Handel as follows:[76] **Population**: Its population is very small. Turkey had a large population in comparison with the population of weak states. Standing at 36.16 million in 1973 it was larger than the population of many middle powers. **Area**: Its are is very small. Turkey's area, too, is relatively big. (780 thousand sq. km.) **Economy**: 1- Its GNP is small in absolute terms. Turkey's GNP per capita was very small even among weak states. (340 dollars in 1973) However, its total GNP was relatively high among weak states. (12.16 billion dollars in 1973.) 2- It has little or no heavy industry. Turkey generally lacked large heavy industry. Its crude steel production (1.312 thousand metric tons in 1971), energy production (11.01 million metric tons equiv. of coal), and energy consumption (18.65 metric tons equiv. of coal in 1971) were very low in comparison with middle and great powers. 3- It has high degree of specialization in a narrow range of products. Turkey largely exported agricultural products and specialized in a few industrial products such as textiles. 4- Its domestic market is small, hence it has high dependency on foreign markets for imports and exports. Turkey's domestic market was relatively large, but it was still dependent on exports and imports to strengthen its economy. Its dependence on "high-tech" technological products was considerable. 5- It has high dependence on foreign capital.

Military: 1- It cannot defend itself against external threats by its own strength; high or total dependence on external help. Turkey was not too weak to defend itself against small and middle regional powers but it needed US and NATO protection against the Soviet threat. 2- It is totally (or highly) dependent on weapon acquisition in foreign countries. Almost all Turkey's weaponry came from the West, especially from the USA. 3- It has a high proportion of strength always mobilized or at its disposal; longer-range war potential very low. Turkey kept a very big army but lacked modern weaponry.

The International System: 1- The scope of its interests limited (usually to neighboring and regional areas). 2- It has little or no influence on the balance of power (or the nature of the system). 3- It is mainly passive and reactive in foreign policy. 4- It tends to minimize risks, especially vis-a-vis the great powers. 5- It can be penetrated relatively easily. 6- It demonstrates strong support for international law and norms of international organizations. Turkey had regional interests rather than global ones, but it had the potential to influence big power relations because of its strategic importance. It continued to be a member of NATO in spite of the displeasure of the other superpower, but it tried not to provoke the Soviet Union

---

[76] Handel, *Weak States in the International System*, pp. 52-53. See also ibid., pp. 36, 41-45, Rothstein, "On the Problems of Being Small and Poor", p. 29. The information in paragraph 2.5.1 is based on the 1973 figures. It should be noted that Turkey's situation is not static and there have been dramatic changes in some of the characteristics since World War II. Handel divides states into four categories; great, middle, weak (including Turkey), and mini; and gives figures on the military and economic capabilities of states. Handel, *Weak States in the International System*, pp. 15-17, 25-26, 32-35, 49.

especially in the 1960s and 1970s. Turkey allowed the stationing of U.S. experts on its territory, but it is hard to prove that it was deeply penetrated. Turkish leaders always announced support for international law and international organizations, but they did not hesitate to criticize them when they seemed to be unfair in dealing with Turkish interests.

As a conclusion it might be said that Turkey could be considered a small power especially in comparison with European middle powers. But its level among small states should be very high. Holbraad put Turkey's place as the eighth-strongest small state of Europe though it qualified as a middle power among Asian states according to his criteria.[77] Handel mentioned that Annette Baker Fox called Turkey a small state but Vital, Barston and Kuznets did not even consider it as a member of this category because it had a population of over 30 million. In Handel's opinion, Turkey quite clearly fell short of the middle powers in terms of her overall capabilities.[78]

Characteristics of the patron-client state relationship, which are mentioned by scholars, are as follows:[79] 1- There must be a sizeable difference between the military capabilities of the two states. The bargaining power of the patron is greater than that of the client because of the resources it has. 2- The client plays an important role in patron (superpower) competition. Its position is determined by the availability of other patrons who can render the client the same protection and material support, the mobility of the clients between alternative patrons and the degree to which the patron is dependent on the client's services. 3- The patron and the client are closely tied to each other for a recognizable period of time. In almost every issue, the client follows the patron's lead either to get immediate positive rewards or to accumulate goodwill and credit for the future. Sometimes it is asked to do so, more frequently the client knows what is expected of it by the patron and adjusts its policy accordingly. In the patron-client relationship, coercion, manipulation and authority exist implicitly in the background, but they are not always necessarily dominant. 4- Security transactions from the patron to the client are more prominent in the relationship. At a low level of threat to the client, other goals such as economic development, regional leadership, and international prestige may gain importance. Arms transfers are powerful tools of influence for the patron. 5- Elite of the client state absorbs the patron's perceptions of the world through foreign or domestic education. 6- The patron's goals in continuing the relationship are more complicated: ideological goals (demands for changes in the client's political, economic and social structure), international solidarity (voting cohesion in the United Nations, signing of international agreements, visits between senior statesmen, client announcements of support for the patron), strategic goals (demands for bases).

1- Military capabilities of the United States were clearly much greater than those of Turkey. Since the USA was the main military and economic aid supplier of Turkey, she had more bargaining power. However, Turkey's strategic importance gave its rulers the capability to affect U.S. decisions in some issues. (The U.S. unwillingness to take forceful action against Turkey on the Cyprus question can be cited as an example.) 2- Turkey played quite an important role in superpower competition with its geographical location controlling vital

---

[77] Carsten Holbraad, *Middle Powers in International Politics*, London: Macmillan Press, 1984, pp. 85-86, 89.

[78] Handel, *Weak States in the International System*, pp. 31-33.

[79] Christopher C. Shoemaker and J. Spanier, *Patron-Client State Relationships*, New York: Praeger, 1984, pp. 13-15, 18-22, Handel, *Weak States in the International System*, pp. 132-137, Bruce E. Moon, "Consensus or Compliance? Foreign Policy Change and External Dependence", *International Organisation*, vol. 39, No. 2, Spring 1985, pp. 308-309.

outlets of the Soviet Union. The United States attributed importance to keeping Turkey in the Western camp. Western European powers were potentially alternative of patrons for Turkey's security and economy, but Turkish rulers believed that they could not get from anywhere else the protection and material support which they obtained from the USA. U.S. officials, too, did not consider leaving Turkey, believing that Turkey's services for the USA were important. This situation practically decreased the mobility of both sides between different alternatives. 3- Turkey and the United States were closely tied to each other between 1947 and 1975 though this closeness was more dominant in the 1950s. Especially in the 1950s and in the first half of the 1960s, Turkey closely followed the lead of the USA in the international arena though the USA did not always demand her support. Turkish leaders proudly acted in this way, seeing it as a requirement of the Western alliance. From 1965, they acted more independently, taking some actions against the U.S. stance (supporting the Arabs in the Arab-Israeli conflict is one example). The United States did not use direct pressures against Turkish rulers. The Johnson letter in 1964, which forced the Turks not to intervene in Cyprus, and the U.S. Congress's decision to impose an arms embargo on Turkey were exceptions in this regard and they caused a deterioration in the two countries' relations. Indirect U.S. pressures forced Turkish rulers to prohibit opium cultivation in 1971, but three years later the Ecevit government reversed the decision in spite of strong U.S. protests.

4- U.S. military assistance to Turkey was prominent in their relationship. The Turks valued it very highly, but in the détente period, they paid more attention to economic development and accepted the aid of the Soviet Union for this purpose. They even risked the loss of U.S. aid with their policies on Cyprus and opium. The U.S. Congress tried to influence Turkish policies by using the leverage of military and economic assistance (the U.S. administration generally opposed the Congress pressures but in some cases such as opium they were privately happy about it), but it was not able to change Turkish attitudes dramatically. 5- The Turkish elite had the same perceptions of the world with U.S. rulers through foreign and mostly domestic education but they always announced that it was their choice to adopt Western values. 6- The United States obviously wanted Turkey to adopt a democratic system, capitalist economy and Western social structure. But it is hard to claim that U.S. officials forced the Turks in this regard because Turkish rulers themselves chose this way when they established their republic in 1923. U.S. rulers generally asked for Turkey's support when they faced international crises, but this was not directed to achieving a continuous show of international solidarity. The Turks themselves chose to vote with the USA in the United Nations, felt pleasure with the visits of U.S. statesmen and the U.S. Sixth Fleet and frequently announced support for the USA in international crises. The Turks were also happy with the U.S. use of bases on their territory. When Turkey voted with Third World countries on the Arab-Israeli conflict and colonial issues and when the reduction of U.S. Sixth Fleet visits to Turkish ports were demanded because of public demonstrations, the United States did not protest against Turkey.

As a conclusion, it might be said that the U.S.-Turkish relationship bore some characteristics of the patron-client relationship, but this was not enough to fit this categorization. Especially after 1965, it cannot be said that Turkey followed U.S. policy step by step. Nevertheless, the United States was generally happy with the Turkish government's general attitude until July 1975 when the functioning of U.S. bases in Turkey was halted.

b) Dependency Theories

Dependency theories are mainly related to economic aspects of the patron-client state relationship. General characteristics of dependent countries are explained by scholars as follows:[80] The internal market of the dependent country is internationalized and its economy is incorporated into the global capitalist system. A large share of needs are supplied externally, a large share of markets are foreign and the ratio of foreign to domestic capital, technology, production facilities, etc. is high. Development of the economy is conditioned by the development and expansion of another economy and by the attitude of multinational corporations. Domestic firms buy their equipment and other capital goods from outside. The national bourgeoisie are not completely abandoned by external powers, but it is not given a full opportunity to develop. There is an alliance between local and international capital and the state, derived from mutual interests. In fact, the flows of trade and investment invoke the interests of the elite more than the masses. The dependent state is specialized in the export of a few products and its export is heavily reliant upon few trading partners. Internally, the following factors are prominent: lack of integration across economic sectors, shortage of large-scale industry based on mass-production, little investment in research and development, lack of responsiveness of production structures to increased or decreased demand, etc.

In a global world, in which all national economies are dependent on each other, it is hard to find out which economy is dependent on which other economy. However, it should be noted that Turkey's situation generally fitted the characteristics of developing states' economies, which are largely dependent on and under the influence of developed countries and multinational corporations. The United States was surely one of the major powers which affected the situation of world economies and which owned giant multinational corporations. It is obvious that U.S. rulers would try to maximize their economic gains and would care about interests of U.S. firms in their dealings with Turkey. However, it is hard to claim that the Turkish economy was totally dependent on the United States because Turkey also had important economic contacts with other Western powers, Middle Eastern and Eastern bloc countries and international organizations such as the IMF and the World Bank. It is also a fact that U.S. economic assistance to Turkey dramatically decreased at the end of the 1960s and in the first half of the 1970s whereas Turkey became the recipient of the largest economic assistance of the USSR outside Eastern bloc countries in the same period. To study complicated economic relations between countries and to reach a conclusion is beyond the scope of this thesis.

Some scholars' studies are directed to finding a correlation between the U.S. aid allocations to developing states and voting agreements of these states with the United States in the United Nations.[81] Witkoff, Richardson and Moon concluded that UN voting patterns of nations that were linked to the USA through substantial trade or aid were likely to resemble

---

[80] Peter Evans, *Dependent Development*, Princeton: Princeton University Press, 1979, pp. 26, 28, 31-32, 34-43, James A. Caporaso, "Dependence, Dependency, and Power in the Global System: A Structural and Behavioral Analysis", *International Organisation*, vol. 32, No. 1, Winter 1978, pp. 25-26, Neil R. Richardson, "Political Compliance and U.S. Trade Dominance", the American Political Science Review, vol. 70, No. 4, December 1976, pp. 1099, 1100n, 1102, Handel, *Weak States in the International System*, pp. 228-229, Moon, "Consensus or Compliance?...", pp. 306, 308.

[81] Eugene R. Witkoff, "Foreign Aid and United Nations Votes: A Comparative Study", *The American Political Science Review*, vol. 67, No. 3, September 1973, pp. 868-888, Richardson, "Political Compliance and U.S. Trade Dominance", pp. 1098-1109, Moon, "Consensus or Compliance?...", pp. 297-329.

the voting of the USA, especially on cold war issues. Witkoff's study shows that Turkey's General Assembly roll-call relative agreement scores with the United States in 1963 were the highest among the UN members while its score in 1967 was still high, but they came fifteenth.[82] At the 15th session of the UN (1961), Turkey's voting coincidence with the USA was 75.1 percent of the total votes cast (109 of 145); in the 16th session this figure rose to 80.8 percent (101 of 125): (in cold war issues 33 of 37 in the 15th session, 20 of 22 in the 16th session; in issues of disarmament 7 of 8 and 28 of 34; in issues of colonialism 28 of 38 and 31 of 38; in the Arab-Israeli conflict 3 of 8 and 8 of 9.)[83] In 1967, in the fifth special, fifth emergency special and twenty-second sessions of the UN Turkey's voting coincidence with the USA was 30 out of 65 (in the Arab-Israeli conflict 3 of 15, in colonial issues 1 of 17, in cold war issues 19 of 19, in disarmament issues 5 of 5.)[84]

c) Influence

In his book, Couloumbis put forward some propositions of influence that could be applied to the U.S.-Turkish relationship:[85] 1- Potential influence increases as elite in A perceive a greater need to influence and elite in B perceive a need to accept A's influence. (After the World War II the USA came to the position of influencing other states as a result of its global policy. As proud and obstinate people the Turks were frequently resistant to influence.) 2- The greater the convergence of ideological orientations and the greater the coincidence of threat perceptions among the elite in A and B, the greater the receptivity of A's influence by B. (Ideological closeness with Western powers made Turkish elite more receptive to U.S. influence especially in the 1950s. The Soviet threat gave more leverage to the USA to influence Turkish elite.) 3- The potential of A's influence in B is modified by A and B leaders' personalities and mentalities. (Johnson was more interventionist. Bülent Ecevit seemed less receptive to U.S. influence.) 4- The greater the dependency of B upon A for its economic stability and growth, the greater the potential of influence of A upon B. (Turkey's economic problems increased its receptivity to U.S. influence.) 5- The greater the dependency of B upon A for sophisticated weaponry, the greater the potential for A's influence over B. (This was very much case for Turkey.) 6- The greater the dependency of B on any actors other than A for the importation of vital energy sources, the less the potential for A's influence over B. (After 1973, Turkey pursued more pro-Arab policies outside the U.S. influence because of its dependence on oil.)

7- High-quality diplomatic services maximize capability to transform potential influence into actual influence. (Turkish diplomacy's quality decreased the U.S. influence, especially on the Cyprus question.)[86] 8- A's potential of influence in B increases when B is ruled by military regimes. (Turkish military regimes were more responsive to U.S. requests as it was seen in the opium question. Anti-American leftist opposition was silenced during the military-backed governments.) 9- The potential influence of A over B is proportional to the degree of internal cohesiveness and foreign policy consensus within B. (Public consensus on the Cyprus

[82] Witkoff, "Foreign Aid and United Nations Votes...", pp. 879-880.

[83] *Middle East Record*, vol. 2, 1961, pp. 4, 7-13.

[84] *Middle East Record*, vol. 3, 1967, pp. 91-103.

[85] Theodore A. Couloumbis, *The United States, Greece and Turkey*, New York: Praeger, 1983, pp. 171-195. A stands for the USA and B for Turkey in the following explanations.

[86] The author's interview with former Turkish foreign minister Ü. Haluk Bayülken.

question decreased Turkey's responsiveness to U.S. influence on the matter.) 10- A's potential influence in B is proportional to benign public attitudes in B regarding the image and reputation of A. (Turkish public anger against the USA on the Cyprus question decreased the U.S. leverage to influence Turkey.) 11- Perception in A with respect to the importance of the strategic location of B relate to the degree of influence A wishes to exert in B. (The USA did not put heavy pressure on Turkey after the Turkish intervention in Cyprus partly because of Turkey's strategic importance for it.) 12- A's influence over B is proportional to the number of powerful states and the level of tension in the international arena. (In the 1950s, Turkey was more receptive to U.S. influence than in the détente years.)

It would be wrong to say that Turkey was under the constant influence of the United States in the 1960-1975 period because this influence varied in accordance with the factors mentioned above. It might be generally said that U.S. influence in Turkey in the late 1940s was significant, but it gradually decreased until 1974.

5. THE EXAMPLES OF U.S. INFLUENCE ON TURKEY

Many Turkish scholars and politicians believed that, since the Truman Doctrine of 1947, Turkish foreign policy had been totally dependent on American policy-makers' desires and decisions. In their eyes, especially in the 1950s, Turkey seemed to have no foreign policy interests outside its alliance with the West and it just followed her Western allies' decisions and actions. Feroz Ahmad claims that "throughout the fifties, Ankara pursued the foreign policy objectives set in Washington or London with conviction and without complaint."[87] Ferenc A. Vali explains that the Turks threw themselves into the arms of their rich friend, the USA, and tied themselves to the USA in many ways by signing bilateral agreements. In his opinion, "Turkey seemed to feel that... what the United States wanted should not be questioned."[88] Gönlübol makes his accusation much sharper: "Turkey found itself following the policies of the United States almost step by step both within and outside NATO, thus reducing herself to the position of a satellite."[89] Ahmet Ş. Esmer summarizes Turkish foreign policy in the 1950s as follows:

> [After joining NATO and being an ally of America] we signed numerous bilateral agreements with the United States and left our business in her hands. Our military is under the command of NATO, our bases are in the hands of the Americans, our security is dependent on America, and our economic development is dependent on American aid. We saw it as our duty to support France, America and Britain in their dealings with the Algerian, Vietnam and Suez problems. We also felt it our responsibility to defend Western colonialism in the Bandung Conference of non-aligned countries. In the United Nations votings, we look at the arm of American representative. We do not have the initiative in foreign policy.[90]

The United States was accused by Turkish critics of penetrating into every sector of Turkish life by using its economic and military aid, by providing American education to thousands of Turks and also by inserting a lot of U.S. experts into the Turkish military and

---

[87] Feroz Ahmad, *The Turkish Experiment in Democracy*, London: The Royal Institute of International Affairs, 1977, p. 395.
[88] Ferenc A. Vali, *Bridge Across the Bosporus*, Baltimore: the John Hopkins Press, 1971, pp. 356, 38, 71, 116.
[89] Gönlübol, "NATO, USA and Turkey", p. 22.
[90] Ahmet Ş. Esmer, "Uyduluk Siyasetine Son", *Milliyet*, 24 December 1965.

civil service.[91] American Peace Corps volunteers, university lecturers and any kind of U.S. experts were regarded by leftists as U.S. agents collecting secret information on Turkey and influencing ruling elite. While describing U.S. control, Turkish Labor Party leader Mehmet Ali Aybar said: "Like God, America's eyes, ears and hands are everywhere in Turkey."[92]

While the criticism of some authors reflected more or less the truth, accusations of leftists were much more exaggerated propaganda aiming at attracting the public's attention to their movement.

a) Economic Dependence

Turkish critics put forward the following claims on Turkey's economic dependence on the USA: American economic aid to Turkey was used mostly by pro-American Turkish economic elite, multinational and American companies to strengthen their position and helped them to exploit Turkey's economic resources and to control the Turkish economy. This was the Americans' intention as well.[93] The Turkish economy fell wholly under the influence of the American economy with American aid and foreign investment. American economic elite used Turkey's raw materials and labor force for their own interests and deliberately tried to prevent the development of the Turkish economy.[94] The consortium which was established by several countries to supply economic aid to Turkey[95] and the American aid agency, AID,[96] used their power to control and direct the Turkish economy and to intervene in Turkey's domestic politics. The United States used its aid to Turkey as a means of pressure to force Turkey to fulfil some American demands as was seen in the Cyprus and opium questions.[97]

b) The U.S. Intervention in Turkish Politics

Some Turkish politicians and intellectuals, especially leftist ones, believed that the United States intervened in Turkey's internal politics by supporting rightist parties against leftist groups. The Republican People's Party leaders opposed the U.S. aid to Turkey in 1958[98] and the U.S.-Turkish agreement in 1959 because they suspected that the USA was trying to save the Democrats from falling from power.[99] When the American Acheson plan on the Cyprus question was rejected by the Turkish government in August 1964, some rumors erupted in Turkey, claiming that the United States was looking for another prime minister in

---

[91] Jacob M. Landau, *Radical Politics in Modern Turkey*, Leiden: E. J. Brill, 1974, pp. 80-82.

[92] "Dış Politikamız Nasıl Olmalıdır?", interview by Y. Çetiner, *Cumhuriyet*, 17 October 1964.

[93] In *Cumhuriyet*: İ. Selçuk, "2000 Yılına Kadar", 9 August 1965, p. 2, "Bayramlık", 12 April 1965, p. 2, "Manzara-i Umumiye", 7 January 1966, p. 2.

[94] İ. Selçuk, "NATO'ya Göbeğimizden Bağlıyız", *Cumhuriyet*, 5 November 1967, p. 2, R. Özarda, *MMTD*, 29 April 1969, term 2, sess. 4, vol. 36, p. 105, B. Boran, *Türkiye ve Sosyalizm Sorunları*, İstanbul: Tekin Yayınevi, 1970, p. 267, A. Kabaklı, "Faydası Ne?", *Tercüman*, 30 August 1964.

[95] İ. Selçuk, "Manzara-i Umumiye", *Cumhuriyet*, 7 January 1966, p. 2.

[96] T. Z. Ekinci and S. Aren, *MMTD*, 1 March 1968, term 2, sess. 3, vol. 27, p. 29, ibid., 4 March 1968, p. 158, R. Özarda, ibid., 29 April 1969, term 2, sess. 9, vol. 36, p. 104.

[97] For the author's opinion on the subject see the section on dependency theories in this chapter.

[98] *Keesing's Contemporary Archives*, 1959-1960, vol. 12, p. 16636.

[99] Harris, *Troubled Alliance*, pp. 69, 81, 83. It should be noted that some Democrat Party politicians subsequently claimed that the USA wanted the DP to fall in 1960.

Turkey, who would accept American plans rejected by Prime Minister İnönü.[100] Metin Toker, İsmet İnönü's son-in-law, claimed that, in August 1964, President Johnson sent General Porter to Turkey for this purpose. He reasoned that the CIA was aware of a radical change in Turkey's foreign policy and was trying to prevent it.[101] In January 1965, İnönü denied the rumors by saying: "I myself do not worry about it. America has given definite assurances in this subject."[102] However, the visit of U.S. Ambassador Raymond Hare to the opposition leaders just before the parliamentary vote on 13 February 1965, which brought down the İnönü government, caused the accusation that he was giving orders to the leader of the Justice Party, Süleyman Demirel, to topple the government.[103] İnönü denied the claims again in his speech in Parliament on 1 March 1965: "I will not agree that a shadow be cast on an honest and serious person because of a bad coincidence. In sum, at the time we relinquished our official duties we were in complete and mutual confidence with the American government and its ambassador."[104] Ambassador Hare told Turkish journalists: "As decided a long time ago, I paid ceremonial visits to the leaders of the two opposition parties. At the same time, an unexpected political crisis came about in Turkey. There is no relation between the two events apart from chronological coincidence. We, the Americans, who have interest in Turkey's development pursue, the policy of keeping ourselves away from Turkey's internal politics. Internal politics is your business, not ours."[105]

After the Justice Party (JP) came to power in the elections of 1965, the left accused it of having received American support during the election campaigns and claimed that America financially supported rightist groups against leftist ones and always wanted a rightist government in Turkey.[106] Republican MP Bülent Ecevit told his party's parliamentary caucus in June 1966 that America acted as if it was the ally of the JP, not Turkey, and that big American companies worked like partners of the JP.[107] He mentioned the CIA's activities in other countries, hinting that it could do same thing in Turkey:

> In America it has been disclosed with what dirty games the CIA is involved affecting domestic politics in friendly and allied countries. It pours money into elections in order to bring those it wants into power and to unseat those it does not want... In order to prepare a pretext for smashing legal and democratic opposition, it has claimed that there was a great communist danger; or else in order to prepare justification for armed American intervention it has claimed that there was a danger of unarmed and indirect aggression and has organized demonstrations, sabotage and civil war.[108]

---

[100] A. Kabaklı, "Zararlı Faaliyetler", *Tercüman*, 29 August 1964, "Başyazı", *Forum*, 1 September 1964, p. 3.

[101] M. Toker, "İsmet Paşa ile 4 Buhranlı Yıl", *Milliyet*, 11 February 1969, p. 5. See also A. Haluk Ulman and R. H. Dekmejian, "Changing Patterns in Turkey's Foreign Policy, 1959-1967", *ORBIS*, vol. 11, Fall 1967, p. 782.

[102] *Milliyet*, 8 January 1965.

[103] D. Avcıoğlu, "Asıl Muhalefet şimdi Başlıyor", *Yön*, 19 February 1965, p. 3.

[104] Harris, *Troubled Alliance*, p. 132.

[105] *Cumhuriyet*, 24 February 1965, p. 1, *Milliyet*, 10 August 1965.

[106] İ. Selçuk, "Hayallerden Silkinmek", *Cumhuriyet*, 22 June 1966, p. 2, İ. Selçuk, "Bir İki, Üç Dört, Üstünü Ört", ibid., 17 December 1968, p. 2, Harris, *Troubled Alliance*, pp. 136-137. Fahir Armaoğlu, retired Turkish academic and columnist, told the author that in the cold war period the United States always supported rightist rules, democratic or dictatorial. He argued that Turkey was not an exception in this regard and that the JP enjoyed the American support. Armaoğlu further claimed that the USA affected Turkish politics through different methods and that this was the fate of small countries.

[107] *Cumhuriyet*, 21 June 1966, p. 7.

[108] Translated by Harris, *Troubled Alliance*, p. 136.

By mentioning the big increase in the number of rightist organizations, newspapers and magazines Ecevit hinted that their financial support had come from America.[109]

National Unionist Senator Haydar Tunçkanat claimed that he found a document consisting of correspondence between Turkish and American officials on preventing the increase of the left's power and supporting pro-American Turkish groups.[110] Turkish Labor Party MP Behice Boran wrote in her book that ruling elite and the United States had made every kind of effort to prevent the success of the Turkish socialist movement and its party.[111]

When U.S. Ambassador Parker Hart claimed in January 1966 that the United States never prevented the planned Turkish military intervention in Cyprus[112] while a heated debate was going on between rival Turkish political groups on whether the government should explain the content of the Johnson letter of June 1964; the opposition groups attacked Hart, accusing him of joining an internal Turkish political debate on the side of the governmental party and acting like a high commissioner or prime minister of Turkey.[113] Some Turkish critics believed that the United States played a part in the Turkish military coup by memorandum on 12 March 1971.[114]

These unproven claims cannot be taken as facts since they were made by biased anti-American critics. Some of these critics such as Bülent Ecevit denied any foreign intervention in Turkish politics when they were in power. The only thing which can be said is that the United States wanted rightists to come into power in Turkey as she did in other countries because anti-Communist rightists were more likely to pursue policies which would be compatible with U.S. interests. This does not necessitate direct U.S. intervention.

c) The Recognition of China

Some Turkish critics claimed that Turkish rulers did not recognize communist China until 1971 merely to please their American friends though the Americans did not put forward any open demand and did not force the Turkish government on this matter to act in a certain way. It was argued that Turkey's recognition of communist China would not be a radical one because some other NATO members such as Britain had already recognized China and it would bring trade benefits.[115] In August 1971, Turkey suddenly decided to extend its official recognition to China after the American rulers initiated some actions to restore normal relations with the Chinese.[116] There was a speculation that the USA influenced the decision by putting pressure on Turkish rulers. Turkish Deputy Prime Minister Sadi Koçaş denied it:

---

[109] *Cumhuriyet*, 21 June 1966, p. 7.

[110] *Cumhuriyet*, 11 July 1966, p. 1, Ulman and Dekmejian, "Changing Patterns in Turkey's Foreign Policy, 1959-1967", p. 782.

[111] Boran, *Türkiye ve Sosyalizm Sorunları*, p. 211.

[112] *Dışişleri Bakanlığı Belleteni*, January 1966, pp. 37-38.

[113] In *Cumhuriyet*: E. Güresin, "Amerika'nın Esef Verici Tutumu", 5 January 1966, p. 1, İ. Selçuk, "Amerikan Elçisine Açık Mektup", 6 January 1966, p. 2; "Amerikan Elçisinin Siyasi Komiser Edası", Forum, 15 January 1966, p. 6; H. Uysal, "Tehlikeli Alakalar", *Akis*, 15 January 1966, p. 5.

[114] See the section on U.S. efforts to eradicate Turkey's opium production in Chapter VIII.

[115] *MMTD*, 20.2.1968, term 2, sess. 3, vol. 25, p. 469, İ. Çamlı, "Yanlış Kavramlar ve Kalıplaşmış Yargılar", *Cumhuriyet*, 17 April 1971, p. 2.

[116] *Keesing's Contemporary Archives*, 1971-1972, vol. 18, p. 24794.

"Our decision was taken strictly in the light of Turkish interests. No foreign country influenced or advised us while taking this decision."[117]

As Turkey's voting patterns in the United Nations showed, Turkey always followed the U.S. lead in cold-war matters even in the periods when it was not on good terms with it. The recognition of China by Turkey was one of the examples, which fitted this trend. Turkish leaders waited until the U.S. initiative gave them the green light to extend recognition to a communist regime in a country where nationalist forces also claimed to represent the state. It is a classic example of the Turkish lack of confidence in communist rulers. While they had some problems with the United States on some of their national interests, Turkish rulers did not want to fall in disagreement with the Americans in cold-war issues as well, which did not directly affect Turkish interests. The removal from İnönü's letter to Johnson in 1964 of the part criticizing the U.S. policy in Vietnam[118] strengthens this observation. Therefore, it might be said that Turkey wanted to please the United States with its policy on the recognition of China, but its action cannot be presented only as an example of U.S. influence.

d) The Komer Event

The appointment of Robert Komer as the American ambassador to Turkey at the end of 1968 was an event that was been frequently cited as an example of Turkey's dependence on the USA and of the American dominance to the point where they felt no need to consider Turkish sensitivities. The appointment was strongly criticized by Turkish leftist groups on the ground that Komer, who had been involved in the American pacification program in Vietnam, was sent to Turkey to break the power of the leftist movement. They claimed that Washington considered Turkey its backyard like Vietnam and, therefore, it did not hesitate to appoint an ex-CIA agent as ambassador to Turkey. Some other Turkish critics argued that sending an ex-CIA agent to Turkey at a time when anti-Americanism was rife among Turkish people was a mistake. They were of the opinion that it would cause the humiliation of the Turkish government and the deterioration of U.S.-Turkish relations. When Komer visited on 9 January 1969 the Middle Eastern Technical University in Ankara, which was established with American financial aid, leftist students strongly protested against his visit and set fire to his car.[119] President Nixon's decision to replace Komer with William Handley in April 1969 was considered a response to the campaign of leftist groups. But it is more likely that the American action was actually aimed at easing the position of the Turkish government against public criticism.

The Komer event seems a propaganda action of leftists to stimulate public antagonism toward the United States. It is hard to expect the U.S. and Turkish governments to listen to demands of a small minority in such a matter. Since most diplomats are involved in intelligence matters somehow, being a member of the CIA could scarcely be an excuse to reject ambassadors. Therefore, the U.S. insistence on sending Komer cannot be seen as an act of U.S. influence. If the Turkish government had wanted the withdrawal of Komer's

---

[117] *Cumhuriyet*, 7 August 1971, p. 1, Ahmad, Ahmad, *The Turkish Experiment in Democracy*, p. 429n.

[118] The author's interview with former Turkish foreign minister Ü. Haluk Bayülken. The incident will be mentioned in the section on the Johnson letter in Chapter VI.

[119] Mehmet Ali Birand et al., *12 Mart*, Ankara: İmge Kitabevi, 1994, pp. 151-152.

appointment after public leftist protests on the subject, it would have seemed yielding to far leftists' pressures.

6. THE REJECTION OF U.S. INFLUENCE ACCUSATIONS

Regardless of their political orientation, leftist or rightist, all Turkish authorities rejected the claim that Turkey was a satellite of the United States. Their denials were so frequent that one can easily ask why Turkish officials needed so many denials; these denials had the effect of increasing the suspicions of Turkey's dependence on America.[120] In his press conference in August 1962, Bülent Ecevit, who was then the minister of labor, firmly criticized actions of American trade unionist M. Thalmayer, who came to Turkey to support Turkish workers in their struggle against American companies. Ecevit said: "some people try to present the flow of foreign capital from our friendly allies to our country as colonialism or imperialism. Mr. Thalmayer seems to lead this propaganda campaign against an imaginary American colonialism... No Turkish government allows the foreign capital to turn into a form of colonialism."[121]

Some American politicians joined the defense of Turkey's independence in order to give the impression that the United States did not intend to violate Turkey's sovereignty for the sake of its own interests. At the dinner welcoming Turkish President Cevdet Sunay on 3 April 1967, U.S. Secretary of State Dean Rusk said that Turkey and the United States were not allies who merely followed one another, but they were close friends and allies who independently tried to protect their national interests.[122] Ambassador Komer told Turkish daily *Milliyet*'s correspondent that the claim of Turkey's dependence on America was a myth made up by leftist propagandists. He claimed that in comparison with Turkey's position in the aftermath of the Second World War, the Turkey of 1969 was much more independent, much stronger and less dependent on others' help.[123] A high-ranking American officer in NATO in Paris said that Turkey acted independently within NATO by giving the example that Turkey rejected the implementation of NATO's Orient Express operation on its territory.[124] The apparent reason for the Turkish rejection was to avoid annoying the Middle Eastern countries at a time when some important events took place in the region.

---

[120] Prime Minister Demirel's press conference, *Dışişleri Bakanlığı Belleteni*, November 1966, pp. 73, 75-76; Foreign Minister Çağlayangil's speech in Parliament, *MMTD*, term 2, sess. 2, vol. 11, p. 127; Deputy Foreign Minister Faruk Sükan's speech in Parliament, *Cumhuriyet Senatosu Tutanak Dergisi (CSTD)*, term 1, sess. 6, vol. 42, p. 21; President Cevdet Sunay's Victory Day speech, *Cumhuriyet*, 31 August 1968, p. 7; Foreign Minister Osman Olcay's speech in a private dinner, ibid., 28 May 1971, p. 7.

[121] *Cumhuriyet*, 27 August 1962, p. 5.

[122] *Dışişleri Bakanlığı Belleteni*, April 1967, p. 50, *Amerika'da Onbir Gün*, p. 10.

[123] *Milliyet*, 18 April 1969.

[124] *Cumhuriyet*, 26 November 1968, p. 7.

Chapter 3

FOREIGN POLICY FORMATION IN TURKEY AND THE USA

This chapter analyses the structure and determinants of Turkish and U.S. foreign policies between 1960 and 1975 in order to help the reader assess correctly events of the two countries' relations, which will be mentioned in the following chapters. It provides necessary information about factors and the formal framework that affected opinions, decisions and actions of policy-makers on both sides. It tries to illuminate the internal and international atmosphere in which relations of the two countries took place. In order to achieve this, it mentions a number of preoccupation of each country that were not of primary concern to the other but nevertheless influenced the background against which their mutual relationships were conducted (for example the Vietnam war which was of enormous importance to the USA but not to Turkey).

1. DETERMINANTS OF TURKISH FOREIGN POLICY

a) Independence and Security

The most important goal of Turkish foreign policy is to preserve Turkey's national independence and sovereignty and its territorial integrity.[1] The Turks attribute much more importance to these aspects than other nations generally do because they believe that their loss or limitation during the last centuries of the Ottoman Empire caused great damage to Turkish national interests. They know that economic, judicial and political privileges granted by the Ottoman Empire to foreigners greatly limited the independence of the empire and damaged its economic life. They are also aware that foreign countries accelerated the collapse of the empire by intervening in its internal affairs in the name of protecting ethnic and religious minorities. Especially in the first two and half decades of the new Turkish Republic, in order to ensure genuine independence and sovereignty, Turkish leaders were reluctant to

---

[1] Ferenc A. Vali, *Bridge Across the Bosporus*, Baltimore, London: John Hopkins Press, 1971, p. 69, James E. Sowerwine , *Dynamics of Decision Making in Turkish Foreign Policy*, Ph.D. Thesis, University of Wisconsin, Madison, 1987, p. 14.

enter into alliance relations with other countries or grant them economic privileges.[2] In the 1960s and 1970s, Turkey's relations with the United States and NATO were criticized severely on the ground that they violated Turkey's independence. Even today, Turkish leaders always claim that their first priority in pursuing foreign policy is to avoid any kinds of acts, which might damage Turkey's complete independence.

The Turks are also very concerned about guaranteeing their national security. The belief that about 50 countries, which were under Ottoman rule for centuries, have hostile thoughts against Turkey has led Turkish rulers to assign great importance to security. It was the national security concern which played the most important part in forcing the Turks to seek the military alliance with the West after the Second World War, and it is mainly the same concern which has made Turkey chose to remain within the NATO pact despite changes in the international arena.

b) Moral Values

Another important goal of Turkish foreign policy is to achieve the long-lived dream of being recognized as an equal and respected member of the Western community of "civilized" nations with the assimilation of Turkish people into Western civilization.[3] Since the foundation of the Turkish Republic in 1923, Turkish ruling elite has believed that Turkey can reach the level of advanced countries only if it follows the path of Western countries and joins their political, economic and cultural organizations. They have therefore directed their efforts towards having close relations with the West and avoided having clashes with the West in any arena. We can say that modernization and Westernization efforts at home greatly affected Turkey's general foreign policy line. Especially after 1945, the main plank of Turkey's foreign policy was its alliance with the West. Turkish rulers have always attributed great importance to attaining full participation in all Western organizations and supported main Western initiatives in the international arena.

It is a traditional claim of Turkish policy-makers that their foreign policy aims at having friendly relations with every country and helping the establishment and protection of peace in the international arena. On every occasion, they declare that Turkey sincerely respects international law and international treaties and supports all peace initiatives in every part of the world. The saying of Kemal Atatürk, "peace at home, peace in the world" is a widely accepted principle of Turkish foreign policy. But this principle is also interpreted as preparedness for war against possible enemy attacks and willingness to use armed force in case of need to secure national security and interests.[4] This principle did not prevent the Turks from intervening in Cyprus militarily, annexing Hatay and arming the Turkish Straits.

The Atatürkism, which means following the main principles of the founder of the Turkish Republic, Kemal Atatürk, has its impact on Turkish foreign policy, too. Since the death of Atatürk, all main actors in Turkish political arena have claimed that they have followed the path of Atatürk and worked for the survival of his principles. As Ferenc A. Vali states, "Turkish statesmen, politicians, professors, and even common people still quote him and

[2] Vali, *Bridge Across the Bosporus*, pp. 24-25.
[3] Vali, *Bridge Across the Bosporus*, pp. 35-36, 56, 69, 70, 318, Metin Tamkoç, *The Warrior Diplomats*, Salt Lake City: University of Utah Press, 1976, p. 298.
[4] Tamkoç, *The Warrior Diplomats*, p. 301.

profess to follow his directions."[5] The main principles of the Atatürkism, which were endorsed in 1937 by the constitution, are known as the "Six Arrows": nationalism, secularism, republicanism, populism, etatizm, and revolutionism.[6] These principles and their interpretations are regarded by Turkish policy-makers as main references in foreign policy-making as well as domestic policy-making.

Other moral values, too, have affected minds of Turkish foreign policy-makers. Anti-communism and co-operating with other states against communist expansion was one of their main concerns. They like to be seen as champions of democracy in their dealings with other states. To gain the support of the Muslim world for Turkish interests, they emphasize the Islamic identity of the Turkish nation.

c) Economic Development

Economic development and modernization also constitute an important part of Turkish foreign policy aims. For most Turkish ruling elite, acquiring the technological and economic strength of the Western advanced states has been an aim of both domestic and foreign policy making. Economic considerations played an important part in main Turkish foreign policy decisions such as joining NATO and making alliance with the Western powers. Turkey's needs for foreign economic assistance affected its relations with money supplying countries. Especially after the Second World War, Turkish leaders struggled to obtain maximum possible assistance of the West for its economic development and modernization. Attaining full membership in the European Economic Community also remained as an unchanged foreign policy aim after 1959.

d) Strategic Location

Scholars who study main determinants of Turkish foreign policy give a special place to the geographical location of Turkey.[7] It is a widespread belief among scholars and Turkish politicians that Turkish foreign policy is under the inevitable influence of its geopolitical location. It is claimed that Turkey cannot afford to pursue a neutral policy outside the general superpower competition because of its strategic place between Europe and Asia. The Turkish Straits connecting the Black Sea with the Aegean and Mediterranean Seas constitute a potential source of power as well as threat for Turkey because they are key points for the main sea powers for their presence in the Black Sea and the Mediterranean. With its geographical position, Turkey has the potential to act both as a bridge and barrier between Europe and the Soviet Union (Russia), and between Europe and the Middle East. Turkish politicians put a special emphasis on the bridge position of Turkey between the two continents and between different cultures, expecting thereby to increase the role of Turkey in world politics. Turkey's closeness to the Middle East, so long the center of conflict among

---

[5] Vali, *Bridge Across the Bosporus*, p. 27.
[6] Sowerwine , *Dynamics of Decision Making in Turkish Foreign Policy*, p. 15.
[7] Vali, *Bridge Across the Bosporus*, p. 43, Sowerwine , *Dynamics of Decision Making in Turkish Foreign Policy*, p. 24, Richard D. Robinson, *The First Turkish Republic*, Cambridge, Mass.: Harvard University Press, 1963, pp. 164-165, Nuri Eren, *Turkey, NATO and Europe*, Paris: Atlantic Institute for International Affairs, 1977, pp. 10-11.

super and regional powers, has also been an important factor influencing Turkish foreign policy-making.

e) Cyprus

Since the second half of the 1950s the Cyprus question has been a constant factor and problem of Turkish foreign policy, affecting decisions of policy makers in other matters as well. For the Turks, Cyprus is a matter of national honor and prestige, and policies towards it cannot be decided by a few top officials on their own without regard for public opinion.[8] When the Cyprus issue showed in the 1960s that Turkey was isolated in the international arena and "betrayed" by even her allies, Turkish foreign policy became subject to public debate perhaps for the first time in Turkish history. Thus, the Cyprus problem played a catalyst role in attracting people's attention to matters of foreign relations and encouraging them to express their views on foreign policy.[9] The developments on the Cyprus question also led the Turkish government to re-examine its foreign policy and pursue a more flexible one aiming at putting an end to Turkey's isolation in the international arena and gaining support of the Soviet bloc and Third World countries on the Cyprus issue.

f) Continuity of Foreign Policy

It is widely believed among scholars and Turkish politicians that fundamentals of Turkish foreign policy have not changed since the foundation of the Republic in spite of slight changes in the composition of policy-makers and in the methods and means used in foreign relations.[10] Continuity is regarded as one of the main characteristics of Turkish foreign policy. Main political actors in the Turkish political arena including political parties, influential political figures, interest groups, the press and the military have an undeclared consensus on main Turkish foreign policy goals mentioned above though they attack each other on other matters. For Turkish ruling elite, the main direction and line of Turkish national policy is so correct that trying to alter this line or even criticize it is unpatriotic and unacceptable.[11] In the 1960s, foreign policy became subject to parliamentary and public debate and was criticized by many politicians and intellectuals, but the official line of the government's policy remained unchanged.[12] In spite of heated discussions, a lot of noise and emotion on foreign policy matters, the government stood firm in pursuing its policy without reformulating it. For example, in spite of all pressures from different groups, the Turkish government did not sever its relations with the United States and did not think of leaving NATO.[13] Even during the rule of weak coalition and military-supported governments in the 1970s, special attention was paid to foreign policy in order to prevent radical changes and the post of foreign minister was

---

[8] Vali, *Bridge Across the Bosporus*, p. 242.
[9] Mehmet Gönlübol, "NATO, USA and Turkey" in Kemal H. Karpat (ed.), *Turkey's Foreign Policy in Transition*, Leiden: E. J. Brill, 1975, p. 32.
[10] Vali, *Bridge Across the Bosporus*, pp. 68, 78, 79, 352, Dankwart A. Rustow, *Turkey: America's Forgotten Ally*, New York: Council on Foreign Relations, 1987, pp. 84, 85, Tamkoç, *The Warrior Diplomats*, p. 298.
[11] Vali, *Bridge Across the Bosporus*, p. 358.
[12] Gönlübol, "NATO, USA and Turkey", p. 22.
[13] Feroz Ahmad, *The Turkish Experiment in Democracy*, London: the Royal Institute of International Affairs, 1977, p. 407.

given to respected figures from one of the major centrist parties or experienced career diplomats.[14]

2. FOREIGN POLICY-MAKING IN TURKEY BEFORE 1960

From the foundation of the Turkish Republic to the military coup of 1960, Turkey's foreign policy was made exclusively by the executive branch with minimum participation of other branches and groups.[15] At least until 1945, the leadership of the Republican People's Party (RPP) single-handedly directed foreign policy of the country by using the power of the executive branch.[16] Although the constitution of 1924 gave the ultimate power to the Grand National Assembly, in practice, the government formed by the top leadership of the RPP decided and implemented all domestic and foreign policy activities of the state.[17] Under the presidencies of Kemal Atatürk and İsmet İnönü foreign policies were determined by the president and a small circle of advisers.[18] While the president took final decisions, "the members of the Council of Ministers, the General Staff of the armed forces, a few top Foreign Ministry officials and a few party members in the Assembly including the Head of the Parliamentary group of the RPP and the Chairman of the Committee on Foreign Affairs" were, from time to time, called upon to express their views on foreign policy matters.[19]

The first president of the Turkish Republic, Kemal Atatürk, saw foreign policy matters exclusively within his realm of authority and concern. In a sense, he acted as the chief diplomat of his country.[20] The second president, İsmet İnönü, "was his own prime minister and foreign minister. He was in absolute control of foreign relations of Turkey from 1938 to the middle of 1950."[21] Holding all powers exclusively in his hand, he appointed and dismissed prime ministers and ministers and maintained a strict control over the election of deputies to the Grand National Assembly.[22] Foreign policy-making patterns remained unchanged under the administration of the Democrat Part government, which stayed in power in the 1950s. Foreign policy activities of the state were conducted exclusively by the executive branch headed by President Celal Bayar and Prime Minister Adnan Menderes.[23] Bayar and Menderes took the decision to send troops to the Korean war in consultation with only the Minister of Defense, the Chief of the General Staff and the commanders of the armed forces. The secret bilateral accords with the United States in the 1950s were reached without consultation or ratification by the Parliament. Turkey's Middle East policy in the 1950s was determined only by Bayar and Menderes.

---

[14] Rustow, *Turkey*, p. 85.

[15] Sowerwine , *Dynamics of Decision Making in Turkish Foreign Policy*, p. 165, Gönlübol, "NATO, USA and Turkey", p. 16.

[16] Sowerwine , *Dynamics of Decision Making in Turkish Foreign Policy*, p. 163.

[17] Ibid., p. 164.

[18] Vali, *Bridge Across the Bosporus*, pp. 41, 43.

[19] Sowerwine , *Dynamics of Decision Making in Turkish Foreign Policy*, p. 165, Tamkoç, *The Warrior Diplomats*, p. 221.

[20] Sowerwine , *Dynamics of Decision Making in Turkish Foreign Policy*, p. 166, Tamkoç, *The Warrior Diplomats*, p. 127.

[21] Tamkoç, *The Warrior Diplomats*, p. 221.

[22] Ibid., p. 33.

[23] Sowerwine , *Dynamics of Decision Making in Turkish Foreign Policy*, p. 173.

Before 1960, foreign policy of the Turkish governments was rarely discussed and criticized by the opposition parties and the press.[24] In this period, foreign policy was considered a national issue, which could not be questioned by the public. There was a widespread belief that the official foreign policy represented the unanimous will of the whole nation.[25] Even after transition to multi-party democracy in 1950, foreign policy was not made subject to political debates between the parties in spite of their severe disagreements in domestic politics.[26] The government's Middle East policy in 1958 was the first foreign policy issue, which was criticized by the opposition party.

The military coup on 27 May 1960 and the constitution of 1961 brought about a new political atmosphere in Turkey. Under the constitution, the exercise of sovereignty was divided among the three main branches, the legislative (the bicameral Grand National Assembly), the executive (headed by the President and Council of Ministers) and an independent judiciary.[27] The new constitution provided a more pluralistic electoral system based on proportional representation, giving more place and effectiveness to smaller parties. In the new system, trade unions and voluntary associations gained legitimacy and the autonomy of universities, the press, and the national radio and television increased.[28] In the atmosphere of greater freedom and democracy, the foreign policy of the government as well as ideological foundations of the regime were questioned and criticized by political parties in the parliament, journalists and columnists in the press and academics in the universities. Thus, the former taboo regarding discussion of foreign policy was lifted,[29] and national consensus on foreign policy was broken.[30] Ideology entered into Turkish politics as an important factor affecting foreign policy debates especially among radical groups. The changes mentioned above also played a part in widening the Turkish foreign policy-making circle, providing more political participation in the domestic and foreign policy-making process.[31]

3. THE STRUCTURE OF TURKISH FOREIGN POLICY-MAKING PROCESS

In theory, a wide range of political actors seemed to have the potential to participate in formulating foreign policy decisions or at least to affect them in the 1960s and 1970s. In practice, however, the impact of these groups on foreign policy-making differed in accordance with their real power and policy-making was generally concentrated in the hands of the top leadership in conjunction with a few directly involved officials.

---

[24] Karpat (ed.), *Turkey's Foreign Policy in Transition,* p. 7.
[25] Vali, *Bridge Across the Bosporus,* p. 41, Tamkoç, *The Warrior Diplomats,* p. 297.
[26] Ahmad, *The Turkish Experiment in Democracy,* p. 390.
[27] *The Turkish Constitution as Amended,* Ankara: Başbakanlık Basımevi, 1978, Articles 4, 5, 6, 7, pp. 8-9.
[28] Sowerwine , *Dynamics of Decision Making in Turkish Foreign Policy,* p. 178.
[29] Vali, *Bridge Across the Bosporus,* pp. 40-41, 57-58, 71.
[30] Eren, *Turkey, NATO and Europe,* p. 9.
[31] Tamkoç, the Warrior Diplomats, pp. 297-298.

a) The President

The Turkish political system created by the constitution of 1961 gave predominantly ceremonial responsibilities to the president, leaving actual policy-making and implementation to the prime minister and the Council of Ministers.[32] Almost all political decisions were ratified by the president as the ultimate nominal power, but the real responsibility for taking decisions and implementing them remained in the hands of the government. According to the constitution, the president was the head of the state, representing the whole state and nation in the international arena and he was also the Commander-in-Chief of the Armed Forces. The president had the right to preside over the Council of Ministers and the National Security Council when he felt it necessary. He was empowered to appoint a member of the parliament to form a government and to reject laws accepted by the parliament and send them back for reconsideration. The candidate for prime ministry selected by the president was the person whose position was more suitable to form a government and the president had to ratify laws re-enacted by Parliament. The president had the right to appoint the chief of the general staff upon recommendation by the prime minister.[33] In the foreign policy arena, the president was authorized to receive representatives of foreign states, to appoint the diplomatic representatives of his own country and to ratify and publish international agreements and laws.[34]

According to the constitution of 1982, the president has more or less the same rights and responsibilities. Acting as the commander-in-chief of the armed forces, playing a limited role in deciding the use of the armed forces, appointing the chief of the general staff, calling the National Security Council to meet and presiding it are still among the important authorities of the president. Nevertheless, he has no official responsibility toward any state authority on his actions.[35]

In the 1960s and 1970s, the presidents continued to be very close to the real decision-making centers and had the opportunity to affect real policy-makers, but they had not been in the position of making and implementing foreign policy decisions bypassing the power of the government. Foreign policy making was under the control of the prime ministers and the ministers in the 1980s and 1990s. However, some presidents such as Turgut Özal and Süleyman Demirel were more active in the foreign policy field because of the opportunities created by the end of the Cold War and the emergence of new independent Turkic states in the Caucasus and Central Asia. Their bold initiatives affected the state's general foreign policy line to a great extent. The role played by Özal during the Gulf Crisis and War of 1990-1991 will always remembered as an example demonstrating the great potential of the president in affecting foreign policy of the state.

---

[32] Sowerwine , *Dynamics of Decision Making in Turkish Foreign Policy,* pp. 181-182, Richard C. Campany, *Turkey and the United States,* New York, London: Praeger, 1986, p. 41, Rinn S. Shinn, "Government and Politics" in Richard F. Nyrop (ed.), *Turkey,* Washington D.C.: The American University, 1980, p. 195.

[33] Sowerwine , *Dynamics of Decision Making in Turkish Foreign Policy,* p. 181.

[34] Tamkoç, *The Warrior Diplomats,* p. 128, Shinn, "Government and Politics", p. 195.

[35] *The Turkish Constitution of 1982,* Articles 104 and 105.

b) The Council of Ministers

The Council of Ministers, headed by the prime minister and advised by the Ministry of Foreign Affairs, was the chief foreign policy-making body of Turkey in the system introduced by the 1961 constitution.[36] In time of crises or in case of discussing major national issues, the president and the chief of the general staff were allowed to attend the meetings of the Council of Ministers.[37] The prime minister was the most important actor in shaping foreign policy of Turkey with his duty of implementing the general government policy with the assistance of other ministers. Some prime ministers such as Bülent Ecevit played a more active role in foreign policy decisions. All other ministers had collective responsibility regarding the government's general foreign policy to the parliament.[38] In general, the council of ministers was more likely to reach foreign policy decisions by consensus and if a decision was taken by a majority vote, other ministers were obliged to support this decision. The provisions of the constitution of 1982 grant more or less the same responsibilities and powers to the council of ministers.

Especially from the second half of the 1960s, the cabinet felt compelled to inform and consult leaders of political parties on essential questions and to defend its foreign policy before the parliament and the electorate.[39] The vulnerability of the government in domestic and foreign policy issues increased during the coalition governments since the cabinet could be dismissed from power by the parliament if its actions were unacceptable to the majority in the parliament. When the Turkish political system passed through great crises and the ministers of foreign affairs were changed in short intervals in the 1990s, the council of ministers could not formulate necessary foreign policies and could not respond to developments effectively.

c) The Ministry of Foreign Affairs

The foreign ministry headed by the foreign minister is the major foreign policy-making body apart from the cabinet, which formulated main foreign policy decisions.[40] Implementation of foreign policy decisions and day-to-day management of foreign affairs are in practice handed over to the foreign ministry and its minister. As Vali states, "the ministry of foreign affairs and its minister are in the position of exercising independent authority in matters of political detail and are able to influence the higher level decision-making process."[41] They are able to assist and advise top foreign policy-makers and are charged with preparing the government's foreign policy program. The foreign minister holds a unique position in deciding many foreign policy matters independently and has the final say in all matters which does not concern the council of ministers.[42] The foreign minister's top advisers including the secretary general of the ministry and the general directors of the various divisions within the ministry and other high-ranking career foreign service officers have also

---

[36] Shinn, "Government and Politics", p. 195, Vali, *Bridge Across the Bosporus*, p. 73.
[37] Vali, *Bridge Across the Bosporus*, p. 73, Tamkoç, *The Warrior Diplomats*, pp. 250-251.
[38] Shinn, "Government and Politics", pp. 195-196.
[39] Vali, *Bridge Across the Bosporus*, pp. 72, 79.
[40] Ibid., p. 74, Sowerwine, *Dynamics of Decision Making in Turkish Foreign Policy*, p. 194.
[41] Vali, *Bridge Across the Bosporus*, p. 74.
[42] Sowerwine, *Dynamics of Decision Making in Turkish Foreign Policy*, p. 196.

great influence in foreign policy decisions.[43] The career diplomats of the Turkish Foreign Ministry have a special place in the Turkish political system, assuring the continuity of traditional Turkish foreign policy line for decades. They are "the best educated, the most Westernized, and also the most aristocratic" group among the civil service,[44] fully dedicated to the aim of integrating Turkey with the Western world.[45]

d) The Military

The Ministry of National Defense and its minister play a vital role in shaping foreign policy decisions related to Turkey's national security. They are empowered to prepare the government's program on national defense. The minister of national defense has the final power in deciding national security matters, which are not too important to attract the attention of the cabinet.[46] However, the defense minister is not the boss of the military, having no voice in the command and control of the armed forces. Actual military policy is shaped by the commanders of the armed forces.[47]

The military in Turkey has potentially great power in deciding the direction of Turkish political system. The 1960-1973 period saw the Turkish military playing an extensive part in ruling Turkey. Frequent interventions by the military in politics were based on the view that Kemal Atatürk had bequeathed to the military the duty of protecting the Republic and the reforms he had initiated. When the military felt that politicians were unable to rule the country effectively and that Atatürk's reforms were under threat, it saw taking over the rule of the country and putting the train back on the track as its legitimate right and duty.[48] The majority of military officers were in favor of a democratic regime and they were against politicizing the armed forces through intervention in domestic politics,[49] but, at the same time, officers expected politicians to carry out Atatürk's reforms and take necessary measures against the extreme right and left.

The officers of the 27 May 1960 coup[50] did not allow lower-rank officers to halt the democratic process,[51] but they pressurized the governments and political parties in order to protect their revolution and reforms and to prevent revenge of anti-coup politicians.[52] They forced party leaders to elect General Cemal Gürsel as president and İsmet İnönü as prime minister by threatening to prohibit all political parties.[53] On 12 March 1971, military officers

---

[43] Tamkoç, *The Warrior Diplomats*, p. 255.

[44] Karpat(ed.), *Turkey's Foreign Policy in Transition*, p. 7.

[45] Vali, *Bridge Across the Bosporus*, p. 75.

[46] Sowerwine , *Dynamics of Decision Making in Turkish Foreign Policy*, pp. 187-188.

[47] Campany, *Turkey and the United States*, pp. 41-42.

[48] Roger Paul Nye, *The Military in Turkish Politics*, Ph.D. Thesis, Washington University, 1974, pp. 18, 66-67, 77, 248, Campany, *Turkey and the United States*, p. 42, Rustow, *Turkey*, pp. 62, 119.

[49] Nye, *The Military in Turkish Politics*, pp. 17, 121, 133, 248.

[50] For detailed information about the 27 May coup see *Keesing's Contemporary Archives, 1959-1960*, vol. 12, pp. 17501-17505, Ergun Özbudun, *The Role of Military in Turkish Politics*, Occasional Papers, No. 14, Center for International Affairs, Harvard University, November 1966.

[51] On the coup attempt of Colonel Aydemir see *Keesing's Contemporary Archives*, 1963-1964, vol. 14, pp. 19656-19657, Mehmet Ali Birand et al., *12 Mart*, Ankara: İmge Kitabevi, 1994, pp. 55-70, 84-95.

[52] Nye, *The Military in Turkish Politics*, pp. 27, 252.

[53] Ahmad, *The Turkish Experiment in Democracy*, pp. 178-179.

caused the resignation of the Demirel government by delivering a stern memorandum[54] and ruled the country for the next two and half years behind the scenes through the above-party governments. They suppressed extreme groups[55] and passed some laws in Parliament, but they could not persuade deputies to elect their candidate General Gürler as president.[56]

The army commanders prefer to stay outside the policy-making process in foreign affairs. They do not intervene in the structure of the Foreign Ministry and leave the job of foreign policy-making to famous political figures or career diplomats. It might be said that particularly in the time of civilian rule the army acts as a pressure group rather than policy determiner.[57] However, when issues of national security and defense come to consideration, the government has to consider the views of the army commanders.[58] Especially the Supreme Military Council headed by the chief of the general staff and attended by the commanders of the army, navy, air forces, and gendarmerie has influence on policy-makers during the crises in which use of armed forces is considered. For example, during the Cyprus crises in 1963-64 and 1967 the top military leadership was actively involved in the adoption of important decisions.[59] In the 1990s, Turkey's relations with Israel were improved mainly because of the initiatives of the Turkish military. The process of capturing the leader of the separatist PKK, Abdullah Öcalan, was initiated by the army commanders, who adopted a harsh attitude toward Syria. The military officials did not hesitate to make statements on main foreign policy issues of the state. The military's role in foreign and domestic politics in the late 1990s underlines its potential in foreign policy making.

e) The National Security Council

Turkey maintains a National Security Council, which is headed by the president when present or by the prime minister and includes the deputy prime minister; the ministers of foreign affairs, national defense, interior affairs, finance, communication, labor, industry; the chief of the general staff; the commanders of the Army, Navy and Air Forces and the secretary of the NSC, who is a general. The main functions of the council are to advise the president and the Council of Ministers on national security matters, to co-ordinate all activities of national mobilization and defense and to prepare national security plans and programs.[60] Although the president has the right to preside over the council when at present, generally the prime minister directs activities of the council. The council has become an important policy-making body on the matters of national security and seems to carry more weight in taking decisions on important occasions than other bodies do.[61] Although it is an organ of consultation and although the influence of the military in Turkish politics has to be diminished as a necessity for the future membership in the European Union, the effect of the

---

[54] For detailed information on the subject see *Keesing's Contemporary Archives,* 1971-1972, vol. 18, pp. 24637-24642.

[55] Ibid., p. 24642.

[56] Ibid., 1973, vol. 19, pp. 25853-25854.

[57] Sowerwine , *Dynamics of Decision Making in Turkish Foreign Policy,* p. 191.

[58] Campany, *Turkey and the United States,* p. 42.

[59] Tamkoç, *The Warrior Diplomats,* p. 249.

[60] Vali, *Bridge Across the Bosporus,* pp. 76-77, Sowerwine , *Dynamics of Decision Making in Turkish Foreign Policy,* p. 185, Tamkoç, *The Warrior Diplomats,* p. 250, Shinn, "Government and Politics", p. 196, H. D. Nelson and I. Kaplan, "National Security" in Nyrop (ed.), *Turkey,* p. 262.

[61] Tamkoç, *The Warrior Diplomats,* p. 249.

NSC in Turkey's internal and foreign policies increased greatly toward the end of the 1990s. The NSC meetings, which had been considered as routine activities previously, became number one item in Turkey's domestic and foreign agenda in this period.

f) The Grand National Assembly

Before 1960, the Turkish parliament acted as the legitimiser of the government's foreign policy by accepting all governmental actions with minimum discussion or resentment.[62] In the 1960s and the 1970s, the political parties, which had different ideological views and interests, were able to gain representation in the parliament. The political system gave the political parties the chance of presenting their views to the public through various means such as the parliamentary debates, the press and radio and TV broadcasting.[63] Throughout the 1960s and the 1970s, the Turkish parliament openly discussed foreign policy issues, criticized the government's foreign policy and influenced the government in re-examining some of its policies. At least, the government had to consider the reaction of the parliament while taking foreign policy decisions. The possibility of dismissing the government from power through a vote of no confidence by the parliament forced the governments, especially the coalition governments, to act more carefully in foreign affairs. However, Parliament was not directly involved in the foreign policy-making process and did not cause radical changes in the general direction of Turkish foreign policy.

According to the constitution of 1961, the Turkish Grand National Assembly (GNA), consisting of the Senate and the National Assembly, was empowered to ratify or reject international treaties and laws[64] and the budget of the Foreign Ministry. The authority to permit the use of armed forces, to send troops to foreign countries and to allow the stationing of foreign troops in Turkey was also given to the GNA.[65] The Assembly endeavored to check and control the government's foreign policy activities through debates on the Foreign Ministry budget, general debates, and parliamentary investigations, inquiries and interpellations.[66] The National Assembly had much more direct influence on the foreign policy-making process than the Senate had. The Assembly had direct means to supervise foreign policy activities whereas the Senate had more general authorities such as electing the president from among its own members, delaying or postponing bills passed by the National Assembly and accepting or rejecting a declaration of war.[67]

According to the constitution of 1982, the GNA is empowered with vast authorities such as deciding on war, ratifying international agreements and checking all activities and actions of the government. However, in practice, the parliament has little effect in determining the foreign policy line of the state and in forcing the government to act in a certain way in foreign policy issues. It mainly serves as a mechanism supporting the government in national causes. For example, the GNA extended the assignment period of the international force stationed in

---

[62] Sowerwine , *Dynamics of Decision Making in Turkish Foreign Policy,* p. 165, Karpat (ed.), *Turkey's Foreign Policy in Transition,* p. 7.
[63] Sowerwine , *Dynamics of Decision Making in Turkish Foreign Policy,* p. 249.
[64] Ibid., p. 200, Tamkoç, *The Warrior Diplomats,* p. 259, Shinn, "Government and Politics", p. 193.
[65] Tamkoç, *The Warrior Diplomats,* p. 259.
[66] Ibid., p. 259, Sowerwine , *Dynamics of Decision Making in Turkish Foreign Policy,* p. 202.
[67] Campany, *Turkey and the United States,* pp. 40-41.

Turkey to protect the safe heaven in the northern Iraq whenever it was requested in the 1990s though the majority of the MPs openly declared their opposition to the force.

g) Political Parties and Groups

Republican People's Party(RPP): The RPP was founded by Kemal Atatürk and ruled the country single-handedly between 1923 and 1950. It always saw itself as a supporter and protector of the Turkish democratic and capitalist system, but its actions sometimes seemed at variance with this professed role of champion of democracy. The RPP's top leadership approved the military coup on 27 May 1960[68] and the Commanders' Memorandum on 12 March 1971.[69]

The main problem for the RPP in the 1960s was to gain support of peasants, workers, intellectuals and students who were being drawn into newly emerged leftist movements. For this purpose, party leader İsmet İnönü claimed that his party was on the left of center.[70] Secretary-General Bülent Ecevit furthered the idea of "left-of-center" and presented it to masses as the policy of the RPP.[71] RPP leaders condemned the policies and anti-NATO and anti-American protests of extreme leftists and limited their effect on the Turkish public. Ecevit himself claimed that "the left of center is the strongest wall and the most effective barrier against the flood of the extreme left."[72]

The Republicans seemed to pay more attention to a planned economy in which the state sector would be the leading force, but they always felt it necessary to declare that the private sector would be encouraged and would not be interfered.[73] Specifically Ecevit's aim was to establish a social democratic regime such as some Scandinavian regimes, in which peasants and workers could be protected against large-scale capitalism.[74] However, as a whole, Ecevit's policy merely strove to help the survival of the capitalist system under Turkey's special conditions.

Republicans were always staunch supporters of the Kemalist principles and Turkey's Western connection.[75] However, they did criticize relations with the United States and NATO and Western attitudes toward the Cyprus question when they were in opposition in the second half of the 1960s. Some Republicans believed that the USA took some actions to prevent the RPP from coming to power and gave support to rightist parties.[76] The RPP's leader in the 1970s, Ecevit, seemed to be an advocate of a more independent policy in dealings with the West and improved relations with the Eastern bloc.[77] However, in the end RPP leaders

---

[68] Suna Kili, *Cumhuriyet Halk Partisinde Gelişmeler*, İstanbul: Boğaziçi Üniversitesi Yayınları, 1976, pp. 136, 186, *Keesing's Contemporary Archives*, 1959-1960, vol. 12, p. 17505.

[69] Kili, *Cumhuriyet Halk Partisinde Gelişmeler*, p. 271, Ahmad, *The Turkish Experiment in Democracy*, p. 261, *Keesing's Contemporary Archives*, 1971-1972, vol. 18, p. 24641.

[70] *Milliyet*, 29 July 1965.

[71] Bülent Ecevit, *Ortanın Solu*, İstanbul: Tekin Yayınevi, 1973.

[72] Ibid., p. 28.

[73] Ahmad, *The Turkish Experiment in Democracy*, pp. 272-273.

[74] Ibid., pp. 255-256, 329.

[75] Ibid., p. 213, Mehmet Gönlübol et al., *Olaylarla Türk Dış Politikası*, Ankara: SBF Yayınları, No. 407, 1977, pp. 337-338, İsmail Arar, *Hükümet Programları*, İstanbul: Burçak Yayınevi, 1968, pp. 339-340, 369, 399.

[76] George S. Harris, *Troubled Alliance*, Washington D. C.: American Enterprise Institute, 1972, pp. 69, 81, 83, 119, 132, 136, Kili, *Cumhuriyet Halk Partisinde Gelişmeler*, p. 207, Ecevit, *Ortanın Solu*, pp. 16-17.

[77] Ahmad, *The Turkish Experiment in Democracy*, pp. 419, 421, 422, Ecevit, *Ortanın Solu*, p. 150.

stressed that Turkey should be a part of the West and NATO[78] and when they were in power they took great care not to harm relations with the West.

The RPP still exists in the Turkish political system with its leftist and socialist tendencies though it has to water down its etatist aspects and its opposition to traditional elements. The other main leftist party, the Democratic Leftist Party, which became influential under veteran politician Bülent Ecevit in the 1990s with its position in the coalition governments, was disintegrated and faced a heavy defeat in the 2002 elections.

The Justice Party (JP): The JP, the main moderate rightist party, was established on 11 February 1961 and ruled the country between 1965 and 1971 single-handedly. It, too, was an advocate of the Kemalist principles and Western-style democracy and economic system.[79] It favored a mixed economy in which the private sector would be the leading force, guided but not controlled or restricted by the state.[80] In spite of their strong stand for secularism, JP leaders addressed the religious feelings of the Turkish people to gain their support and accused the RPP of encouraging atheism.[81] They also expected electoral gains from condemning socialist and leftist movements and accusing the RPP of co-operating with extreme leftists.[82]

The JP was a staunch supporter of Turkey's special relations with the West[83] and its membership of NATO.[84] Ironically it was also the JP government, which was pushed by internal and international factors (such as the Cyprus issue, isolation in international arena, and détente) towards pursuing a more flexible foreign policy, improving relations with the Eastern bloc and Third World and making some important changes in relations with the USA.[85] JP leader Demirel dared to declare, "no Turkish Prime Minister said 'no' to the United States as much as I did."[86] However, the JP government's actions were mainly directed to appeasing the angry Turkish public opinion. JP leaders always maintained their pro-American stand and feared that the U.S. commitment, and along with it U.S. military and economic aid, to Turkey might be reduced because of the anti-American atmosphere at home.

The True Path Party represented the tradition of the JP in the 1980s and 1990s with some successes in elections and with its position in coalition governments. However, the party (along with the other rightist party in the center, the Motherland Party, which was ruled the country in the 1980s) gradually lost its public support at the advantage of the traditionalist and Islamist elements, which eventually came to power in the 2002 elections with the claim that they would represent the right of the center.

The Extreme Left: The Turkish Labor Party (TLP), established on 13 February 1962, was the main representative of socialist groups in the 1960s. When Mehmet Ali Aybar

---

[78] Bülent Ecevit, "Batı'nın Bunalımı ve Türkiye", *Özgür İnsan*, June 1975.

[79] Arar, *Hükümet Programları*, p. 431, Ferruh Bozbeyli, *Parti Programları*, İstanbul: Ak Yayınları, 1970, p. 3, Süleyman Demirel, *1971 Buhranı ve Aydınlığa Doğru*, Ankara, 1973.

[80] Bozbeyli, *Parti Programları*, p. 9, Arar, *Hükümet Programları*, p. 445, Ahmad, *The Turkish Experiment in Democracy*, pp. 238-239, Süleyman Demirel, *Büyük Türkiye*, İstanbul: Dergah Yayınları, 1975, p. 236.

[81] Ahmad, *The Turkish Experiment in Democracy*, pp. 242, 383-384, Demirel, *1971 Buhranı*, p. 293.

[82] Demirel, *1971 Buhranı*, pp. 22-23, 73-74, 170, 198-200, 359, Ahmad, *The Turkish Experiment in Democracy*, p. 199, Harris, *Troubled Alliance*, p. 140.

[83] Bozbeyli, *Parti Programları*, pp. 38-40, Demirel, *1971 Buhranı*, pp. 165, 327, 360, Demirel, *Büyük Türkiye*, pp. 300, 302, 314, 422, 434-435, Gönlübol et al., *Olaylarla Türk Dış Politikası*, p. 540, Arar, *Hükümet Programları*, p. 481.

[84] Demirel, *Büyük Türkiye*, pp. 412-413, 433-435, Harris, *Troubled Alliance*, pp. 230, 235, 237-238, Arar, *Hükümet Programları*, pp. 479, 487.

[85] Some JP actions in this regard can be seen in the chapters on military relations and opium.

[86] Gönlübol et al., *Olaylarla Türk Dış Politikası*, p. 520.

became chairman of the party in February 1962, TLP's character changed greatly, attracting workers, intellectuals and students who were dissatisfied with the current regime and influencing Turkish politics out of proportion to its size and representation in Parliament. In spite of its achievement of winning fifteen seats in the 1965 elections, the TLP had never been a strong and homogenous party. The Soviet invasion of Czechoslovakia in 1968 caused ideological and factional disagreements within the party.[87] After the military's intervention in politics in March 1971, the TLP was dissolved on 20 July 1971 by the Turkish constitutional court because it allegedly violated the law on political parties and the constitution. Its leaders were found guilty of encouraging leftist subversive activities against the regime.

Leftist leaders believed that Turkey could develop economically only under a socialist regime which would make the state sector the leading force in the economy, implement a strict development plan and nationalize vital economic sectors.[88] They condemned foreign capital, foreign aid and foreign debt as the means of outside powers and the internal elite of making Turkey dependent on foreign countries.[89]

Foreign policy provided a good means for leftist groups to increase their political influence by strongly opposing NATO and the West, especially the United States. In their opinion, the United States penetrated deeply into every part of Turkish administration and dominated all Turkey's domestic and foreign policies by using NATO and bilateral arrangements.[90] If Turkey withdrew from NATO and ended her special relations with the USA, she would have regained her complete independence and the possibility of U.S. intervention against socialist groups would have been reduced, giving way to the establishment of socialism in Turkey. Leftist leaders spent a great deal of time explaining the disadvantages of NATO for Turkey.[91] Apart from the TLP, leftist newspapers such as *Yön*, *Ant*, *Devrim*, *Akis*, *Akşam* and *Türk Solu*,[92] students, workers and trade union DİSK (the Confederation of Revolutionary Workers' Union) joined the condemnation of the West.

The poor performance of the TLP in the 1969 elections alienated a large section of the extreme left from the parliamentary system and pushed them to try extra parliamentary actions, particularly terror and violence, to attract the attention of the masses. Workers and students became increasingly more violent, paralyzing factories and universities. A band of student extremists, believed to be a part of terrorist Dev-Genç organization, started a terror campaign against American personnel and American activities in Turkey, announcing that they would struggle until the country was cleared from "imperialist" foreigners. When the Israeli Consul General was kidnapped and murdered by those leftist terrorists in May 1971, the Turkish government took harsh measures against leftist radicals. Suspected leftist activists

---

[87] Jacob M. Landau, *Radical Politics in Modern Turkey*, Leiden: E. J. Brill, 1974, pp. 129-130, Harris, *Troubled Alliance*, p. 143.

[88] Behice Boran, *Türkiye ve Sosyalizm Sorunları*, İstanbul: Tekin Yayınevi, 1970, pp. 238, 241, 243, 246, 250, Mehmet Ali Aybar, *Bağımsızlık, Demokrasi ve Sosyalizm*, İstanbul: Gerçek Yayınevi, 1968, pp. 192, 193, 203, 361, 407, 408, Bozbeyli, *Parti Programları*, pp. 283, 289, 291, 317, 331, Landau, *Radical Politics in Modern Turkey*, pp. 138, 145, 150, 151.

[89] Boran, *Türkiye ve Sosyalizm Sorunları*, pp. 241, 269-270, 286, 289-291, Aybar, *Bağımsızlık, Demokrasi ve Sosyalizm*, pp. 203, 335, 338, 339, Ahmad, *The Turkish Experiment in Democracy*, p. 413.

[90] Boran, *Türkiye ve Sosyalizm Sorunları*, pp. 267-268, Aybar, *Bağımsızlık, Demokrasi ve Sosyalizm*, pp. 388, 402-403, 417, 462, 465, 498.

[91] Boran, *Türkiye ve Sosyalizm Sorunları*, pp. 271-273, 276, 279, 297, Aybar, *Bağımsızlık, Demokrasi ve Sosyalizm*, pp. 325-326, 340, 379, 459-460, 463, 560, 561, 580, 582, 591, 592, 605, 617, 623.

[92] For a good summary of leftist columnists' views see Duygu Sezer, *Kamuoyu ve Dış Politika*, Ankara: SBF Yayını, 1972, pp. 358-362, 367-369, 374-378, 452-453, 455, 458-461.

and a number of professors, politicians and journalists who were accused of inspiring those leftist guerrillas were arrested, leftist periodicals were closed down and the TLP was dissolved.[93]

There are still a number of radical leftist parties in the Turkish political system, including the communist party, which was allowed in the 1980s with changes in the constitution. Leftist parties have little public support and try to become influential with violent demonstrations and anti-Americanism. The ones, which try to obtain support of the people having Kurdish origins, obtain considerable amount of votes, but they cannot be represented in the parliament because of the electoral system.

The Extreme Right: The Republican Peasants Nation Party (RPNP), later renamed the Nationalist Action Party (NAP), followed the nationalistic line. Its leader in the post-1965 period, Alparslan Türkeş, a colonel who was actively involved in the 27 May 1960 Revolution and was then expelled from the National Union Committee because of his opposition to early parliamentary elections, almost single-handedly directed the party and determined its policies. The party won 15 seats in the 1965 elections and one in 1969 though it increased its proportionate vote slightly. The NAP had influence in the political arena mainly because of activities of its youth organizations such as the Union of Homes of Ideals (Ülkü Ocakları Birliği), the Association of Young Idealists (Genç Ülkücüler Teşkilatı) and later Idealist Youth of Turkey (Türkiye Ülkücü Gençlik Teşkilatı).

The Nationalists believed that Turkey could not be developed by copying the regimes of other countries such as capitalism and communism. In their opinion, Turkey needed a completely national regime based on its own history, national traditions and spirit, that was the regime of the Nine Lights (Dokuz Işık) whose principles were explained by Türkeş.[94] They proposed a mixed economic system in which the state would direct development and control main sectors.[95] In the thinking of nationalists, religion (Islam) held a secondary place and was seen not as a way of life but as an integral and important component of Turkish culture.[96] They addressed religious feelings of people to gain their support.[97] Nationalists saw international communism and its agents at home as the most dangerous threats to Turkey's independence and fought against them.[98] A well-disciplined para-military organization called the commandos or Grey Wolves (Bozkurtlar) clashed with leftists, broke up their meetings and demonstrations.[99]

The NAP leadership supported Turkey's alliance with NATO and the USA as necessary components of Turkish security and favored having close relations with the West.[100] They

---

[93] *Keesing's Contemporary Archives*, 1971-1972, vol. 18, pp. 24642, 24753-24755, 25143, 25329-25331, ibid., 1973, vol. 19, pp. 25854-25855.

[94] Alparslan Türkeş, *Temel Görüşler*, İstanbul: Dergah Yayınları, 1975, pp. 30, 37-38, 45, 52, 80, 146,147, 178,179, Alparslan Türkeş, *Yeni Ufuklara Doğru*, İstanbul: Kutluğ Yayınları, 1974, pp. 11, 15, 37-38, 53-54, 93.

[95] Türkeş, *Temel Görüşler*, pp. 84, 90, 91, 194, 196, 211-214, Türkeş, *Yeni Ufuklara Doğru*, pp. 21, 22, Bozbeyli, *Parti Programları*, pp. 186, 187, 223, 225-227.

[96] Landau, *Radical Politics in Modern Turkey*, pp. 193, 199, 202.

[97] Türkeş, *Temel Görüşler*, pp. 42, 179-180, Türkeş, *Yeni Ufuklara Doğru*, pp. 16, 17, 30, Bozbeyli, *Parti Programları*, p. 181.

[98] Türkeş, *Yeni Ufuklara Doğru*, pp. 36-37, 41, 62, 66, 88, 91, Türkeş, *Temel Görüşler*, pp. 61, 65, Landau, *Radical Politics in Modern Turkey*, pp. 229, 254-255, 265, 274.

[99] Landau, *Radical Politics in Modern Turkey*, pp. 215-216, Metin Toker, *Solda ve Sağda Vuruşanlar*, Ankara: Akis Yayınları, 1971, pp. 157, 160.

[100] For Türkeş's views on NATO see Türkeş, *Temel Görüşler*, pp. 263-275.

paid a special attention to the situation of the Turks living outside Turkey (the Outer Turks)[101] and strongly supported a Turkish military intervention in Cyprus to protect Turkish Cypriots.[102]

The NAP is still active in Turkish politics with a considerable amount of public support. They have more or less the same opinions and tendencies. The failure of the centrist parties in satisfying demands of the public increased the power basis of the nationalists in some periods and even gave them the opportunity to rule the country as coalition partners.

The Islamist Groups: Islamist groups were less active and effective in the political arena in the 1960s. Their activities were limited to publishing Islamic books, magazines and newspapers, arranging mass praying and trying to organize themselves. Among them, the Mücadelecis were the most active, clashing with leftists and campaigning against so-called imperialists.[103] The Islamists attacked communism as a godless system challenging Islamic principles and Muslims and condemned "the international Jewish plot", worldwide freemasonry and missionary activities.[104] Some considered Western imperialism equally as dangerous as communism and praised Islam as a system and civilization, which could compete with Western civilization.

In the political arena, Necmettin Erbakan organized Islamists. He had been a member of the Justice Party heading a more conservative, Islamic-minded faction. After his candidacy for parliament was vetoed by the JP, he was elected to the parliament as an independent candidate in the 1969 elections. The National Order Party founded by Erbakan on 26 January 1970 was closed down on 20 May 1971 on the ground that it violated articles of the Constitution related to secularism.[105] Erbakan's party re-emerged in October 1972 under the name of the National Salvation Party (NSP), won 48 seats in Parliament (11.8 percent of total votes) in the 1973 elections and joined the coalition government in 1974. Seven of it members served as ministers in the cabinet.

The NSP clearly stood for religion and made Islam the basis of its policies. Since the Salvationists were restricted by the law in using Islamic terms, they used unclear moral and traditional terms in explaining their ideas. They talked of moral recovery and progress, i.e. Islamisation of the people. They seemed to have accepted secularism as a pillar of the state but, they rejected the interpretation of secularism in a way that would restrict religious freedoms and put religious people under pressure.[106] They were opposed to communism and capitalism as products of Christian Europe[107] and proposed a mixed economy model in which the state would play the most important part under a development plan.[108]

The NSP leadership was in favor of having close economic and political relations with the Muslim world rather than the West. Erbakan was strongly opposed to Turkey's membership of the European Economic Community, which he regarded as a Christian club

---

[101] Ibid., pp. 34, 294, 297, Türkeş, *Yeni Ufuklara Doğru*, pp. 19, 75, 80, 82, Landau, *Radical Politics in Modern Turkey*, pp. 194-198.
[102] Türkeş, *Temel Görüşler*, pp. 310-320.
[103] Toker, *Solda ve Sağda Vuruşanlar*, pp. 103-105, 107, 111-112, 119-120, 126.
[104] Ahmad, *The Turkish Experiment in Democracy*, p. 376.
[105] *Keesing's Contemporary Archives*, 1971-1972, vol. 18, p. 24640.
[106] Bozbeyli, *Parti Programları*, p. 399.
[107] Ibid., pp. 397, 414.
[108] Ibid., pp. 414-415, 417-418.

protecting the interests of only Christians and Jews.[109] He claimed that it would be to Turkey's advantage to lead the establishment of a Muslim Common Market by disassociating itself from the West.[110] When they were in government Salvationists agreed with the RPP that Turkey should remain within the Western security system and existing alliances.[111]

The success of Erbakan's party, the Welfare Party, in general elections in the mid-1990s, caused a crisis in the Turkish political system, eventually giving way to the indirect intervention of the military. While their party was dissolved by the Constitutional Court and their activities were restricted, the traditionalists increasingly became pro-Western and supported Turkey's membership in the European Union. The great victory of the faction, which emerged from Erbakan's party, in the 2002 elections with a almost two third majority in the parliament reminded the victory of the Democrat Party in 1950 in the aftermath of a period in which the people had been seriously alienated from the system.

h) Public Opinion

From 1964 onward, the Turkish press played a special role in starting foreign policy discussions outside official circles for the first time and in stimulating other private groups and the general public to join the general foreign policy discussion.[112] As the most influential public opinion creator, the press became a forum for columnists, experts and well-known personalities to express their views on foreign policy matters. The government and other official policy-makers saw the press both as an important channel of information and a gauge of public opinion. Although the press had the potential to influence the views of both the general public and the official circles with its power to express and spread its views openly,[113] it did not achieve any radical foreign policy changes.

After 1965, university students were actively involved in the discussion of foreign policy matters and tried to influence the determination of foreign policy decisions by using various methods such as holding press conferences and public forums, organizing demonstrations and boycotts, delivering their own literature and even resorting to violence.[114] Student groups played a part in fuelling public discussion on foreign policy and forced the government to have a more flexible attitude in foreign policy, but they were not able to influence the government to change its basic foreign policy line.[115] University lecturers also joined the discussion of foreign policy by issuing joint statements. Individually lecturers took part in foreign policy discussions by expressing their views in newspaper columns.[116]

Labor unions, too, contributed to the radicalization of the public opinion in the 1960s and 1970s.[117] They tried to affect the official foreign policy especially in economic matters by

---

[109] Mehmet Yaşar Geyikdağı, *Political Parties in Turkey*, New York: Praeger Publishers, 1984, p. 123, Landau, *Radical Politics in Modern Turkey*, p. 192.

[110] Ahmad, *The Turkish Experiment in Democracy*, pp. 333, 382-383, Bozbeyli, *Parti Programları*, pp. 421, 432.

[111] Ahmad, *The Turkish Experiment in Democracy*, p. 337.

[112] Harris, Troubled Alliance, p. 129, for the role of the press see also Sowerwine, *Dynamics of Decision Making in Turkish Foreign Policy*, pp. 264-268.

[113] Sezer, *Kamuoyu ve Dış Politika*, p. 307.

[114] Ibid., pp. 346, 348.

[115] Gönlübol, "NATO, USA and Turkey", p. 23, Sowerwine , *Dynamics of Decision Making in Turkish Foreign Policy*, pp. 292-294.

[116] Sezer, *Kamuoyu ve Dış Politika*, pp. 353, 354.

[117] Harris, *Troubled Alliance*, p. 130, Eren, *Turkey, NATO and Europe*, pp. 8-9.

organizing strikes and boycotts and sometimes resorting to violence. They used influential figures in political parties to put pressure on the government. Business associations were also well positioned to affect the official circles through their financial and political resources.

Despite the widespread discussion and criticism of the government's foreign policy by the political parties, the press, the intelligentsia, students and workers, the interest of the average Turkish citizen in foreign policy matters remained very little throughout the 1960s and the 1970s.[118] In general, the passive part of the Turkish public opinion, which represented the majority of people, did not feel any concern about foreign policy issues unless those issues affected its national and religious feelings. Questions affecting national honor or religious feelings were more likely to attract the attention of the general public.[119] The general public was also sensitive to foreign interferences in domestic affairs.[120] Especially in the second half of the 1960s, the general Turkish public opinion sharply criticized the United States and Turkey's other NATO allies over Cyprus and other issues,[121] but it did not go so far as the radical groups did in criticizing the government's policies.

4. FACTORS AFFECTING U.S. FOREIGN POLICY 1960-1975

a) Anti-Communism

In the 1960-1975 period, American foreign policy continued to be affected by the opposition of American policy-makers to communism and their desire to contain so-called communist expansion in different parts of the world. Almost all the presidents and chief policy-makers saw communism directed by the Soviet Union and China as the most important threat to the United States and other countries of the "free world". They took the communist threat so seriously that even nationalist movements were perceived as communist-inspired subversive activities. In the 1960-1975 period, cold war clashes occurred between the United States and communist countries such as the Soviet Union and China and American interventions took place in some small countries where communism was seen as a threat by the Americans. However, especially in the beginning of the 1970s, American politicians realized that cold war conflict was not the only option in pursuing foreign policy and that the USA also could get benefits from relaxing its relations with communist countries.

Presidents John F. Kennedy, Lyndon B. Johnson and Richard Nixon were sincere anti-Communists, trying to strengthen American power vis-a-vis the power of communist states. During his presidential campaign, Kennedy accused his predecessors of not taking effective actions against Soviet moves and frequently emphasized the missile gap between the USA and USSR, which was not real at that time.[122] He was strongly in favor of increasing American military capacity against an imaginary Soviet superiority in this arena. It was also Kennedy who advocated American superiority over the Russians in space by launching

---

[118] Vali, *Bridge Across the Bosporus,* p. 100.
[119] Ibid., p. 100.
[120] Ibid., p. 360.
[121] Rustow, *Turkey*, p. 84.
[122] Maldwyn A. Jones, *The Limits of Liberty*, Oxford: Oxford University Press, 1983, p. 544.

expensive space projects.[123] Kennedy took a very tough stance on the Vietnam issue, deciding not to give any concessions to the Vietnamese communists in order to isolate the People's Republic of China and to stop communist expansion in East Asia.[124] He thought that if Vietnam was lost to communists, this victory would encourage communist movements and therefore the West would have to deal with similar challenges throughout the world. The Cuban missile crisis demonstrated Kennedy's determination in opposing Soviet moves. He could not accept Soviet nuclear missiles on the doorstep of America.[125] Kennedy failed to realize the true character of national liberation wars by regarding them as communist expansionist actions.[126] In relations with the West, Kennedy placed considerable importance on strengthening the capability, unity and effectiveness of the NATO alliance. He also encouraged the Western Europeans to promote their union under the Common Market.[127]

Lyndon B. Johnson, too, believed that communism was the most important threat to the "free world" and that the USA should have the responsibility of halting its advance all over the world.[128] He seemed a more moderate leader during the presidential campaign in comparison with the Republican candidate, Barry M. Goldwater, who advocated a total struggle against communism and even suggested using tactical nuclear weapons in the Vietnamese war.[129] However, after coming to power, Johnson also struggled for an American victory in Vietnam against communists by escalating the war. According to R. J. Barnet, Johnson held the view that the United States must oppose all newly-established communist or communist-leaning governments in the world even if they came to power by election.[130]

Richard Nixon had the same cold-war mentality in spite of his achievements in relaxing relations with the Soviet Union and communist China. Throughout his political career Nixon remained a sincere anti-Communist, always seeking American superiority over communist states.[131] Realizing the limits of the American power in continuing the war in Vietnam and remaining under the pressure of public opinion, Nixon decided to stop the war, but it had to be an honorable withdrawal for the USA, therefore, in order to achieve this aim, Nixon did not hesitate to attack Cambodia and Laos to put pressure on the Vietnamese. His détente policy did not mean the end of U.S.-Soviet confrontation in different parts of the world, especially in Third World countries.

To summarize, the opposition to communism was the main characteristic of both American conservatives and liberals, and of both Republican and Democrat administrations.[132] As J. W. Fulbright, a former chairman of the Senate Foreign Relations Committee, stated, the fatal mistake of American policy-makers in this period was to regard

---

[123] Robert A. Divine, *Since 1945 Politics and Diplomacy in Recent American History*, New York, London: John Wiley and Sons, Inc., 1975, p. 115, Jones, *The Limits of Liberty*, p. 545.

[124] Divine, *Since 1945 Politics and Diplomacy in Recent American History*, p. 116, Dewey W. Grantham, *The United States Since 1945*, New York: London: McGraw Hill, Inc., 1976, p. 189.

[125] Divine, *Since 1945 Politics and Diplomacy in Recent American History*, pp. 128-131.

[126] Grantham, *The United States Since 1945*, p. 177.

[127] Ibid., p. 189.

[128] Jones, *The Limits of Liberty*, pp. 554-555, Grantham, *The United States Since 1945*, p. 230.

[129] Jones, *The Limits of Liberty*, p. 551, Paul Y. Hammond, *Cold War and Détente*, New York: Harcourt Brace Jovanovich, Inc., 1975, p. 227.

[130] Richard J. Barnet, *Intervention and Revolution*, London: Paladin, 1972, p. 23.

[131] Henry Brandon, *The Retreat of American Power*, London: The Bodley Head, 1973, p. 270.

[132] James Dull, *The Politics of American Foreign Policy*, Englewood Cliffs, New Jersey: Prentice-Hall, Inc., 1985, pp. 177-178, 209.

communism as an absolute evil and to give their opposition to communism priority over their support for nationalist movements in the Third World.[133]

b) World Leadership

American leaders saw the United States as the leader of the "free world", having a global mission to protect countries of the world against the expansion of monolithic communism. In their opinion, the United States was the most powerful state in the free world, therefore it could not afford to avoid helping and protecting other countries against evil forces. It was the moral duty of the United States to intervene in affairs of other countries if necessary to protect freedoms. In this sense, America appeared to undertake the job of world policeman and this concept of world leadership strongly affected American foreign policy decisions.

John F. Kennedy was a convinced believer in the American world leadership. On 17 September 1960, he declared that "our responsibility is to be the chief defender of freedom at a time when freedom is under attack all over the globe."[134] In a television speech during the presidential campaign, Kennedy presented the USA as "the sentinel of the gates of freedom around the world" and said that "if we succeed, freedom succeeds. If we fail, freedom fails".[135] In his inaugural address Kennedy stated that the USA "would pay any price, bear any burdens, meet any hardship, support any friend, oppose any foe to assure the survival and success of liberation."[136] He accelerated U.S. military projects to fulfil the world leadership role and formed the Peace Corps to help Third World countries as a part of America's global mission.[137]

Lyndon B. Johnson devoted most of his energy to winning the war in Vietnam, thus he wanted to keep the confidence of world nations in American leadership and American protection.[138] Realizing dangers of direct commitments of the United States all over the world, the Nixon administration tried to carry on American world leadership by applying more indirect commitments, giving the duty of actual defense to local powers and helping them economically and militarily and encouraging them in facing evil forces. The Nixon Doctrine is the expression of this aim.[139] Nixon's national security adviser Kissinger stated that "the Nixon Doctrine is our realistic way of remaining committed to the rest of the world. It can lay a basis for a continuing practical relationship, not a basis for a total withdrawal".[140]

American governments tried to blockade revolutionary movements in the Third World in the name of her global mission to protect the present system. They extended economic and military assistance to governments of some Third World countries to preserve stability and the status quo.[141] American leaders saw themselves in a position where they could determine whether a movement anywhere in the world constituted a threat to the interests of the United

---

[133] J. William Fulbright, *The Arrogance of Power*, New York: Random House, 1966, pp. 77, 78, 106-107, 119.

[134] Henry Fairlie, *The Kennedy Promise*, New York: Doubleday and Company, Inc., 1973, p. 68.

[135] Divine, *Since 1945 Politics and Diplomacy in Recent American History*, p. 105.

[136] Jones, *The Limits of Liberty*, p. 545.

[137] Ibid., p. 545.

[138] Divine, *Since 1945 Politics and Diplomacy in Recent American History*, p. 161, Jones, *The Limits of Liberty*, p. 555.

[139] David Landau, *Kissinger: the Uses of Power*, London: Robson Books Ltd., 1974, pp. 112-114, Grantham, *The United States Since 1945*, p. 257.

[140] Landau, *Kissinger*, p. 112.

[141] Barnet, *Intervention and Revolution*, pp. 21-22.

States and the international community and felt that they could handle it in a way which they wished. In most cases, they even did not need to consult other countries or international organizations. The Americans saw their world leadership as a unique opportunity to promote the ideals of democracy and capitalism throughout the world.[142]

c) Realism

The Nixon administration made some important changes in U.S. foreign policy by decreasing the influence of ideology and the containment of communism on foreign policy. In particular, Nixon's national security adviser Henry Kissinger, who taught foreign relations at Harvard University, played an important role in shifting the direction of American foreign policy with his "realist" views. He believed that ideology should not dominate relations between states and determine the general line of a country's foreign policy. He and Nixon realized that the world at the beginning of the 1970s was different from the world in the 1960s. The old polarity between the United States and the Soviet Union had undergone a radical change with the rise of such new centers of power and influence as China, Japan, France and the Third World bloc. They knew that the USA could not carry on cold war confrontations with communist powers throughout the world as it had before and that it could not undertake commitments, which would lead her to, armed conflicts. The Vietnam war had showed that it was not in American interests to carry out wars abroad on behalf of regional powers. The results of this kind of thinking were the détente policy which aimed at having better relations with ideological opponents and the Nixon Doctrine, which was intended to restrict American commitments, particularly military ones, abroad.

Believing that the United States and the Soviet Union could have some common interests and that it could be to American advantage to have normal trade relations and increased contacts with the Russians, Nixon tried to make some changes in U.S.-Soviet relations. As a sign of his realist views, Nixon said that "we have to live with communist powers and we have no illusion about communism, but we must accept the realities."[143] Strategic Arms Limitation Treaty I between the USA and the USSR was the most important result of Nixon's détente policy. Nixon's visit to Moscow and his sincere efforts to ease tensions between the two superpowers made this kind of agreement real. Another Nixon revolution in American foreign policy was to open relations with China. He was the first American president to visit communist China.

The Nixon Doctrine was a clear realization of the limits of American power by the American President. American retreat from different parts of the world in the military sense was necessary and Nixon wanted to carry out this retreat without damaging U.S. interests and prestige. In his inaugural address, Nixon announced that "the time has passed, when America will make every other nation's conflict our own, or make every other nation's future our responsibility, or presume to tell the people of other nations how to manage their own affairs".[144] Kissinger expressed the doctrine as follows: "The United States alone cannot make itself responsible for every part of the world at every moment of time against every

---

[142] Dull, *The Politics of American Foreign Policy*, p. 209.
[143] Brandon, *The Retreat of American Power*, p. 184.
[144] Grantham, *The United States Since 1945*, p. 276.

danger and to capitalize every opportunity."[145] According to the doctrine, the United States would continue to support its allies against their enemies by supplying economic aid and weapons, but its allies would undertake more burdens and would face opponents and carry out military struggle on their own.[146] It might be said that the main goal was to preserve the position of American power in the world by establishing a new system in which American soldiers would not be involved directly. In this sense, the doctrine did not restrict U.S. commitments throughout the world and did not reduce her determination to face communist threats,[147] but it changed ways of fulfilling commitments.

d) Other Moral Values

Certain moral values helped to shape U.S. foreign policy or, at least, American policy makers used these values to justify their actions. Linked with the world leadership concept, honor and prestige affected American leaders in some of their actions. American presidents tried to save the prestige and honor of the United States by escalating the war in Vietnam. In their minds, an American defeat against a Third World power would be humiliating for the United States before the world community.[148] Such ideas as democracy and anti-totalitarianism, freedom and liberty, free enterprise and capitalism and anti-imperialism also affected the minds of American policy-makers to some extent.[149] American politicians always supported these ideas at home and abroad and claimed that one of their major goals in foreign policy was the acceptance of those ideas by the world community. However, in most cases American governments gave practical national interests priority over moral values. Many of the governments that had received U.S. economic and military aid and political support were totalitarian regimes violating civil liberties. American administrations also did not criticize, but they recognized and supported many military coups in various friendly countries.[150]

e) Vietnam

In the second half of the 1960s and at the first half of the 1970s, the major concern of the American administrations was to gain an honorable victory in Vietnam. In this period, the preoccupation with the war in Vietnam affected many aspects of U.S. foreign policy deeply. The subject common to the electoral campaigns of presidential candidates was the American military involvement in Vietnam.[151] Some suggested tough actions in Vietnam while others presented themselves as men of peace. To secure the support of more voters, the candidates accused other candidates on the Vietnamese issue and gave promises to the American people on the matter. His failure in handling the Vietnamese issue forced President Johnson not to become a candidate for the presidency a second time. President Nixon spent most of his

---

[145] Landau, *Kissinger*, p. 112.
[146] Brandon, *The Retreat of American Power*, pp. 80-81, Barnet, *Intervention and Revolution*, pp. 276-277.
[147] Landau, *Kissinger*, pp. 113-114.
[148] Fulbright, *The Arrogance of Power*, p. 17.
[149] Dull, *The Politics of American Foreign Policy*, p. 179.
[150] Barnet, *Intervention and Revolution*, p. 274.
[151] Divine, *Since 1945 Politics and Diplomacy in Recent American History*, p. 148, Grantham, *The United States Since 1945*, pp. 245-246, 249, 272.

energy and time trying to achieve an honorable end of the war. The continuation of the war divided and radicalized the American public and made it more conscious of foreign affairs. The presidents' way of the handling the war aroused the opposition of Congress to the presidents' foreign policy activities and led Congress to seek the restoration of its constitutional authorities in foreign affairs. The war in Vietnam caused some damage to America's relations with its allies and prevented the United States for a certain time from relaxing its relations with communist China and the Soviet Union.[152]

f) The Third World

Relations with Third World countries constituted a considerable part of American policy. In the 1960-75 period, the American administrations undertook commitments in the Third World in the name of facing the threat of communist expansion and defending freedom against totalitarianism.[153] The United States provided economic, military and political support to some Third World countries to preserve the existing regimes[154] and it sometimes did not hesitate to interfere in their internal affairs. Competition with the USSR in extending influence to Third World countries and getting their support in the international arena affected U.S. foreign policy.[155] American policy makers pursued some moral values such as advancing development and democracy and defending freedoms in their dealings with the Third World.[156]

Economic and military aid, especially to Third World countries, was used as an instrument of U.S. foreign policy.[157] It became a tool of the American administration in legitimizing the U.S. presence in developing countries and the U.S. involvement in domestic affairs of these states. It was used to protect American military, political and economic interests in the recipient countries. For example, the Congress tried to affect Turkey's opium policies by threatening to cut off aid to this country. As a part of aid programs, the Kennedy administration established a voluntary organization in March 1961, called the Peace Corps. Voluntary peace corpsmen worked in developing countries to help them in such fields as education, sanitation, irrigation, and agriculture.[158] It was presented as evidence of the claim that the United States was fulfilling the world leadership role in a positive way.[159]

5. THE STRUCTURE OF U.S. FOREIGN POLICY-MAKING PROCESS

A wide range of organizations, groups and individuals are involved in making and conducting American foreign policy : the president, staff men in the White House, the members of the cabinet, especially the secretaries of State and Defense and their departments,

---

[152] Fulbright, *The Arrogance of Power*, p. 181.
[153] Grantham, *The United States Since 1945*, p. 185.
[154] Barnet, *Intervention and Revolution*, pp. 22, 29.
[155] Grantham, *The United States Since 1945*, pp. 185, 230.
[156] Fulbright, *The Arrogance of Power*, p. 18.
[157] Ibid., pp. 232, 237.
[158] Grantham, *The United States Since 1945*, p. 17, Dull, *The Politics of American Foreign Policy*, p. 61.
[159] Fairlie, *The Kennedy Promise*, pp. 284, 287, 288.

the National Security Council, the Chairman of the Joint Chiefs of Staff, the Director of the Central Intelligence Agency, many other sections of the executive branch, members and relevant committees of the Congress, occasionally local governments of the USA, and intergovernmental and international organizations to which the United States belongs.[160] The press, pressure groups, research organizations, specialists and experts in universities and occasionally public opinion also affect American foreign policy decisions.

a) The Presidency

At the top of the American foreign policy mechanism stands the American President. It is the president who is the center of power, who controls the whole foreign policy making process and who takes final decisions.[161] For most Americans, the President represents American national interests abroad, he is "the single source, the symbol and the spokesman of American policy".[162] If he wants to do so, the president has enough means and authority to dominate foreign policy, in fact he has more freedom of action and power in foreign policy than he has in domestic policy. The American constitution gives a wide range of authority to the president.[163] It authorizes him, with the advice and consent of the Senate, to negotiate and sign treaties with foreign countries, and appoint American ambassadors and receive ambassadors of other countries. The constitution also empowers the president with the role of commander-in-chief of the armed forces. The president also can use the powers of making executive agreements[164] and recognizing foreign governments in conducting foreign policy.

Since he is elected by the entire population, the president can stand out in most cases as the representative of the whole nation and deal with some foreign issues single-handedly, seeing it unnecessary to consult the other branches of the American government. Moments of crisis, especially, present unique opportunities to the president to increase his power[165] because almost every American recognizes that in emergency situations the president should act quickly and secretly to face the threat immediately even without securing the approval of other government officials.[166] Cold war confrontations between the United States and the communist bloc in the 1950s and the 1960s provided the American presidents with opportunities to increase their power in conducting foreign policy by securing the support of the Congress and the American people.[167] The emergence of the United States as a world power, the adoption of containment strategy for facing communist expansionism, the need for handling serious crises quickly, the emotion of the American people in supporting the

---

[160] Dull, *The Politics of American Foreign Policy*, p. 22, Roger Hilsman, *The Politics of Policy Making in Defense and Foreign Affairs*, New York: Harper and Row Publishers, 1971, pp. 118-119, 147.

[161] Dull, *The Politics of American Foreign Policy*, pp. 22, 296, Cecil V. Crabb and Pat M. Holt, *Invitation to Struggle*, Washington D.C.: Congressional Quarterly Inc., 1980, pp. 3, 5, Hilsman, *The Politics of Policy Making in Defense and Foreign Affairs*, pp. 17, 18, 21.

[162] Dull, *The Politics of American Foreign Policy*, p. 21.

[163] For detailed information see Crabb and Holt, *Invitation to Struggle*, pp. 9-16.

[164] Arthur M. Schlesinger, Jr., *The Imperial Presidency*, London: Andre Deutsch, 1973, pp. 312-313, Agron Wildavsky, "The Two Presidencies" in Douglas M. Fox (ed.), *The Politics of U.S. Foreign Policy Making*, Pacific Palisades, California: Goodyear Publishing Company, Inc., 1971, p. 178, Hilsman, *The Politics of Policy Making in Defense and Foreign Affairs*, p. 74.

[165] Fulbright, *The Arrogance of Power*, p. 45.

[166] Hilsman, *The Politics of Policy Making in Defense and Foreign Affairs*, p. 27.

[167] Fulbright, *The Arrogance of Power*, p. 45.

presidents against communist forces, all helped the concentration of the power in the hands of a very few people in the presidency.

John F. Kennedy came to power with a strong determination to use the fullest power and authority of the presidency in order to make important revisions in foreign policy. He believed in a strong and active presidency. In his speech on 25 January 1960 to the National Press Club, Kennedy declared that the president "must above all be the Chief Executive in every sense of the word. He must be prepared to exercise the fullest powers of his office."[168] On 3 September 1960 he claimed that the president "is the only one who can speak for the people of the United States."[169] In his article in the November issue of the Catholic World, Kennedy wrote that "if Washington is the capital city of the world, the President must be its leader... The President must be the man capable of acting as Commander-in-Chief of the grand alliance."[170] During his term of presidency, Kennedy took bold actions extending presidential power. Without consulting Congress, he allowed the CIA to implement the Bays of Pigs landing to topple the Cuban regime,[171] he deepened the American involvement in Vietnam, he challenged Soviet Premier Khrushchev over Berlin[172] and he risked a nuclear war in the Cuban missile crisis.[173]

Lyndon B. Johnson increased presidential power especially by his tactics of handling the Vietnam war. He took important decisions without involvement of Congress or other governmental bodies. His group of advisers was very small and he overwhelmed almost all of them with his personality in taking decisions. Like President Kennedy, he kept important decisions for himself and for the group of the Tuesday lunches, which included the Secretaries of State and Defense and the director of the CIA[174] Johnson continued the consolidation of power in the presidency by securing the support of the Congress in escalating the war in Vietnam. With the Gulf of Tonkin resolution in 1964, the Congress almost unanimously decided to empower the president to "take all necessary measures to repel any armed attack against forces of the United States and to prevent further aggression in Southeast Asia."[175] The resolution was adopted by the Senate by a vote of 88 to 2 and by the House of Representatives by a vote of 416 to 0.[176] It was considered by many scholars a blank cheque by the Congress, giving the President wide war-making powers without having to consult the Congress first. Johnson used the resolution to justify his actions of escalating the war in Vietnam and to share responsibilities with Congress. Johnson also ordered 22,000 American troops to the Dominican Republic in the spring of 1965 without consulting the Congress.

The presidential power reached its peak during the Nixon administration, which succeeded in centralizing power in the White House. Nixon and his national security adviser Kissinger both distrusted the professional foreign policy organizations and therefore preferred a system of foreign policy making which is dominated by the president and his advisers.[177] Nixon clearly wanted to be his own Secretary of State and therefore appointed one of his

---

[168] Fairlie, *The Kennedy Promise*, p. 66.
[169] Ibid., p. 67.
[170] Ibid., p. 69.
[171] Schlesinger, *The Imperial Presidency*, p. 172.
[172] Ibid., p. 173.
[173] Ibid., p. 173, Fulbright, *The Arrogance of Power*, pp. 48-49.
[174] Brandon, *The Retreat of American Power*, pp. 47-48.
[175] Divine, *Since 1945 Politics and Diplomacy in Recent American History*, p. 555.
[176] For Senator Fulbright's views on the resolution see Fulbright, *The Arrogance of Power*, pp. 50-52.
[177] Robert J. Strong, *Bureaucracy and Statesmanship*, New York: University Press of America, 1986, pp. 20, 57.

friends reliable but inexperienced in foreign affairs, William P. Rogers, as his Secretary of State. Nixon reduced the power of the Cabinet and the Congress in foreign affairs to the minimum point.[178] His adviser Kissinger was far more influential in making foreign policy than the Secretaries of State and Defense. Nixon did not consult the Congress when he ordered the American troops to invade Cambodia and Laos. Using the concept of national security Nixon established a presidential secrecy system,[179] preventing the public from learning many activities of the administration in domestic affairs as well as in foreign affairs. The Nixon administration also extended the concept of executive privileges in order to refuse to testify before congressional committees.[180] The excessive use of presidential power in foreign affairs by Nixon led the Congress to compete with the Presidency to regain its powers in foreign affairs and to pass some acts to limit the presidential power. When, as a result of the Watergate Scandal,[181] it was known that Nixon used the secrecy system to defeat his political opponents at home, public pressure forced him to resign from the presidency.

Jimmy Carter's memoirs illuminate how a president can manipulate foreign policy even in the aftermath of the Congress's forceful actions to bring the president into line. He explains that final decisions on basic foreign policy were made by himself, not the State Department, and that he discussed major foreign policy issues with only few people (the National Security Adviser, the Vice-President and the Secretaries of State and Defense) to the extent that the Cabinet meetings on foreign policy became almost unnecessary.[182] Carter also states that his administration carried out negotiations with the Chinese to reach an agreement and prepared the plan of hostage rescue from Iran without informing congressmen and public.[183] However, Carter admits that he faced the opposition of congressmen, public and formidable lobbies in many issues and that many worthy agreements were rejected because of the effective power of a small group in the Senate.[184] While explaining how he struggled to gain support of public, congressmen, lobbies and even officials of his own administration for the Panama Canal treaties, Carter reveals that he talked to one hundred senators privately and that he gained the vote of Jim Abourezk, a Lebanese descent, through the Prince Sultan of Saudi Arabia.[185]

b) The Congress

The Congress has, too, wide powers in foreign policy, sufficient to check and balance the presidential power. If it wants to do so, the Congress can block many foreign policy actions of the president and it can affect the general line of American foreign policy. Some

---

[178] Divine, *Since 1945 Politics and Diplomacy in Recent American History*, p. 212, Arthur M. Schlesinger, *The Cycles of American History*, Boston: Houghton Mifflin Company, 1986, p. 280, Grantham, *The United States Since 1945*, pp. 265, 277, Schlesinger, *The Imperial Presidency*, pp. 198, 200-201, 220, 246.

[179] Schlesinger, *The Cycles of American History*, pp. 280-281, Strong, *Bureaucracy and Statesmanship*, pp. 61, 63, 70.

[180] Jones, *The Limits of Liberty*, p. 563, Schlesinger, *The Cycles of American History*, p. 277.

[181] *Keesing's Contemporary Archives*, 1973, vol. 19, pp. 25917-25923, 26069-26080, 26109-26114, 26229-26233, ibid., 1974, vol. 20, pp. 26290-26291, 26462-26464, 26537-26540, 26645-26650, 26677-26779, 26723-26724.

[182] Jimmy Carter, *Keeping Faith: Memoirs of a President*, London: Collins, 1982, pp. 52, 55-56, 60.

[183] Ibid., pp. 199-200, 511.

[184] Ibid., pp. 83, 225.

[185] Ibid., pp. 156-157.

constitutional prerogatives of the Congress in foreign affairs are as follows:[186] (a) The advice and consent prerogative: The Senate has the authority to give advice to the president in negotiating and making treaties and to give consent to treaties. Treaties have to be approved by a two-thirds vote of the Senate to take affect, but executive agreements do not require the approval of the Senate. (b) The confirmation of appointments: Appointment of ambassadors and high officials, too, has to gain senatorial approval. (c) The power of the purge: the Congress has the right to reduce, maintain or refuse foreign policy allotments suggested by the executive branch. The House of the Representatives can legitimize, cut or refuse the executive budget. (d) War powers: The Congress is authorized to raise and support armed forces, to provide and maintain a navy and to declare war against an enemy. (e) Economic powers: The Congress is empowered with the authority of regulating commerce with foreign nations. Informally the Congress constitutes a forum for national debate on foreign affairs. Discussion of foreign affairs in the Congress, testimonies of specialists and experts and responsible officials before the Congress affect the Presidency and the public opinion.

In spite of its wide constitutional authorities the Congress did not have a powerful voice in determining American foreign policy in the post-World War II period. Until the late 1960s, the Congress's role in foreign affairs remained very small.[187] It generally served as an organ justifying foreign policy actions of the American administrations. It was regarded as a duty of the Congress to give prompt support and consent to the presidents on matters of foreign relations. The Congress did not exploit the right of confirming diplomatic appointments as an instrument of policy and because the president could make executive agreements without the consent of Congress, the prerogative of approving treaties was of little effect. It made small cuts in the military budgets of the governments, but the presidents generally succeeded in getting what they wanted. Congress did not reject the executive budgets. The example of how far Congress remained under the control of the Presidency is the Gulf of Tonkin Resolution, with which Congress gave a blank cheque to the executive in committing American troops abroad.

When it appeared that Johnson's tactics of handling the Vietnam war were not good enough to solve the problem, some Congressmen, especially some members of Johnson's own party, began to oppose the president's actions in Vietnam. Democrat senators William Fulbright, Frank Church, Eugene McCarthy and Vance Hartke bitterly attacked the escalation of American military involvement in Vietnam.[188] At the end of 1968, the Congress, especially the Senate Foreign Relations Committee, started a campaign to reassert its constitutional powers in foreign affairs, which it had lost, to the Presidency since the end of the World War II.[189] Congressmen had felt humiliated by the way President Johnson had used their approval for escalating the war in Vietnam.

After Nixon came to power, Congress increased its initiatives to challenge Nixon's struggle to concentrate power in the White House. In June 1969, the Senate passed a resolution, which asked the President not to commit the American armed forces to hostilities

---

[186] For detailed information see Crabb and Holt, *Invitation to Struggle*, pp. 38-49.
[187] Fulbright, *The Arrogance of Power*, p. 45, Dull, *The Politics of American Foreign Policy*, p. 297, Crabb and Holt, *Invitation to Struggle*, p. 51.
[188] Divine, *Since 1945 Politics and Diplomacy in Recent American History*, p. 161, Jones, *The Limits of Liberty*, p. 556, Grantham, *The United States Since 1945*, p. 241.
[189] Brandon, *The Retreat of American Power*, pp. 11-12.

on foreign territory without affirmative action by the Congress.[190] When Nixon sent American troops to Cambodia in December 1970, the Senate passed another law forbidding the President to use funds to introduce American ground combat troops or military advisers into Cambodia, Thailand and Laos.[191] In 1970, the Congress also repealed the Gulf of Tonkin Resolution. In November 1971, the Senate completely rejected the foreign aid authorization bill.[192] The Senate Foreign Relations Committee set up special committees to investigate the activities of the American administration. These committees inquired into American security agreements and commitments[193] and uncovered many unknown facts such as the American secret defense pact with Thailand and excessive American involvement in Laos.

The Congress's most important act in opposing the presidential power in foreign affairs is the War Powers Act of 1973, which was designed to restrain the President from taking the nation into armed conflicts and to provide Congressional participation in decisions of involving American troops abroad. The Congress overrode a presidential veto in passing the act. According to the new act, the President was forced to report to the Congress within 48 hours of starting an American armed involvement abroad and to withdraw the troops if the Congress refused to agree with it.[194] As a sign of its determination to affect foreign policy, the Congress refused the extension of the most favorable nation status to the Soviet Union, it embargoed arms sales to Turkey in 1975, and in early 1975 it rejected the appeal of the Ford administration to provide emergency military aid to the South Vietnamese regime.

Although the Congress showed some signs of affecting American foreign policy in the 1970s, the general trend in American tradition is the domination of foreign policy by the president. In general, the Congress can indirectly control the upper and lower limits of foreign policy and it can amend or block individual actions of the Presidency. But it has very little power to force the presidency to make changes in the general direction of American policy. It is generally believed that congressmen lack information and experience to make correct decisions and therefore foreign policy cannot be left to them.

As individual united political bodies, political parties in the American tradition have very little effect in shaping foreign policy. One party does not generally support or oppose foreign policy actions, but some congressmen from different political parties take initiatives in foreign policy. Party loyalty and party unity is very rare in foreign policy matters. There are many basic foreign policy principles on which the political parties agree. In the past, particularly in the post-world War II period, a considerable part of American foreign policy was bipartisan. The views of an American political party are not radically different from those of the other party. During elections, the parties feel compelled to present to the electorates different foreign policy options, different policy style and perceptions to appeal to as many voters as possible. But after the elections, they return to their state and local forms and pay very little attention to foreign policy matters and they exercise very little influence on policy-making process.[195]

[190] Ibid., p. 145.
[191] Ibid., pp. 146-147, Schlesinger, *The Imperial Presidency*, op. cit., p. 194.
[192] Brandon, *The Retreat of American Power*, p. 149.
[193] Ibid., p. 148, Schlesinger, *The Imperial Presidency*, op. cit., p. 201.
[194] Brandon, *The Retreat of American Power*, p. 211, Schlesinger, *The Imperial Presidency*, pp. 301-304.
[195] Dull, *The Politics of American Foreign Policy*, p. 135.

c) The Secretaries of State and Defense

The secretaries of state and defense are close advisers of the president in conducting foreign policy.[196] But their effect on foreign policy-making process depends on the president's willingness to consult them in shaping the policy and their personal capabilities. Some presidents may bypass the secretaries of state and defense and formulate foreign policy with his special advisers. Secretary of State of the Nixon administration, William Rogers, had less effect on foreign policy than national security adviser Kissinger. The secretaries of state and defense possess the potential to affect foreign policy decisions, provided by the important position of their departments. They have the power to formulate policies and take decisions within their departments, disregarding views of department officials and professionals. Channels are available for them to express their views to the president directly. But at the final stage, their effectiveness depends on the president's will.

d) The National Security Council

The National Security Council might be influential in foreign policy making in the sense that its members have the potential to be close special advisers of the president. President Kennedy benefited from the NSC in centralizing power in the White House and dealing with foreign policy matters. When the Cuban missile crisis erupted, he set up an executive committee of the NSC to deal with the problem.[197] During the Kennedy and Johnson administrations, the NSC served as an advisory body. As a whole, the council did not directly intervene in foreign policy making process, but some of its members attended decision-making meetings as advisers.[198]

The unique position of Henry Kissinger in shaping American foreign policy is a good example of how far a national security adviser can affect the conduct of foreign policy. Throughout the Nixon administration period, Kissinger remained as Nixon's principal foreign policy adviser, his chief negotiator and his leading foreign policy spokesman.[199] Having no trust in the bureaucracy, the public and the Congress in the formulation of foreign policy,[200] Kissinger structured the NSC in a new way so that it could dominate other state bodies in affecting decisions.[201] But Kissinger remained chief director of the NSC, denying freedom of actions to the council. He dominated American foreign policy during his service and served as *de facto* Secretary of State towering over the Secretaries of State and Defense.[202]

---

[196] Ibid., pp. 43-48.

[197] Ibid., p. 41.

[198] Edward A. Kolodziaj, "The National Security Council: Innovations and Implications" in Fox (ed.), *The Politics of U.S. Foreign Policy Making*, pp. 187-188.

[199] Brandon, *The Retreat of American Power*, p. 24, Strong, *Bureaucracy and Statesmanship*, pp. 53, 64.

[200] Brandon, *The Retreat of American Power*, p. 32, Landau, *Kissinger*, p. xiv, Dull, *The Politics of American Foreign Policy*, pp. 21, 52, John G. Stoessinger, *Crusaders and Pragmatists*, New York: W. W. Norton and Company, 1979, pp. 237, 238, 239.

[201] Brandon, *The Retreat of American Power*, p. 46, Landau, *Kissinger*, p. 140, Dull, *The Politics of American Foreign Policy*, pp. 41-42.

[202] Landau, *Kissinger*, p. 4, *Strong, Bureaucracy and Statesmanship*, p. xii. Jimmy Carter's NSC adviser, Zbigniew Brezizinski, too, was influential in foreign policy-making process. Carter, *Keeping Faith*, pp. 51-52, 55. Carter cites: "I hardly know the desk officers and others in State [Department], but work very closely with NSC people." Ibid., p. 450.

e) The CIA

The Central Intelligence Agency can be influential if it is allowed to be by the president. It was originally established to co-ordinate all American intelligence and counter-intelligence services and to perform services for the National Security Council. The director of the CIA is one of the closest associates of the president. Using his position, he can make recommendations to the president in foreign affairs and if he gains confidence of the president he can play role in making foreign policy. The CIA is famous for its plots to overthrow foreign governments. At the very beginning of his presidency, Kennedy was persuaded by the CIA to give permission for the Bay of Pigs operation designed to overthrow the Cuban communist regime.[203] After the failure of the operation, activities of the CIA diminished and the power of the agency decreased, but the CIA continued to have the potential to exercise considerable power.[204] The Senate investigations in the 1970s of the CIA activities revealed that from the time of the Kennedy administration onward the CIA had plotted to overthrow some foreign governments and assassinate their leaders and secretly watched the activities of individuals, groups, parties and radical political movements.[205]

f) The Military

The American military has the potential to influence foreign policy decisions because there is a strong relationship between defense and foreign policy in the modern world and the United States has been able to assume the world leadership because of its military power.[206] During war periods, the military is more likely to affect decisions. The secretary of defense is the boss of the Pentagon, he can impose control over the military. The secretary of defense of the Kennedy and Johnson administration, Robert McNamara, established a civilian control over the Pentagon. During the term of McNamara and Clark M. Clifford, the Pentagon had a powerful hand in formulating foreign policy.[207] However, in the Nixon administration era, the Secretary of Defense, M. R. Laird, and the Pentagon lost their influence on foreign policy though they prevented Kissinger from imposing his control over the military.[208] As Kissinger stated, "under the leadership of Secretary Laird, the Pentagon had not attempted to assert a prerogative in wide areas of foreign policy. It has confined itself more to strictly military considerations than has been the case at least in the two previous administrations."[209] The Chairman of the Joint Chiefs of Staff, too, has a powerful position in affecting foreign policy initiatives.

---

[203] Dull, *The Politics of American Policy*, p. 81.
[204] Hilsman, *The Politics of Policy Making in Defense and Foreign Affairs*, pp. 65-66.
[205] Jones, *The Limits of Liberty*, p. 565, Dull, *The Politics of American Foreign Policy*, pp. 78, 219.
[206] Dull, *The Politics of American Foreign Policy*, p. 62.
[207] Brandon, *The Retreat of American Power*, pp. 203, 209.
[208] Ibid., p. 212.
[209] Landau, *Kissinger*, p. 139.

g) The Public Opinion

The president has to consider the reaction of the public before formulating policies. The public sometimes might force the president to change his policies. But it is generally too weak to oppose and challenge the president's foreign policy actions. In fact, the president has more power of manipulating the public in foreign matters than he has in domestic matters. The great mass of the public generally shows no concern on a foreign issue unless that issue affects its interests. When the escalation of the war in Vietnam by President Johnson committed more American troops, American public opinion increasingly turned against the war and wanted an immediate end to it. The continuing escalation gave momentum to the anti-war and peace movements. It polarized public opinion and politicized and radicalized many groups, especially the youth. Students, religious groups, and civil right activists attended anti-war protests arranged throughout the country.[210] Growing public opposition to his policies over the Vietnam issue severely dented Johnson's prestige and forced him to decide not to run for the presidency for a second term.

During the Nixon administration, anti-war activists continued to harass the regime. The invasion of Cambodia and Laos caused an eruption of violence and turmoil throughout the United States and brought about student riots in college and university campuses. Under public pressure, President Nixon felt compelled to seek a way of terminating the war. As an immediate step, he began to withdraw a considerable number of the American troops from Vietnam. Opponents of the war did not get what they wanted from the Nixon administration. Nixon did not terminate the war immediately, on the contrary, to gain an "honorable peace", he escalated the war and spread it to Cambodia and Laos. However, the public influenced Nixon's policy by forcing him to Vietnamise the war that is to leave the war effort to the Vietnamese rather than to increase American troops in the battlefield.[211]

In the American political system, few pressure and interest groups are concerned with foreign policy decisions. Interest group structure is very weak in foreign affairs[212] and lobbying in the field of foreign relations is relatively rare. The most organized and effective pressure groups are ethnic associations whose members have strong ties with a country.[213] Those organized national minorities lobby in order to affect American foreign policy decisions to the advantage of their homeland and they are supported and funded by the foreign countries with which they have ethnic ties. The American Jewish community has worked for the interests of Israel and tried to influence foreign policy decisions related to Israel. The Turkish-American and the Greek-American communities have also worked to secure the American support for the cause of their ethnic groups in Cyprus.[214] Activities of interest groups in foreign affairs are directed towards the Congress as well as the government to affect the Congress decisions on matters of particular concern to their group. The president may also use some agencies to lobby on his behalf to ensure the acceptance of the laws supporting his policies and programs by the Congress.

---

[210] Grantham, *The United States Since 1945*, pp. 241-243.

[211] Hilsman, *The Politics of Policy Making in Defense and Foreign Affairs*, p. 104.

[212] Agron Wildavsky, "the Two Presidencies" in Fox (ed.), *The Politics of U.S. Foreign Policy Making*, p. 180, Hilsman, *The Politics of Policy Making in Defense and Foreign Affairs*, pp. 69-70.

[213] Wildavsky, "the Two Presidencies", p. 180, Hilsman, *The Politics of Policy Making in Defense and Foreign Affairs*, p. 70.

[214] Dull, *The Politics of American Foreign Policy*, p. 146. For more detailed information on the role of lobby groups see the section on the Johnson letter in Chapter VI and on the arms embargo in Chapter VII.

Sometimes senators may exert an influence on American foreign policy for reasons that have little or nothing to do with the particular foreign policy issue but arise from reaction to the President's domestic policies or other matters. President Carter's memoirs are illuminating in this connection. In his account of difficulties he faced in getting senators to accept the Panama Canal Treaties in 1979, he records: "Jim Abourezk says that because of the closed conference meetings in energy from which he is excluded, he's considering voting against the Panama Canal Treaty... Even my friend Senator Jim Sasser of Tennessee sent me word that he could not vote for the second treaty because of some of his home-state issues on which we disagreed."[215]

The American business, too, has great interests in influencing foreign policy decisions. Since its investment abroad and its worldwide trade and business contacts are very important for the fate of its companies, the American business asks the administration to pursue a foreign policy protecting business interests abroad. In the opinion of James Dull, "American foreign policy since the World War II has been designed, in part, to promote American business interests abroad." He also claims that "business is a major actor in the political process, and decision makers cannot easily disregard its voice".[216] Big business has a great power to influence the general policy making process because it provides financial support for candidates for the presidency and the Congress and its members serve in the administration. G. William Domhoff goes so far as to say that "... American foreign policy during the post war era was initiated, planned and carried out by the richest, most powerful and most international-minded owners and managers of major corporations and financial institutions".[217] Clearly, the American president is expected to pursue the sort of foreign policy that will benefit American business interests abroad.

---

[215] Jimmy Carter, Keeping Faith, p. 175.
[216] Dull, *The Politics of American Foreign Policy,* p. 143.
[217] G. William Domhoff, "Who Made American Foreign Policy 1945-1963?" in Fox (ed.), *The Politics of U.S. Foreign Policy Making,* p. 95.

Chapter 4

U.S.-TURKISH MILITARY RELATIONS 1960-1980

Military contacts certainly constituted the most important aspect of the Turkish-American relationship because the two countries came together mainly as a result of security concerns. While mutual security interests brought about a special close alliance between the two states, the character of the relationship ended up with Turkey's military dependence on the United States. This chapter tries to explain how this relationship was established and took this character during the course of time. It notes the course of events in the development of this military relationship in the 1960s and 1970s, the problems that arose and their causes and mentions the heated public discussion on Turkey's alliance relations in Turkish domestic politics. It particularly emphasizes the Turkish administration's attempts to alter its image as the satellite of the USA and questions how far it succeeded in these efforts. In order to establish a sound basis for understanding, the true character of the military relationship and for assessing U.S. influence on Turkey, the chapter further considers why each country was important to the security and defense of the other. (Turkey's strategic importance for the USA and U.S. military assistance to Turkey.)

1. THE FORMATION OF THE FORMAL MILITARY RELATIONSHIP

Immediately following the Second World War, in response to a threat from the Soviet Union, Turkey began to seek an alliance with the United States.[1] In 1945, the Soviet Union informed Turkey of its intention not to extend the Treaty of Neutrality and Non-Aggression between the two countries, which was due to expire in November 1945, demanded military bases on the Straits and the secession of two north-eastern Turkish provinces to it, and sought in international forums the revision of the Montreaux Convention regulating the status of the Straits.[2] Although the United States did not offer help to Turkey in the early stages when Soviet pressures were more prominent, U.S. policy-makers gradually came to the conclusion

---

[1] Theodore A. Couloumbis, *The United States, Greece and Turkey*, New York: Praeger, 1983, pp. 12-13, 200.

[2] Duygu B. Sezer, "Turkey's Security Policies" in Jonathan Alford (ed.), *Greece and Turkey*, Aldershot: Gower, 1984, p. 54, Richard C. Campany, *Turkey and the United States*, New York: Praeger, 1986, p. 80, Mehmet Gönlübol, "NATO, USA and Turkey" in Kemal H. Karpat (ed.), *Turkey's Foreign Policy in Transition*, Leiden: E. J. Brill, 1975, p. 13.

that the fall of Turkey would further encourage Soviet expansion in the eastern Mediterranean and thus would harm specific U.S. interests in the region as well as the general ones in the context of the newly-emerging superpower competition. Believing that the loss of Turkey and Greece would bring the loss of the whole Middle Eastern region,[3] the Americans decided to undertake responsibilities in Greece and Turkey, which were about be relinquished by the British because of financial problems.

As a confirmation of the new policy, the U.S. battleship Missouri visited Turkey on 5 April 1946, carrying the body of Turkish Ambassador Minür Ertegün, who died in Washington during the war. Then, the United States sent a note to the Soviet Union on 9 August 1946, stating that any attack or threats of attack against the Turkish Straits would be a matter for the UN Security Council.[4] At the joint session of the Congress on 12 March 1947, President Truman asked the Congress to provide authority for assistance to Greece and Turkey.[5] Truman's aid proposal was approved in the Senate with a vote of 67 to 23 on 22 April and in the House with a vote of 287 to 107 on 22 May. Truman considered the doctrine his most important decision since the decision to drop the atomic bomb on Hiroshima; it certified the U.S. determination to resist any Soviet aggression against Turkey with all means at its disposal, including the force of arms.[6] In his memoirs, Harry Truman wrote:

> The alternative was the loss of Greece and the extension of the Iron Curtain across the eastern Mediterranean. If Greece was lost, Turkey would become an untenable outpost in a sea of communism... The ideals and the traditions of our nation demanded that we come to the aid o Greece and Turkey and that we put the world on notice that it would be our policy to support the cause of freedom wherever it was threatened.[7]

The Truman doctrine marked the beginning of U.S.-Turkish defense relationship on the basis of the containment of Soviet and communist expansionism.[8] The military assistance agreement on 12 July 1947[9] established the first official military contact between the two countries. Under the agreement, the United States supplied Turkey with weaponry and other military equipment, personnel for instruction, and financial aid and technical advice for construction programs of road, harbor and strategic installations.[10] On 4 July 1948, the United States signed another agreement with Turkey in order to supply economic aid in accordance with the Marshall Plan, which was designed to help the reconstruction of European countries whose main industry and infrastructure were destroyed by the war.

After the North Atlantic Treaty Organization was established in 1949, Turkish officials made the utmost efforts to join the organization for the following reasons: Turkey needed the guarantee of NATO, especially the United States, which was the most powerful state and

---

[3] George McGhee, *The U.S. Turkish NATO Middle East Connection*, London: MacMillan, 1990, pp. 20-22.

[4] Bruce R. Kuniholm, *The Origins of the Cold War in the Near East*, Princeton, N. J.: Princeton University Press, 1980, p. 362, Dean Acheson, *Present at the Creation*, London: Hamish Hamilton Ltd., 1970, p. 196.

[5] John M. Collins, *Greece and Turkey: Some Military Implications Related to NATO and the Middle East*, Report Prepared for Special Committee on Investigations of Committee on Foreign Affairs, 94th Congress, 1st Session, February 28, 1975, Washington: U.S. Government Printing Office, 1975, pp. 19-22, Dankwart A. Rustow, *Turkey: America's Forgotten Ally*, New York: Council on Foreign Relations, 1987, p. 89.

[6] Bruce R. Kuniholm, "Turkey and NATO: Past, Present and Future", *ORBIS*, Summer 1983, p. 422.

[7] H. S. Truman; *Memoirs, Years of Trial and Hope*, vol. II, Garden City: Doubleday, 1956, pp. 100-101.

[8] Campany, *Turkey and the United States*, p. 2, Couloumbis, *The United States, Greece and Turkey*, p. 13.

[9] For its text see Appendix A, Campany, *Turkey and the United States*, pp. 96-99, George S. Harris, *Troubled Alliance*, Washington D.C.: American Enterprise Institute, 1972, pp. 213-215.

[10] Ferenc A. Vali, *Bridge Across the Bosporus*, Baltimore: The John Hopkins Press, 1971, pp. 125-126.

leader of the Western camp, to counter the threat of its big neighbor, the Soviet Union.[11] The NATO membership would guarantee and institutionalize the Western aid, which was essential for socio-economic development of Turkey and modernization of its armed forces. The acceptance by the Atlantic alliance would also confirm that Turkey was an integral part of the Western world and would strengthen organic relations with the European family of nations.[12] In Vali's words, "identification with that part of the world and with the civilization represented by it was to guarantee security, development, and acculturation."[13]

It was clear that the Turks would not be satisfied with a membership of an alliance of Mediterranean or Middle Eastern states, which would be sponsored by Western powers. In order to gain the trust of the Western states for NATO membership, Turkey sent a 4,500-man unit to the Korean War in 1950 to fight with U.S. troops.[14] The Turkish brigade, which was the third largest contingent after the American and South Korean forces, performed well during the war and earned high praise.[15] In spite of a general hesitation within NATO and opposition of some members,[16] NATO states gave approval to the membership of Turkey mostly as a result of the U.S. request for it. On 15 May 1951, the United States proposed to NATO members that Greece and Turkey be accepted as full members.[17] The proposal was accepted at the meeting of the NATO Council in September 1951 in Ottawa[18] and finally Turkey became an official member of NATO with the protocol of accession[19] coming into force on 18 February 1952.

To NATO countries, specifically the United States, Turkey's membership of NATO offered considerable advantages at that time:[20] Firstly, the south-eastern flank of NATO would be protected against hostile forces, and Soviet aggression and expansion would be further contained. Secondly, additional twenty-two Turkish divisions, which were the least costly forces to maintain in the alliance, would make an important contribution to NATO's deterrent force. Thirdly, the presence of Turkish forces along its southern border would force the Soviet Union to divert significant forces from Central Europe to commit against Turkey. Fourthly, Turkey's strategic location would be a valuable asset to prevent the Soviet expansion to the Middle East, whose oil held vital importance for the Western states. As

---

[11] Sezer, Sezer, "Turkey's Security Policies", pp. 54-55, Couloumbis, *The United States, Greece and Turkey*, p. 20, Campany, *Turkey and the United States*, p. 26.

[12] Harris, *Troubled Alliance*, p. 44, Vali, *Bridge Across the Bosporus*, p. 115, Rustow, *Turkey*, p. 91.

[13] Vali, *Bridge Across the Bosporus*, p. 115.

[14] Ibid., p. 37, Harris, *Troubled Alliance*, pp. 39-40.

[15] U.S. President Johnson and Secretary of State Dean Rusk praised Turkey's Korean effort during Turkish President Sunay's visit to the USA in 1967, *Amerika'da Onbir Gün*, Ankara: Yarın Yayınları, 1967, pp. 10, 16.

[16] Monteagle Stearns, *Entangled Allies*, New York: Council on Foreign Relations Press, 1992, pp. 74-75. Stearns, who was serving in the U.S. embassy in Ankara in the summer of 1950, argues that the high possibility of Soviet attack against Turkey at the time of the Korean crisis led Western leaders to invite Greece and Turkey to NATO. Ibid., p. 75. He cites, "the military threat to Turkey was thought to be so grave after the outbreak of the Korean War that an evacuation plan for U.S. residents was prepared, and a handful of officials were designated to remain behind in the event of a Soviet occupation of Ankara." Ibid., p. 170n.

[17] Harris, *Troubled Alliance*, p. 42.

[18] Gönlübol, "NATO, USA and Turkey", pp. 26-27.

[19] For the text see Collins, *Greece and Turkey*, pp. 29-31.

[20] Harris, *Troubled Alliance*, pp. 42, 50, Gönlübol, "NATO, USA and Turkey", p. 26, Mehmet Gönlübol et al., *Olaylarla Türk Dış Politikası*, Ankara: A.Ü. S.B.F. Yayını, 1977, p. 238, Vali, *Bridge Across the Bosporus*, p. 117, Bruce R. Kuniholm, "U. S. Policy in the Near East: the Triumphs and Tribulations of the Truman Administration" in Micheal J. Lacey (ed.), *The Truman Presidency*, Cambridge: Cambridge University Press, 1991, pp. 309, 316, 317.

Omar Bradley, Chairman of the U.S. Joint Chiefs of Staff, told the Foreign Relations Committee of the U.S. Senate on 15 January 1952: "Turkey, astride the Bosporus and Dardenelles, guards the approach by water from the Black Sea to the Mediterranean and to the Suez Canal and Egypt farther south. Turkey flanks the land routes from the North to the strategically important oil fields of the Middle East."[21] Finally, Turkish airfields would be available for NATO allies for important missions.

2. RELATIONS IN THE 1950S

Once Turkey entered NATO, this connection served as the general basis for the whole range of military relations between Turkey and the United States. Under the NATO arrangement, mainly the Americans were involved in the Turkish military establishment. American military advisers directed works to co-ordinate Turkey's defense plans with those of other NATO states and tried to train, equip and organize Turkish armed forces under the American model to increase their efficiency.[22] Together with arming of Turkish military forces with U.S. weapons, this heavy American involvement in the Turkish military structure certainly played an important role in Turkey's military dependence on the USA, which was more clearly realized when the U.S. Congress imposed an arms embargo on Turkey in 1975. This situation also led to the accusation that Turkey was a satellite of the USA.

Under Article III of the North Atlantic Treaty and the NATO Status of Forces Agreement of June 1951, Turkey and the United States entered a wide range of bilateral military arrangements.[23] Article III states: "In order more effectively to achieve the objectives of this Treaty, the Parties, separately and jointly, by means of continuous and effective self-help and mutual aid, will maintain and develop their individual and collective capacity to resist armed attack."[24] Some of these arrangements were full-fledged agreements, openly published and ratified by the Turkish parliament, such as the Status of Forces Agreement of June 1954, which provided privileges and immunities for non-diplomatic U.S. personnel in Turkey.[25] There were also public and secret exchanges of notes and executive agreements, which were negotiated between U.S. and Turkish officials in different ranks and ministries and not ratified by the Turkish parliament. The Military Facilities Agreement of June 1954 was the most important of these. Apart from formal understandings, U.S. and Turkish officials often worked out their own mutually agreeable procedures to fill gaps or implement a general agreement.[26]

These bilateral agreements dealt with "such specific matters as (a) U.S. force deployments; (b) military exercises by U.S. forces; (c) the legal and administrative status of

---

[21] McGhee, *The U.S. Turkish NATO Middle East Connection*, pp. 88-89.

[22] Harris, *Troubled Alliance*, pp. 53-54, Charlotee Wolf, *Garrison Community*, Westport: Greenwood, 1969, pp. 42-43.

[23] Gönlübol, "NATO, USA and Turkey", p. 35, Gönlübol *et al.*, *Olaylarla Türk Dış Politikası*, pp. 244, 525.

[24] Richard F. Grimmett, *United States Military Installations and Objectives in the Mediterranean*, Report for Subcommittee on Europe and the Middle East of the Committee on International Relations, U. S. Congress, March 27, 1977. Washington: U.S. Government Printing Office, 1977, p. 57.

[25] For the text see Appendix B, Harris, *Troubled Alliance*, pp. 217-220, Campany, *Turkey and the United States*, pp. 100-102.

[26] Harris, *Troubled Alliance*, pp. 54-55, Gönlübol, "NATO, USA and Turkey", pp. 35,36, Gönlübol *et al.*, *Olaylarla Türk Dış Politikası*, pp. 244, 525, Grimmett, *United States Military Installations and Objectives in the Mediterranean*, p. 6, 41.

U.S. forces; (d) intelligence activities; (e) operations plans for U.S. forces; (f) operations plans for joint force commands."[27] The agreements which granted U.S. personnel immunity from the Turkish tax and law system and which allowed various kinds of U.S. facilities to operate free from Turkish taxes, rules or laws were subjected to heavy criticism by Turkish public opinion later in the 1960s. The number of U.S. personnel and dependants, who came to Turkey under the bilateral agreements, reached 24,000 at its height. Some of them were military advisers belonging to JUSMMAT, Joint United States Military Mission for Aid to Turkey, which was originally established in 1947.[28] The civilian group included members of the U.S. diplomatic and consular missions, the U.S. Information Service, the Agency for International Development, the Peace Corps and various private business or educational organizations.[29] TUSLOG, The United States Logistics Group, which was established in 1955, regulated all activities of U.S. personnel such as hospital, dental, veterinary, legal, weather, chaplain, mortuary, and postal services; the exchange and commissionary services, recreational facilities, intelligence groups, all means of communication, the dependant schools, transportation, security, law enforcement, control of the estate, etc.[30]

In formulating bilateral arrangements Turkish and U.S. officials made some mistakes which brought about the severe criticism of the U.S. and NATO by Turkish public opinion in the 1960s. Former U.S. official George Harris wrote in his book:

> Neither state exercised close and comprehensive control over American activity in Turkey. There were no full records of the verbal understandings to which either was committed; knowledge of some of the more sensitive activities was extremely closely held on both sides. The Turkish General Staff was not organized to provide centralized co-ordination of U.S. activities in Turkey. Nor, indeed, was any responsible senior American commander named to oversee all the various U.S. military elements in Turkey.[31]

Perhaps not surprisingly, in such an atmosphere of close friendship Turkish officials and military officers belonging to different departments fulfilled requests of their American counterparts without applying bureaucratic procedures, but this resulted in a web of written and oral bilateral agreements concluded by different government offices, each not knowing what the others were doing.[32]

During the 1950s, seeing no way of staying outside the East-West conflict and alliances in a bipolar world and seeing no defense policy outside NATO,[33] the Turkish governments identified Turkey's security interests with those of NATO, especially the United States. It is striking that Turkey's entry into NATO was approved in the Turkish Parliament by a vote of 404 to 0, with one abstention. Foreign Minister Fuat Köprülü told the Turkish Parliament in December 1951: "Our national interests are identical from every standpoint with the joint interests of NATO and with its geographic and military requirements."[34] In the 1950s, Turkey

---

[27] Grimmett, *United States Military Installations and Objectives in the Mediterranean*, p. 6.

[28] Wolf, *Garrison Community*, pp. 42-43.

[29] Vali, *Bridge Across the Bosporus*, p. 137.

[30] Wolf, *Garrison Community*, pp. 44-45.

[31] Harris, *Troubled Alliance*, p. 55.

[32] Gönlübol, "NATO, USA and Turkey", pp. 35-36, Sezai Orkunt, *Türkiye-ABD Askeri İlişkileri*, İstanbul: *Milliyet* Yayınları, 1978, p. 258, the author's interview with retired Turkish academic and columnist Fahir Armaoğlu, Ali Halil, *Atatürkçü Dış Politika ve NATO ve Türkiye*, İstanbul, 1968, p. 205.

[33] Harris, *Troubled Alliance*, p. 51.

[34] Ibid., p. 45. See also speeches of Köprülü in 1955 and President Celal Bayar in 1956, which considered Turkey's NATO connection a national policy in Gönlübol *et al.*, *Olaylarla Türk Dış Politikası*, pp. 321-322.

supported and joined Western initiatives in different parts of the world.[35] It played a major role in the establishment of the abortive Middle East Command and the Baghdad and Balkan Pacts,[36] it acted as the spokesman of the West at the Bandung Conference of non-aligned states in 1955 and it gave full support to the West during some events in the Middle East such as the Suez crisis of 1956, the Eisenhower doctrine[37] and the Syrian crisis of 1957, the Lebanese and Jordanian events[38] and the Iraqi revolution of 1958.

The United States, in return, frequently reiterated its commitment to Turkey's security. After the Suez crisis, on 29 November 1956, the USA declared that threats to the territory of the Baghdad Pact members (including Turkey) would be viewed "with utmost gravity."[39] When Turkey was threatened by Moscow during the Syrian crisis, U.S. Secretary of State Dulles assured Turkish rulers that, in case of a Soviet attack, the United States would not limit itself to a "purely defensive operation."[40] After the Iraqi revolution, at the request of Turkish officials, the United States signed with Turkey the Cooperation Agreement on 5 March 1959, which stated that "in case of aggression against Turkey" the United States "will take such appropriate actions, including the use of armed forces" to assist Turkey.[41] The Turkish opposition, the Republican People's Party, severely criticized the agreement on the ground that it included the concept of "indirect aggression", which could be used by the government to call U.S. intervention against the internal opposition as Lebanese President Chamoun did in 1958.[42] Later in the 1960s, some Turkish critics claimed that the agreement did not bring any additional guarantee for Turkey's security, but it constituted a threat for its independence, being a constant reminder of the U.S. control of Turkey.[43]

In the 1950s, the Eisenhower administration accepted "massive retaliation" as the strategy of NATO, which required a total nuclear response to Soviet aggression on any scale against a member of the alliance.[44] The Turks thought that the strategy provided enough deterrence to the Soviet threat against Turkey. The strategy seemed reasonable in an age when the Soviet Union had considerable advantage over Europe on conventional forces and

---

[35] Gönlübol, "NATO, USA and Turkey", p. 30, George S. Harris, "Turkey and the United States" in Karpat *(ed.)*, *Turkey's Foreign Policy in Transition*, pp. 54-55, Vali, *Bridge Across the Bosporus*, pp. 126-127.

[36] *Documents on International Affairs* 1951, the Royal Institute of International Affairs, Oxford University Press, p. 65, ibid. 1953, pp. 264-266, *Foreign Relations of the United States* 1952-1954, Washington D.C.: the U.S. Government Printing Office, 1986, pp. 138-140, McGhee, *The U.S. Turkish NATO Middle East Connection*, pp. 154-156.

[37] R. P. Magnus, *Documents on the Middle East*, Washington D.C.: American Enterprise Institute, 1969, pp. 86-94, *Documents on International Affairs* 1957, p. 259.

[38] *Documents on International Affairs* 1958, p. 295.

[39] *Documents on American Foreign Relations*, New York: Harper Brothers, 1957, p. 378, *Documents on International Affairs* 1956, pp. 341-342.

[40] Vali, *Bridge Across the Bosporus*, pp. 126-127.

[41] For the text see Appendix C, *Keesing's Contemporary Archives*, 1959-1960, vol. 12, p. 16749, Harris, *Troubled Alliance*, pp. 221-223, *Documents on International Affairs* 1959, pp. 343-345, *United States Security Agreements and Commitments Abroad*, Greece and Turkey, Hearings Before the Subcommittee on United States Security Agreements Abroad of the Committee on Foreign Relations, U.S. Senate, 91st Congress, 2nd Session, Part 7, June 9 and 11, 1970, Washington: U.S. Government Printing Office, 1970, pp. 1857-1858.

[42] MP Bülent Ecevit was particularly outspoken in this subject. Harris, *Troubled Alliance*, pp. 67, 69, Gönlübol *et al.*, *Olaylarla Türk Dış Politikası*, pp. 319-320, *Cumhuriyet*, 6 February 1960, p. 5, A. Haluk Ulman and R. H. Dekmejian, "Changing Patterns in Turkish Foreign Policy, 1959-1967", *ORBIS*, vol. 11, Fall 1967, pp. 773-774. Turkish columnist Fahir Armaoğlu told the author that "indirect aggression" meant internal subversive activities.

[43] Saffet Ural, *Cumhuriyet Senatosu Tutanak Dergisi (CSTD)*, 4 February 1968, term 1, sess. 7, vol. 45-3, p. 452, Edip Çelik, "İkili Andlaşmalardan Biri", *Cumhuriyet*, 2 March 1966, p. 2.

[44] Harris, *Troubled Alliance*, p. 51, Gönlübol, "NATO, USA and Turkey", p. 41.

neither of the superpowers had long-range missiles to hit the other side from their own countries. The absence of long-range missiles gave importance to U.S. bases in Turkey to check Soviet military activities and to hit Soviet territory with short-range missiles.[45] When the Soviets seemed to take the lead on inter-continental strategic missiles with the launching of Sputnik in 1957, the United States tried to fill the missile gap by deploying intermediate range strategic missiles (Jupiters and Thors) to NATO's European allies[46] The story of the Jupiter missiles which had implications for U.S.-Turkish military relations will be mentioned in Chapter VI.

Turkish initiatives in the 1950s, which in effect advanced U.S. interests in the Middle East, and U.S. announcements of support for Turkish security, too, strengthened Turkey's image as a faithful follower of U.S. policies.

3. THE TURKISH JUNTA PERIOD

The Turkish military officers, who seized power on 27 May 1960, did not make any changes in Turkey's military relations. They proclaimed in their first public declaration that they believed in NATO and CENTO and were loyal to them.[47] They held their predecessor's view on the cold war, seeing the Soviet Union as a threat to Turkey's security and considering the U.S. and NATO connection in the interests of Turkey. In the eyes of military rulers, U.S. economic and military aid was vital to achieve economic development, to keep a strong army and to improve the situation of military officers.[48] Therefore, the 27 May regime was more dependent on the United States than the Menderes government had been, thus it, too, was open to U.S. influence. In his reply to Soviet Premier Khrushchev's letter, which proposed good relations between the two countries provided that Turkey embarked upon neutrality, Turkish President Cemal Gürsel reiterated Turkey's loyalty to her commitments stemming from NATO and CENTO.[49] The new Turkish regime's attitude toward its alliances was welcomed by the U.S. President in his message to the Turkish premier on 11 June 1960.[50]

The Turkish military regime seemed willing to make some changes in bilateral military arrangements with the United States. In his press conference on 17 September 1960, Turkish President Gürsel hinted that the implementation method of the NATO Status of Forces Agreement should be changed.[51] Some inter-ministerial studies were conducted to deal with difficulties stemming from the use of U.S. bases in Turkey and the Turkish Foreign Ministry gave its opinion that all principles of non-secret bilateral agreements should be collected in a

---

[45] Orkunt, *Türkiye-ABD Askeri İlişkileri*, p. 246.

[46] Gönlübol, "NATO, USA and Turkey", p. 41, Sezer, "Turkey's Security Policies", p. 62, Oral Sander, "Turkey: the Staunchest Ally of the United States?", *Turkish Yearbook of International Relations*, vol. 15, 1975, p. 19.

[47] *Cumhuriyet*, 27 May 1960, Vali, *Bridge Across the Bosporus*, pp. 40, 127, Gönlübol *et al., Olaylarla Türk Dış Politikası*, p. 333. See also Foreign Minister Selim Sarper's 1961 budget speech praising NATO and CENTO in Gönlübol *et al., Olaylarla Türk Dış Politikası*, pp. 334-335.

[48] Harris, *Troubled Alliance*, p. 86, Gönlübol, "NATO, USA and Turkey", pp. 14-15, Feroz Ahmad, *Turkey's Experiment in Democracy*, London: C. Hurst and Company, 1977, p. 401. In his memoirs published in Turkish newspaper *Sabah* on 22 June 1994 Colonel Alparslan Türkeş, who was among the military leadership of the 27 May coup, confirmed this point.

[49] For the texts of letters dated June 28, 1960 and July 8, 1960 see *Middle Eastern Affairs*, vol. 11, No. 10, November 1960, pp. 317-320.

[50] Gönlübol *et al., Olaylarla Türk Dış Politikası*, pp. 333-334, *Cumhuriyet*, 17 June 1960, p. 5.

[51] Gönlübol *et al., Olaylarla Türk Dış Politikası*, p. 336.

document.[52] Military rulers showed particular interest in restricting the privileges and immunities of U.S. personnel. To obtain the right to decide the duty status of U.S. personnel committing a crime, the junta formed a special inter-ministerial commission and proposed to U.S. authorities changes in this issue. Since the Americans did not want to surrender this important right, no development was achieved.[53] While failing to obtain concessions from U.S. authorities, the Turkish military junta brought a new legal mechanism under the 1961 constitution, which would facilitate the legalization of secret and public executive agreements with the United States. With the new arrangement, "implementing agreements pursuant to an international agreement... do not require approval by the Turkish Grand National Assembly."[54] A parliamentary committee specifically noted that this article would permit the government "to carry out some necessarily secret arrangements of the free world defense system which we joined..."[55]

4. THE JOHNSON LETTER

U.S. President Johnson's famous letter to Turkish President İnönü in June 1964 caused changes in the Turkish perception of the Atlantic alliance.[56] Firstly, Johnson stated that "adhesion to NATO... means that NATO countries will not wage war on each other" and that therefore a war between Turkey and Greece was unthinkable. This was interpreted as meaning that only the United States could determine who could be Turkey's enemy and that Turkey could have no enemy other than the Soviet Union. If a NATO country violated Turkey's rights, NATO's interests would prevent it from taking any action.[57] Secondly, Johnson stated that the United States would not agree to the use of any U.S.-supplied military equipment for a Turkish intervention in Cyprus and reminded İnönü that "under Article IV of the Agreement with Turkey of July 1947, your government is required to obtain United States consent for the use of military assistance for purposes other than those for which such assistance was furnished."[58] The Turks realized that their alliance with the USA brought some limitations to Turkey's freedom of action and sovereignty.[59] Their army was equipped predominantly with U.S. weaponry and they would not able to use them to defend themselves against threats, which were not approved by the United States.

Finally and most importantly, Johnson warned that "your NATO allies have not had a chance to consider whether they have an obligation to protect Turkey against the Soviet Union if Turkey takes a step which results in Soviet intervention without the full consent and understanding of its NATO allies." The Turks were really shocked because they had based all their security on the guarantee provided by NATO and now doubts began to emerge about the credibility of the NATO umbrella in case of a Soviet attack. It seemed that the U.S.-Turkish

---

[52] Orkunt, *Türkiye-ABD Askeri İlişkileri*, p. 255, Haydar Tunçkanat, *CSTD*, 3 February 1967, term 1, sess. 6, vol. 38-3, p. 569.

[53] Harris, *Troubled Alliance*, pp. 88-89.

[54] Article 65 of the constitution cited by ibid., p. 89.

[55] Ibid., p. 89.

[56] For the texts of both premiers' letters see Appendix D and *Middle East Journal*, vol. 20, Summer 1966, pp. 386-393. The Johnson letter was also mentioned in the Chapter VI in the context of the Cyprus question.

[57] Gönlübol, "NATO, USA and Turkey", pp. 18, 35.

[58] For the full text of Article IV see Appendix A and Harris, *Troubled Alliance*, pp. 214-215.

[59] Ecvet Güresin, "Amerika Dikkat Etmeli", *Cumhuriyet*, 25 August 1964, p. 1.

alliance was favoring one side; the Turks had taken risks to support the USA (Cuba and Korea), but the Americans did not even agree to the implementation of the NATO commitment for Turkey's survival.[60] In Sezer's words, Johnson "reserved to himself the right to define when and under what conditions the Soviet Union could be a threat to the security of Turkey."[61] Johnson's remarks compelled Turkish Prime Minister İnönü to conclude in his letter to Johnson "there are between us wide divergences of views as to the nature and basic principles of the North Atlantic Alliance. I must confess that this has been to us the source of great sorrow and grave concern. If NATO's structure is so weak as to give credit to the aggressor's allegations, then it means that this defect of NATO needs really to be remedied." The Johnson letter led the Turks to begin a wide-ranging re-evaluation of their alliance with NATO and to be more cautious in their dealings with both the USA and the USSR.

5. Turkish Initiatives to Gain More Independence

a) Improving Relations with the Countries outside the West

The disappointment over the Western attitude toward the Cyprus question led the Turks to try to normalize their relations with the Eastern bloc and Third World countries. The Soviet Union had renounced its claims on some Turkish territories in 1953[62] and made some overtures to Turkey to relax relations. All major NATO countries had already mended their fences with the Soviet Union. However, Turkey, seeing Soviet gestures as tactical changes, had stayed behind as the last inflexible "Cold Warrior."[63] With the realization that NATO did not provide firm and automatic security, Turkish rulers began to avoid getting involved in superpower politics and provoking the Soviet Union unnecessarily.[64] They thought that rapprochement with the USSR would bring economic assistance, increasing détente in military confrontation, hence greater security,[65] and more international support in matters involving national interests, especially in the Cyprus question.[66] The result was intensive exchanges of state visits and parliamentary delegations between Turkey and the Eastern bloc countries and USSR economic assistance to Turkey.[67] After returning from his visit to Moscow in September 1967, Prime Minister Demirel said: "I think we have entered a new era in our dealings with the Russians. As is known, there had been great strain between our

---

[60] Harris, "Turkey and the United States", pp. 59-60. Fahir Armaoğlu rightly commented that Turkey had entered NATO mainly to gain the commitment of the USA (not any other NATO members) and that if the USA was telling Turkey now that "NATO might not protect you", this was a total collapse of Turkey's security policy.

[61] Sezer, "Turkey's Security Policies", pp. 65-66.

[62] Gönlübol, "NATO, USA and Turkey", p. 27.

[63] Ibid., pp. 28, 29, 30, Vali, *Bridge Across the Bosporus*, pp. 133, 356.

[64] Sezer, "Turkey's Security Policies", pp. 66, 76.

[65] Harris, *Troubled Alliance*, p. 127.

[66] Ulman and Dekmejian, "Changing Patterns in Turkish Foreign Policy, 1959-1967", p. 779.

[67] *Keesing's Contemporary Archives*, 1963-1964, vol. 14, p. 20500, ibid., 1965-1966, vol. 15, p. 20936, ibid., 1967-1968, vol. 16, pp. 21881, 22335, 22672, ibid., 1969-1970, vol. 17, p. 23632, Yuluğ Tekin Kurat, *Elli Yıllık Cumhuriyetin Dış Politikası, 1923-1973*, Ankara: Türk Tarih Kurumu, 1975, pp. 299-304, Mehmet Gönlübol and A. Haluk Ulman, "Türk Dış Politikasının Yirmi Yılı 1945-1965", *SBF Dergisi*, vol. 21, No. 1, March 1966, pp. 174-175. On the improvement of Turkey's relations with the USSR see also George Harris, "Cross-Alliance Politics: Turkey and the Soviet Union", *Turkish Yearbook of International Relations*, vol. 12, 1972, pp. 1-32.

countries over the years, and in the period after World War II we had no relations at all. Now that gap has been bridged, I am not suggesting that all the doubts are gone, but I think the hostility is gone."[68] In the international arena, contrary to Western attitudes, Turks gave more support to the Arabs in the Arab-Israeli conflict and to Third World countries in colonial issues.[69] Turkish rulers' new policy softened their rigid evaluation of the Soviet threat and thus affected their perception of the alliance with NATO countries.[70] However, they never considered making the Soviet Union a defense partner as an alternative to NATO. They wanted only normalization of relations between the two countries.[71]

b) The Turkish Withdrawal from MLF

A multilateral force had been suggested by the United States to cope with anxieties of its European allies over the control of nuclear arms. It would include Polaris missile-equipped submarines with crews of mixed nationalities. Although Turkey did not have any special interest in joining the force, it had accepted the idea and sent a crew to the Working Group. In January 1965, the Turkish government declared that it would not participate in the MLF and would withdraw its crew serving on the USS Claude V. Ricketts.[72] Official sources presented financial considerations and the refusal of some other NATO members to join the force as the reasons for the decision,[73] but it cannot be denied that Soviet objections to the plan and Turkish resentment toward the USA because of its attitude toward the Cyprus question played an important role in the decision.[74]

c) The U-2 Flights

In 1956, Turkey allowed U.S. forces in the İncirlik airbase near Adana to operate "scientific" U-2 flights, but it did not have detailed information on them.[75] Until 1960, the United States secretly carried out the U-2 program of high-altitude overflights of the Soviet Union from the İncirlik base to take photographs of Soviet missile activities. When the U-2 plane, which took off from İncirlik and which was used by U.S. pilot Gary Powers, was shot down by the Soviets over their territories on 1 May 1960,[76] U-2 flights became a subject of

---

[68] *Milliyet*, 14 October 1967, translated by Vali, *Bridge Across the Bosporus*, p. 179.

[69] Ulman and Dekmejian, "Changing Patterns in Turkish Foreign Policy, 1959-1967", p. 784, Kurat, *Elli Yıllık Cumhuriyetin Dış Politikası*, pp. 303-304. On the improvement of Turkey's relations with Arab countries see Ömer Kürkçüoğlu, *Türkiye'nin Arap Ortadoğusuna Karşı Politikası*, 1945-1970, Ankara: SBF Yayını, 1972.

[70] Harris, *Troubled Alliance*, pp. 127-128.

[71] Harris, "Turkey and the United States", p. 61.

[72] *Milliyet*, 10, 15, 16 January 1965, *Hürriyet*, 17 January 1965, *Dışişleri Bakanlığı Belleteni*, January 1965, p. 56, Halil, *Atatürkçü Dış Politika ve NATO ve Türkiye*, pp. 159-160.

[73] Deputy Prime Minister Kemal Satır's statement, *Millet Meclisi Tutanak Dergisi (MMTD)*, 26 January 1965, term 1, sess. 4, vol. 35, pp. 173-174.

[74] Harris, *Troubled Alliance*, p. 151, Vali, *Bridge Across the Bosporus*, p. 121, Gönlübol *et al., Olaylarla Türk Dış Politikası*, pp. 522-523, Orkunt, *Türkiye-ABD Askeri İlişkileri*, pp. 392-408, "Durum", *Milliyet*, 15 January 1965, p. 1.

[75] Orkunt, *Türkiye-ABD Askeri İlişkileri*, p. 360, Gönlübol *et al., Olaylarla Türk Dış Politikası*, p. 325.

[76] For details of the events and statements of both the U.S. and USSR governments see *Keesing's Contemporary Archives*, 1959-1960, vol. 12, pp. 17425-17429.

public discussion in Turkey. Soviet Premier Khrushchev's speech on 7 May[77] and the Soviet note to Turkey on 13 May warned Turkish officials over their "allowing foreign military aircraft to use their airspace for the preparation and execution of intrusions into Soviet airspace."[78] While the Turkish government announced that it "has never authorized any American aircraft to fly over Russian territory for reconnaissance flights or any other reason,"[79] Turkish politicians and newspaper columnists criticized the United States over the timing of the Powers flight, but they generally blamed Khrushchev for sabotaging the Paris summit under the pretext of the incident and defended the necessity of the U-2 flights.[80] Later in the second half of the 1960s, in the atmosphere of heavy criticism of the United States, Turkish critics mentioned the Powers incident frequently to warn against Turkey's involvement in an unwanted conflict because of the U-2 flights.

In December 1965, another U.S. reconnaissance plane, which started its journey in İncirlik, accidentally crashed in the Black Sea while flying over international waters. The Soviet government and press complained that Turkey was allowing its territory to be used for dangerous missions.[81] Turkish military authorities particularly felt resentment since the flight of the plane occurred without their knowledge.[82] On 28 December 1965, the Demirel government asked the United States to stop all reconnaissance flights carried out from Turkish bases.[83] The United States tried to persuade the Turks to reverse their decision through the visit of the U.S. commander in NATO to Turkey,[84] but such flights were not resumed in the 1965-1975 period.[85] This Turkish attitude showed how serious the Turks were in their decision to be more cautious in their dealings with the superpowers. It was also an act aimed at easing intensive public criticism directed toward the government on its military relations with the USA.

d) The Use of the İncirlik Base for non-NATO Purposes

During the landing of U.S. marines in Lebanon in 1958, the United States dispatched 1,600 U.S. Army troops in Germany to İncirlik to prepare to join in the Lebanese action. U.S. authorities notified Turkish officials of the troops' movement only after the fact, rather than consulting with them prior to the action.[86] The Turkish opposition criticized the deployment of U.S. troops to İncirlik on the grounds that they came on the initiative of Washington, not

---

[77] Khrushchev said: "The Governments... of Turkey must be clearly aware that they were accomplices of this flight because they permitted the use of their airfields against the Soviet Union. This is a hostile act on their part against the Soviet Union." Ibid., p. 17427.

[78] Ibid., p. 17429, Gönlübol *et al., Olaylarla Türk Dış Politikası*, p. 328, Orkunt, *Türkiye-ABD Askeri İlişkileri*, pp. 368, 374, *Cumhuriyet*, 14 May 1960, p. 1.

[79] *Keesing's Contemporary Archives*, vol. 12, p. 17430.

[80] Harris, *Troubled Alliance*, p. 57.

[81] Ibid., pp. 165-166.

[82] Orkunt, *Türkiye-ABD Askeri İlişkileri*, pp. 377-378.

[83] Prime Minister Süleyman Demirel's press conference on 7 February 1970, *Dışişleri Bakanlığı Belleteni*, February 1970, pp. 101, 106.

[84] Orkunt, *Türkiye-ABD Askeri İlişkileri*, p. 380, Çağlayangil's interview with Cem in İsmail Cem, *Tarih Açısından 12 Mart*, İstanbul: Cem Yayınevi, 1980, pp. 303-304.

[85] Demirel's press conference, p. 106.

[86] Harris, *Troubled Alliance*, pp. 66-67, Couloumbis, *The United States, Greece and Turkey*, p. 35, Orkunt, *Türkiye-ABD Askeri İlişkileri*, p. 266, J. W. Lewis, Jr., *The Strategic Balance in the Mediterranean*, Washington D. C.: The American Enterprise Institute, 1976, p. 30.

Ankara.[87] In the second half of the 1960s, Turkish critics stated that the 1958 incident showed that the United States, whenever it wished, could use the İncirlik base for military purposes other than NATO defense plans and thus it could drag Turkey into a war against its will or at least could harm Turkey's relations with its neighbors.[88]

The Demirel government took the position that the joint defense bases could be used only against an attack from the enemy camp under the NATO agreement.[89] When the Arab-Israel war broke out in June 1967, the Turkish Foreign Minister told the Turkish Parliament that the bases could not be used without the explicit permission of Turkey.[90] Reportedly, in the 1967 war, Turkey allowed the United States to use communications stations, but it did not allow it to use bases for refueling or supply activities.[91] During the Lebanese disturbances of October 1969, Turkish Prime Minister Demirel openly said that Turkey would not let the United States use the İncirlik base for a landing in Lebanon, recalling the principle that the joint bases could not serve for operations to interfere in internal affairs of other states.[92] When the Jordanian government suppressed the Palestinian commando uprising in September 1970, Turkish authorities showed the same sensitiveness toward the possible use of bases by the United States.[93] However, at that, time Turkey allowed the USA to use bases for the evacuation of U.S. citizens in Jordan and transfer of supplies from İncirlik to Amman.[94]

These Turkish actions demonstrate that the Turkish government did not want deterioration of its relations with other states because of its contacts with the United States, which threatened that it might not come to Turkey's help if she was attacked by the Soviet Union. Turkish rulers also apparently wanted to prove that their defense policy was not totally dependent on the USA and that they could reject important demands of the Americans even in the security area. One cannot predict how Turkish authorities would have acted if the United States really needed to use the Turkish bases for its operations in the Middle East. However, it is certain that the Americans felt displeasure with the Turkish attitudes mentioned above. U.S. officials and politicians sometimes cited these attitudes while they claimed that Turkey was not co-operating with the USA adequately in the defense area.

e) The Duty Status Issue

The NATO Status of Forces Agreement of 1951 certified that in case of "offences arising out of any act or mission done in the performance of official duty" a NATO country would surrender jurisdiction to the allied country whose personnel were charged with the crime.[95] The real problem was the definition of duty status and of the right to determine it. Turkish Law no. 6816 of 16 July 1956 clarified that the words of "in the performance of official duty"

---

[87] Gönlübol et al., Olaylarla Türk Dış Politikası, pp. 315-316.
[88] Cem, Tarih Açısından 12 Mart, p. 273, Türkkaya Ataöv, Amerika, NATO ve Türkiye, Ankara: Aydınlık Yayınevi, 1969, pp. 218, 219, Osman Bölükbaşı, MMTD, 19 February 1969, term 2, sess. 4, vol. 34, p. 42, Doğan Avcıoğlu, "Türkiye'deki Amerikan üsleri", Yön, 25 November 1966, pp. 8-9, Nihat Arda "Türkiye'deki Amerikan üsleri", ibid., p. 7, Abdi İpekçi, "Üsler Sorunu", Milliyet, 21 May 1970, p. 1.
[89] United States Security Agreements, p. 1862.
[90] MMTD, 8 June 1967, term 2, sess. 2, vol. 18, p. 168.
[91] Kuniholm, "Turkey and NATO", p. 426.
[92] Cumhuriyet, 31 October 1969, pp. 1,7.
[93] Harris, Troubled Alliance, p. 166, Cem, Tarih Açısından 12 Mart, p. 273.
[94] Kuniholm, "Turkey and NATO", op. cit., p. 426, Collins, Greece and Turkey, p. 17.
[95] Harris, Troubled Alliance, p. 57.

meant "while on a general duty status."[96] On 31 July 1956, the Turkish Ministry of Justice sent instructions to judicial authorities throughout Turkey that jurisdiction would be left to U.S. officials upon certification by the senior American commander that the offender was on duty when the crime was committed.[97] Thus, the initial U.S.-Turkish arrangements left the interpretation of what constituted "duty" to the U.S. commander.

A major incident which caught the attention of Turkish public opinion was the traffic accident in November 1959 in which Lieutenant Colonel Allen I. Morrison ran into a contingent of the Presidential Guard, killing one and injuring eleven others. Morrison was tried by U.S. authorities since he was considered on duty at the time of accident and fined 1,200 dollars.[98] Finding it inadequate, the Turkish press protested against the punishment[99] and later publicized all actions of U.S. personnel including incidents involving Turkish national symbols such as the Turkish flag and the statues of Atatürk.

In the 1960s, Turkey's sacrifice of jurisdiction over U.S. personnel was heavily criticized by Turkish newspaper columnists and politicians as a breach of sovereignty reminiscent of the old capitulations. It was claimed that the exemption of U.S. personnel from Turkish justice went beyond NATO's general agreements, keeping the limits of related personnel and the "duty" concept too wide. It was believed that U.S. personnel were abusing their rights under the present arrangement at the expense of Turkish citizens.[100] It should be noted that American personnel felt that Turkish law was irrational and unfairly applied to them.[101]

Starting in the early 1960s, Turkish and U.S. officials held long-lasting negotiations on the duty status issue,[102] revolving around the Turkish right to reject the certificate of the U.S. commander. Finally, on 24 September 1968, the United States and Turkey signed the Duty Status Agreement formulating procedures to be followed by the Turkish General Staff if it rejected the duty certificate.[103] Turkish rulers declared that the new agreement, which was published in July 1969, constituted the most suitable solution to the duty status problem[104] because it gave Turkish officers the right of objecting to certificates given by Americans. However, as Turkish critics claimed, the Americans had the final say in the matter.[105] Thus, in the duty status issue, Turkish authorities could not obtain the result which they wanted to obtain, but they hoped that the new arrangement would improve their image in the eyes of Turkish people as a government which could force the Americans to make changes in the previous defense arrangements.

---

[96] Ibid., p. 58, Haydar Tunçkanat, *İkili Anlaşmaların İçyüzü*, İstanbul: Tekin Yayınevi, 1975, pp. 237-238.

[97] Harris, *Troubled Alliance*, p. 58, Tunçkanat, *İkili Anlaşmaların İçyüzü*, pp. 238-240.

[98] Harris, *Troubled Alliance*, p. 59.

[99] *Cumhuriyet*, 9-17 March 1960.

[100] Gönlübol, "NATO, USA and Turkey", p. 243, the author's interview with Fahir Armaoğlu, Ataöv, *Amerika, NATO ve Türkiye*, p. 215, Saffet Ural, *CSTD*, 4 February 1968, term 1, sess. 7, vol. 45-3, p. 451, Mehment Ali Aybar, *MMTD*, 7 November 1965, term 2, sess. 1, vol. 1, pp. 176-177; in *Cumhuriyet*, Hamza Eroğlu, "ABD İle Aramızdaki Andlaşmaların Yeniden Gözden Geçirilmesi", 7 September 1964, G. Güneri, "Resmi Görev Dolayısıyla İşlenen Suçlar", 23-24 November 1965, B. Akel, "Amerikan Üsleri ve İkili Anlaşmalar", 18 December 1965, Ahmet Kabaklı, "Faydası Ne?", *Tercüman*, 30 August 1964.

[101] Wolf, *Garrison Community*, pp. 191-192.

[102] Süleyman Demirel, *MMTD*, 9 November 1965, term 2, sess. 1, vol. 1, pp. 289-290.

[103] Appendix E, Harris, *Troubled Alliance*, pp. 225-228, Tunçkanat, *İkili Anlaşmaların İçyüzü*, pp. 244-248, Gönlübol *et al.*, *Olaylarla Türk Dış Politikası*, pp. 532-533.

[104] Demirel's press conference, op. cit., pp. 108-109.

[105] Harris, *Troubled Alliance*, pp. 168-169, Tunçkanat, *İkili Anlaşmaların İçyüzü*, pp. 249-250, Edip Çelik, "İkili Anlaşmalar", *Cumhuriyet*, 25 March 1970, p. 2, Abdi İpekçi, "Durum", *Milliyet*, 25 May 1970, p. 11.

f) Problems Related to U.S. Personnel

Turkish public opinion attacked customs and tax privileges granted to U.S. personnel,[106] U.S. PX shops (Post of Exchanges) and Army Postal Service (APO), claiming that Americans, staying out of Turkish control, carried out large-scale black-market activities and illegal currency trafficking and smuggled Turkish historic and cultural treasures out of Turkey. Turkish critics stated that activities of U.S. personnel harmed the Turkish economy, deprived Turkey of an important income source and affected social life of Turkish society in a negative way.[107] Arrests of some Americans carrying out black-marketeering gave ammunition to Turkish people for their criticism.[108]

The radical left showed their anger toward Americans by demonstrating against visits of the U.S. Sixth Fleet, attacking its personnel,[109] and targeting U.S. personnel and facilities in Turkey.[110] The Sixth Fleet visits were seen by leftists as an U.S. demonstration of its influence on Turkey.[111] They protested, sometimes violently, against each visit of the Fleet in the second half of the 1960s. The intervention of police and rightist groups in demonstrations resulted in serious clashes and the death of some people.[112] While Turkish authorities saw nothing wrong in visits of a friendly country's fleet,[113] the U.S. administration continued the Sixth Fleet visits in spite of violent demonstrations, but it eventually reduced the number of visits toward the end of the 1960s upon the advice of the U.S. ambassador to Turkey.[114]

Labor strikes in U.S. bases brought some clashes between U.S. personnel and Turkish workers. Concerned with the situation of U.S. personnel affected by the strikes, some U.S. senators came to Turkey and held talks with Turkish authorities on the issue.[115] The Turkish government's decision to postpone the strike of the Harb-İş trade union in U.S. bases on the ground that the strike would damage national security at a time when a NATO operation would take place caused angry protests of Turkish critics who claimed that the government came under U.S. influence and cared about U.S. interests rather than those of Turkish workers.[116]

As a result of the anti-American atmosphere in Turkey, the United States took some measures to make the U.S. presence in Turkey less obvious. It shifted some irritant elements in Ankara such as the Post of Exchange and the American school to isolated locations.

---

[106] For the text of the U.S.-Turkish tax exemption agreement of 1954 see Tunçkanat, *İkili Anlaşmaların İçyüzü*, pp. 251-270.

[107] Harris, *Troubled Alliance*, p. 60, Gönlübol, "NATO, USA and Turkey", p. 37, Tunçkanat, *İkili Anlaşmaların İçyüzü*, pp. 271, 294, Rıfat Baykal, *MMTD*, 24 February 1966, term 2, sess. 1, vol. 4, p. 463, "Modern Kapitülasyonlar ve Amerikan Kaçakçılığı", *Yön*, 3 December 1965, pp. 8-9, Kenan Esengin "Türkiye'deki Amerikan Personeli", *Cumhuriyet*, 10 April 1965, p. 2, Ulman and Dekmejian, "Changing Patterns in Turkish Foreign Policy, 1959-1967", p. 781.

[108] Harris, *Troubled Alliance*, p. 60, *Cumhuriyet*, 4 December 1965, pp. 1,7.

[109] Harris, *Troubled Alliance*, pp. 169-171, Vali, *Bridge Across the Bosporus*, p. 143, *Cumhuriyet*, 16-19 July 1968, 11-17 February 1969, 20-22 December 1969, *United States Security Agreements and Commitments Abroad*, p. 1832, *Keesing's Contemporary Archives*, 1971-1972, vol. 18, p. 24637.

[110] *Cumhuriyet*, January-March 1971.

[111] İlhan Selçuk, "Pencere", *Cumhuriyet*, 17 October 1967, p. 2, Türkkaya Ataöv, "Altıncı Filo Defol", *Forum*, 1 August 1968, p. 14.

[112] Mehmet Ali Birand et al., *12 Mart*, Ankara: İmge Kitabevi, 1994, pp. 148-150, 153-154.

[113] President Sunay's Victory Day speech, *Cumhuriyet*, 31 August 1968, p. 7, Prime Minister Demirel's statement, *Dışişleri Bakanlığı Belleteni*, September 1968, p. 58.

[114] *United States Security Agreements and Commitments Abroad*, p. 1864.

[115] *Cumhuriyet*, 23, 26 September 1967, 18 April- 31 May 1969.

[116] *Cumhuriyet*, 29 September 1967, pp. 1, 7, Abdi İpekçi, "Ertelenen Grev", *Milliyet*, 1 October 1967, p. 1.

Economic pressures at home, too, forced the Americans to reduce the number of U.S. personnel in Turkey and to transfer some facilities to the Turks.[117] The Anadolu Kavağı and Manzaralı joint defense installations near Ankara (1968), radar sites in Trabzon and Samsun and the Çiğli airbase near İzmir (1970) were turned over to Turkish authorities.[118] The number of U.S. personnel and their dependants was cut down from 24,000 in 1968 to 16,000 in 1970.[119]

Turkish authorities saw the Sixth Fleet events and the labor strikes as actions of far-leftist groups and therefore they did not demand any response from the Americans. Neither apparently did they make any demands to U.S. officials on the subjects of the number of U.S. personnel, their high profile in big cities and the transfer of some facilities to Turkey. But they warmly welcomed U.S. initiatives in these issues, which eased their position before Turkish public opinion. To counter public criticism of tax privileges of U.S. personnel, the Turkish government signed an agreement with the United States in May 1967, making the Americans subject to Turkish custom arrangements.[120]

g) The Passage through Straits

Until January 1966 Turkish authorities had permitted American ships armed with missiles to pass through the Straits. But beginning in 1966, the Turks changed their interpretation of the limitations imposed by the Montreaux agreement and no longer permitted the passage of U.S. ships armed with anti-aircraft missiles.[121] They seemed determined not to treat the United States specially in this issue as well, as a part of their policy of being more cautious in their contacts with the Americans.

h) NATO's New Strategy

Appreciating the threat of annihilation for both superpowers in a global conflict with nuclear weapons, the Kennedy administration suggested in 1961 that NATO should meet Soviet aggression with a flexible response rather than an all-out attack. In December 1967, the NATO Defense Planning Committee formally gave approval to the strategy of flexible response.[122] Turkey officially supported the U.S. position on the new strategy, but some Turkish officials and senior military officers expressed doubts about it. The strategy implied a

---

[117] The statement of Robert J. Pranger, Deputy Assistant Secretary of Defence, *United States Security Agreements and Commitments Abroad*, p. 1861.

[118] Demirel's press conference, op. cit., p. 107, *Dışişleri Bakanlığı Belleteni*, June 1968, pp. 34-35, 38-41, Gönlübol *et al., Olaylarla Türk Dış Politikası*, pp. 533-534, *Cumhuriyet*, 15 June 1968, 1 July 1970.

[119] Harris, *Troubled Alliance*, p. 167, *United States Security Agreements and Commitments Abroad*, p. 1860. Demirel stated in his press conference in February 1970 that the number of U.S. personnel in Turkey in 1970 was 7,000, op. cit., p. 107. According to Collins there were 6,570 U.S. personnel in Turkey in November 1974, Collins, *Greece and Turkey*, p. 3n.

[120] *Cumhuriyet*, 7 May 1967, pp. 1, 7.

[121] *Cumhuriyet*, 28 April 1966, pp. 1,7, Harris, *Troubled Alliance*, pp. 171-172, Ulman and Dekmejian, "Changing Patterns in Turkish Foreign Policy, 1959-1967", p. 781, Gönlübol and Ulman, "Türk Dış Politikasının Yirmi Yılı 1945-1965", p. 175.

[122] Harris, *Troubled Alliance*, p. 149, Gönlübol *et al., Olaylarla Türk Dış Politikası*, pp. 537-538, Orkunt, *Türkiye-ABD Askeri İlişkileri*, pp. 247-248, Demirel's press conference, op. cit., pp. 118-120, Gönlübol, "NATO, USA and Turkey", pp. 43-44.

difference between "wing" and "center"; the center would be defended at its perimeter, but a localized Soviet attack on Turkey would be met in depth, sacrificing Turkish territories, or Turkey would be left to the aggressor for the sake of central regions.[123] To counter the weakness of the strategy, NATO defense planners proposed various schemes such as the ACE Mobile Force for immediate deployment, atomic demolition munitions for mining the borders with atomic bombs and an integrated naval unit in the Mediterranean.[124] But none of them allayed Turkish anxieties. Nevertheless, the Turks had no choice but to accept the flexible response strategy and to try to obtain guarantees for Turkey's security in accordance with this strategy.

NATO's flexible response strategy was subjected to heavy criticism by Turkish politicians, newspaper columnists, academics and retired military officers.[125] The new strategy protected the superpowers almost completely, but it did not provide total security for Turkey. Under NATO planning, large areas of eastern Anatolia would be abandoned and the main defense line would be established along the Zagros and Taurus mountain chains. Thus, the new doctrine left Turkey exposed to aggression and made it a first target and forward front of a possible war. Prime Minister Demirel rejected all these claims in his press conference in February 1970. The new nuclear balance made the change of strategy necessary. An aggressor could not risk a military operation against Turkey because it would result in a change in the balance of Europe and the outbreak of a global war. The new NATO strategy did not see Turkey as a dispensable area nor made any differentiation between the center and wings.[126]

i) Control of Nuclear Weapons

In connection with implications of the flexible response strategy, Turkish critics argued that Turkey did not have the right to use nuclear weapons on its territory, but their presence attracted the Soviet threat.[127] In their opinion, the Soviet Union could bomb the bases armed with nuclear weapons in case of a war with the Western world or as a preventive strike. Or the United States could drag Turkey into a war against its will by using nuclear weapons on Turkish territory, which were not under the control of the Turkish government.[128] It was

---

[123] Harris, *Troubled Alliance*, p. 150, Vali, *Bridge Across the Bosporus*, p. 121.

[124] Harris, *Troubled Alliance*, p. 150, Vali, *Bridge Across the Bosporus*, pp. 121-122, 163, Nuri Eren, *Turkey, NATO and Europe*, Paris: The Atlantic Institute for International Affairs, 1977, pp. 19-20, Prime Minister Demirel praised these schemes in his press conference in February 1970, op. cit., pp. 130-132.

[125] In *MMTD*: F. Güley, 24 February 1968, term 2, sess. 3, vol. 26, p. 342; Behice Boran, 19 February 1966, term 2, sess. 1, vol. 3, p. 573; Behice Boran, 18 February 1967, term 2, sess. 2, vol. 13, p. 396; İsmet İnönü, 22 January 1970, term 3, sess. 1, vol. 2, p. 290; Sezai Orkunt, 24 May 1970, term 3, sess. 1, vol. 5, p. 393; in *CSTD*: M. Ataklı, 31 January 1969, term 1, sess. 8, vol. 50-3, p. 498; Gönlübol in Karpat (*ed.*), *Turkey's Foreign Policy in Transition*, p. 45; Duygu Sezer, *Kamuoyu ve Dış Politika*, Ankara: A.Ü. S.B.F. Yayını, 1972, pp. 377, 414-415, 477; Ataöv, *Amerika, NATO ve Türkiye*, p. 222; Orkunt, *Türkiye-ABD Askeri İlişkileri*, pp. 248-249; in *Cumhuriyet*: M. Ok, "NATO Stratejisi ve Milli Strateji", 20 April 1968, A. Haluk Ulman, "Türkiye ve NATO", 23 May 1968, Ahmet Yıldız, "NATO, İkili Anlaşmalar ve Bilinmesi Gereken Gerçekler", 12 February 1970; Abdi İpekçi, "Esnek Mukabele Nedir?", *Milliyet*, 23 May 1970.

[126] *Dışişleri Bakanlığı Belleteni*, February 1970, pp. 120-121.

[127] Fahir Armaoğlu told the author that this was a Soviet propaganda. He argued that even if there were no nuclear weapons in Turkey, the Soviet Union would still see Turkey as one of first targets during a possible East-West confrontation because of her strategic position.

[128] Sezer, *Kamuoyu ve Dış Politika*, pp. 369, 377, 401, 414-415; Orkunt, *Türkiye-ABD Askeri İlişkileri*, pp. 248-249; Ataöv, *Amerika, NATO ve Türkiye*, p. 219; in *MMTD*: Muzaffer Karınca, 24 February 1966, term 2, sess. 1,

suggested that either Turkish control should be established over nuclear weapons or all nuclear weapons in Turkey should be withdrawn.[129]

Prime Minister Demirel answered these claims in his press conference. Nuclear weapons in Turkey were defensive and short-range, and could not be used without Turkey's consent because they were subjected to the double-key system. The launching devices of weapons and their use after a NATO decision were entirely in the hands of Turkish personnel. Nuclear weapons in İncirlik, which were not subjected to the double-key system, could only be used with the decision of the NATO Council in which Turkey had the power of veto. Military installations in Turkey did not constitute a threat for Turkey or its enemies, but they were legitimate defense bases providing additional deterrence.[130]

From the beginning, Turkey had accepted the close supervision of nuclear weapons by the United States and appreciated the U.S. Atomic Energy Act of 1954.[131] But, in the 1960s, to counter the possibility that their allies might not come to their help in case of an aggression, Turkish military planners demanded an increased role in the planning and decision for the use of nuclear weapons. The Turkish General Staff insisted that one of the revolving seats in the Nuclear Planning Group established by NATO in December 1966 should be allocated to Turkey. The Turkish government requested placing of nuclear mines in the eastern Turkish border hoping that the United States would relax the system of dual control imposed on nuclear arms. But when it was realized that the legal limits of the U.S. system precluded any effective surrender of U.S. control, Turkish rulers dropped the matter officially in May 1969.[132] Thus, they did not obtain any concrete results on the control of nuclear weapons, which they could use against public criticism.

j) Bilateral Agreements

Starting at the end of 1965, Turkish public opinion expressed intense criticism of the U.S.-Turkish bilateral agreements for the following reasons: Bilateral agreements did not have any legal basis since they were not approved by the Turkish Parliament. They were not related to NATO arrangements but mainly served U.S. interests. They included articles, which gave the United States excessive rights at the expense of Turkey's independence, security and economic development. Finally, the United States had complete control over military installations based on bilateral agreements; Turkish authorities had no power to check them.[133] There were widespread calls among Turkish critics for abolition or at least reconsideration of bilateral agreements.

---

vol. 4, p. 471, Behice Boran, 5 January 1967, term 2, sess. 2, vol. 11, pp. 88-89; in *Cumhuriyet*: Sezai Orkunt, "Yine İkili Anlaşmalar", 24 October 1967, M. Ok, "Türkiye Nükleer Bir Hedef midir?", 6 October 1968; Ahmet Şükrü Esmer, "NATO Cenderesi", *Milliyet*, 4 April 1968; Nihat Arda, "Türkiye'deki Amerikan üsleri", *Yön*, 25 October 1966, p. 7.

[129] The RPP's NATO report in 1968 in *Cumhuriyet*, 8 February 1975; Ferda Güley, *MMTD* 24 February 1968, term 2, sess. 3, vol. 26, p. 342, S. Koç, ibid., p. 353; M. Ataklı, *CSTD* 31 January 1969, term 1, sess. 8, vol. 50-3, p. 499.

[130] *Dışişleri Bakanlığı Belleteni*, February 1970, pp. 103, 110, 124-126.

[131] Collins, *Greece and Turkey*, p. 4.

[132] Harris, *Troubled Alliance*, pp. 152-153.

[133] In *MMTD*: Mehmet Ali Aybar, 7 November 1965, term 2, sess. 1, vol. 1, pp. 176, 179, Rıfat Baykal, term 2, sess. 1, vol. 4, pp. 462,463, Kenan Esengin, 12 April 1967, term 2, sess. 2, vol. 16, p. 78, Behice Boran, 20 February 1968, term 2, sess. 3, vol. 25, p. 472; in *CSTD*: H. O. Bekata, 27 June 1967, term 1, sess. 6, vol. 42, p. 20, Saffet Ural, 4 February 1968, term 1, sess. 7, vol. 45-3, p. 452; Sezer, *Kamuoyu ve Dış Politika*, pp. 342,

Turkish rulers countered accusations by claiming that, under the 1961 constitution, bilateral agreements did not need to be approved by the Turkish Parliament and stating that if they really had violated Turkey's interests, the previous governments would have made some changes in them. As for military bases, they were Turkish territories, belonged to Turkey and Turkish authorities had the power to check them at any time. They were established for defensive purposes under NATO arrangements and did not serve a particular country.[134]

Under strong domestic pressure, the Demirel government asked the United States on 7 April 1966 to open negotiations to review and bring up to date existing bilateral arrangements. Washington accepted the proposal on 18 April 1966.[135] Turkish rulers generally admitted that there were some gaps and mistakes in bilateral arrangements that needed to be corrected.[136] Prime Minister Demirel stated in his press conference: "For over ten years preceding 1965, there were scattered agreements concluded by several authorities not based on any principles. We were up against a practice whose legal grounds and content were not known and which led to great difficulty and complaints."[137] According to Harris, former U.S. official, through reconsideration of bilateral agreements,

> the Turkish civilian authorities sought essentially a thoroughgoing reaffirmation of Turkish sovereignty and control over every facet of military co-operation with the United States. To obviate recurrent criticism that some American activities in Turkey fell outside the bounds of NATO, the Ankara authorities wished the agreement to state specifically that all joint defense co-operation would take place pursuant to the NATO Pact and within the limits of NATO commitments. The Turkish side wanted to establish for the record its right to have full and detailed knowledge before granting permission for any American activity... The Ankara government felt an overriding concern to demonstrate that the United States did not operate these facilities as a sovereign lessee, but rather shared them with Turkey for mutually beneficial purposes.[138]

According to statements of Turkish rulers; officials of the Turkish Foreign Ministry and the General Staff, working together, reviewed all bilateral agreements with the United States, prepared a basic draft agreement including general principles on which bilateral accords should be based and submitted it to the U.S. Embassy on 8 September 1966. After the Americans made their own preparations, Turkish Foreign Ministry and U.S. Embassy representatives started negotiations officially on 20 January 1967.[139] Turkish authorities

---

368, 369, 399, 400-404, 406; the RPP's NATO report in *Cumhuriyet*, 8 February 1975; Mehmet Gönlübol, "Türkiye ve İkili Andlaşmalar", *Milliyet*, 12 July 1969; Doğan Avcıoğlu, "Türkiye'deki Amerikan üsleri", *Yön*, 25 November 1966, pp. 8-9; the author's interview with Fahir Armaoğlu; İlhan Selçuk, "Şu Acı Gerçek", *Cumhuriyet*, 26 November 1965, p. 2, Edip Çelik, *Türkiye'nin Dış Politika Tarihi*, İstanbul, 1969, p. 159.

[134] In *MMTD*: P.M. Süleyman Demirel, 8 November 1965, term 2, sess. 1, vol. 1, pp. 257-258, Defence Minister Ahmet Topaloğlu, 24 February 1966, term 2, sess. 1, vol. 18, p. 490, Foreign Minister Çağlayangil, 17 February 1967, term 2 sess. 2, vol. 13, pp. 366-367, 20 February 1968, term 2, sess. 3, vol. 25, p. 489; *Dışişleri Bakanlığı Belleteni*, June 1968, pp. 39, 41.

[135] The Turkish government's press release on 3 July 1969, *The Middle East Journal*, Winter 1970, vol. 24, p. 72. See Appendix F.

[136] Foreign Minister Çağlayangil, *MMTD*, 6 January 1967, term 2, sess. 2, vol. 11, pp. 126, 128, ibid., 19 February 1969, term 2, sess. 4, vol. 34, p. 78, Faruk Sükan, *CSTD*, 27 June 1967, term 1, sess. 6, vol. 42, p. 21, the government's white paper, *Dışişleri Bakanlığı Belleteni*, November 1966, p. 63.

[137] *Dışişleri Bakanlığı Belleteni*, February 1970, p. 106.

[138] Harris, *Troubled Alliance*, pp. 160-161, 162.

[139] Çağlayangil, *CSTD*, 1 February 1967, term 1, sess. 6, vol. 38-3, p. 377; Çağlayangil, *MMTD*, 19 February 1969, term 2, sess. 4, vol. 34, p. 77; Demirel's press conference, *Dışişleri Bakanlığı Belleteni*, February 1970, p. 104; Orkunt, *Türkiye-ABD Askeri İlişkileri*, pp. 257-258; Tunçkanat, *İkili Anlaşmaların İçyüzü*, pp. 302, 304.

occasionally informed Turkish public opinion of developments on the matter.[140] In his various speeches to parliament, Foreign Minister Çağlayangil read out the general principles on which U.S.-Turkish bilateral agreements would be based.[141] Given the diverse nature of arrangements and the sensitivity of the problem, the pace of negotiations proved extremely slow. Many technical questions arose; the removal of files and related officials by the 1960 regime; the status of verbal understandings, Turkish expectation of additional aid, the absence of the U.S. ambassador for some time and changing some agreements completely caused delay.[142]

After two years and four months of extensive and detailed negotiations, on 3 July 1969, Turkish Foreign Minister Çağlayangil and U.S. Ambassador William J. Handley signed the Defense Co-operation Agreement in Ankara.[143] The agreement, which was kept secret from the public under the 1961 constitution, replaced the Military Facilities Agreement of 1954, revised some of the bilateral agreements and attempted to clarify others. It was to be supplemented by individual accords to govern each U.S. activity or facility in Turkey. The Turkish government's press release on 3 July 1969[144] and Prime Minister Demirel's press conference on 7 February 1970[145] gave general information about the agreement and cited its basic principles. No action could be taken from installations without Turkey's consent. Turkey retained property rights of the areas allotted to joint defense installations. Turkish authorities had the full control over and the right to inspect them and to assign their own military or civil personnel to these areas. The Turkish government would be able to restrict American use of bases in the event of a national emergency. The joint management and utilization principle would be applied in these installations.

The 1969 Agreement was the most important effort of Turkish rulers to gain initiative in their military relations with the USA. The published general principles of the agreement showed that they were quite successful in this regard. However, one cannot reach a conclusion because military agreements between the USA and Turkey remained classified. The tone of the general principles leads to the comment that efforts of Turkish authorities were largely directed to appeasing public opinion. The new arrangement was not satisfactory to the mainly leftist anti-American groups[146] but it was more acceptable to moderates.[147] The opposition parties called for a debate and approval of the agreement by the parliament. When the government chose not to seek parliament's approval, the opposition heavily criticized it.[148]

---

[140] Gönlübol et al., Olaylarla Türk Dış Politikası, pp. 528-529, Sezer, Kamuoyu ve Dış Politika, pp. 524-527, Dışişleri Bakanlığı Belleteni, April 1967, p. 84.

[141] MMTD, 6 January 1967, term 2, sess. 2, vol. 11, pp. 125-126; Dışişleri Bakanlığı Belleteni, January 1967, p. 73; MMTD, 20 February 1968, term 2, sess. 3, vol. 25, p. 489; Vali, Bridge Across the Bosporus, pp. 139-140.

[142] Harris, Troubled Alliance, pp. 161-163, Vali, Bridge Across the Bosporus, p. 139.

[143] Keesing's Contemporary Archives, 1969-1970, vol. 17, p. 23484.

[144] For the text see The Middle East Journal, Winter 1970, vol. 24, pp. 72-73, Dışişleri Bakanlığı Belleteni, July 1969, pp. 30-35, Appendix F.

[145] For the text see Dışişleri Bakanlığı Belleteni, February 1970, pp. 98-139, for its English translation see Harris, Troubled Alliance, pp. 229-238, Appendix G.

[146] Tunçkanat, İkili Anlaşmaların İçyüzü, p. 324.

[147] Fahir Armaoğlu told the author that with the 1969 Agreement Turkey established full sovereignty over the bases.

[148] Nihat Erim, MMTD, 23 May 1970, term 3, sess. 1, vol. 5, p. 347.

6. OTHER MATTERS

a) Détente

Although Turkish officials expressed their pleasure with the détente between the two blocs, they had doubts over the West's attitude toward the Soviet camp. They feared that the new approach would destroy the Western sensitiveness toward the Soviet threat, would harm the consolidation of NATO and would encourage communist expansionism.[149] Turkish authorities were particularly concerned about the U.S. troop reduction in Europe in 1968 and subsequent strategic arms limitation and mutual force reduction talks with the Eastern bloc because they thought that Moscow could transfer its troops in Europe to the Turkish border.[150]

b) Military Aid

Turkish defense planners felt that Turkey needed more U.S. aid to modernize the Turkish military establishment. But there was already a wide divergence in 1966 between Turkish expectations and availability of U.S. military aid. In his visit to Turkey in February 1966, the U.S. Assistant Secretary of Defense, John McNaughton, proposed a five-year program of modernization for Turkish armed forces calling for 134 million dollars a year in U.S. aid starting in 1967. Turks were unhappy about the amount of aid and its allocation between different forces. Washington failed to meet even this level in the years following the first year.[151]

7. NATO DISCUSSION IN TURKISH POLITICS IN THE 1960s

a) Views of Those Who Criticized NATO

The following remarks are typical of the criticisms made in Turkey at the time:[152]

All Turkish armed forces were assigned to NATO and put under the command of foreign generals. Even the most senior Turkish generals were under the command of a NATO lieutenant general. Turkey could not use its armed forces and military equipment given by NATO for its national interests which fell outside NATO purposes. The Turkish Army was organized in accordance with NATO's interests and defense strategy, which did not suit Turkey's realities. After Turkey entered NATO, all military equipment was bought from the United States, thus Turkish forces became dependent on the U.S. in every aspect and the national defense industry was destroyed. The present situation, which restricted Turkey's

---

[149] Süleyman Demirel, *Büyük Türkiye*, İstanbul: Dergah Yayınları, 1975, pp. 412-413.

[150] Harris, *Troubled Alliance,* pp. 150-151, Ü. Haluk Bayülken (Turkish foreign minister), "Turkey's Foreign Policy", *Foreign Policy*, No. 1, March 1973, p. 70.

[151] Harris, *Troubled Alliance,* pp. 153-160, Harris, "Turkey and the United States", pp. 65-66.

[152] These criticisms constitute public questioning of characteristics of the U.S.-Turkish alliance, which were mentioned in Chapter II.

freedom of action, was not compatible with Turkey's independence, sovereignty and national defense.[153] Turkey should develop a national force through her own resources to create a local deterrence. The national defense industry should be developed and a national defense strategy should be created.[154]

NATO did not arm the Turkish army with modern weapons and kept it below the NATO standards.[155] Weapons, which were given by NATO, were outdated and did not suit Turkey's defense requirements, their maintenance expenses were high but their firepower was low.[156] NATO provided more military equipment for Greece than it provided for Turkey, and thus it changed the balance between the two countries' military power in favor of Greece.[157] NATO, specifically the United States did not provide enough military and economic aid in comparison with Turkey's contribution to NATO and responsibilities, which she undertook within the alliance.[158] For NATO, Turkey maintained the second largest military force in terms of numbers in the alliance by using its limited resources which should be allocated for

---

[153] Sezer, *Kamuoyu ve Dış Politika*, pp. 267,268, 375,376, 379, 381,382, 413, 417; in *MMTD*: H. Ataman, 9 January 1963, term 1, sess. 2, vol. 10, p. 655, A. Oğuz, 7 September 1964, term 1, sess. 3, vol. 32, p. 312, Rıfat Baykal, 24 February 1966, term 2, sess. 1, vol. 4, pp. 462,463, Muzaffer Karınca, ibid., pp. 470,471, Behice Boran, 5 January 1967, term 2, sess. 2, vol. 11, p. 87, Behice Boran, 18 February 1967, term 2, sess. 2, vol. 13, pp. 395-397, Behice Boran, 24 February 1968, term 2, sess. 3, vol. 26, pp. 358,359, İ. Kabadayı, 19 February 1971, term 3, sess. 2, vol. 11, p. 625; in *CSTD*: Ahmet Yıldız, 1 February 1967, term 1, sess. 6, vol. 38-3, p. 356, Haydar Tunçkanat, ibid., pp. 570,571; in *Cumhuriyet*: İlhan Selçuk, "Mağlup Devletler Gibi", 10 September 1964, "Ordunun İtildiği Çıkmaz", 23 February 1967, "Silahlı Kuvvetler Problemi", 3 February 1969, the RPP's NATO's report, 8 February 1975; Halil, *Atatürkçü Dış Politika ve NATO ve Türkiye*, p. 171. To counter these accusations Turkish authorities claimed that Turkish forces were under Turkish control in the time of peace and would come under NATO's command in the event of a war to defend the region and that Turkey could use its forces at any time for its own interests as the Cyprus crises proved. See in *MMTD*: Süleyman Demirel, 9 November 1965, term 2, sess. 1, vol. 1, p. 288, Defence Minister Ahmet Topaloğlu, 18 February 1967, term 2, sess. 2, vol. 13, p. 412, Süleyman Demirel, 30 September 1968, term 2, sess. 3, vol. 28, p. 714, İhsan Sabri Çağlayangil, 19 February 1969, term 2, sess. 4, vol. 34, p. 76; in *CSTD*: Ahmet Topaloğlu, 3 February 1967, term 1, sess. 6, vol. 38-3, p. 594.

[154] Sezer, *Kamuoyu ve Dış Politika*, p. 359, Muzaffer Karınca, *MMTD*, 24 February 1966, term 2, sess. 1, vol. 4, p. 471; Behice Boran, ibid., p. 573; Ahmet Yıldız, *CSTD*, 1 February 1965, term 1, sess. 4, vol. 24-3, p. 995; Kenan Esengin, "Milli Ordu Ne Demektir?", *Cumhuriyet*, 9 February 1969; the RPP's NATO report, *Cumhuriyet*, 8 February 1975. For this purpose the Turkish press and other groups organized fund-raising campaigns which gained the support of the government. See Harris, *Troubled Alliance*, p. 154, Suha Bölükbaşı, *Superpowers and the Third World*, New York: University Press of America, 1988, p. 123.

[155] Sezer, *Kamuoyu ve Dış Politika*, pp. 376-377, 381, 414, 423, 473-474, Behice Boran, *MMTD*, 17 February 1969, term 2, sess. 4, vol. 33, p. 404, Halil, *Atatürkçü Dış Politika ve NATO ve Türkiye*, p. 171, A. Haluk Ulman, "Türk Ulusal Savunması üzerine Düşünceler", *SBF Dergisi*, vol. 21, No. 4, December 1966, p. 205.

[156] Behice Boran, *MMTD*, 18 February 1967, term 2, sess. 2, vol. 13, p. 395; Ulman, "Türk Ulusal Savunması üzerine Düşünceler", pp. 203-205. The comment of David C. Jones, Chairman of the U.S. Joint Chiefs of Staff, during a Senate hearing: "Over the years, the Turkish Armed Forces have been equipped almost totally with arms and equipment that were being phased out of U.S. and NATO inventories. Due to lack of replacements, Turkey has been compelled to keep in its inventory World War II and Korean vintage arms and equipment far beyond their scheduled phase out. M-47 tanks, F-84, F-100 and F-102 aircraft, and ships over 30 years old are but a few examples." *The Military Aspects of Banning Arms Aid to Turkey*, hearing before the Committee on Armed Services; U.S. Senate, 95th Congress, 2nd session, June 28, 1978, Washington: U.S. Government Printing Office, 1978, p. 45.

[157] Sezer, *Kamuoyu ve Dış Politika*, pp. 473-474, Y. Çetiner, "Atina Ankara'ya Tercih Edildi", *Cumhuriyet*, 29 April 1965.

[158] In *MMTD*: F. Güley, 21 February 1962, term 1, sess. 1, vol. 3, p. 92; A. Tahtakılıç, ibid., p. 142; Z. Dorman, 2 January 1963, term 1, sess. 2, vol. 10, pp. 516-517; H. Ataman, 9 January 1963, ibid., pp. 655-656; A. Oğuz, 11 January 1963, term 1, sess. 2, vol. 11, p. 71; S. Koç, 18 February 1967, term 2, sess. 2, vol. 13, p. 387.

economic development, put its survival under threat, paid for salaries of U.S. personnel and maintenance of NATO installations while not receiving any rent, etc.[159]

As the Cyprus crises and the Johnson letter proved, NATO did not provide total security for Turkey and did not protect it from a Soviet attack.[160] Article V of the North Atlantic Treaty, which called upon members to help the member under attack, was too flexible to require automatic aid of NATO.[161] Events showed that the United States interpreted Article V differently from Turkey.[162] As was seen during the Cyprus crises, NATO restricted Turkey's freedom of action and decision in her national causes.[163] Loyalty to NATO and looking at events from NATO's point of view made Turkey's foreign policy inflexible and alienated it from Muslim Arab countries and the Third World and thus deprived her of their votes in the United Nations.[164]

Turkey was not able to act independently within NATO, it had no say in NATO organs, which decided and implemented policies.[165] Turkey's membership in NATO could drag her

---

[159] Sezer, *Kamuoyu ve Dış Politika*, pp. 377, 379,381; F. Güley, *MMTD*, 21 February 1962, op. cit., p. 92; A. Oğuz, *MMTD*, 11 January 1963, op. cit., p. 71; İlhan Selçuk "Kolombun Yumurtası", *Cumhuriyet*, 31 August 1964, p. 2. The remark of the U.S. Commander in Chief in NATO in 1978, Alexander Haig: "Turkey has historically and traditionally contributed at a relative level above the overall NATO average and at as much as twice the rate of some NATO forces. This created a drag on their economic development efforts..." *The Military Aspects of Banning Arms Aid to Turkey*, p. 17. For ideas claiming that it cost the Americans less to buy security from the Turks than to produce it at home see Eleftherios N. Botsas, "The U.S. Cyprus Turkey Greece Tetragon; the Economics of an Alliance", *Journal of Political and Military Sociology*, vol. 16, No. 2, Fall 1988, pp. 252-253, George E. Gruen, "Ambivalence in the Alliance: US Interests in the Middle East and the Evolution of Turkish Foreign Policy", *ORBIS*, vol. 24, No. 2, Summer 1980, p. 368, Ron Ayres, "Turkish Foreign Relations", *Khamsin*, No. 11, pp. 119, 120. Turkish rulers stated that even if Turkey were not in NATO, she had to keep the size of her army for her defense: Defence Minister İlhami Sancar, *MMTD*, 14 January 1963, term 1, sess. 2, vol. 11, p. 111, Foreign Minister Çağlayangil's speech in the budget committee, *Dışişleri Bakanlığı Belleteni*, January 1969, p. 37, İ. S. Çağlayangil, "NATO ve Türkiye", *Milliyet*, 8 April 1968.

[160] Sezer, *Kamuoyu ve Dış Politika*, pp. 164-165, 376, 413-414, 422-423; in *MMTD*: Ahmet Oğuz, 7 September 1964, term 1, sess. 3, vol. 32, p. 312; Behice Boran, 19 February 1966, term 2, sess. 1, vol. 3, pp. 572-573; Rıfat Baykal, 24 February 1966, ibid., p. 462; Behice Boran, 24 February 1968, term 2, sess. 3, vol. 26, pp. 358, 360.

[161] İsmet İnönü, *MMTD*, 22 January 1970, term 3, sess. 1, vol. 2, pp. 290-291; Haydar Tunçkanat, *CSTD*, 3 February 1967, term 1, sess. 6, vol. 38-3, pp. 570-571; Behice Boran, "NATO Nedir ve Ne Değildir?", *Milliyet*, 5 April 1968. Commenting on the absence of NATO's automatic aid, Prime Minister Demirel said in his press conference: "In a collective security system formed by independent and sovereign states the agreements could not have been otherwise. Like Turkey, other NATO countries are also tied by the provisions of their constitutions and the will of their parliaments... But NATO has taken some measures to counter this shortcoming." *Dışişleri Bakanlığı Belleteni*, February 1970, p. 130.

[162] Collins cites in his report: State Department interpretations submit that shape, extent and timing of U.S. responses "would in the final analysis depend on the nature of the attack, the defensive capacity of the state or states attacked, and other relevant circumstances." According to State Department authorities Article V will be inoperative if Greece attacked Turkey, or vice versa, since it "does not cover an attack by one NATO member on another." Collins, *Greece and Turkey*, p. 3 and 3n. See also the statement of Rodger Davies, Deputy Assistant Secretary of State, in 1970 in this regard in *United States Security Agreements and Commitments Abroad*, pp. 1771, 1855.

[163] Sezer, *Kamuoyu ve Dış Politika*, pp. 164, 374, A. Haluk Ulman, "Ulusal Savunmamızın Sorunları", *Cumhuriyet*, 15 February 1967, p. 2, A. Haluk Ulman, "Türkiye ve NATO", *SBF Dergisi*, vol. 12, December 1967, pp. 163-164.

[164] Sezer, *Kamuoyu ve Dış Politika*, p. 380, Eren, *Turkey, NATO and Europe*, p. 20, İ. Selçuk, "NATO", *Cumhuriyet*, 11 September 1965, p. 2.

[165] İlhan Selçuk, "NATO'ya Girelim", *Cumhuriyet*, 20 June 1973, p. 2. Turkish rulers claimed that Turkey acted independently within the NATO framework. As an example, in October 1968 she refused to allow the Orient Express maneuvers to be held along the Syrian border. Vali, *Bridge Across the Bosporus*, p. 136. They stated that Turkey had equal rights with the other members in all organs of the alliance and had a role in policy making and implementing. Foreign Minister Feridun Cemal Erkin, *MMTD*, 9 January 1963, term 1, sess. 2, vol. 10, pp. 629-630, Defence Minister İ. Sancar, *MMTD*, 14 January 1963, term 1, sess. 2, vol. 11, p. 111.

into a war between the military blocs, which was unrelated to its national interests.[166] The United States kept NATO under its control, determined its strategies and policies and used it for its own interests.[167]

The necessity of keeping an alliance with the West could not be explained by the Soviet threat. Turkey had resisted the post-war Soviet pressures alone without receiving any help from the West.[168] The Soviet Union could not dare to attack Turkey since such an action would bring great dangers for her.[169] The Soviet Union was no longer a threat[170] or the only threat for Turkey[171] or its danger decreased greatly.[172] Turkey should determine its defense policy considering other threats as well, take great care not to provoke the Russians[173] and improve its relations with the Eastern bloc countries.

b) Views of Those Who Defended Turkey's NATO Connection

Turkish politicians, columnists and academics who believed that Turkey should continue to be a member of NATO voiced the following ideas which explain importance of the USA and NATO for Turkey's security quite well. The Soviet Union was a close threat for Turkey as it had been in the past. The recent events such as the invasion of Czechoslovakia, the Brezhnev doctrine, the Soviet involvement in the Middle East and the Soviet naval penetration into the eastern Mediterranean[174] demonstrated that the Soviet policy of expanding its territory and sphere of influence had not undergone any substantial change. Since Turkey was located within the expansion zone of the Soviet Union and since she was not capable of meeting the Soviet expansion with its own resources, Turkey needed the alliance of NATO to balance the Soviet power.[175] Turkey could not remain outside the

---

[166] Sezer, *Kamuoyu ve Dış Politika*, pp. 377, 422; Eren, *Turkey, NATO and Europe*, p. 20; in *MMTD*: Muzaffer Karınca, 24 February 1966, term 2, sess. 1, vol. 4, pp. 469,470, Behice Boran, 5 January 1967, term 2, sess. 2, vol. 11, p. 89, Behice Boran, 24 February 1968, term 2, sess. 3, vol. 26, p. 363, İsmet İnönü, 22 January 1970, term 3, sess. 1, vol. 2, p. 292; in *Cumhuriyet*: A. Haluk Ulman, "Türk-Amerikan İlişkileri", 25 November 1966, p. 2, İlhan Selçuk, "NATO Güvenliğimizi Sağlıyor mu?", 21 July 1967, p. 2. Turkish authorities claimed that NATO could not drag Turkey into a war against her wishes because decisions in the NATO Council were taken unanimously. Çağlayangil's statement to *Bayram Gazetesi* on 13 March 1968, *Dışişleri Bakanlığı Belleteni*, March 1968, p. 43, Vali, *Bridge Across the Bosporus*, p. 135, İhsan Sabri Çağlayangil, *MMTD*, 20 February 1968, term 2, sess. 3, vol. 25, p. 489.

[167] Sezer, *Kamuoyu ve Dış Politika*, pp. 374,375, 379,382, 402, 413, 416; Ataöv, *Amerika, NATO ve Türkiye*, p. 221; in *MMTD*: Ahmet Oğuz, 7 September 1964, term 1, sess. 3, vol. 32, p. 312, Behice Boran, 24 February 1968, term 2, sess. 3, vol. 26, p. 360; Ç. Özek, "Türkiye Amerika NATO", *Milliyet*, 13 September 1964. Turkish rulers rejected the claim that NATO was under the control of the U.S. by stating that all important decisions in NATO were taken by the Council in which every member had the power of veto. P.M. Demirel, *MMTD*, 9 November 1965, term 2, sess. 1, vol. 1, p. 288.

[168] Sezer, *Kamuoyu ve Dış Politika*, pp. 271, 403, 461-462.

[169] Behice Boran, *MMTD*, 17 February 1967, term 2, sess. 2, vol. 13, p. 346, Doğan Avcıoğlu, "Dış Politika Tabuları", *Yön*, 25 March 1966, p. 3, A. Haluk Ulman, "Ulusal Savunmamızın Sorunları", *Cumhuriyet*, 18 February 1967, p. 2.

[170] Sezer, *Kamuoyu ve Dış Politika*, pp. 459-460, 462.

[171] Ibid., pp. 375-376, 413, 423, Behice Boran, *MMTD*, 19 February 1966, term 2, sess. 1, vol. 3, p. 572.

[172] Sezer, *Kamuoyu ve Dış Politika*, pp. 269, 416, 420.

[173] In *MMTD*: Behice Boran, 5 January 1967, term 2, sess. 2, vol. 11, p. 88, Behice Boran, 17 February 1969, term 2, sess. 4, vol. 33, p. 408.

[174] Stearns, *Entangled Allies*, op. cit., pp. 64-65.

[175] Gönlübol, "NATO, USA and Turkey", pp. 47,48; Vali, *Bridge Across the Bosporus*, p. 375; Sezer, *Kamuoyu ve Dış Politika*, pp. 426,427, 444-445, 449-451, 464,465; Fahir Armaoğlu, "Turkey and the United States: A New Alliance", The *Turkish Yearbook of International Relations*, vol. 6, 1965, p. 12; in *MMTD*: İ. S. Çağlayangil, 19 February 1966, term 2, sess. 1, vol. 3, p. 592, İ. Sarıgöz, 24 February 1966, term 2, sess. 1, vol. 4, pp. 476-

conflict of the superpowers because it was located in a strategically important area; geopolitical and historical factors compelled it to join a defense pact (NATO).[176] It did not have enough economic and military power and other elements to be able to pursue a neutralist policy; neutrality did not suit Turkey's interests for the time being.[177]

NATO brought restrictions and responsibilities for Turkey as it did for the other members, but its benefits were much greater. NATO provided security for its members including Turkey since it was established.[178] It maintained balance of power and peace in Europe;[179] it forced the Soviet Union to pursue more moderate policies[180] and to renounce her demands on Turkey.[181] NATO continued to be the most important guarantee of Turkey's defense, deterring its enemies.

NATO provided Turkey with military aid in the form of arms equipment, ammunition, repair parts, construction projects, training and miscellaneous services.[182] From the financial point of view, Turkey's benefits from NATO were far superior to the value of its contribution to the alliance.[183] If Turkey did not receive the NATO aid, it could not have maintained a well-disciplined modern army[184] and it would have to spare more resources for its defense, cutting down its economic development efforts.[185] Since Turkey could not maintain its defense with its own resources it had to rely on the assistance of NATO.[186]

Through its membership in NATO, Turkey became a part and an equal member of the West. It benefited greatly from consultation, discussion and exchange of views in various

---

477, S. Koç, 18 February 1967, term 2, sess. 2, vol. 13, p. 396, İ. Sarıgöz, 17 February 1969, term 2, sess. 4, vol. 33, p. 412, Y. Menderes, term 2, sess. 4, vol. 34, p. 64; Ahmet Kabaklı, "NATO'dan Çıkmak, Çıkmamak", *Tercüman*, 27 May 1968.

[176] Vali, *Bridge Across the Bosporus*, pp. 381-382; Sezer, *Kamuoyu ve Dış Politika*, pp. 427, 432, 451, 462-463; in *MMTD*: İ. Sarıgöz, 24 February 1966, term 2, sess. 1, vol. 4, pp. 476-477; S. Koç, 18 February 1967, term 2, sess. 2, vol. 13, p. 387, Süleyman Arif Emre, 24 February 1968, term 2, sess. 3, vol. 26, p. 396, Cüneyt Kırca, 19 February 1969, term 2, sess. 4, vol. 34, p. 56; C. S. Barlas, "Dış Politika ile Oynanmaz", *Cumhuriyet*, 13 September 1964, p. 2.

[177] Sezer, *Kamuoyu ve Dış Politika*, pp. 302-303, in *MMTD*: Nihat Erim, 9 January 1963, term 1, sess. 2, vol. 10, p. 648, Rıfat Baykal, 24 February 1966, term 2, sess. 1, vol. 4, p. 463, İ .S. Çağlayangil, 17 February 1967, term 2, sess. 2, vol. 13, p. 367; Armaoğlu, "Turkey and the United States", p. 13; Sezer, "Turkey's Security Policies", p. 83.

[178] Gönlübol, "NATO, USA and Turkey", p. 48; İsmet Giritli, *Neden NATO'ya Evet?*, İstanbul: Ak Yayınları, 1968, pp. 12, 51; C. Baban, "NATO'ya Hayır", *Cumhuriyet*, 22 February 1972, p. 2; in *MMTD*: Süleyman Demirel, 9 November 1965, term 2, sess. 1, vol. 1, p. 287, N. Diler, 19 February 1969, term 2, sess. 4, vol. 4, p. 61, Turhan Feyzioğlu, 23 May 1970, term 3, sess. 1, vol. 5, p. 341.

[179] Vali, *Bridge Across the Bosporus*, pp. 162, 163; President Cevdet Sunay's speech in White House on 3 April 1967, *Amerika'da Onbir Gün*, op. cit., p. 26; İ. S. Çağlayangil, "NATO ve Türkiye", *Milliyet*, 8 April 1968.

[180] Sezer, *Kamuoyu ve Dış Politika*, pp. 416, 464, Coşkun Kırca, *MMTD*, 20 February 1968, term 2, sess. 3, vol. 25, p. 450.

[181] Sezer, *Kamuoyu ve Dış Politika*, pp. 432, 442-443, 464, Ahmet Kabaklı, "Yine NATO", *Tercüman*, 14 December 1967.

[182] Collins, *Greece and Turkey*, p. 4, Feridun Cemal Erkin, *MMTD*, 9 January 1963, term 1, sess. 2, vol. 10, p. 630, Botsas, "The U.S. Cyprus Turkey Greece Tetragon; the Economics of an Alliance", p. 252.

[183] Turkey's quota in NATO for the cost sharing is 1.1 percent. Vali, *Bridge Across the Bosporus*, p. 124, Sezai Orkunt, *MMTD*, term 3, sess. 4, vol. 34, p. 443.

[184] Gönlübol, "NATO, USA and Turkey", p. 49; Sezer, *Kamuoyu ve Dış Politika*, p. 445; Vali, *Bridge Across the Bosporus*, p. 124; in *Tercüman*: Ahmet Kabaklı, "Yine NATO", 14 December 1967, "Niçin NATO'dayız?", 25 May 1968.

[185] Vali, *Bridge Across the Bosporus*, p. 162; Sezer, *Kamuoyu ve Dış Politika*, pp. 445-446; İ. S. Çağlayangil, "NATO ve Türkiye", *Milliyet*, 8 April 1968; in *MMTD*: Çağlayangil, 19 February 1969, term 2, sess. 4, vol. 34, p. 76, M. Bilgin, 19 February 1971, term 3, sess. 2, vol. 11, p. 621.

[186] Sezer, *Kamuoyu ve Dış Politika*, pp. 421, 439, 445, 451; in *MMTD*: İ. S. Çağlayangil, 19 February 1966, term 2, sess. 1, vol. 3, p. 592, Ahmet Topaloğlu, 24 February 1966, term 2, sess. 1, vol. 4, p. 489, Çağlayangil, 20 February 1968, term 2, sess. 3, vol. 25, p. 481.

subjects among Western powers.[187] Within the NATO framework, Turkey was continuing its political, economic and cultural relations with the West in a better way.[188] Due to its membership of NATO, Turkey obtained information about modern warfare and equipment. Its general staff gained experience and first-hand knowledge through participating in discussions and exercises at high levels.[189] Turkey could better defend its interests and national causes and influence international developments by remaining in NATO, thus participating political and defense discussions and decisions of NATO.[190]

NATO membership could also dissuade the United States, which had naturally different interests in the region than Turkey, from taking forceful actions against it. If Turkey was not a NATO member, the United States could directly threaten it on the Cyprus issue. If Turkey left NATO, the balance of power between Turkey and Greece would lean in favor of Greece and the Turkish stand on the Cyprus question would be weakened. NATO aid to Greece would be to the disadvantage of Turkey, and Western powers were more likely to support the Greek cause on Cyprus.[191]

The NATO discussion in Turkish domestic politics had been initiated by radical leftist groups, organizations, students and scholars, and the Turkish Labor Party members, who wanted Turkey's complete withdrawal from NATO on the 20th anniversary of NATO's establishment, that is 1969.[192] The reformist, slightly leftist part of Turkish public opinion supported the idea that Turkey should reduce its participation in NATO and disengage itself from the United States.[193] Liberal, pro-Western critics saw NATO as a necessity for Turkey and stated that Turkey's defense ties with the West should be maintained provided that present mistakes in Turkey's relations with NATO and the United States were corrected.[194] Rightists and extreme rightists supported Turkey's NATO and U.S. connection for reasons of Turkish self-interest and security and fear of communism; they accused critics of NATO of trying to make Turkey a satellite of the Soviet Union.[195]

All opposition parties except the TLP were in favor of Turkey's membership of NATO on the condition that relations should be revised.[196] The major opposition party, the Republican People's Party, commissioned a panel chaired by Nihat Erim to report to the party's top policy organ on NATO. The committee's report in spring 1967 weighed the pros and cons of Turkey's NATO membership and recommended that Turkey retain its NATO ties but with substantial change. The RPP's formal policy paper, which was released to the public

---

[187] Vali, *Bridge Across the Bosporus*, pp. 124-125.

[188] İ. .S. Çağlayangil, *MMTD*, 19 February 1969, term 2, sess. 4, vol. 34, p. 75.

[189] Eren, *Turkey, NATO and Europe*, pp. 48-49; Feridun Cemal Erkin, *MMTD*, 9 January 1963, term 1, sess. 2, vol. 10, p. 630; Sezai Orkunt, "NATO, Milli Güvenlik ve Ötesi", *Cumhuriyet*, 10 April 1968, p. 2.

[190] Eren, *Turkey, NATO and Europe*, p. 49; in *MMTD*: Coşkun Kırca, 19 February 1969, term 2, sess. 4, vol. 34, p. 57, Turhan Feyzioğlu, 22 January 1970, term 3, sess. 1, vol. 2, p. 297.

[191] Gönlübol, "NATO, USA and Turkey", pp. 48-49; Vali, *Bridge Across the Bosporus*, p. 161; Sezai Orkunt, "NATO, Milli Güvenlik ve Ötesi", *Cumhuriyet*, 10 April 1968, p. 2; Abdi İpekçi, "NATO Sorunu", *Milliyet*, 20 May 1970; Turhan Feyzioğlu, *MMTD*, 23 May 1970, term 3, sess. 1, vol. 5, p. 343.

[192] Harris, *Troubled Alliance*, p. 141, Sezer, *Kamuoyu ve Dış Politika*, pp. 331, 342, 379, Vali, *Bridge Across the Bosporus*, p. 103.

[193] Vali, *Bridge Across the Bosporus*, p. 102.

[194] Ibid., p. 101, Sezer, *Kamuoyu ve Dış Politika*, pp. 275, 282-284, 384, 387, 415, 417, 463, Sezai Orkunt, "NATO, Milli Güvenlik ve Ötesi", *Cumhuriyet*, 11 April 1968, p. 2.

[195] Vali, *Bridge Across the Bosporus*, p. 104, Sezer, *Kamuoyu ve Dış Politika*, pp. 428, 447, 450, Ahmet Kabaklı, "NATO III", *Tercüman*, 15 December 1967.

[196] In *MMTD*: S. Koç, 24 February 1968, term 2, sess. 3, vol. 26, p. 353, Süleyman Arif Emre, ibid., p. 357, Osman Bölükbaşı, 19 February 1969, term 2, sess. 4, vol. 34, p. 41.

in July 1967, approved the committee's recommendations by watering down the criticism of NATO.[197] RPP leader İsmet İnönü, in his various speeches, expressed his support for Turkey's NATO connection provided that Turkey did not pursue policies, which would provoke any of the superpowers.[198] All the Turkish governments from 1960 to 1971 promised that they would strengthen Turkey's relations with NATO.[199] With the help of some factors such as the invasion of Czechoslovakia, change in France's adamant position within NATO with the fall of De Gaulle and İnönü's stand in favor of NATO, the NATO discussion on Turkish politics lost its momentum after 1969[200] and opinion polls showed that the majority of Turkish people supported Turkey's membership of NATO.[201]

It should be noted that ideas of both critics and supporters of Turkey's NATO connection carried some correct points and their discussion helped the Turkish governments assess their defense policies more realistically. The one who sees the content of the Johnson letter which was mentioned previously in the chapter cannot help appreciating criticisms directed toward Turkey's alliance with the USA and NATO. Turkish critics were right in stating that security could not be entrusted only to NATO. It was obvious that interests of NATO and Turkey could clash with each other in some matters or NATO might decide not to come Turkey' help in case of attack for different reasons. Turkey itself had to ensure its security by taking measures, including modernizing its army, which was equipped with outdated weapons at that time. On the other hand, NATO was certainly a great guarantee for Turkey's security, contributing to different aspects of its defense. Any alliance would bring costs and problems as well as benefits, the important thing was to find the right balance and Turkey could do it by staying within NATO. One important point is that many aspects of Turkey's alliance with NATO, which were subjected to criticism, were hidden in secret arrangements, therefore one could not make any judgements on these issues.

8. MILITARY RELATIONS IN THE 1970S

a) The Arms Embargo

As a reaction to Turkey's military intervention in Cyprus in July and August 1974, the U.S. Congress imposed an arms embargo on Turkey.[202] With the provisions of section 620(x) of the Foreign Assistance Act entering into force on 5 February 1975, "all military assistance, all sales of defense articles and services (whether for cash or by credit, or any other means),

---

[197] Harris, *Troubled Alliance*, pp. 141-142, Vali, *Bridge Across the Bosporus*, pp. 160-161, Sezer, *Kamuoyu ve Dış Politika*, pp. 340-341, *Cumhuriyet*, 10 July 1968, p. 7, 8 February 1975.

[198] Vali, *Bridge Across the Bosporus*, p. 83, İsmet İnönü, *MMTD*, 12 March 1970, term 3, sess. 1, vol. 3, p. 449, *Cumhuriyet*, 19 October 1966, p. 7, 14 January 1968, p. 7, 6 October 1968, p. 7, 2 April 1970, pp. 1,7.

[199] İsmail Arar, *Hükümet Programları*, İstanbul: Burçak Yayınevi, 1968, pp. 311-312, 339-340, 369, 399, 424, 479, 487.

[200] Harris, *Troubled Alliance*, pp. 142-143.

[201] Vali, *Bridge Across the Bosporus*, pp. 112-113, Eren, *Turkey, NATO and Europe*, pp. 46-47, Bölükbaşı, *Superpowers and the Third World*, pp. 122-123. In his report to the Congress, U.S. Secretary of State William Rogers stated that the anti-American Turkish leftists constituted very small percentage of Turkish population and that they targeted the Turkish government as well as America. ABD Dışişleri Bakanı Rogers'ın Kongreye Sunduğu Rapordan Bölümler, Ankara: Amerikan Basın ve Kültür Merkezi, 1972, p. 3.

[202] The arms embargo issue was also mentioned in Chapter VII in the context of the Cyprus question.

and all licenses with respect to the transportation of arms, ammunitions, and implements of war" to the Turkish government were suspended.[203]

Supporters of the arms embargo claimed that Turkey had violated U.S. law by employing U.S. arms and equipment in its military intervention in Cyprus contrary to the provisions of the agreements under which these arms had been sold to it.[204] It was stated that U.S. failure to impose an embargo on Turkey would alienate Greece, a strategically vital ally of the United States.[205] Some congressmen went so far to say that the United States did not need Turkey any more because its strategic value and benefits to NATO and the U.S. had sunk to almost zero.[206]

The U.S. administration opposed the arms embargo for the following strategic reasons: 1- Turkey, whose strategic importance with respect to the Soviet Union and the Middle East remained vital to the Western alliance, could be alienated and consequently Turkey might seek non-NATO resources to satisfy its defense requirements.[207] 2- The suspension of the U.S. activities in some Turkish installations because of the embargo resulted in the loss of some intelligence information on Soviet space, missile and military systems development, operations and training. It hampered the U.S. capability to develop countermeasures to Soviet weapons systems under development and degraded intelligence acquisition used to monitor and verify compliance with the SALT agreements.[208] 3- The embargo had impaired the cohesion and strength of the southeastern flank of NATO.[209] 4- The fighting capability, deterrent posture and material readiness of the Turkish armed forces had been diminished and the Turkish NATO forces had been weakened.[210] 5- The unavailability of Turkish ports for the U.S. 6th Fleet visits had created morale and other problems for the fleet.[211] 6- In the final analysis, the embargo had degraded NATO's overall military capabilities and adversely affected U.S. national security interests.[212]

The Turkish side responded sharply to the embargo, stating that the Congress action constituted a unilateral violation of defense co-operation accords between the two

---

[203] *Legislation on Foreign Relations Through 1979: Current Legislation and Related Executive Orders*, vol. 1, U.S. House of Representatives and Senate, Washington: U.S. Government Printing Office, 1980, p. 113.

[204] Couloumbis, *The United States, Greece and Turkey*, p. 104, Campany, *Turkey and the United States*, pp. 75, 76, Paul Y. Watanabe, *Ethnic Groups, Congress and American Foreign Policy*, London: Greenwood Press, 1984, pp. 113,114. The Foreign Assistance Act of 1961 (PL 87-195) and the Military Sales Act of 1968 (PL 90-629) stipulated that Defence articles and services to any country should be furnished solely for internal security and legitimate self-Defence and that any substantial violation of these provisions should render the violator immediately ineligible for further assistance.

[205] Couloumbis, *The United States, Greece and Turkey*, p. 104.

[206] Sezer, "Turkey's Security Policies", p. 63, Senator Walter Mondale's speech on the opium issue in S. Taşhan, "Turkey's Relations With the U.S.A. and Possible Future Developments", *Foreign Policy*, vol. 8, Nos. 1-2, 1979, pp. 20-21, Gruen, "Ambivalence in the Alliance", p. 372.

[207] Couloumbis, *The United States, Greece and Turkey*, pp. 104-105; Campany, *Turkey and the United States*, p. 77; *The Military Aspects of Banning Arms Aid to Turkey*, pp. 8, 62. In the latter reference, U.S. Secretary of State Cyrus Vance, Secretary of Defence Harold Brown, Chairman of the Joint Chiefs of Staff David C. Jones, Commander in Chief in U.S. European Command Alexander Haig, five former supreme allied commanders and Colonel Phelps Jones presented arguments for the necessity of lifting the arms embargo.

[208] *The Military Aspects of Banning Arms Aid to Turkey*, pp. 8, 26, 48, 49, Watanabe, *Ethnic Groups, Congress and American Foreign Policy*, pp. 109, 131, Laurance Stern, *The Wrong Horse*, New York: Times Books, 1977, pp. 152-154.

[209] *The Military Aspects of Banning Arms Aid to Turkey*, pp. 4, 11,12, 15.

[210] Ibid., pp. 4-5, 7, 9-10, 12, 23-24, 39, 48.

[211] Ibid., p. 48.

[212] Ibid., pp. 4, 10, 62, Watanabe, *Ethnic Groups, Congress and American Foreign Policy*, p. 109.

countries.[213] The embargo was perceived as a hostile act that undermined the capability, preparedness and effectiveness of the Turkish armed forces.[214] On 25 July 1975, the Turkish government declared that the Defense Co-operation Agreement of 1969 and all other related agreements had lost their legal validity and that all U.S. installations in Turkey passed under the full control and custody of the Turkish armed forces. The İncirlik air base was to be used only for direct NATO purposes. The decision also meant the suspension of operations at four intelligence-collecting centers at Karamürsel, Sinop, Diyarbakır and Belbaşı.[215]

On 6 October 1975 the U.S. Congress partially lifted the arms embargo; it exempted from the embargo military deliveries contracted for before the effective day of the embargo, that meant arms worth 185 million dollars.[216] But the Turkish administration did not allow the resumption of functioning of U.S. bases in return.

According to the statement of U.S. Defense Secretary Harold Brown, between 1975 and 1979 Turkey was authorized credits of 425 million dollars under the Foreign Military Sales (FMS) Financing Program.[217] In this period, Turkey also purchased U.S. military repair parts, maintenance services and spares totaling 31.2 million dollars through the NATO Maintenance and Supply Agency (NAMSA)[218] and received about 265 million dollars worth of military equipment from other Western powers.[219] On 26 March 1976, Turkey and the United States signed a new Defense Co-operation Agreement, providing 800 million dollars in FMS and 200 million dollars in grant aid over a four-year period. But it was not approved by the Congress and was never implemented.[220] On 26 July 1978, the U.S. Senate voted to repeal the embargo, the House followed through on August 1.[221] President Carter signed the embargo repeal legislation on 26 September 1978, thus lifting the embargo completely. On 9 October 1978, the Turkish government terminated the suspension measures implemented in U.S. bases and facilities.[222]

On 29 March 1980, Turkey and the United States signed an updated Defense and Economic Co-operation Agreement (DECA).[223] It was a five-year executive agreement, renewable annually, which would implement the NATO treaty. The United States undertook to provide defense equipment, services, and training to the Turks. Turkey, in return,

---

[213] In *MMTD*: M. Altınsoy, 20 February 1975, term 4, sess. 2, vol. 9, p. 369, İ. Müftüoğlu, 21 February 1975, ibid., p. 444, S. Öztürk, ibid., p. 452, H. Ulman, ibid., p. 457, Foreign Minister Melih Esenbel, ibid., p. 460, Foreign Minister İhsan Sabri Çağlayangil, 12 June 1975, term 4, sess. 2, vol. 12, p. 579, H. Savaşçı, 28 April 1976, term 4, sess. 2, vol. 19, p. 120; Prime Minister Sadi Irmak's statement in *Cumhuriyet*, 4 February 1975, p. 7.

[214] Sezer, "Turkey's Security Policies", p. 66, Bülent Ecevit, "Turkey's Security Policies" in Alford (ed.), *Greece and Turkey*, p. 137.

[215] *Cumhuriyet*, 26 July 1975, Couloumbis, *The United States, Greece and Turkey*, p. 151, Grimmett, *United States Military Installations and Objectives in the Mediterranean*, pp. 43-44, *The Military Aspects of Banning Arms Aid to Turkey*, pp. 8, 72.

[216] U.S. Public Law 94-104 in *Current Legislation*, pp. 247-249, Campany, *Turkey and the United States*, p. 63, Rustow, *Turkey*, p. 104, Kuniholm, "Turkey and NATO", p. 440.

[217] *The Military Aspects of Banning Arms Aid to Turkey*, pp. 21-22, 32, Campany, *Turkey and the United States*, p. 63, Kuniholm, "Turkey and NATO", p. 440. For the detailed information about the military equipment received by Turkey in this period see *The Military Aspects of Banning Arms Aid to Turkey*, p. 76.

[218] *The Military Aspects of Banning Arms Aid to Turkey*, pp. 35, 48, 79.

[219] Ibid., p. 33.

[220] Grimmett, *United States Military Installations and Objectives in the Mediterranean*, pp. 44, 88-93 (text), Couloumbis, *The United States, Greece and Turkey*, p. 151, Campany, *Turkey and the United States*, p. 63, Stern, op. cit., pp. 155-156.

[221] U.S. PL 95-384 in *Current Legislation*, p. 320.

[222] Couloumbis, *The United States, Greece and Turkey*, p. 106, Kuniholm, "Turkey and NATO", p. 427n.

[223] For the texts of the main agreement and supplementary agreements see Campany, *Turkey and the United States*, pp. 103-123, Appendix H.

authorized the United States to maintain forces and carry out military activities at specified installations. An U.S.-Turkish Joint Commission was created as a mechanism for discussing how to use Turkey's resources for its security objectives.

The arms embargo and suspension of functioning of military bases in Turkey represented a serious cut-off on U.S.-Turkish military relations though the two states remained allies within NATO. The embargo did not achieve its original declared aim, Turkish concessions on the Cyprus question, but it reminded the Turks that their defense was heavily dependent on the United States. By nullifying the 1969 agreement, the Turks showed that they were not merely a stooge of the United States. But they could not save themselves entirely from military dependence on the USA. U.S. imposed conditions on aid in the following years continued to be a headache for Turkish authorities.

b) The Use of Bases

The use of Turkish territory by the United States for non-NATO purposes continued to be a sensitive issue in the U.S.-Turkish military relations in the 1970s and the 1980s. During the Arab-Israel war in 1973, the Turkish government announced again that the İncirlik airbase could not be used for non-NATO purposes.[224] Allegedly, at that time, Turkey permitted Soviet overflights and naval transit through the Straits to resupply Egypt and Syria (normally the Soviet Union has this right),[225] but it did not allow the United States to use bases for direct combat or logistical support though it permitted the Americans to use communications stations.[226] During the Iranian revolution in 1979, Turkey allowed the use of bases for evacuation of U.S. citizens,[227] but it did not cooperate with the hostage rescue mission to Iran in 1980.[228] The use of the İncirlik base by U.S. planes to attack Iraqi positions during the Gulf War of 1991 showed that the United States could obtain the use of bases for non-NATO purposes if it really needed them.[229]

The Turkish government announced in 1979 that it would not permit U-2 flights from Turkish territory as part of the proposed monitoring of SALT II agreement unless the Soviet Union agreed.[230] One controversial issue in the 1980s was the Rapid Deployment Force (RDF), which was suggested by the Americans to be used in emergency situations in the region. In October 1982, Turkey and the United States signed a co-located operating base

---

[224] *Cumhuriyet*, 17 October 1973, p. 7.

[225] Richard F. Grimmett and Ellen B. Laipson, *Turkey's Problems and Prospects: Implications for U.S. Interests*, Report Prepared for the Subcommittee on Europe and the Middle East of the Committee on Foreign Affairs, U.S. House of Representatives, Washington: U.S. Government Printing Office, 1980, p. 48, Senator Mandela's speech in Taşhan, "Turkey's Relations With the U.S.A. and Possible Future Developments", p. 20, Gruen, "Ambivalence in the Alliance", p. 372, Justin Galen, "Turkey As a Self-Inflicted Wound: the Narrowing Options for U.S. Defence Policy", *Armed Forces Journal International*, June 1980, p. 71.

[226] Kuniholm, "Turkey and NATO", p. 426.

[227] Ibid., Hans Binnendijk and Alfred Friendly, *Turkey, Greece, and NATO: The Strained Alliance*, A Staff Report to the Committee on Foreign Relations, U.S. Senate, March 1980, Washington: U.S. Government Printing Office, 1980, p. 29.

[228] Rustow, *Turkey*, p. 113.

[229] During the Gulf War NATO countries promised Turkey that if she came under attack because of the use of the İncirlik base NATO would come to her help. The author's interview with Fahir Armaoğlu.

[230] Gruen, "Ambivalence in the Alliance", p. 376, Micheal M. Boll, "Turkey's New National Security Concept: What It Means for NATO", *ORBIS*, Fall 1979, p. 611, Binnendijk and Friendly, *Turkey, Greece, and NATO*, p. 12.

agreement, providing for the modernization of the ten Turkish airfields and the construction of two new ones in eastern Anatolia. To counter rumors that the airfields could be used for a Western intervention in the Gulf, Turkish authorities emphasized that the 1982 agreement had no connection with RDF and that the use of the airfields would be limited to NATO missions.[231]

c) The Turkish Perception of NATO

In the 1970s, all the Turkish parties, which had members in the parliament, supported Turkey's membership of NATO provided that Turkey took measures to meet its security needs independent of NATO, was not dragged into conflicts unrelated to her national interests, and maintained its freedom of decision and action.[232] As a result of the American arms embargo, Turkish authorities became aware of Turkey's dependence on the United States in terms of military equipment and came to the conclusion that security could not be totally entrusted to their NATO allies.[233] They developed a new national security concept aiming at expansion of domestic defense industry for self-sufficiency in defense.[234] The REMO plan, which was created to modernize the Turkish armed forces and to manufacture weapons at home, was perceived as a step in this direction.[235]

Turkish rulers also expressed some adverse criticism of NATO:[236] Turkey's dependence on one source (the USA) within NATO constituted a disadvantageous position for Turkey's defense. NATO did not help Turkey to modernize its defense structure in accordance with technological developments. Turkey undertook heavy burden for NATO, allocating to NATO a proportionately greater part of her national income and manpower than any other member did did. Turkey neglected its economy because of its defense burden. Turkey's contribution to NATO should be equal to NATO's contribution to Turkey's security and its position in NATO should not provoke its neighbors.

In the 1970s, Turkey seemed more eager to develop relations with the Soviet Union and its other neighbors, creating an atmosphere of mutual confidence.[237] Although it did not purchase any Soviet military equipment, it received from the Soviet Union economic aid

---

[231] William Hale, "Turkey, NATO, and the Middle East" in Richard Lawless (ed.), *Foreign Policy in the Middle East*, Durham: University of Durham, 1985, pp. 57-58, Kuniholm, "Turkey and NATO", pp. 438-439, George Harris (ed.), *The Middle East in Turkish-American Relations*, Washington: The Heritage Foundation, 1985, p. ix.

[232] Eren, *Turkey, NATO and Europe*, p. 47; in *MMTD*: İ. F. Cumalıoğlu, 21 May 1974, term 4, sess. 1, vol. 4, p. 527, S. Selek, ibid., p. 530, Defence Minister Hasan Esat Işık, ibid., p. 550, H. Ulman, 22 May 1974, ibid., p. 625, Foreign Minister Turan Güneş, ibid., p. 630, Prime Minister Bülent Ecevit, 3 July 1974, term 4, sess. 1, vol. 6, pp. 363-364, H. Ulman, ibid., p. 430, A. Akarca, 21 February 1975, term 4, sess. 2, vol. 9, p. 454, H. Savaşçı, 13 May 1976, term 4, sess. 3, vol. 19, p. 496.

[233] Sezer, "Turkey's Security Policies", pp. 66, 67.

[234] Boll, "Turkey's New National Security Concept", pp. 613-614, Prime Minister Bülent Ecevit's statements in Eren, *Turkey, NATO and Europe*, p. 50, İhsan Gürkan, *NATO, Turkey and the Southern Flank*, New York: National Strategy Information Centre, 1980, p. 36.

[235] In *MMTD*: M. Altınsoy, 20 February 1975, term 4, sess. 2, vol. 9, p. 368, H. Savaşçı, 13 May 1976, term 4, sess. 3, vol. 19, p. 497.

[236] Ecevit, "Turkey's Security Policies", pp. 136-139.

[237] Ibid., p. 138, Gürkan, *NATO, Turkey and the Southern Flank*, pp. 35,36.

worth 650 million dollars between 1974 and 1979.[238] In July 1976, Turkey permitted the Soviet aircraft carrier Kiev to pass through the Straits.[239] In July 1978, Turkish Prime Minister Ecevit paid a much-publicized visit to Moscow, signing there a document on friendly relations and co-operation. Although the document reiterated many of the basic principles of the Helsinki Agreement and fell short of a non-aggression pact, it caused anxieties in the Western powers.[240] In spite of these developments, the Turks still saw the Soviet Union as a threat to Turkish security, and in particular the rising power of the USSR in the Mediterranean worried them.[241] Turkish rulers also continued to express their doubts about détente, mutual troop reduction talks with the Eastern bloc and the possibility of Soviet troop transfers from Europe to the Turkish border.[242]

9. TURKEY'S BENEFITS FROM THE UNITED STATES AND NATO

The following information leads to the conclusion that crucial benefits from the United States in military area compels Turkey to continue its alliance with the USA.

a) Military and Economic Aid

Table. 1 US Assistance to Turkey 1946-1985
(millions of dollars)

Fiscal Year	Military	Economic
1946-1948	68.8	44.5
1949	83.5	
1950	7.3	
1951	43.1	
1952	102.0	
1949-1952		225.1
1953	151.8	
1954	238.2	
1955	178.2	
1956	191.3	
1957	152.4	
1958	249.4	

---

[238] Campany, *Turkey and the United States,* pp. 80-81, Kuniholm, "Turkey and NATO", p. 427, CSIA European Security Working Group, "Instability and Change on NATO's Southern Flank", *International Security,* Winter 1978, p. 172, Grimmett and Laipson, *Turkey's Problems and Prospects,* p. 45.

[239] CSIA, "Instability and Change on NATO's Southern Flank", p. 172, Galen, op. cit., p. 71.

[240] CSIA, "Instability and Change on NATO's Southern Flank", p. 172, Boll, "Turkey's New National Security Concept", p. 621, Galen, op. cit., p. 71.

[241] In *MMTD*: Defence Minister M. İzmen, 20 February 1973, term 3, sess. 4, vol. 34, p. 454, İ. F. Cumalıoğlu, 21 May 1974, term 4, sess. 1, vol. 4, p. 527, Faruk Sükan, ibid., p. 535; CSIA, "Instability and Change on NATO's Southern Flank", p. 151.

[242] Hamit Batu, "New Developments in Turkish Foreign Policy", *Foreign Policy,* vol. 5, No. 4, 1976, pp. 14-15; in *MMTD*: Defence Minister M. İzmen, op. cit., p. 454, Foreign Minister Turan Güneş, 22 May 1974, term 4, sess. 1, vol. 4, p. 630, Prime Minister Bülent Ecevit, 3 July 1974, term 4, sess. 1, vol. 6, p. 364.

Fiscal Year	Military	Economic
1959	196.3	
1960	92.6	
1961	85.9	
1952-1962		1,107.8
1962	156.4	195.9
1963	172.2	165.3
1964	101.6	174.8
1965	118.4	193.0
1966	126.5	160.2
1967	160.8	150.0
1968	121.1	85.8
1969	124.6	91.3
1970	122.8	90.2
1971	142.1	82.7
1972	152.6	66.9
1973	148.6	22.9
1974	147.5	5.5
1975	109.1	4.4
1976		
1977	125.0	0.2
1978	175.4	1.1
1979	180.3	69.6
1980	208.3	198.1
1981	253.0	201.0
1982	403.0	301.0
1983	403.0	491.0
1984	718.0	442.0
1985	704.0	477.0

Sources: Agency for International Development, Statistics and Reports Division, Office of Financial Management, *U.S. Overseas Loans and Grants and Assistance from International Organizations, Obligations and Loan Authorizations,* July 1, 1945- June 30, 1973, p. 28; *Türkiye'ye Amerikan İktisadi Yardımları,* 1949-1968, Ankara: Maliye Bakanlığı, November 1968 (this source gives great detail of U.S. economic assistance to Turkey); Binnendijk and Friendly, *Turkey, Greece, and NATO,* p. 17; Grimmett and Laipson, *Turkey's Problems and Prospects,* p. 38; Harris, *Troubled Alliance,* p. 155; Botsas, "The U.S. Cyprus Turkey Greece Tetragon; the Economics of an Alliance", p. 253; Couloumbis, *The United States, Greece and Turkey,* p. 178.

Tables prepared by Shorter give some idea of the amount of U.S. military assistance to Turkey in comparison with Turkey's Gross National Product and total military expenditure. He converted U.S. aid in dollars to Turkish liras. In the table, "military assistance import" represents the U.S. aid to Turkey.

Table 2: Turkish Military Expenditure and GNP
(Billion TL)

Years	Total Military Expenditure	Military Assistance Import	GNP
1948	0.733	0.203	10.1
1949	0.712	0.156	9.3
1950	0.730	0.131	10.4
1951	0.817	0.165	12.3
1952	1.134	0.409	14.3
1953	1.318	0.491	16.8
1954	1.556	0.620	17.1
1955	1.542	0.465	21.1
1956	1.641	0.482	24.3
1957	2.090	0.824	30.5
1958	3.734	2.264	38.5
1959	3.281	1.128	47.7
1960	3.196	0.786	51.0
1961	3.468	0.750	53.7
1962	4.389	1.419	60.7

Source: F. C. Shorter, "Military Expenditures and the Allocation of Resources" in F. C. Shorter (ed.), *Four Studies on the Economic Development of Turkey*, London: Frank Cass and Co. Ltd., 1967, pp. 38-43.

On average, over the 15-year period (1948-1962), U.S. assistance constituted 34 percent of Turkey's total military expenditure. In 1970, total U.S. aid to Turkey constituted 2.1 percent of Turkish Domestic Product (272 million dollars in 12.8 billion dollars). This percentage became 0.71 in 1980 (406 million dollars in 56.9 billion dollars) and 1.4 in 1985 (734 million dollars in 49.7 billion dollars).[243] U.S. economic aid to Turkey between 1950 and 1964 was equivalent to 17 percent of total gross investment and 35 percent of total public investment in Turkey,[244] and it contributed to Turkey's economic growth substantially. However, too much emphasis on security led Turkish rulers to attribute secondary importance to economic development.[245]

Immediately after World War II, the United States was the most important trading partner of Turkey, but it was replaced by the Federal Republic of Germany after 1951. The USA's share in Turkey's trade constantly fell between 1960 and 1978: 24.2 percent in 1960-65, 15.4 percent in 1966-72 and 8.4 percent in 1973-78. Between 1956 and 1966 and between 1969 and 1972, the United States shipped grain and other products to Turkey under Public Law 480, which allows the sale of surplus agricultural products to Third World countries against payment in local currency. Clearly, the EEC countries were more important trade partners for Turkey than the USA was. Their share in Turkey's trade continuously increased, reaching 46 percent in 1973-1978.[246]

---

[243] Rustow, Turkey, op. cit., pp. 136-137.

[244] Leo Tansky, *U.S. and USSR Aid to Developing Countries*, New York: Frederick A. Praeger Publishers, 1967, pp. 60-62.

[245] Ibid., pp. 60, 167, 177.

[246] William Hale, *The Political and Economic Development of Modern Turkey*, London: Croom Helm, 1981, pp. 234, 240, 244-245, *Industrialization and Trade Strategy*, Washington: the World Bank, 1982, pp. 417-418, A.

In the 1980s, Turkey was the third largest recipient of the U.S. military and economic aid after Israel and Egypt. The U.S. Congress had a pattern of conditioning aid on good Turkish behavior on the Cyprus question and limiting it to a ratio (10:7) between the assistance given to Turkey and Greece.[247]

b) Military Equipment

Table 3 at the end of this chapter gives some idea on the military equipment provided by the USA for Turkey.

According to Military Assistance Program Data of U.S. Defense Security Agency, the United States delivered the following military material to Turkey as of 7 August 1974:[248] (a) Tactical aircraft (some tactical aircraft, plus all 8 inch howitzer, and Honest John rockets can be used for tactical nuclear purposes): 965. (b) Destroyers: 2. (c) Submarines: 7. (d) Tanks (all types): 3,915. (e) Armored personnel carriers: 1,827. (f) Self-propelled artillery: 861. (g) Towed artillery: 1,127. (h) NIKE missiles: 540. (i) Honest John missiles: 831. (j) Recoilless rifles (90-106 mm); 2,044. (k) Mortars (81 mm- 4.2 in): 1,248. (l) Machine-guns: 14,296. (m) Rifles: 320,450. (n) 1:4 ton trucks: 22,588. (o) Two and half ton trucks: 23,928. (p) Tactical radios: 21, 811.

10. IMPORTANCE OF TURKEY FOR THE USA

The information in the following sections, which was derived from articles, books and speeches of scholars and Turkish and American officials, considers mostly the period before the disintegration of the Soviet Union, and, therefore, it provides the viewpoints concerned as they were stated at the time. Some of the points made then might be applied to the post-Soviet Union period as well.

a) Importance of Turkey's Strategic Position

Under the provisions of the Montreaux Convention, Turkey has control over the Straits of the Dardanelles and the Bosphorus, which link the Black Sea to the Mediterranean. It was in the unique position of being able to close the Straits and thereby deny the Soviet Black Sea Fleet access into the Mediterranean and cut off all Soviet naval vessels operating in the Mediterranean from their homeports and lines of communications. If the Turkish control over passage through the Straits was abrogated, Soviet naval vessels would enjoy a significant surge capacity in times of international crises or war and thus NATO forces would have to contend with much greater Soviet power in the Mediterranean. The Straits were the major

---

O. Krueger, *Foreign Trade Regimes and Economic Development: Turkey*, New York: Columbia University Press, 1974, pp. 183-184, Z. Y. Hershlag, *Turkey: the Challenge of the Growth*, Leiden: E. J. Brill, 1968, pp. 253, 373, Vali, *Bridge Across the Bosporus*, pp. 326, 332.

[247] Richard N. Haas, "Managing NATO's Weakest Flank; the United States, Greece and Turkey", *ORBIS*, vol. 30, No. 3, Fall 1986, p. 466. For a detailed study of the 10:7 ratio see Stearns, *Entangled Allies*, pp. 40-50.

[248] Cited by Collins, *Greece and Turkey*, p. 50. The wide discrepancies between above lists and this list may be accounted for by the fact that the latter list refers to outright U.S. grants to Turkey whereas the former lists include items purchased.

routes used by the Soviet navy and merchant ships to reach the Mediterranean, North Africa and the Middle East. With the Straits and the Suez Canal open, Soviet ships could easily reach the Indian Ocean and the Atlantic. Turkey had the potential to deny these vital opportunities to the Russians. The requirements to give advance notice to warship transit and to traverse only on the surface by submarine in the Straits provided continuing intelligence opportunities for the West in peacetime. Soviet ships could easily be monitored in this way.[249]

Turkey has control over the high plateau of Anatolia, which commands the entire Fertile Crescent down to the Persian Gulf and Red Sea. It lies along the roads from the Balkans to the Middle East and from the Caucasus to the Persian Gulf and it commands land, sea and air communications in much of the Balkans and the Middle East. It controlled the ideal Soviet land route to oilfields of the Persian Gulf.[250] Turkey was also in a position to regulate and deny Soviet overflights to the Middle East.[251] It served as an obstacle and powerful deterrence to any Soviet aggression directed toward Southern Europe, the Middle East and North Africa.[252]

Apart from Norway, Turkey was the only NATO country, which shared a long border (1500-mile) with the Soviet Union.[253] It was vital to the security and stability of NATO's southern flank and constituted the first line of defense for the flank.[254] The Turkish armed forces strengthened NATO in the eastern Mediterranean, enabling it to control the region and giving to it superiority against the Soviet power in the area.[255] Turkey contributed the second largest land force to NATO; 490,000 men, 15 divisions and 20 air squadrons.[256] The Turkish forces tied down 50 Warsaw Pact divisions on the east of Turkey and Baltic fronts, which could otherwise be concentrated against other areas of NATO, including the central sector.[257] Turkey served as a staging ground for counterattacks against the Soviet Union and provided facilities for NATO forward tactical operations and support activities.[258] And, finally, Turkey

---

[249] *The Military Aspects of Banning Arms Aid to Turkey*, pp. 7, 16, 24, 41, 47; Vali, *Bridge Across the Bosporus*, pp. 46, 216-217; Couloumbis, *The United States, Greece and Turkey*, pp. 137, 187; Campany, *Turkey and the United States*, pp. v-vi; McGhee, *The U.S. Turkish NATO Middle East Connection*, p. 170; Margaret Krahenbuhl, *Turkish-American Relations: An Affair to Remember*, Santa Monica: Rand Corporation, 1974, p. 2; Haas, "Managing NATO's Weakest Flank", p. 458; Gürkan, *NATO, Turkey and the Southern Flank*, p. 13; Lewis, *The Strategic Balance in the Mediterranean*, pp. 28, 31-32, 70-72; Collins, *Greece and Turkey*, pp. 5-6, 15,17; *United States Security Agreements*, p. 1817; Stearns, *Entangled Allies*, pp. 53, 59.

[250] Karpat *(ed.)*, *Turkey's Foreign Policy in Transition*, p. 2, Vali, *Bridge Across the Bosporus*, pp. xi-xii, Campany, *Turkey and the United States*, pp. v-vi, McGhee, *The U.S. Turkish NATO Middle East Connection*, pp. 88-89, L. V. Thomas and R. N. Frye, *The United States and Turkey and Iran*, Cambridge, Mass.: Harvard University Press, 1951, p. 145.

[251] Sezer, "Turkey's Security Policies", p. 63, Collins, *Greece and Turkey*, p. 17, *The Military Aspects of Banning Arms Aid to Turkey*, p. 3.

[252] McGhee, *The U.S. Turkish NATO Middle East Connection*, pp. 88-89, Sezer, "Turkey's Security Policies", p. 63, Thomas and Frye, *The United States and Turkey and Iran*, p. 145, Collins, *Greece and Turkey*, p. 5, *The Military Aspects of Banning Arms Aid to Turkey*, pp. 6,9, 16,74.

[253] *The Military Aspects of Banning Arms Aid to Turkey*, p. 3, Gürkan, *NATO, Turkey and the Southern Flank*, pp. 14-15.

[254] Vali, *Bridge Across the Bosporus*, pp. xi-xii, 373, Campany, *Turkey and the United States*, p. v, Sezer, "Turkey's Security Policies", p. 63, Krahenbuhl, *Turkish-American Relations*, p. 2, *The Military Aspects of Banning Arms Aid to Turkey*, p. 6.

[255] McGhee, *The U.S. Turkish NATO Middle East Connection*, p. 170, Collins, *Greece and Turkey*, pp. ix, 9.

[256] *The Military Aspects of Banning Arms Aid to Turkey*, pp. 3,16, 62,74, Collins, *Greece and Turkey*, p. 9.

[257] *The Military Aspects of Banning Arms Aid to Turkey*, pp. 6,9, 10,17, 24,47,74, Collins, *Greece and Turkey*, pp. 9,16, McGhee, *The U.S. Turkish NATO Middle East Connection*, p. 170, Haas, "Managing NATO's Weakest Flank", p. 458.

[258] *The Military Aspects of Banning Arms Aid to Turkey*, p. 6.

provided a valuable link between the Islamic World and the West as a member of both the Islamic Conference and NATO.[259]

b) Importance of the U.S. Bases in Turkey

The United States had 61 military facilities in Turkey as of June 30, 1976.[260] The following conflation of American assessments of some of them illustrates the importance of these facilities to the USA.

Intelligence-collection stations:[261] 1- Sinop (on the Black Sea coast in north central Turkey almost directly opposite Yalta): A radar monitoring and communications facility, manned by personnel from the Army Security Agency (ASA), a component of the National Security Agency (NSA). It collected data on the Soviet Union's air and naval activities in the Black Sea area, as well as that country's missile testing activities. 2- Samsun (on the Black Sea coast in north-central Turkey): A communications site, associated with Sinop, manned by personnel of the U.S. Air Force Security Service (USAFSS), also a component of NSA. Radar at Samsun had been tracking down Soviet missile test shots from Kapustin Yar (east of Volgograd) since 1955 - including SLBMs.[262] 3- Karamürsel Air Station (located on the south-east shore of the Sea of Marmara and south-east of İstanbul): A communications and monitoring installation which tracked Soviet naval traffic in the western Black Sea area and the area surrounding the Straits. It was manned by USAFSS personnel. 4- Diyarbakır Air Station (in south-eastern Turkey near the Syrian border): A long-range radar and communications complex that tracked Soviet missile launches from various Soviet testing sites and monitored other Soviet military activities. Its activities were carried out by personnel of USAFSS. 5- The Belbaşı Station (near Ankara in central Turkey): A seismographic detection base, which monitored Soviet nuclear tests.

Intelligence collection installations were vital to monitor Soviet military activity in the southeastern military districts of that country, development of certain Soviet weapons systems, Soviet nuclear explosions and missile tests, and Soviet compliance with SALT treaties, ABM and Test Ban treaties.[263] U.S. Secretary of Defense Harold Brown stated that some of these facilities were irreplaceable and more important than those in Greece.[264] The former NATO Supreme Commander, Gen. Lyman Lemnitzer, described their importance as follows: "There is no area in the world comparable to Turkey as a vital base of intelligence-gathering operations against the Warsaw Pact... These bases when fully operational are capable of providing valuable and irreplaceable intelligence coverage for which no substitute is available."[265]

---

[259] Campany, *Turkey and the United States*, p. vi.

[260] *Grimmett, United States Military Installations and Objectives in the Mediterranean*, p. 8n.

[261] Ibid., p. 39, Couloumbis, *The United States, Greece and Turkey*, pp. 135-136, Lewis, *The Strategic Balance in the Mediterranean*, pp. 29-30. For the following information on bases see also Grimmett and Laipson, *Turkey's Problems and Prospects*, pp. 15-23, Binnendijk and Friendly, *Turkey, Greece, and NATO*, pp. 8-9.

[262] Collins, *Greece and Turkey*, p. 13.

[263] *The Military Aspects of Banning Arms Aid to Turkey*, pp. 16, 26,65, Collins, *Greece and Turkey*, p. 13, Grimmett, *United States Military Installations and Objectives in the Mediterranean*, pp. 37, 46-47, Lewis, *The Strategic Balance in the Mediterranean*, pp. 30-31, Gruen, "Ambivalence in the Alliance", p. 367.

[264] *The Military Aspects of Banning Arms Aid to Turkey*, p. 26.

[265] Campany, *Turkey and the United States*, p. 57.

The U.S. Defense Communication System (DSC) terminals: 6 in European Turkey, 5 in Ankara area, 13 in İzmit area, 3 in İzmir area, 7 in Diyarbakır area, 2 in İncirlik area, 3 in Malatya area, 1 in Sinop and 1 in Samsun.[266] The Yamanlar facility in western Turkey just north of İzmir connected Turkey with Greece through the Mt. Pateras terminal, located south of Athens. It was also connected to the Şahin Tepesi terminal, which linked the Karamürsel-Yalova communications terminals with a number of European Turkey DSC sites and with the Elmadağ terminal, which was located northeast of Ankara. The Elmadağ terminal was linked to the Samsun communications facility near the Black Sea coast and the Karataş terminal near the İncirlik Air Base, which was connected with the Malatya terminal in east-central Turkey. The Malatya terminal was linked to the Diyarbakır terminal, which housed a Defense Satellite Communications System earth terminal that was connected with Lakehurst Naval Air Station in Lakehurst, NJ[267]

NADGE (NATO's Air Defense Grand Environment) early-warning radar sites: They were spread throughout Turkey: Ankara, İzmit, Eskişehir, Lüleburgaz, Bartın, Diyarbakır, Merzifon, Perşembe, Pazar, Erzurum, Mardin, Çanakkale, Sarıkışla, Kargapazar.[268] 19 fully integrated, semi-automatic sites astride the Aegean centralized missile and aircraft warning efforts in that area and directed air defense actions in response to proven and possible threats.[269] For Soviet aircraft overflying near either Greece or Turkey, warning could be provided while these aircraft were over Bulgaria or the Black Sea. Early warning was critical to the operation of the U.S. Sixth Fleet.[270]

Airbases, stations: 1- The İncirlik Air Base (located near the city of Adana in south-central Turkey): The major tactical fighter base in Turkey, where USAFE (U.S. Air Forces, Europe) F-4 squadrons from Torrefon Air Base in Spain and Avaino Air Base in Italy serve on a rotational basis. U.S. fighters located at İncirlik are the most forward deployed land-based American aircraft in the eastern Mediterranean that are capable of launching a tactical nuclear airstrike in the event of conflict in the region.[271] 2- Karamürsel Air Base (near the city of İzmit): It might be used to guard against any threat to the Straits.[272] 3- The Ankara Air Station: Ankara also housed The Joint U.S. Military Mission for Aid to Turkey (JUSMMAT) and the U.S. Logistic Group (TUSLOG), which was the central logistical and support command for all U.S. supply services in the eastern Mediterranean and the Middle East.[273] 4- The İzmir Air Station (in west-central Turkey off the Aegean coast) and the Çiğli Air Base: İzmir was the site of an air support base for USAFE, as well as the headquarters of NATO's Allied Land Forces, South-eastern Europe (LANDSOUTHEAST) and the Sixth Allied

---

[266] Collins, *Greece and Turkey*, pp. 62-63.

[267] *Grimmett, United States Military Installations and Objectives in the Mediterranean*, pp. 39, 41.

[268] Collins, *Greece and Turkey*, p. 62.

[269] Ibid., p. 12.

[270] *The Military Aspects of Banning Arms Aid to Turkey*, pp. 6,62.

[271] Grimmett, *United States Military Installations and Objectives in the Mediterranean*, p. 41, Collins, *Greece and Turkey*, p. 10, Couloumbis, *The United States, Greece and Turkey*, p. 136.

[272] Lewis, *The Strategic Balance in the Mediterranean*, p. 30.

[273] Grimmett, *United States Military Installations and Objectives in the Mediterranean*, p. 41, Collins, *Greece and Turkey*, p. 12, Couloumbis, *The United States, Greece and Turkey*, pp. 135, 136, Lewis, *The Strategic Balance in the Mediterranean*, p. 30.

Tactical Air Force (SIXATAF). A USAFE tactical airbase was located in Çiğli, north of İzmir.[274]

ACE High communications sites: 12 communications sites in Turkey were associated with NATO's tropospheric scatter network (ACE High): Ankara, İzmir, Eskişehir, Elmadağ, Amasra, Merzifon, Perşembe, Pazar, Sivas, Diyarbakır, Mardin, Adana.[275]

Storage facilities: İskenderun and Yumurtalık are the most important supply, and storage centers for U.S. military forces in the extreme eastern Mediterranean.[276]

The Kargaburun U.S. Navy LORAN (long-range aid to navigation) station, located on the northern shore of the Sea of Marmara, was an installation which assisted U.S. military aircraft in fixing their positions in the eastern Mediterranean from long ranges through electronic radio-navigational devices.[277]

The report of Grimmett claims that in the event that the United States had to withdraw from its bases in Turkey,

> Greece would be able to provide the most viable and useful base sites for relocation from Turkey of naval and air support installations and facilities for tactical fighter aircraft... Certain defense communications installations currently in Turkey could be replaced by use of other communications systems, including those that presently interconnect with Greece, and through the use of satellites. All of the above, of course, would require the approval of the Greek government.[278]

Mentioning the views of U.S. policy-makers that some intelligence facilities in Turkey could not be replaced, Grimmett's report states: "Yet since collection of intelligence data on the Soviet Union's military activities by the United States does not depend upon Turkish installations alone... the essential problem... would be a loss of information that could strongly confirm data... obtained from other sources." As alternatives he gives satellites, Crete, Greece and Iran (unavailable after 1979).[279] These opinions cannot change the fact that U.S. officials attributed great importance to their facilities in Turkey.

c) Turkey's Position With Respect to the Middle East

Turkey's importance to the United States with respect to the Middle East can be understood better if U.S. stated aims in the Middle East are mentioned: 1- To deter Soviet armed aggression against the region. 2- To secure NATO's southern flank. 3- To encourage stability in the Middle East. 4- To support friendly states like Israel. 5- To maintain western supply lines in the Mediterranean. 6- To ensure continued access to Middle Eastern oil.[280]

---

[274] *Grimmett, United States Military Installations and Objectives in the Mediterranean*, p. 41, Collins, *Greece and Turkey*, p. 12, Couloumbis, *The United States, Greece and Turkey*, pp. 135, 136, Lewis, *The Strategic Balance in the Mediterranean*, p. 30.

[275] Collins, *Greece and Turkey*, pp. 12, 62.

[276] *Grimmett, United States Military Installations and Objectives in the Mediterranean*, p. 41.

[277] Ibid., p. 41, Couloumbis, *The United States, Greece and Turkey*, p. 135.

[278] *Grimmett, United States Military Installations and Objectives in the Mediterranean*, p. 45.

[279] Ibid., pp. 46-47. See also Collins, *Greece and Turkey*, p. 17.

[280] *Grimmett, United States Military Installations and Objectives in the Mediterranean*, p. 5, Collins, *Greece and Turkey*, p. 2.

Turkey protected the Middle East against Soviet expansion and influence by constituting a barrier between the Soviet Union and the region.[281] The United States would lose substantially its political and military posture and influence in the Middle East without the collaboration of Turkey.[282] In the absence of the Turkish barrier, "Soviet support for and accessibility to such countries as Syria and Iraq would have been much more pervasive and potentially threatening to U.S. interests in the region"[283] and Israel would not be able to "maintain its status as a regional power and cope with continuing Arab hostility without the risk of facing... the full force of the Red Army."[284] Turkey neutralized potential risks of the Middle Eastern region for U.S. global strategy,[285] contributed to the stability of the region, which was essential for U.S. interests[286] and provided an important access to the Middle East and Africa.[287] The İncirlik air base in Turkey served as a staging base for U.S. contingents for use in the Middle East and an important stopover for transport airport en route to the Persian Gulf.[288]

Some developments in the 1980s increased Turkey's importance to the United States vis-a-vis the Middle East: 1- The Middle East continued to be NATO countries' main source of energy (oil and gas) and raw materials which were essential to their economic well-being.[289] 2- Soviet military build up in its southern military districts, the invasion of Afghanistan, the expansion of Soviet influence to Aden and Ethiopia, and growing Soviet military presence in Syria threatened the regional balance. 3- The Iranian revolution in 1979 and the growth of Islamic fundamentalism in its aftermath posed threats to the stability of the region. 4- The Iranian hostage crisis. 5- The Iran-Iraq war in the 1980s.[290] 6- The upgrading of some airfields in eastern Turkey in the early 1980s made Turkey more valuable as a possible base for rapid deployment in the Middle East.[291] 7- The important role played by Turkey in the allied coalition against Iraq in 1991 led U.S. officials to assess Turkey's strategic significance in its Middle East context once again.[292]

---

[281] McGhee, *The U.S. Turkish NATO Middle East Connection*, pp. xvi, 174, 176,177, B. Lewis's Preface in Rustow, *Turkey*, pp. vii, ix, Rustow, *Turkey*, pp. 107, 110, Taşhan, "Turkey's Relations With the U.S.A. and Possible Future Developments", pp. 21, 22, *The Military Aspects of Banning Arms Aid to Turkey* op. cit., pp. 6, 75. Former U.S. ambassador Stearns claims that the hope that Turkey would help discourage Soviet take-overs in the Middle East was exaggerated. He argues that as was proved by the Gulf War Turkey is likely to play the role of stepping stone rather than a barrier in the context of the Middle East. Stearns, *Entangled Allies*, pp. 52-53.

[282] Vali, *Bridge Across the Bosporus*, p. 372, Collins, *Greece and Turkey*, p. ix.

[283] B. R. Kuniholm, "Turkey and the West", *Foreign Affairs*, vol. 70, No. 2, Spring 1991, p. 39.

[284] Rustow, *Turkey*, p. 110.

[285] Ibid., p. 111.

[286] *The Military Aspects of Banning Arms Aid to Turkey*, p. 15.

[287] Ibid., p. 3.

[288] Collins, *Greece and Turkey*, p. 16.

[289] Richard Burt, "Turkey and the Reagan Administration" in Harris (ed.), *The Middle East in Turkish-American Relations*, p. 19, Gürkan, *NATO, Turkey and the Southern Flank*, pp. 4, 34, *The Military Aspects of Banning Arms Aid to Turkey*, pp. 24,47.

[290] Burt, "Turkey and the Reagan Administration" p. 19, Barry Rubin, "Middle East Policy in the Turkish Context" in Harris (ed.), *The Middle East in Turkish-American Relations*, pp. 75,78.

[291] Rustow, *Turkey*, pp. 113-114.

[292] Kuniholm, "Turkey and the West", op. cit., pp. 34,43.

11. CONCLUSION

The close military relationship in the 1950s opened the way for U.S. influence on Turkey and eventually brought about the anti-American atmosphere of the 1960s in Turkey. The closeness of the relationship during honeymoon period in the 1950s was for beyond that is seen in normal inter-state relations. The excessive confidence of Turkish rulers in the United States as a close companion who would do anything to protect her "dear" partner against hostile forces led them to entrust the Turkish military establishment to American experts. The presence of U.S. military officers and the flow of U.S. military equipment were enthusiastically welcomed. Together with a firm stance in favor of Western powers in international forums, this situation caused the portrayal of Turkey's image as the satellite of the United States in the eyes of international community.

The following factors brought about the spread of anti-Americanism among Turkish people in the 1960s: Misconduct by officials on both sides who exceeded their authority by signing of various bilateral military agreements; misuse of their rights and privileges by U.S. personnel in Turkey; the U.S. use of Turkish territory for secret reconnaissance flights; free political discussion atmosphere in Turkey, which was introduced by the 1960 constitution; apparent U.S. indifference to the fate of Turkish Cypriots at the hands of the Greek Cypriots; President Johnson's bitter letter, which stated that NATO might not protect Turkey against a Soviet attack and which warned that Turkish rulers should not use U.S.-supplied weapons for purposes not approved by the USA.

Public pressures and the disappointing attitude of the USA led Turkish rulers to take some actions to gain initiative in their military relations with the Americans. Their actions, which displeased U.S. officials to some extent, surely showed that they were not merely a puppet of the United States and that they might reject important U.S. demands if these demands were not compatible with Turkish interests. However, it should be stated that changes brought about by these actions were not radical and that the real character of the U.S.-Turkish military relationship which was hidden in secret bilateral agreements continued to be a mystery. Turkey's military dependence on the United States has also continued up to now though Turkish rulers has sought alternative defense partners and sources. U.S. officials sometimes felt disappointment with some Turkish attitudes in the defense area such as the use of bases and U-2 flights, but they were generally pleased with Turkey's commitment to NATO and the availability of Turkish bases for their general use. Nevertheless, U.S. authorities knew that Turkey could take drastic measures against them in the defense area if it was forced to do so.

Table 3: Military Equipment of Turkish Armed Forces

Item	Number	Supplier
Aircraft		
Lockheed T-33 A-N	36	USA
Lockheed RT-33A	18	FR Germany
Lockheed T-33 A-N	30	USA
Beech T-34 Mentor	24	Canada
Cessina T-37C	25	USA

Item	Number	Supplier
Lockheed T-33	12	FR Germany
Lockheed T-33	9	USA
Cessina T-410	20	USA
Beech T-42 Boron	5	USA
Republic F-84F	(130)	USA
Republic F-84F	42	FR Germany
Republic F-84F	42	FR Germany
Republic RF-84F	(30)	USA
Republic RF-84F	(5)	France
NA F-86D Sabre	50	USA
NA F-86K Sabre	(65)	Netherlands
NA F-100C SuperSabre	260	USA
NA F-100C SuperSabre	40	USA
NA F-100F SuperSabre	(25)	USA
Convair F-102A Delta Dagger	36	USA
Convair TF-102	3	USA
Lockheed F-104 Straight fighter	32	USA
F-104 Straight fighter	113	
F-104D	45	
F-104S	18	
TF-104	12	
TF-104G	4	
F-4E Phantom	80	USA
RF-4E	7	USA
Northrop F-5 Freedom fighter	140	
Beech C-45	(8)	USA
C-47A	64	
Douglas C-54	3	USA
Lockheed C-130 Hercules	10	USA
Transall C-160	20	FR Germany
Piper L-18 Super Cub	200	USA
Canadair CL-13 Sabre Mk4	25	UK
Canadair CL-13 Sabre	82	Canada
Cessna 421	20	
Cessna U-17A	20	USA
Cessna 206	8	USA
Dornier Do-27	15	FR Germany
Dornier Do-27	3	FR Germany
Dornier Do-28	14	FR Germany
Dornier Do-28B-1	5	FR Germany
Bell 47G	(5)	USA
Agusta-Bell 47	20	Italy
Agusta-Bell 204B	13	Italy

Item	Number	Supplier
Agusta-Bell 204B	7	Italy
Agusta-Bell 205Iraquois	3	USA
Agusta-Bell 206AJetRanger	(35)	
Grumman S-2 Tracker	8	Netherlands
Grumman S-2 Tracker	12	USA
Grumman TS-2	2	USA
Srat 223 Flamingo	15	FR Germany
Britten-Norman BN-2Islander	2	UK
Missiles		
Nike Ajax	75	USA
Nike Hercules	(75)	USA
Usamicon MGR-1 Honest John	(24)	USA
NWC Sidewinder	(600)	USA
MBB Bo 810 Cobra2000	(300)	FR Germany
MBB Bo 810 Cobra2000	(500)	FR Germany
Martin Bullpup (AGM-128)	300	USA
Nord SS.11	(100)	France
Hughes TOW(BGM-71A)		USA
Penguin		
Naval Vessels		
Submarine GuppyIA,II,IIA,III	9	USA
Submarine Gur Class	7	USA
Submarine rescue ship	1	USA
Submarine depot ship	1	USA
Destroyer Gearing class	9	USA
Destroyer AllanMSummer	1	USA
Destroyer Fletcher class	5	USA
Destroyer Milne class	4	UK
Motor torpedo boat Jaguar	7	FR Germany
Torpedo boat Nasty	4	FR Germany
Patrol boat Akhisar	5	USA
Patrol boat Ashwlle	2	USA
Coastal escor Batia	9	Canada
Coastal mine layer	6	USA
Mine layer	1	Denmark
Mine layer	2	FR Germany
Coastal mine sweeper MCB	4	Canada
Coastal mine sweeper Adjutant	12	USA
Coastal mine sweeper MSC	3	USA
Cape inshore mine sweeper	4	USA
Motor launch	4	USA
Motor launch	9	FR Germany
Repair ship	1	USA

Item	Number	Supplier
Boom defense vessel	2	USA
Boom defense vessel	1	France
Gunboat	7	USA
Fleet ocean tug	1	USA
Barracks craft	1	USA
Supply ship	1	FR Germany
Armored fighting vehicles		
M-36	(25)	USA
M-26 Pershing	(100)	USA
M-24 Chaffee	(50)	USA
M-47 main battle tanks	500	USA
M-48A1 main battle tanks	2,775	USA
M-48A5 main battle tanks	180	USA
Leopard IA3 main battle tanks	77	FR Germany
M-60A1 main battle tanks		USA
M-41 Lighttank	(100)	USA
M-113 armored personnel carrier	1,400	USA
M-59 armored personnel carrier	(400)	USA
V-150 commando vehicle		USA
M-44 and M-52	24	FR Germany
M-74	69	FR Germany
M-59 155mm towed guns	150	USA
M-107 175mm self-propelled guns	36	USA
M-101A-1 105mm howitzer	600	USA
M-114A1 155mm howitzer	400	USA
M-7 105mm howitzer	345	USA
M-44 155mm howitzer	108	USA
M.110 203mm howitzer		USA
M-1A1 40mm antiaircraft gun	900	USA
M-51 75mm antiaircraft gun		USA
M-118 90mm antiaircraft gun		USA
M-117 90mm antiaircraft gun		USA

Sources: Stockholm International Peace Research Institute (SIPRI), *Arms Trade Registers*, Stockholm: Almqvist and Wiksel International, 1975, pp. 126-130; *Journal of Defence and Diplomacy*, vol. 3, No. 9, September 1985, pp. 34-35; Binnendijk and Friendly, *Turkey, Greece, and NATO*, p.15; Christopher F. Foss, *Jane's Pocket Book of Towed Artillery*, London: MacDonald and Jane's, 1977, pp. 31, 87, 133, 135, 197, 239, 247, 251, 253; Ronald Pretty, *Jane's Pocket Book of Missiles*, London: MacDonald and Jane's, 1978, pp. 49, 64, 84, 149, 201; John W. R. Taylor, *Jane's Pocket Book 2 Major Combat Aircraft*, London: MacDonald and Jane's, 1978, pp. 23, 49, 51, 97, 131, 149, 151, 185, 191; John E. Moore, *Jane's Pocket Book 1 Major Warships*, London: MacDonald and Jane's, 1978, pp. 20, 44-46, 125-127, 146, 181, 189, 209; Christopher F. Foss, *Jane's Pocket Book Modern Tanks and Armoured Fighting Vehicles*, London: Jane's, 1981, pp. 21, 57, 59, 61, 63, 149, 207, 209, 215, 259, 263, 265, 267, 269; Lewis, *The Strategic Balance in the Mediterranean*, pp. 130, 136, 143, 150, 152, 153. For claims that equipment of the Turkish army is antiquated and that its control systems are inefficient see Kuniholm, "Turkey and NATO", pp. 440-441, Galen, "Turkey As a Self-Inflicted Wound: the Narrowing Options for U.S. Defence Policy", p.66-67, *Journal of Defence and Diplomacy*, op. cit., p.34.

Chapter 5

THE BAGHDAD PACT AND
TURKISH-AMERICAN RELATIONS

1. INTRODUCTION

Founders of the Republic of Turkey aimed at integrating Turkey with the Western world and tried to westernize all aspects of Turkish society by carrying out various reforms. Their Western-orientated policies led them to seek good relations with the West in their foreign affairs. Although Turkey signed a pact of mutual assistance with Britain and France in May 1939 and was under pressure of the Allied powers to join the Second World War on their side, it chose to stay out of the war until the last moment. Nevertheless, Turkish policy-makers could not afford to be isolated from the Western world. They decided to declare war on Germany and Japan on 23 February 1945 to be able to participate in the San Francisco Conference and to become a member of the United Nations.

Soviet demands on Turkey in the 1945-1946 period regarding the status of the Turkish straits and Armenian and Georgian territorial claims on two eastern provinces of Turkey, Kars and Ardahan, led Turkish leaders to seek the American security guarantee. The Soviet Union was urging important changes in the Montreaux Convention of 1936 regarding the Turkish straits[1] and the Soviet republics of Georgia and Armenia were claiming that Kars and Ardahan, which were left to Turkey by the new communist regime of Russia after its withdrawal from the First World War, should be returned to them. Turkish leaders saw the United States, which emerged from the war as the most powerful Western state, as a possible ally against the Soviet pressures.

The Truman Doctrine of 1947 was the turning point for Turkish foreign policy since it put Turkey into the Western bloc in the newly emerged cold war atmosphere. The doctrine was a result of the British decision of ending military and economic assistance to the weakened Greek government. Intending to hold a firm line against Soviet actions in various places of the world, the United States decided to replace Britain in supporting the Greek government against communist threat, and extended its help to Turkey since it saw this country as a bulwark against a possible Soviet expansion towards the Near and Middle East.

---

[1] Kemal H. Karpat, "Turkish-Soviet Relations" in Kemal H. Karpat (ed.), *Turkey's Foreign Policy in Transition 1950-1974*, Leiden: E. J. Brill, 1975, pp. 83-84.

Recognizing the Soviet threat as the number one danger, Turkish policy-makers aimed at consolidation of political, military and economic links with the West. Turkey's intention was to receive a considerable amount of economic aid from the West, particularly from the USA, to support its development plans.[2] While the Marshall Plan strengthened the Turkish position within the Western world, Turkey became more ready to support and join various Western attempts to defend the Western bloc against the communist world. The Turkish aim of consolidating relations with the West was considerably strengthened by the Democrat Party's coming to power since its leaders were prepared to struggle for joining all the Western organizations and to support all Western policies globally. The Turkish policy towards the Baghdad Pact of 1955, which was originally an American proposal, was determined by this general line of Western-orientated Turkish foreign policy.

Turkey was in fact reluctant to become involved in Middle Eastern politics since it was determined to join the West and to keep itself away from the unstable Arab world. After voting against the partition of Palestine in the United Nations in 1947, Turkey became the first Muslim country to recognize Israel in 1949 and maintained political and trade links with Israel. In Arab eyes, Turkey was a part of the imperialist Western world and it was opposed to their cause in facing the western control.[3] Turkey, therefore, was unlikely to think of undertaking any special mission in the Arab world without prompting from its Western partners.

In this chapter, the origins, establishment and end of the Baghdad Pact will be discussed. The main focus is the Turkish role in defense plans for the Middle East. The chapter will concentrate on Turkish attempts to draw the Arab world into an alliance with the West in facing international communism, which was indeed a price Ankara was ready to pay in return for the American support for its NATO membership and for its close relations with the USA.

2. THE MIDDLE EAST COMMAND PROPOSAL

a) Turkey's Precondition

The main problem of Turkish foreign policy in the early 1950s was to gain membership of the newly established Western military organization, i.e. NATO. As a first step, Turkish policy-makers expressed their intention of joining a Mediterranean pact, which might be an extension of the North Atlantic Alliance to the Eastern Mediterranean. They considered a Mediterranean pact as a means of entering the North Atlantic alliance through the back door. In February 1949, Necmettin Sadak, the Turkish foreign minister, said that the Turkish government would be interested in a Mediterranean security alliance in which Turkey, Greece, Italy, France and Britain would be members.[4]

Turkish attempts to join NATO, however, did not find a positive response from the West. The most important obstacle to Turkish efforts was Britain's intention to establish a Middle Eastern organization to preserve its position in the region, which was based on bilateral

---

[2] George S. Harris, Turkey, *Coping with Crisis*, London: Westview Press, 1985, p.184.
[3] J. C. Hurewitz, Middle *East Dilemmas*, New York: Russell & Russell, 1953, p. 156.
[4] Halfrod L. Hoskins, The *Middle East*, New York: MacMillan Company, 1956, pp. 278-279, Yaacov Ro'i, From *Encroachment to Involvement*, New York: John Wiley & Sons, 1974, p. 67.

agreements with various Arab countries. The British government requested Turkey to have a key role in this project and suggested that the Turkish and Greek forces should be assigned to a British general under a separate command which would include the Eastern Mediterranean and Arab countries. They hoped, with this project, that they could strengthen the deteriorating British prestige among the Arab states. They also saw it as a means of restoring their uneasy relations with Egypt and to maintain their position in the strategic Suez Canal Zone.[5]

The United States did not challenge these British ideas because the American statesmen thought that a Western defense of the Middle East should be led by Britain and should be based on the British bases in the Middle East. The major American concern was the increasing use of the Suez Canal by American petroleum companies, which had important interests in Saudi Arabia.[6] In the American eyes, to keep the Canal Zone in friendly hands was vital to American interests and they thought that a multilateral arrangement on the pattern of NATO might provide an effective solution to British difficulties in Egypt and for the defense of the Middle East as a whole.[7]

In the British project for the defense of the Middle East, Turkey had a key role together with Egypt. Turkey's military and economic power and its strategic geographical location were important for any defense organization of the region. Moreover, Turkey's involvement in the Western project as a Middle Eastern and Muslim country was expected to make the project more acceptable to the Arab countries.[8] However, Turkey put joining NATO at the top of the agenda and did not feel any enthusiasm for the Western projects for the Middle East. The Turks strongly resisted the idea that they should belong to a Middle East defense grouping and preferred to be included in Washington's defense plans for Europe. The Turkish government was eager to keep its distance from Muslim neighbors and to emphasize the Western, secular character of the Turkish political system.[9] They tried to show Turkey's determination to be included in the Western organizations by joining the European Council in 1949, by applying for NATO membership in May 1950 and by sending troops to the Korean conflict in September 1950. On the other hand, the Turkish government did not show any enthusiasm for the Egyptian attempt to establish a regional defense pact that would include Turkey. They rejected it because the Egyptian aim was to create a neutral bloc in the Middle East while Turkey was struggling to gain admission to NATO.[10]

Britain dropped its objection to the Turkish application for NATO membership and Turkey was accepted to NATO in the autumn of 1951 as a full member. When this occurred, Turkish statesmen began to look at Western projects for the Middle East positively and to support it. On 18 July 1950, the British foreign secretary, Herbert Morrison, in his speech to the House of Commons, declared Britain's intention to support the admission of Greece and Turkey to NATO. He stated that "at the same time, they (HMG) are most anxious that Turkey shall play her appropriate part in the defense of the Middle East. The Turkish government

---

[5] G. S. Harris, *Troubled Alliance*, Washington D.C.: American Enterprise Institute, 1972, p. 43, John C. Campbell, *Defence of the Middle East*, New York: Harper & Brothers, 1960, pp. 15-16, Hoskins, *The Middle East,* p. 260.

[6] Campbell, *Defence of the Middle East,* p. 39, Thomas A. Bryson, *American Diplomatic Relations with the Middle East*, Metuchen NJ: the Scarecrow Press Inc., 1977, pp. 178-179.

[7] *Hurewitz, Middle East Dilemmas,* p. 92.

[8] Campbell, *Defence of the Middle East.* p. 41.

[9] Ibid., p. 41, Dankwart A. Rustow, *Turkey: America's Forgotten Ally*, New York: Council on Foreign Relations, 1987, pp. 90-91.

[10] George Lenczowski, *The Middle East in World Affairs*, Ithaca & London: Cornell University Press, 1980, p. 519.

share this view and I hope that arrangements will soon be made to associate her fully with plans for the safety of that important part of the world".[11] It was understood that Turkey was persuaded to join British efforts for Middle East defense in return for the British acceptance of the Turkish membership in NATO. In the following period, Turkey supported all the Western attempts to establish a Middle Eastern alliance.[12]

b) The Middle East Command Proposal and Turkey

On 8 September 1951, the British and American leaders agreed to establish a Middle East Command (MEC), consisting of a Supreme Allied Commander with Headquarters at Cairo, who would be assisted by a staff committee made up of American, British, French and Turkish advisers. On 13 October 1951, the British, American, French and Turkish ambassadors at Cairo jointly presented the MEC proposal to the Egyptian government. The designers of the project believed that Egyptian membership in the command was essential for the success of the MEC since the Suez base was in Egypt and Egypt was trying to be leader of the Arab world. If Egypt agreed, the other powers of the region would follow it.[13]

The purpose of the plan, as presented, was to defend Egypt and other Middle Eastern countries against aggression from outside. France, Turkey, Britain and the United States were prepared to participate with other interested countries in establishing a Middle East command. They invited Egypt to participate as a founder of the MEC on the basis of equality and partnership with the other founder members. If Egypt joined the plan fully, Britain, for its part, would be willing to agree to withdraw from Egypt the British forces which were not allocated to the Allied Middle East Command by the agreement. The present British base in Egypt would be formally handed over to the Egyptians on the understanding that it would simultaneously become an allied base. In return, Egypt would agree to furnish to the proposed Allied MEC Organization strategic defense and other facilities on its soil.[14]

The main aim of the proposal was to keep the Suez base in the hands of the Western Powers and to bring about a solution to British problems with the Egyptians. But the planners ignored the force of Arab nationalists, who saw the proposal as an instrument for British occupation of the Arab territories. The timing of the proposal was extremely bad because, at that time, the Egyptians had already declared their intention to denounce the Anglo-Egyptian Treaty of 1936. As expected, two days later the proposal was rejected by the Egyptian government.[15]

The proposal increased Turkey's isolation from the Arab world and caused deterioration in its relations with Egypt and other Arab countries. Turkey did not have any interest in joining the proposal, but it wanted to contribute to the Western attempts generally. The Turkish foreign minister Fuad Köprülü declared on 20 July 1951 in his speech to the Grand

---

[11] *Documents on International Affairs 1951*, R.I.I.A., Oxford University Press, p. 65.

[12] Mehmet Gönlübol, "NATO, USA and Turkey" in Karpat (ed.), *Turkey's Foreign Policy in Transition*, pp. 26,30, Ömer Kürkçüoğlu, *Turkiye'nin Arap Orta Doğusuna Karşı Politikası 1945-1970*, Ankara: Sevinç Matbaası, 1972, pp. 44-45.

[13] Campbell, *Defence of the Middle East*, p. 42, Hoskins, *The Middle East*, p. 270, Bryson, *American Diplomatic Relations with the Middle East*, p.179.

[14] *Documents on International Affairs 1951*, pp. 425-427.

[15] Elizabeth Monroe, *Britain's Moment in the Middle East*, London: Chatto & Windus, 1964, p. 174, Campbell, *Defence of the Middle East*, p. 43, Hoskins, *The Middle East*, p. 282, Bryson, *American Diplomatic Relations with the Middle East*, p. 180.

National Assembly that Turkey would play its role in the defense of the Middle East.[16] But the Arab countries saw the Turkish attempts as siding with the imperialists against the Arab world. Almost all Arab countries were opposed to the proposal. On 8 November 1951, the Secretary General of the Arab League announced that the Arab world was unanimously opposed to the Middle East defense pact suggested by the Western powers.[17] Turkish-Soviet relations were also affected when the Soviet Union delivered a sharp protest note in November 1951 against Turkey's attempts to involve the Middle East in the military maneuvers of NATO.[18]

c) Other Attempts to Establish a Middle East Defence Organization

In spite of the Egyptian rejection of the MEC proposal, the Western powers did not give up trying to promote the idea of the Middle East Defence Organization. On 10 November 1951, the Four Powers announced an eleven-point statement, in which they stated that defense of the Middle East was vital to the free world and its defense against outside aggression could be secured only by cooperation of all interested states. They presented the MEC as the center of cooperative efforts for the defense of the area as a whole. Arms and equipment would be made available to the states of the area willing to join on a basis of equality in its defense.[19]

By August 1952, the MEC project had been abandoned in favor of a Middle East Defence Organization (MEDO) sponsored by the United States, Britain, France and Turkey, together with Australia, New Zealand and the Union of the South Africa.[20] Egypt was still a formidable obstacle to the efforts since it insisted on the British withdrawal from its territories before any organization was established. In Egyptian eyes, MEDO looked like another attempt to reconstruct the old British mechanism of power under a new name. They tried to improve the Arab League Collective Security Pact, whose aim was to integrate Arab military planning in the event of another contest with Israel, as a counterproposal to MEDO.[21]

Turkey continued to hold a key position in the Middle East defense project because of its special geographical location and its special relations with the Middle Eastern countries. According to the United States ambassador at Ankara, George McGhee, the association of Turkey, as a neighbor with strong Middle East ties and no suspicion of colonial intention, should greatly assist Western efforts. Turkey was "the only significant military power in the Middle East" and its troops were "the only ones available for land defense of the Middle East". The Turks were "in a unique position to provide military training for the Middle Eastern countries" and "to sell arms to the Middle East states".[22]

On the other hand, the deteriorating appeal of the Turks in Arab eyes, which was a result of the Turkish attempts to be integrated with the West, made the Turkish involvement in the

---

[16] Mehmet Gönlübol et. al., *Olaylarla Türk Dış Politikası*, Ankara: A.Ü. S.B.F. ve Basın-Yayın Yüksekokulu Basımevi, 1987, p. 232.

[17] Bryson, *American Diplomatic Relations with the Middle East*, p. 180.

[18] *Survey of International Affairs* 1951, R.I.I.A., Oxford University Press, p.259, *Documents on International Affairs* 1951, pp. 432-433.

[19] *Documents on International Affairs* 1951, pp. 427-429.

[20] *Foreign Relations of the United States (FRUS)*, 1952-1954, Washington D.C.: the United States Printing Office, 1986, p. 252.

[21] James W. Spain, "The Middle East Defence", *The Middle East Journal*, vol. 8, Summer 1954, p. 253.

[22] *FRUS* 1952-1954, p. 202.

defense projects a negative element. As American Acting Regional Planning Adviser Hoskins stated, "Turkey's weakened position stems from the fact that a growing number of people in the Arab states feel that Turkey has decided to orient itself heavily toward Europe and NATO rather than primarily as a Middle East and Asian power. Furthermore they feel that Turkey has been induced to accept and to help to enforce decisions. For the moment, Turkish support of any idea or plan is almost kiss of death".[23] Although the Turkish statesmen were eager to promote the MEDO project even if Arabs would not play any role,[24] the American government was more careful not to antagonize the Arabs completely.[25] While the MEDO project failed because of Arab opposition, Turkey found itself face to face with Arab nationalism.

3. THE BAGHDAD PACT

a) The Northern Tier Concept

From the beginning of 1953, United States policy towards the Middle East began to change considerably. As the importance of the Middle East for the United States continued to increase because of the region's strategic location and oil resources, and the British-orientated projects of regional defense failed, the United States gradually became more anxious to take the lead in Middle East defense. In the new American approach, the containment of the Soviet Union in its southern borders held an important place. The Soviet threat of expansion towards the Middle East led the American statesmen to organize the neighboring Middle Eastern states of the Soviet Union within a Western-sponsored alliance.[26] After the establishment of the South-East Asian Treaty Organization (SEATO), the only gap in the containment policy remained between Pakistan and Turkey and this would be filled by the Baghdad Pact later.[27]

The new American policy towards the Middle East appeared clearly after the visit of the Secretary of State, John Foster Dulles, to the Middle Eastern countries in May 1953. With Britain and Egypt at an impasse, Dulles decided that a new approach must be taken for the defense of the Middle East and toured the Middle East between 9 and 29 May visiting Egypt, Israel, Jordan, Syria, Lebanon, Iraq, Saudi Arabia, India, Pakistan, Turkey, Greece and Libya. In his visit to Egypt, the Egyptians clearly confirmed their position that they would not join any defense organization as long as the British influence remained in Egypt. The Egyptian Prime Minister thought that the Arab League Collective Security Pact of 1950 might be developed into something useful.[28] The Pakistani Prime Minister Muhammad Ali expressed his opinion to Dulles that a regional grouping could be created to prevent Soviet expansion towards the Arabian Gulf.[29]

---

[23] Ibid., p. 257.
[24] Ibid., p. 296.
[25] Ibid., pp. 272-273.
[26] Rouhullah K. Ramazan, *The Northern Tier*, Princeton, NJ: D. von Nastrand Comp. Inc., 1966, p. 117.
[27] *Survey of International Affairs* 1955-1956, p. 23, *Survey of International Affairs* 1954, pp. 202-203, William R. Polk, "A Decade of Discovery: America in the Middle East" in Albert Hourani (ed.),*The Middle Eastern Affairs,* St. Anthony's Papers, No: 11, London: Chatto & Windus, 1961, p. 62.
[28] *FRUS* 1952-1954, pp. 11-12, 21-22, 26-28.
[29] Ibid., pp. 135-136.

While the purpose of his trip was originally to visit the Arab capitals and the south-Asian countries, Dulles also accepted the invitation extended by the Turkish government for him to stop in Ankara.[30] He found Turkish politicians extremely anxious to take part in a regional defense organization. According to the memorandum of the counselor of the American Embassy in Turkey, in his talks with Dulles, Turkish Prime Minister Adnan Menderes said that "the hope of having the Arab countries accept MEDO should be abandoned at this time" and "in the defense of the Middle East, the backbone must be Turkey". He also stated that Turkey would continue to try every way to establish a regional organization including Pakistan for the Middle East defense.[31]

On 1 June 1953, Dulles explained the impressions, which he got from his visit to the Middle East. He said that most peoples in the Near East and the South Asia are deeply concerned about their and their neighbors' political independence. They were suspicious of the colonial powers.[32] In his opinion, "many of the Arab League Countries are so engrossed with their quarrels with Israel or with Britain or France that they pay little heed to the menace of the Soviet communism. However, there is more concern where the Soviet Union is near. In general the northern tier of the nations shows awareness of the danger"[33] Dulles finally stated that "there is a vague desire to have a collective security system. But no such system can be imposed from without. It should be designed and grow from within out of common destiny and common danger".[34]

b) The Turkish Contribution to the Establishment of the Baghdad Pact

When the American policy-makers decided to establish a regional defense alliance based on the northern tier concept, the most suitable regional country to lead the project was Turkey, which had the largest army in the Middle East and was a member of NATO. Turkey seemed to be only firm base from which the Western alliance system could be extended into the Middle East. The Turks were also anxious to take the lead in the project since they considered their independence was closely linked to the United States.[35]

The Turks undertook to negotiate the series of agreements with their regional partners, which resulted in the formation of the Baghdad Pact of 1955. As a first step, Turkey tried to achieve an alliance with Iraq or Pakistan considering the Egyptian cause was opposed to the interests of the free world. In the Turkish view, the Egyptian attempt to present the Suez Canal issue as a struggle for independence and freedom should be secondary to the importance that the canal zone had to the entire free world. The Turkish opinion was completely different from that of Egypt in that Turkey believed that the canal area defenses should be well maintained and that zone should not be evacuated unless and until suitable alternative arrangements were made.[36] In the eyes of the Turks, "since the Arab governments are far from stable and subject to frequent revolutionary changes, the defense of the Middle

---

[30] Ibid., p. 137.
[31] Ibid., pp. 138-140.
[32] *Documents on International Affairs* 1953, p.264.
[33] Ibid., p. 266.
[34] Ibid., p. 266.
[35] Campbell, *Defence of the Middle East,* p. 50, *Survey of International Affairs* 1953, p. 117.
[36] *FRUS* 1952-1954, p. 139, 149.

East should be organized without Arab participation" and "the NATO powers should take drastic measures to organize the Middle Eastern defense".[37]

In the early months of 1954, Turkey and the United States took separate initiatives to conclude an agreement with Pakistan. The Pakistanis were anxious to strengthen their country's military and political position, particularly against India by gaining the support of the United States. Turkish-Pakistani talks about the possibility of a bilateral defense arrangement began in December 1953 and they were encouraged by the US government.[38] On 2 April 1954 in Karachi, Turkey and Pakistan signed a treaty of friendship and cooperation for security. It was not a full military alliance since it only provided that the parties would study the means and the extent of cooperation necessary for collective defense should an unprovoked attack occur against them from outside. The important point about the agreement was that it was open to accession by other states, which provided a basis for the establishment of the Middle Eastern alliance.[39]

Although the Turks did not expect the immediate adherence of the Arab countries to the agreement, they hoped that they would get general support in the Arab world. Turkish Foreign Minister Fuad Köprülü announced to the press that the agreement was an open invitation to the Middle Eastern countries to join their efforts.[40] The Arab countries, however, were strongly opposed to the agreement since they considered it as a Western effort. At the meeting of the Arab League Council in April, referring to the Turco-Pakistani treaty, the member states declared that they would not accept any responsibility undermining their sovereignty and independence or incompatible with their responsibilities as the members of the Arab League.[41] While France totally rejected the idea of a regional pact, the Soviet Union warned Turkey that the Turkish-Pakistani treaty had a direct relationship to the Soviet security and that Turkey would have to undertake the responsibility for consequences of its actions.[42]

As a second step, Turkey began to seek the Iraqi participation in the Turkish-Pakistani agreement. Iraqi Premier Nuri al- Said was determined to achieve an alliance with the West and considered that Iraq had the right to do so because of its proximity to the Soviet Union.[43] After the visit of the Egyptian Minister of National Guidance, Salah Salim, to Baghdad in August 1954, Nuri al-Said went to Cairo for talks with Colonel Abdal-Nasser, the Egyptian premier, in September. During the talks Nasser explained the Egyptian determination not to join any Western alliance while Nuri insisted that the Arab League Security Pact could be linked with the West and could be used as the basis for a defense pact.[44]

At the end of September 1954, Nuri al-Said visited Turkish Prime Minister Menderes in İstanbul. Recognizing that the security of Turkey and Iraq made necessary the establishment of cooperation with their neighbors, the two statesmen agreed to seek Egyptian participation in their grouping and to keep touch in the hope of arranging talks with Syria, Iran and

---

[37] Ibid., p. 388.
[38] Ibid., p. 440, 458-459, 489, 506.
[39] *Documents on International Affairs* 1953, pp. 185-186.
[40] Gönlübol et al., *Olaylarla Türk Dış Politikası*, p. 254.
[41] Spain, "The Middle East Defence", p. 257.
[42] Ibid., pp. 264-265.
[43] Campbell, *Defence of the Middle East*, p. 53, Waldemar J. Gallman, *Iraq Under General Nuri*, Baltimore: the John Hopkins Press, 1964, p. 25.
[44] Ro'i, *From Encroachment to Involvement*, p. 135, *Survey of International Affairs* 1954 p. 211, Gallman, *Iraq Under General Nuri*, pp. 23-24.

Pakistan.[45] This led Nasser to take the initiative in the Arab world to prevent Nuri from joining the Turkish-Pakistani alliance. However, at the ordinary session of the Arab League Council of November 19- December 12, Nasser could not get a resolution condemning the Iraqi actions.[46]

Nuri and Menderes had talks in Baghdad from January 6 to January 12, 1955 and at the close of their discussions they issued a communiqué announcing that Turkey and Iraq decided to conclude a treaty as soon as possible to enforce and expand the existing cooperation between them for the stability and security of the Middle East.[47] In his press statement, Menderes explained that their objective was not to sign a bilateral agreement but to arrange a multilateral cooperation and that it was the proof of the importance, which they attributed to the entire Arab World.[48]

The announcement caused great criticism of Iraq in Egypt. Nasser called the premiers of the Arab League states for a conference to discuss the Iraqi actions. In the conference which opened on 22 January 1955 and which was not attended by Nuri, the premiers suggested a commission be sent to Baghdad to mediate, but the visit of commission to Baghdad did not bring about any agreement. The conference ended without producing any resolution.[49] Nasser also initiated a propaganda campaign against Turkey and Iraq. At a press conference, Major Salem claimed that "this is a serious development which may threaten the existence of the Arab League and expose Arab nationalism to grave dangers".[50] Cairo Radio accused Nuri of leaving the Arab bloc to tie his country to Israel and imperialists and reminded the Iraqi King of anti-Arab actions undertaken by the Turks in the past and at that time.[51] The Egyptian government organ, al-Cumhuriyya, claimed that the Iraqi action was in complete contradiction to the spirit of the Arab League Charter.[52]

Finally, the Turkish-Iraqi Pact was signed in Baghdad on 24 February 1955 by the King of Iraq and the President of Turkey. With this pact, the two parties agreed to cooperate for their security and defense and to take measures to give effect to this cooperation. They promised not to interfere in each other's internal affairs and not to enter into any international obligation incompatible with the present pact. The two countries also accepted the pact to be open for accession to any member of the Arab League or any other state actively concerned with the security and peace in the region and which was fully recognized by both parties. Intending to set up a regional organization, they decided that a permanent council at ministerial level would be established when at least four countries became parties to the pact.[53]

In the exchange of the interpretive letters, the premiers of Turkey and Iraq agreed that "the pact would enable the two countries to cooperate in resisting any aggression directed

---

[45] Gallman, *Iraq Under General Nuri*, p. 26.
[46] Lenczowski, *The Middle East in World Affairs*, p. 744, John Marlowe, *Arab Nationalism and British Imperialism*, London: the Cresset Press, 1961, pp. 84-85.
[47] Gallman, *Iraq Under General Nuri*, p. 33, *Documents on International Affairs* 1955, p.287.
[48] Gallman, *Iraq Under General Nuri*, p. 35.
[49] *Lenczowski, The Middle East in World Affairs*, pp. 284-285, George E. Kirk, *Contemporary Arab Politics*, London: Methuen, 1961, p. 34, Ro'i, *From Encroachment to Involvement*, p. 136.
[50] *Documents on International Affairs* 1955, pp. 313-314.
[51] Gallman, *Iraq Under General Nuri*, p. 39.
[52] Kirk, *Contemporary Arab Politics*, p. 34.
[53] Ralph H. Magnus, *Documents on the Middle East*, Washington D.C.: American Enterprise Institute, 1969, pp. 81-83, *Documents on International Affairs* 1955, pp. 287-288, *Western Powers and the Middle East*, R.I.I.A., Oxford University Press, 1958, pp. 5-7.

against either party and that the two parties would cooperate to make the UN resolutions on Palestine effective". It was an attempt by Nuri al-Said to appease Arab public opinion and was accepted by Menderes as a price of concluding the agreement.[54]

c) The Establishment of the Baghdad Pact Organization

The Baghdad Pact agreement was joined by the three countries, Britain, Pakistan and Iran, in a short time and it was turned into a regional organization. Different considerations affected these countries in their participation in the pact. Turkey's signing the agreement was because of its special relations with the West, particularly because of the American encouragement of Turkey to play a key role in the northern tier concept.

Iraqi Premier Nuri al-Said was a Western-minded Arab politician and was anxious to get Iraq involved in a Western-sponsored security system against the Soviet and Iranian threats. His main concern was to get the Western economic and military support for his country. Moreover, he aimed at terminating the Anglo-Iraqi Treaty of 1936 before it expired under the framework of a regional organization so that he could increase his prestige at home.[55] Nuri saw the position of Iraq as different from that of Egypt because of its proximity to the USSR, Turkey and Iran and he did not want to meet the security needs of his country within Arab security plans.[56]

At the beginning, Great Britain had not been enthusiastic about the American defense projects based on the northern tier since its projects for the Middle East were founded on the British bases in the region. But when the Baghdad Pact was signed and it provided adherence of other powers concerned with the security of the region, Britain saw the pact as an opportunity to preserve its influence in the region, particularly in Iraq. Its 1930 treaty with Iraq would expire and it was unlikely to be renewed. After the British withdrawal from Egypt became definite, Britain got more determined not to leave its bases in Iraq.[57]

According to Anthony Eden, the British Prime Minister, the Baghdad Pact could grow into a NATO for the Middle East and defense arrangements between Britain and Iraq, which were to the advantage of both countries, would be better placed in a wider agreement between equals. It was true that by acceding to the pact Britain would undertake obligations to cooperate with Turkey and Iraq for their security and defense, but Britain had such obligations already, under NATO and under the Anglo-Iraqi treaty.[58]

On 20 March 1955, Eden informed the House of Commons of the British decision to join the pact. He explained Britain's aim to establish a new association with Iraq, which would bring Anglo-Iraqi relations into line with those, which already exist with Turkey and other NATO members. The agreement, which Britain reached with the Iraqi government, would carry out that aim. He welcomed "the part, which our Turkish allies have played to make this new arrangement possible," and expressed his hope that "it will eventually include other countries in the area".[59]

---

[54] Gallman, *Iraq Under General Nuri*, p. 52, Lenczowski, *The Middle East in World Affairs*, p. 285.
[55] Lenczowski, *The Middle East in World Affairs*, p. 284.
[56] Marlowe, *Arab Nationalism and British Imperialism*, p. 84, Campbell, *Defence of the Middle East*, p. 53.
[57] Campbell, *Defence of the Middle East*, p. 57, Ramazani, *The Northern Tier*, p. 118, *Survey of international Affairs 1955- 1956*, p. 28, Gallman, *Iraq Under General Nuri*, p. 61.
[58] Anthony Eden, *Full Circle*, London: Cassell, 1960, p. 220.
[59] Ibid., pp. 221-222, *Documents on International Affairs 1955*, pp. 290-292.

On 4 April 1955, Britain officially adhered to the Baghdad Pact and, at the same time, it signed a special treaty with Iraq, which was provided by Article 5 of the Baghdad Pact. The British adherence to the pact brought about an important change. The idea of regional alliance based on the northern tier concept was originally an American idea, but, by joining the pact as the only Western member, Britain naturally assumed the leadership of the pact.[60]

Pakistan had been anxious to join a Western-sponsored regional alliance and, therefore, it had signed a treaty with Turkey in April 1954. After the Baghdad Pact was formed and it was considered as the basis of a regional organization, the Pakistanis expressed their support for the pact and their willingness to join it. Pakistan's main concern was to strengthen her military and political position against India. It also hoped to get Western economic aid for its development by joining the Baghdad Pact.[61] On 4 April 1955, the Iraqi and Turkish governments issued a statement calling on Pakistan to join the Baghdad Pact. Accepting the invitation, Pakistani Prime Minister Muhammad Ali declared his government's decision on 1 July 1955 to join the pact. Pakistan officially joined the pact on 23 September 1955.

Iran's choice to join the pact constituted a revolutionary change in Iranian foreign policy, breaking with the country's traditional neutrality policy. It was decided by the Shah, who believed that internal and external threats could be met only by a strong army strengthened with the Western arms. After the Musaddiq rule, the Shah chose to approach the West, particularly the United States, to strengthen his authority at home and Iran's power abroad against the Soviet Union. He decided to join the Baghdad Pact, because he saw it as an American plan and hoped to get the American protection of Iran and modern American arms for his army.[62] On 11 October, Iranian Premier Ala announced his government's decision to sign the pact and, on 3 November, Iran officially joined the pact.

The premiers of the pact's Middle Eastern signatories and the foreign secretary of Britain met at Baghdad on November 20-22, 1955 to set up a formal organization, including a council of ministers and special committees for military planning, economic cooperation, communication and counter-subversion. They established a permanent secretariat with headquarters at Baghdad, selected Awni Khalidi as its first secretary general and appointed an advisory staff.[63]

d) The Baghdad Pact and The United States

The United States was the original creator of the northern tier concept and it was Washington, which inspired and encouraged the regional countries to establish a defense organization. All the member countries except Britain considered future American participation as a vital element of their membership in the pact. However, the United States did not become a full member of the pact though it supported the pact members on various occasions and contributed to pact's actions considerably. This American behavior disappointed the Baghdad Pact members and diminished the success of the pact.

---

[60] Campbell, *Defence of the Middle East,* pp. 57-58.
[61] Ibid., pp. 234-235.
[62] Ibid., p. 60, Lenczowski, *The Middle East in World Affairs,* p. 200, Ramazani, *Iran's Foreign Policy,* Charlottesville: University Press of Virginia, 1975, p. 276.
[63] *Documents on International Affairs* 1955, pp. 307-309, Gallman, *Iraq Under General Nuri,* pp. 66-68.

The USA chose not to join the Baghdad Pact because it feared that official participation in the pact would damage its global interests in the Middle East. Its general policy towards the Middle East was to avoid taking part officially in Middle Eastern groupings. It did not want to abandon completely its contacts with Egypt and Saudi Arabia. These countries were strongly opposed to the grouping. Besides, the USA did not want to damage its relations with Israel. The American statesmen also feared that by joining the pact they would provoke the Soviet Union in turning its attention towards the Middle East. As J. C. Campbell pointed out "the United States did not relish the prospect of a debate in the Senate on ratification, which might throw its whole Middle Eastern policy into the arena of domestic politics".[64]

Although the United States did not participate in the pact officially, it did not completely keep itself away from it. On the contrary, it participated extensively in activities of the pact, contributing financial support and taking part actively in its various organs. The United States welcomed the Turkish-Iraqi declaration of 12 January 1955 and expressed its willingness to assist the Turkish and Iraqi efforts to achieve an effective defense arrangement. On 18 January 1955, J. F. Dulles stated that "as those countries take their place to close the gap in between Turkey and Pakistan, we believe the security of area will be greatly improved".[65] At the meeting of the Baghdad Pact Council of November 1955, the United States expressed its intention to establish permanent military and political liaison with the council and had an observer at the organizational meeting of the economic committee.[66] At the Baghdad Pact Council meeting at Teheran in April 1956, the United States reaffirmed its support of the pact and promised that it would continue to support individual and collective efforts of the member nations to attain political, defensive, economic and social objectives of the pact and became a member of the Economic Committee and Counter Subversion Committee.[67] On 29 November 1956, the United States expressed its support for the pact and the principles and objectives of the collective security on which it was based and stated that " a threat to the territorial integrity of political independence of the members would be viewed by the United States with the utmost gravity".[68]

However, the pact members would not be satisfied with these contributions unless the USA became a full member of the pact. The failure to do so diminished their willingness to refer more roles to the pact.[69] On 23 February 1955, Turkish Foreign Minister Fatin Rüştü Zorlu demanded an early American adherence to the pact by claiming that Iraq and Turkey would be in a stronger position in their approach to the Arab states and the future of the pact would be brighter.[70] Turkish Prime Minister Menderes never abandoned his hope for American participation and he once stated: " obviously its participation will be beyond sending observers and being kept informed, it is only right and natural that this should occur at a time when the United States itself deems it convenient and appropriate".[71]

---

[64] Lenczowski, *The Middle East in World Affairs*, p. 286, Campbell, *Defence of the Middle East*, p. 60, Gallman, *Iraq Under General Nuri*, p. 73.

[65] Gallman, *Iraq Under General Nuri*, pp. 45-46.

[66] *Documents on International Affairs* 1955, p. 307.

[67] *Documents on American Foreign Relations 1956*, New York: Harper & Brothers, 1957, p. 376, *Documents on International Affairs* 1956, pp. 41-42.

[68] *Documents on American Foreign Relations 1956*, p. 378, *Western Powers and the Middle East*, p. 9, Magnus, *Documents on the Middle East*, p. 83, *Documents on International Affairs* 1956, pp. 341-342.

[69] Eden, *Full Circle*, pp. 335-336.

[70] Gallman, *Iraq Under General Nuri*, p. 51.

[71] Ibid., p. 70.

4. THE EFFECT OF THE BAGHDAD PACT ON TURKISH FOREIGN POLICY

a) Relations with the Arab World

The immediate effect of the Baghdad Pact on Turkish foreign policy was to place Turkey and the Arab world in opposite sides. Propaganda of radical Arab states against Turkey and the Baghdad Pact caused isolation of Turkey from the Arab world. For radical Arabs, Turkey was a part of the imperialist Western world since it was a member of NATO and the Baghdad Pact. On the other hand, Turkish policy-makers believed that the Arab world except Iraq did not realize the danger of the communist threat to the region and that the Arabs helped the expansion of the Soviet influence towards the region.

The Soviet factor was perceived by radical Arabs and Turkey differently. For the Arab peoples, the Soviet threat was not a close danger; they were much more concerned about the establishment of the state of Israel and the continuing influence of Western colonialism in the Arab World. They suspected that the Baghdad Pact was an instrument of the West to pressurize the Arabs to make peace with Israel.[72] The general tendency in the Arab World at the time was anti-Westernism. Radical Arabs espoused neutralism to obtain the support of the Third World regarding the Palestinian question. A military alliance with the West did not occupy their minds as an immediate necessity.[73] The Arabs were also anxious to maintain their united front in their opposition against Israel and the Western world as the sponsors of the state of Israel. If any Arab state broke the unity by joining the Baghdad Pact, this would divide the Arab front and give relatively more strength to Israel's resistance.[74]

On the other hand, for Turkey, the Soviet threat was much more real because of its long frontier with the Soviet Union and the post-war Soviet pressure on Turkey regarding the Turkish straits and two eastern provinces of Turkey, Kars and Ardahan.[75] Turkey also had no reason to oppose the West. On the contrary, it needed to have good relations with the West to obtain Western military and economic assistance.

Egypt took the lead in opposing the Baghdad Pact and in trying to isolate Iraq and endeavored to gain the leadership of the Arab world by rejecting Western plans for the region. Egyptian President Nasser emerged as the champion of neutralism in the Arab World, leading an attack on the Iraqis since they damaged Arab unity by joining a Western-sponsored project. Nasser could not ignore Egyptian public opinion, which was opposed to arrangements with the West because of the former British influence on Egypt. The Egyptian-Israeli hostility also led Nasser to strengthen relations with the West. He tried to obtain modern Western weapons against Israel and the Western money to build the Aswan Dam, but when the West refused to give him credit, he turned totally against the West and began to improve relations

---

[72] Campbell, *Defence of the Middle East,* pp. 18-19, 46-47, George Lenczowski, *Soviet Advance in the Middle East,* Washington D.C.: American Enterprise Institute, 1971, pp. 56, 160, *Documents on International Affairs* 1955, p.284.

[73] Walter Z. Laqueur, *The Soviet Union and the Middle East,* London: Routledge & Kegan Paul, 1959, pp. 191-192.

[74] Michael Ionides, *Divide and Lose,* London: Geoffrey Bles, 1960, p. 111.

[75] Lenczowski, *Soviet Advance in the Middle East,* p. 160.

with the Soviet bloc. His attacks on the Baghdad Pact were a result of his anti-Western policy and his rivalry for the leadership of the Arab World with Iraq.[76]

Saudi Arabia joined Nasser in condemning the Baghdad Pact. The Saudi aims were to keep its prestige in the Arab World by opposing a foreign pact and to prevent the Iraqi Hashemite dynasty, which was its traditional enemy, from extending its influence in the Arab World.[77] In Syria, the growing strength of nationalist and leftist groups led the country to oppose the Baghdad Pact strongly. The visit of Menderes to Damascus after signing the Baghdad Pact had caused a serious government crisis in Syria, where the opposition to the pact became a unifying factor among the various Syrian groups. As Egypt did, Syria launched an anti-Western campaign and tried to improve its relations with Egypt and the Soviet bloc. Neutralism and pan-Arabism became the main elements in the state policy.[78]

After their failure to prevent Iraq from signing a pact with Turkey; Egypt, Saudi Arabia and Syria decided to promote a new tripartite security pact, which would constitute a counterweight to the Baghdad Pact. On 6 March 1955, the three countries issued a statement announcing their decision to sign an agreement, which would strengthen the economic, political and military structure of the Arab World and declared their agreement not to join the Baghdad Pact.[79] The Egyptian-Syrian Mutual Defence Pact was signed on 20 October 1955 and Saudi Arabia and Egypt signed the same kind of agreement on 27 October 1955. These pacts placed the armed forces of the three countries under a joint command headed by Egyptian generals.[80]

The Arab reaction to the Baghdad Pact took Turkish leaders by surprise because they had thought that Egypt, which signed a treaty with Britain in 1954, would drop its opposition to Western projects for Middle East defense and would cooperate with the West. Despite strong opposition to the Baghdad Pact, the Turkish government continued to hope to draw Egypt, Syria and Saudi Arabia to the new grouping. On 21 October 1955, Turkish Prime Minister Menderes declared his extreme willingness to have talks with the Egyptian premier and demanded Egyptian support for the pact. Turkish authorities miscalculated the importance of the Anglo-Egyptian Treaty for Egyptian radicals and did not correctly appreciate the real attitude of Arab radicals towards the West.[81]

Turkey's signing an alliance with Iraq increased anti-Turkish feelings in the Arab World and exacerbated its image in the eyes of the Arab nations. Anti-Western and anti-Baghdad Pact demonstrations took place in various Arab countries, accusing Turkey and Iraq of being agents of imperialism. Turkey had aimed at drawing the Arab countries into line against the Soviet Union, but the Baghdad Pact pushed Egypt and Syria to have closer ties with the Soviet Union by strengthening their economic and trade links and encouraging them to conclude an arms deal with this country.

[76] Lenczowski, *The Middle East in World Affairs*, pp. 527-529, P. J. Vatikiotis, "The Soviet Union and Egypt" in Ivo J. Lederer (ed.), *The Soviet Union and the Middle East*, Stanford, California: Hoverd Institution Press, 1974, pp. 125-126, Laqueur, *The Soviet Union and the Middle East*, p. 213, *Lenczowski, Soviet Advance in the Middle East*, p. 78, Albert Hourani, "The Middle East and Crisis of 1956" in *Middle Eastern Affairs*, St. Anthony's Papers No. 4, London: Chatto & Windus, 1958, p. 24.

[77] Lenczowski, *The Middle East in World Affairs*, p. 590.

[78] Ibid., pp. 337, 341-342.

[79] Gönlübol et. al., *Olaylarla Türk Dış Politikası*, p. 261, Ro'i, *From Encroachment to Involvement*, p. 136, *Documents on International Affairs* 1955, pp. 326-327.

[80] Ibid., pp. 328-331.

[81] Kürkçüoğlu, *Turkiye'nin Arap Orta Doğusuna Karşı Politikası 1945-1970*, pp. 62-64.

b) Relations with The USSR

Turkish-Soviet relations in the aftermath of the Second World War had been extremely tense because of the Soviet territorial demands on Turkey and Turkey's participation in NATO. After Stalin's death, the new Soviet leadership decided to improve their relations with other countries by pursuing the policy of peaceful coexistence. They also tried to restore their relations with Turkey by renouncing the Armenian and Georgian territorial claims on Turkey and the Soviet demands for special privileges in the Turkish Straits. However, the Soviet declaration of 30 May 1953 aimed at creating good neighborly relations[82] was not well received by Turkey. Turkey's reply of 18 July 1953 was formal and unpromising.[83]

The formation of the Baghdad Pact fuelled the Soviet-Turkish confrontation by sharpening their opposition in the cold-war conflict. Turkey was suspicious of the improvement of the relations of the Soviet Union with Egypt and Syria and saw it as a part of the Soviet intention to dominate the Middle East. In the eyes of the Turks, the Egyptian-Czech arms deal of 1956 and the Soviet economic and military assistance to Egypt and Syria were the movements aimed to advance international communism. Turkish representatives in the NATO councils took the lead in condemning the Soviet activities in the Middle East as both dangerous and provocative.[84]

On the other hand, the Soviet Union accused Turkey of serving as the gendarme of the United States and NATO in the Middle East and dividing the Arab World by carrying the cold war conflict to the region. The Soviet Union denounced the Baghdad Pact as the revival of Western colonialism in the Middle East and as the extension of NATO to the region. In February 1955, in a speech before the Supreme Soviet, Soviet Foreign Minister Molotov expressed the desire of having good neighborly relations with Turkey and complained about Turkey's negative attitude towards their gestures.[85] A statement of the Soviet Ministry of Foreign Affairs on 16 April 1956 declared that "the role which the Western Powers allocate Turkey in establishing military blocs in the Near and Middle East, arouse legitimate fears in the Arab countries".[86] In a Soviet note to Iran on 25 November 1955, it was stated that Turkey was being converted under the guidance of the United States into a military strategic bridgehead directed against the peace-loving neighboring states.[87] Soviet Premier Khrushchev said on 14 February 1955 "SEATO and NATO are not only aggressive military and political alignments, but also instruments of enslavement, a new colonial-type form of exploitation of underdeveloped countries".[88]

The Baghdad Pact also caused deterioration of Turkish-Israeli relations, which had developed since the Turkish recognition of the Israeli state in 1949. The Israelis considered the letter, which was exchanged between Nuri and Menderes, a hostile action towards Israel. On 26 February 1955, the Israeli Foreign Ministry issued a statement expressing the Israeli concern: "The text of the pact is at once noteworthy for the absence of an article by which the

---

[82] *Documents on International Affairs* 1953, pp. 277-278, Ferenc A. Vali, *Bridge Across the Bosporus, Baltimore: London: the John Hopkins Press,* 1971, pp. 174-175.
[83] *Documents on International Affairs* 1953, p. 278.
[84] Harris, *Troubled Alliance,* p. 63, Harris "The Soviet Union and Turkey" in Lederer (ed.), *The Soviet Union and the Middle East,* pp. 36, 39.
[85] Laqueur, *The Soviet Union and the Middle East,* pp. 205-206.
[86] *Documents on International Affairs* 1955, pp. 300-304.
[87] Ibid., p. 311.
[88] Ro'i, *From Encroachment to Involvement,* p. 161.

two contracting parties undertake to refrain from the use of force and threats of force in international relations". Thus, Turkey not only failed to get the support of the Arab World, but it also caused some deterioration in its relations with Israel.[89]

c) A Brief Balance Sheet of the Baghdad Pact

The Baghdad Pact was established as a military organization, which would unite the Middle Eastern countries against the Soviet expansion under the sponsorship of the West. But it lacked some important elements vital for a military organization. First of all, the aims of its members were considerably different in joining the pact and their perceptions of a common threat also differed greatly. Turkey had achieved a guarantee of its security by joining the main Western military organization, NATO, and it did not need membership in another organization to strengthen its defense. Pakistan was preoccupied with its defense against India rather than the Soviet Union. Britain had joined the pact to save its position in Iraq and its influence in the Middle East. For Iran and Iraq, to join the organization was much more related to their need of the Western economic and military assistance rather than to secure their defense against the Soviet Union.

From the start, the Baghdad Pact did not meet any special need and did not have enough power to carry out its planned function. If the so-called Northern States needed modern arms, military training and general improvement of their armies, that could be done without the mechanism of the Baghdad Pact by bilateral and multilateral arrangements. If the main aim was to provide economic and technical cooperation among the member states, again that could be achieved by special arrangements without giving it a military aspect.[90] The pact was not effective as a defense organization. Turkey, which had already put its forces under NATO command, could not contribute to the defense of the Middle East. The military strength of Iraq and Iran was fairly weak, Pakistan was absorbed in its disputes with India and Britain was not prepared to have military commitments in the Middle East.[91]

The Baghdad Pact, contrary to its original aim, split the Arab world into two different camps and made the Arab World ripe for Soviet penetration. It also strengthened the pan-Arabist and neutralist movements in the region.[92] The Egyptian-Iraqi conflict, which was fuelled by the Baghdad Pact, became the dominant event in the Arab World from 1954 to 1958. Egypt took the lead in the Arab World in condemning the Western-sponsored projects and pursuing the neutralist policy. Provoked by the Baghdad Pact, Syria and Egypt sought Russian military and economic assistance.

The Baghdad Pact did not serve as a barrier against Soviet penetration into the Middle East. The Soviet Union easily improved its relations with the Arab countries, which were antagonized by the Baghdad Pact. The pact was exploited by the Russians to reduce Western prestige in the Middle East and to present themselves to the Arab peoples as their true

---

[89] *Documents on International Affairs* 1955, p. 290, Gönlübol, et. al., *Olaylarla Türk Dış Politikası*, pp. 262-263, Kürkçüoğlu, *Turkiye'nin Arap Orta Doğusuna Karşı Politikası 1945-1970*, p. 67.

[90] Lenczowski, *The Middle East in World Affairs*, p. 796.

[91] Campbell, *Defence of the Middle East*, pp. 61, 242.

[92] Lenczowski, *The Middle East in World Affairs*, p. 145, Kürkçüoğlu, *Turkiye'nin Arap Orta Doğusuna Karşı Politikası 1945-1970*, pp. 65-66.

friends.[93] The pact did not prevent the Soviet Union from arming Egypt and Syria and provoking them against the Northern Tier States.

For Turkey, the Baghdad Pact represented a departure from the traditional policy of not committing itself in the Middle East. It provided Turkey with more American support in its relations with the Soviet bloc, but its also increased dangers to its national defense. The Soviet military and economic assistance to Egypt and Syria greatly worried Turkish statesmen.

5. THE TURKISH ROLE IN THE MIDDLE EAST AS A MEMBER OF THE PACT

a) The Question of the Jordanian Participation in the Pact

After the establishment of the Baghdad Pact Organization with five members, it was Turkey, which undertook to extend the pact into other Arab countries. Turkish Prime Minister Menderes tried to achieve Lebanese membership and even hoped to reach an understanding with Egypt. He also put pressure on Syria to accept membership by threatening it and concentrating troops on the Syrian border.[94] Menderes did not give up his hope of obtaining American participation until the Baghdad Pact came to an end.

The Turkish president, Celal Bayar, took several initiatives to draw some Arab countries into the Baghdad Pact. He invited Lebanese President Camille Chamoun to Ankara and had talks with him from April 1 to 6, 1955 to urge him to agree to Lebanese participation in the pact. Bayar himself paid a six-day visit to Lebanon in June 1955 to persuade Lebanese politicians, but Lebanon declined to join the pact. Bayar also went to Iran in September and to Jordan in November to urge the Shah and King Hussein to participate in the pact.[95]

In the meeting of the Baghdad Pact powers at Baghdad in November 1955, the Turkish representatives urged British Foreign Secretary Macmillan to take the initiative to bring Jordan into the pact.[96] At the time, it was generally assumed that Jordan, which was a close ally of Britain, would follow Iraq in joining the Baghdad Pact. The Jordanian leaders had been in favor of the Baghdad Pact and on 16 November 1955 Jordan handed the British ambassador its formal proposal on the pact membership.[97] In the Baghdad Pact meeting of November 1955, Britain agreed to send General Sir Gerald Templer, the Chief of the British Imperial General Staff, to Jordan to urge Jordan's immediate adherence to the pact. The British government was prepared to offer Jordan, as a price for joining the pact, a revision of the Anglo-Jordanian Treaty of 1946 and an increased subsidy.[98]

The achievement of Jordanian membership for the Pact was extremely important for the future. In the autumn of 1955, the pact looked healthy with the participation of the three new

---

[93] Lenczowski, *The Middle East in World Affairs,* pp. 780-781, 796, Frank Tachau, *Turkey,* New York: Preager Publishers, 1984, p.180.

[94] Campbell, *Defence of the Middle East,* p. 56, *Survey of International Affairs* 1955-1956, p. 27.

[95] Metin Tamkoc, *The Warrior Diplomats,* Salt Lake City: University of Utah Press, 1976, pp. 237- 238.

[96] Monroe, *Britain's Moment in the Middle East,* p. 188.

[97] Erskine B. Childers, *The Road to Suez,* London: MacGibbon & Kee, 196). p. 143, Eden, *Full Circle,* p. 341.

[98] Eden, *Full Circle,* p. 343.

members, but the other Arab countries led by Egypt were also active to stop the expansion of the pact's influence. If Jordan joined the pact, its prestige would increase considerably and it would be a great victory against the Egyptian anti-pact propaganda. However, when Templer arrived in Jordan and the Jordanian government declared its intention of joining the pact, serious riots occurred in Amman and other towns. The Jordanian people provoked by the Egyptian propaganda and supported by Saudi Arabian funds protested against foreign pacts and attacked many foreign and international institutions. The opposition parties joined in condemning any further link with the West. Syria, Egypt and Saudi Arabia promised aid to King Hussein in return for his refusal to participate in the Baghdad Pact.[99] The Jordanian government had to resign and the new premier promised not to adhere to any foreign pacts. Further riots compelled King Hussein to dismiss the commander of the Arab Legion, Lieutenant-General John Bagot Glubb on March 1, 1956 and to order his expulsion from the country.[100]

This unexpected rise of the Jordanian people took the Baghdad Pact members by surprise and led them to declare in the Baghdad Pact Council meeting of 19 April 1956 in Tehran their determination to strengthen the defensive capacity of the Middle East. They also felt it necessary to explain that "criticism and attacks from the neutralist and other sources directed against the Baghdad Pact created to provide for legitimate defense and peaceful development of their member nations springs largely from the lack of knowledge and misunderstanding of its true purposes".[101]

b) The Suez Crisis, the Eisenhower Doctrine and Turkey

The Suez war of October 1956 between Egypt and Israel and the British and French landing in Egypt became a serious threat to the existence of the Baghdad Pact. One of its members, Britain, was involved in the war and the whole Arab World was opposed to the British and French landing. During the crisis, Turkey followed the American line and joined the other Muslim members of the pact in condemning the actions against Egypt.

To prevent the collapse of the Baghdad Pact, its Muslim members met at Tehran on 7 November 1956. On 8 November, they issued a joint communiqué condemning the British role in the events. They invited the British and French governments to stop fighting, to withdraw their troops from the Egyptian territory and to respect the sovereignty, territorial integrity and independence of Egypt.[102] Although Turkey joined the Arab countries in the condemnation of the Suez invasion and withdrew its ambassador in Israel on 6 November 1956, it also tried in the Tehran meeting and other forums to save the British position within the pact and avoided taking any direct action against Britain.[103]

The Suez Crisis severely reduced the British influence in the Middle East and, in the eyes of the Americans, it left a gap in the region, which might be filled by the Soviet Union. As a response to the insistent demands of the Baghdad Pact members for American participation in

---

[99] *Documents on International Affairs* 1956, pp. 34-36.
[100] Lenczowski, *The Middle East in World Affairs,* pp. 481-483, Childers, *The Road to Suez,* p. 143, Eden, *Full Circle,* pp. 344-346.
[101] *Documents on American Foreign Relations 1956,* pp. 373-374.
[102] Gönlübol et. al., *Olaylarla Türk Dış Politikası,* pp. 282-285, *Documents on International Affairs* 1956, p. 313.
[103] Gallman, *Iraq Under General Nuri,* pp. 76-77, Kürkçüoğlu, *Turkiye'nin Arap Orta Doğusuna Karşı Politikası 1945-1970,* p. 98.

the pact, President Eisenhower felt it necessary to take an action which would satisfy the Middle Eastern countries that were under Soviet threat. The result was the Eisenhower Doctrine, which was originally the message of the President to Congress asking authority to give economic and military aid to any Middle Eastern state requesting it and to use military forces to protect Middle Eastern countries in the event of aggression and subversion.[104] On 9 March 1957, the Congress ratified Eisenhower's demands with slight changes.[105]

The Eisenhower Doctrine, which represented a radical change in the American policy towards the Middle East by committing the United States to use armed force for the defense of the region, was warmly welcomed by Turkey as well as the other Muslim countries of the Baghdad Pact. In their joint statement of 21 January 1957, Turkey, Iran, Iraq and Pakistan expressed their support for Eisenhower's proposals as the best means to maintain peace in the Middle East and to advance the economic well-being of the region's nations. They noted "with satisfaction that Eisenhower's plan for the Middle East recognized the threat posed by the communist aggression and subversion to the countries of the Middle East".[106]

The Arab grouping led by Egypt saw the doctrine as a continuation of the imperialist Western efforts to keep their influence in the region and condemned it as a tactic of the cold war. In their eyes, the doctrine implied a degree of interference in internal affairs of the Arab countries and aimed at helping some unpopular regimes to hold on to power.[107] On 19 January 1957, at a conference at Cairo, the Arab leaders issued a joint statement declaring that Arab nationalism was the only principle which could be respected by their countries and that they would not allow themselves to be in a sphere of influence for any foreign power.[108]

c) The Syrian Crisis of 1957

The Syrian crisis of 1957 was Turkey's first direct confrontation with an anti-Western Arab country since the formation of the Baghdad Pact. When Syria accused Turkey and the USA of attempting to interfere in Syrian internal affairs and Turkey concentrated troops on the Syrian border, the event extended to a global crisis concerning NATO, the Warsaw Pact and the United Nations. The whole event was in fact an extension of the East-West conflict into the Middle East.

Turkish statesmen were suspicious of Soviet actions in making Syria a puppet state to exploit against its neighbors. They considered Syria a growing threat to Turkish national security.[109] In December 1956, the Turkish foreign minister explained the Turkish anxiety that Syria had received more arms from the USSR than it could use given its present

---

[104] Campbell, *Defence of the Middle East,* pp. 122-125, Ro'i, *From Encroachment to Involvement,* pp. 198-199, Arthur M. Schlesinger (ed.), *A Dynamics of World Power,* vol. V, New York: Celsea House Publishers, 1973, pp. 408-411, Gallman, *Iraq Under General Nuri,* p. 80, Magnus, *Documents on the Middle East,* pp. 86-93.

[105] Schlesinger, *A Dynamics of World Power,* pp. 414-415, *Western Powers and the Middle East,* pp. 11-13, Magnus, *Documents on the Middle East,* pp. 93-94.

[106] Ro'i, *From Encroachment to Involvement,* p. 211, Gönlübol et. al., *Olaylarla Türk Dış Politikası,* pp. 288-289, *Documents on International Affairs* 1957, p.259.

[107] Lenczowski, *The Middle East in World Affairs,* pp. 797-798, Marlowe, *Arab Nationalism and British Imperialism,* p. 160

[108] Ro'i, *From Encroachment to Involvement,* p. 211.

[109] Kemal H. Karpat, "Turkish and Israeli-Arab Relations" in Karpat (ed.), *Turkey's Foreign Policy in Transition,* p. 120, Kürkçüoğlu, *Turkiye'nin Arap Orta Doğusuna Karşı Politikası 1945-1970,* pp. 104-105.

capabilities. The Turkish authorities felt encircled by the communist danger on both their northern and southern borders.[110]

The United States, too, was worried about increasing Soviet influence in Syria. The American authorities feared that Syria was becoming a Soviet military base and the situation was becoming ripe for a Soviet-sponsored revolution. The United States unhappiness reached its climax when the Syrian government expelled four American officials in August 1957 on the charges of planning with Turkey and Iraq to overthrow the Syrian regime. The United States retaliated by declaring the Syrian ambassador in Washington a *persona non grata*.

At that time, in the summer of 1957, it was claimed that Turkey was concentrating troops on the Syrian frontier. The Syrian and Egyptian governments loudly accused Turkey and the United States of planning armed intervention in Syria and to replace the Ba'athist regime by a free Syrian government. Meanwhile, at the end of August, the American government sent Loy Henderson, the Deputy Undersecretary of State, to the neighboring countries of Syria to examine events on the spot. On 4 September, Henderson reported to the American administration that all of Syria's neighbors feared that the Soviet Union might bring down the regime of each country after exploiting the Syrian crisis. During Henderson's trip to Turkey, the Turkish press pledged that an action should be taken against Syria, it was announced that Turkish military maneuvers would take place near Syria and Ankara Radio declared that Turkey was taking necessary measures to defend its security.[111]

The Soviet Union increasingly held a firm line against Turkey and the United States, warning the Turkish government that it would respond with necessary actions if Turkey attacked Syria. On 10 September 1957, Soviet Prime Minister Bulganin sent a letter to Turkish Prime Minister Menderes, containing a strong warning in which a Soviet invasion of Turkey was threatened in the event of Turkish occupation of Syria. He clearly stated that "we are convinced that should military action against Syria be started and a war began in the Middle East, Turkey would undoubtedly only suffer as a result of participation in such aggression".[112] In his reply to Bulganin's letter, Menderes noted that "although we did not receive any complaint from our neighbor Syria... Soviet Russia has adopted Syria and the Syrian question"[113] and added "Turkey takes these measures exclusively for its defense. Such an action is our right and duty."[114]

The Arab countries were almost united in opposing the anti-Syrian actions of Turkey and the United States. On 27 September, King Saud announced that there was no threat to other Arab states from Syria and that Saudi Arabia would aid Syria against any aggression. Lebanon and Jordan expressed their devotion to the Arab solidarity.[115] In mid-October, two battalions of the Egyptian troops were sent to Syria as a gesture of solidarity and a month later forty members of the Egyptian Parliament visited Damascus. In their joint session with the Syrian Chamber, a resolution was passed, inviting the two governments to negotiate

---

[110] Harris, *Troubled Alliance*, pp. 63-64, Lenczowski, *The Middle East in World Affairs*, p. 145.

[111] Campbell, *Defence of the Middle East*, p. 132, Harris," the Soviet Union and Turkey", p. 39, H. N. Howard "Syria-Lebanon" in Lederer (ed.), *The Soviet Union and the Middle East*, pp. 143-144, Ro'i, *From Encroachment to Involvement*, pp. 237-238.

[112] *Kirk, Contemporary Arab Politics*, p. 99, Ro'i, *From Encroachment to Involvement*, pp. 238-240, for the letter see *Documents on International Affairs* 1957, pp. 333-337.

[113] Ro'i, *From Encroachment to Involvement*, p. 242, *Documents on International Affairs* 1957, p. 340.

[114] *Documents on International Affairs* 1957, p. 341.

[115] Ro'i, *From Encroachment to Involvement*, p. 244, *Survey of International Affairs* 1956-1958, p. 180, Ionides, *Divide and Lose*, p. 231.

federal union of the two countries. The Syrian crisis, thus, provided the impetus for the establishment of a federal union between Egypt and Syria.

The United States stood on the side of Turkey during the crisis and reiterated its promise to come to Turkey's help in the event of attack resulting from the Soviet infiltration of Syria. The United States air forces were sent from Europe to the American base at Adana in Turkey. On October 10, Eisenhower declared that both the Eisenhower doctrine and NATO would be used to protect Turkey from Syrian aggression.[116] On 25 October, Eisenhower and Harold MacMillan issued a communiqué at the close of their talks, stating that "Soviet threats directed against Turkey give solemn significance to obligation under the Article 5 of the North Atlantic Treaty, to consider an armed attack against any member of the alliance as an attack against all".[117]

On October 15, the Syrian foreign minister sent a letter to United Nations Secretary-General Hommarsjkold, requesting urgent inclusion in the United Nations General Assembly agenda of an item entitled 'complaints about threats to the security of Syria and international peace'.[118] Soviet Foreign Minister Gromyko, too, sent a letter on 16 October to the chairman of the General Assembly, strongly criticizing Turkey and asking for a special United Nations commission to be set up to make a close examination of the situation on the Syrian-Turkish frontier.[119] The debate on the Syrian crisis was held in the General Assembly from 25 October to 1 November, but it did not produce any resolution.

By the beginning of 1958, the Syrian crisis had been over. Khrushchev declared that there would be no war between Turkey and the Soviet Union;[120] Turkey and Syria stopped using aggressive language in their communications and Turkey welcomed the establishment of the United Arabic Republic and recognized it on 11 March 1958 since it realized that the Baa'thist group chose to unite the country with Egypt to prevent a communist takeover and considered that this would limit the Soviet influence in Syria.[121]

d) The Iraqi Revolution and the Lebanese and Jordanian Events

The Iraqi revolution of 14 July 1958 was the most important blow to the existence of the Baghdad Pact and to the Western attempts to unite the Middle Eastern states under their sponsorship. The new Iraqi leadership issued a declaration on the day of the revolution, announcing that they founded the Republic of Iraq, which would protect national unity, would establish friendly relations with the other Arab countries and would be loyal to the United Nations Charter, the decisions of the Bandung Conference and all agreements which were compatible with Iraqi interests.[122]

First, the Western World saw the Iraqi Revolution as an expansion of the pan-Arabist movement, which was provoked by Egypt and as a plot by Egyptian Premier Nasser. The

---

[116] Howard, "Syria-Lebanon", p. 145.
[117] Ro'i, *From Encroachment to Involvement*, p. 245.
[118] *Documents on International Affairs* 1957, pp. 343-345.
[119] *Documents on International Affairs* 1957, pp. 345-347.
[120] Kürkçüoğlu, *Türkiye'nin Arap Orta Doğusuna Karşı Politikası 1945-1970*, p. 112.
[121] Karpat "Turkish and Arab-Israeli Relations", p. 121, Kürkçüoğlu, *Türkiye'nin Arap Orta Doğusuna Karşı Politikası 1945-1970*, pp. 113-114.
[122] Gönlübol et. al., *Olaylarla Türk Dış Politikası*, pp. 300-301, *Documents on International Affairs* 1958, pp. 285-286.

revolution came as a shock to the American administration, which considered Iraq the bulwark of peace and stability in Middle East. It represented the loss of a valuable and essential link in the Baghdad Pact. But when the United States and Britain realized that the Iraqi revolution was not totally an anti-Western action and much more related to Iraqi internal events, they extended their recognition to the new Iraqi regime in August 1958.

When the Iraqi revolution took place, Baghdad Pact members were about to meet in Istanbul for an ordinary Baghdad Pact meeting. Iraqi King Faysal was in Baghdad Airport planning to fly to Istanbul when he was arrested by the new regime. He, Prince Abdullah and Nuri al- Said were killed. Iran, Pakistan and Turkey issued a joint communiqué on 17 July 1958 after their talks in Ankara and Istanbul. "They noted with deep concern the latest manifestation of subversive activities, inspired from outside, in an allied country" and expressed their determination "to support in all possible ways the measures which are necessary to stop international banditry in this region".[123] The Baghdad Pact members held a ministerial meeting in London on 28 July 1958 to reexamine their position in the light of the recent events and concluded that the need which caused the establishment of the pact was greater than ever. They declared their determination to maintain their collective security and to resist aggression, direct or indirect, and reaffirmed their determination to strengthen further their united defense posture in the area.[124]

The Iraqi revolution was perceived differently by the Turkish government and the Turkish opposition party. The revolution was a serious blow to the government's Middle Eastern policies, which they had pursued since the beginning of 1950s. They saw the revolution as an act of international communism and feared that the communist threat would spread to Turkey. There were rumors in Turkey that the Turkish authorities considered invading Iraq to restore the old regime.[125] But leaders of the Turkish opposition party, the Republican People's Party, regarded the revolution as an act of a national liberation movement and believed that the withdrawal of Iraq from the Baghdad Pact was likely to strengthen, not weaken, the alliance by removing the opposition of the Arab World to the pact.[126] The Menderes government eventually gave up its hesitancy and extended Turkish recognition to the new Iraqi regime.[127]

On 15 July 1958, American troops landed in Lebanon at the request of Lebanese Prime Minister Camille Chamoun, who feared that Lebanon would face the same fate as the old Iraqi regime. At the time, there were rumors that the United Arab Republic was preparing plans to overthrow the Lebanese and Jordanian regimes. President Eisenhower announced that the American troops had landed in Lebanon to protect American lives and to encourage the Lebanese government in the defense of the Lebanese sovereignty and integrity.[128] On 17 July 1957, British troops landed in Jordan in response to an appeal from King Hussein.

The Turkish government supported the American and British actions during the Lebanese and Jordanian events and gave its full approval to their operations.[129] But there were some critics on the opposition side, condemning the use of the American base at İncirlik in Turkey

---

[123] Ibid., p. 295.
[124] Ibid., pp. 369-370.
[125] Tachau, *Turkey*, p.181, Kürkçüoğlu, *Türkiye'nin Arap Orta Doğusuna Karşı Politikası 1945-1970*, pp. 131-132.
[126] Harris, *Troubled Alliance*, pp. 65-66, Harris, "The Soviet Union and Turkey", p. 42, Tachau, *Turkey*, p. 182.
[127] Kürkçüoğlu, *Türkiye'nin Arap Orta Doğusuna Karşı Politikası 1945-1970*, pp. 133-134.
[128] *Documents on International Affairs* 1958, pp. 287-288, Magnus, *Documents on the Middle East*, pp. 95-97.
[129] Kürkçüoğlu, *Türkiye'nin Arap Orta Doğusuna Karşı Politikası 1945-1970*, pp. 134-135.

by the American troops to prepare for the Lebanese operation. The Turkish government joined the other Baghdad Pact members in issuing a joint communiqué on 17 July 1958, declaring that "they welcome with satisfaction the initiative taken by the United States for upholding the integrity and independence of free and peace-loving countries and in particular the practical support given to the legally-constituted government of Lebanon".[130]

The Jordanian and Lebanese events and the Iraqi revolution marked the end of a phase in Middle Eastern history. In 1950s, the West had tried to draw the Arab countries into the system of the Western alliances by exaggerating the Soviet threat. But the expected Soviet danger never materialized and the Arab countries rejected the Western plans and followed the pan-Arabist line led by Nasser.

e) The End of the Baghdad Pact

After the Iraqi revolution, Baghdad Pact members put more pressure on the United States to join the pact in order to strengthen it at such a critical time. The United States refused their invitation because its policy was not to participate in Middle Eastern groupings to preserve its interests in the region. However, it promised the pact members in their London ministerial meeting of 28 July 1958 to cooperate with them for their security and defense and to enter into agreements designed to give effect to this cooperation.[131] Secretary of State Dulles joined this meeting to demonstrate American support for the pact members and signed the joint communiqué with the others.

Although the new Iraqi regime did not officially withdraw from the pact, it was obvious that their new policy was opposed to entering foreign pacts and they would withdraw soon. On 23 October 1958, the Baghdad Pact members announced that the headquarters and organization of the pact would be moved from Baghdad to Ankara. The sixth session of the pact ministerial council took place in Karachi on 28 January 1959. In the final communiqué, the members "emphasized the value of the pact in providing not only for defensive military cooperation but also for economic and technical cooperation" and " noted with concern that international communism continued its efforts to dominate the pact area".[132]

To fulfil its promise in July 1958, the United States signed, on 5 March 1959, identical bilateral agreements of cooperation with Pakistan, Turkey and Iran. In its agreement with Turkey, it was stated in Article I that "in case of aggression against Turkey, the government of the USA, will take such appropriate actions, including the use of armed forces... in order to assist the Government of Turkey at its request".[133] The agreements did not increase the American commitments to the pact members but aimed at pacifying them.

Iraqi President General Kassem declared his country's withdrawal from the Baghdad Pact on 24 March 1959. After expressing his fear that the pact might be used as a means for interfering in Iraqi affairs, Kassem announced that "the policy of the state, based on neutrality, does not agree with its remaining a party to a pact, a military aggressive bloc".[134] Following the Iraqi withdrawal, the Baghdad Council decided in August 1959 to change its

---

[130] *Documents on International Affairs* 1958, p. 295.
[131] Ibid., p. 370.
[132] *Documents on International Affairs* 1959, pp. 324-326.
[133] Ibid., pp. 343-345.
[134] Ibid., p. 303.

name to the 'Central Treaty Organization' (CENTO). In the final communiqué of the meeting of the CENTO Ministerial Council in Washington in October 1959, it was stated that this name "signifies that the countries occupying a central area between NATO and SEATO regions have confirmed their decision to join together for mutual defense and economic development".[135] From that time onward, CENTO continued to provide a forum for regular high-level contact particularly for economic assistance and cooperation. It served more as an economic organ than as a military one.

6. CONCLUSION

Turkish policy towards the Middle East and Turkey's role in the Baghdad Pact Organization was closely linked with its relations with the Western world. Turkey's expectation of military and economic assistance from the West and its general policy of integrating itself with the West led it to support Western projects for Middle East defense. The Turkish approach to the Middle East in 1950s was mainly a result of demands of their partners within the NATO alliance. The Menderes government, which held power from 1950 to 1960, determined its policies towards the Middle East by following the line of the United States, which was its closest military and political ally.

In the 1950s, Turkey approached the Arab world with a cold-war mentality and tried to persuade the Arabs that the most important and serious danger for the Middle East was communist expansion. However, at that time, the Arab countries except Iraq did not perceive any threat coming from the Soviet Union because of their relative remoteness from the USSR. Their concern was mainly to end Western influence in the Middle East and to strengthen their position against Israel. Together with these factors, the effect of pan-Arabist radicals in the Arab world caused the failure of Turkish and Western attempts to establish a strong military alliance in the region against the USSR.

After the Iraqi withdrawal from the Baghdad Pact, the Arab aspect of the pact came to an end and Turkey returned to its traditional policy of keeping herself out of Middle East politics. Thus, the Turkish adventure in the Middle East, which was a result of Western demands, ended. Turkey's membership of the Baghdad Pact and its actions in the Middle East as a member of the pact had caused a complete isolation of Turkey from the Arab world, which appeared obviously in the 1960s as a lack of Arab support to Turkey in UN debates on Cyprus.

---

[135] Ibid., p. 357.

Chapter 6

THE CUBAN MISSILE CRISIS OF
OCTOBER 1962 AND TURKEY

The Cuban missile crisis in October 1962 came to a point, which concerned Turkey's very survival. The crisis started in mid-October 1962 when American U-2 planes spotted some Soviet SAMs (surface-to-air missiles) on Cuban soil and President Kennedy decided to enforce a naval blockade of Cuba. While the two superpowers approached the brink of armed conflict, probably a nuclear war, the removal of the Jupiter missiles in Turkey in return for the Soviet removal of its missiles from Cuba seemed to many an appropriate way to end the crisis. At the peak of the crisis, on 27 October 1962, Soviet Premier Nikita Khrushchev officially proposed such a solution. The Cuban crisis presents a good example of evaluating different aspects of the U.S.-Turkish alliance, which were mentioned in Chapter II. In this chapter, events and discussions surrounding the Jupiters during the crisis will be studied in order to explore how Turkey's alliance with the United States made it a party to a superpower conflict and put its survival under threat.

1. THE HISTORY OF THE JUPITERS

When the Soviets successfully launched the first Sputnik in 1957, the Eisenhower administration feared that the Soviets were leading the West in nuclear armament and that deterrence or at least a confidence gap was emerging. To strengthen NATO both militarily and psychologically, the United States gained unanimous approval of NATO members for stationing American-made intermediate-range ballistic missiles in Europe.[1] However, most NATO allies declined to accept deployment of missiles on their territories because they were fearful of provoking Soviet aggression, becoming a target of a nuclear war and provoking domestic opposition.[2] Only Britain, Italy and Turkey consented to take these missiles.[3]

---

[1] *The Times*, 29 October 1962, p. 8, Barton J. Bernstein, "The Cuban Missile Crisis: Trading the Jupiters in Turkey?", *Political Science Quarterly*, vol. 95, No. 1, Spring 1980, pp. 98-99, Michael R. Beschloss, *Kennedy v. Khrushchev*, London and Boston: Faber and Faber, 1991, p. 439.

[2] Bernstein, "The Cuban Missile Crisis", p. 99, "Başyazı", *Forum*, 1 June 1964, p. 4.

[3] Beschloss, *Kennedy v. Khrushchev*, p. 439, Raymond L. Garthoff, *Reflections on the Cuban Missile Crisis*, Washington D.C.: The Brookings Institution, 1989, p. 71n.

The agreement for installing fifteen Jupiters in Turkey was signed in October 1959 between the USA and Turkey. According to the agreement, "the missiles would be owned by the United States...; the weapons could be launched only on the order of the Supreme Allied Commander in Europe (an American) on the approval of both American and Turkish governments; and the sites would be manned by soldiers of both nations."[4] The Turkish government did not make this agreement public though Foreign Minister Fatin Rüştü Zorlu promised in January 1959 that the Turkish Parliament would be informed when the Jupiter agreement was concluded.[5] The Jupiters went to Turkey at about the time of Soviet Premier Khrushchev's visit to the United States in 1959.[6] Preliminary installation arrangements were accomplished during the era of the Menderes government, which was toppled by a military coup on 27 May 1960.[7] Despite strong Soviet objections to these activities, the new Turkish military regime went along in carrying out preliminary works at the same speed. Turkish crews were sent to America for special training and installations for the missiles were constructed in the İzmir area in the west of Turkey. As George Harris stated, "the Turkish military rulers appeared far more eager to receive these missiles than Washington to provide them."[8]

The Jupiters were installed in Turkey in late 1961 by the Kennedy administration to implement the 1959 agreement. They became fully operational in about July 1962.[9] But the actual transfer of the first Jupiter missile (warheads remained under American control) to Turkish armed forces took place on 22 October 1962, on the same day Kennedy announced the quarantine of Cuba.[10]

2. U.S. Attempts to Remove the Jupiters from Turkey

As early as 11 February 1961, a report of the Joint Congressional Committee on Atomic Energy, entitled "the Study of US and NATO Nuclear Arrangements", recommended that "construction should not be permitted to begin on the Jupiter sites in Turkey. Instead of placing obsolete liquid-fuel IRBMs in Turkey, an alternative system such as Polaris submarines should be assigned to NATO."[11] Unlike the Jupiters, which were inaccurate and vulnerable, "the Polaris would add to deterrence and better protect the United States, NATO and Turkey" since they were "mobile, concealed and thus virtually immune from a Soviet attack."[12]

U.S. President John Kennedy raised the question of the Jupiters in a National Security Council meeting on 29 March 1961. According to a NSC memorandum on this meeting, which was dated 6 April 1961, the president instructed a committee consisting of officials of

---

[4] Bernstein, "The Cuban Missile Crisis", p. 99.
[5] George S. Harris, *Troubled Alliance*, Washington D. C.: American Enterprise Institute, 1972, p. 92.
[6] Beschloss, *Kennedy v. Khrushchev*, p. 439.
[7] George S. Harris, "Turkey and the United States" in Kemal H. Karpat (ed.), *Turkey's Foreign Policy in Transition*, Leiden: E. J. Brill, 1975, p. 58.
[8] Ibid., p. 58.
[9] Bernstein, "The Cuban Missile Crisis", p. 100, Thomas C. Reeves, *A Question of Character: A Life of John F. Kennedy*, New York: The Free Press, 1991, p. 375, Harris, *Troubled Alliance*, p. 92.
[10] James G. Blight and David A. Welch, *On the Brink*, New York: Hill and Wang, 1989, p. 172.
[11] Graham T. Allison, *Essence of Decision*, Boston: Little, Brown and Co., 1971, pp. 311n, 312n, Blight and Welch, *On the Brink*, p. 172, Bernstein, "The Cuban Missile Crisis", p. 100.
[12] Bernstein, "The Cuban Missile Crisis", p. 100.

Departments of State and Defence and the CIA to review the issue of stationing IRBMs in Turkey.[13] A member of this committee, George McGhee, reports in his book that in a meeting he was asked by the president, "if I thought the Turks would permit us to take the IRBMs out. I replied that I doubted it..."[14] In his book McGhee also cites that in their talk during a CENTO meeting the Turkish foreign minister strongly opposed the removal of the IRBMs because Turkey "had put a good deal of money into the installations of the Jupiters, which had just come into place", and therefore "it would be difficult for the Turkish people to understand their removal without any compensating additions to their security."[15] McGhee's report on 22 June 1961 to McGeorge Bundy, Kennedy's special assistant for national security, argued against the cancellation of the Jupiters project; "in the aftermath of Khrushchev's hard posture at Vienna, cancellation... might seem a weakness,"[16] moreover, the Turkish military was unwilling to abandon the project.[17] General Lauris Norstad, Supreme Commander of Allied Forces in Europe, warned that the Turks could feel insulted if the Jupiters were removed and that this could cause some problems within NATO.[18]

In Dean Rusk's account, in their meeting in May 1961, Selim Sarper, the Turkish foreign minister, told him that "they had just gotten from their parliament the appropriations for the Turkish side of the cost of those missiles, and it would be very embarrassing to go right back to them and say that they were being taken out... It would be very bad for the morale of Turkey as a member of NATO if they were taken out before Polaris submarines were in the Mediterranean to take their place."[19] In fact, as Secretary of Defence McNamara confirmed, there were no extra Polaris submarines at that time to offer the Turks.[20] A study of the American administration on the Jupiters, which was completed in early 1962, deduced that these missiles were worthless, and therefore should be phased out.[21]

It seems that Turkish military leaders who were anxious to obtain modern weaponry believed that the Jupiters, which were a part of their military asset, increased Turkey's military capabilities and strengthened its security against the Soviet Union. The newly installed civilian government was in no position to insist on withdrawing missiles over the opposition of the Turkish armed forces.[22] Turkish officials probably did not think about strategic liabilities of the missiles. For them, the Jupiters "added prestige, emphasized

---

[13] Blight and Welch, *On the Brink*, pp. 100-101.

[14] George McGhee, *The US Turkish NATO Middle East Connection*, London: MacMillan Press Ltd., 1990, p. 166.

[15] Ibid., p. 166.

[16] Bernstein, "The Cuban Missile Crisis", p. 101, David Detzer, *The Brink: Cuban Missile Crisis 1962*, London: J. M. Dent and Sons Ltd., 1979, p. 157, Beschloss, *Kennedy v. Khrushchev*, p. 439.

[17] Bernstein, "The Cuban Missile Crisis", p. 101.

[18] Detzer, *The Brink*, p. 157, Beschloss, *Kennedy v. Khrushchev*, pp. 439-440.

[19] Blight and Welch, *On the Brink*, p. 173. See also Allison, *Essence of Decision*, pp. 141, 226, Robert F. Kennedy, *Thirteen Days*, New York: W.W. Norton and Company Inc., 1971, p. 72, Bernstein, "The Cuban Missile Crisis", p. 102, Hafner, "Bureaucratic Politics and Those Frigging Missiles", pp. 318-319. Former Turkish foreign minister Ü. Haluk Bayülken confirmed Sarper's response. According to him, Sarper agreed with the Americans but thought that Turkish military rulers who recently overthrew the government could misunderstand the U.S. proposal. Bayülken told the author that he himself heard the U.S. proposal from Dean Rusk.

[20] Bernstein, "The Cuban Missile Crisis", pp. 101-102.

[21] Allison, *Essence of Decision*, p. 141, Elie Abel, *The Missile Crisis*, Philadelphia: Lippincott, 1966, p. 190, Donald L. Hafner, "Bureaucratic Politics and Those Frigging Missiles", *ORBIS*, vol. 21, No. 2, Summer 1977, p. 318.

[22] Harris, *Troubled Alliance*, pp. 92-93.

Turkey's role in NATO, and exaggerated the warmth of relations with a great power, the United States. The missiles were political assets abroad and possibly at home."[23]

In August 1962, during a National Security Council meeting, President Kennedy ordered U.S. officials to investigate what action could be taken to get the Jupiters out of Turkey in the light of the new Soviet bloc activity in Cuba.[24] It is clear that Kennedy linked the Jupiter missiles in Turkey to the Cuban problem, presumably concerning that the Soviets might justify an arming of Cuba with nuclear arms by pointing to the Jupiters in Turkey. In the late summer of 1962, when Secretary of State Rusk was in Europe, President Kennedy pressed Undersecretary of State George Ball to push forward the issue.[25] During their talks, the Turkish ambassador to Washington told Ball that removal of the Jupiters would have harmful effects on Turkish public opinion.[26] After this initiative, State Department officials decided not to pursue the issue so as not to allow relations with the Turks to deteriorate.

Some authors claim that before the Cuban crisis erupted Kennedy had already ordered the removal of the Jupiter missiles from Turkey and Italy and erased this issue from his mind assuming that his orders had been carried out. According to these authors, Khrushchev's proposal of Turkey-for-Cuba trade on 27 October 1962 made Kennedy aware of the fact that his orders had not been implemented by American bureaucrats. However, as most authors who studied the Cuban missile crisis argue, although President Kennedy several times gave instructions to review the matter of removing the Jupiter missiles, he never actually ordered their removal and knew that they were still in Turkey when the Cuban crisis broke out.[27] The NSC Action Memorandum of 23 August 1962, the last move of the Kennedy administration before the Cuban crisis to remove the Jupiters, ordered State Department officials only to study what actions could be taken to get the missiles out of Turkey. Even if it had ordered their removal, it would be practically impossible to finish the job by the time when the Cuban crisis came about.[28] During the crisis the Turkey-for-Cuba trade was discussed by American officials and Kennedy was aware of it and he was himself involved in some of these discussions.[29]

3. THE ROLE OF JUPITERS IN THE RUSSIAN MOVE IN CUBA

To explore the role of the Jupiters in the Soviet action to arm Cuba with nuclear weapons will show to what extent Turkey contributed to a major move of a superpower with nuclear missiles on its territory, whose warheads belonged to another superpower.

Soviet Premier Nikita Khrushchev began questioning encirclement of the Soviet Union by American military bases as early as 1958 when he complained to Adlai Stevenson, the Kennedy administration's ambassador to the United Nations, that "we see ourselves

---

[23] Bernstein, "The Cuban Missile Crisis", pp. 99, 100.

[24] Reeves, *A Question of Character*, p. 375, Bernstein, "The Cuban Missile Crisis", pp. 102-103.

[25] Bernstein, "The Cuban Missile Crisis", p. 102, Allison, *Essence of Decision*, pp. 142, 226, Kennedy, *Thirteen Days*, pp. 72-73, Abel, *The Missile Crisis*, pp. 190-191.

[26] Abel, *The Missile Crisis*, p. 191, Allison, *Essence of Decision*, p. 142.

[27] Reeves, *A Question of Character*, p. 375, Garthoff, *Reflections on the Cuban Missile Crisis*, p. 71n, Bernstein, "The Cuban Missile Crisis", pp. 103-104, Detzer, *The Brink*, pp. 157, 244, George W. Ball, *The Past Has Another Pattern*, New York: W. W. Norton, 1982, p. 501n.

[28] Bernstein, "The Cuban Missile Crisis", p. 103.

[29] McGeorge Bundy's recollection approves this point. Ibid., p. 104, Reeves, *A Question of Character*, p. 375.

surrounded by military bases... The Americans have bases in England, Turkey, Greece... What would the Americans think if the Russians set up bases in Mexico or some other place? How would you feel?"[30] In June 1959, Khrushchev expressed his feeling of humiliation by the American nuclear bases close to the Soviet border during his conversation with Averell Harriman, two-time American presidential candidate who had served as Franklin Roosevelt's wartime envoy to Stalin.[31]

In the summer of 1959, U.S. President Eisenhower predicted that placing the Jupiters near the Soviet Union could lead the Russians to take actions in other places: "If Mexico or Cuba had been penetrated by the communists and then began getting arms and missiles from [the Soviets], we would be bound to look on such developments with the gravest concern and in fact... it would be imperative for us to take... offensive military action."[32] In the same summer, Premier Khrushchev complained to U.S. Vice President Richard Nixon about the American plan to station the Jupiters in Turkey.[33]

When some rumors erupted in February 1961 that the Americans were planning to transfer ownership of the Jupiter missiles to the Turks, Nikita Ryzhov, the Soviet ambassador in Ankara, asked the Turkish foreign minister to tell him what was going on.[34] During their summit meeting in June 1961, Khrushchev told Kennedy: "can six million people really be a threat to the mighty United States? If the United States felt threatened by tiny Cuba, what was the Soviet Union to do about Turkey and Iran? These two countries are followers of the United States. They march in its wake, and they have U.S. bases and rockets."[35] In his interview with American columnist Drew Pearson in August 1961, Khrushchev pointed to the American bases in Turkey; "maybe they are going to blow us up here."[36]

It was suggested that Khrushchev first got the idea of deploying nuclear missiles to Cuba in April 1962 during his talk with Defence Minister Marshal Rodion Malinovsky in Crimea.[37] Malinovsky told him that nuclear missiles in Turkey, just across the Black Sea, "could in a short time destroy all our southern cities... The Americans have surrounded us with bases on all sides, and we have no possibility and right to do the same."[38]

During his visit to Bulgaria in May 1962, Khrushchev strongly criticized the installation of the Jupiter missiles in Turkey.[39] The Soviet government issued a public statement on 11 September 1962 complaining that

> The whole world knows that the United States has ringed the Soviet Union and other socialist countries with bases... They have brought armaments there in their ships, and these armaments stationed along the frontier of the Soviet Union - in Turkey, Iran, Greece, Italy, Britain, Holland, Pakistan and other countries belonging to the military blocs of NATO, CENTO and

---

[30] Beschloss, *Kennedy v. Khrushchev*, pp. 381-382.
[31] Ibid., p. 382.
[32] Barton R. Bernstein, "Reconsidering the Missile Crisis: Dealing with the Problems of the American Jupiters in Turkey" in James A. Nathan (ed.), *The Cuban Missile Crisis Revisited*, New York: St. Martin's Press, 1992, p. 58.
[33] Ibid., pp. 58-59.
[34] Beschloss, *Kennedy v. Khrushchev*, p. 65.
[35] Ibid., p. 200.
[36] Ibid., pp. 290, 382.
[37] Garthoff, *Reflections on the Cuban Missile Crisis*, p. 12.
[38] Beschloss, *Kennedy v. Khrushchev*, p. 381.
[39] Garthoff, *Reflections on the Cuban Missile Crisis*, p. 11.

SEATO... They consider this their right! But to others the United States does not permit this even for defense...[40]

Under this awareness of what American bases and missiles around the Soviet Union meant, the Soviets were struck with the idea of using the same American tactic to prevent the Americans from toppling the Castro regime in Cuba.[41] In a memoir attributed to himself, Khrushchev stated: "We had to establish a tangible and effective deterrent to American interference in the Caribbean. But what exactly? The logical answer was missiles. The United States had already surrounded the Soviet Union with its own bomber bases and missiles. We knew that American missiles were aimed against us in Turkey and Italy."[42] In a meeting of Soviet officials, Soviet Premier Khrushchev favored missile deployment to Cuba "to repay the Americans in kind for surrounding the Soviet Union with military bases and missiles" and to teach them "what it is like to live under sights of nuclear weapons." Khrushchev thought that "faced with a fait accompli of secretly installed missiles the pragmatic Americans would not dare to take irrational risks and would learn to live with them just as the Soviet Union had learned to live with American missiles in Turkey, Italy and West Germany."[43]

Before the Cuban crisis, the last time Soviet Premier Khrushchev expressed his sharp objections to the installation of Jupiter missiles in Turkey and Italy was during his meeting with Foy Kohler, the new American ambassador to Moscow, on 16 October 1962.[44] Unlike the American leaders, Khrushchev was aware of the fact that in a few days the first Jupiter missile launch position in Turkey would be turned over to the Turks[45] and perhaps the misunderstanding that the Turks would gain the ability to trigger the missiles led him to attribute too much importance to the matter.[46] He told Kohler: "Just because I am building a fishing port in Cuba, you want to go to war. After all I'm not doing anything you haven't done to me in Turkey and Iran."[47]

After the Cuban missile crisis broke out Soviet officials in the United Nations, Britain and the USA urged a trade-off between Soviet missiles in Cuba and the Jupiters in Turkey.[48] Soviet ambassador Ryzkov raised the issue in his meeting with Turkish Foreign Minister Feridun C. Erkin on 25 October 1962.[49] In his letter to Kennedy on 27 October 1962, Khrushchev stated:

...your actions, in effect, mean that you have surrounded the Soviet Union with military bases... literally around our country... You say that Cuba worries you because it lies at a distance of ninety miles across the sea from the shores of the United States. However, Turkey lies next to us... You have stationed devastating rocket weapons... in Turkey literally right next to us.[50]

[40] Allison, *Essence of Decision*, p. 43, Hafner, "Bureaucratic Politics and Those Frigging Missiles", p. 318.
[41] Bruce Miroff, *Pragmatic Illusions*, New York: David McKay Company Inc., 1976, pp. 85-86.
[42] Nikita Khrushchev, *Khrushchev Remembers*, London: Andre Deutsch, 1971, p. 493.
[43] Garthoff, *Reflections on the Cuban Missile Crisis*, p. 15.
[44] Ibid., p. 28, Allison, *Essence of Decision*, pp. 43-44, Beschloss, *Kennedy v. Khrushchev*, p. 439.
[45] Garthoff, *Reflections on the Cuban Missile Crisis*, p. 60, Beschloss, *Kennedy v. Khrushchev*, p. 439.
[46] Beschloss, *Kennedy v. Khrushchev*, p. 440.
[47] Ibid., p. 8.
[48] Allison, *Essence of Decision*, p. 44.
[49] Garthoff, *Reflections on the Cuban Missile Crisis*, p. 79.
[50] Kennedy, *Thirteen Days*, pp. 161-162.

It is clear that the Soviets were always worried about nuclear weapons in Turkey, very close to their country. They also used the issue for propaganda in their confrontations with the Western camp. In any case, Turkey was considered a threat by the Soviet Union, therefore, it was at the top of the Soviet defense agenda. It is also fair to say that by giving the idea to them, the presence of the Jupiters in Turkey contributed to the Soviet decision to deploy missiles to Cuba, which brought the world to the edge of a nuclear war. Thus, Turkey became an indirect cause of a superpower conflict. However, it should be stated that the Soviets did not originally intend to trade the Cuban missiles for the Jupiters.[51] When they faced a difficult situation arising from the strong American response, by offering a trade-off, Soviet officials probably wanted to gain something from a bad situation and to appease military hawks at home.

4. MISSILE TRADE DISCUSSIONS DURING THE CRISIS

From the beginning of the Cuban missile crisis, American officials predicted that the Soviets might propose a trade-off between Turkish and Cuban missiles, and they made preparations bearing this possibility in their mind.[52] Even before Soviet missiles were spotted in Cuban territory, a National Security Council staff member prepared an argument rejecting similarities between Turkish and Cuban missiles in the case of a Soviet demand to trade them: Soviet weapons in Cuba were offensive and deployed secretly, American weapons in Turkey were defensive and deployed openly.[53]

According to the notes of Theodore Sorensen, Kennedy's close counsel, in the initial meetings of the Executive Committee (ExCom), which was established by Kennedy to deal with the Cuban crisis, "the removal of our missile bases in Turkey in exchange for the removal of the Cuban missiles [was discussed]... as a possibility which Khrushchev was likely to suggest if we did not."[54] In the meeting on Tuesday, October 16, some members suggested that Khrushchev might be preparing to trade off the Cuban missiles for the Jupiters in Turkey and Italy.[55] On Wednesday, October 17, even hawkish members who were in favor of an air strike against Cuba proposed making a deal with the Soviets, withdrawing all American nuclear forces based in Turkey - aircraft as well as missiles - in return for removal of Soviet missiles from Cuba.[56] On the same day, Adlai Stevenson, the American ambassador to the United Nations, warned President Kennedy that the world opinion would equate American missiles in Turkey with Soviet missiles in Cuba and recommended that "you should [make] it clear that the existence of nuclear missile bases anywhere is negotiable before we start anything."[57]

According to Kennedy's special assistant Arthur Schlesinger's quotations from minutes of the ExCom meeting on Friday, October 19, "more than once during the afternoon Secretary

---

[51] Garthoff, *Reflections on the Cuban Missile Crisis,* p. 22, Hafner, "Bureaucratic Politics and Those Frigging Missiles", p. 330.

[52] Ball, *The Past Has Another Pattern,* p. 295.

[53] Bernstein, "The Cuban Missile Crisis", p. 104.

[54] Hafner, "Bureaucratic Politics and Those Frigging Missiles", p. 313.

[55] "White House Tapes and Minutes of the Cuban Missile Crisis", *International Security,* Summer 1985, vol. 10, No. 1, p. 178, Abel, *The Missile Crisis,* p. 47, Bernstein, "Reconsidering the Missile Crisis", pp. 68-69.

[56] Detzer, *The Brink,* p. 157, Reeves, *A Question of Character,* p. 376.

[57] Bernstein, "The Cuban Missile Crisis", pp. 104-105.

[of Defence] McNamara voiced the opinion that the United States... would at least have to give up our missile bases in Italy and Turkey and would probably have to pay more besides... to get the Soviet missiles out of Cuba." On Saturday and Monday, McNamara voiced the same opinion again and emphasized that the United States would be lucky to get out of the crisis with only a trade of the Turkish missiles. Nobody in these meetings raised objection to McNamara's remarks.[58]

On Saturday, October 20th, in the meeting of the ExCom, Adlai Stevenson recommended that the United States should establish a bargaining position and should consider offering to abolish the American naval base at Guantanamo and to withdraw its Turkish and Italian Jupiter missile bases if the Soviets would withdraw their Cuban bases, and to send UN inspection teams to all the foreign bases maintained by both sides to prevent their use in a surprise attack while the dismantling was being carried out.[59] In Stevenson's opinion, it was almost certain that the Soviets would propose the trade and world opinion "would ask why it was right for the United States to have bases in Turkey, but wrong for the Russians to have bases in Cuba."[60] He was not proposing a simple trade, but he was thinking that to accomplish the significant goal of removing all Russian presence from the Caribbean the United States ought to pay some price such as giving up some bases of debatable military value.[61]

According to A. M. Schlesinger, who saw the classified ExCom minutes, after hearing Stevenson's proposal almost every participant of the meeting "jumped on Stevenson."[62] Most participants feared that Stevenson's suggestion, by starting with concessions, would legitimize Khrushchev's action and give him an easy triumph. It would mean offering to pay Russia to take the missiles out and looking weak and backing down against the Soviet Union.[63] Robert Kennedy, the brother and Attorney General of President Kennedy, was among those who strongly objected to Stevenson's proposal.[64] He told Stevenson's aide Schlesinger on Monday, 22 October, that "we will have to make a deal at the end, but we must stand absolutely firm now. Concessions must come at the end of negotiations, not at the beginning."[65] He also warned President John Kennedy that "he [Stevenson] is not strong or tough enough to be representing us at the United Nations at a time like this."[66] President Kennedy replied: "I think Adlai Stevenson showed plenty of strength and courage, presenting that viewpoint at the risk of being called an appeaser... Maybe he went too far when he suggested giving up Guantanamo, but... I admire him for saying what he did."[67]

In the ExCom meeting in which Stevenson made his proposal, President Kennedy rejected his ideas.[68] From his point of view, accepting the removal of the Jupiters would cause

---

[58] Abram Chayes, *The Cuban Missile Crisis*, London: Oxford University Press, 1974, p. 95.

[59] Allison, *Essence of Decision*, p. 209, *Miroff, Pragmatic Illusions*, p. 90, Reeves, *A Question of Character*, p. 375, Kennedy, *Thirteen Days*, p. 27, Abel, *The Missile Crisis*, p. 95, Bernstein, "The Cuban Missile Crisis", p. 105, Detzer, *The Brink*, pp. 155-156, Beschloss, *Kennedy v. Khrushchev*, p. 468, Arthur M. Schlesinger, *A Thousand Days*, London: Andre Deutsch, 1965, p. 690.

[60] Abel, *The Missile Crisis*, p. 95.

[61] Ibid., p. 96, Detzer, *The Brink*, p. 156.

[62] Bernstein, "The Cuban Missile Crisis", p. 105, *Kennedy, Thirteen Days*, p. 27, Abel, *The Missile Crisis*, p. 95.

[63] Bernstein, "The Cuban Missile Crisis", p. 105, Detzer, *The Brink*, p. 156.

[64] Kennedy, *Thirteen Days*, p. 28.

[65] Bernstein, "The Cuban Missile Crisis", p. 105.

[66] Reeves, *A Question of Character*, p. 376, Detzer, *The Brink*, p. 159.

[67] Detzer, *The Brink*, p. 159.

[68] Allison, *Essence of Decision*, p. 209, Miroff, *Pragmatic Illusions*, p. 97, Abel, *The Missile Crisis*, p. 95.

loss of American prestige, damage trust of NATO members in America and seem to confirm the idea Charles De Gaulle planted that the United States would sacrifice the interests of its allies to protect its own security. According to ExCom minutes reported by Schlesinger, "Kennedy agreed that at an appropriate time we would have to acknowledge that we were willing to take strategic missiles out of Turkey and Italy if this issue was raised by the Russians. But he was firm in saying that we should only make such a proposal in the future."[69]

On October 21, W. Averell Harriman, the assistant secretary of state, counseled President Kennedy about Khrushchev's position at home and likely Soviet purposes and hinted that offering a trade of the Cuban and Turkish missiles might rescue Khrushchev from taking a radical action to appease hawkish military leaders. Harriman informed Kennedy that "there has undoubtedly been greatest pressure on Khrushchev for a considerable time to do something about our ring of bases, aggravated by our placing Jupiter missiles in Turkey."[70]

A State Department group working on UN aspects of the Cuban missile crisis headed by Ambassador Adlai Stevenson met with Secretary of State Dean Rusk on Sunday, 21 October. During the meeting a proposal for a UN Security Council resolution embracing mutual concessions for both American and Soviet sides, perhaps including a missile trade, was put forward by Stevenson and seconded by Secretary Rusk. There was a feeling among the participants that "if the missiles were to be given up anyway, it might make sense, from the viewpoint of UN planning, to offer that concession to gain a tactical advantage in the Security Council."[71] According to Chayes, proposals were ultimately abandoned not because they added up to a 'Munich' but because they had great tactical disadvantages. One could not be sure that they would really satisfy demands of the Soviets. "All the proposals would have required consultation with other affected parties. The United States could hardly propose... drastic changes in the Turkish defense posture without talking to this ally first."[72]

After Kennedy's speech on Tuesday, October 22, announcing a naval blockade of Cuba, some American officials expressed their strong objections to a possible trade-off of the Jupiters in Turkey. According to Bernstein, one American official warned, "the danger in Turkey can be especially acute... If the alliance or the United States seems to be pulling away from [Turkey] it could lead to the fall of the present government."[73]

On Wednesday, October 24, George Ball drafted and sent duplicate telegrams to the American ambassador in Turkey and the American NATO delegation in Fontainebleau.[74] The telegrams stated that the administration considered "that a negotiated solution for removal of Cuban offensive threat may involve dismantling and removal of the Jupiters" and requested these American diplomats to assess the political situation in Turkey and smooth the way for such an operation, without harming America's relations with an important ally, Turkey. Ball's telegram also asked if Turkey would consent to withdrawal of the Jupiters if there was some military replacement such as deployment of an American-controlled Polaris submarine or establishment of a Multilateral Nuclear Force (MLF) within NATO.[75]

---

[69] Bernstein, "The Cuban Missile Crisis", p. 106, Beschloss, *Kennedy v. Khrushchev,* p. 468.
[70] Bernstein, "The Cuban Missile Crisis", p. 105.
[71] Chayes, *The Cuban Missile Crisis,* pp. 81-82.
[72] Ibid., p. 82.
[73] Bernstein, "The Cuban Missile Crisis", pp. 107-108.
[74] Ball, *The Past Has Another Pattern,* p. 295.
[75] Bernstein, "The Cuban Missile Crisis", p. 108, Detzer, *The Brink,* p. 243.

Bernstein cites the reply of Raymond Hare, U.S. ambassador to Turkey, to Ball as follows:

> [Hare responded that] removal of the Jupiters as part of an explicit trade would weaken NATO and injure American relations with Turkey... Turkish officials would greatly resent that 'their interests were being traded off in order to appease an enemy.' They were proud that, unlike the Cubans, they were not the stooge of a great power. Both Turkey's political and military power were at stake... and the Jupiters fulfilled both needs... Hare reluctantly suggested a secret Soviet-American arrangement (without Turkey's knowledge) and then the prompt dismantling of the missiles.[76]

The American ambassador to NATO, Thomas Finletter, also replied to Ball's telegram that the Turks would resent the idea greatly. He warned State Department officials that making a trade-off with the Russians could encourage them to initiate other adventures and frighten other NATO members by leading them to think that the next time they could be asked to give up some military capability to appease the Soviets.[77]

Meanwhile, the idea of a missile trade had been discussed in European press and United Nations corridors from the beginning of the week. The British newspaper, *The Guardian* predicted that a Soviet countermove against the Jupiter bases in Turkey was possible[78] and suggested "what is sauce for Cuba, is also sauce for Turkey."[79] In fact, as Chayes states, "British newspapers of all political shades had been urging the dismantling of the Turkish missiles as a basis for settlement from the first announcement of the crisis."[80] The editorial of *The Times* of London on 26 October 1962 stated:

> If it could be brought about there seems to be one way which President Kennedy could secure the elimination of the missile bases in Cuba. That is by opening up the broader question of precautions against surprise attack. Comparisons between the Cuban and the Turkish bases are hotly and quite rightly resented by most Americans. The history and the whole extent are, indeed, different. Even so a case can be made for banishing offensive missiles from each base.[81]

The British Labor Party leader, Hugh Gaitskell, complained about American insistence on continuing the crisis by pointing to American missiles in Turkey: "If indeed there were to be an American attack on Cuba on these grounds, it would be difficult to see how the Russians would not able to justify a similar attack on Turkey. If the ground for attack is that there are nuclear bases in neighboring territories, I am afraid this seems to follow."[82]

A more open proposal to trade Turkish for Cuban missiles as a way of ending the crisis came from *Washington Post* columnist Walter Lippmann. In his column on Thursday, 25 October, Lippmann stated:

> The way [of ending the crisis] is to try to negotiate a face-saving agreement. The only place that is truly comparable with Cuba is Turkey. This is the only place where there are strategic

---

[76] Bernstein, "The Cuban Missile Crisis", p. 108.
[77] Ibid., pp. 108-109.
[78] Abel, *The Missile Crisis,* p. 129.
[79] Detzer, *The Brink,* p. 203.
[80] Chayes, *The Cuban Missile Crisis,* p. 97.
[81] *The Times,* 26 October 1962, p. 11.
[82] *The Times,* 26 October 1962, p. 6.

weapons right on the frontier of the Soviet Union... The Soviet missile in Cuba, like the U.S. NATO base in Turkey, is of little military value. The Soviet military base in Cuba is defenseless and the base in Turkey is all but obsolete. The two bases could be dismantled without altering the world balance of power.[83]

It was likely that Soviet leaders, who probably thought that Lippmann's column spoke for the President, assumed that the White House was sending up a trial balloon through Lippmann.[84] Beschloss speculates that

> once Lippmann made his Thursday proposal, Kennedy may have thought it useful to call Khrushchev's attention to one route by which they could negotiate an end to the crisis. Had he wished to warn Khrushchev away from such a route of bargaining, he could have easily asked Salinger [his press secretary] to issue a statement to the effect that the United States could not accept the suggestion of a Turkey-for-Cuba trade that had appeared in public prints. Knowing Khrushchev might assume that Lippmann was proposing the trade on his behalf, the President let the column stand.[85]

On Thursday, October 25, a special National Security Council committee recommended the withdrawal of Turkish missiles in return for removal of Soviet missiles from Cuba. Not to antagonize the Turks and other NATO members such an offer "might be expressed in generalized form, such as withdrawal of missiles from territory [near] the other [great power]."[86]

On Friday, October 26, Assistant Secretary of State Harlan Cleveland proposed that only nuclear powers should station nuclear weapons in their territories, thus the United States and the Soviet Union should withdraw their nuclear arms from non-nuclear countries including Turkey and Cuba. Endorsing Cleveland's resolution, Averell Harriman suggested that "agreement should not be put forward as a trade over Cuba [and Turkey] but as a first and important step towards disarmament."[87] On the same day, to provide a face-saving solution for the Soviets a special NSC committee recommended suggesting "a summit conference, to be preceded by the agreement of NATO and Turkey to accept a Multilateral Force and to remove missiles from Turkey and Italy."[88] Director of the Policy Planning Council Walt W. Rostow's solution was to secure NATO's speedy approval for MLF with an agreement to dismantle the Jupiters. He thought the Soviets "could read it [dismantling the Jupiters] as a way of helping them off the hook."[89] In the ExCom meeting in Friday morning, Ambassador Adlai Stevenson predicted that the Soviets would ask the United States to guarantee the territorial integrity of Cuba and to dismantle U.S. strategic missiles in Turkey. John McCone, director of the CIA, strongly objected the linkage of Cuban missiles with Turkish missiles.[90]

According to Garthoff, several recent Soviet disclosures revealed that there was a previously unreported meeting of Attorney General Robert Kennedy with the Soviet

---

[83] *Washington Post*, 25 October 1962, p. A-25, col. 1.

[84] Garthoff, *Reflections on the Cuban Missile Crisis*, p. 70, Detzer, *The Brink*, p. 243, Beschloss, *Kennedy v. Khrushchev*, p. 529, Abel, *The Missile Crisis*, pp. 188-189.

[85] Beschloss, *Kennedy v. Khrushchev*, p. 530.

[86] Bernstein, "The Cuban Missile Crisis", p. 109.

[87] Ibid., p. 109.

[88] Ibid., p. 110.

[89] Ibid., pp. 110-111.

[90] Ibid., p. 111, Beschloss, *Kennedy v. Khrushchev*, p. 508, "White House Tapes and Minutes of the Cuban Missile Crisis", p. 195.

ambassador to Washington, Anatoly Dobrynin, at the Soviet Embassy on Friday, October 26. In this meeting, when Dobrynin complained about American double standards in considering the presence of American missiles in Turkey legitimate while denying legitimacy of Soviet missiles in Cuba, Robert Kennedy asked if the Turkish missiles were really important for the Soviet Union and informed Dobrynin that President Kennedy was planning to phase out the Jupiter missiles in Turkey. "He, then, left the room to talk with the president, and upon his return confirmed the president's intention to remove the missiles from Turkey if the overall situation was normalized. Dobrynin then reported this possibility to Moscow."[91]

It is clear that all U.S. officials were willing to trade the Jupiters in Turkey with Soviet missiles in Cuba on the condition that the Turks and other NATO members would not know about it and/or would not show resentment against it. Most of U.S. officials were even in favor of risking resentment of NATO members to oust the Soviets from the Caribbean in a peaceful way whereas some of them were really worried about its repercussions for U.S. relations with Turkey and NATO. In any case, Turkey was on the discussion table, being a part of the missile crisis, and Turkish authorities did not know about it.

5. THE RUSSIAN MOVES TO END THE CRISIS PEACEFULLY

The first Soviet initiative to find a peaceful solution for the Cuban crisis came on Friday, 26 October, through an unofficial channel. Alexander Fomin, a counselor of the Soviet embassy in Washington, lunched with John Scali, the diplomatic reporter of the American ABC TV, and asked him if the United States "would be interested in settlement of the Cuban crisis along these lines: Bases [in Cuba] would be dismantled under the UN's supervision and Castro would pledge not to accept offensive weapons of any kind, ever, in return for U.S. pledge not to invade Cuba."[92] When President Kennedy heard Fomin's proposal, he agreed with Secretary of State Dean Rusk that it was an acceptable basis for the settlement and told Scali: "Tell them you've gotten a favorable response from the highest authority in the government"[93] adding, "without attributing it to the President". John Scali then informed Fomin that "I have reason to believe that the United States government sees real possibilities in this and supposes that the representatives of the Soviet Union and the United States in New York can work this matter out with [UN Secretary General] U Thant and with each other."[94] Fomin, then, promised that this information would be passed on immediately to the highest levels.

Soviet Premier Khrushchev's long personal letter to Kennedy in the evening of the same day repeated the same general proposal made by Alexander Fomin. The letter stated: "If assurances were given that the president of the United States would not participate in an attack on Cuba and the blockade lifted, the question of the removal or the destruction of the missile sites in Cuba would then be an entirely different question."[95]

---

[91] Garthoff, *Reflections on the Cuban Missile Crisis,* p. 87, see also L. Chang, "The View from Washington and the View from Nowhere: Cuban Missile Crisis Historiography" in Nathan (ed.), *The Cuban Missile Crisis Revisited,* pp. 150-151.

[92] Pierre Salinger, *With Kennedy,* London: Jonathan Cope, 1967, p. 274.

[93] Detzer, *The Brink,* p. 238.

[94] Salinger, *With Kennedy,* p. 275.

[95] Kennedy, *Thirteen Days,* pp. 66-67.

These acceptable Soviet proposals made American officials optimistic about ending the crisis peacefully and caused a great relief. But when the ExCom met in the morning of Saturday, October 27, a new message from Khrushchev arrived. Khrushchev's new letter added a new element to the solution of the crisis: the removal of American missiles from Turkey in return for the Soviet withdrawal from Cuba. Roger Hilsman, the State Department intelligence chief, later recalled that "it was the blackest hour of the crisis."[96]

The proposal in Khrushchev's second letter was as follows:

> We agree to remove those weapons from Cuba, which you regard as offensive weapons. We agree to do this and to state this commitment in the United Nations. Your representatives will make a statement to the effect that the United States, on its part, bearing in mind the anxiety and concern of the Soviet state, will evacuate its analogous weapons from Turkey... Of course it is necessary that the governments of Cuba and Turkey would allow these [UN] representatives to come to their countries and check fulfillment of this commitment, which each side undertakes... We, having assumed this commitment in order to give satisfaction and hope to the peoples of Cuba and Turkey and to increase their confidence in their security, will make a statement in the Security Council to the effect that the Soviet government gives a solemn pledge to respect the integrity of the frontiers and the sovereignty of Turkey, not to intervene in its domestic affairs, not to invade Turkey, not to make available its territory as a place d'armes for such invasion and also will restrain those who would think of launching an aggression against Turkey either from Soviet territory or from the territory of other states bordering on Turkey.[97]

The American government would give exactly same assurances regarding Cuba.

The reasons for Soviet Premier Khrushchev including a missile trade in a settlement of the crisis could be summarized as follows: Firstly, in their meeting on 26 October, Robert Kennedy told Dobrynin that the American president was willing to phase out the Jupiter missiles in Turkey and Dobrynin reported this exchange to Moscow. Secondly, a missile trade to end the crisis was popular in the Western press and UN corridors and the Soviets knew this. Thirdly, Walter Lippmann's open proposal of a missile trade might have been seen by the Soviet rulers as a trial balloon of the Americans. Finally, it is possible that hawkish Soviet military leaders put pressure on Khrushchev for radical action and that Khrushchev proposed the missile trade to appease them.

On why Khrushchev did not propose the Turkey-for-Cuba trade in his first letter Beschloss states:

> Georgi Kornienko [a counselor at the Soviet Embassy in Washington in 1962] and other Soviet officials suggested in 1991 that on Friday night [26 October 1962], the Chairman [Khrushchev] was convinced that a U.S. invasion of Cuba was imminent and that to achieve a quick settlement, he dropped his intention to demand removal of the Turkish missiles... By Saturday, surrounded by his generals, Khrushchev considered such an assault more remote and thus included the demand in the second letter.[98]

With Khrushchev's proposal Turkish missiles were put on the bargaining table, thus Turkey became a direct part of the crisis outside the knowledge and intention of its rulers.

---

[96] Bernstein, "The Cuban Missile Crisis", p. 113.
[97] Kennedy, *Thirteen Days*, pp. 162-163.
[98] Beschloss, *Kennedy v. Khrushchev*, p. 526.

6. THE DANGER OF A NUCLEAR WAR AND TURKEY

It was considered highly possible by American officials that if America attacked Soviet missiles in Cuba and thus killed Soviet citizens there, the Soviet Union would retaliate by attacking the Jupiter missiles and American bases in Turkey.[99] As early as Tuesday, October 23, Secretary Rusk had told George Ball that "we have won a considerable victory. You and I are still alive." In that morning, the Secretary of State's fears had not been realized. The Russians had not blocked the autobahn to Berlin. They had not bombed the Jupiter bases in Turkey or moved to close the Dardanelles.[100] In the ExCom meeting on Saturday, October 27, President Kennedy said that the NATO countries did not realize that if the USA carried out an air strike against Cuba probably in two or three days and the Soviet Union answered by attacking Turkey all NATO was going to be involved. The president, then, would have to decide whether he would fire nuclear missiles in Turkey.[101]

When a Soviet SAM missile shot down an American U-2 reconnaissance plane over Cuba on 27 October, killing its pilot, Major Rudolf Anderson, Jr., a nuclear war between two super powers seemed even more imminent. Earlier in the week, the ExCom had decided that if a U-2 were shot down, the United States would retaliate against a single SAM site. If a second U-2 were attacked, the United States would destroy all SAM sites in Cuba. According to Allison and Robert Kennedy "in the ExCom [meeting on Saturday, 27 October], there was almost unanimous agreement that the United States had to attack early the next morning" with bombers and fighters and destroy the SAM sites.[102] Kennedy's counsel Theodore Sorensen later wrote that "our little group seated around the cabinet table in continuous session that Saturday felt nuclear war to be closer on that day than at any time in the nuclear age."[103]

In spite of the eagerness among top American officials for an attack, President Kennedy decided to stand back and give one more chance to the Soviets.[104] The president held back on the order until they could be sure that the U-2 plane had not accidentally crashed but had been shot down by a Soviet missile.[105] His most important concern at that moment of the crisis was a nuclear holocaust causing a human tragedy all over the world. He told the ExCom members that "it isn't the first step that concerns me, but both sides escalating to the fourth and fifth step - and we do not go to the sixth because there is no one around to do so."[106] According to Allison, this process of escalating to a nuclear war would directly involve Turkey at the beginning.[107]

Robert Kennedy described those critical moments and President Kennedy's concern about involvement of other countries in his memoir as follows:

His mind went to other areas of the world... If we attacked Cuba and the Russians reciprocated with an attack on Turkey, would or should the Turkish missiles be fired? He ordered

[99] Hafner, "Bureaucratic Politics and Those Frigging Missiles", p. 312.
[100] Abel, The Missile Crisis, p. 127.
[101] Allison, Essence of Decision, p. 227, Beschloss, Kennedy v. Khrushchev, pp. 527-528, Kennedy, Thirteen Days, p. 74.
[102] Allison, Essence of Decision, pp. 224-225, Kennedy, Thirteen Days, p. 76, "White House Tapes and Minutes of the Cuban Missile Crisis", p. 203.
[103] Reeves, A Question of Character, p. 387.
[104] Allison, Essence of Decision, p. 225.
[105] Reeves, A Question of Character, p. 387, Salinger, With Kennedy, p. 272, Kennedy, Thirteen Days, p. 76.
[106] Kennedy, Thirteen Days, p. 76.
[107] Allison, Essence of Decision, p. 217.

preparations taken to defuse missiles with atomic warheads, so that he personally would have to give permission before they were used. What role Turkey and the rest of NATO have in determining our response? Within a very short time, they might be faced with decisions of life and death. Before that happened, should they not have a right to learn what we were deciding to do, particularly if that was likely to affect them in such a rapid and possibly devastating way? These hourly decisions, necessarily made with such rapidity, could be made only by the president of the United States, but any of them might close and lock doors for peoples and governments in many other lands, we had to be aware of this responsibility at all times, he said, aware that we were deciding, the president was deciding, for the United States, the Soviet Union, Turkey, NATO and really for all mankind.[108]

Thus, the presence of the Jupiters on its territory positioned Turkey under a direct threat of a nuclear war and put its fate in the hands of the Americans and the Soviets. It could be one of very few targets, which would be seriously damaged, in a limited nuclear war, which would be halted before escalating to involve the whole humanity. In the event of an all-out nuclear war, Turkey's situation would not constitute a special, different case than others.

7. THE ROLE OF THE JUPITERS IN RESOLVING THE CRISIS

In the Saturday morning meeting of the ExCom (October 27), President Kennedy was really frustrated with hearing the new Soviet proposal. The Turkish missiles had put him in a very difficult situation. Because of them, Kennedy was confronted with one of two difficult choices: to give in to this Soviet demand and look weak and shake the Western alliance or refuse the Soviet proposal and possibly bring about a thermonuclear war.[109] In one point of the discussions, Kennedy boiled with anger and reportedly shouted: "Get those frigging missiles off the board!"[110] Hafner suggests that "the President, in his anger that Saturday morning, seemed to think that if the Jupiters had not been there, no Soviet proposal for a trade-off would have been possible. That is unlikely."[111] There were other bargaining points and it was easy for the Soviets to come with another trade proposal.

At that moment of the crisis, President Kennedy had come to a point that he was now utterly determined to withdraw the American missiles from Turkey in order to remove a target that the Soviets could legitimately strike in retaliation for an American action or subject to a trade again in the future. He seemed to be ready to come to terms with Khrushchev's proposal. The President privately talked with Secretaries McNamara and Rusk at the close of the morning session of the ExCom (27 October), instructing them to consider the possibility of missile trade very carefully. He did not want to offend or frighten Turkey and other NATO members. He assigned McNamara's deputy Roswell Gilpatric to spend the afternoon in McGeorge Bundy's office at the White House with representatives of the State Department and the Joint of Chief Staff and prepare a scenario for withdrawing the Jupiters from Turkey and Italy in the possible earliest time.[112]

In the afternoon meeting, President Kennedy pondered upon the notion of bargaining. Although he was willing to get rid of the Turkish missiles, President Kennedy regretted that

---

[108] Kennedy, *Thirteen Days,* p. 77.
[109] Ibid., p. 73.
[110] Allison, *Essence of Decision,* p. 142, Detzer, *The Brink,* p. 244.
[111] Hafner, "Bureaucratic Politics and Those Frigging Missiles", p. 330.
[112] Abel, *The Missile Crisis,* pp. 194-195, Detzer, *The Brink,* p. 245.

"the Russians had made the Turkish proposal in the most difficult way."[113] "It's not as if it was a private proposal, which would give us an opportunity to negotiate with the Turks. Khrushchev has put it out in a way that the Turks are bound to say they don't agree to this."[114] Kennedy also said:

> ... we are now in the position of risking war in Cuba and Berlin over missiles in Turkey, which are of little military value. From the political point of view, it would be hard to get support on an airstrike against Cuba because many would think that we would make a good trade if we offered to take the missiles out of Turkey... We cannot propose to withdraw the missiles... but the Turks could offer to do so. [They] must be informed of the great danger in which they will live during the next week and we have to face up to the possibility of some kind of a trade over the missiles.[115]

In the ExCom meeting after 4 p.m., Kennedy expressed his feeling that "we would not be in a position to offer any trade for several days... If we could succeed in freezing the situation in Cuba and rendering the strategic missiles inoperable, then we would be in a position to negotiate with the Russians." When Bundy warned that "if we sound as if we wanted to make this trade to our NATO people and to all the people who are tied to us by alliance, we are in real trouble", the President replied, "yes, but if we refused to discuss such a trade and then take military action in Cuba, we would also be in a difficult situation."[116] In the meeting, some members and the Joint of Chiefs staff suggested a military action: reject the trade, defuse the Jupiters in Turkey, inform the Soviets, and then attack Cuba. Kennedy did not like the idea because "if the Russians do attack the NATO countries [in retaliation], we do not want them [NATO allies] to say that they had not been consulted about the actions we were taking."[117] At one point President Kennedy said, "the best position now was to let Khrushchev know that the United States was glad to discuss Turkish missiles with them once we get a positive indication that they've ceased their work in Cuba."[118]

In late afternoon in the cabinet room Kennedy suggested again, "I think... I'll just say [to Khrushchev], 'of course we ought to try to go to the first route which you suggest'... But it seems to me we ought to have this discussion with NATO about these Turkish missiles."[119] In an informal discussion following the afternoon meeting, Vice President Lyndon B. Johnson asked George Ball "why we were not prepared to [accept the trade proposal] if we were prepared to give up the use of U.S. missiles in Turkey?" Ball responded that "last week we thought it might be acceptable to trade the withdrawal of the missiles in Turkey if such action would save Berlin. Why not now? We can... replace the missiles in Turkey by assigning Polaris submarines to the area".[120]

[113] Bernstein, "The Cuban Missile Crisis", p. 118.
[114] Beschloss, *Kennedy v. Khrushchev*, p. 527, "White House Tapes and Minutes of the Cuban Missile Crisis", pp. 197. 198.
[115] "White House Tapes and Minutes of the Cuban Missile Crisis", p. 199, Bernstein, "The Cuban Missile Crisis", p. 118.
[116] "White House Tapes and Minutes of the Cuban Missile Crisis", Bernstein, "The Cuban Missile Crisis", pp. 119-120, Beschloss, *Kennedy v. Khrushchev*, p. 527.
[117] Bernstein, "The Cuban Missile Crisis", pp. 119-120.
[118] Beschloss, *Kennedy v. Khrushchev*, p. 527.
[119] Ibid., p. 533.
[120] Ibid., p. 535, Bernstein, "The Cuban Missile Crisis", p. 120, "White House Tapes and Minutes of the Cuban Missile Crisis", p. 203.

As for the issue of preparing a response to Khrushchev's letters, American officials differed. State Department officials generally were in favor of sending a letter openly rejecting the trade proposal. In the morning session of the ExCom meeting, Assistant Secretary of Defence Paul Nitze had said, "it would be an anathema to the Turks to pull the missiles out... The next Soviet step would be a demand for denuclearization of the entire NATO area." McGeorge Bundy's view was that "we cannot get into the position of appearing to sell out an ally... to serve our own interests, i.e., getting the Soviet missiles out of Cuba."[121] Rusk and Ball predicted that such a trade "would undermine the faith of the whole alliance in America's pledged word" and State Department's Soviet expert Llewellyn Thompson argued that "the Russians would certainly interpret the President's acceptance as proof of weakness."[122] In the afternoon session, Rusk and Ball submitted a draft letter, having the character of a response from the American President to Khrushchev, answering arguments of Khrushchev's latest letter, rejecting a missile trade and demanding a halt to work on the missiles in Cuba.[123] The other members, including Robert Kennedy, objected to the draft by arguing that "it would be difficult for the administration to persuade world opinion, and perhaps opinion at home as well, that prolonging or intensifying the crisis was preferable to withdrawing obsolete missiles from Turkey."[124]

Robert Kennedy and Theodore Sorensen came up with the idea that President Kennedy should ignore Khrushchev's second letter and respond to the terms of the first letter. With the President's instruction, Robert Kennedy and Sorensen left the room, drafted a letter consisting of their proposal, and submitted it to the ExCom. With minor changes the committee accepted the letter and gave consent to sending it to Khrushchev.[125] The deal, which was proposed by Kennedy's letter to Khrushchev on October 27, was as follows:

> 1- You would agree to remove these weapons systems from Cuba under appropriate United Nations observation and supervision; and undertake, with suitable safeguards, to halt the further introduction of such weapon systems into Cuba. 2- We, on our part, would agree -upon the establishment of adequate arrangements through the United Nations to ensure the carrying out and continuation of these commitments- (a) to remove promptly the quarantine measures now in effect and (b) to give assurances against an invasion of Cuba. I am confident that other nations of the Western Hemisphere would be prepared to do likewise.[126]

Although the letter did not mention the Jupiter missiles specifically, it left the door open for some future arrangement about them. It stated:

> The effect of such a settlement on easing world tensions would enable us to work toward a more general arrangement regarding 'other armaments', as proposed in your second letter which you made public... If your letter signifies that you are prepared to discuss a détente affecting NATO and the Warsaw Pact, we are quite prepared to consider with our allies any useful proposals.

---

[121] Bernstein, "The Cuban Missile Crisis", p. 118, "White House Tapes and Minutes of the Cuban Missile Crisis", p. 197.

[122] Allison, *Essence of Decision*, p. 226.

[123] Ibid., p. 227, Kennedy, *Thirteen Days*, p. 79.

[124] Garthoff, *Reflections on the Cuban Missile Crisis*, p. 85.

[125] Allison, *Essence of Decision*, p. 227, Kennedy, *Thirteen Days*, pp. 79-80, Reeves, *A Question of Character*, pp. 387-388.

[126] Kennedy, *Thirteen Days*, p. 165.

But Kennedy's letter also warned: "The continuation of this threat, or a prolonging of this discussion concerning Cuba by linking these problems to the broader questions of European and world security would surely lead to an intensified situation on the Cuban crisis and a grave risk to the peace of the world."[127]

After sending this letter to Khrushchev, in order to ensure world peace, President Kennedy asked his brother Robert Kennedy to make a private arrangement with Soviet Ambassador Dobrynin on the Jupiters. This secret decision was taken by the President in the Oval Office in the presence of Rusk, Bundy, McNamara, Sorensen and Robert Kennedy after the afternoon meeting of the ExCom on October 27.[128] It was Dean Rusk who proposed it. According to McGeorge Bundy's notes, "the fact that Rusk, stalwart on interests of the NATO alliance, made the proposal encouraged rapid consensus and presidential decision... Rusk was aware of the President's own favorable inclination and saw it as appropriate to assist the President in using this diplomatic asset."[129]

Robert Kennedy's memoir cites his meeting with Dobrynin as follows:

> [I told Dobrynin:] We had to have commitment by tomorrow that these bases would be removed ... He should understand that if they did not remove those bases, we would remove them... Perhaps his country might feel it necessary to take retaliatory action; but before that was over, there would be not only dead Americans but dead Russians as well. He [Dobrynin] raised the question of our removing the missiles from Turkey. I said that there could be no quid pro quo or any arrangement made under this kind of threat or pressure, and that in the last analysis this was a decision would have to be made by NATO. However, I said, President Kennedy had been anxious to remove these missiles from Turkey and Italy for a long period of time. He had ordered their removal some time ago, and it was our judgement that, within a short time after the crisis was over, these missiles would be gone.[130]

Robert Kennedy also warned that the understanding would be cancelled at once if the Soviets tried to claim public credit for removing the Turkish missiles.[131]

Robert Kennedy's message to Dobrynin had double characteristics, an ultimatum coupled with a way out. It threatened an American attack on Cuba unless the Soviets agreed with terms of the American proposal. On the other hand, it showed a way out to the Soviets by stating the American pledge not to invade Cuba in return for the removal of Soviet missiles from Cuba. The American concession of withdrawing the Jupiter missiles in Turkey was aimed at saving the face of the Soviets and smoothing the way for them to accept a peaceful solution. It had to be kept secret, otherwise the American administration would come under attack from several sides, including the Republicans, the Pentagon, militant ExCom members and America's NATO allies.

When Dobrynin complained in 1989 that the Americans were still refusing to acknowledge that the Jupiters were part of an explicit Soviet-American deal to settle the missile crisis, Sorensen made the following statement:

---

[127] Ibid., p. 165.
[128] Beschloss, *Kennedy v. Khrushchev*, p. 535, Garthoff, *Reflections on the Cuban Missile Crisis*, p. 88, Bernstein, "Reconsidering the Missile Crisis", p. 95.
[129] Garthoff, *Reflections on the Cuban Missile Crisis*, p. 88.
[130] Kennedy, *Thirteen Days*, pp. 86-87.
[131] Beschloss, *Kennedy v. Khrushchev*, p. 537.

Ambassador Dobrynin felt that Robert Kennedy's book did not adequately express that the 'deal' on the Turkish missiles was part of the resolution of the crisis. And here I have a confession to make... I was the editor of Robert Kennedy's book... His diary was very explicit that this was part of the deal; but at that time it was still a secret even on the American side, except for the six of us who had been present at that meeting. So I took it upon myself to edit that out of his diaries and that is why the Ambassador is somewhat justified in saying that the diaries are not as explicit as his conversation.[132]

In the Saturday night meeting of the ExCom, the participants agreed not to tell other NATO countries and Turkey about the private missile deal. Kennedy told the ExCom members what should be said to the U.S. ambassador to Turkey:

Let's give him an explanation of what we're trying to do. We're trying to get it back on the original proposition of last night... because we don't want to get into this [Jupiters] trade. If it's unsuccessful, then... it's possible that we may have to get back on the Jupiter thing. If we do, then we would of course want it to come from the Turks themselves and NATO, rather than just the United States. We're hopeful, however, that that won't come. If it does, his judgement on how it should be handled... we're prepared to do the Polaris and others, does he think this thing can be made?[133]

Meanwhile a special message was sent to Finletter for Sunday's NATO meeting, emphasizing that he should not "hint of any [American] readiness to meet the Soviet Jupiter exchange proposal."[134]

In Sunday morning, October 28, Khrushchev responded to Kennedy's letter by accepting its terms without referring to the Jupiter missiles in Turkey. The crisis was over now.[135]

According to more recent revelations of Dean Rusk in 1987, in the evening of 27 October 1962 after Robert Kennedy's departure to see Dobrynin, President Kennedy privately asked Secretary Rusk to deliver a secret message to Andrew Cordier, former UN parliamentarian. Rusk's statement is as follows:

[T]here is a postscript, which I only can furnish. It was clear to me that President Kennedy would not let the Jupiters in Turkey become an obstacle to the removal of the missile sites in Cuba because the Jupiters were coming out in any event. He instructed me to telephone the late Andrew Cordier, then at Columbia University, and dictate to him a statement which would be made by U Thant, the Secretary General of the United Nations, proposing the removal of both the Jupiters and the missiles in Cuba. Mr. Cordier was to put that statement in the hands of U Thant only after further signal from us. That step was never taken and the statement I furnished to Mr. Cordier has never seen the light of day. So far as I know, President Kennedy, Andrew Cordier and I were the only ones who knew of this particular step.[136]

As was understood from this revelation, the United States, as the last resort, would accept an open trade, which was literally proposed by an independent person. It is clear that President Kennedy was ready to pay the political price rather than go to war. Dean Rusk said

---

[132] Bernstein, "Reconsidering the Missile Crisis", p. 96.
[133] Ibid., pp. 92-93.
[134] Ibid., p. 93.
[135] For Khrushchev's letter see Kennedy, *Thirteen Days*, p. 168.
[136] Blight and Welch, *On the Brink*, pp. 83-84, see also ibid., pp. 114-115, 170-171, Reeves, *A Question of Character*, p. 387, Garthoff, *Reflections on the Cuban Missile Crisis*, pp. 95-96, Beschloss, *Kennedy v. Khrushchev*, p. 538, Bernstein, "Reconsidering the Missile Crisis", p. 100.

in 1987 that he felt the Cordier ploy "would have been used before we landed troops in Cuba, because landing those troops... would have been a major escalation from the Soviet point of view."[137]

On Monday, 29 October, Soviet Ambassador Dobrynin brought Robert Kennedy an unsigned draft letter from Khrushchev to Kennedy, spelling out their secret agreement on the Turkish missiles. Dobrynin's original aim was to ensure a formal American pledge to withdraw the Jupiter missiles in Turkey and to get a presidential letter fulfilling this purpose.[138] According to Dobrynin's account of this meeting "Robert Kennedy told him that it would be very hard for the United States to accept the letter, since withdrawal of the Turkish missiles had to be sanctioned by NATO. This would take time. He renewed his guarantee, on behalf of the President, that the missiles would be gone within four to five months."[139] After studying the letter with President Kennedy, the next day Robert Kennedy told Dobrynin that they could not accept any such written exchange. There could be no quid pro quo in this matter. He said: "Take back your letter, reconsider it and if you feel it is necessary to write letters then we will also write one which you cannot enjoy. Also if you should publish any document indicating a deal then it is off and also if done afterward will further affect the relationship [of the two countries]." Although Robert Kennedy assured Dobrynin that the missiles would be gone in a near future, he emphasized that "it was important not to publicize it" because he and the President would appear to be "purveying a falsehood to the American public."[140]

The secret initiatives of the American administration, which were mentioned above, were known to only few people close to President John Kennedy. The other members of the ExCom, the American Congress, the American people and America's allies believed that the President was determined not to bargain with the Soviets on the Jupiter missiles in Turkey. American officials publicly claimed that the Jupiter missiles did not play any kind of role whatsoever in resolving the Cuban crisis. On 29 October 1962, Rusk cabled Ambassadors Hare and Finletter that "no 'deal' of any kind was made involving Turkey." In 1963, McNamara told the House Appropriations Committee: "without any qualifications whatsoever there was absolutely no deal between the Soviet Union and the United States regarding the removal of the Jupiter weapons from either Italy or Turkey."[141] In his testimony in an executive session of the Senate Foreign Relations Committee in January 1963, Dean Rusk told the senators that the administration had long been planning to phase out the Jupiters and that their removal was "not the basis of any deal or agreement". When Senator Bourke Hickenlooper asked whether the Secretary meant that the removal of the missiles from Turkey "was in no way, shape or form, directly or indirectly, connected with the settlement, the discussion or manipulation of the Cuban situation," Rusk replied: "that is correct, sir."[142]

It is clear from revelations that the Jupiters were a part of the U.S.-Soviet deal in ending the crisis. Kennedy had secretly pledged to scrap the Turkish missiles without informing the Turks. American authorities were even prepared to make the trade openly if it was necessary.

---

[137] Blight and Welch, *On the Brink*, pp. 173-174.
[138] Ibid., p. 174, Garthoff, *Reflections on the Cuban Missile Crisis*, 95n.
[139] Beschloss, *Kennedy v. Khrushchev*, p. 546.
[140] Ibid., pp. 546-547.
[141] Bernstein, "Reconsidering the Missile Crisis", p. 98.
[142] Garthoff, *Reflections on the Cuban Missile Crisis*, pp. 132-133n.

Turkish response and interests obviously held secondary place for the Americans who were anxious to see the end of the crisis.

8. TURKEY'S ATTITUDE DURING THE CRISIS

From the outset of the Cuban missile crisis, Turkey stood staunchly behind its ally, the United States, and without hesitation gave its full support to all the American actions during the crisis. Turkey was one of the first countries, which announced that it would comply with the American decision to establish a naval blockade of Cuba.[143] On 22 October 1962, Turkish President Cemal Gürsel, Prime Minister İsmet İnönü, Foreign Minister Feridun Cemal Erkin and Chief of the General Staff Cevdet Sunay met in the presidential palace. They confirmed that Turkey was one of the first targets of a possible war and discussed what precautions could be taken to minimize the loss in Turkey if a war broke out. Prime Minister İnönü said that his government was going to support America without condition until the last moment of the crisis. In his opinion, America was right in its worries about Cuba and should be supported by Turkey as a requirement of Turkey's commitments to the NATO alliance.[144]

In his speech to the Turkish Parliament on 24 October 1962, İnönü said:

> Turkey's whole hope is that the dispute could be solved by peaceful means. But if one of our allies asked us to do our duty, we shall of course fulfil our obligations. We are keeping steadily in mind as a faithful ally the complaint and serious anxiety of the United States... We are quite sure that the American nation is sincerely trying to achieve a peaceful solution as befits a great nation, which sincerely desires to live in peace.[145]

On the same day, President Gürsel told journalists: "America is our friend and ally. We have to sympathize with the American attitude [towards the Cuban crisis]. We, the Turkish nation, are determined in respecting alliances to which we belong, therefore there is nothing odd in our attitude of supporting our friends in their difficult times."[146]

After the Cuban crisis, Turkish officials continued to express their sympathy with America's attitude during the crisis. In his speech to the Turkish National Assembly on 19 January 1963, Foreign Minister Erkin praised the American action which "prevented the crisis from developing to more dangerous stages and abolished the miscalculation of the enemy side that the United States was not determined enough to protect vital interests of the West." Erkin also proudly mentioned that the speech of the Turkish Prime Minister in front of the parliament, which declared open support for America, strengthened the feelings of trust and gratification of America and other NATO members towards Turkey.[147]

The Turkish public, too, supported America during the Cuban crisis. But the Turkish people did not know that the crisis put Turkey under a great danger. Most Turks were not even aware before the crisis that there were American-made Jupiter missiles on the Turkish territory. On behalf of the main opposition party, MP Fethi Tevetoğlu told the Turkish press that the Justice Party had endorsed the government's attitude, which suited "Turkey's alliance

---

[143] Mehmet Gönlübol, et al., *Olaylarla Türk Dış Politikası*, Ankara: A.Ü. S.B.F. Yayınları, No. 407, 1977, p. 338.
[144] Metin Toker, "İsmet Paşa ile 4 Buhranlı Yıl", *Milliyet*, 4 February 1969, p. 5.
[145] *Millet Meclisi Tutanak Dergisi (MMTD)*, 24 October 1962, term 1, sess. 1, vol. 8, p. 246.
[146] *Cumhuriyet*, 25 October 1962, p. 5.
[147] *MMTD*, 9 January 1963, term 1, sess. 2, vol. 10, pp. 628-629.

relations and its important place within NATO."[148] Youth organizations issued statements backing America and the Turkish government's attitude and sent a Turkish flag and a letter to American President Kennedy, supporting his policy. According to Metin Toker, the Turkish government was receiving messages approving its position on the crisis from all over the country.[149]

While supporting the American side during the Cuban crisis, the Turks greatly resented ideas making comparisons between Cuba and Turkey and proposing a trade-off between the Turkish and Cuban missiles as a way of ending the crisis. Accepting the missile trade under Soviet pressure was impossible for the Turks. They were proud that they were not the stooge of a great power and could not stomach the bargaining of their interests by a great power to appease an enemy state.

When Khrushchev's official proposal of the missile trade was made public, Turkish officials did not make any comment on it. *The Times* correspondent interpreted this situation as follows: "Behind the almost complete silence one can detect a certain irritation that Turkey was not consulted or, it seems, hardly even informed, before the American-Soviet exchange of messages involving Turkey's defense arrangements and vital interests." As the correspondent stated, Turkish officials followed the American line in interpreting the proposal of missile trade: "There is no similarity between the Cuban and the Turkish bases, not only because of the complete different fashion in which they were set up [the Cuban missiles were deployed secretly while the Turkish ones were deployed openly], but also because the Turkish bases are NATO bases and are part of a well-publicized Western defense network." The correspondent cited the view of a source close to the Turkish Foreign Ministry: "The question of any withdrawal of missile bases from Turkey is a matter not for Turkey alone but for the whole of NATO to decide."[150]

On 31 October 1962, in his statement to the press, Turkish Foreign Minister Feridun C. Erkin indirectly commented on the Soviet demands of withdrawal of American missiles from Turkey: "Those who have demanded the abolition of our bases first should themselves promise to abolish their bases which constituted a threat to Turkey."[151] Later, on 9 January 1963, Erkin told the Turkish Parliament that during the Cuban crisis the Soviets tried to bargain the Jupiter missiles in Turkey with Cuban missiles, but this Soviet proposal was flatly rejected by the Americans. He also added that no decision concerned Turkey could be taken without its participation.[152]

The Turkish press showed great anger against Khrushchev's official proposal of a missile trade-off. Earlier, on 24 October 1962, *Cumhuriyet* columnist Ecvet Güresin had warned that in order to put the Americans in a difficult situation, the Soviet Union could try to initiate a bargaining on the NATO bases in Turkey.[153] Other newspaper columnists claimed that it was not fair to make comparisons between the Cuban and Turkish missiles because while the former was offensive and changed the status quo, the latter was defensive and kept the status quo which was established in 1957. Therefore, the press comments suggested that neither

---

[148] *Cumhuriyet*, 26 October 1962, p. 5.
[149] Metin Toker, , "İsmet Paşa ile 4 Buhranlı Yıl", *Milliyet*, 5 February 1969, p. 5.
[150] *The Times*, 29 October 1962, p. 8.
[151] *Cumhuriyet*, 1 November 1962, p. 5.
[152] *MMTD*, 9 January 1963, term 1, sess. 2, vol. 10, p. 629.
[153] Ecvet Güresin, "Küba Olayları Karşısında Ankara'daki Akisler", *Cumhuriyet*, 24 October 1962.

Turkey nor America could take the Soviet proposal into consideration.[154] In fact, Turkish officials and Turkish people were almost sure that their ally, the United States, would not make such a concession which would harm the cohesion of the NATO alliance.

9. THE IMPLICATIONS OF THE CRISIS FOR TURKEY

When the Soviet-American deal on the Cuban and Turkish missiles was known by the world, it caused a deep resentment and apprehension in Turkish public opinion and led to accusations that the United States decided to withdraw the Jupiters as a part of its deal with the Soviets without consulting the Turkish government, which actually owned the missiles (but not their warheads), for the sake of its own interests, pushing the Soviets out of the Caribbean and preventing an armed combat with them. It was felt that it treated Turkey as a client state whose interests were negotiable with enemy states. It was clear that, in the future, when American interests demanded, the United States would not hesitate to engage in deals with other powers at the expense of Turkey.[155]

The Turkish prime minister in 1962, İsmet İnönü, made the following remarks in the Turkish Parliament later in January 1970: The Americans told the Turkish leaders that they wanted to remove the Jupiter missiles in Turkey because they were outdated and obsolete and to replace them with Polaris submarines carrying nuclear missiles. The Turkish rulers found the American proposal reasonable, therefore, they accepted it without hesitation. But later they found out that the Americans had made a deal with the Soviets on the missiles. Keeping this fact in mind, the present Turkish leaders should be careful about not allowing the Americans to involve Turkey in unwanted crisis situations against its will.[156]

Another implication of the Cuban crisis for the Turks was that Turkey might become a target for a Soviet nuclear attack because of the American bases and nuclear weapons on its territory. Soviet Premier Khrushchev's letter to Kennedy on 27 October 1962 had stated as a part of its proposal that the Soviet Union would give a solemn pledge to respect the integrity of the frontiers and sovereignty of Turkey, not to intervene in its domestic affairs and not to invade it. It means that if the United States did not accept the Soviet proposal the Soviet Union might do the opposite. In fact, according to Metin Toker's account of the Cuban crisis, the Turkish leaders felt that their country together with the United States was on the brink of a nuclear war. İsmet İnönü was fearing that it would be too difficult this time to keep Turkey out of the war if a conflict erupted between the two superpowers.[157] During the crisis, Turkey went through almost a state of war for few days. The Soviet ambassador in Ankara, Ryzhov, was threatening Turkish politicians by saying that a nuclear war was at the door of Turkey. The Turkish rulers were thinking that if a nuclear war erupted, the Hiroshimas of this nuclear war would be İstanbul and Ankara.[158]

During the Cuban crisis, probably for the first time, the Turkish rulers realized that increased military force did not mean increased security. The crisis showed that having

---

[154] Duygu Sezer, *Kamuoyu ve Dış Politika*, Ankara: A.Ü. S.B.F. Yayınları, No. 339, 1972, p. 131.
[155] Turkish columnist Fahir Armaoğlu rightly commented that the Turkish response to U.S. attitude on the Cyprus question after 1963 was so strong mainly because of U.S. attitude on the Cuban missile crisis.
[156] *MMTD*, 22 January 1970, term 3, sess. 1, vol. 2, pp. 291-292.
[157] Toker, "İsmet Paşa ile 4 Buhranlı Yıl", *Milliyet*, 4 February 1969, p. 5.
[158] Ibid., 5 February 1969, p. 5.

nuclear missiles and being part of NATO might not deter enemies. Danger of war could arise without warning and Turkey's alliance ties might not be able to do anything about it. This was a serious blow to the long-held security perception of Turkish leaders. It made them accept the withdrawal of the Jupiter missiles without voicing strong complaints. The Turks also understood that a decision taken by Washington might jeopardize Turkey's security and its very existence. The lives of 30 million Turkish people might come under threat because of a disagreement between the two superpowers in a region, which was thousands of miles away from Turkey.

10. The Removal of the Jupiters and its Implications for Turkey

Immediately after the Cuban crisis was over, American officials began to take necessary actions for the removal of the Jupiters. Defence Secretary Robert McNamara said later that at the end of the Cuban crisis, "right away I went back to the Pentagon and ordered them [the Turkish missiles] withdrawn, cut up and photographed so that I could personally see that those missiles had been destroyed."[159] Reportedly McNamara told John McNaugton, the general counsel of the Defence Department: "I'm going to tell you something. I don't want you to ask any questions about it. I don't want you to say to anybody else why it's being done, because I'm not going to tell you, I just want you to do it, and I want every single missile removed out of Turkey."[160] On Monday, 29 October 1962, an interdepartmental task force was assembled to work on the removal of the Jupiters under the chairmanship of McNaughton, who said in the first meeting: "Those missiles are going to be out of there by April 1, [1963] if we have to shoot them out."[161]

On 9 November 1962, Dean Rusk advised President Kennedy that the Jupiters in Turkey and Italy should not be withdrawn in the near future on the grounds that "they were useful sponges in the event of a Soviet first strike because the 45 missiles would be targets for Soviet weapons that would otherwise be aimed at Western Europe... If the Jupiters were soon removed, American credibility would be found wanting, and allies besides Turkey and Italy might no longer trust the United States. But as modern and effective weapons systems come into being... and as the Cuban missile crisis recedes, the phasing out of the [Jupiters] would at a later time be entirely feasible."[162] Rusk's argument was not incompatible with the U.S. promise to the Soviets that the missiles would go in about five months. In early November 1962 and January 1963, McBundy's aide Robert Komer, ignorant of the deal, strongly advised against the withdrawal of the missiles from Turkey, pointing to uncertainties in Turkish political outlook.[163]

In January 1963, Turkish and American officials discussed what should be done about the Jupiter missiles in Turkey. On 9 January 1963, Turkish Foreign Minister Erkin informed the Turkish National Assembly that Turkey would join the joint discussions in NATO, which would consider the value of NATO's present weapon systems. He said that if NATO decided

---

[159] Beschloss, *Kennedy v. Khrushchev*, p. 588n.
[160] Bernstein, "Reconsidering the Missile Crisis", p. 98.
[161] Chayes, *The Cuban Missile Crisis*, p. 98n, Hafner, "Bureaucratic Politics and Those Frigging Missiles", p. 319.
[162] Bernstein, "Reconsidering the Missile Crisis", pp. 98-99.
[163] Ibid., p. 99.

to replace some weapon systems with others because of technological changes it would strengthen the security of NATO and Turkey and, therefore, Turkey would accept it.[164]

Eventually Erkin declared in the Turkish Parliament on 17 February 1963 that the Turkish government officially informed the American ambassador in Ankara that Turkey accepted the American proposal to replace the Jupiter missiles in Turkey with Polaris submarines which would be placed in the Mediterranean.[165] In April 1963, the United States and Turkey exchanged notes for this end.[166] On 25 April, U.S. Defence Secretary McNamara informed President Kennedy, "the last Jupiter came down [in Turkey] yesterday", and it would be flown out at the end of the week. A Polaris submarine with 16 missiles was deployed to the area.[167]

The removal of the Jupiters was met by the Turkish public opinion with a certain degree of caution. Some articles appeared in the press, expressing doubts that the removal of the Jupiters would weaken Turkey's defense system and cause a security gap in deterring the Soviet Union. Some newspaper columnists warned that after the Jupiters were gone, Turkey's strategic importance might seem decreased, therefore foreign aid to Turkey might be reduced.[168] In his speeches to the Turkish Parliament, Foreign Minister Erkin stated that these kinds of doubts expressed by Turkish writers were baseless. He explained that Polaris submarines had many advantages in comparison with the Jupiters, therefore in terms of Turkey's security and defense, the deployment of Polaris submarines was a success for the Turkish government. Denying the loss of Turkey's strategic importance, Erkin also said that American officials gave assurances on the continuity of aid.[169]

In fact, the removal of the intermediate range Jupiters from Turkey did cause a change in its strategic importance. Turkey no longer had nuclear missiles in its territory, which could reach the Soviet Union. Thus it ceased to present a kind of danger to the Soviets, which would attract the first strike in the event of conflict. It no longer held the position of extreme importance in the cold war conflict, which it had occupied in the past.[170] The Turkish military continued to welcome the American strike aircraft, equipped with nuclear weapons, which were stationed in Turkey in accordance with a tactical rotation agreement concluded in February 1957. But these aircraft did not pose such a compelling threat for the Soviets since they had effective surface-to-air missiles to face strike aircraft. In the eyes of the Turkish military leaders, strike aircraft served to assure the American involvement in defending Turkey in the event of a Soviet attack.[171]

---

[164] Sezer, *Kamuoyu ve Dış Politika*, p. 133.

[165] *MMTD*, 17 February 1963, term 1, sess. 2, vol. 13, pp. 222-223.

[166] Harris, *Troubled Alliance*, p. 94.

[167] Bernstein, "Reconsidering the Missile Crisis", p. 99.

[168] Sezer, *Kamuoyu ve Dış Politika*, p. 134, "Durum", *Milliyet*, 4 and 13 February 1963, p. 1, Ecvet Güresin, "NATO'da Görüş Değişikliği ve Toplantılar", *Cumhuriyet*, 20 January 1963.

[169] *MMTD*, 9 January 1963, term 1, sess. 2, vol. 10, p. 629, ibid., 17 February 1963, term 1, sess. 2, vol. 13, pp. 222-225. Former Turkish foreign minister Bayülken told the author that Foreign Ministry officials did not deplore the removal of the Jupiters because they would go any way since they were outdated.

[170] George S. Harris, "Turkey and the United States" in Karpat (ed.), *Turkey's Foreign Policy in Transition*, pp. 58-59, Harris, *Troubled Alliance*, p. 95.

[171] Harris, "Turkey and the United States", pp. 58-59, Harris, *Troubled Alliance*, pp. 94-95.

11. CONCLUSION

The Cuban missile crisis was one of the most important influences on U.S.-Turkish relations during the period of our concern. In particular, it played a part in the cautious attitude of Turkish rulers in military relations with the USA from 1965. It also sharpened the Turkish disappointment over the American attitude toward the Cyprus problem.

It is instructive to consider the relevance of theoretical explanations to this crisis in the light of historical account we have outlined above. The crisis constituted a very good example of costs and dangers of the U.S.-Turkish alliance for its smaller partner, Turkey. The Turks had entered into alliance relations with the USA to protect their security against more powerful enemies, especially the Soviet Union. They had also welcomed the stationing of the Jupiters on their territory, thinking that it would help the defense of Turkey and the whole NATO region. But the crisis showed that alliance relations with one superpower and allowing the presence of its weapons and forces in the country might also attract and increase the threat of the other superpower and drag Turkey into a terrible nuclear war over an issue in the outbreak of which she actively played no role. The Soviets would prefer to attack Turkey as a first step because the similarity between the Cuban and Turkish missiles would justify their action and also attacking the weakest, the smallest link in the Western alliance might have prevented escalation of the conflict.

The crisis also showed difficulties of having alliance relations with a big power for a small state. U.S. authorities had easily put Turkey on the bargaining table without consulting with Turkish rulers. This was totally the opposite of the Turkish attitude of consulting with the Americans even in matters, which did not concern the USA. In cold-war matters the Turks would not dare to take one step before informing U.S. rulers. In this context, the Cuban crisis shows that U.S.-Turkish contacts bore the characteristics of the patron-client relationship at that time. Turkish expectation of reward and praise from the Americans for their steadfast support for the USA during the crisis also fits this pattern. This unconditional Turkish support for the big ally without considering national interests first constitutes another aspect of the patron-client relationship.

The Cuban crisis also reflects the Turkish perception of their alliance with the USA. The Turks had thought that the apparent close relationship between the two countries, which depended on having same ideological principles, required unconditional support for each other. That was why they supported America wholeheartedly during the crisis. They would not expect from the Americans to bargain interests of an ally with the enemy. They would be proved to be wrong in their opinion for the second time later during the Cyprus crises.

The Cuban crisis also confirmed the idea that the agreement between superpowers could be to the disadvantage of small powers. Finally, it should be stated that as was explained earlier, Turkey's strategic location (the stationing of the Jupiters near the Soviet Union) contributed to the outbreak of a conflict between the two superpowers and that the removal of the Jupiters decreased strategic importance of Turkey, thus reduced its bargaining power vis-a-vis the United States.

Chapter 7

THE CYPRUS QUESTION BETWEEN 1960 AND 1965 AND ITS EFFECT UPON TURKISH-AMERICAN RELATIONS

The Cyprus question and the U.S. attitude toward it were major influences on Turkish foreign policy, and undoubtedly played an important role in shaping Turkish-American relations and affected the alliance between the two countries in the 1964-1975 period. It is, therefore, necessary to study the Cyprus question to comprehend characteristics of the two countries' relations and alliance. For the sake of clarity, it is convenient to divide our consideration of this topic into two chapters, each marking separate critical developments in Cyprus that had profound but different influences on Turkish-U.S. relations. The first of these two chapters will examine the effects of the breakdown in 1964-65 of the 1960 constitutional regime. The following chapter will cover the 1974 Sampson coup and the subsequent Turkish military intervention. In the present chapter, the events between 1960 and 1965 will be reviewed briefly and then Cyprus policies of Turkey and the United States and the impact of the Cyprus issue on relations and the alliance between the two countries and on foreign policies of each state, especially Turkey, will be analyzed.

1. THE 1960-1963 PERIOD

The Zurich-London settlement of the Cyprus question in 1959[1] and the subsequent declaration of the independent Republic of Cyprus on 16 August 1960[2] were welcomed by the United States. For American policy-makers a serious matter, which threatened the co-operation of the three NATO, powers, Greece, Britain and Turkey, had been eliminated and thus the stability of the Western alliance had been saved.[3] President Eisenhower praised the settlement as a "a victory for common sense", an "imaginative and courageous act of

---

[1] *Keesing's Contemporary Archives*, 1959-1960, vol. 12, pp. 16643-16647, 16657-16661. (The source gives details of negotiations and agreements.)

[2] Ibid., p. 17730.

[3] Van Coufoudakis, "United States Foreign Policy and the Cyprus Question" in Michael A. Attalides (ed.), *Cyprus Reviewed*, Nicosia: Jus Cypri Association, 1977, p. 108.

statesmanship" and a "splendid achievement".[4] Deputy Under-Secretary of State Murphy endorsed it as a happy solution and the statesmanlike action of America's allies.[5] Subsequently, the Americans expected that Cyprus would join Britain, Greece and Turkey to form a solid bulwark against communism and allow the United States to use its existing communication facilities in Cyprus and the British sovereign base areas on the island.[6]

Turkey was pleased with the settlement of the Cyprus issue since Turkish Cypriots were granted constitutional guarantees, which would protect their existence as a separate community and would provide their participation in the administration effectively.[7] Moreover, Turkey's fears that Cyprus could fall into hands of a hostile state and threaten Turkey's security seemed to be eliminated by the Treaty of Guarantee, which authorized Turkey to intervene militarily in the island to protect the status quo.[8]

It soon became clear that the Turkish and Greek Cypriot communities would not cooperate sufficiently to enable the new regime to work successfully. As early as the summer of 1961, the American administration had worried that the system of guarantees assuring the stability of Cyprus would break down soon. In August 1961, Kennedy said: "It seems to me if the situation is as desperate as we hear it is, we cannot continue to rely upon our policy of hoping that the guarantor powers will shoulder the principal share of the Western burden."[9] In 1962, Kennedy and Vice-President Johnson separately urged Cypriot leaders to act to deter the growth of the communist movement in Cyprus.[10] Nevertheless, the Americans were extremely reluctant to intervene directly in the matter, fearing to alienate their allies, Turkey and Greece.[11] When inter-communal disputes in Cyprus worried the State Department officials in February 1963, Secretary of State Rusk sent a cable to the American Ambassador in London, stating,: "We want Britain to emphasize to Greeks and Turks similarities [in] their present positions and guide them to a common stance and coordinated three-power pressure on Cypriot communities."[12]

The Turkish response to disputes between Turkish and Greek Cypriots on violations of the Cypriot constitution was to send notes warning the Greek side that Turkey would not allow any change in the constitution,[13] but Turkish warnings were mild in order not to cause a crisis.

---

[4] John Reddaway, *Burdened with Cyprus*, London: K. Rustem and Brother, 1986, p. 124.

[5] Elen B. Laipson, "Cyprus: A Quarter Century of U.S. Diplomacy" in John T. A. Koumoulides (ed.), *Cyprus in Transition 1960-1985*, London: Trigraph, 1986, p. 58.

[6] Thomas W. Adams and Alvin J. Cottrell, *Cyprus Between East and West*, Baltimore: John Hopkins Press, 1968, p. 56.

[7] *Keesing's Contemporary Archives*, vol. 12, p. 17069.

[8] Suha Bölükbaşı, *Superpowers and the Third World*, New York: University Press of America, 1988, p. 38. Former Turkish foreign minister Ü. Haluk Bayülken told the author that experienced, high-quality Turkish diplomats obtained successful results on the Cyprus question in the UN in the 1950s and succeeded in getting a favorable solution of the problem so that Turkey was able to have a say in the future of Cyprus in the following years.

[9] H. W. Brands, Jr., "America Enters the Cyprus Tangle, 1964", *Middle Eastern Studies*, vol. 23, No. 3, July 1987, p. 350.

[10] Ibid., p. 350, Bölükbaşı, *Superpowers and the Third World*, p. 54, Adams and Cottrell, *Cyprus Between East and West*, pp. 59-60.

[11] Brands, "America Enters the Cyprus Tangle, 1964", pp. 349, 350-351.

[12] Bölükbaşı, *Superpowers and the Third World*, p. 55.

[13] İnönü's Address in the Turkish National Assembly on 5 May 1964 as quoted by S. Bilge et al., (eds.), Cyprus: Past, Present, Future, Ankara, 1964, pp. 97-99, Foreign Minister Erkin's speech in Parliament on 9 January 1963, *Keesing's Contemporary Archives*, 1963-1964, vol. 14, p. 19257.

2. THE CYPRUS CRISIS OF DECEMBER 1963

On 30 November 1963, Cypriot President Makarios submitted to Turkish Vice-President Küçük a memorandum proposing thirteen substantive amendments to the Cypriot constitution.[14] On 16 December, the Turkish government rejected the entire memorandum as totally unacceptable and insisted that no change whatsoever could be made in the constitution.[15] On 21 December, widespread shootings and killings began in Cyprus when the Turkish community was targeted by the Greek police and ex-terrorist irregulars who wanted the unification of the island with Greece (enosis).[16]

The Turks were convinced that the Greek side had tried to achieve constitutional changes and ultimately enosis by force under a pre-planned program, the Akritas plan.[17] Turkish rulers informed Western states that they took the events in Cyprus seriously and threatened to intervene in the island as a guarantor of the Cyprus system.[18] On 25 December, Turkish jets flew over Cyprus to warn the Greek Cypriots.[19] The Turkish warnings had their effect on 26 December. The Greek Cypriots accepted the establishment of a joint peace force consisting of the Turkish, Greek and British forces on the island.[20]

As the hostilities began and spread over Cyprus, the immediate American concern was to bring about a cease-fire or at least contain the fighting and thus to prevent a military clash between Turkey and Greece and to save the southeastern flank of NATO.[21] The Americans did not want the breakdown of the political system of the Cyprus Republic because it could create conditions that might be exploited by AKEL (the Cypriot Communist Party) and the Russians. The United States also opposed the internationalization of the Cyprus question through the discussion of the problem in the United Nations and preferred its solution within a Western setting securing Western strategic interests. To fulfil these purposes, U.S. officials

---

[14] Bölükbaşı, *Superpowers and the Third World,* pp. 55-56, *Keesing's Contemporary Archives,* vol. 14, p. 20113, Metin Tamkoç, *The Turkish Cypriot State,* London: K. Rustem and Brother, 1988, p. 73, Zenon Stavrinides, *The Cyprus Conflict,* Loris Stavrinides Press, 1976, p. 12.

[15] Robert Stephens, *Cyprus,* London: Pall Mall Press, 1966, p. 180, Dimitri S. Bitsios, *Cyprus: the Vulnerable Republic,* Thessaloniki, Greece: Institute for Balkan Studies, 1975, p. 125, *Keesing's Contemporary Archives,* vol. 14, p. 20113.

[16] Reddaway, *Burdened with Cyprus,* pp. 137-138, Nancy Crawshaw, *The Cyprus Revolt,* London: G. Allen and Unwin, 1978, pp. 366-367, Stephens, *Cyprus,* pp. 182-184, *The Historical Background of Cyprus and the Turkish Republic of Northern Cyprus,* Ankara: The Cyprus-Turkish Cultural Association, pp. 23-24, 31-32, *Keesing's Contemporary Archives,* vol. 14, pp. 20113-20114.

[17] Nihat Erim, *Bildiğim ve Gördüğüm Ölçüler İçinde Kıbrıs,* Ankara: Ajans-Türk, 1975, p. 207, Rauf R. Denktash, *The Cyprus Triangle,* London: K. Rustem and Brother, 1988, pp. 26-27, Bölükbaşı, *Superpowers and the Third World,* p. 57, Nihat Erim, "Reminiscences on Cyprus", *Foreign Policy,* vol. 4, Nos. 2-3, February, 1975, p. 158, Tamkoç, *The Turkish Cypriot State,* p. 74, Yuluğ Tekin Kurat, *Elli Yıllık Cumhuriyetin Dış Politikası 1923-1973,* Ankara: Türk Tarih Kurumu, 1975, pp. 294-295. Independent observers and even Greek Cypriots confirmed the existence of the plan. Clement H. Dodd, *The Cyprus Issue: A Current Perspective,* Huntingdon: the Eothen Press, 1994, p. 4.

[18] Erim, *Bildiğim ve Gördüğüm Ölçüler İçinde Kıbrıs,* p. 208, Bilge, et al. (eds.), *Cyprus,* p. 5, Stephens, *Cyprus,* p. 184, *Keesing's Contemporary Archives,* vol. 14, p. 20114.

[19] Bilge, et al. (eds.), *Cyprus,* p. 7.

[20] Thomas Ehrlich, *Cyprus: 1958-1967,* London: Oxford University Press, 1974, p. 58, Stephens, *Cyprus,* p. 185, Crawshaw, *The Cyprus Revolt,* p. 367, *Keesing's Contemporary Archives,* vol. 14, p. 20114.

[21] Coufoudakis "United States Foreign Policy and the Cyprus Question", p. 110, Joseph S. Joseph, *Cyprus; Ethnic Conflict and International Concern,* New York: Peter Lang, 1985, p. 127, Adams and Cottrell, *Cyprus Between East and West,* p. 56.

urged restraint on all sides and particularly asked the Turks not to intervene in Cyprus[22] though they did not condemn the action of Turkish jet fighters, which were provided under NATO auspices and assigned to the NATO command.[23] To tone down the Turkish threats to invade Cyprus, President Johnson sent a letter on 26 December 1963 to Turkish President Cemal Gürsel, stating that the United States was ready "to support any and all actions proposed by the three guarantor powers which offer any reasonable hope of assisting in a peaceful solution."[24]

The State Department's policy directive to the U.S. representatives in the United Nations on 27 December shows that the United States did not want to get too closely involved in the Cyprus question:

> The U.K., Greece and Turkey have treaty responsibilities. We look to [the] U.K. to take [the] lead to keep debate in constructive channels... The U.S. should take a back seat during debate but should discreetly seek [to] keep discussion in [a] moderate key, particularly when chair... We assume, however, it will be necessary for the U.S. to speak. Our statement should not discuss [the] merits of Cypriot complaint against Turkey or of background issues which brought on recent communal violence, but should stress [the] need for those concerned to work out their differences... [The United States] did not want to do anything to abet [the] Greek Cypriots in their efforts [to] bypass [the 1959] treaties.[25]

W. Averell Harriman, the undersecretary of state for political affairs, summarized his impressions and worries after the UN Security Council meeting on 27 December 1963 in a cable to various American embassies: "The results of this meeting were to weaken current efforts to reestablish law and order on Cyprus, to strengthen the hands of extremists in both communities on Cyprus and in Greece and Turkey and to provide an opportunity for Soviet and other anti-Western propaganda initiatives."[26]

3. THE NATO PLAN OF JANUARY-FEBRUARY 1964

On 25 January 1964, the British Ambassador to Washington, Sir David Ormsby-Gore, informed U.S. Undersecretary of State George Ball that Britain could no longer undertake primary responsibility alone for keeping peace in Cyprus[27] and said that "Her Majesty's government has concluded that it is best to establish an international force on Cyprus, and early rather than later."[28] Such a force could be broadly based, but should include detachments only from NATO countries.[29] When George Ball responded that the United Stated did not want to get involved because it "had far too much on [its] plate", the

---

[22] Bölükbaşı, *Superpowers and the Third World,* pp. 58, 60, Johnson's letter to Turkish and Greek Cypriot leaders in Halil İbrahim Salih, *Cyprus: the Impact of Diverse Nationalism in a State,* Alabama: University of Alabama Press, 1978, p. 35, Brands, "America Enters the Cyprus Tangle, 1964", p. 351.

[23] George S. Harris, *Troubled Alliance,* Washington D.C.: American Enterprise Institute, 1972, p. 108.

[24] Salih, *Cyprus,* p. 35.

[25] Quoted by Bölükbaşı, *Superpowers and the Third World,* p. 61.

[26] Brands, "America Enters the Cyprus Tangle, 1964", p. 351.

[27] George W. Ball, *The Past Has Another Pattern,* New York, London: W. W. Norton, 1982, p. 340, Brands, "America Enters the Cyprus Tangle, 1964", p. 349.

[28] Edward Weintal and Charles Bartlett, *Facing the Brink,* London: Hutchinson, 1967, p. 18.

[29] Ball, *The Past Has Another Pattern,* p. 340.

ambassador warned that if such a NATO force could not be summoned, Britain would turn the Cyprus question over to the United Nations.[30]

On the same day George Ball told Secretary of Defence Robert McNamara and General Maxwell Taylor, "we must tell the British that we have other responsibilities, which we will continue to bear. They must bear theirs."[31] McNamara, too, was reluctant to broaden American responsibilities but "he was fully aware that an exploding Cyprus could not only endanger... Mediterranean position [of America] but undermine the whole southern flank of NATO."[32] In the evening, Ball discussed the matter with President Johnson. The President was reluctant to accept the British proposal, but, since he understood the seriousness of the Cyprus question, he directed Ball to draw up an acceptable solution.[33] Half an hour later George Ball told Ormsby-Gore that the United States would support a NATO force diplomatically and logistically, but that no American troops would be committed.[34] He said, "[we] did not wish [to] move into another political problem with no end in sight... We are prepared to do what we could with Greeks and Turks but [we are] not sure what could be said that [is] new... [The] U.K. should understand that we viewed getting involved with greatest reluctance."[35]

Under constant pressures from Turks that they would invade Cyprus unless the USA did something,[36] the U.S. administration revised its decision in a few days. In order to appease hawkish Turkish commanders and also to warn the Turks on the fatal consequences of unilateral intervention, President Johnson dispatched General Lyman Lemnitzer, the American commander of NATO, to Ankara and Athens on 28 January 1964.[37] By 29 January 1964 President Johnson had decided to approve a plan for the American participation in a peace force.[38] The conditions for participating in the NATO plan were summarized by George Ball to McNamara: "We should insist... 1- that the duration of the force be limited to three months, 2- that the Greeks and Turks agree not to use their unilateral intervention rights for three months, and 3- that they agree on a mediator who was not representative of any of the three guarantor powers but from another NATO European country."[39]

Even after the Greek Cypriot side rejected the NATO plan on 4 February 1964,[40] the United States tried to achieve the implementation of the plan. On 7 February, Secretary of State Dean Rusk stated in a press conference that the United States was willing to participate in a peacekeeping operation in Cyprus with other NATO partners.[41] George Ball was dispatched by President Johnson from 9 February 1964 to Athens, Ankara and Nicosia to sell the plan. In the first stage of his visit, Ball stopped in London on 9 February 1964 to talk to

---

[30] Brands, "America Enters the Cyprus Tangle, 1964", p. 349, Weintal and Bartlett, *Facing the Brink*, p. 18.

[31] Brands, "America Enters the Cyprus Tangle, 1964", p. 352.

[32] Ball, *The Past Has Another Pattern*, p. 341.

[33] Ibid., p. 341.

[34] Brands, "America Enters the Cyprus Tangle, 1964", p. 352.

[35] Bölükbaşı, *Superpowers and the Third World*, p. 63.

[36] Ibid., pp. 63-64, Ball, *The Past Has Another Pattern*, p. 341.

[37] Salih, *Cyprus*, p. 34, Brands, "America Enters the Cyprus Tangle, 1964", p. 352.

[38] Brands, "America Enters the Cyprus Tangle, 1964", p. 352.

[39] Ball, *The Past Has Another Pattern*, p. 341. For the full text of the Anglo -American proposal for a NATO force, which was submitted to the parties concerned on 31 January 1964, see *Keesing's Contemporary Archives*, vol. 14, p. 20116.

[40] For Makarios's note to Britain and the USA see *Keesing's Contemporary Archives*, vol. 14, p. 20116.

[41] Salih, *Cyprus*, p. 33.

British officials. In London, Ball also talked to the Cypriot foreign minister, Sypros Kyprianou. Kyprianou was so adamant in rejecting the NATO plan that, as Brands states,

> Ball came convinced that the idea was futile... He began to fear that even if such a force made it to the island, the American contingent would be singled out for attack by Cypriot terrorists - an opinion seconded by the CIA. However, because the United States had made a commitment to the NATO force, Ball did not want the Johnson administration to be seen as backing out... As he described to Johnson, his plan was to place on Makarios' shoulders the primary onus for... [America's] non-participation.[42]

On 10 February, George Ball talked to Turkish Prime Minister İsmet İnönü in Ankara and persuaded him to accept the NATO plan.[43] İnönü insisted that the United States must "move swiftly; Turkish patience was running out. Given the excited state of public opinion, any overnight flare up of killing on the island might force the Turkish military to intervene... So long as nothing was done to impair Turkey's right of intervention to protect the Turkish Cypriot population, the Turkish government was prepared to go along with the Anglo-American proposal for a NATO force."[44] Meanwhile, on 10 February, the U.S. State Department clarified that the United States had no intention of imposing any solution on any side on the Cyprus question and that it "has no preconceptions or preference as to the shape or form of final solutions that might be developed for the Cyprus problem... The United States must emphasize that it does have a major interest in the maintenance of peace in the eastern Mediterranean... It will do whatever it can to assure that objective."[45]

During their meeting on 12 February, Makarios, the Greek Cypriot President, rejected Ball's proposal for a NATO peace force and suggested that the whole matter of peacekeeping force must be submitted to the UN Security Council. In George Ball's view, "Makarios's central interest was to block off Turkish intervention so that he and his Greek Cypriots could go on happily massacring Turkish Cypriots. Obviously we would never permit that."[46] Ball warned Makarios that if he continued to block a solution that would eliminate Turkey's reason for intervening, "the Turks... would inevitably invade, and neither the United States nor any other Western power would raise a finger to stop them."[47] In the evening, Ball cabled President Johnson and Dean Rusk that "overwhelming pressure must be brought on Makarios to frighten him sufficiently to consider some move to halt the killing."[48]

Meanwhile, on 12 February, Greek Cypriots broke a cease-fire agreement and launched a massive attack against the Turkish positions in Limassol. Rumors then spread that Turkish ships were sailing for Cyprus and later that a military invasion had been prevented by American diplomatic efforts and the deliberate obstruction of the U.S. Sixth Fleet.[49] Secretary of State Rusk instructed George Ball to return to Turkey "to keep [the Turks] at home."[50] In their meeting, Ball wanted İnönü not to intervene in Cyprus until the UN Security Council discussed the issue and assured him that the United Nations would take no action nullifying

[42] Brands, "America Enters the Cyprus Tangle, 1964", p. 353.
[43] Metin Toker, "İsmet Paşa ile 4 Buhranlı Yıl", *Milliyet*, 7 February 1969, p. 5.
[44] Ball, *The Past Has Another Pattern*, p. 343.
[45] Salih, *Cyprus*, p. 33, *Cumhuriyet*, 11 February 1964, p. 7.
[46] Ball, *The Past Has Another Pattern*, pp. 344-345.
[47] Ibid., pp. 342, 345.
[48] Ibid., p. 345.
[49] Stephens, *Cyprus*, p. 189.
[50] Bölükbaşı, *Superpowers and the Third World*, p. 71.

Turkey's intervention right and that Makarios would get a severe lesson at the UN.[51] In Ball's words, "İnönü reluctantly agreed, but emphasized that if there were further serious violence on the island, Turkey would no longer stand still."[52]

When he left Ankara, Ball was convinced that Turkey was seriously thinking of intervening in Cyprus. He cabled to President Johnson from London on 16 February: "we can count on only a few days. Even that time could be foreshortened by a major incident in Cyprus. The Turks are not bluffing."[53] "Both the governments and people of Turkey and Greece want peace, but.. they cannot, by their own unaided efforts, avoid catastrophe. They can be pushed off a collision course only by some outside agency... The Greek Cypriots do not want a peacemaking force; they just want to be left alone to kill Turkish Cypriots."[54] As a last minute attempt, Ball proposed to bypass Makarios entirely and organize a joint peace force composed of Greek, Turkish and British units. It would be an action of the three guarantor powers to exercise their rights of intervention under Article 4 of the Treaty of Guarantee.[55] President Johnson accepted the proposal and asked British Prime Minister Sir Alec Douglas-Home to convene a summit conference to implement the plan,[56] but the British refused to go along with the plan.[57] When Ball reported this to President Johnson, "Johnson agreed that the United States had gone as far as we should try to deflect a tribal conflict. Now our only available course was to work through the United Nations."[58]

The Americans certainly would have liked the discussion of the Cyprus problem within the NATO framework. In this way, they could assert their influence more easily and the involvement of the Eastern bloc and non-aligned countries in a matter, which mainly concerned NATO powers, could be prevented. However, since Makarios was adamant in rejecting it and he was supported by Greek rulers, the Americans saw no way other than allowing the discussion of the matter in the UN.

The Turks had accepted the NATO plan mainly because it provided for American participation. They hoped that the Americans would deter the Greek Cypriots from continuing their atrocities. The spokesman of the Turkish government, A. İhsan Göğüş, expressed pleasure with the U.S. decision of participating in the peace force: "Our great ally America has recognized the importance of the Cyprus question and, therefore, has decided to work for the restoration of peace and security in Cyprus."[59] For Turkish Prime Minister İnönü the U.S. involvement would make it easier for him to call for U.S. mediation during crisis situations and resist the pressures of pro-intervention circles at home.[60] Moreover, the plan would provide for a temporary solution in the absence of Turkish military intervention, which stemmed from Turkey's technical insufficiency.[61] The Turks also preferred the involvement

---

[51] Ball, *The Past Has Another Pattern*, p. 347, Prime Minister İnönü's letter to President Johnson, 13 June 1964, Appendix D, *Middle East Journal*, vol. 20, summer 1966, pp. 386-389, Toker, "İsmet Paşa ile 4 Buhranlı Yıl", *Milliyet*, 7 February 1969, p. 5.

[52] Ball, *The Past Has Another Pattern*, p. 347.

[53] Bölükbaşı, *Superpowers and the Third World*, p. 71.

[54] Brands, "America Enters the Cyprus Tangle, 1964", p. 354, Ball, *The Past Has Another Pattern*, p. 347.

[55] Brands, "America Enters the Cyprus Tangle, 1964", p. 354, Bölükbaşı, *Superpowers and the Third World*, p. 71.

[56] Bölükbaşı, *Superpowers and the Third World*, p. 71, Weintal and Bartlett, *Facing the Brink*, p. 21.

[57] Brands, "America Enters the Cyprus Tangle, 1964", p. 354, Weintal and Bartlett, *Facing the Brink*, p. 21.

[58] Ball, *The Past Has Another Pattern*, p. 348.

[59] *Cumhuriyet*, 30 January 1964, p. 7.

[60] Bölükbaşı, *Superpowers and the Third World*, p. 65.

[61] Toker, "İsmet Paşa ile 4 Buhranlı Yıl", *Milliyet*, 7 February 1969 p. 5.

of NATO rather than the United Nations, which was the aim of the Greek side, fearing that the UN could abolish their role as guarantor power.[62]

4. THE UN SECURITY COUNCIL MEETING ON CYPRUS

Before the UN Security Council met to discuss the Cyprus problem, the United States tried to dissuade Greeks from taking the matter to the UN and working for a resolution which would support mainly the Greek cause and alienate Turkey. Allegedly, U.S. officials threatened the Greek delegation in the UN with not preventing Turkish intervention in Cyprus and proposed to them a draft resolution, which seemed to support the Turkish viewpoint.[63] However, according to Greek representative Bitsios's accounts, on 17 February, he received the following statement from America's UN ambassador, Adlai Stevenson: "Press reports from London that the United States is seeking to isolate Archbishop Makarios, and favors settlement of the communal conflict in Cyprus by partition, are untrue... The United States has no position on the terms of any settlement."[64]

During the 1096th meeting of the Security Council in February 1964,[65] U.S. ambassador Stevenson made the following points: "the Treaty of Guarantee forms an integral part of the organic arrangements that created the Republic of Cyprus. In fact, it is so-called a basic article of the Constitution of Cyprus... This treaty or any international treaty cannot be abrogated, cannot be nullified, cannot be modified either in fact or in effect by the Security Council of the UN"[66]

> The major business before the Council... was the restoration of communal peace and order. His government had no position as to the shape of a final settlement of the Cyprus problem. The leaders of the two communities had to work out their differences together but in the present climate this was patently impossible. The Security Council had therefore to make an effective contribution to the reestablishment of conditions in which a long-term political solution could be sought with due regard to the interests, the rights and the responsibilities of all parties concerned... [The United States] was [not] even proposing that the international force be comprised only of NATO military units [but] recommended that the Council, in consultation with the Secretary General, appeal to the parties concerned to move ahead quickly in working out peace-keeping arrangements to which other states could make a contribution[67].

As the first part of Stevenson's speech supported mainly the Turkish theory of the validity of the London-Zurich agreements, its second part sought a more balancing attitude, which aimed to accommodate the views of both sides.

On 4 March 1964, UN Security Council accepted a different resolution from the Anglo-American proposal, which regarded the London-Zurich agreements as the basis of the independence of Cyprus and which mentioned the rights of the guarantor powers to intervene

---

[62] Philip Windsor, *NATO and the Cyprus Crisis*, London: the Institute for Strategic Studies, 1964, pp. 10-11.

[63] Bitsios, *Cyprus*, pp. 141-146.

[64] Ibid., pp. 142-143.

[65] *Keesing's Contemporary Archives*, vol. 14, pp. 20118-20119.

[66] Salih, *Cyprus*, p. 37.

[67] "Cypriot Complaint of Turkish Aggression and Interference in its Internal Affairs", *International Organisation*, vol. 18, 1964, p. 482.

in Cyprus.[68] Yet the American officials did not consider it a defeat for the United States. They reasoned that their aim, which was endorsed by the resolution, was "to install a UN force as quickly as possible, while assuring that the resolution did not nullify the intervention rights of the guarantor powers, since the Turks would not stand still for that. We sought also to keep the Soviet Union as far as possible out of the action." It was in fact a success for the United States because both sides were happy; "Makarios regarded it as foreclosing the Turkish right to intervene, the Turks saw it as preserving their intervention rights."[69]

The United States endorsed the Security Council resolution which required the establishment of the UN Force in Cyprus (UNFICYP) and the appointment of a mediator. It pledged financial support for the force and help with the airlift of its troops.[70] In the eyes of American officials, UNFICYP "was a satisfactory substitute for a direct NATO presence on the island, since the participating countries did not include any eastern bloc nations."[71] However, the appointment of a mediator did not satisfy American officials entirely, therefore they sought alternative peace mediation ways in the following months.

The Turkish side, too, seemed happy with the acceptance of the Security Council resolution. They welcomed the resolution in their public statements, noting that it did not abrogate Turkey's right of intervention and but would hopefully help the restoration of peace and stability in Cyprus.[72]

When Greek Cypriots attacked Turkish positions in Paphos, Nicosia and Kyrenia on 8 March 1964,[73] the Turkish government sent a strong ultimatum to the Greek Cypriots and informed the United States that it would invade the island if the attacks did not stop.[74] In order to prevent the Turkish action, U.S. officials secured the quick arrival of the UN contingent to Cyprus through intensive diplomatic efforts. Subsequently tension eased and the Turks postponed their action.[75]

5. THE JOHNSON LETTER OF JUNE 1964

a) The Johnson Letter

The Greek Cypriot administration's rapid militarization efforts and its decision to introduce military conscription caused another Cyprus crisis.[76] On 2 June 1964, the Turkish

---

[68] Reddaway, *Burdened With Cyprus*, p. 159. For the text see *Keesing's Contemporary Archives,* vol. 14, p. 20119.

[69] Ball, *The Past Has Another Pattern,* p. 348.

[70] Laipson, "Cyprus: A Quarter Century of U.S. Diplomacy", p. 60.

[71] Ibid., p. 61. On the UNFICYP see also Thomas W. Adams and Alvin J. Cottrell, "American Foreign Policy and the UN Peace Keeping Force in Cyprus", *ORBIS,* vol. 12, No. 2, Summer 1968, pp. 490-503, James M. Boyd, "Cyprus: Episode in Peacekeeping", *International Organisation,* vol. 20, 1966, pp. 1-17, Rosalyn Higgins, "Basic Facts on the U.N. Force in Cyprus", *The World Today,* vol. 20, January-December 1964, pp. 347-350.

[72] Mehmet Gönlübol et al., *Olaylarla Türk Dış Politikası,* Ankara: A.Ü. S.B.F. Yayınları, No. 407, 1977, p. 396.

[73] Bölükbaşı, *Superpowers and the Third World,* p. 72.

[74] Erim, *Bildiğim ve Gördüğüm Ölçüler İçinde Kıbrıs,* pp. 256-257, 264, Bölükbaşı, *Superpowers and the Third World,* p. 73, Bitsios, *Cyprus,* p. 159, *Cumhuriyet,* 13 March 1964, p. 7, Stephens, *Cyprus,* p. 191, *Keesing's Contemporary Archives,* vol. 14, p. 20120.

[75] Bölükbaşı, *Superpowers and the Third World,* p. 73, Prime Minister İnönü's response to President Johnson, Appendix D, *Middle East Journal,* op. cit., p. 389.

[76] *Keesing's Contemporary Archives,* vol. 14, p. 20125, Erol Mütercimler, *Kıbrıs Barış Harekatının Bilinmeyen Yönleri,* İstanbul: Yaprak Yayınevi, 1990, p. 97, Erim, *Bildiğim ve Gördüğüm Ölçüler İçinde Kıbrıs,* p. 298, Theodore A. Couloumbis, *The United States, Greece and Turkey,* New York: Praeger, 1983, p. 62.

National Security Council decided to intervene in Cyprus militarily.[77] Nevertheless, Turkish Prime Minister İnönü decided to consult with American officials before starting military operations, though his foreign minister, F. Cemal Erkin, opposed him, arguing that if the United States were informed of the action it would certainly stop it.[78] On 4 June 1964, İnönü said to U.S. Ambassador Raymond Hare: "all GOT [Government of Turkey] has in mind is [to] occupy part of [the] island and stop there. Greeks could [also] occupy part [of it] and [the UN] force could remain between them. From that position one could get down to meaningful discussion."[79] Hare asked for a twenty-four hour delay of Turkish action to consult with his administration and İnönü accepted it.

Meanwhile, the United States took some actions apparently to prevent a Turkish action. The U.S. commander of NATO, General Lemnitzer, warned Turkish military leaders about possible harmful results of a Turkish military intervention in Cyprus for NATO interests. Allegedly, the Americans positioned a Carrier Task Force of the Sixth Fleet between Cyprus and Turkey to prevent a movement of Turkish troops onto the island[80] and used electronic means to block Turkish communications so that Turks could not carry out the military operations successfully. Rodger Davies, U.S. Deputy Assistant Secretary of State, denied these allegations in his testimony before a Senate committee in 1970. He promised to senators to supply the information where the Sixth Fleet was at that time, but, later, it was recorded in the Senate papers that this information was classified.[81]

In Washington, Secretary of State Dean Rusk, aided by Assistant Secretary of State Harlan Cleveland and his deputy Joseph Sisco, prepared a letter to be sent to the Turkish premier. In the view of Undersecretary of State George Ball, who saw the letter before it was submitted to Johnson, the letter was "the most brutal diplomatic note" which he had ever seen and "the diplomatic equivalent of an atomic bomb." He said to Rusk: "I think that may stop İnönü from invading but I don't know how we'll ever get him down off the ceiling after that. The Secretary looked at me with a sweet smile. 'That'll be your problem' he said."[82] On 5 June 1964, the letter was signed by President Johnson and sent to Turkish Prime Minister İnönü.

In the letter,[83] President Johnson expressed his grave concern on the Turkish decision to intervene by military force to occupy a portion of Cyprus and stated that "such a course of action by Turkey, fraught with such far-reaching consequences, is [not] consistent with the commitment of your government to consult fully in advance with us... I must... first urge you

[77] Weintal and Bartlett, *Facing the Brink*, pp. 21-22, Erim, *Bildiğim ve Gördüğüm Ölçüler İçinde Kıbrıs*, pp. 300, 309.
[78] Cüneyt Arcayürek, *Yeni Demokrasi, Yeni Arayışlar*, Ankara: Bilgi Yayınevi, 1984, p. 274, Mehmet Ali Birand et al., *12 Mart*, Ankara: İmge Kitabevi, pp. 104-105, the author's interview with former Turkish foreign minister Ü. H. Bayülken. Former Turkish diplomat and MP Kamran İnan and Turkish academic Seyfi Taşhan supported Erkin's argument.
[79] Bölükbaşı, *Superpowers and the Third World*, p. 75.
[80] Ibid., p. 76, İlhan Selçuk, "Pencere", *Cumhuriyet*, 9 April 1965, p. 2.
[81] *United States Security Agreements and Commitments Abroad: Greece and Turkey*, Hearings Before the Subcommittee on United States Security Agreements and Commitments Abroad of the Committee on Foreign Relations, U.S. Senate, 91st Congress, 2nd Session, Part 7, June 9 and 11, 1970, Washington: U.S. Government Printing Office, 1970, p. 1831.
[82] Ball, *The Past Has Another Pattern*, p. 350. Former U.S. ambassador Stearns calls the letter, "a startling specimen of diplomatic overkill." Monteagle Stearns, *Entangled Allies*, New York: Council on Foreign Relations Press, 1992, p. 36.
[83] For its text see Appendix D and *Middle East Journal*, vol. 20, Summer 1966, pp. 386-388. The Johnson letter was also studied in Chapter IV in the context of military relations.

to accept the responsibility for complete consultation with the United States before any such action is taken." Johnson claimed that Turkey's action was inconsistent with the Treaty of Guarantee because it did not consult with other guarantor powers and its action would result in partition of the island, which was excluded by the Treaty. Calling İnönü's attention to the possibility of a war between Turkey and Greece as a result of Turkish action, Johnson reminded him that a war between the two countries was unthinkable. He warned that NATO might not help Turkey in case of the Soviet involvement and stated that the USA could not allow the use of U.S.-supplied military equipment by Turkey in its intervention in Cyprus. Finally, Johnson assured İnönü that the United States had "no intention of lending any support to any solution of Cyprus which endangers the Turkish Cypriot community" and would remain "deeply concerned about the interests of Turkey and of the Turkish Cypriots." Johnson also invited İnönü to Washington to discuss the Cyprus question.

In the opinion of American officials, the harshness of Johnson's letter was necessary to deter the Turks effectively from invading Cyprus and thus to prevent likely fatal results.[84] Although the letter aroused bitter resentment in Turkey, American leaders did not regret it and believed that the letter had its desired effect since no Turkish military action was taken. They had the feeling that they had chosen the lesser evil, i.e. alienating the Turks rather than having a war between Greece and Turkey.[85]

It should be noted that the intensive and organized campaigning of Greek-Americans on the Cyprus question influenced at least the timing of the Johnson letter and its undiplomatic, brutal tone because Greek-American votes held importance in the approaching presidential elections.[86] Greek-American individuals and various associations of Greek people including the Orthodox Church had bombarded President Johnson with letters and cables urging him to pressurize Turkey not to invade Cyprus. Many messages referred to Johnson's candidacy for presidency. President Johnson was aware of the importance of Greek-American votes. Greek-Americans were far more numerous than Turkish ones and were located in some of the big urban centers that controlled large numbers of electors. Some Democrats, including Johnson, were concerned that Republican candidate Goldwater would gain their votes by trading on the Cyprus question.

The Turks interpreted the Johnson letter as the abandonment of Turkey by the United States in favor of Greece. Prime Minister İnönü was reported to have said to his cabinet: "Our friends and our enemies have joined hands against us."[87] The letter was perceived as an ultimatum, forcing Turkey to act in a certain way and thus constituting a clear U.S. intervention in Turkey's sovereign affairs.[88] In MP Nihat Erim's words, it included every kind of threat except only one sentence, that was that if Turkey did not comply with the letter's content in a short time, the U.S. Sixth Fleet would have bombed the Turkish ports.[89] According to former Turkish foreign minister Bayülken, high-level Foreign Ministry officials saw Johnson's threat as bluff because they believed that the United States could not let the

---

[84] Weintal and Bartlett, *Facing the Brink*, p. 24, Haluk Şahin, *Gece Gelen Mektup*, İstanbul: Cep Kitapları, 1987, pp. 48-50, Harris, Troubled Alliance, op. cit., p. 115.

[85] Rodger Davies' statement in *United States Security Agreements and Commitments Abroad*, pp. 1834-1835.

[86] For detailed information see Jacob M. Landau, *Johnson's 1964 Letter to İnönü and Greek Lobbying at the White House*, Jerusalem: The Hebrew University Press, 1979.

[87] Ferenc A. Vali, *Bridge Across the Bosporus*, Baltimore: John Hopkins Press, 1971, p. 132.

[88] "Amerikan Elçisinin Siyasi Komiser Edası", *Forum*, 15 January 1966, p. 6, Abdi İpekçi, "Mektup mu, Ültimatom mu?", *Milliyet*, 15 January 1966, p. 1, Bülent Ecevit, "Mektuplar", *Akis*, 22 January 1966, pp. 8-9.

[89] *MMTD*, 29 December 1965, term 2, sess. 1, vol. 2, p. 164.

Soviet Union attack Turkey since it would harm U.S. interests first. This explanation does not reflect the general political atmosphere in Turkey and the tone of Turkish rulers' statements at that time and it does not eliminate the fact that the Turks really feared that they could be abandoned by the West. But the explanation coincides with İnönü's real intention, which will be mentioned later in this chapter.

The Johnson letter was kept secret from the public, but Turkish people knew that it had prevented Turkish military intervention in Cyprus. When the text of the letter was released by the White House in January 1966,[90] the anti-Americanism was already popular among Turkish people. Leftist circles saw it as confirmation of the fact that Turkey was merely a satellite state of the United States.[91] Other people thought that the United States went too far in pressurizing Turkey while not preventing the Greek side from violating rights of the Turkish Cypriots.

The question of why Turkey complied with the Johnson letter should be dealt with here very briefly. One reason might be the fear of Turkish leaders that U.S. military assistance would be suspended. Even American "refusal to furnish repair and replacement parts might have been almost as effective within a short period as the removal of equipment already provided" and might have mutilated Turkish military forces.[92] Secondly, Turkish leaders could not act against the will of the two super-powers, that was why no Turkish MPs suggested intervening in Cyprus and ignoring the American warning during the closed session of the Turkish parliament.[93] The Turks could not afford to have a major rupture in their relations with the USA.[94]

However, the most important reason lies in Turkish Prime Minister İnönü's reluctance to intervene in Cyprus militarily.[95] He was not sure that the Turkish armed forces would achieve a decisive military victory in Cyprus because they were neither trained and equipped nor positioned to undertake a landing on Cyprus.[96] İnönü also feared that a Turkish military intervention in Cyprus might endanger Turkey's security by involving the Soviet Union in the matter.[97] Soviet leaders had already warned Turkey not to invade Cyprus and had announced their support for Makarios in case of an outside aggression. The best option for İnönü was to consult with American rulers and to seek their approval for a military intervention in Cyprus. This could eliminate at least the alienation of the United States. American leaders could give their consent to a limited Turkish military operation and they could prevent an outbreak of war between Turkey and Greece.

Some suggest that İsmet İnönü deliberately informed American leaders of the decision to intervene in Cyprus and he deliberately leaked preparations of the Turkish armed forces to the public. He was sure that the United States would step in and warn Turkish rulers not to resort

---

[90] On the occasion of the release of Johnson and İnönü's letters, the U.S. ambassador to Turkey, Parker T. Hart, stated that U.S.-Turkish relations continued to be friendly even after the exchange of these letters. He showed İnönü's visit to Washington in June 1964 and the joint communiqué at the end of this visit as the proofs of this fact. *Dışişleri Bakanlığı Belleteni*, January 1966, p. 60.

[91] İlhan Selçuk, "Pencere", *Cumhuriyet*, 14 January 1966, p. 2.

[92] Ehlrich, *Cyprus*, p. 84.

[93] Nihat Erim, *MMTD*, 7 October 1964, term 1, sess. 3, vol. 32, p. 327.

[94] *United States Security Agreements and Commitments Abroad*, pp. 1834-1835.

[95] Toker, "İsmet Paşa ile 4 Buhranlı Yıl", *Milliyet*, 7 February 1969, p. 5.

[96] Harris, *Troubled Alliance*, p. 107, Şahin, *Gece Gelen Mektup*, pp. 104-105, Birand et al., *12 Mart*, p. 104. Former Turkish foreign ministers Osman Olcay and Bayülken confirmed this point.

[97] Bölükbaşı, *Superpowers and the Third World*, p. 76.

to military action.[98] Then, İnönü would cancel the military operation and blame the United States for his own inactivity.[99] Thus, he would be able to appease pro-intervention public opinion and military leaders at home. İsmet İnönü also might have assumed that apparent Turkish insistence on military intervention would lead American leaders to put more pressure on the Greek and Greek Cypriot side[100] and would deter Greek Cypriots from attacking the Turkish community in Cyprus.[101] Other instances of İnönü's political acumen lend plausibility to this interpretation.

b) İnönü's Response to Johnson

Writing to Johnson on 13 June 1964,[102] İnönü pointed out that the Turkish government had, at American request, postponed its decision to exercise its right of unilateral action in Cyprus, which was granted by the Treaty of Guarantee. Johnson's message, "both in wording and content", had therefore been disappointing for an ally like Turkey, which had always given the most serious attention to its relations with the United States. Johnson's letter had "brought to the fore substantial divergences of opinion in various fundamental matters pertaining to these relations." Contrary to Johnson's claim, on several occasions, Turkey did consult with the United States and the other guarantor powers on its decision to intervene in Cyprus, and complied with American demands not to intervene though no positive development was achieved in the Cyprus question. However, this did not mean that Turkey gave up its right to intervene in Cyprus. Finally, the Turkish premier stated:

> As a member of the [NATO] alliance our nation is fully conscious of her duties and rights. We do not pursue any other aim than the settlement of the Cyprus problem in compliance with the provisions of the existing treaties. Such a settlement is likely to be reached if you lend your support and give effect with your supreme authority to the sense of justice inherent in the character of the American nation.

At the end of his letter İnönü accepted Johnson's invitation to Washington to discuss the Cyprus problem.

c) Short Evaluation

The Johnson letter constitutes the most important event of U.S.-Turkish contacts on the Cyprus question, which affected the subsequent situation of relations between the two countries. It is clear that the Americans heavily pressured Turkish authorities to prevent their intervention in Cyprus. The Turks had expected U.S. opposition to their planned action, but the severe tone of the U.S. warning certainly disappointed them to the extent they began to have doubts on the value of their alliance with the USA. Up to that point, they had not faced an U.S. action, which appeared to treat Turkey as a satellite. As proud people, the Turks could

---

[98] Metin Toker's statement to a Turkish television documentary, Birand et al., *12 Mart*, p. 105.

[99] Bölükbaşı, *Superpowers and the Third World*, pp. 75-76, Harris, *Troubled Alliance*, p. 114, Şahin, *Gece Gelen Mektup*, p. 105.

[100] Harris, *Troubled Alliance*, p. 114.

[101] Metin Tamkoç, *The Warrior Diplomats*, Salt Lake City: University of Utah Press, 1976, pp. 266-267.

[102] For the letter's text see Appendix D and *Middle East Journal*, vol. 20, Summer 1966, pp. 388-393.

not stomach Johnson's threats putting Turkey in a position of puppet state, which was expected to listen to advice from its big partner. The most unacceptable thing for Turkish rulers was the use of the U.S.-Turkish alliance (which was supposed to serve Turkish interests) by the Americans as a threat to prevent their action in a vital national interest. The Americans probably made a mistake by ignoring realities of Turkish politics and interests and by concentrating only on prevention of Turkish intervention which was expected to bring grave dangers for NATO and U.S. interests.[103]

6. THE AMERICAN MEDIATION EFFORTS ON THE CYPRUS PROBLEM

a) George Ball's Visit to Greece and Turkey

From the outset of the Cyprus crisis, the United States tried to pursue a policy, which would not alienate both Greece and Turkey. After sending a harsh letter to the Turks, President Johnson felt that an equally severe presentation should be made to Greek rulers, warning them not to provoke the Turks on the Cyprus question. Johnson also thought that neither the NATO machinery nor the United Nations mediation efforts would provide a solution to the Cyprus issue, and that therefore the United States should intervene in the matter directly, offering its mediation between the concerned parties. He considered it necessary to encourage Turkey and Greece to find a solution to the problem through bilateral talks. In order to achieve these aims, Undersecretary of State George Ball was dispatched to Greece and Turkey in mid-June 1964.

In Athens, on 10 June 1964, Ball told Greek Prime Minister Papandreou that "disaster was avoided only by President Johnson's forceful intervention and his adamant insistence that there could be no war between NATO allies"[104] and that if Greece did not show greater co-operation, the United States would not take such a hard line again.[105] When Papandreou complained about Turkish intervention threats, Ball said that "nobody could determine how the threat of intervention contributed to the turbulence over Cyprus, nor how the turbulence gave reality to the intervention threat."[106] Reiterating that the United States had no formula for a Cyprus settlement and was committed to no side in the matter, Ball informed Papandreou that President Johnson was of the opinion that only the prime ministers of Turkey and Greece could work out a satisfactory formula for a settlement through mutual concessions. Pressing the Greek prime minister to undertake talks with the Turkish prime minister, Ball said: "If you, Mr. Prime Minister, and the Turkish government, take no immediate and effective action, the Cyprus crisis can expand into war, or open the way to communism in the eastern Mediterranean."[107] Papandreou seemed unmoved, he did not accept Ball's proposal. In Ball's words, "against all the evidence, he [Papandreou] still seemed to assume that Greece could pursue its goal of enosis without danger of the Turks invading Cyprus, since he apparently took it for granted that the United States would always

---

[103] Stearns, *Entangled Allies*, p. 24.

[104] Weintal and Bartlett, *Facing the Brink*, pp. 25-26.

[105] Ball, *The Past Has Another Pattern*, p. 353, Andreas Papandreou, *Democracy at Gunpoint*, London: Andre Deutsch, 1970, p. 101.

[106] Weintal and Bartlett, *Facing the Brink*, p. 26.

[107] Weintal and Bartlett, *Facing the Brink*, p. 26, Ball, *The Past Has Another Pattern*, p. 353, Papandreou, *Democracy at Gunpoint*, p. 101.

stand ready to thwart the Turks."[108] Nevertheless, Ball persuaded Papandreou to visit the United States to have talks with President Johnson.[109]

In his meeting with Prime Minister İnönü in Ankara on 11 June,[110] in his own words, Ball "reassured him regarding the warmth of America's friendship for Turkey and our desire to cooperate closely with the Turks in resolving a festering quarrel... America, I told him, was not partial to the Greek side; indeed, we recognized that the Greek Cypriot majority had largely created the problem by terrorizing the Turkish Cypriots. I made clear that we totally mistrusted Makarios... İnönü was deeply troubled and personally hurt by the scolding he had received from President [Johnson]." After Ball gave reassurances, İnönü said that the American "attempt to promote a settlement based on strong principles is an encouraging development, but experience had shown that principles are sometimes abandoned when the time comes to translate them into concrete measures."[111] İnönü also told Ball that Johnson's letter included "all the juridical thunderbolts that could be assembled. And, of course, as a result, you have committed some errors and some unjust things. Our foreign office will answer the thunderbolts."[112] The U.S.-Turkish joint communiqué on the same day stated that America believed that any solution of the Cyprus problem should be compatible with the interests of both Turkey and Greece.[113]

b) The Visits of the Turkish and Greek Prime Ministers to the USA

İnönü's visit to the United States took place between 22 and 26 June 1964. The joint Turkish-American communiqué on 23 June reaffirmed the validity and binding effects of the existing treaties on Cyprus as a starting point for a new solution.[114] This was considered a great success by Turkish rulers because the validity of the Cyprus treaties was their main viewpoint. In his press conference in New York on 25 June, İnönü stated: "We believe in the present regime in Cyprus, which is based on the Cypriot constitution and the international agreements on Cyprus. But we even accept enosis on the condition that it should be implemented with its original form, i.e. one part of the island is left to Turkey, another to Greece."[115] According to accounts by Nihat Erim, who was in İnönü's official delegation, officials from the State Department inquired the opinion of the Turkish delegation on the proposal of leaving Cyprus to Greece in return for a Greek island on the Aegean Sea.[116] The Americans also showed that they were not worried about the arrival of pro-enosist Greek General Grivas in Cyprus, arguing that he had gone there to fight communists, not the Turks.[117] It seems that enosis in return for some concessions to Turks was on the agenda even at that time.

---

[108] Ball, *The Past Has Another Pattern*, p. 353.
[109] Papandreou, *Democracy at Gunpoint*, p. 101.
[110] *Cumhuriyet*, 12 June 1964.
[111] Ball, *The Past Has Another Pattern*, p. 354.
[112] Weintal and Bartlett, *Facing the Brink*, p. 28.
[113] *Cumhuriyet*, 12 June 1964.
[114] Erim, *Bildiğim ve Gördüğüm Ölçüler İçinde Kıbrıs*, p. 329, *Dışişleri Bakanlığı Belleteni*, July 1964, pp. 16-17, *Keesing's Contemporary Archives*, vol. 14, p. 20268.
[115] Erim, *Bildiğim ve Gördüğüm Ölçüler İçinde Kıbrıs*, p. 330, Murat Sarıca et al., *Kıbrıs Sorunu*, İstanbul: İstanbul Üniversitesi Yayınları, 1975, p. 76.
[116] Erim, *Bildiğim ve Gördüğüm Ölçüler İçinde Kıbrıs*, p. 328.
[117] Ibid., p. 334.

During Greek Prime Minister Papandreou's visit to Washington on 24 and 25 June 1964, President Johnson and other high-level U.S. officials allegedly pressured him to have direct talks with Turkish Prime Minister İnönü on the Cyprus problem by threatening that otherwise they would not prevent a Turkish military intervention in the island.[118] But Papandreou remained unmoved. In Ball's words, Johnson "liked Prime Minister İnönü, with whom he could talk straight forwardly. If the Greek leader had shown anything like the same understanding, serious progress could have been made."[119] On 26 June, George Ball proposed to the Greek delegation that Greek and Turkish representatives meet separately in Geneva with Dean Acheson, former secretary of state.[120] After UN Secretary-General U Thant gave consent to the plan on the condition that talks would be held under the chairmanship of the UN mediator, Greeks, too, accepted it.[121]

In order to ensure that Greek-Turkish bilateral talks would take place, Johnson sent a letter to Papandreou on 2 July 1964, urging him to send delegates to Geneva.[122] Papandreou responded harshly against the United States, asserting that Johnson's letter was an ultimatum of the same kind Greece had received from the Nazis in 1940.[123] Nevertheless, he reiterated his promise to send delegates to Geneva.

While encouraging the Turks and the Greeks to have direct talks under the auspices of American mediation, American officials emphasized that their efforts were not intended to forestall the UN mediation. When the U.S. administration was criticized in the UN because of its attempt, the White House issued a statement claiming that the American initiative was not incompatible with the UN mediation efforts. The statement noted that the peacekeeping and peace-making role belonged entirely to the United Nations and the only aim of the American efforts was to prevent an armed combat in the eastern Mediterranean.[124]

c) The Acheson Mission

The Geneva talks between Turkish and Greek representatives began on 8 July 1964 under the chairmanship of UN mediator Sakari Tuomioja. No Cypriot representative had been called to the talks. Dean Acheson was present at Geneva as the special envoy of President Johnson, but he undertook the actual mediation responsibility. On 14 July, Acheson submitted his proposals, the Acheson plan, to the Turkish and Greek delegations headed by Nihat Erim and Nicolareisis: Cyprus was to be free to choose to unify itself with Greece (enosis). On the Carpas peninsula in the northeast of Cyprus a territory was to be given to Turkey. This territory was to become an indivisible part of Turkey and Turkey was to have full sovereignty over it and to have the right of stationing as large a military force as it wished on the territory.

---

[118] Papandreou, *Democracy At Gunpoint,* pp. 102-104. Greeks had received the same warnings from the U.S. ambassador to Athens and President Johnson through the Greek ambassador in Washington in the first two weeks of June. Brands, "America Enters the Cyprus Tangle", p. 355.

[119] Ball, *The Past Has Another Pattern,* p. 355. See also *Keesing's Contemporary Archives,* vol. 14, p. 20268.

[120] Papandreou, *Democracy at Gunpoint,* p. 103.

[121] Ball, *The Past Has Another Pattern,* pp. 355-356, Weintal and Bartlett, *Facing the Brink,* pp. 28-29.

[122] Coufoudakis, "United States Foreign Policy and the Cyprus Question", *Cyprus Reviewed,* p. 113, Salih, *Cyprus,* p. 47.

[123] Ball, *The Past Has Another Pattern,* p. 356, Weintal and Bartlett, *Facing the Brink,* p. 30.

[124] Bitsios, *Cyprus,* p. 166.

The Greek island of Kastellorizion (Meis) was to be ceded to Turkey.[125] In Acheson's own words, his plan was to bring about the union of Cyprus with Greece, but it would also provide for Turkey "a military presence unhampered by the need for tripartite consent at every turn. A sequestered base for ground, air and sea forces not only could be a defense for Cyprus but prevent its being used against Turkey, could defend the sea approaches to the south Turkish seaports, and be a constant reminder on the island of Turkish presence and interests."[126]

It seemed that the Acheson plan could solve the Cyprus problem permanently to the advantage of the United States and the West. If it were implemented, Cyprus would be removed from the non-alignment camp and would be placed in the NATO sphere. The power of Makarios and AKEL, which were thought to be harmful to Western interests, would be neutralized. The friction between two NATO allies would be eliminated and the alienation of Turkey and Greece from the Western alliance would be prevented. The extension of Soviet influence to the region would be blocked.[127]

For Turkish rulers, the Acheson plan seemed to satisfy Turkey's interests. Hence, the Turkish government authorized the Turkish delegation to continue negotiations on the basis of the Acheson plan and to try to achieve the enlargement of Turkish sovereign base area.[128] During the talks, while Nihat Erim emphasized Turkey's security interests on Cyprus and the necessity for Turkish control over a portion of the island, Turkish commander Turgut Sunalp claimed that the base area offered to Turkey was too small to provide for enough space for Turkey's military activities.[129] The Greek delegation totally opposed the secession of Cypriot territory to Turkey and instead they offered to lease a small base to Turkey for twenty-five years.[130] Meanwhile, the talks were interrupted by the outbreak of new violence in Cyprus.

It should be noted that during the summer of 1964 American officials considered exploiting the hostility between Greek Cypriot leader Makarios and Greek General Grivas to solve the Cyprus problem. American intelligence had reported that the antipathy between the two persons still existed and was growing. "Though Grivas was... a passionate advocate of enosis", George Ball thought that "he might be easier to work with than Makarios" and established an underground contact with Grivas through Socrates Iliades, the chief lieutenant to Grivas.[131] Ball and Grivas agreed that Cyprus would be united with Greece and as compensation some bases would be turned over to Turkey. Makarios, who was the chief obstacle to such designs, would be ousted.[132] When clashes broke out in Cyprus in August, all these schemes were upset.

---

[125] Erim, *Bildiğim ve Gördüğüm Ölçüler İçinde Kıbrıs,* pp. 351-359, Salih, *Cyprus,* pp. 47-48. Articles, which are related to only Cyprus, were ignored.

[126] Polyvious G. Polyviou, *Cyprus: the Tragedy and the Challenge,* Washington: American Hellenic Institute, 1975, p. 47, Salih, *Cyprus,* p. 50, Adams and Cottrell, *Cyprus Between East and West,* p. 66.

[127] Couloumbis, *The United States, Greece and Turkey,* p. 47, Michael A. Attalides, *Cyprus: Nationalism and International Politics,* Edinburgh: Q Press ltd., p. 19, P. N. Vanezis, *Makarios,* London: Abelard-Schuman, 1974, p. 133.

[128] Erim, *Bildiğim ve Gördüğüm Ölçüler İçinde Kıbrıs,* pp. 360, 372.

[129] Ibid., pp. 347-350, 359-362.

[130] Ibid., pp. 363-366, 372-373, 376-378.

[131] Ball, *The Past Has Another Pattern,* p. 357.

[132] Ibid, p. 357, Coufoudakis, "United States Foreign Policy and the Cyprus Question", p. 116, Attalides, *Cyprus,* p. 70, Brands, "America Enters the Cyprus Tangle, 1964", p. 357, Weintal and Bartlett, *Facing the Brink,* p. 32.

d) The August 1964 Fighting in Cyprus

On 6 August 1964, the Greek Cypriot forces under the command of General Grivas[133] launched a major attack from land and sea against the Turkish positions in the Kokkina-Mansoura area in the northwestern part of the island.[134] The Turkish leaders feared that, encouraged by Turkey's inactivity, Greek Cypriots would try to resolve the Cyprus question by force and remove the major pockets of Turkish Cypriot resistance. Nihat Erim told Prime Minister İnönü that he had the impression from his talks with American mediator Acheson that the Americans would not oppose a limited military action to give a lesson to Archbishop Makarios.[135] On 8 August, Turkish jet fighters, which were bought from the United States, bombed the positions of Greek forces around Kokkina.[136]

American officials moved to contain the fighting in Cyprus and prevent a possible Greco-Turkish war. At the night of 8 August 1964, President Johnson sent identical letters to Makarios, Papandreou and İnönü, urging the greatest possible restraint.[137] Dean Rusk's cable to Papandreou asked him to cooperate with General Grivas in neutralizing Makarios, who was threatening a general massacre in Cyprus unless the Turkish air raids were stopped. On August 9, Rusk sent a cable to the U.S. ambassador to Greece, Henry Labouisse, stating that while the USA was pressuring the Turks to halt their air raids, Papandreou must abandon "horsetrading or equivocation or passionate oratory and act decisively to restore peace in Cyprus".[138]

In New York the UN Security Council accepted a resolution which was prepared by U.S. and British representatives.[139] The resolution requested the interested parties to establish a cease-fire and to refrain from any action liable to aggravate the situation. During Security Council talks U.S. Ambassador Adlai Stevenson emphasized that all hostilities should stop because as long as any of them continued all would continue and it would mount up to a dangerous international war.[140] With Soviet Premier Khrushchev's urging,[141] Makarios accepted the UN's cease-fire call. In spite of strong opposition by members of the Turkish National Security Council, Turkish Prime Minister İnönü, too, ordered the cessation of aerial bombing.[142]

---

[133] Grivas had secretly returned to Cyprus with the knowledge of the Greek government. He openly announced that his intention was to unify Cyprus with Greece. *Keesing's Contemporary Archives*, vol. 14, p. 20270.

[134] Ehlrich, *Cyprus*, pp. 62-63, Stephens, *Cyprus*, p. 196, Crawshaw, *The Cyprus Revolt*, p. 371, Salih, *Cyprus*, p. 50, *Keesing's Contemporary Archives*, vol. 14, p. 20265.

[135] Erim, *Bildiğim ve Gördüğüm Ölçüler İçinde Kıbrıs*, p. 381.

[136] Sarıca et al., *Kıbrıs Sorunu*, p. 81, Bölükbaşı, *Superpowers and the Third World*, pp. 82-83, Bitsios, *Cyprus*, p. 170, Salih, *Cyprus*, p. 51, Weintal and Bartlett, *Facing the Brink*, pp. 32-33, *Keesing's Contemporary Archives*, vol. 14, p. 20270.

[137] Weintal and Bartlett, *Facing the Brink*, p. 33, Brands, "America Enters the Cyprus Tangle, 1964", p. 357, *Keesing's Contemporary Archives*, vol. 14, p. 20266.

[138] Weintal and Bartlett, *Facing the Brink*, pp. 33-34.

[139] *Keesing's Contemporary Archives*, vol. 14, p. 20265.

[140] Bitsios, *Cyprus*, pp. 173-174.

[141] Weintal and Bartlett, *Facing the Brink*, p. 34.

[142] Erim, *Bildiğim ve Gördüğüm Ölçüler İçinde Kıbrıs*, p. 393, Arcayürek, *Yeni Demokrasi Yeni Arayışlar*, p. 283, Tamkoç, *The Warrior Diplomats*, p. 275, *Keesing's Contemporary Archives*, vol. 14, p. 20266.

e) The Second Acheson Plan

On 15 August 1964, the Greek and Turkish representatives met again with the UN mediator and Dean Acheson in Geneva. On 20 August, Dean Acheson put forward his so-called Second Acheson Plan whose main aim was to overcome the objections of the Greek side: 1- Cyprus was to be free in choosing enosis. 2- A military base on the Carpas peninsula was to be leased to Turkey for fifty years. 3- The Greek government was to give strong guarantees to the Turkish Cypriot community regarding human and minority rights. 4- With the consent of the Greek and Turkish governments, a high commissioner from an international organization was to be appointed for Cyprus.[143]

On 21 August, the Turkish delegation informed Acheson that the Turkish government decided to reject the plan because the renting of a small territory in return for enosis did not meet Turkey's long-term security interests.[144] Acheson told the Turkish representatives that he was not going to press the Greeks to make more concessions. The plan was the last opportunity to find a peaceful solution to the problem with the help of the American administration. If the Turks rejected it, no NATO countries would appreciate Turkey's position.[145] The Greek side, too, rejected the plan because of Makarios's opposition.[146]

On 18 August 1964, Dean Acheson had sent a message to George Ball, suggesting that he should "liquidate" the Geneva effort. Ball responded that this would encourage Makarios to drive the island into another crisis and bring about Turkish military intervention. In his next cable to Ball, Acheson stated that the United States should stop irritating the Turks and Greeks by trying to pressure them into a Cyprus agreement. If the United States walked away, both sides would realize that they alone were responsible for finding a way out. Finally Acheson said that if an American retreat from Cyprus brought on a showdown with Makarios, "then let it come."[147] After the rejection of the second Acheson plan by both sides, the American administration adjourned its Geneva efforts on 31 August 1964 by calling Acheson to Washington.

f) The Aftermath of the Geneva Talks

In September 1964, at a meeting of top U.S. officials including President Johnson, Dean Acheson stated that a stalemate was reached in the Cyprus question because of Makarios's adamant attitude and that a violent and uncontrolled Turkish invasion of the island would be inevitable unless something was done. Acheson and Ball argued that the only solution to the problem was the *fait accompli* of a controlled Turkish invasion of the island. In their plan, the Turks would seize the part of Cyprus, which they would have received under the first Acheson plan and then the Greek and Greek Cypriots would instantly proclaim the unification of the rest of Cyprus with Greece.[148]

---

[143] Erim, *Bildiğim ve Gördüğüm Ölçüler İçinde Kıbrıs*, pp. 399-400, Sarıca *et al.*, *Kıbrıs Sorunu*, pp. 82-83, Salih, *Cyprus*, p. 49.

[144] Erim, *Bildiğim ve Gördüğüm Ölçüler İçinde Kıbrıs*, p. 401.

[145] Ibid., pp. 402-404, Toker, "İsmet Paşa ile 4 Buhranlı Yıl", *Milliyet*, 11 February 1969, p. 5.

[146] *Keesing's Contemporary Archives*, vol. 14, p. 20269.

[147] Weintal and Bartlett, *Facing the Brink*, pp. 34-35.

[148] Brands, "America Enters the Cyprus Tangle, 1964", pp. 358-359.

In fact, Acheson had raised the issue with the Turks during the Geneva talks. On 4 August 1964, he told the Turkish delegation that he did not advise them to resort to military force, but if they did so, America would not oppose them.[149] After the rejection of the second Acheson plan, Acheson said to the Turkish delegation again: "I am privately and friendly telling you: If you can invade the part of Cyprus which was reserved for you without causing too much bloodshed, the Sixth Fleet does not obstruct your way but protects you." Turkish commander General Turgut Sunalp took the proposal to İnönü the next day. İnönü rejected it by saying that he could not initiate such an adventure without the official approval of the American administration.[150]

In the September meeting, Acheson and Ball told President Johnson that the Turks liked their scheme and all that was required to put the plan into motion was a signal from Washington. When Johnson summed up the scheme by saying that a resort to force was inevitable and that the only question was "whether it should be messy and destructive or controlled and eventually productive, in accordance with a plan," Acheson agreed that this was a fair summary. Initially Johnson seemed interested in the proposal, but, in the end, he rejected it. The Vietnam War was already a major trouble for him, he could not consent to the outbreak of another one. He thought that Turkish invasion might not be as clean as Acheson and Ball expected and that it might escalate to a major war. At least, the next few months would not be a good season for a war because of the approaching presidential election.[151]

American officials were generally of the opinion that the Greek side was primarily responsible for the failure of the Geneva talks. A few months later Dean Acheson wrote to the U.S. ambassador to Egypt:

> We came to close an understanding which might have cropped the Archbishop's whiskers and solved the idiotic problem of Cyprus to your Mr. Nasser's disappointment and chagrin. Our weakness was Papandreou's weakness... He gave away our plans at critical moments to Makarios... A little money, which we had, the Greek 7th Division in Cyprus, which the Greeks had, and some sense of purpose in Athens, which did not exist, might have permitted a different result. The Turks could not have been more willing to cooperate.[152]

In his speech before the Chicago Bar Association on 24 March 1965, Dean Acheson said:

> There was little doubt that from a legal point of view the treaties were binding upon the parties... Merely to restrain the Turks from intervention would be, in fact, to intervene against them... Time was running strongly against the Turks, due to the military build up on the island and the Archbishop's increasing pressure to crush Turkish Cypriot resistance to his imposed regime... The Turks were quite willing to pick up discussions at the point where the Kokkina fighting interrupted them. But they saw that in making any further concession to unresponding Greeks, they would merely be negotiating with themselves.[153]

President Johnson scolded the Greek ambassador to Washington harshly because of the Greek stubbornness on the problem.[154]

---

[149] Erim, *Bildiğim ve Gördüğüm Ölçüler İçinde Kıbrıs*, p. 369.
[150] Ibid., p. 406.
[151] Brands, "America Enters the Cyprus Tangle, 1964", pp. 359-360.
[152] Ibid., p. 358.
[153] Seyfi Taşhan, "Turkish-US Relations and Cyprus", *Foreign Policy*, vol. 4, Nos. 2-3, February 1975, pp. 168-169.
[154] Brands, "America Enters the Cyprus Tangle, 1964", p. 358.

In September 1964, the UN Security Council, too, discussed the Cyprus question. U.S. ambassador Stevenson stated that the United States disapproved any air attacks on Cyprus launched from outside, hinting Turkish air attacks against the island. He also clarified that the United States had never agreed to the use of arms furnished under its military assistance for any purpose not specified in assistance agreements.[155]

7. THE U.S. POLICY TOWARD THE CYPRUS QUESTION

The main American concern on the Cyprus question was to contain the conflict and to prevent it from escalating to a greater war between Greece and Turkey. The deterioration of relations and outbreak of an armed combat between Turkey and Greece, which were strategically important allies of the USA,[156] contained the following dangers: Firstly, NATO could be destabilized and weakened in facing the enemy camp and its southeastern flank could collapse. Secondly, the political, military and economic co-operation between the United States, Greece and Turkey could be undermined and thus the presence of American bases and facilities in these countries could be threatened. Thirdly, the Soviet Union could have the opportunity to destabilize the Western camp by involving itself in a matter concerning NATO countries. Finally, the prestige of the Western alliance could be harmed since the hostility would be a great embarrassment to the Western bloc and a symbol of the Western disunity.

As a result of this thinking, American officials paid attention to the possibility that the Cyprus question could push Turkey and Greece to sever their ties with NATO and to seek better relations with the Soviet Union to the extent that they could fall under Soviet influence. Turkey's efforts in this direction led the Americans to be more careful in not alienating the Turks with their attitude on the Cyprus question. They sought assurances from Turkish leaders that these efforts would not weaken their ties with the Western alliance.

The United States had strategic concerns over Cyprus in the 1960s. The island is located at the crossroads of the three continents and the major routes connecting the West with the East. It is 44 miles south of Turkey, 64 miles west of Syria, 130 miles northwest of Israel, and 240 miles north of Egypt and the Suez Canal.[157] Cyprus commanded the outlets of the pipelines on the coasts of Syria, Lebanon, Israel and Egypt, the northern entrance of the Suez Canal and the line of containment of the Soviet Union along its southern borders.[158] Some developments in the 1960s seemed to increase the strategic importance of the island: "the growth of Soviet political and military missions in various Arab states, the growth of the Soviet fleet in the area; the continuing Arab-Israel crisis; the increasing American concern about Middle Eastern oil supplies and the protection of oil shipping routes; the prospect of a reopened Suez Canal and the loss of American bases and base rights in the area."[159] Cyprus could provide useful bases in the eastern Mediterranean for the West.

---

[155] *International Organisation*, vol. 19, 1965, p. 87.
[156] H. J. Psomiades, "the United States and the Mediterranean Triangle; Greece, Turkey and Cyprus: a New Phase" in Attalides (ed.), *Cyprus Reviewed*, p. 201, Couloumbis, Couloumbis, *The United States, Greece and Turkey*, pp. 24, 28.
[157] Joseph, *Cyprus*, p. 119.
[158] Stephen G. Xydis, " Cyprus: What Kind of Problem" in Attalides (ed.), *Cyprus Reviewed*, p. 28.
[159] Coufoudakis, "United States Foreign Policy and the Cyprus Question", p. 109.

The British retained two sovereign Cyprus bases, Dhekelia and Akrotiri, and enjoyed the privileges of military use of Cypriot air space, transport and land. They could allow the United States to benefit from the same facilities whenever they wanted. Akrotiri especially was a very important RAF base and could be used by the United States and NATO to support operations in the Middle East and to defend NATO's southeastern flank.[160] Makarios had already allowed the United States to use communication facilities in Cyprus, including radio listening and broadcasting stations and the horizon radar installations for the detection of ICBM launches in the Soviet Union and communications between Middle Eastern and Eastern bloc countries.[161] It was important for the Americans to prevent Cyprus from falling into the hands of enemies. They would have preferred the island to come under NATO control (as a consequence of enosis or partition) than to remain under the Cypriot administration that pursued a policy of non-alignment. But their priority lay in having good relations with Greece and Turkey. The U.S. position in the eastern Mediterranean was much more dependent on Greek and Turkish bases than the Cypriot ones.[162]

In the minds of U.S. officials, the first thing, which should be done on the Cyprus question, was to bring the violence and clashes in Cyprus to an end. This could open a way to negotiations between the interested parties to find a political settlement. The Americans pressurized the parties to the conflict from time to time to refrain from taking any actions which would worsen the situation in Cyprus. They particularly put pressure on the Turks to deter them from invading the island. In order to maintain peace, the United States also supported the United Nations peacekeeping force in Cyprus diplomatically and materially. U.S. leaders preferred all attempts to seek a solution to be made through quiet diplomacy. They did not want a problem concerning Western states to be aired in international forums, thinking that it would provide an opportunity to enemies to undermine and humiliate the Western bloc.

American leaders were generally reluctant to put forward a proposal for the Cyprus question because they feared that their proposal would alienate at least one ally. They frequently announced that the United States was in favor of a settlement, which would protect the interests of all the interested parties. They thought that only an agreed settlement between Greece and Turkey through bilateral talks could bring a permanent solution to the problem because the two states had the power to influence the Cypriot communities. For this purpose, the United States pressed Turkish and Greek officials especially in the summer of 1964 to come together to find a peaceful way of the Cyprus problem. During these bilateral talks, the United States came up with a proposal to be discussed by the two sides, which could be called enosis, partition or double enosis. It seemed that the present position of independent Cyprus did not suit Western and American interests because it was very likely that it could attract Soviet influence to the region and cause a war between Turkey and Greece.

The unification of the island with Greece (enosis) with some concessions to Turkey could solve the problem in accordance with the Western interests. In this way, Cyprus would be put into NATO's ranks, a communist take over in the island would be prevented and Greece and Turkey would be kept happy. The Geneva talks and the Acheson plans were directed to achieving this aim. When it was understood that this scheme would not be successful,

---

[160] Attalides, *Cyprus,* p. 158.
[161] Ibid., p. 13, Pierre Oberling, *The Road to Bellapais,* New York: Columbia University Press, 1982, p. 124.
[162] John C. Campbell, "The United States and the Cyprus Question, 1974-1975" in Van Coufoudakis (ed.), *Essays on the Cyprus Conflict,* New York: Pella Publishing, 1976, p. 14.

American policy shifted to the acceptance of a unitary independent Republic of Cyprus so long as the NATO alliance was not damaged by the situation in the island. But American politicians always kept the enosis scheme as an alternative in case other solutions failed and encouraged the Greek and Turkish governments to hold secret bilateral talks on the question.

Another American concern related to the Cyprus question was to prevent communist influence from advancing in the Mediterranean region. At that time, it seemed that the Soviets had changed the balance of power and gained the upper hand in the Middle East by having a close relationship with non-aligned, anti-Western Arab regimes. If Cyprus fell under Soviet influence, the Western interests in the eastern Mediterranean and the Middle East could be damaged greatly. To restore the balance of power in the region it was vital to keep the Soviet influence away from Cyprus.

American officials had already been alerted by the policies of the Cypriot administration. The Makarios regime had appealed to the Soviet Union for support on the Cyprus question and showed readiness to rely on the Soviet support to protect its security. It signed trade agreements with the Soviet Union and made contacts to obtain Soviet weapons. The Cypriot government also pursued a non-aligned policy in its foreign relations and had close contacts with the non-aligned countries, especially with Nasser of Egypt, who seemed to pursue anti-Western policies. It rejected all Western designs for the Cyprus problem, gave communists a respectable political role in the state machinery, announced that it rejected all military alliances and declared that it would not allow the use of Cypriot bases against the Arabs in case of fighting between Arabs and Israel.[163] The strength of the Cyprus communist party, AKEL, also worried Americans. The party was well organized, had substantial popular support and was an influential actor in Cyprus politics. It was opposed to the presence of Western nuclear bases on the island and had tried to turn public opinion against Britain and the United States. If it gained political control, it could allow the Soviet fleet to use the Cyprus ports.

In order to prevent Cyprus from becoming a threat to Western interests, American policy was directed, to some extent, to the elimination or at least neutralization of political capability of Makarios and the communist elements. American contacts with Greece and Cyprus aimed at finding a solution to the Cyprus problem, excluding Makarios and AKEL.

The overall U.S. policy on Cyprus mentioned above made it necessary to prevent any Turkish intervention in Cyprus and to pressure the Turks to act in this way when required. American authorities were not able to control the Greek Cypriots entirely to prevent their actions against Turkish Cypriots. But a Turkish intervention in Cyprus presented more dangers for them, i.e. a Greek-Turkish war and damage to NATO. It was therefore imperative for U.S. rulers to check Turkish actions on Cyprus. However, they failed to predict how the Turks would respond to their warnings, which were, maybe unnecessarily, too harsh for an independent state. U.S. officials might have been deceived by the fact that until that time the Turks always became the most loyal ally within NATO and always attributed great importance to pleasing their American ally with their actions. It seems that the Americans did not understand the pride of Turkish authorities. One reason for the severe U.S. warning to Turkey might be that as a result of being a superpower the United States expected that a small country such as Turkey should listen to its advice in a matter which could concern the whole

---

[163] Attalides, *Cyprus*, p. 15.

Western camp. Scolding of the Greek ambassador by Johnson strengthens this view.[164] However, when U.S. officials realized that they could alienate the Turks and eventually lose their alliance, which was important for U.S. interests, they acted more cautiously.

8. THE TURKISH POLICY ON THE CYPRUS QUESTION

The Cyprus question was a national cause for Turkey, concerning its national prestige, self-esteem and honor. The problem addressed deep-rooted feelings of the Turks. Since it gained its independence, Greece had expanded at the expense of Turkey's territories. The Turks had saved their mainland, Asia Minor, from the occupation of Greece but lost important Aegean islands to her. The island of Crete had been gradually weaned away from them under the pretext of self-government and finally surrendered to Greece. The Turks were determined not to allow the same thing happen again. In their minds, modern Turkey was no longer a sick man whose just claims could be ignored.[165] Turkish Prime Minister İnönü said in Parliament: "Cyprus is a national cause for us, concerning each home and each individual in this country. We are right and we are determined to find a just solution for this problem. It will be solved in conformity with the honor and dignity of the Turkish nation. Any solution contrary to this will be beyond the capacity of any power to force us to accept."[166]

In the eyes of Turkish leaders, Cyprus had a great strategic importance to Turkey.[167] It is located in a position overlooking the southern ports of Turkey, lying just over forty miles from the Turkish coast, and therefore it controlled Turkey's vital strategic approaches and consequently had fundamental importance to its defense. The Turks argued that if Cyprus were controlled by an enemy power or a weak state such as Greece, in case of war Turkey would be in a dangerous situation, isolated from the outside world. If Cyprus passed to Greece, Turkey's entire Aegean and Mediterranean coastlines would be controlled by an unfriendly Greece, which was a traditional enemy.

> In their dealings with the Cyprus question, Turkish officials always stated that their main aim was to protect the lives and rights of Turkish Cypriots. They claimed that this responsibility had been given to Turkey by the international agreements on Cyprus. In their opinion, Turkey had to act as protector of Turkish Cypriots who had the same ethnic origin, cultural and religious background and who had nobody else to rely on in saving them from discrimination by the Greek majority.

For the Turks, the most suitable solution to the Cyprus problem was the partition of the island between the Turks and the Greeks and the separation of the two ethnic communities in Cyprus. In their view, the hatred between the two communities, which stemmed from having absolutely different national identities with different cultural, political and religious values,

---

[164] Johnson told the ambassador: "America is an elephant. Cyprus is a flea. Greece is a flea. If those two fellows continue itching the elephant, they may just get whacked by the elephant's tail. If your Prime Minister gives me talk about democracy, parliament and constitution, he, his government and his constitution may not last very long." Brands, "America Enters the Cyprus Tangle, 1964", p. 358.

[165] Vali, *Bridge Across the Bosporus*, p. 242.

[166] *MMTD*, 5 May 1964, term 1, sess. 3, vol. 30, p. 210.

[167] M. A. Ramady, "The Role of Turkey in Greek-Turkish Cypriot Communal Relations" in Coufoudakis (ed.), *Essays on the Cyprus Conflict*, p. 2, Psomiades in Attalides(ed.), *Cyprus Reviewed*, p. 203, Vali, *Bridge Across*

was so great that it would be dangerous and unreasonable not to separate them. The harrowing experiences, which Turkish Cypriots suffered at the hands of Greek Cypriots in 1963, and the following years had shown that the Greek majority rule in Cyprus would not protect rights of the Turkish community. That was why Turkey accepted the first Acheson plan as the basis of negotiating a solution for Cyprus. The plan would have also satisfied Turkey's security concerns. The Turks were convinced that short of partition only federal government could give Turkish Cypriots security.[168]

Turkish leaders believed that their Cyprus cause was just and that it was the Greek side which caused all the troubles and atrocities. They expected that their Western allies, especially the United States, which was the leader of the West, would show a decisive reaction to the Greek attacks against the Turkish Cypriots and pressurize Greece and Makarios to stop their violence.[169] Turkey had supported its Western allies in all situations even by putting its own security in danger and it was now the West's turn to support its faithful ally Turkey in its just cause. This kind of action would also be a requirement of Western principles such as justice and human rights. However, instead of pressuring the Greek side, the Americans demanded more concessions from Turkey each time Makarios rejected a new proposal and the violence in Cyprus continued. Consequently, Turkish leaders grew impatient.[170] In their view, this was an abandonment of Western principles by the West itself since the victims were non-Christian Turks.

Turkish rulers began to hint of changes in Turkey's traditional Western-oriented foreign policy. In his interview with *Time* magazine in mid-April 1964, Prime Minister İnönü stated that while Turkey had done its best to preserve its alliance with the West, its allies had been competing with enemies in destroying the Western alliance and warned that "if our allies do not change their attitude, the Western alliance will break up and then a new kind of world order will be established under new conditions, and in this world Turkey will find itself a place. I had faith in the leadership of America, which has responsibility within the Western alliance, I am suffering now as a result of this attitude."[171]

The Turks began to think that the monolithic pro-U.S. and pro-Western foreign policy did not meet Turkey's national interests entirely. They realized that the interests of Turkey and the Western powers would not always be identical and that they could clash with each other in some situations. The Cyprus question created a conflict between Turkey's interests and its commitment to the NATO alliance and manifested that NATO could restrict Turkey's

---

the Bosporus, p. 242, Bilge, "the Cyprus Conflict and Turkey" in Karpat (ed.), *Turkey's Foreign Policy in Transition,*, pp. 142, 183.

[168] Prime Minister İnönü's speech in Parliament on 3 September 1964, *Keesing's Contemporary Archives,* 1965-1966, vol. 15, p. 20267, Gönlübol et al., *Olaylarla Türk Dış Politikası,* p. 400, Foreign Minister İhsan Sabri Çağlayangil, *Cumhuriyet Senatosu Tutanak Dergisi (CSTD),* 1 February 1967, term 1, sess. 6, vol. 38-3, p. 376.

[169] Turkish Prime Minister İnönü's statement to AP agency correspondent: "The USA should know all facts about the Cyprus question and undertake its responsibilities." *Cumhuriyet,* 26 January 1964, p. 1. Turkish radio's broadcast: "The United States, which is the spokesman of peace cause in the world should have warned her ally Greece on her illegal actions in Cyprus." *Cumhuriyet,* 9 June 1964, p. 7.

[170] Metin Toker, "Türkiye Yol Ağzında", *Akis,* 4 April 1964, p. 7, Metin Toker, "İsmet Paşa ile 4 Buhranlı Yıl", *Milliyet,* 19 February 1969, p. 5. Statements of President C. Gürsel, Defence Minister İlhami Sancar and the Turkish radio in *Cumhuriyet,* 17, 18 and 22 April 1964, the author's interview with Turkish columnist Fahir Armaoğlu.

[171] *Cumhuriyet,* 17 April 1964, *Milliyet,* 16 April 1964, Sarıca et. al, *Kıbrıs Sorunu,* p. 67, the statement of Turkish journalist M. Ali Kışlalı, who was present at the meeting as Times' Turkish representative, to a Turkish TV documentary, Birand et al., *12 Mart,* p. 104.

freedom of action in matters that concerned it. It also became apparent to Turkish leaders that Turkey was isolated in the international arena and had no support in its national causes. Consequently, Turkish policy-makers began to reassess Turkey's foreign policy, its relations with the United States and its position within NATO. Knowing that the ties between the West and Turkey were based on complementary interests rather than identical ones, they tried to be more flexible in their dealings with the West, the Warsaw Pact and the Third World.[172]

It would be wrong to conclude that Turks really considered making radical changes in their traditional pro-Western foreign policy and in their relations with the USA. When such an interpretation circulated among Turkish political circles, Turkish leaders were quick to deny it. Prime Minister İnönü said in the Turkish parliament:

In their dealings in connection with the Cyprus question our allies have from time to time created the impression that they are not interested in the problem or have no influence on it. In complaining about these actions of our allies we have been obliged from time to time to use such expressions as would indicate the psychological mood of a sincere and sorrowful friend. Beyond this, the interpretation to the effect that we are to depart from the main course of our foreign policy which we have followed and that we are to abrogate our treaties are untrue... We sincerely hope that our allies will take a stance, which distinguishes the guilty from the innocent, and show their loyalty to the [Western] alliance, legal principles and justice.[173]

During his visit to Washington in June 1964, İnönü also stated that "our allies in NATO have neither left nor betrayed us. They only insist that Turkey and Greece should agree on a solution. We want our allies help us. Any change in Turkey's foreign policy is out of the question."[174] Opposition MPs expressed doubts about the implications of İnönü's statement to *Time*. Faruk Sükan and Gökhan Evliyaoğlu warned that any changes in foreign policy would bring fatal results.[175]

9. TURKISH PUBLIC OPINION ON THE CYPRUS QUESTION

The Cyprus question had a great impact on Turkish public opinion. For the first time, Turkey's foreign policy became a subject of public discussion, and anti-Americanism gained popularity among Turkish people. Leftist circles, university students, intellectuals and the press loudly criticized the United States. Mass demonstrations were arranged.[176] U.S. personnel and buildings in Turkey were attacked and the shouting of "Yankee, go home!" was heard in Turkish streets for the first time.

The following criticism was common among Turkish critics: While the United States herself was bombing North Vietnam under no international agreement, it was preventing Turkey from using its legal intervention right to save lives of the Turkish Cypriots and to stop the bloodshed in Cyprus.[177] The tone of American dissuasion was reminiscent of the tactics of

---

[172] The author's interview with F. Armaoğlu.
[173] *MMTD*, vol. 30, term 1, sess. 3, 5 May 1964, p. 210.
[174] *Cumhuriyet*, 26 June 1964, p. 7, Erim, *Bildiğim ve Gördüğüm Ölçüler İçinde Kıbrıs*, pp. 335-336.
[175] *MMTD*, 5 May 1964, vol. 30, term 1, sess. 3, pp. 231-232, 295-297.
[176] *Keesing's Contemporary Archives*, vol. 15, p. 20627.
[177] M. F. Fenik, "Nazi Kampından Beter", *Son Havadis*, 31 March 1964 quoted by Duygu Sezer, *Kamuoyu ve Dış Politika*, Ankara: SBF Yayını, No. 339, 1972, p. 184, Ali Rıza Alp, "Haçlı Zihniyetinin Yaşadığı Devirdeyiz", *Tercüman*, 21 September 1964, O. Z. Dorman, *MMTD*, 7 September 1964, term 1, sess. 3, vol. 32, p. 306,

the eastern bloc countries and colonial powers.[178] American attitude tilted to the Greek side and encouraged them in their violence against the Turkish Cypriots. The Second Acheson plan proposed pure enosis (unification of the whole Cyprus with Greece). While threatening Turkey not to intervene in Cyprus, Americans did not warn the Greeks over their shipment of arms and men to Cyprus and their use of U.S.-supplied arms against the Turks.[179] The United States, which was opposed to communism all over the world, did not care about the increase of the strength of the Cypriot communists under Makarios's political protection because the victims were Muslim Turks.[180]

Turkey had given steadfast support to the United States in international crises such as Korea, Cuba and Vietnam and always been a faithful ally of the West, but the USA did not show the same sensitivity toward Turkey's just cause.[181] The U.S. attitude was not compatible with Western principles to which Turkish leaders attributed great importance. The Americans tolerated violation of basic human rights by the Greek side and only watched the massacre of the Turkish Cypriots.[182] Turkey should stop consulting with the Western powers and intervene in Cyprus militarily to solve the problem permanently.[183] It was also high time for Turkey to reconsider its friendship, alliance and agreements with the West, which did not protect Turkish interests adequately.[184]

Ahmet Bilgin, *MMTD*, 25 May 1965, term 1, sess. 4, vol. 40, p. 559, C. Odyakmaz, Ibid., p. 561, Ahmet Yıldız, *CSTD*, 6 January 1966, term 1, sess. 5, vol. 31, p. 423.

[178] C. Talas, "Kıbrıs, Avrupa, NATO, Amerika", *Forum*, 15 September 1964, p. 9, Fahir Armaoğlu, "Dış Politikada Değişiklik Zorunludur", *Cumhuriyet*, 2 September 1964, p. 2, Ahmet Kabaklı, "Zararlı Faaliyetler", *Tercüman*, 29 September 1964.

[179] "Başyazı", *Forum*, 15 September 1964, p. 3, O. Okyar, "Dış Politikada Revizyon", *Forum*, 15 September 1964, p. 10, Talas, "Kıbrıs, Avrupa, NATO, Amerika", p. 9, Metin Toker, "İsmet Paşa ile 4 Buhranlı Yıl", 9 February 1969, p. 5, A. Artus, "Kıbrıs ve Amerika'nın Tutumu", *Milliyet*, 4 September 1964, "Durum", *Milliyet*, 2 September 1964, p. 1, Nihat Erim *MMTD*, 25 May 1965, term 1, sess. 4, vol. 40, p. 550, Yıldız, op. cit., p. 411, H. Uysal, "Tehlikeli Alakalar", *Akis*, 15 January 1966, p. 5, S. Ural, *CSTD*, 4 February 1968, term 1, sess. 7, vol. 45-3, pp. 452-453, Ali Rıza Alp, "Kıbrıs Meselesinde Johnson'ın Hesabı", *Tercüman*, 4 September 1964, Mehmet Gönlübol and Haluk Ulman, "Türk Dış Politikasının Yirmi Yılı, 1945-1965", *SBF Dergisi*, vol. 21, No. 1, March 1966, p. 177.

[180] M. F. Fenik, "Bu Gafletin Cezasını Bütün Dünya çeker" *Son Havadis*, 31 March 1964, Fenik, "Amerikan Nasihati", Ibid., 9 May 1964, O. S. Orhon, "Kıbrıs ve Ötesi", ibid., 6 January 1964 quoted by Sezer, *Kamuoyu ve Dış Politika*, pp. 182-185, Dorman, *MMTD*, term 1, sess. 3, vol. 30, p. 278, Kabaklı, "Bakışlar", *Tercüman*, 4 January 1964.

[181] Okyar, op. cit., p. 10, Metin Toker, "Kral Kadar Kralcı", *Akis*, 9 September 1964, p. 7, Kabaklı, "Cepheler", *Tercüman*, 19 April 1964, Dorman, *MMTD*, 6 May 1964, term 1, sess. 3, vol. 30, p. 278, R. Aşçıoğlu, "Böyle Oyun Olur mu?", *Tercüman*, 15 January 1965, Ecvet Güresin "Amerika'nın Tutumu", *Cumhuriyet*, 6 June 1964, İ. Baran, *MMTD*, 5 May 1964, term 1, sess. 3, vol. 30, p. 244.

[182] Erim, *MMTD*, 5 May 1964, term 1, sess. 3, vol. 30, p. 223, C. Baban, ibid., p. 236, Dorman, 6 May 1964, ibid., p. 278, Erim, *MMTD*, 25 May 1965, term 1, sess. 4, vol. 40, pp. 549-550, "Başyazı", *Forum*, 1 May 1964, p. 4, Talas, op. cit., p. 9, Kayhan Sağlamer, "Dünyada Bugün", *Cumhuriyet*, 30 April 1964, p. 3, Bahri Savcı, "Amerika'nın Kısır, Haksız Politikası", *Cumhuriyet*, 8 September 1964, p. 2, the author's interview with Fahir Armaoğlu.

[183] Harris, Troubled Alliance, op. cit., p. 112, Couloumbis, *The United States, Greece and Turkey*, p. 61, A. Oğuz, *MMTD*, 7 September 1964, term 1, sess. 3, vol. 32, p. 309.

[184] Erim, *MMTD*, 5 May 1964, term 1, sess. 3, vol. 30, p. 223, M. Karınca, ibid., 24 February 1966, term 2, sess. 1, vol. 4, p. 469, S. Karaman, *CSTD*, 7 May 1965, term 1, sess. 5, vol. 27-2, p. 185, Haydar Tunçkanat, ibid., 3 February 1967, term 1, sess. 6, vol. 38-3, pp. 568-570, *Forum*, 15 September 1964, p. 7, Dorman, *MMTD*, 7 September 1964, term 1, sess. 3, vol. 32, p. 307, Bilgin, *MMTD*, 25 May 1965, term 1, sess. 4, vol. 40, p. 559, "Durum", *Milliyet*, 21 April 1964, p. 1, Oğuz, op. cit., p. 312, Ekrem Alican, *MMTD*, 7 September 1964, term 1, sess. 3, vol. 32, p. 314, Sadi Koçaş, *CSTD*, 8 May 1965, term 1, sess. 5, vol. 27-2, p. 261.

It should be noted that there were also some Turkish critics who warned that Turkey should not alienate the West by criticizing it harshly on the problems which stemmed from its own mistakes.[185]

10. EPILOGUE

The barrage of criticism at home and the U.S. attitude toward the Cyprus question led Turkish rulers to initiate some actions such as the bombing of Cyprus in August 1964 to demonstrate that they were not under the influence of the United States in their actions on the Cyprus issue. However, Turkish authorities did not want to cause the deep resentment in the USA because they needed its alliance. They tried to limit the damage done by public criticism to the alliance with the United States and NATO. While explaining the Acheson talks and the American attitude toward the Cyprus question to the Turkish Parliament on 3 September 1964, Turkish Prime Minister İnönü preserved a calm and detached tone:

> The United States has reconfirmed that it has tried sincerely to find a way of settlement for the Cyprus question, which could be accepted by both sides... We have wanted the United States to play an active role in finding a solution to the problem, not to be indifferent to it... The main American concern has been to prevent a war between two NATO allies... They believed that the problem would be solved through cooperating with the leaders of Turkey, Greece and Cyprus... The main reason for the failure of American efforts is that the United States misjudged the characteristics of the Greek and Cypriot administrations... and that the two governments misled the American leaders.[186]

U.S. rulers, too, did not want to alienate the Turks and lose the alliance with Turkey, since the alliance served U.S. interests. They tried to heal the wounds with Turkey and to appease the angry Turkish public opinion. The U.S. administration issued public statements renewing its commitment to protect Turkey's security, and promising continuity of economic and military assistance.[187] When the Turkish government rejected UN mediator Galo Plaza's plan on Cyprus and Galo Plaza himself as mediator,[188] the United States did not raise any objection to Turkey. It tacitly agreed with Turkey that the UN mediation would bring no solution to the problem.

In December 1965, the United States voted against the UN General Assembly resolution which appeared to support Makarios's claim for the independence of Cyprus and to discount the Turkish claim to the right of intervention in Cyprus based on the Treaty of Guarantee. The resolution recognized that "the Republic of Cyprus, as an equal member of the United Nations, is, in accordance with the Charter, entitled to and should enjoy full sovereignty and complete independence without any foreign intervention or interference."[189] The resolution was passed by 47 votes to 5 with 54 abstentions. The Western and Eastern bloc countries abstained, while the Third World countries of Africa, Asia and South America voted in favor

---

[185] Fahir Armaoğlu, "Batı İttifakından Ayrılamayız", *Cumhuriyet*, 29 April 1964, Faruk Sükan, *MMTD*, 5 May 1964, term 1, sess. 3, vol. 30, pp. 231-232, Gökhan Evliyaoğlu, ibid., pp. 295-297, Saadettin Bilgiç, ibid., 7 September 1964, term 1, sess. 3, vol. 32, pp. 321-322.

[186] *Cumhuriyet*, 4 September 1964, p. 7, *Dışişleri Bakanlığı Belleteni*, October 1964, pp. 53-56.

[187] Harris, *Troubled Alliance*, p. 120.

[188] *Keesing's Contemporary Archives,* vol. 16, p. 20989.

[189] Ibid., p. 21237, *Foreign Policy*, vol. 4, Nos. 2-3, February 1975, p. 217.

of the resolution. The countries who voted against it were Turkey, the United States, Albania, Iran, and Pakistan.[190]

The American opposition to the resolution was justified by American officials on the ground that it seemed to violate the existing treaties on Cyprus and to favor only one side of the problem. But the main American concern was to restore the prestige of the United States in Turkey, which was shaken by the Johnson letter. During the UN General Assembly talks on Cyprus between 11 and 17 December 1965, American representative Charles W. Yost made the following points:

> The Security Council had recognized that a solution to the Cyprus problem could not be imposed but should be reached by negotiation, accommodation and mediation. The Assembly should therefore refrain from any action inconsistent with the measures already taken by the Security Council, and it should in particular refrain from passing judgement on the positions of the parties or on the issues in dispute. The United States had no preferred formula for a settlement of the Cyprus problem. It merely hoped that the parties would move toward the agreed solution envisaged in the Council's resolution of March 4, 1964.[191]

In his speech to the UN Security Council in August 1965, Yost had reconfirmed the American consideration that the London-Zurich agreements were still valid. His main points were as follows:

> The government of Cyprus had not been content with extending the mandate of its House of Representatives but had gone one step further and amended the electoral law. This was inconsistent with the London-Zurich agreements and the constitution of Cyprus. However, whatever legal rights any of the parties might claim, his delegation joined the Secretary General in urging all those concerned to refrain from any action or threat of action likely to worsen the situation in Cyprus or to endanger international peace.[192]

The American vote against the UN General Assembly resolution did not undo the negative impression of the USA in Turkey. Some Turkish critics claimed that America could have influenced other states to vote against the resolution if it had wished, but the American representatives in the UN did not make any effort in this direction.[193] In fact, during the UN General Assembly talks the exercise of American influence on behalf of Turkey was not out of the question. The Greek and Greek Cypriot representatives feared that such an American initiative would be disastrous for their attempt to pass a resolution supporting their cause. Hence, they made strong representations to the U.S. mission twice, when they thought that the United States was attempting to persuade Latin American states to support Turkey. These

---

[190] *Keesing's Contemporary Archives*, vol. 15, p. 21237, Sarıca et al. *Kıbrıs Sorunu*, pp. 109-112.
[191] *International Organisation*, vol. 20, 1966, pp. 308-309.
[192] Ibid., vol. 19, 1965, p. 987.
[193] H. Uysal, op. cit., p. 5, *Cumhuriyet*, 28.12.1965, p. 7.

Greek actions were generally successful because the United States did not engage actively in the struggle to pass a resolution on Cyprus.[194]

---

[194] Robert O. Keohane, "The Study of Political Influence in the General Assembly", *International Organisation*, vol. 21, 1967, p. 232.

Chapter 8

THE CYPRUS QUESTION BETWEEN 1965 AND 1975 AND ITS EFFECT UPON TURKISH-AMERICAN RELATIONS

This chapter covers serious developments such as the Turkish intervention in Cyprus and the U.S. embargo on Turkey and concludes with an assessment of their effect upon the relationship and the theoretical implications.

1. U.S. EFFORTS TO PROMOTE TALKS
BETWEEN TURKEY AND GREECE

American rulers hoped that a small concession (probably a military base) by the Greeks to Turkey could solve the Cyprus problem to the advantage of all Western powers, including Greece and Turkey, with unification of the island with Greece. Therefore, they encouraged Greek and Turkish officials to have bilateral talks. The Americans certainly disliked the excessive Greek Cypriot opposition to such plans and the Greek support for this opposition. This was probably the reason for apparent U.S. pressures on the Greek side after 1965.

Allegedly, U.S. authorities put enormous pressure on the Greek governments between 1965 and 1967 and on the Greek junta after 1967 to have secret bilateral talks with Turkey to find a solution to the Cyprus problem along the Acheson plan lines. It was also claimed that their dislike for George Papandreou's attitude toward the Cyprus question led the Americans to play a role in ousting his government in July 1965 and the Greek military coup in April 1967.

Among other reasons,[1] U.S. officials disliked Andreas Papandreou, son of Greek Prime Minister Papandreou and minister in the cabinet, because of his open support for Greek Cypriot President Makarios's policies.[2] The Greek right wing press had attacked A.

---

[1] Theodore A. Couloumbis, *The United States, Greece and Turkey*, New York: Praeger, 1983, p. 49, Halil İbrahim Salih, *Cyprus: the Impact of a Diverse Nationalism on a State*, Alabama: University of Alabama Press, 1978, p. 54, M. Goldbloom, "United States Policy in Post-War Greece" in Richard Clogg and George Yannopoulos (eds.), *Greece Under Military Rule*, London: Secker and Warburg, 1972, pp. 234, 237.

[2] Michael A. Attalides, *Cyprus: Nationalism and International Politics*, Edinburgh: Q Press Ltd., 1979, p. 72.

Papandreou over his alleged role in the Greek rejection of one version of the Acheson plan, which would bring the union of at least the major portion of Cyprus with Greece.[3] He had told Eric Rouleou of *Le Monde*: "Certain Western powers have attempted to create a rift between President Makarios and our government by asking us to condemn his policies... An agreement based on enosis and a Turkish military base must be excluded as long as the Cyprus government is against it." The statement further deepened the friction between the U.S. and Greek governments. American diplomats loudly protested against it and consequently A. Papandreou resigned from his post.[4]

In March 1965, the U.S. embassy in Athens was alarmed by the news that a ship carrying Soviet ground-to-air missiles had left Egypt and was on its way for delivery to Cyprus. Upon American protests, Greek Defence Minister Garoufalias went to Cyprus to discuss the matter.[5] Greek Cypriot leader Makarios declared that Garoufalias's action was ordered directly by U.S. Secretary of Defence McNamara. He claimed that obeying the Pentagon's instructions, Garoufalias prevented the delivery of Soviet missiles to Cyprus and withdrew from Cyprus all Greek officers who could have trained their Cypriot counterparts to handle the missiles.[6]

As a result of American pressures, Greek Foreign Minister Stavros Costopoulos and his Turkish counterpart Işık held talks on the Cyprus question at the meeting of NATO foreign ministers in London in May 1965.[7] Makarios condemned the talks, stating that they could lead to the partition of Cyprus. In July 1965, Greek Prime Minister Papandreou resigned because of his disagreement with the King over his undertaking the defense minister post. It was claimed that the USA took part in this development by supporting the King mainly because of its dislike for Papandreou's Cyprus policy.[8] Given the general U.S. suspicion that leftist powers, including Papandreou's party, would harm American interests, this claim needs to be taken cautiously.

The next Greek minority government under the premiership of Stephanopoulos seemed to attribute more importance to its ties with NATO. Hence it was inclined to solving the Cyprus problem through talks with Turkey for the sake of NATO's interests. Encouraged by the Americans, Greek rulers sought union of Cyprus with Greece with some compensation to Turkey.[9] On these lines, the Greek and Turkish foreign ministers had contacts in May,[10] June and December 1966. Since the Greeks did not give consent to Turkey's having full sovereignty over a Cypriot territory, no agreement was achieved.[11]

It was claimed that the United States, if not involved directly, at least gave consent to the Greek military coup on 21 April 1967, which forestalled the inevitable election victory of George Papandreou's Center Union Party disliked by the Americans, among other reasons,

---

[3] Laurance Stern, *The Wrong Horse*, New York: Times Books, 1977, p. 33.

[4] Andreas Papandreou, *Democracy At Gunpoint*, London: Andre Deutsch, 1970, pp. 105-106.

[5] Ibid., p. 108.

[6] Ibid., p. 206.

[7] Ibid., p. 109, Salih, *Cyprus*, p. 54, Robert Stephens, *Cyprus: A Place of Arms*, London: Pall Mall Press, 1966, p. 203, *Keesing's Contemporary Archives*, 1965-1966, vol. 15, p. 20809.

[8] Papandreou, *Democracy At Gunpoint*, pp. 137-138, Goldbloom, "United States Policy in Post-War Greece", p. 237.

[9] Papandreou, *Democracy At Gunpoint*, pp. 205-207.

[10] *Keesing's Contemporary Archives*, vol. 15, p. 21540.

[11] Salih, *Cyprus*, pp. 55-56, Suha Bölükbaşı, *Superpowers and the Third World*, New York: University Press of America, 1988, p. 132, Attalides, *Cyprus*, p. 71, *Keesing's Contemporary Archives*, 1967-1968, vol. 16, p. 21947.

because of its Cyprus policy.[12] According to Stern, CIA station chief Maury in the American Embassy in Athens disclosed that "senior members of the CIA country team met in January 1967... We concluded that a victory by the Papandreous would seriously damage vital U.S. interests in the eastern Mediterranean area, weaken the southern flank of NATO and seriously destabilize Greek-Turkish relations then severely strained by the Cyprus situation."[13] The new Greek junta regime, too, supported by Americans, was in favor of having bilateral talks with the Turks to solve the Cyprus problem in a way, which would be compatible with NATO interests.[14]

On 9 and 10 September 1967, the prime ministers of Turkey and Greece, Süleyman Demirel and Kollies, met in the Turkish and Greek border towns, Keşan and Alexandroupolis (Dedeagatch). Kollies's proposal was the union of Cyprus to Greece (enosis) and territorial adjustments on the Greco-Turkish border in favor of Turkey. The Turks rejected enosis and demanded either a return to the 1960 regime or double enosis (secession of some Cypriot territory to Turkey).[15] After returning to Turkey, Demirel declared in his press conference that Turkey rejected enosis and insisted on the validity of the London-Zurich agreements on Cyprus.[16] In Andreas Papandreou's words, "Demirel's statement fell like a bombshell in Greece. Papadopoulos and the junta government had had a resounding defeat."[17] In Turkey, opposition MPs criticized the Kesan-Alexandroupolis talks on the ground that they were held under the influence of foreign powers and sought union of Cyprus with Greece.[18]

2. THE 1967 CYPRUS CRISIS

a) The November 1967 Fighting in Cyprus

On 15 November 1967, Greek Cypriot forces under the command of General Grivas attacked and occupied the Turkish Cypriot villages of Ayios Theodhoros (Boğaziçi) and Kophinou (Geçitkale).[19] The Turkish side believed that Greek attacks were organized attempts to achieve the enosis recently rejected by Demirel.[20] Reportedly, the Greek Cypriot offensive was arranged by Grivas on orders from the Greek junta.[21]

---

[12] Goldbloom, "United States Policy in Post-War Greece", p. 238, Attalides, *Cyprus*, pp. 146-147, Couloumbis, *The United States, Greece and Turkey*, pp. 50-51, Papandreou, *Democracy At Gunpoint*, pp. 187, 191-192.

[13] Stern, *The Wrong Horse*, p. 37.

[14] Papandreou, *Democracy At Gunpoint*, pp. 200, 201, 208.

[15] Van Coufoudakis, "United States Foreign Policy and the Cyprus Question" in Michael A. Attalides (ed.), *Cyprus Reviewed*, Nicosia: Jus Cypri Association, 1977, p. 142n, *Keesing's Contemporary Archives*, vol. 16, p. 22282.

[16] Salih, *Cyprus*, p. 57, Murat Sarıca et al., *Kıbrıs Sorunu*, İstanbul: İstanbul Üniversitesi Yayınları, No. 2071, 1975, p. 139.

[17] Papandreou, *Democracy At Gunpoint*, p. 209.

[18] Sarıca et al., *Kıbrıs Sorunu*, pp. 138-140.

[19] Papandreou, *Democracy At Gunpoint*, pp. 209-210, Bölükbaşı, *Superpowers and the Third World*, pp. 133-134, Rauf R. Denktash, *The Cyprus Triangle*, London: K. Rustem and Brother, 1988, p. 50, Thomas Ehlrich, *Cyprus: 1958-1967*, London: Oxford University Press, 1974, p. 98, Nancy Crawshaw, *The Cyprus Revolt*, London: G. Allen and Unwin, 1978, p. 377.

[20] Denktash, *The Cyprus Triangle*, p. 50, Crawshaw, *The Cyprus Revolt*, p. 373, Bölükbaşı, *Superpowers and the Third World*, p. 134. UN Secretary-General U Thant's report confirmed the Turkish belief. *Keesing's Contemporary Archives*, vol. 16, p. 22435.

[21] Attalides, *Cyprus*, p. 98, Papandreou, *Democracy At Gunpoint*, p. 211.

The Turkish government issued a public statement condemning the attacks strongly and warning that the crisis might go beyond the borders of Cyprus.[22] The Turkish ultimatum to Makarios, which threatened aerial bombardment, brought about the withdrawal of the Greek forces from the two Turkish villages.[23] By the end of November 17, the UN force in Cyprus had achieved a cease-fire.[24] However, staying under strong public pressure, especially from the press, military commanders and parliament, to intervene in Cyprus,[25] on November 17, Turkish Prime Minister Süleyman Demirel sent an ultimatum-like note to Greece, making certain demands.[26]

It seemed that Turkey was poised to invade Cyprus if Greece did not accept its demands. Between November 17 and 22, a war atmosphere rapidly developed.[27] The Turkish armed forces lacking enough equipment and trained personnel were not ready for a landing in Cyprus and Turkish rulers were not willing to launch a military intervention. However, they seemed determined to resort to military option if necessary to save Turkey's prestige.[28]

b) The Vance Mission

The main American concern was to restore peace in Cyprus and thus to prevent an outbreak of a Greco-Turkish war. American officials tried to restrain both sides from taking any action, which would worsen the situation. The U.S. ambassador to Turkey, Parker Hart, told Turkish Foreign Minister Çağlayangil that President Johnson requested Turkey not to intervene in Cyprus but chose not to send a written message because of the Turkish public's reaction to the Johnson letter in 1964.[29] A task force of the U.S. Sixth fleet was deployed close to the shores of Cyprus, apparently to deter the Turkish invasion.[30] On 22 November, the United States joined Britain and Canada in proposing a settlement formula.[31]

When the Greek government rejected the Turkish demands on 22 November, President Johnson dispatched Cyrus Vance, the former deputy secretary of defense, as his special envoy to mediate between the sides of the conflict. Cyrus Vance "was told that Turkish troops were already at the embarkation port and were expected, according to intelligence, to invade Cyprus the next morning. This would mean war between Greece and Turkey." President Johnson instructed Vance: "Do what you have to to stop the war. If you need anything, let me know."[32]

As a first step, Cyrus Vance maneuvered to gain time to be able to mediate between the sides. In his meeting with Turkish Prime Minister Demirel on November 23, Vance obtained

---

[22] Ehlrich, *Cyprus*, pp. 98, 105.
[23] Bölükbaşı, *Superpowers and the Third World*, p. 135, Sarıca et al., *Kıbrıs Sorunu*, p. 143.
[24] Ehlrich, *Cyprus*, p. 105.
[25] Bölükbaşı, *Superpowers and the Third World*, p. 136, Erol Mütercimler, *Kıbrıs Barış Harekatının Bilinmeyen Yönleri*, İstanbul: Yaprak Yayınevi, 1990, p. 117, *Keesing's Contemporary Archives*, vol. 16, p. 22435.
[26] Coufoudakis, "United States Foreign Policy and the Cyprus Question", p. 142n, Papandreou, *Democracy At Gunpoint*, pp. 211-212.
[27] Quotations from *Washington Post* and *The Daily Telegraph* in Papandreou, *Democracy At Gunpoint*, pp. 211-212.
[28] Bölükbaşı, *Superpowers and the Third World*, p. 135, Mütercimler, *Kıbrıs Barış Harekatının Bilinmeyen Yönleri*, pp. 120, 137.
[29] Bölükbaşı, *Superpowers and the Third World*, p. 137.
[30] Ibid., p. 137, Sarıca et al., *Kıbrıs Sorunu*, p. 144.
[31] Ehlrich, *Cyprus*, p. 110.
[32] Bölükbaşı, *Superpowers and the Third World*, p. 139.

the Turkish government's promise that it would not invade Cyprus in the next few days.[33] Then, Vance shuttled between Athens and Ankara to find a settlement formula agreed by both sides. Subsequently, Makarios could be put in the position of either accepting the settlement or being the isolated cause of a continuing crisis. Although Vance pressed the Turkish side as well as the Greeks, this time there would be no repetition of the Johnson letter in 1964. A Johnson letter-like threat could cause total alienation of Turkey from the United States. This time, it was the Greek side which caused the crisis and thus threatened the cohesion of NATO, therefore it should make major concessions to end the crisis. Nevertheless, Greece should be approached properly to provide it with a ladder it could climb down.[34]

The official American position was that Vance acted only as a mediator and did not threaten sanctions against either side. But there were some rumors that the United States would cut off its military aid to both sides. Ehlrich rightly suggests that "even if Vance did not directly discuss future military assistance for Greece and Turkey, the issue must have been very much in the minds of leaders in those countries, for both depended on American assistance to maintain their armed forces."[35] In Ankara, reportedly, Vance reminded Turkish officials of the American view that the use of U.S.-supplied military equipment by Turkey in its operation against Cyprus was not compatible with the assistance agreements between the two countries.[36] In Athens, he pressured the Greeks by saying that the United States was unwilling to continue deterring the Turks from invading Cyprus.[37]

The Greek colonels seemed prepared to compromise because they did not want to worsen their already uneasy position in NATO by a conflict with Turkey.[38] By 30 November, Cyrus Vance had persuaded the Greek junta to agree with the Turks on the following points: 1- The demobilization of Turkish armed forces that had been poised for war. 2- The gradual withdrawal of Turkish and Greek forces over the number authorized by the 1959 London-Zurich agreements. 3- Compensation to the Turkish Cypriots in Ayios Theodhoros and Kophinou for their losses resulting from the Greek Cypriot attacks. 4- Expansion of the size and powers of the UN force in Cyprus to prevent repetition of fighting. 5- The disbandment of the 20,000 member Greek Cypriot National Guard. 6- The recall of Greek General Grivas to Athens. 7- The authorization for Turkish Cypriots to form their own local governments and police forces in their enclaves. 8- Disengagement where the fighting was taking place.[39]

On the same day, Cyrus Vance took his plan to Makarios. But he was unable to overcome Makarios's refusal to dismantle the National Guard.[40] The crisis was over when both Greece and Turkey announced on 3 December 1967 that they would comply with the appeal of UN Secretary General U Thant, which called for the withdrawal of all foreign troops illegally introduced into Cyprus and the dismantling of paramilitary forces on the island.[41]

---

[33] Ehlrich, *Cyprus,* pp. 111-112.

[34] Thomas W. Adams and Alvin J. Cottrel, *Cyprus Between East and West,* Baltimore: John Hopkins Press, 1968, p. 72.

[35] Ehlrich, *Cyprus,* pp. 111-112.

[36] Sarıca et al., *Kıbrıs Sorunu,* pp. 146-147, Mütercimler, *Kıbrıs Barış Harekatının Bilinmeyen Yönleri,* p. 124.

[37] Salih, *Cyprus,* p. 59.

[38] George S. Harris, *Troubled Alliance,* Washington D.C.: American Enterprise Institute, 1972, p. 123.

[39] Salih, *Cyprus,* p. 59, Papandreou, *Democracy At Gunpoint,* pp. 212-213, Metin Tamkoç, *The Turkish Cypriot State,* London: K. Rustem and Brother, 1988, p. 94, *Keesing's Contemporary Archives,* vol. 16, p. 22436.

[40] Bölükbaşı, *Superpowers and the Third World,* pp. 140-141, Joseph S. Joseph, *Cyprus: Ethnic Conflict and International Concern,* New York: Peter Lang, 1985, pp. 141-142.

[41] Bölükbaşı, *Superpowers and the Third World,* p. 141, Ehlrich, *Cyprus,* pp. 114-115, *Keesing's Contemporary Archives,* vol. 16, p. 22437.

Concerns, aims and tactics of the Americans during the 1967 Cyprus crisis were almost same as those in 1964 when Turkey threatened to resort to military force. The only difference was that U.S. rulers acted more cautiously this time in order not to alienate Turkey. They succeeded in preventing Turkish intervention in 1967 without causing deterioration of U.S.-Turkish relations, but their mediation effort increased the Turks' determination to solve the Cyprus question in their own way because U.S. intervention brought no important changes in the Cyprus situation from their own point of view. The Turkish intervention in 1974 was the eventual outcome.

c) The Reaction of Turkish Public to U.S. Mediation

Since the memory of the American prevention of Turkish military intervention in Cyprus in 1964 had not yet faded from the minds of Turkish people, when the United States became involved in the November 1967 crisis, the Turks, especially leftist circles, assumed that the United States would block Turkish action again. During the crisis, leftist university students organized anti-American demonstrations. U.S. mediator Vance could not land on the civilian Esenboğa airport in Ankara because of the demonstrations but had to land on the military Mürted airport.[42] Leftists claimed that the Americans forced Turkish rulers not to launch military intervention for which a real opportunity was created by the Greek Cypriot attacks and thus prevented a permanent solution of the Cyprus problem.[43]

The majority of Turkish critics thought that this time the American attitude was totally different from its stance during the 1964 Cyprus crisis. They believed that the Americans now distinguished the guilty from the innocent and pressed Athens to accept the Turkish demands and thus favored the Turkish position.[44] Turkish authorities claimed that they acted independently during the crisis and did not come under American pressure. They denied the claim that the decision not to intervene was a result of U.S. pressures[45] and proudly announced that they used Turkish forces and bases assigned to NATO for Turkish interests during the crisis.[46]

3. THE GREEK-TURKISH SECRET TALKS ON CYPRUS (1967-1974)

After the November 1967 crisis, both the Turkish and Greek governments were still willing to have secret bilateral talks to find a political settlement to the Cyprus problem. The Greek junta, which was largely dependent on the United States for its survival, seemed to attribute more importance to its membership of NATO. The Greek colonels were willing to

---

[42] Bölükbaşı, *Superpowers and the Third World*, p. 140.

[43] İlhan Selçuk, "Pencere", 26-28 November 1967, *Cumhuriyet*, p. 2, Behice Boran, *Millet Meclisi Tutanak Dergisi (MMTD)*, 4 December 1967, term 2, sess. 2, vol. 22, pp. 330-331, ibid., 20 February 1968, term 2, sess. 3, vol. 25, p. 468.

[44] Ecvet Güresin, "Günün Notları", *Cumhuriyet*, 23 November 1967, p. 1, "Durum", *Milliyet*, 11 December 1967, p. 1, Coşkun Kırca, *MMTD*, 20 February 1968, term 2, sess. 3, vol. 25, p. 454, T. Feyzioğlu, *MMTD*, 23 January 1969, term 2, sess. 4, vol. 31, p. 425, A. Haluk Ulman and R. H. Dekmeijian, "Changing Partners in Turkey's Foreign Policy 1959-1967", *ORBIS*, vol. 11, Fall 1967, p. 784.

[45] Foreign Minister İ. S. Çağlayangil, *MMTD*, 20 February 1968, term 2, sess. 3, vol. 25, pp. 482, 487.

[46] Defence Minister Ahmet Topaloğlu, *Cumhuriyet Senatosu Tutanak Dergisi*, 4 February 1968, term 1, sess. 7, vol. 45-3, p. 489.

find a solution to the Cyprus question, based on the lines of the Acheson plan, i.e. enosis in return for some compensation to Turkey. This kind of solution would satisfy their traditional aim of unifying Cyprus with Greece and please their American allies. They made public statements to this effect.[47] By late 1969, Greece and Turkey had resumed their secret talks on the Cyprus question.[48] The talks between the Turkish and Greek foreign ministers, Olcay and Palamas, during the Lisbon meeting of NATO foreign ministers on 3-4 July 1971 seemed rather promising.[49] Reportedly the two sides had moved closer to a consensus on some form of double enosis.[50] However, extreme pro-enosist elements in Greece and Cyprus resorted to terrorist acts at this time and prevented the achievement of a solution[51] because their activities soured relations between the Greek and Greek Cypriot governments and also between the Turkish government and the Greek regime.

Greek contacts with the Turks did not please the Greek Cypriots. In fact, there was a strong enmity between the Makarios regime and the Greek junta between 1967 and 1974 because of their different approaches to the Cyprus question. While the Greek junta tried to achieve enosis with some compensation to the Turks in order not to harm its ties with the Western alliance,[52] Makarios was in favor of pure enosis, strongly opposing any Turkish involvement.[53] Makarios's non-aligned policy and good relations with the eastern bloc was also an important reason for the Greek dislike for him.[54] Allegedly, in order to achieve enosis, Greece tried to overthrow the Makarios regime by actively supporting the pro-enosis terrorist organizations in Cyprus and taking part in many assassination attempts against Makarios.[55] In September 1971, George Grivas escaped from his house arrest in Athens and secretly entered Cyprus to head the fight for enosis, allegedly with the knowledge of the Greek rulers. He reactivated the terrorist organization EOKA in the form of EOKA-B and assumed its leadership.[56]

---

[47] Greek Premier Caramanlis' interview with *Le Monde* and *The Times* in Papandreou, *Democracy At Gunpoint*, pp. 219-220, Greek P. M. Papadopoulos' statement to *Milliyet* in Attalides, *Cyprus*, p. 132, Stephen G. Xydis, "The Military Regime's Foreign Policy" in Clogg and Yannopoulos (eds.), *Greece Under Military Rule*, p. 203.

[48] Coufoudakis, "United States Foreign Policy and the Cyprus Question", p. 125.

[49] Bölükbaşı, *Superpowers and the Third World*, pp. 172-173. Monteagle Stearns, the former U.S. ambassador to Greece, describes the Lisbon meeting as "the closest the two communities have come to an agreement." Monteagle Stearns, *Entangled Allies*, New York: Council on Foreign Relations Press, 1992, pp. 113-115.

[50] Stern, *The Wrong Horse*, p. 90, Couloumbis, *The United States, Greece and Turkey*, p. 78, p. 126, Attalides, *Cyprus*, pp. 132, 153-154.

[51] Stern, *The Wrong Horse*, pp. 113-115.

[52] Couloumbis, *The United States, Greece and Turkey*, p. 78, P. N. Vanezis, *Cyprus: the Unfinished Agony*, Cyprus: Abelard-Schuman, 1977, p. 46, Van Coufoudakis, "The Dynamics of Political Partition and Division in Multiethnic and Multireligious Societies; the Cyprus Case" in Van Coufoudakis (ed.), *Essays on the Cyprus Conflict*, New York: Pella Publishing Company, 1976, p. 46.

[53] Denktash, *The Cyprus Triangle*, p. 55. Makarios's address to a mass rally in Nicosia on 8 February 1973 in *Keesing's Contemporary Archives*, 1973, vol. 19, p. 25778.

[54] Stern, *The Wrong Horse*, p. 86, Couloumbis, *The United States, Greece and Turkey*, p. 77.

[55] Bölükbaşı, *Superpowers and the Third World*, p. 168, Coufoudakis, "United States Foreign Policy and the Cyprus Question", pp. 125-126.

[56] Coufoudakis, "United States Foreign Policy and the Cyprus Question", p. 126, Denktash, *The Cyprus Triangle*, pp. 60-61, Stern, *The Wrong Horse*, pp. 115-116, *Keesing's Contemporary Archives*, 1971-1972, vol. 18, p. 25033. On the EOKA terror see *Keesing's Contemporary Archives*, vol. 19, pp. 25778, 25979-25980, 26115, ibid., 1974, vol. 20, p. 26603.

4. TURKEY'S CYPRUS POLICY (1967-1974)

As was understood from the statements of Turkish officials, their Cyprus policy between 1967 and 1974 contained the following elements: 1- Turkey's security concerns had to be considered. 2- Cyprus could not be unified with another state unilaterally. 3- The international agreements on Cyprus could not be abrogated or changed by one side unilaterally. 4- One community in Cyprus could not impose its own regime over the other. 5- The power balance in the Mediterranean and the Aegean region, which was established by the Lausanne treaty, could not be changed in favor of one side.[57] In this period, the Turkish government paid little attention to developments in Cyprus since it was preoccupied with domestic problems. The Turkish rulers gave the impression that they were happy with the inter-communal talks and preferred the solution of the problem in a way acceptable to the Greek side as well.[58] The Ecevit-Erbakan coalition government, which came to power at the beginning of 1974, considered that the most suitable solution for the Cyprus question was federation giving autonomy to Turkish Cypriot enclaves, but excluding territorial separation of the two ethnic communities in Cyprus.[59]

5. THE U.S. POLICY TOWARD CYPRUS (1967-1974)

After the November 1967 Cyprus crisis, the United States stopped its diplomatic efforts to find a solution to the Cyprus problem. The negotiations between the representatives of Greek and Turkish Cypriots, Glafkos Clerides and Rauf Denktash, which began on 24 June 1968,[60] seemed to suit American interests since they brought a relative calm to the Cyprus issue. Thanks to the inter-communal talks, whose main aim was to make the 1960 constitution work in a way that would protect Turkish minority rights and also permit the Cyprus government to function, an international conflict would disappear from the agenda of the American administration at least for the time being. Therefore, the United States endorsed and gave support to these talks.[61] American policy turned to support for the Makarios regime and the independence of Cyprus.[62] The long-held anti-Makarios American view seemed to be replaced with a favorable attitude to the Archbishop.[63]

The United States also seemed to favor the Turkish side's position. During Turkish President Cevdet Sunay's visit to Washington in April 1967, President Johnson officially supported the two community concept of the Turkish side, rejecting the terms of "majority" and "minority" for Cypriot groups.[64] The joint Turkish-American communiqué, which was

---

[57] Sarıca et al., *Kıbrıs Sorunu*, pp. 129, 139, 150, Demirel's press conference, *Dışişleri Bakanlığı Belleteni*, April 1967, p. 85.

[58] Bölükbaşı, *Superpowers and the Third World*, pp. 147, 171.

[59] Sarıca et al., *Kıbrıs Sorunu*, p. 173, Bölükbaşı, *Superpowers and the Third World*, p. 178.

[60] On the inter-communal talks see *Keesing's Contemporary Archives*, vol. 16, p. 22883, ibid., 1969-1970, vol. 17, pp. 23635, 24041, 24117, ibid., vol. 18, pp. 24398, 24673-24674, 25032-25033, 25367, ibid., vol. 19, pp. 25700, 25979, ibid., 1974, vol. 20, pp. 26310, 26603.

[61] Coufoudakis, "United States Foreign Policy and the Cyprus Question", pp. 119-120, 123, Attalides, *Cyprus*, p. 153, Stern, *The Wrong Horse*, p. 91.

[62] Coufoudakis, "United States Foreign Policy and the Cyprus Question", p. 127.

[63] Ellen B. Laipson, "Cyprus: A Quarter Century of U.S. Diplomacy" in John T. A. Koumoulides (ed.), *Cyprus in Transition 1960-1985*, London: Trigraph, 1986, p. 67.

[64] Attalides, *Cyprus*, p. 153, Adams and Cottrell, *Cyprus Between East and West*, p. 68.

issued at the end of this visit, stated that the two Presidents agreed that the existing treaties on Cyprus had binding effects and would continue to be an essential element in seeking a settlement formula.[65]

American rulers also supported bilateral talks between Greece and Turkey on the Cyprus question. These talks would reduce American involvement in the conflict, put greater responsibility on the regional powers[66] and make it easier to reach a settlement since Greek and Turkish Cypriot communities were dependent on Greece and Turkey. While the inter-communal talks and Greek-Turkish bilateral talks continued, but reached nowhere, American officials became more worried about the situation in Cyprus. In 1973, there were reports that the United States pressurized the parties to the conflict to reach a quick solution.[67]

In spite of their policy mentioned above, the Americans continued to prefer the unification of Cyprus with Greece in return for compensation to the Turks and the overthrow of the Makarios regime. They believed that Makarios would accept double enosis if confronted with something worse as an alternative. A consensus was reached among these officials that the Makarios problem must be left to Greece.[68] Some Greek critics accused the United States of taking part in anti-Makarios activities in Cyprus.[69] U.S. intelligence services in Cyprus were particularly condemned because of their alleged role in the assassination attempt against Makarios in March 1970.[70] It was claimed that American officials, at least, were well-informed of anti-Makarios terrorist activities supported by the Greek junta, but chose to do nothing about it.[71] The U.S. ambassador to Cyprus appealed to the State Department to condemn the assassination attempts against Makarios, but the appeal was ignored by Secretary of State Kissinger and was opposed by the American ambassador to Greece.[72]

It should be noted that there was a special relationship between the Greek junta and the U.S. administration in the 1967-1974 period. While the United States became the main source of support for the increasingly isolated Greek junta in the international arena,[73] Athens provided important bases and facilities to the USA.[74] Consequently, the Greek regime became

[65] *Dışişleri Bakanlığı Belleteni*, April 1967, p. 61, *Amerika'da Onbir Gün*, Ankara: Yarın Yayınları, 1967, p. 32. During Turkish P.M. Erim's visit to the USA in March 1972 U.S. authorities reiterated the same opinion. *Resmi Temaslar, Sayın Başbakan ve Bn. Erim'in Amerika'yı Ziyareti*, 18-23 March 1972 (no publisher, place and date), p. 63.

[66] Laipson, "Cyprus: A Quarter Century of U.S. Diplomacy", p. 66.

[67] Attalides, *Cyprus*, p. 103.

[68] Attalides, *Cyprus*, p. 154, Coufoudakis, "United States Foreign Policy and the Cyprus Question", p. 126.

[69] Attalides, *Cyprus*, pp. 155, 156-157, Coufoudakis, "United States Foreign Policy and the Cyprus Question", pp. 128, 144n, P. M. Kitromilides, "From Coexistence to Confrontation: the Dynamics of Ethnic Conflict in Cyprus" in Attalides (ed.), *Cyprus Reviewed*, pp. 58-59. As early as March 1965 Greek Cypriot newspaper Agon alleged that U.S. intelligence agents and certain Greek Cypriots had plotted to overthrow Makarios. *Keesing's Contemporary Archives*, vol. 15, pp. 20630-20631.

[70] Sarıca et al., *Kıbrıs Sorunu*, pp. 165-166.

[71] Attalides, *Cyprus*, p. 133.

[72] Ibid., p. 131.

[73] Xydis, "The Military Regime's Foreign Policy", pp. 195-196, 200, Couloumbis, *The United States, Greece and Turkey*, p. 52, Attalides, *Cyprus*, p. 130, Papandreou, *Democracy At Gunpoint*, p. 294.

[74] John C. Campbell, "The United States and the Cyprus Question 1974-1975" in Coufoudakis (ed.), *Essays on the Cyprus Conflict*, pp. 16-17, Salih, *Cyprus*, p. 71, Papandreou, *Democracy At Gunpoint*, p. 295, Xydis, "The Military Regime's Foreign Policy", p. 204, Couloumbis, *The United States, Greece and Turkey*, p. 54.

more open to pressures from the Americans, who wanted solution of the Cyprus problem without alienating the Turks.[75]

6. THE MILITARY COUP IN CYPRUS

a) The Cypriot Coup and the United States

In 1974, the enmity between the Greek and Greek Cypriot administrations reached its peak. Makarios began to take actions against terrorist organizations and Greek elements in Cyprus.[76] On 2 July, he sent a letter to Greek President Gizikis, asking for the withdrawal of Greek officers staffing the National Guard in Cyprus.[77] On 15 July, the National Guard, led by Greek officers and aided by EOKA-B units attacked the Cypriot presidential palace. Makarios escaped death and left the island with the British help.[78] Nikos Sampson, a rightist journalist and a leading figure in EOKA-B, was declared president.

Allegedly, the United States had enough information to predict the coup against the Makarios regime. The American intelligence service, the CIA, had close and constant contact with the Greek intelligence and therefore had known what was going on in Athens. Makarios himself and the Cypriot press publicized the fact that a coup against the Cypriot administration was being prepared. In March 1974, the Cypriot ambassador to the United States, Nikos Dimitriou, informed State Department officials Rodger Davies and Thomas Boyatt that an assassination attempt would be made against Makarios.[79] Subsequently, some working level State Department officials appealed to the higher level officials to express their opposition to assassination attempts against Makarios. But their appeals were ignored.[80]

On 20 June, General Ioannides, the head of the Greek junta, informed a CIA officer in Athens that his administration decided to overthrow the Makarios regime and asked U.S. opinion about it.[81] Subsequently, a CIA report mentioning this serious development was dispatched to Washington. The State Department instructed U.S. ambassador to Greece, Henry Tasca, to convey Washington's opposition to the use of violence in Cyprus to Ioannides personally.[82] Since he did not regard the situation as critical, Tasca chose not to see Ioannides personally, but to pass the message through government channels.[83] On 3 July, the CIA passed a message to Washington from a new and untested source that Greek General

---

[75] Polyvious G. Polyviou, *Cyprus: Conflict and Negotiation 1960-1980*, London: Duckworth, 1980, p. 127, Attalides, *Cyprus*, p. 99.

[76] Sarıca et al., *Kıbrıs Sorunu*, pp. 178-179.

[77] Quoted in R. Denktash, *The Cyprus Triangle*, pp. 174-179, *Keesing's Contemporary Archives*, vol. 20, pp. 26661-26662.

[78] Couloumbis, *The United States, Greece and Turkey*, p. 88, Polyvious G. Polyviou, *Cyprus: the Tragedy and the Challenge*, Washington D.C.: American Hellenic Institute, 1975, p. 55, *Keesing's Contemporary Archives*, vol. 20, p. 26662. Makarios told the UN Security Council on 19 July that the coup was organised by the Greek junta. Ibid., pp. 26664-26665.

[79] Stern, *The Wrong Horse*, p. 94, Attalides, *Cyprus*, p. 166.

[80] Laipson, "Cyprus: a Quarter Century of U.S. Diplomacy" in Koumoulides (ed.), *Cyprus in Transition 1960-1985*, p. 68, Attalides, *Cyprus*, pp. 166-167.

[81] Attalides, *Cyprus*, p. 163.

[82] Couloumbis, *The United States, Greece and Turkey*, p. 86, Stern, *The Wrong Horse*, pp. 99-100.

[83] Attalides, *Cyprus*, p. 167, Couloumbis, *The United States, Greece and Turkey*, p. 86, Campbell, "The United States and the Cyprus Question 1974-1975", p. 18, Bölükbaşı, *Superpowers and the Third World*, p. 182.

Ioannides decided to abandon his coup action against the Cypriot administration.[84] The resignation of Greek Foreign Minister Tetenes on 8 July because of his opposition to a coup in Cyprus did not attract the attention of U.S. officials.[85] On 14 July, the CIA reported again that Ioannides had been dissuaded from attempting a coup in Cyprus. British military intelligence also believed that Ioannides had been forced to back off by diplomatic pressures.[86] Under these circumstances, Bell rightly suggests that "the CIA was deceived rather than deceiving, and that Ioannides believed himself to have enough diplomatic leverage to induce Washington to restrain the Turks, just as they had done in the crises of 1964 and 1967."[87]

Some Greek critics accused American officials of encouraging Ioannides in his coup plot by assuring him that they would not oppose the overthrow of Makarios and would prevent a Turkish invasion of Cyprus.[88] It was argued that the USA could prevent the Cyprus coup if it took a strong action against the Greek junta in the early stages when rumors erupted.[89] Secretary of State Henry Kissinger was particularly criticized because of his failure to register a strong disapproval of the Greek junta's actions.[90] Allegedly, he rejected Senator William Fulbright's suggestion to prevent the Greek plot.[91] Kissinger denied these accusations in his press conference on 22 July 1974: "The information concerning an impending coup was not exactly lying around the streets."[92] The Cyprus Country Director in the State Department, Thomas Boyatt, said in this subject in a conference on 22 February 1975:

> I am prepared to accept that U.S. policy was inadequate... and that there have been mistakes made... [But] I absolutely reject the devil theory, the proposition that this government, through any of its arms, somehow bluntly and clandestinely developed a situation with General Ioannides that he would take an action which in the last analysis would have the result which is so totally disastrous for the United States.[93]

It seems that U.S. rulers had continued their policy of leaving the Makarios problem to the Greeks. In spite of sufficient warnings on the Greek junta's action, they did not want to get involved in disagreements between the Greek and the Greek Cypriot administrations by condemning the one side. The Americans would pay more attention to not alienating the Greek junta because of U.S. interests in Greece. However, they might have failed to predict the exact time of the Cypriot coup to take effective action to prevent it.

---

[84] Attalides, *Cyprus*, pp. 167-168, Stern, *The Wrong Horse*, pp. 101-102.

[85] Bölükbaşı, *Superpowers and the Third World*, p. 183, Paul Y. Watanabe, *Ethnic Groups, Congress and American Foreign Policy*, London: Greenwood Press, 1984, p. 88.

[86] Coral Bell, *Diplomacy of Detente*, London: Martin Robertson, 1977, pp. 146-147, Stern, *The Wrong Horse*, p. 102.

[87] Bell, *Diplomacy of Detente*, pp. 146-147, see also Kemal H. Karpat, "War on Cyprus: the Tragedy of Enosis" in Kemal H. Karpat (ed.), *Turkey's Foreign Policy in Transition 1950-1974*, Leiden: E. J. Brill, 1975, p. 195.

[88] Attalides, *Cyprus*, pp. 170-171, Bölükbaşı, *Superpowers and the Third World*, p. 185.

[89] Couloumbis, *The United States, Greece and Turkey*, p. 88, Polyviou, *Cyprus: the Tragedy and the Challenge*, p. 85.

[90] Stern, *The Wrong Horse*, p. 101, Attalides, *Cyprus*, p. 167, Watanabe, *Ethnic Groups, Congress and American Foreign Policy*, p. 88.

[91] Bölükbaşı, *Superpowers and the Third World*, pp. 183-184.

[92] Watanabe, *Ethnic Groups, Congress and American Foreign Policy*, p. 87.

[93] "U.S. Foreign Policy Toward Greece: Panel Discussions" in Theodore A. Couloumbis and Sallie M. Hicks (eds.), *U.S. Foreign Policy Toward Greece and Cyprus*, Washington D.C.: Center for Mediterranean Studies, 1975, p. 140.

b) The U.S. Attitude in the Aftermath of the Cyprus Coup

In the first few days of the Cypriot coup, the United States followed a wait-and-see policy and avoided showing any reaction to the developments in Cyprus. It did not condemn the coup and its organizers, did not criticize the Athens junta for its alleged involvement in the coup, did not call for the withdrawal of Greek officers from Cyprus and did not make clear its position on who represented official authority in Cyprus.[94] It seemed that the United States was ready to accept the new situation in Cyprus. It was reported that U.S. officials felt great relief when they learned of the removal of Makarios.[95]

State Department Spokesman Robert Anderson refused to comment on the recognition of legal Cypriot regime and avoided criticizing any side in the conflict. His statements were far from making the U.S. position clear.[96] In his meeting with Turkish Prime Minister Ecevit on 17 July, U.S. ambassador William B. Macomber had the same attitude and concentrated mainly on the possibility of a Greco-Turkish war.[97] In the United Nations and NATO, U.S. representatives worked rather for softening criticism against the Greek regime and blocking harsh resolutions condemning the coup organizers.[98] On 18 July, the U.S. ambassador to Cyprus, Rodger Davies, received the foreign minister of the new regime, Dimis Dimitrou, at the latter's request. Thus, the United States became the only state, which established official contact with the short-lived Sampson regime.[99]

It seems that the main American concern after the Cyprus coup was to prevent the outbreak of a war between Turkey and Greece rather than to restore the status quo in Cyprus.[100] The Americans particularly feared that if they took a stance against the Cyprus coup, the Greek junta regime could be alienated, anti-Western young Greek officers could be encouraged to overthrow it and that thus U.S. strategic interests in Greece including bases could be jeopardized.[101]

As Kissinger notes in his memoir, many American officials in the State Department and the Secretary of Defence wanted the United States to adopt a stance against the Greek junta and thus accelerate its fall.[102] But in Kissinger's view, "Turkey's demands left little doubt that it was planning to intervene... the Greek government was unlikely to survive its follies. That

---

[94] Campbell, *Diplomacy of Detente*, p. 19, Nikolas A. Stavrou, "Kissinger's Tilt on Cyprus, the New Style of Crisis Diplomacy" in Couloumbis and Hicks (eds.), *U.S. Foreign Policy Toward Greece and Cyprus*, p. 100, Laipson, "Cyprus: a Quarter Century of U.S. Diplomacy", p. 69, Polyviou, *Cyprus: Conflict and Negotiation 1960-1980*, p. 156, Couloumbis, *The United States, Greece and Turkey*, p. 88, Kryriacos C. Markides, *The Rise and Fall of the Cyprus Republic*, New Haven, Conn. and London: Yale University Press, 1977, p. 180.

[95] Watanabe, *Ethnic Groups, Congress and American Foreign Policy*, pp. 90-91, Haluk Ulman, "Geneva Conferences", *Foreign Policy*, vol. 4, Nos. 2-3, February 1975, p. 50, Couloumbis, *The United States, Greece and Turkey*, pp. 88-89.

[96] C. Hackett, "Ethnic Politics in Congress: the Turkish Embargo Experience" in Abdul A. Said (ed.), *Ethnicity and U.S. Foreign Policy*, New York: Praeger Publishers, 1977, p. 21, Stern, *The Wrong Horse*, p. 112, Polyviou, *Cyprus: Conflict and Negotiation 1960-1980*, p. 156, Bölükbaşı, *Superpowers and the Third World*, p. 186.

[97] Sarıca et al., *Kıbrıs Sorunu*, p. 186.

[98] Attalides, *Cyprus*, p. 171, Stavrou, "Kissinger's Tilt on Cyprus, the New Style of Crisis Diplomacy" p. 101.

[99] Stavrou, "Kissinger's Tilt on Cyprus, the New Style of Crisis Diplomacy", p. 101, Couloumbis, *The United States, Greece and Turkey*, p. 89, Laipson, "Cyprus: a Quarter Century of U.S. Diplomacy", p. 69.

[100] Karpat, "War on Cyprus: the Tragedy of Enosis", p. 197.

[101] J. Reyton's article in International Herald Tribune on 18 July 1974 quoted by Seyfi Taşhan, "Turkish-U.S. Relations and Cyprus", *Foreign Policy*, vol. 4, Nos. 2-3, February 1975, p. 172, Markides, *The Rise and Fall of the Cyprus Republic*, p. 180, Pierre Oberling, *The Road to Bellapais*, New York: Columbia University Press, 1982, p. 161, Stern, *The Wrong Horse*, p. 113.

[102] Henry Kissinger, *Years of Upheaval*, London: Weidenfeld and Nicolson and Micheal Joseph, 1982, p. 1190.

made it all the more necessary that the United States not to be seen in Greece as the agent of its humiliation."[103] Such an American action also could be used by Turks to justify their intervention in Cyprus.[104] It is difficult to say under these circumstances that the U.S. attitude aimed to encourage a Turkish intervention, which could cause the loss of Greece for America and could bring unpredicted grave dangers for U.S. interests.

Anyway, the U.S. attitude pleased neither the Turks nor the Greeks. The Turks claimed that if they did not act quickly the United States would recognize the Sampson regime and the *fait accompli* in Cyprus would be legalized.[105] The Greek side was of the opinion that the U.S. inactivity against the Cyprus coup gave Turkey a good pretext for its invasion of Cyprus.[106]

7. THE TURKISH MILITARY INTERVENTION IN CYPRUS

a) The Sisco Mission

The Turkish government publicly announced and informed the USA that the Cyprus coup was an intervention by Greece in Cyprus and that Turkey would not tolerate it.[107] In its meeting on 15 July, the Turkish National Security Council secretly decided to land armed forces in Cyprus on 20 July.[108] In order to complete the legal procedure under the Treaty of Guarantee before intervention, Turkish Prime Minister Bülent Ecevit went to Britain for consultations and proposed to the British a joint military intervention in Cyprus.[109] The British were of the opinion that peaceful alternatives had not yet been exhausted.

At the night of 17 July 1974, when Ecevit and the British authorities were having talks, U.S. Undersecretary of State Joseph Sisco was dispatched by Secretary of State Henry Kissinger to defuse the crisis. In Kissinger's words, "Sisco's mission was to help Britain start a negotiating process that might delay a Turkish invasion and enable the structure under Sampson in Cyprus to fall of its own weight."[110] However, this American move was too little and too late to prevent a Turkish intervention in Cyprus. The Turks, at that stage, were virtually unstoppable.[111] The U.S. decision not to condemn the Greek junta's actions and the Cypriot coup had robbed Sisco of much needed leverage in dealing with the Turkish leaders.[112]

---

[103] Ibid., pp. 1190-1191.

[104] Oberling, *The Road to Bellapais*, p. 162, Stern, *The Wrong Horse*, p. 113.

[105] Oberling, *The Road to Bellapais*, p. 162, Mehmet Ali Birand, *30 Sıcak Gün*, 4th Edition, İstanbul: *Milliyet* Yayınları, 1976, p. 30.

[106] Stavrou, "Kissinger's Tilt on Cyprus, the New Style of Crisis Diplomacy", p. 101, Polyviou, *Cyprus: Conflict and Negotiation 1960-1980*, pp. 156-157, Polyviou, *Cyprus: the Tragedy and the Challenge*, p. 85, Couloumbis, *The United States, Greece and Turkey*, p. 89.

[107] Couloumbis, *The United States, Greece and Turkey*, p. 90, Sarıca et al., *Kıbrıs Sorunu*, pp. 180-181.

[108] Bölükbaşı, *Superpowers and the Third World*, pp. 188-190, Bülent Ecevit's statement to Kurtul Altuğ's program, Bunalımlı Yıllar, on Turkish TV, 1993.

[109] Couloumbis, *The United States, Greece and Turkey*, p. 90, Bölükbaşı, *Superpowers and the Third World*, p. 191, Ü. Haluk Bayülken, "The Cyprus Question and the United Nations", *Foreign Policy*, vol. 4, Nos. 2-3, February 1975, pp. 119-120, Sarıca et al., *Kıbrıs Sorunu*, p. 186, *Keesing's Contemporary Archives*, vol. 20, p. 26663.

[110] Kissinger, *Years of Upheaval*, p. 1191.

[111] Couloumbis, *The United States, Greece and Turkey*, p. 91.

[112] Watanabe, *Ethnic Groups, Congress and American Foreign Policy*, p. 94.

During their meeting in London on 18 July 1974, Sisco assured Ecevit that U.S. military assistance to Turkey, which was reduced during the last weeks as a result of American displeasure over Turkey's decision to resume poppy cultivation, would be resumed in full.[113] But he also warned that a Turkish intervention in Cyprus might cause a bigger war involving Greece and the Soviet Union and that consequently Turkish-American relations might be damaged.[114] Ecevit reminded Sisco that the U.S. prevention of Turkish interventions in the past harmed the U.S. image in Turkey.[115]

The next day, Sisco was in Athens, pressurizing the Greek colonels to replace Sampson with a more moderate Greek Cypriot and to withdraw Greek officers from Cyprus.[116] The Greek authorities offered only to replace rather than withdraw the Greek officers on a phased timetable.[117] Sisco then flew to Ankara on the same day to inform Ecevit of the Greek answer. Ecevit was determined to initiate the military intervention. He rejected Sisco's demand for a forty-eight hour delay in Turkish operation. Ecevit said: "The United States and Turkey both have made mistakes - the United States by preventing Turkish military action and Turkey by complying with it. We should not make the same mistakes again."[118] At 3.00 a.m. on 20 July 1974, Ecevit informed Sisco of the Turkish intervention: "We have done it your way for ten years, and now we are going to do it our way."[119]

b) The U.S. Ineffectiveness to Prevent the Turkish Intervention

Some critics accused the United States of not being sincere in trying to prevent the Turkish intervention in Cyprus.[120] They showed the statements of Turkish officials as proofs of their claim.[121] In his press conference on 16 August 1974, Turkish Prime Minister Ecevit praised the American attitude as being less emotional than Britain's and refraining from taking sides and putting pressures on the parties to the problem.[122] Turkish Foreign Minister Turan Güneş later acknowledged that the United States resorted to diplomatic methods to persuade Turkish rulers not to intervene, but did not use any threats because it knew that if it acted in this way it would lose Turkey completely.[123]

American officials themselves declared that they did not threaten Turkey to deter it from intervening in Cyprus. In his press conference on 22 July 1974, Kissinger said:

> I made clear on Saturday in San Clemente [at a July 20 news briefing] that no war would be fought between NATO allies with an open American supply line so this put a limit to the escalation that could be conducted. As to the other steps that were taken, there were no

---

[113] Birand, *30 Sıcak Gün*, p. 48, Stavrou, "Kissinger's Tilt on Cyprus, the New Style of Crisis Diplomacy", p. 102.
[114] Bölükbaşı, *Superpowers and the Third World*, p. 192.
[115] Birand, *30 Sıcak Gün*, p. 48.
[116] Salih, *Cyprus*, p. 91, Haluk Şahin, *Gece Gelen Mektup*, İstanbul: Cep Kitapları, 1987, pp. 57-59.
[117] Couloumbis, *The United States, Greece and Turkey*, p. 92, Stern, *The Wrong Horse*, pp. 118-119.
[118] Birand, *30 Sıcak Gün*, p. 64, Couloumbis, *The United States, Greece and Turkey*, p. 92, Stern, *The Wrong Horse*, p. 119.
[119] Couloumbis, *The United States, Greece and Turkey*, p. 93, Stern, *The Wrong Horse*, p. 120.
[120] Polyviou, *Cyprus: the Tragedy and the Challenge*, pp. 83, 84, 85, Watanabe, *Ethnic Groups, Congress and American Foreign Policy*, p. 93.
[121] Attalides, *Cyprus*, p. 172.
[122] Watanabe, *Ethnic Groups, Congress and American Foreign Policy*, p. 119, for another statement of Ecevit see *Cumhuriyet*, 8 September 1974, p. 7.
[123] *Cumhuriyet*, 25 July 1975.

specific threats made. It was very clear that we would consider a continuation of a military confrontation between NATO allies as a very grave matter.

While answering a question, he stated that they did not threaten Turkey with cutting off military aid.[124] On 19 August 1974, Kissinger explained the reasons for this attitude:

> We are giving economic and military aid as a reflection of our common interest in the defense of the eastern Mediterranean. Once such a decision is taken, it will have the most dramatic consequences... It was judged that the United States would be both ineffective and counterproductive to threaten the cut off aid. Short of this, however, we made the most repeated and urgent representations to Turkey in order to prevent the military action that happened.[125]

Allegedly, U.S. officials including Sisco did threaten Turkey with cutting off aid,[126] but as some authors rightly put it, this was not a sufficient weapon because the flow of aid to Turkey had been reduced to the minimum as a result of budgetary adjustments and Congress's displeasure with the Turkish decision to resume poppy cultivation. Moreover, the Turks were determined not to listen the advice of the United States unlike the 1964 and 1967 crises.[127] Preventing a Turkish intervention with threats only would have caused an irreparable damage to U.S.-Turkish relations.[128]

It was reported that U.S. Ambassador in Athens Henry Tasca urged the Pentagon to deploy the Sixth Fleet to the Mediterranean to discourage Turkey. Secretary of State Kissinger intercepted the message and cabled Tasca that the idea was "hysterical." This would undermine Turkish-American relations and would make the United States the supporter of the Sampson regime.[129] It seems that Kissinger was sure about a Turkish invasion and therefore believed that any American pressure, which was brought on the Turks, would be counter-productive in terms of wider American strategic interests.[130] In his own words,

> it had become since an article of faith in Turkish politics that this submission to American preferences [in 1964 and 1967] had been unwise and would never be repeated. I thought it was most unlikely that Turkey would tolerate the union of Cyprus with Greece. That Turkey was driving toward a showdown was obvious... We could not without cost resist a Turkish invasion because that would be considered as objectively supporting the Greek junta. In any case, only the threat of American military action could have prevented a Turkish landing on the island; this was an impossibility. My consultations with Congressional leaders produced the unanimous advice that we should not get involved at all. We could not avoid diplomatic

---

[124] A. A. Fatouros, "How to Resolve Problems by Refusing to Acknowledge They Exist -Some Legal Parameters of Recent U.S. Policy Toward Greece and Cyprus" in Couloumbis and Hicks, (eds.), *U.S. Foreign Policy Toward Greece and Cyprus*, p. 46n, *Milliyet*, 24 July 1974.

[125] Fatouros, "How to Resolve Problems by Refusing to Acknowledge They Exist -Some Legal Parameters of Recent U.S. Policy Toward Greece and Cyprus", pp. 34-35, for State Department spokesman Anderson's statement in the same meaning see *Cumhuriyet*, 19 September 1974, p. 1.

[126] Ulman, "Geneva Conferences", p. 50, Salih, *Cyprus*, p. 92.

[127] Watanabe, *Ethnic Groups, Congress and American Foreign Policy*, p. 95, Bell, *Diplomacy of Detente*, p. 149.

[128] Taşhan, "Turkish-U.S. Relations and Cyprus", p. 173, Karpat, "War on Cyprus: the Tragedy of Enosis", p. 198.

[129] Markides, *The Rise and Fall of the Cyprus Republic*, p. 181, Birand, *30 Sıcak Gün*, p. 58, Karpat, "War on Cyprus: the Tragedy of Enosis", pp. 198-199.

[130] Polyviou, *Cyprus: Conflict and Negotiation 1960-1980*, p. 156, Stern, *The Wrong Horse*, p. 113.

engagement in a NATO crisis, but in the last three weeks of Nixon's Presidency we were in no position to make credible threats or credible promises.[131]

U.S. failure to prevent the Turkish intervention in Cyprus seems to be the most important example of the United States' inability to enforce Turkey to act in a certain way. The Americans had not opposed the secession of a Cypriot territory (a base) to Turkey and even thought about a controlled invasion of a part of Cyprus by the Turks. However, they certainly did not want an uncontrolled Turkish intervention in Cyprus, which was very likely to lead to a Greco-Turkish war. Therefore, U.S. rulers applied diplomatic pressures, which were eventually unsuccessful, to stop the Turks. But, as was apparent from the events, the Americans were not altogether determined to prevent the Turkish intervention. They had shown the same attitude toward the Greek coup, which weakens the claim that the Turks effectively defied the U.S. influence. The U.S. regime at that time was preoccupied with the Watergate scandal and impeachment of the president, so it was not in a powerful position to deter the Turks. Moreover, the Turkish intervention in Cyprus was likely to bring less damage to general U.S. interests than the Turkish alienation by U.S. intervention provided that the USA could prevent a Greco-Turkish war whose possibility was reduced by the Greek unpreparedness.

c) The Turkish Military Intervention in Cyprus

The Turkish naval and aerial landing on Cyprus started at 5.30 a.m. on 20 July 1974.[132] Turkish authorities announced that they took this action as their legal right under the Cyprus treaties to restore the independence and constitutional order of Cyprus.[133] On the same day, the UN Security Council adopted resolution 353, which demanded an immediate end to foreign military intervention in Cyprus.[134]

At that stage, the danger of a major war between Greece and Turkey was so acute that American officials concentrated all their efforts on averting this possibility. Joseph Sisco continued his shuttle diplomacy between Athens and Ankara. He and Ambassador Tasca took a very strong stance against the Greek junta's decision to declare war on Turkey.[135] Secretary of State Kissinger established continuous telephone contact with European leaders and Turkish Prime Minister Ecevit, urging him to cease-fire immediately.[136] Meanwhile, the Greek army chiefs opposed a war with Turkey, thinking that it would be against interests of Greece, causing the loss of the Aegean islands to Turkey. Their initiative caused the replacement of the Greek junta with a civilian government under the premiership of

---

[131] Kissinger, *Years of Upheaval*, pp. 1190-1191.

[132] *Keesing's Contemporary Archives*, vol. 20, pp. 26663-26664.

[133] Statements of Ecevit and the Turkish government in *Foreign Policy*, vol. 4, Nos. 2-3, February 1975, pp. 224-227. For opinions defending the Turkish action see also Kamran İnan, "Cyprus, 1974 Crisis", *Foreign Policy*, vol. 4, op. cit., p. 67, Bayülken, "The Cyprus Question and the United Nations", p. 119, Tamkoç, *The Turkish Cypriot State*, pp. 99, 105, Denktash, *The Cyprus Triangle*, p. 68.

[134] For full text see *Foreign Policy*, vol. 4, op. cit., pp. 218-219, *Keesing's Contemporary Archives*, vol. 20, p. 26665.

[135] Salih, *Cyprus*, p. 93, Stern, *The Wrong Horse*, pp. 120-122, Couloumbis, *The United States, Greece and Turkey*, p. 94, Sarıca et al., *Kıbrıs Sorunu*, p. 198, Bölükbaşı, *Superpowers and the Third World*, p. 198.

[136] Bölükbaşı, *Superpowers and the Third World*, p. 199, Campbell, *Diplomacy of Detente*, p. 20.

Constantine Caramanlis on 22 July.[137] In the evening, the Turkish government announced its decision to agree to a cease-fire.[138] Subsequently, the puppet Sampson regime in Cyprus collapsed and Glafkos Clerides, the President of the Cyprus House of Representatives, assumed the duties of president.[139] Clerides was viewed by American officials in Nicosia "as a satisfactory alternative to Makarios, whose political fortunes they thought and/or hoped were finished."[140]

There are different views on why Turkey accepted the cease-fire on 22 July. Kissinger claimed in his memoirs: "During the night of Jul 21-22, we forced a cease-fire by threatening Turkey that we would move nuclear weapons from forward positions - especially where they might be involved in a war with Greece. It stopped Turkish military operations while Turkey was occupying only a small enclave on the island."[141] Bölükbaşı disagrees with this claim by noting that the Turkish government accepted the cease-fire only after it secured a bridgehead in Cyprus.[142] In Birand's opinion, the main reason for the Turkish decision was the fear that the two superpowers could act together in stopping the Turkish intervention.[143] In his press conference on 22 July 1974, Turkish Prime Minister Ecevit denied that U.S. pressures brought about the cease-fire: "There has been no pressure from any country. Pressure tactics are and should be out of the question between friendly countries. I had a friendly conversation with Kissinger, whom I have known for a long time. We made joint effort for peace and agreed on the necessity of establishing peace in the region."[144] It is, however, almost certain that Turkey stopped its operations before achieving its real aims because of international opposition, especially the U.S. opposition.

d) The U.S. Attitude toward the Turkish Intervention

As U.S. authorities did not condemn the Cyprus coup not to alienate the Greek junta, they showed almost the same attitude toward the Turkish intervention in Cyprus. They did not issue any statement openly denouncing the Turkish intervention and did not press the Turks to reverse their action.[145] It was clear that the Turks would not leave Cyprus under any conditions. Given the alienation of the Greeks from the USA, pressing the Turks would cause only the loss of another strategic ally in the eastern Mediterranean. The only thing, which could be done, was to contain the Turkish action within the limits acceptable to the Greeks.[146]

Kissinger was opposed to taking forceful actions against Turkey because the crisis had been started by Greece, taking a one-sided position would prevent the USA from easing the conflict between two strategic allies in the eastern Mediterranean and the U.S. government

---

[137] Couloumbis, *The United States, Greece and Turkey*, p. 94, Campbell, *Diplomacy of Detente*, pp. 20-21, Salih, *Cyprus*, p. 93, Stern, *The Wrong Horse*, p. 124, *Keesing's Contemporary Archives*, vol. 20, pp. 26666-26668.

[138] Ecevit's statement quoted by *Foreign Policy*, vol. 4, op. cit., pp. 228-229.

[139] Polyviou, *Cyprus: the Tragedy and the Challenge*, p. 56, Couloumbis, *The United States, Greece and Turkey*, p. 95, *Keesing's Contemporary Archives*, vol. 20, p. 26666.

[140] Laipson, "Cyprus: a Quarter Century of U.S. Diplomacy", p. 70.

[141] Kissinger, *Years of Upheaval*, p. 1192.

[142] Bölükbaşı, *Superpowers and the Third World*, pp. 199-200.

[143] Mehmet Ali Birand, *Diyet*, İstanbul: Ağaoğlu Yayınevi, 1979, p. 28.

[144] *Foreign Policy*, vol. 4, op. cit., p. 229, Sarıca et al., *Kıbrıs Sorunu*, p. 197.

[145] Polyviou, *Cyprus: the Tragedy and the Challenge*, p. 86, Watanabe, *Ethnic Groups, Congress and American Foreign Policy*, p. 97.

[146] Oberling, *The Road to Bellapais*, pp. 169-170, Ulman, "Geneva Conferences", p. 50.

which was on the verge of the collapse was not in a position to take such actions. "The preoccupation with Watergate had reached a point where we were losing even the ability to transmit papers bearing on vital foreign policy matters... between the president and the White House."[147]

8. THE GENEVA CONFERENCES

The first Geneva conference on the Cyprus crisis was held between 25 and 30 July 1974 and was attended by the foreign ministers of Turkey, Greece and Britain; Turan Güneş, George Mavros and James Callaghan. The United States sent to the conference a special representative, Assistant Secretary of State William Baffum.[148] The joint declaration issued at the end of the conference, on 30 July 1974,[149] was seen by the Turks as supporting their viewpoint.[150]

The Second Geneva conference was held between 8 and 14 August and was also attended by Turkish Cypriot leader Rauf Denktash and Greek Cypriot President Glafcos Clerides. The Turkish side proposed a federal system based on the geographical separation of the two ethnic communities in Cyprus.[151] When the Greek delegation rejected the proposal, Kissinger persuaded Turkish Prime Minister Ecevit to put a cantonal system proposal on the table.[152] The new Turkish proposal, which suggested establishment of six autonomous Turkish region covering 34 percent of Cyprus, too, was rejected by the Greeks.[153] Allegedly, on 13 August, Callaghan informed the Greek delegation that Kissinger could not exert any further pressure on Turkey to prevent a further Turkish expansion in Cyprus unless the Greeks accepted the Turkish proposal as the basis of negotiations.[154] Believing that the Greeks were employing delaying tactics and their position in Cyprus was deteriorating, on 13 August, the Turks demanded an immediate yes-or-no answer to their proposals. With the Turkish rejection of the Greek demand of 36 hours to answer, the negotiations broke down.[155]

Toward the end of the second Geneva conference, the American attitude seemed increasingly favoring the Turkish position. The Turkish cantonal proposal contained heavy inputs from the Americans and apparently gained their support. The State Department's statement on 13 August also implied the U.S. support for Turkish position:

> U.S. position is as follows: we recognize that the position of the Turkish community in Cyprus requires considerable improvement and protection. We have supported a greater degree of autonomy for them. The parties are negotiating on one or more Turkish autonomous

---

[147] Kissinger, *Years of Upheaval*, pp. 1191-1192.

[148] For a detailed account of the conference see Ulman, "Geneva Conferences", pp. 52-59.

[149] For the text of the declaration see *Foreign Policy*, vol. 4, op. cit., pp. 230-232, *Keesing's Contemporary Archives*, vol. 20, p. 26709.

[150] Ulman, "Geneva Conferences", p. 47, Bölükbaşı, *Superpowers and the Third World*, p. 201.

[151] Ulman, "Geneva Conferences", pp. 60-61. Former Turkish foreign minister Ü. H. Bayülken told the author that new conditions compelled Turkey not to bring the former regime, which was required by the treaties on Cyprus.

[152] Birand, *Diyet*, p. 27, Ulman, "Geneva Conferences", p. 62.

[153] Ulman, "Geneva Conferences", p. 63, Birand, *Diyet*, p. 29, Bölükbaşı, *Superpowers and the Third World*, p. 205.

[154] Polyviou, *Cyprus: Conflict and Negotiation 1960-1980*, pp. 175-176.

[155] Bölükbaşı, *Superpowers and the Third World*, pp. 206-207, Ulman, "Geneva Conferences", pp. 59-60, 64, Denktash, *The Cyprus Triangle*, p. 73, Couloumbis, *The United States, Greece and Turkey*, p. 97, *Keesing's Contemporary Archives*, vol. 20, pp. 26709-26710.

areas. The avenues of diplomacy have not been exhausted and therefore the United States would consider a resort to military action unjustified. We have made this clear to all parties.[156]

Turkey's strategic importance for U.S. interests played a crucial role in this U.S. attitude.[157]

In Ecevit's account, the Turkish side made a further interim proposal to prevent the breakdown of the conference: If the Greeks would agree in principle to the Turks' basic demand for a cantonal or bizonal system, to the establishment of a buffer zone around the area held by the Turkish Armed Forces (the area to include a line from Nicosia to Kyrenia and to the Turkish part of Famagusta), and to the immediate withdrawal of their forces in 17-18 percent area of the island to be handed over to Turkish Cypriot administration, Turkey would not place troops there while negotiations were in progress and it would wait for the boundaries of other cantons to be fixed. If the Greeks had accepted this proposal and evacuated their troops from the region Turkish rulers would have been prepared to wait not 36 hours but 36 days before taking further action. Kissinger liked the idea and tried to sell it to the other side. But Callaghan's negative attitude prevented the success of the plan.[158]

Apart from Callaghan's attitude and the U.S. failure to exert heavy pressure on the Turks,[159] the incompatibility of Turkish and Greek demands and the Turkish determination to strengthen their position in Cyprus with further military operations[160] played a role in the breakdown of the Geneva talks. By the end of 13 August, the Turks had realized that the negotiations would bring no favorable results and that if they did not act swiftly international public opinion would totally turn against them and they would have to be content with the seven percent of Cyprus.

9. THE SECOND TURKISH INTERVENTION AND THE U.S. ATTITUDE

Accusing the Greek side of intentionally obstructing a peaceful solution and violating security of Turkish Cypriot people, the Turkish government resumed its military operations in Cyprus on 14 August.[161] By 16 August, the Turkish forces had captured 36 percent of the territory of Cyprus, displacing thousands of Cypriot people.[162]

As a reaction to the new development, the United States announced that if Turkey and Greece fought with each other it would cut off its military aid and arms sales to both countries,[163] but did not explicitly condemn the Turkish action.[164] It seemed to be happy with the geographical separation of Cypriot communities with the Turkish action.[165] Kissinger

---

[156] Couloumbis, *The United States, Greece and Turkey*, pp. 96-97, Polyviou, *Cyprus: Conflict and Negotiation 1960-1980*, p. 181.

[157] Campbell, *Diplomacy of Detente*, p. 22, Stern, *The Wrong Horse*, p. 130.

[158] Ecevit's letter to Denktash quoted in Denktash, *The Cyprus Triangle*, pp. 369-373.

[159] Campbell, *Diplomacy of Detente*, pp. 21-22, Polyviou, *Cyprus: Conflict and Negotiation 1960-1980*, p. 199.

[160] Campbell, *Diplomacy of Detente*, p. 21, Bölükbaşı, *Superpowers and the Third World*, p. 207.

[161] Sarıca et al., *Kıbrıs Sorunu*, pp. 207-208, Ecevit's statement in Bayülken, "The Cyprus Question and the United Nations", p. 122, the Turkish government's statement in Foreign Policy, vol. 4, op. cit., pp. 233-234, *Keesing's Contemporary Archives*, vol. 20, p. 26710.

[162] Bölükbaşı, *Superpowers and the Third World*, p. 211.

[163] Birand, *Diyet*, p. 39.

[164] Polyviou, *Cyprus: Conflict and Negotiation 1960-1980*, p. 201, Polyviou, *Cyprus: the Tragedy and the Challenge*, p. 87.

[165] Attalides, *Cyprus*, p. 176, Polyviou, *Cyprus: the Tragedy and the Challenge*, pp. 195-196n.

reportedly stated that the United States would not resort to forceful actions to intervene in the matter because it was not the policeman of the world.[166] Only Secretary of Defence Schlesinger criticized the Turks by saying that their action went beyond what any of its friends would have accepted. He raised the possibility of an aid cut-off and the return of some of the Cyprus territory, which the Turks had captured.[167]

It should be noted that, at that time, American officials were preoccupied with the resignation of President Nixon and the change of the administration. The only thing, which Kissinger could do, was to recommend immediate resumption of talks between the concerned parties and to offer his services as mediator.[168] U.S. strategic interests in the eastern Mediterranean led American officials to try to remove Cyprus as a source of friction in the region by forcing both sides to compromise rather than condemning only one side.[169]

Meanwhile, the U.S. failure to stop the Turkish intervention alienated the Greeks greatly.[170] On 14 August 1974 the Greek government withdrew from the military area of NATO.[171] In the anti-American demonstration in Nicosia on 19 August, U.S. Ambassador Rodger Davies was killed.[172] The Greek Americans arranged large demonstrations in front of the White House.[173]

10. THE ARMS EMBARGO AND TURKISH-AMERICAN RELATIONS

a) The Imposition of the Arms Embargo

On 15 August 1974, a delegation of Greek-American congressmen led by Representative John Brademas visited Secretary of State Kissinger. They blamed him for the U.S. failure to stop the Turkish intervention and requested that the administration cut off its military assistance to Turkey until its troops were withdrawn from Cyprus.[174] In Kissinger's eyes, the intervention of the Greek-American Congressmen, who were merely instruments of the Greek foreign office, in the formulation of U.S. foreign policy could not be accepted.[175] He largely blamed Callaghan for the failure of the second Geneva conference and claimed that the USA was doing enough to restrain the Turks.[176]

---

[166] *Cumhuriyet*, 22 August 1974, p. 1.

[167] Ibid., 19 August 1974, Thomas M. Franck and Edward Weisband, *Foreign Policy by Congress*, Oxford: Oxford University Press, 1979, p. 36, Attalides, *Cyprus*, p. 177.

[168] Salih, *Cyprus*, pp. 97-98.

[169] Van Coufoudakis, "United States Foreign Policy and the Cyprus Question" in Attalides (ed.), *Cyprus Reviewed*, p. 131, Bell, *Diplomacy of Detente*, p. 153.

[170] Oberling, *The Road to Bellapais*, p. 182, Zenon Stavrinides, *The Cyprus Conflict*, Loris Stavrinides Press, 1976, p. 92.

[171] Couloumbis, *The United States, Greece and Turkey*, p. 97, Salih, *Cyprus*, p. 98, *Keesing's Contemporary Archives*, vol. 20, p. 26710.

[172] Salih, *Cyprus*, p. 98, *Keesing's Contemporary Archives*, vol. 20, p. 26753.

[173] Couloumbis, *The United States, Greece and Turkey*, p. 98.

[174] Stern, *The Wrong Horse*, pp. 140-141, Birand, *Diyet*, pp. 42-43.

[175] K R. Legg, "Congress as Trojan Horse, the Turkish Embargo Problem, 1974-1978" in John Spanier and Joseph Nogee (eds.), *Congress, the Presidency and American Foreign Policy*, New York: Pergaman Press, 1981, p. 117, Birand, *Diyet*, p. 41.

[176] Birand, *Diyet*, p. 42, Stern, *The Wrong Horse*, p. 141.

At a news conference on 19 August 1974, Kissinger promised to get expert opinion about the legality of Turkish use of U.S.-supplied military equipment in Cyprus.[177] Although the administration kept the result of a legal team's study on the matter secret from the public,[178] it leaked it to Senator Thomas Eagleton through his aide Brian Adwood. The legal memo concluded that by no stretch of the statues or the legal imagination of the State Department's attorneys could military aid to Turkey be continued.[179] Subsequently, some congressmen decided to plunge into battle with the administration on the issue of law and order in the context of the legality of U.S. aid to Turkey.

In spite of Kissinger's warnings that cutting off aid to Turkey could jeopardize U.S. interests and bases in Turkey,[180] the U.S. Congress passed a series of resolutions requesting the President to stop arms sales to Turkey.[181] Initially, President Ford vetoed such bills, but the strong support for the embargo in the Congress forced him to sign a resolution banning U.S. assistance to Turkey from 5 February 1975 if it did not make concessions in the Cyprus issue. The Turks seemed to be willing to soften their attitude in Cyprus. They accepted the UN General Assembly resolution on 1 November 1974 and decided to reduce the number of Turkish troops in Cyprus. But the disagreement between the coalition partners on the Cyprus issue resulted in the resignation of the government on 19 September 1974.[182] After both Bülent Ecevit and Süleyman Demirel had been unable to form a new government, President Korutürk asked Sadi Irmak to do so. Irmak's cabinet of mostly independent senators and technocrats was announced on 17 November, but failed to gain a vote of confidence. Nevertheless, at this difficult time, Irmak remained Prime Minister until 31 March 1975 when he was succeeded by Demirel, who led a "national front" coalition.

On 5 February 1975, the Congress's embargo action came into effect. Deliveries for over 200 million dollars in arms purchases and grants, which had been scheduled for transfer to Turkey, was frozen.[183] The ban included 78 million dollars worth of equipment already paid for.[184] The Turks harshly condemned the action and declared that U.S. pressures would not affect their Cyprus policy.[185]

In the aftermath of the embargo resolution, U.S. authorities stated that they supported political negotiations between the sides of the Cyprus conflict[186] and pressed the Turks to make territorial concessions in Cyprus if they wanted to reverse the embargo.[187] When the

---

[177] Hackett, "Ethnic Politics in Congress: the Turkish Embargo Experience", p. 23, Legg, "Congress as Trojan Horse, the Turkish Embargo Problem, 1974-1978", p. 117.

[178] Ellen B. Laipson, *Congressional-Executive Relations and the Turkish Arms Embargo*, Washington: U.S. Government Printing Office, June 1981, p. 14, Fatouros, "How to Resolve Problems by Refusing to Acknowledge They Exist -Some Legal Parameters of Recent U.S. Policy Toward Greece and Cyprus", p. 35.

[179] Stern, *The Wrong Horse*, pp. 143-144, Laipson, *Congressional-Executive Relations and the Turkish Arms Embargo*, p. 14.

[180] Kissinger's meeting with some congressmen on 19 September 1974 in Stern, *The Wrong Horse*, p. 145, Birand, *Diyet*, p. 56, Laipson, *Congressional-Executive Relations and the Turkish Arms Embargo*, p. 19, Hackett, "Ethnic Politics in Congress: the Turkish Embargo Experience", pp. 22-23.

[181] For the Congress actions on the Turkish arms embargo see Theodore A. Couloumbis and Sallie M. Hicks, "the Impact of Greek Americans Upon United States Foreign Policy" in Attalides (ed.), *Cyprus Reviewed*, pp. 165-171, *Keesing's Contemporary Archives*, 1975, vol. 21, p. 26886.

[182] Birand, *Diyet*, pp. 79, 81-82, *Keesing's Contemporary Archives*, vol. 21, pp. 26885-26886.

[183] Couloumbis, *The United States, Greece and Turkey*, p. 105.

[184] Legg, "Congress as Trojan Horse, the Turkish Embargo Problem, 1974-1978", p. 121.

[185] Statements of the Turkish Prime Minister and NSC in Polyviou, *Cyprus: the Tragedy and the Challenge*, pp. 210-211, Birand, *Diyet*, p. 100.

[186] The State Department's statement in Salih, *Cyprus*, p. 186n.

[187] Kissinger's meetings with Turkish rulers in the first half of 1975 in Birand, *Diyet*, pp. 118-128.

House of Representatives defeated the partial lifting of the embargo on 24 July 1975, the Turkish government announced that the Defence Cooperation Agreement of 1969 and all other related agreements between the United States and Turkey had lost their legal validity.[188] The Congress decision to lift the embargo partially in October 1975[189] did not impress the Turks. They did not terminate suspension measures in the bases until the complete lifting of the embargo in September 1978.[190]

b) Arguments of the U.S. Congress on the Arms Embargo

In the eyes of U.S. congressmen, the second Turkish military operation in Cyprus was an unacceptable aggressive act whereas its first action could be justified as a defensive act, aimed at protecting lives of Turkish Cypriots and restoring the status quo in the island.[191] Their main argument for imposing an embargo on Turkey was that Turkey used in its military operations in Cyprus U.S. arms and military equipment contrary to the American law and the provisions of the agreements under which these arms had been granted or sold to it.[192] They also reasoned that an arms embargo was necessary to force Turkey to make concessions to the Greek side and thus to accelerate the process of finding a peaceful settlement to the Cyprus question. Failing to do so would mean rewarding the Turkish aggression and allowing the Turks to dictate their solution of the Cyprus problem by the force of arms.[193] Even George Ball and Cyrus Vance, the former American mediators on the Cyprus question, testified in favor of retaining the linkage between Turkey's security assistance program and demonstrated progress on Cyprus.[194] The pro-embargo forces also claimed that failing to impose the embargo would alienate Greece, a strategically vital ally of the United States.[195]

However, the main reasons of congressmen for opposing the American administration on the embargo issue stemmed from the uneasy relationship between the legislative and executive branches. The American policies toward Vietnam, Cambodia, Chile, the Soviet Union and Pakistan had caused the gradual loss of Congressional confidence in the practices of the administration. As the years passed, the Congress became more and more suspicious of the motives and practices of the executive branch. Finally, the Watergate scandal resulted in an almost complete breakdown of Congressional trust in the Presidency. In the eyes of congressmen, the American administration had become a body, which did not care about the rule of law and the power of the Congress. Congressmen believed that they had to give a lesson to the executive branch to break its arrogance. The Cyprus issue simply provided this

---

[188] Ibid., p. 175, Couloumbis, *The United States, Greece and Turkey*, p. 151, *Cumhuriyet*, 26 July 1975, *Keesing's Contemporary Archives*, vol. 21, p. 27337.

[189] *Keesing's Contemporary Archives*, vol. 21, p. 27450.

[190] Couloumbis, *The United States, Greece and Turkey*, p. 106.

[191] Congressman D. Riegle's statement quoted by Watanabe, *Ethnic Groups, Congress and American Foreign Policy*, p. 100, see also Hackett, "Ethnic Politics in Congress: the Turkish Embargo Experience", p. 25.

[192] Couloumbis and Hicks, "the Impact of Greek Americans Upon United States Foreign Policy", p. 146, Couloumbis, *The United States, Greece and Turkey*, p. 104.

[193] Richard F. Grimmett, *Turkish-U.S. Defense Relationship: the Arms Embargo Issue*, the Library of Congress, Congressional Research Service, 1978, p. 4, Representative B. Rosenthal's statement in Bölükbaşı, *Superpowers and the Third World*, pp. 216-217.

[194] Laipson, "Cyprus: a Quarter Century of U.S. Diplomacy", p. 73.

[195] Rosenthal's statement in Bölükbaşı, *Superpowers and the Third World*, p. 217.

opportunity.[196] The opposition to Kissinger as a former member of the now discredited Nixon administration, too, played an important role in the Congress's insistence on the arms embargo.[197] The Turkish embargo issue offered an opportunity for Kissinger's congressional critics to question some major tenets of his domestic and foreign policies, his methods and his style of careful manipulation of the Congress and public opinion.

For many congressmen, to work for imposing an arms embargo on Turkey was a part of the struggle to have a greater voice and control in foreign affairs. In reality what Congress challenged was the strong executive dominance over the foreign policy process.[198] For some Congressmen who were highly critical of the Turkish government's decision to resume poppy cultivation, the arms embargo was a good opportunity to express their disapproval over the Turkish decision and punish Turkey.

c) Arguments of the U.S. Administration on the Embargo

The arguments of anti-embargo forces, the American administration and some congressmen, could be summarized as follows:[199] Firstly, putting pressure on only one side in a complicated problem would not help its solution. Imposing an arms embargo on Turkey would be destructive to U.S. efforts to bring about a peaceful solution the Cyprus question by rendering the proud and independent-minded Turks less flexible on future Cyprus negotiations.[200] Secondly, the embargo would cause alienation of Turkey, whose strategic importance was vital to NATO and Western security designs. The United States might lose its strategic military and communication facilities in Turkey and the American position in the strategic eastern Mediterranean region might weaken.

Thirdly, the arms embargo was an act of Congress, which represented an abuse of congressional authority in foreign policy and violated the principle of separation of power in the state structure. Foreign policy making and its tactical (day-to-day) applications were largely the prerogative of the administration. Congress's excessive involvement in the example of the arms embargo restricted the administration's executive capabilities in protecting U.S. interests. While imposing an arms embargo against Turkey, congressmen could not take a responsible, statesmanlike posture in an important issue because they were influenced and manipulated by an agitated group of politically active Greek Americans.[201]

Finally, apparently to prompt the opposition of the mighty Israeli lobby, the American administration claimed that an arms embargo against Turkey could also hurt Israel. Israel, too, might be caught by a strict interpretation of the non-defensive use provisions of the law

---

[196] Richard E. Campany, *Turkey and the United States*, New York: Praeger, 1986, p. 78, Laipson, "Cyprus: a Quarter Century of U.S. Diplomacy", p. 71, Laipson, Congressional-Executive Relations... , p. 30.

[197] Laipson, *Congressional-Executive Relations and the Turkish Arms Embargo*, p. 29.

[198] Campany, *Turkey and the United States*, p. 78.

[199] Statements of President Ford, Secretary of State Kissinger, the Senate majority leader and State Department spokesman Anderson in Watanabe, *Ethnic Groups, Congress and American Foreign Policy*, pp. 107, 109, Salih, *Cyprus*, pp. 100-101, 187n, Polyviou, *Cyprus: the Tragedy and the Challenge*, p. 211, Kissinger, *Years of Upheaval*, p. 1192, Stern, *The Wrong Horse*, p. 152, Grimmett, *Turkish-U.S. Defense Relationship: the Arms Embargo Issue*, p. 4, *Keesing's Contemporary Archives*, vol. 21, pp. 27035, 27337.

[200] Couloumbis, *The United States, Greece and Turkey*, p. 105.

[201] Laipson, *Congressional-Executive Relations and the Turkish Arms Embargo*, p. 30.

because Israel had used American weapons in its struggle against the Arabs.[202] Moreover, the U.S. bases in Turkey, which were threatened by the arms embargo, were important for Israel's defense.[203]

d) The Role of the Greek Americans in the Imposition of the Embargo

The Greek Orthodox Church in North America was very active in communicating a deep concern over Cyprus to its members and in activating Greek American population to force American officials and legislators for anti-Turkish actions.[204] The expected role of the Orthodox Church on the arms embargo was so great that in October 1974 Ford and Kissinger met with Archbishop Iakovos in the Oval Office in order to persuade him to calm his community.[205] Greek American lobby groups, too, played a crucial role in activating the Greek-American population and putting pressure on congressmen and the American administration on the arms embargo issue.[206]

It seems that congressmen were influenced by the efforts of Greek Americans in their votes on the embargo issue because they wanted to secure the support of Greek Americans in the approaching congressional elections in November 1974.[207] No congressmen would like the agitated Greek-American groups, which constituted a politically and socially activated segment of the U.S. population, lobbying against him. Many congressmen would incline toward accommodating such an important ethnic group in a symbolic vote.[208] But it should be noted that in the embargo issue congressmen were also affected by other factors, which were mentioned above, and they used efforts of the Greek-Americans for their own political aims.[209]

Whatever its reasons were, the arms embargo was the most important action of the United States after the Johnson letter to force Turkey to act in a certain way. The Turks felt the negative consequences of the embargo, but they did not change their policies toward Cyprus. The U.S. administration's opposition to the embargo might have played a role in this Turkish attitude. But it is also a fact that U.S. officials asked the Turks to make concessions in Cyprus to help the lifting of the embargo. The Turkish reaction was to suspend U.S. activities in military bases in Turkey rather than yield to U.S. pressures.

---

[202] Hackett, "Ethnic Politics in Congress: the Turkish Embargo Experience", p. 26, Legg, "Congress as Trojan Horse, the Turkish Embargo Problem, 1974-1978", p. 118, Birand, *Diyet*, p. 70.

[203] Hackett, "Ethnic Politics in Congress: the Turkish Embargo Experience", p. 26.

[204] Couloumbis and Hicks, "The Impact of Greek Americans Upon United States Foreign Policy", p. 152, Bölükbaşı, *Superpowers and the Third World*, p. 214.

[205] Couloumbis and Hicks, "The Impact of Greek Americans Upon United States Foreign Policy", p. 155.

[206] Ibid., pp. 162-163, Bölükbaşı, *Superpowers and the Third World*, pp. 214-215, Legg, "Congress as Trojan Horse, the Turkish Embargo Problem, 1974-1978", pp. 117, 120, Hackett, "Ethnic Politics in Congress: the Turkish Embargo Experience", p. 29.

[207] Bölükbaşı, *Superpowers and the Third World*, pp. 215-216, Legg, "Congress as Trojan Horse, the Turkish Embargo Problem, 1974-1978", p. 118.

[208] Hackett, "Ethnic Politics in Congress: the Turkish Embargo Experience", p. 29.

[209] Couloumbis and Hicks, "The Impact of Greek Americans Upon United States Foreign Policy", p. 174, Laipson, *Congressional-Executive Relations and the Turkish Arms Embargo*, p. 5.

e) Arguments of Turkish Rulers against the Embargo

Firstly, Turkish authorities claimed that their military operations in Cyprus were just and in conformity with international law and agreements and that, therefore, the arms embargo, which aimed at punishing Turkey for its Cyprus action, was unjust. Secondly, Turkish authorities argued that the arms embargo was an obstacle to the negotiation process on Cyprus in many ways: 1- It encouraged the uncompromising attitude of the Greek side. 2- It brought Turkey under psychological pressure. If it made concessions in this situation it would seem yielding under U.S. pressure.[210] 3- The embargo changed the balance between the positions of the two sides by putting pressure on only one side and thus it undermined the peace negotiations from the outset.[211]

Thirdly, Turkish rulers always stressed that the Cyprus question and the bilateral defense cooperation between Turkey and the United States were separate issues and could not be linked with each other.[212] Fourthly, they pointed out that the supply of American arms to Turkey was not a favor, but an essential obligation under a military defense alliance.[213] Fifthly, Turkish authorities argued that the arms embargo would harm the NATO defense system by causing the destruction of its southeastern flank and the weakening one of its members.[214] Sixthly, they warned that the arms embargo could cause the total breakdown of U.S.-Turkish relations. Finally, Turkish officials claimed that the arms embargo was a discriminatory act of the United State toward Turkey because it did not apply the same U.S. laws against other countries such as Greece and Cyprus, which used U.S.-supplied military equipment for non-defensive purposes.[215]

f) Turkish Public's Reaction to the Intervention and Embargo

Some Turkish people, especially leftist ones, believed that the Cyprus coup was a plot organized under the auspices of the United States.[216] In their opinion, the United States expected that the Cyprus coup would solve the chronic Cyprus problem to its advantage by removing anti-American Makarios and unifying Cyprus with pro-American Greece. They also alleged that the Americans predicted that Turkish Prime Minister Bülent Ecevit with anti-American and leftist inclinations would not be able to resist the Cyprus coup, and thus he would lose his credibility at home and would be replaced by a more pro-American politician.

---

[210] Speeches of the Turkish foreign ministers, Turan Güneş and Melih Esenbel, in Turkish Parliament in *Cumhuriyet*, 26 October 1974, p. 1, 18 December 1974, p. 7.

[211] Foreign Minister Melih Esenbel, *Millet Meclisi Tutanak Dergisi (MMTD)*, 21 February 1975, term 4, sess. 2, vol. 9, pp. 459-460.

[212] Turkish P.M. Demirel's talk to Kissinger in Birand, *Diyet*, p. 124, Grimmett, *Turkish-U.S. Defense Relationship: the Arms Embargo Issue*, p. 2, Melih Esenbel, *MMTD*, 21 February 1975, op. cit., pp. 459-460 , Foreign Minister İhsan Sabri Çağlayangil, *MMTD*, 12 June 1975, term 4, sess. 2, vol. 12, p. 579.

[213] Esenbel, *MMTD*, 21 February 1975, op. cit., p. 460, Turkish P.M. Sadi Irmak's statement to journalists in *Cumhuriyet*, 4 February 1975, p. 7, Turkey's National Security Council's statement in *Cumhuriyet*, 17.6.1975, p. 9.

[214] Turkish P.M. Demirel's talk with President Ford in Birand, *Diyet*, p. 126.

[215] Turkish Defence Minister Hasan Işık's statement on the Turkish TV in *Cumhuriyet*, 27 September 1974, Turkish P.M. Demirel's talk with Kissinger in Birand, *Diyet*, p. 182.

[216] Birand, *30 Sıcak Gün*, pp. 30, 80, in *Cumhuriyet*: Oktay Akbal, "Paylaşmaya Doğru mu?", 20 July 1974, İlhan Selçuk, "Pencere", 24 July 1974 p. 2, Ali Sirmen "Dünyada Bugün", 26 July 1974, p. 3.

The Turkish military intervention in Cyprus received unanimous support from Turkish public opinion. There was no other issue, domestic or foreign, on which there was such unanimity in Turkey. All Turkish major parties and the domestic press supported the Turkish military action. There were no MPs and no editorials in any major newspapers and magazines criticizing the move and calling for the withdrawal of Turkish troops from Cyprus. Turkish public opinion unanimously condemned the arms embargo as an anti-Turkish move and deplored the use of arms supplies as a tool to exert influence on Turkish policy. Nobody suggested withdrawing from Cyprus or making any compromise.[217] Even the Turkish armed forces, which were the most affected element of the Turkish political structure by the arms embargo, did not favor any concessions under the American pressure. Only a small group of leftist radicals, intellectual Marxists, opposed Turkey's military intervention because they felt that Turkey was acting as an imperialist state.[218]

11. CONCLUSION

The Cyprus question was a test of the U.S.-Turkish alliance in a matter, which did not the concern common security interests that constituted the basis of the alliance. The problem mainly concerned Turkish national interests and foreign policy. The United States interested in the development of the matter because of global, strategic interests and policies, stemmed from being a superpower. This proves that the U.S.-Turkish relationship was a small-big state relationship. Turkey would not advise or try to influence the United States in its policy toward Vietnam.

The Johnson letter in 1964 had claimed that Turkish rulers had the commitment to consult with the U.S. administration before taking any action in Cyprus. In fact, Turkish authorities always complied with this advice by informing the Americans on their action on Cyprus before initiating them. This situation gives the impression that the U.S.-Turkish alliance bore some characteristics of the patron-client relationship. But it is also related to the Turkish perception that close allies should consult with each other in every matter concerning each state. Another reason for this attitude might be Turkish rulers' intention to use U.S. opposition to appease agitated public opinion.

It is not true, as some Turks had claimed that the United States was particularly opposed to the Turkish cause on Cyprus and supported the Greek side. It was mainly concerned with its own interests while reacting to developments in the Cyprus question. When it thought that pressuring Turkey was necessary it did not hesitate to act in this way. U.S. pressures on Turkey before 1965 were really heavy and forced the Turks to abandon their proposed intervention in Cyprus. However, the Americans also had to consider the possibility of losing Turkey's alliance. Therefore, they did not take direct forceful actions such as the active involvement of the U.S. Sixth Fleet in stopping Turkish ships. They also acted more cautiously after 1964 not to alienate the Turks, being aware of the severe official Turkish response and the anti-Americanism among Turkish people. Turkey could threaten to leave NATO in the face U.S. pressures, but had to consider the consequences of its action. It certainly did not wish to be left alone against the Soviet threat; it needed U.S. and NATO

---

[217] Discussions in Parliament, *MMTD*, 20 February 1975, term 4, sess. 2, vol. 9, pp. 367-372, 21 February 1975, ibid., pp. 444-457.

[218] *Campany, Turkey and the United States,* pp. 52-53.

support for its security, and it did not want to weaken its position on Cyprus by losing all Western sympathy and understanding.

The U.S. attitude toward the Cyprus problem before 1965 led Turkish rulers to be more cautious in their relations with the USA, suspecting that their interests could be adversely affected by U.S. actions. It also inspired the Turks to have a more independent and flexible foreign policy by improving relations with the Eastern bloc, the Third World and neighboring countries. So both the U.S.-Turkish alliance and Turkish foreign policy were affected by developments in the Cyprus question.

The Americans managed to prevent Turkish intervention in Cyprus in November 1967. However, this time they took great care not to antagonize the Turks. Their influence was not too heavy at that time. But, at the end, the Americans achieved their objective of preventing Turkish intervention.

In 1974, the United Stated failed to prevent the Turkish intervention in Cyprus. Its influence apparently did not work this time. But the Americans were not too determined in this direction. Turkey's strategic importance for U.S. interests played a role in this attitude. The weakness of the U.S. government because of Watergate was another factor. The Turks were not entirely free in their actions in Cyprus because of U.S. pressures and opposition. They stopped their first intervention before achieving their original aims and after capturing 36 percent of Cyprus faced the punishment of the U.S. congress (the embargo and later conditioning of U.S. assistance) whose effects have continued up to now. The embargo did not succeed in forcing the Turks to change their Cyprus policies radically, but affected their future defense policies and increased their isolation in the international arena. The suspension of U.S. activities in Turkish bases was Turkey's proof that it was not a satellite of the USA.

Chapter 9

THE OPIUM ISSUE AND TURKISH-AMERICAN RELATIONS

The opium controversy between the United States and Turkey broke out as a result of the American administration's campaign against the drug addiction problem among American youth. U.S. rulers made great efforts to persuade Turkey to decrease its opium production and even to ban it completely. Turkey's failure to fulfil American demands satisfactorily because of domestic reasons made the issue one of the most important matters of Turkish-American relations at the end of the 1960s and at the beginning of the 1970s. The opium question was a matter outside the formal defense alliance between the two countries, but touched the feelings of both American and Turkish people. Like the Cyprus question, it would have been a test of the Turkish-American alliance in a matter, which did not concern common strategic interests. However, the issue was forestalled by the Turkish intervention in Cyprus in July 1974 and ceased to be an important matter after the U.S. Congress imposed an arms embargo on Turkey because of its actions in Cyprus and the Turkish government took effective measures preventing Turkish opium from falling into illicit hands.

1. THE OPIUM ISSUE BEFORE THE NIXON ADMINISTRATION

a) The Period before 1960

Opium had been grown by Turkish peasants in Anatolia for centuries. Turkey had long been a major exporter of opium for the licit medicinal market. The first contact between Turkey and the United States involving opium occurred at the beginning of the nineteenth century. When the British East India Company forbade its ships to carry opium to China in 1805, American ships moved into the opium trade from Turkey to China and held a monopoly of it for fifteen years to the extent that one Chinese official in Canton thought that Turkey was a part of the United States.[1]

In the early 1900s, the growing concern for drug addiction at home and the dislike for the dirty trade abroad led American officials to take up the opium issue in the international arena.

---

[1] James W. Spain, "The United States, Turkey and the Poppy", *Middle East Journal*, Summer 1975, vol. 29, No. 3, p. 295.

The United States played a leading role in convening an international opium commission in Shanghai in 1909[2] and in drawing up The Hague International Opium Convention in 1912.[3] In 1923, the American Consul General in İstanbul suggested that Turkey could be persuaded to eliminate opium production if a suitable crop such as silk could be substituted for poppy.[4] The memorandum of the U.S. ambassador to Turkey, Joseph C. Grew, on his farewell conversation with the Turkish foreign minister on 29 February 1932 stated: "I observed that there was still one unfortunate element which could exact an adverse effect on relations; namely the continued clandestine traffic in narcotics from Turkey to the United States."[5]

In spite of her dislike for the League of Nations, the United States cooperated with the League's Advisory Committee on the Traffic of Opium and Other Dangerous Drugs and participated actively in preparation of a draft convention focusing primarily on controlling opium at its source.[6] The American Congress's Joint Resolution No. 241 which was approved by the President on 1 July 1944 (Public Law 400, 78th Congress) urged all poppy-growing nations to enter into an international agreement to reduce the production of opium to the medical and scientific needs of the world.[7]

Turkey adhered to the League of Nations convention to control the production and sale of narcotics in 1932 and made the production and marketing of opium a state monopoly in 1933.[8] According to the information which was given by a Turkish official to Harvey R. Wellman, the Special Assistant for Narcotic Matters to the U.S. Secretary of State in 1971, Turkish President Kemal Atatürk advocated as early as 1937 the replacement of the cultivation of opium by sugarbeets because he was concerned that Turkish opium was circulating as a poison in the world.[9] On 14 May 1945, the İnönü government explained Turkey's position that opium production should be restricted to a few countries including Turkey. It also gave assurances that Turkey would consent to every limitation of production, which might be contemplated under equal conditions for all producers.[10]

After the Second World War, the United States played the leading role in international efforts to control production and marketing of narcotic drugs. In 1953, the Opium Protocol was signed under United Nations auspices, limiting the authorization to produce opium for export to seven named producers, including Turkey.[11] Both Turkey and the United States signed and ratified the protocol. In the same year, Turkey licensed opium-growing farmers for the first time and made the opium production and exportation the responsibility of the Turkish Soil Products Office.[12]

In 1958, 42 of Turkey's 67 provinces were growing opium, which contained the highest raw morphine in the world. U.S. Secretary of State Christian B. Herter was informed at that

---

[2] Ibid., p. 296, Harvey R. Wellman, "Drug Abuse: A Challenge to U.S.-Turkish Cooperation in the Seventies", *Department of State Bulletin*, vol. 64, 1 February 1971, p. 142.

[3] Spain, "The United States, Turkey and the Poppy", p. 296, Wellman, "Drug Abuse: A Challenge to U.S.-Turkish Cooperation in the Seventies", p. 143.

[4] Spain, "The United States, Turkey and the Poppy", pp. 296-297.

[5] Ibid., p. 297.

[6] Ibid., p. 297.

[7] Joseph L. Zentner, "The 1972 Turkish Opium Ban: Needle in the Haystack Diplomacy", *World Affairs*, vol. 136, Summer 1973, p. 37.

[8] Ibid., p. 38, George S. Harris, *Troubled Alliance*, Washington D.C.: American Enterprise Institute, 1972, p. 191.

[9] Wellman, "Drug Abuse: A Challenge to U.S.-Turkish Cooperation in the Seventies", p. 144.

[10] Harris, *Troubled Alliance*, p. 191.

[11] Wellman, "Drug Abuse: A Challenge to U.S.-Turkish Cooperation in the Seventies", p. 143, Zentner, "The 1972 Turkish Opium Ban", p. 37.

[12] Zentner, "The 1972 Turkish Opium Ban", p. 38.

time that too much Turkish opium was entering the illicit traffic and that therefore Turkey should begin seriously to control its production.[13] During a CENTO meeting in Washington in 1959, reportedly Herter and CIA Director Dulles asked Turkish Prime Minister Adnan Menderes to prohibit opium cultivation in Turkey, but Menderes strongly rejected their demand and proposed that Turkey and the USA should establish an opium industry in Turkey together and build a joint opium factory whose products would be sold to Europe.[14]

b) The Opium Issue in the 1960s

In 1961, the Single Convention on Narcotic Drugs was signed under United Nations auspices. The Convention, which came into force in 1964, aimed at consolidating existing treaties and bringing all narcotic substances under control. Under the Single Convention, the International Narcotics Control Board was authorized to administer the system of estimates and statistical control of all transactions concerning narcotic substances. As for the prevention of the illicit drug traffic, the Board's authority was limited to surveillance, investigation, publicity and recommendations. The responsibility for preventing opium from falling into illicit channels lay mainly with the treaty members.[15] The United States attributed great importance to the Single Convention and always drew attention to this treaty while pressurizing Turkey on opium.

In the mid-1960s, U.S. President Lyndon B. Johnson began to stress the opium issue in the U.S. relations with Turkey and thus linked the domestic issue of drug abuse with the foreign policy objective of controlling opium production in producer nations.[16] In Spain's words, Johnson was "hoping to salvage part of his dream of "the Great Society" from the inroads of the Vietnam War" by achieving success in the increasing heroin addiction problem.[17]

Turkey initially showed no enthusiasm toward American demands. The İnönü government officially rejected the American demand to prohibit opium cultivation.[18] In 1963, the Turkish Parliament passed Law No. 245, which reiterated Turkey's promise to fight against illicit opium traffic and to maintain strict control on opium.[19] The Demirel government, which came to power in November 1965, showed more willingness to cooperate with the United States in fighting against the illegal opium trade.[20] The Turkish Parliament ratified the Single Convention on Narcotics in December 1966 and Turkey formally acceded to this treaty on 22 June 1967.[21]

---

[13] Ibid., p. 39.
[14] Cüneyt Arcayürek, *Çankaya'ya Giden Yol 1971-1973*, Ankara: Bilgi Yayınevi, 1985, p. 146, Özgen Acar, "Afyon Raporu", *Cumhuriyet*, 20 July 1970.
[15] Wellman, "Drug Abuse: A Challenge to U.S.-Turkish Cooperation in the Seventies", p. 143.
[16] Michael Allan Turner, *The International Politics of Narcotics*, Ph.D. Thesis, Kent State University, 1975, p. 106.
[17] Spain, "The United States, Turkey and the Poppy", p. 297.
[18] Arcayürek, *Çankaya'ya Giden Yol 1971-1973*, p. 147.
[19] Turkish Agriculture Minister İlhami Ertem, *Millet Meclisi Tutanak Dergisi* (*MMTD*), 24 July 1970, term 3, sess. 1, vol. 8, p. 631.
[20] Harris, *Troubled Alliance*, p. 192, Turner , *The International Politics of Narcotics*, pp. 122-123.
[21] Harris, *Troubled Alliance*, pp. 192-193.

2. U.S. PRESSURES ON TURKEY ON OPIUM 1969-1971

a) Views of the Americans on Turkey's Opium Production

The following section is largely based on opinions of American officials and American public opinion.

Drug addiction was a serious problem in the United States at the end of the 1960s and in the 1970s.[22] It was threatening the whole of American society in cities and suburbs. The number of drug addicts was increasing dangerously. The Director of the Bureau of Narcotics and Dangerous Drugs (BNDD), John E. Ingersoll, gave some figures in his statement on 26 October 1970: "Ten years ago we estimated there were 60,000 narcotic addicts in the United States; today we believe there are two to three times that amount. Ninety-seven percent of the addicts are addicted to heroin. Our list of addicts is growing by several thousand each year, and in 1969 the number of new addicts doubled from the previous year."[23] It was estimated in 1973 that there were about 600,000 heroin addicts in the United States and that half of them lived in New York.[24]

American law enforcement officials believed that there was a direct link between heroin addiction and increase of crime.[25] They claimed that at least half of all street crimes and burglaries in New York City were committed by addicts who stole to maintain their habits.[26] The BNDD estimated that a typical male addict needed 50 milligrams of heroin a day to maintain his habit and that this cost him about 29 dollars a day and 10,556 dollars a year. Thus heroin was a huge industry pushing people to crime.[27] John Ingersoll's figures on crime related to heroin addiction was as follows: "In 1965 there were less than 50,000 arrests in the United States for drug-related offences; in 1969 there were 233,690 such arrests. Almost 20 percent of these arrests were in suburban areas, where drug problems had not existed in previous years. Arrest trends for all drug-law violations increased nearly 500 percent during the last ten years. During the same period the arrest trends for persons under 18 years of age increased nearly 2500 percent."[28]

Deaths caused by heroin addiction also increased in the United States. In New York City alone three or four persons were dying because of drug-related causes per day.[29] According to one estimate, in the whole of America, people were dying of drug addiction at the rate of 8 to 10 per day.[30]

The number of families who were affected by drug addiction problems, too, was increasing greatly. Statistical figures showed that almost one third of American families complained about heroin addiction of their children.[31] The rise of heroin addiction among the sons and daughters of the American elite led the American administration to attribute the

---

[22] Wellman, "Drug Abuse: A Challenge to U.S.-Turkish Cooperation in the Seventies", p. 141.
[23] Ibid., p. 141.
[24] The Staff and Editors of Newsday, *The Heroin Trail*, London: Souvenir Press, 1975, pp. xi, 186, Özcan Köknel, "Haşhaş Ekimi ve ABD", *Milliyet*, 4 November 1975, Zentner, "The 1972 Turkish Opium Ban", p. 47n.
[25] Turner , *The International Politics of Narcotics*, pp. 9, 11-12.
[26] *The Heroin Trail*, pp. xi-xii.
[27] Ibid., p. 187.
[28] Wellman, "Drug Abuse: A Challenge to U.S.-Turkish Cooperation in the Seventies", p. 141.
[29] Ingersoll's statement, ibid., p. 141, Spain, "The United States, Turkey and the Poppy", p. 298.
[30] Ragıp Üner, "Afyon Sorunu ve Amerika", *Cumhuriyet*, 18 March 1971.
[31] Arcayürek, *Çankaya'ya Giden Yol 1971-1973*, p. 146.

utmost importance to the matter.[32] Ingersoll voiced the complaint of American families in his statement:

> I speak for over 200 million human beings who are alarmed, distressed, and even outraged about a calamitous problem they did not create and which they cannot solve alone. They do not understand why the nations of the world cannot bring an end to the waste and devastation that drug abuse, particularly opiate addiction, is causing our people. There is growing unity of opinion among the various and diverse segments of our population: Illicit narcotics must go.[33]

The Americans believed that the real cause of their sufferings was the availability of heroin, which was derived from illegally, supplied foreign opium.[34] Source countries, and not the United States, were considered the real cause of the American drug disease. Among the producer countries Turkey was the most notorious for the Americans. The Bureau of Narcotics and Dangerous Drugs alleged that 80 percent of heroin illegally consumed in the United States was derived from Turkish opium.[35] American drug officers claimed that they reached this conclusion because they could identify Turkish opium with its high percentage of morphine.[36]

According to American sources, Turkish opium reached the United States in the following way: Turkish villagers, who had very low incomes, were tempted to sell opium gum to illegal buyers because, while the government paid about 10 dollars for a kilogram of opium gum, illegal drug smugglers paid three times more for the same amount.[37] Collectors who were usually well known to villagers collected opium gum and took it to secret depots.[38] It was changed to morphine base easily by a simple chemical process before leaving Turkey.[39] Changing 10 kilograms of opium worth 300 dollars into 1 kilogram of morphine increased its value to 500 dollars.[40] Turkish patrons smuggled morphine base abroad through custom points like Kapıkule[41] and passed it through Bulgaria in return for a price. They were expected to occasionally reciprocate by providing the smuggling of guns and ammunition from Bulgaria to Turkish revolutionaries and supplying intelligence information to the

---

[32] George Harris, "Turkey Between Alliance and Alienation", *Foreign Policy*, vol. 8, Nos. 3-4, 1980, p. 121.

[33] Wellman, "Drug Abuse: A Challenge to U.S.-Turkish Cooperation in the Seventies", p. 140.

[34] Ibid., p. 141.

[35] Turner , *The International Politics of Narcotics,* pp. 3, 106, Harris, *Troubled Alliance,* p. 192, Oakley S. Roy, *Drugs, Society and Human Behaviour,* Saint Louis: the C. V. Mosby Company, 1972, p. 193, *The Heroin Trail,* pp. xiii, 7, *ABD Dışişleri Bakanı William Rogers'ın Kongre'ye Sunduğu Rapordan Bölümler,* Ankara: Amerikan Basın ve Kültür Merkezi, 1972, p. 4.

[36] İsmail Cem's interview with former Turkish foreign minister İ. S. Çağlayangil in İsmail Cem, *Tarih Açısından 12 Mart,* İstanbul: Cem Yayınevi, 1980, pp. 311-312. Later some Turkish newspapers reported that American officials misled American people on the source of heroin used in the United States. Reportedly, in 1975 the former chairman of the Congress's commission on dangerous drugs, Walter Minnick, told congressmen that the U.S. Congress and people had been badly misled by American officials on the source of heroin and claimed that Turkey was chosen as scapegoat because she could be pressurized easily. Ali Sirmen "Dünyada Bugün: Afyonlama", *Cumhuriyet,* 8 March 1975. In another report it was claimed that John Ingersoll deliberately tried to present Turkey as the source of American drug addiction problem to divert public anger from the administration. Selahattin Güler, "ABD Kongresini Türkiye'de Görevli Ajanlar Yanılttı," *Cumhuriyet,* 24 March 1975.

[37] Roy, *Drugs, Society and Human Behaviour,* p. 193, *The Heroin Trail,* p. 2, Wellman, "Drug Abuse: A Challenge to U.S.-Turkish Cooperation in the Seventies", p. 44.

[38] *The Heroin Trail,* p. 11.

[39] Ibid., pp. xiii, 11, Roy, *Drugs, Society and Human Behaviour,* p. 194.

[40] Roy, *Drugs, Society and Human Behaviour,* p. 194.

[41] *The Heroin Trail,* pp. 20-42.

Bulgarian secret police.[42] After morphine was converted to heroin in Marseilles laboratories in southern France through a more complicated chemical process which required sophisticated techniques, modern equipment and chemical expertise, the price of a kilogram heroin went up to 4000 to 6000 dollars.[43]

Heroin was then smuggled into the United States by a number of routes, especially through Latin America.[44] Professional smugglers easily passed heroin through the U.S. Bureau of Customs.[45] A large portion of the smuggled heroin ended up in the New York metropolitan area, where it was either adulterated and sold wholesale to dealers throughout the eastern United States or was adulterated, put into bags or packages and sold to the numerous addicts in the area.[46] While one kilogram of heroin was delivered in the United States for 15,000 dollars, it was then sold to distributors who might pay 30,000 to 40,000 dollars for the same amount. The dilution was so great that retail price of a kilogram of heroin might be a quarter of a million dollars at street level.[47]

In the light of these facts, American officials were convinced that their fight against drug addiction at home would not be successful unless the source of heroin, Turkey, was shut off. In their opinion, Turkey had ratified the Single Convention and thus undertook the responsibility to implement the most effective measures in order to eliminate illegal production and sale of opium in Turkey.[48] They further argued that Turkey should totally ban opium production[49] because a country was obliged to eradicate its opium cultivation if it could not successfully prevent the diversion of opium into illegal channels.[50]

b) The Nixon Administration's Fight against Opium

After becoming president, Richard Nixon immediately launched an all-out war against drug addiction at home[51] and opium production abroad. He had come to office with a strong commitment to ending violence in the street, which was growing as drug addicts turned to crime to finance their habits. As a part of this campaign, from 1969 onwards, the American administration pressured Turkey publicly to close down all of its opium fields,[52] making the issue a high priority in relations between the two countries.[53] It also made bilateral

---

[42] Ibid., p. 53.
[43] Roy, *Drugs, Society and Human Behaviour*, p. 194.
[44] *The Heroin Trail*, p. 167.
[45] Ibid., p. 156.
[46] Ibid., p. xii.
[47] Roy, *Drugs, Society and Human Behaviour*, p. 194, Wellman, "Drug Abuse: A Challenge to U.S.-Turkish Cooperation in the Seventies," p. 144, *International Aspects of the Narcotics Problem*, Hearings Before the Subcommittee on Foreign Affairs, House of Representatives, 92nd Congress, 1st Session, July 7,8,9, and 30, 1971, Washington: U.S. Government Printing Office, 1971, p. 5.
[48] Wellman, "Drug Abuse: A Challenge to U.S.-Turkish Cooperation in the Seventies", pp. 143, 145.
[49] Spain, "The United States, Turkey and the Poppy", p. 298.
[50] Harris, *Troubled Alliance*, p. 195, Turner , *The International Politics of Narcotics*, p. 128.
[51] For U.S. domestic measures against drug addiction see Wellman, "Drug Abuse: A Challenge to U.S.-Turkish Cooperation in the Seventies", pp. 141-142, *The Heroin Trail*, pp. xii, xiii, *Keesing's Contemporary Archives*, 1971-1972 vol. 18, p. 25227.
[52] Harris, *Troubled Alliance*, p. 193.
[53] Spain, "The United States, Turkey and the Poppy", pp. 298, 303.

arrangements with other states such as France, Mexico and Canada to fight against the illicit drug traffic.[54]

In his message to Congress on 17 June 1971, President Nixon said:

> If we cannot destroy the drug menace in America, then it will surely in time destroy us, I am not prepared to accept this alternative... I am proposing appropriation of additional funds to meet the cost of rehabilitating drug abusers, and I will ask for additional funds to increase our enforcement efforts to further tighten the noose around the necks of drug peddlers, and thereby loosen the noose around the necks of drug users... I am proposing additional steps to strike at the supply side of the drug equation - to halt the drug traffic by striking at the illegal producers of drugs, the growing of those plants from which drugs are derived, and trafficking in these drugs beyond our borders.[55]

In order to coordinate international efforts on illegal opium production and trafficking President Nixon created the Cabinet Committee on International Narcotics Control in September 1971.[56]

c) U.S. Efforts to Eradicate Turkey's Opium Production

It was reported that several times the United States approached Turkey to buy its whole opium crop. In mid-1969, President Nixon dispatched D. Patrick Moynihan to Turkey with a virtual blank cheque to buy the entire 1969 crop, but the Turks rejected the offer flatly.[57] Later the American ambassador to Turkey, William J. Handley, proposed to Foreign Minister Çağlayangil to pay for the whole opium crop. The reply came from Prime Minister Demirel through Çağlayangil: Opium had been grown in Turkey for centuries, there was even a city, which was named after opium. Turkey could not stop opium cultivation, but could restrict it.[58] Handley was not satisfied with the answer, he wanted to see Demirel personally.[59] In their meeting, Handley proposed to Demirel: Turkey would announce an end to opium production and plough up its 1970 crop in exchange for 5 million dollars to compensate the growers.[60] Demirel rejected the offer and said that he could not find any Turk who would drive bulldozers to destroy poppy fields.[61]

In April 1970, U.S. Under Secretary of State Elliot Richardson visited Ankara. In his press conference at the Esenboğa airport on 23 April, Richardson praised the Turkish government for showing understanding toward the drug addiction problem of the United States. When a reporter asked whether Turkey would reduce its opium-growing provinces to seven in return for an additional three million dollars of U.S. aid, Richardson confirmed that

---

[54] *Keesing's Contemporary Archives*, vol. 18, p. 24693, *The Heroin Trail*, p. 90, Ragıp Üner, "Afyon Sorunu ve Amerika", Wellman, "Drug Abuse: A Challenge to U.S.-Turkish Cooperation in the Seventies", p. 142.
[55] *Keesing's Contemporary Archives*, vol. 18, pp. 24692-24693.
[56] Turner, *The International Politics of Narcotics*, p. 202.
[57] Turner, *The International Politics of Narcotics*, pp. 126, 139-140.
[58] Demirel's statement to a Turkish TV documentary in Mehmet Ali Birand et al., *12 Mart*, Ankara: İmge Kitabevi, 1994, p. 169.
[59] İhsan Sabri Çağlayangil, *Anılarım*, İstanbul: Yılmaz Yayınları, August 1990, p. 324.
[60] Turner, *The International Politics of Narcotics*, p. 126, Arcayürek, *Çankaya'ya Giden Yol 1971-1973*, p. 150, Çağlayangil's interview with İsmail Cem in Cem, *Tarih Açısından 12 Mart*, p. 312.
[61] Arcayürek, *Çankaya'ya Giden Yol 1971-1973*, p. 150.

among other things they negotiated measures which would prevent opium from falling into illicit channels and a further decrease in Turkey's opium production.[62]

Richardson's visit to Ankara publicized the opium issue in Turkish domestic politics. The Turkish press reported that Richardson's talks with Turkish officials were aimed at forcing Turkey to eliminate both legal and illegal opium production. Fierce criticism of the United States appeared in opinion columns of leftist and rightist newspapers. Further criticism was heard when a story in the *New York Times* triggered the rumor that American narcotics officials advocated withholding the requested 40 million dollar economic aid to Turkey in order to force a ban on opium production.[63]

Subsequently, U.S.-Turkish discussions on opium continued intensively. During the CENTO meeting in the United States in May 1970, Turkish Foreign Minister Çağlayangil told Richardson that Turkey could not undertake to ban opium cultivation.[64] In May 1970, high-level BNDD officials, Andrew Tartaglino and John Cusack, visited Turkey.[65] In June 1970, the U.S. President's special envoy, Moynihan, told Turkey's NATO representative Muharrem Nuri Birgi that Turkey should ban opium cultivation if it wanted to avoid harming Turkish-American cooperation in all areas.[66]

The most important event, which triggered an explosion of widespread Turkish anger toward the United States, was U.S. Attorney General John Mitchell's testimony before the House Ways and Means Committee on 20 July 1970. In his testimony, Mitchell gave approval to the concept of economic sanctions in order to shut off opium traffic from countries including Turkey. During the committee meeting, Congressman Vanik proposed to impose economic and trade sanctions against the countries, which did not cooperate with the United States on preventing illegal opium trafficking. Mitchell replied that his government, mainly the State Department, was negotiating with these countries and recently made an initiative in the framework of NATO and he added that if these initiatives were not successful the United States should take further measures.

When the Director of BNDD, John Ingersoll, claimed that 80 percent of the opium illegally introduced to the United States came from Turkey, Vanik stated that economic sanctions might be the best tool to combat the problem. He suggested to Attorney General Mitchell that "we ought to set up a system that would provide for an embargo, or suspension of trade, or even suspension of relationships" until Turkey should "control the problems" of drug traffic. Thereupon Mitchell said that he quite agreed with the concept: "we are all for cutting off the source in any way that is in the best interest of this country." He mentioned some measures taken by Turkey to cut opium production and to prevent illegal trafficking, but he said that he did not think these measures would be successful and that this situation did not prevent him from taking other forceful measures to stop the flow of opium. Mitchell finally added "any legislation or administrative action that can cut down the production and... the illicit traffic of opium... be the country Turkey or another, we, at the Justice Department, would be in favor of it..."[67]

---

[62] *Dışişleri Bakanlığı Belleteni*, April 1970, p. 133.
[63] Harris, *Troubled Alliance*, p. 194, Turner , *The International Politics of Narcotics*, pp. 126-127.
[64] Arcayürek, *Çankaya'ya Giden Yol 1971-1973*, p. 153.
[65] *Cumhuriyet*, 17 May 1970, p. 1.
[66] Arcayürek, *Çankaya'ya Giden Yol 1971-1973*, p. 153.
[67] Harris, *Troubled Alliance*, p. 194n, *Milliyet*, 23 July 1970, *Cumhuriyet*, 23 July 1970, p. 7.

Mitchell's threat of economic sanctions was immediately denounced by the Turkish government. On 22 July 1970, the Turkish Foreign Ministry issued a statement expressing disappointment over Mitchell's remarks and declaring that those kinds of irresponsible statements would harm Turkish-American friendship and cast suspicion on the American attitude.[68] Turkish Prime Minister Süleyman Demirel told reporters that if there were such a statement Turkey would feel sorry about it and added that statements, which were not compatible with the sovereignty of states, could not be tolerated.[69] In the parliament, Turkish Ministers Turhan Bilgin and İlhami Ertem declared that no country could punish Turkey and intervene in its affairs. They accused people who publicized Mitchell's statement of deliberately trying to show that Turkey was under the influence of the United States.[70] MP Celal Kargılı said that the Turkish nation was in deep sorrow because it was scolded by the Attorney General of the U.S. government in a manner, which would fit colonies.[71]

Turkish newspaper columnists voiced the following criticism of Mitchell's statement: The statement clearly showed that Turkey was dependent on the United States and was its satellite. The Americans considered Turkey their colony and therefore did not hesitate to pressurize Turkish rulers to stop opium cultivation. The United States itself failed to take drastic measures at and within its borders to stop heroin smuggling, but tried to hide its incompetence by attacking Turkey. Mitchell's statement showed that the Americans cared only about their own interests. In this context, it was reminiscent of the famous Johnson letter and demonstrated inequality in the U.S.-Turkish relationship.[72]

As Harris stated, the Mitchell statement had not caused as sharp a dividing line in Turkish-American relations as the Johnson letter had. It further strained relations between the two countries, but it did not bring about a dramatic change. "The opium issue had risen too suddenly to seriously affect Turkish public opinion and was not in any case the basic national issue that Cyprus had been." Unlike the reaction to the 1964 Cyprus crisis, Turkish people were no longer shocked by the realization that even allies could have fundamental differences. In fact, after Mitchell made his statement, the American Department of State promptly denied any intention of applying economic sanctions against Turkey.[73]

At the UN Narcotics Committee meeting in Geneva in September 1970, the Turkish representative explained that regulation, not eradication, of opium production was the Turkish government's aim and that Turkey would not accept any obligation outside the present treaties on opium.[74] On 8 October 1970, John Ingersoll brought a personal letter of President Nixon to Turkish Prime Minister Demirel, urging the Turkish government to help the United States on the drug abuse problem. Demirel's letter to Nixon, which was dated 10 November 1970, stated that Turkey was aware of the gravity of the problem and would cooperate with the United States to fight against it. However, the letter did not make any promise to ban opium cultivation completely.[75] In fact, President Nixon had sent another personal and secret

---

[68] *Cumhuriyet*, 23 July 1970, p. 7.

[69] Ibid.

[70] *MMTD*, 24 July 1970, term 3, sess. 1, vol. 8, p. 630-632.

[71] Ibid., pp. 626-629.

[72] In *Cumhuriyet*: Oktay Akbal, "Amerikasız da Yaşanır", İlhan Selçuk, "Düşün" 24 July 1970, p. 2, Cihad Baban, "Demirel Haklı", 28 July 1970, p. 2; Abdi İpekçi, "Türkiye Cezalandırılacakmış", *Milliyet*, 22 July 1970, pp. 1 and 9.

[73] Harris, *Troubled Alliance*, p. 195, Turner, *The International Politics of Narcotics*, pp. 141-142.

[74] Harris, *Troubled Alliance*, p. 195, *Cumhuriyet*, 4 October 1970, p. 1.

[75] Arcayürek, *Çankaya'ya Giden Yol 1971-1973*, pp. 148-149.

letter to Demirel in January 1969. In this letter, Nixon reminded Demirel that when the Soviet Union threatened Turkey after the Second World War, the United States had come to Turkey's rescue. It was now Turkey's turn to help the United States on the opium issue, which posed a similar threat to American people.[76]

Allegedly, the U.S. dislike for the Demirel government on the opium issue played a role in the Turkish military "coup by memorandum" on 12 March 1971.[77] Turhan Bilgin, who was state minister in the Demirel government, later claimed that the CIA had prepared plans in the framework of NATO to topple the Turkish government. He further asserted that one high-level American official had said at that time that the American drug abuse problem could be solved only through the fall of the Demirel government.[78] According to İsmail Cem, during their talk on 7 February 1974, Çağlayangil, the foreign minister of the Demirel government, made the following remarks: The United States was not pleased with the Demirel government because of certain matters such as opium, the flights of American U-2 planes and the use of American bases in Turkey. The government had been weakened by its internal problems and was expected to fall in the near future. The United States correctly assessed the situation and accelerated the process of the Demirel government's fall. When it fell, Turkey's anti-NATO stance came to an end, leftists and the opposition to NATO were crushed and opium production was banned, thus the United States and NATO were pleased.[79]

It is not likely that the Turkish military would have halted the normal democratic process only or mainly to prohibit opium cultivation to please the Americans because it would be difficult to maintain agreement among top Turkish military officers in such an issue. It is even hard to prove the claim that U.S. displeasure with the Turkish government was one of reasons for the 12 March move because documents on both sides are classified. The only thing, which could be said, is that the United States had reasons for not being happy with the situation in Turkey at that time. One can easily see this fact by looking at widespread attacks against Americans in Turkey.[80]

d) U.S. Pressure upon Turkey on the Opium Issue

The Americans applied pressure tactics, for instance, they used the issue of economic and military assistance as leverage against Turkey to force her to comply with American demands on opium. Most authors agree with this conclusion.[81] Turkish public opinion was convinced of the existence of U.S. pressure. Members of the then Turkish government admitted that they were subjected to strong pressures by the United States on the opium issue.[82]

---

[76] Turhan Bilgin, "12 Mart", *Milliyet*, 24 March 1976 quoted by Cem, *Tarih Açısından 12 Mart*, pp. 294-295, Turner, *The International Politics of Narcotics*, pp. 125-126.

[77] Birand et al., *12 Mart*, p. 169.

[78] T. Bilgin, op. cit. quoted by Cem, *Tarih Açısından 12 Mart*, pp. 295-296.

[79] Cem, *Tarih Açısından 12 Mart*, pp. 299-300, 313-314. In Kurtul Altuğ's program on Turkish TV, Bunalımlı Yıllar, a high-level RPP member, Besim Üstünel, claimed that in a dinner in the U.S. embassy in Ankara one week before the 12 March move a high-level U.S. official from the State Department told him that deputy chairman of RPP's parliamentary caucus, Nihat Erim, promised the Americans to prohibit opium cultivation if the RPP came to power.

[80] *Keesing's Contemporary Archives*, vol. 18, pp. 24637-24639.

[81] Van Coufoudakis, "Turkey and the United States: the Problems and Prospects of a Post-War Alliance", *Journal of Political and Military Sociology*, vol. 9, No. 2, Fall 1981, p. 187, Roger Morris, *Uncertain Greatness*, London: Quartet Books, 1977, p. 272.

[82] Cağlayangil's interview with Cem in Cem, *Tarih Açısından 12 Mart*, p. 300.

It seems that the U.S. administration did not openly and officially use threats against Turkey, but advocated indirect pressures through prudent diplomacy. U.S. public officials, including BNDD members, called on the White House to use its leverage of military and economic aid on Turkey. They reasoned that the United States was subsidizing its allies at the expense of the moral and physical health of American citizens.[83] The Nixon administration, the Departments of State and Defence were opposed to such pressure diplomacy, claiming that it would harm the vital U.S.-Turkish alliance, and subsequently U.S. and NATO interests. They suggested that the United States should be helping the Turkish government rather than threatening it.[84] However, in Turner's words,

> American diplomats did not block the transmission of threatening messages to the Turks. Publicly, the administration objected to the holding of congressional hearings on some sixty bills calling for an end to military and economic aid to Turkey. Yet these same bills and the remarks of American legislators were indirectly utilized to emphasize the seriousness of the situation to the Turks. The Turks knew that the Americans would take some type of action if the opium crop were not brought under control... The Turks were aware that general reductions in American aid and personnel could have direct implications for them at a time of much needed improvement in their military hardware.[85]

The reasons for the U.S. administration's pressure on Turkey might be explained with the publicity, which the opium issue gained in domestic politics. The American government could not be indifferent to a matter, which concerned almost the whole American society, and which was closely followed by the Congress, the media and other public opinion groups. Since Turkey was believed to be the source of the U.S. heroin and since it was a weaker ally of the United States, it was natural and easy for U.S. rulers to direct their efforts against Turkey.

U.S. Congressmen took the lead in calling for measures to force Turkey to abandon its opium cultivation. They argued: The United States had given considerable military and economic aid to Turkey since the Second World War. The Turks surely owed the Americans a favor, therefore, they should be willing to give up the 5 million dollars a year they earned from legal opium production, which constituted less than one third of one percent of Turkey's total foreign trade.[86] In 1970 and 1971, congressmen continuously threatened to terminate all aid to Turkey if it did not stop opium production. They argued that this threat would force Turkey to cooperate with the United States on the matter.[87] Section 506 of the Foreign Assistance Act of 1971, passed by Congress, read as follows: "The use of funds herein appropriated to assist any country shall be suspended by the President in whole or in part when the President determines that the government of such country has failed to take appropriate steps to prevent narcotic drugs..."[88] It should be noted that congressmen were

---

[83] Turner, *The International Politics of Narcotics*, pp. 116-117, 197.

[84] Ibid., pp. 117, 120, 132-133, 138, 198. See comments of U.S. congressmen and officials in *International Aspects of the Narcotics Problem*, pp. 12, 17, 22, 75, 76.

[85] Turner, *The International Politics of Narcotics*, p. 121.

[86] Harris, *Troubled Alliance*, p. 196, Spain, "The United States, Turkey and the Poppy", p. 303, Arcayürek, *Çankaya'ya Giden Yol 1971-1973*, p. 145, Zentner, "The 1972 Turkish Opium Ban", p. 43, *Turkish Opium Ban Negotiations*, Hearing Before the Committee on Foreign Affairs, House of Representatives, 93rd Congress, 2nd Session, July 16, 1974, Washington: U.S. Government Printing Office, 1974, pp. 3, 32, 33, 50, 59.

[87] *International Aspects of the Narcotics Problem*, pp. 13, 42.

[88] Turner, *The International Politics of Narcotics*, p. 130.

mainly trying to placate their home constituencies by indicating they were indeed doing something about the situation.[89]

U.S. newspapers and magazines, too, contributed to the publicity of the opium issue by debating it intensively in their columns. They featured articles on the theme, "Let's Halt Heroin at the Source", calling the administration to shut off the flow of Turkish opium.[90] American public; parents, social workers, doctors, and police put great pressure on the U.S. administration to deal firmly with Turkey's opium production. American people had been convinced that the real cause of the drug abuse problem was Turkish opium and that Turkey was not doing enough to prevent its opium from poisoning American youth.[91]

Under the constant pressure from all sides, President Nixon felt that he had to do something about the drug problem. At least, he had to appear to be doing something. He was the candidate for the 1972 presidential elections and the most important and prominent matter for the American people at that time was the drug problem. If Nixon succeeded in forcing Turkey to stop its opium production, this would be a great victory for him and would increase his chance of winning the election.[92]

The Americans were justified in asking the Turks to do more in controlling their opium production. However, they probably made a mistake by directing all their efforts to achieving the prohibition of Turkish opium cultivation and seeing the issue as a means to further their political gains at home. U.S. rulers should have known that only halting the flow of Turkish opium would not end the drug addiction problem and that the elected Turkish governments could not ban a traditional means of earning a living under public pressure of the USA.

3. THE OPIUM ISSUE FROM TURKEY'S POINT OF VIEW

a) Turkish Actions to Control Opium Production

Turkey's Justice Party government committed itself to reducing poppy acreage and the number of provinces where poppy cultivation was legal. While the number of opium-growing provinces was 42 in 1960, this number was reduced in the 1961-62 harvest year to 30, in 1963-64 to 25, in 1966-67 to 21, in 1967-68 to 18, in 1968-69 to 11 and in 1969-70 to 9. The government decree on 30 June 1970 permitted the cultivation of opium crop in 7 provinces for the 1970-71 year and announced a further reduction to 4 for 1971-72.[93] On 20 and 24 July 1970, Turkish Agriculture Minister İlhami Ertem told the Turkish Parliament that the government's aim in reducing the number of poppy-growing provinces was to eliminate opium cultivation in the exterior, frontier provinces where control was difficult and diversion was easy and to concentrate production in a diminishing number of interior provinces for

---

[89] Ibid., pp. 277-278.

[90] Arcayürek, *Çankaya'ya Giden Yol 1971-1973*, pp. 149-150, Acar, "Afyon Raporu", 19 July 1970.

[91] In Ragıp Üner's opinion, American public came to this conclusion because of the intensive and effective propaganda of the Greek and Armenian Americans. Ragıp Üner, "Afyon Sorunu", *Cumhuriyet*, 18 March 1971.

[92] Cem, *Tarih Açısından 12 Mart*, p. 293, Birand et al., *12 Mart*, p. 169, the author's interview with former Turkish foreign minister Osman Olcay.

[93] Acar, "Afyon Raporu", 6 July 1970, Arcayürek, *Çankaya'ya Giden Yol 1971-1973*, p. 148, *Facts on Turkish Poppy*, Directorate General of Press and Information (of Turkey), p. 6, *Cumhuriyet*, 1 July 1970, p. 1, Wellman, "Drug Abuse: A Challenge to U.S.-Turkish Cooperation in the Seventies", p. 145, Zentner, "The 1972 Turkish Opium Ban", p. 39.

more effective supervision. He explained that this did not mean reducing opium production and that the government would continue to permit legal production under certain conditions which would prevent illegal production and trafficking.[94]

Turkish Foreign Minister Çağlayangil later stated that their ultimate aim was to permit opium cultivation only in the province of Afyon, which took its name from opium.[95] There was one report in 1967 that Turkish Prime Minister Demirel had agreed to end all poppy cultivation by 1971.[96] According to another report, on 1 August 1970, Demirel stated that "Turkey cannot ignore [the fact] that humanity... is being destroyed by drugs" and that since it was unable to stop the smugglers it had no option other than replacing the opium poppy with substitute crops in the long run.[97] U.S. official Wellman said in his speech to the American Turkish Society on 14 December 1970 that in Turkey "crop substitution, the development of alternative and more beneficial uses of land, labor, and capital, is still considered the fundamental solution to the problem of illicit opium production."[98]

As the number of provinces with legal cultivation was reduced, it was anticipated that the Turkish government would also reduce the total area under production.[99] However, it was claimed that Turkey's opium production was not being curtailed proportionately because the four grower provinces, Afyon, Burdur, Isparta and Kütahya, were the most productive provinces where more intensive cultivation and illegal planting were made.[100] According to *Newsday* reporters, Turkey produced 60 metric tons of opium crop in the 1969-70 harvest year, 149 metric tons in 1970-71 and 75 tons in 1971-72.[101] Reportedly even the total area under production was not reduced considerably. According to the figures given by Wellman, hectareage of the production area was reduced from 24,000 hectares in 1966 to 20,000 hectares in 1967, and to 13,000 hectares in 1968. The estimated land area was 13,000 hectares in 1969 and 15,300 hectares in 1971. The explanation for this apparent increase in land use for the opium poppy was that in the absence of a licensing and control law, existing controls did not limit land use for poppy cultivation in the provinces where opium production was legal.[102]

In fact, the Turkish government had long been criticized because of its failure to enact a licensing and control law on the opium production. In a meeting of the UN Commission on Narcotic Drugs Turkey gave a pledge that it would enact a strict licensing and control law in accordance with the Single Convention. When the Demirel government was forced out of office by the Turkish military on 21 March 1971, such a law had been prepared and was before the Grand National Assembly for approval.[103]

Among other measures taken to deal with illegal opium production and trafficking, the Turkish administration increased the government price for legal opium and expanded the

---

[94] *MMTD*, term 3, sess. 1, vol. 8, pp. 566, 630-632.

[95] Cem, *Tarih Açısından 12 Mart*, p. 312.

[96] Harris, "Turkey and the United States" in Kemal H. Karpat (ed.), *Turkey's Foreign Policy in Transition*, Leiden: E. J. Brill, 1975, p. 68, Turner, *The International Politics of Narcotics*, p. 124.

[97] Suha Bölükbaşı, *Super Powers and the Third World*, New York: University Press of America, 1988, p. 173.

[98] Wellman, "Drug Abuse: A Challenge to U.S.-Turkish Cooperation in the Seventies", p. 144.

[99] Ibid., p. 145.

[100] Roy, *Drugs, Society and Human Behaviour*, p. 193.

[101] *The Heroin Trail*, p. 15.

[102] Wellman, "Drug Abuse: A Challenge to U.S.-Turkish Cooperation in the Seventies", p. 145, *International Aspects of the Narcotics Problem*, p. 119.

[103] Wellman, "Drug Abuse: A Challenge to U.S.-Turkish Cooperation in the Seventies", p. 144, Spain, "The United States, Turkey and the Poppy", pp. 298, 305.

official collection organization in order to improve control.[104] It established heavy punishments for use and smuggling of heroin, reportedly heavier than U.S. and European punishments for the same crimes. In spite of its limited equipment and resources, the Turkish police showed considerable success in capturing heroin smugglers.[105] To fight against illicit opium production, the Turkish government stationed over 1,000 Turkish national police and gendarmes in the opium growing areas from 1967. In 1969, narcotics police sections and bureaus were organized, trained and equipped.[106]

In Spain's words, "the [Turkish] government [also] had from the beginning cooperated with American narcotics agencies, even subordinating national pride and permitting the stationing in Turkey of more American Drug Enforcement Agency personnel than in any other countries except Mexico and Thailand."[107] American narcotics agents worked closely with the Turkish control authorities to facilitate the exchange of information, experience and techniques, and organizational expertise.[108] They had joined Turkish police in tracking down opium diverted into illicit channels as early as the autumn of 1966.[109] In 1968, the United States gave "a 3 million dollar loan to the Turkish government to defray the foreign exchange costs for research into substitute crops and for vehicles and other equipment needed to implement the restrictions on the opium trade."[110] In Çağlayangil's account, the interior minister was anxious to accept the offer because he saw it as an important opportunity to make good shortages of Turkish police.[111]

In the international arena, Turkey signed all the treaties on opium and other dangerous drugs and joined all organizations established to deal with narcotic drugs.[112] It gave support to any proposals by the United States, which would strengthen the Single Convention and cooperated with it in the UN Commission on Narcotic Drugs.[113]

In spite of its willingness to cooperate with the United States on the opium issue, the Demirel government did not comply with the American demand to ban poppy cultivation completely for the following reasons: Drug addiction was not a problem for the Turkish nation. Therefore, there was no domestic pressure at all on the Turkish government to end poppy production.[114] Indeed, the situation in Turkey was quite the reverse: the poppy crop was the primary source of living for a section of Turkish population. If the Demirel government had banned opium cultivation, it would have brought adverse social and economic results for traditional producers.[115] At that time, the Demirel government had a very thin margin of support in the parliament because the conservative wing had left the Justice Party[116] and formed the Democratic Party in early 1970. Demirel was understandably

---

[104] Spain, "The United States, Turkey and the Poppy", p. 305.

[105] Acar, "Afyon Raporu", 16 July 1970.

[106] Wellman, "Drug Abuse: A Challenge to U.S.-Turkish Cooperation in the Seventies", p. 145, Richard F. Nyrop (ed.), *Turkey; A Country Study, Third Edition*, Washington D.C.: American University, 1980, p. 285, Zentner, "The 1972 Turkish Opium Ban", p. 43, Acar, "Afyon Raporu", 16 July 1970.

[107] Spain, "The United States, Turkey and the Poppy", p. 305.

[108] Wellman, "Drug Abuse: A Challenge to U.S.-Turkish Cooperation in the Seventies", p. 145.

[109] Harris, *Troubled Alliance*, p. 193, Turner, *The International Politics of Narcotics*, p. 124.

[110] Harris, *Troubled Alliance*, p. 193, Acar, "Afyon Raporu", 16 July 1970, *ABD Dışişleri Bakanı William Rogers'ın Kongre'ye Sunduğu Rapordan Bölümler*, p. 4, *International Aspects of the Narcotics Problem*, p. 119.

[111] Cem, *Tarih Açısından 12 Mart*, p. 312.

[112] Özcan Köknel, "Haşhaş Ekimi ve ABD", *Milliyet*, 4 November 1975.

[113] Wellman, "Drug Abuse: A Challenge to U.S.-Turkish Cooperation in the Seventies", pp. 145-146.

[114] Harris, *Troubled Alliance*, p. 192.

[115] Ibid., p. 192, Spain, "The United States, Turkey and the Poppy", p. 298.

[116] *Keesing's Contemporary Archives*, 1969-1970, vol. 17, p. 23956, ibid., vol. 18, p. 24640.

reluctant to initiate measures totally eliminating opium cultivation, especially as the votes of the opium-producing provinces were essential to the survival of his party's parliamentary majority.[117] Furthermore, "constant U.S. pressure... made the issue public and, therefore, increased Demirel's difficulties in handling the question of concessions."[118] If Demirel had banned opium cultivation, he would have seemed to be yielding to U.S. pressures.

The unwillingness of Turkish rulers to prohibit opium production can be understood. But it was a fact that their measures were not effective to prevent the diversion of opium into illicit channels and, therefore, Turkey's reputation in the international arena was damaged. They did not appreciate the fact that the continuity of illicit opium production and trafficking gave the Americans opportunity to pressurize Turkey.

b) Turkey's Arguments on the Opium Issue

Turkish officials believed that Turkish opium was not the only or even the primary source of the U.S. drug addiction problem. They thought that if the supply of heroin were the real source of drug addiction, it would be Turkey, which suffered most from this problem. If Turkey banned opium cultivation, the drug abuse problem of the United States would not come to an end. As long as there was a strong demand for narcotic drugs, they would be supplied somehow.[119] There were already other opium producer countries whose opium reached the United States: India, Pakistan, China, the Soviet Union, Yugoslavia, Thailand, Laos, etc. Marseilles was the center point of the heroin traffic, but the United States did not press France as much as it did Turkey.[120] Figures showed that even if all opium produced in Turkey in a year found its way to the United States it would meet the needs of American addicts only for a few weeks.[121]

In spite of all these facts, Turkey would do its best and cooperate with any country in this matter out of its humanitarian concerns.[122] However, the United States should stop its pressure tactics against Turkey, which constituted interference in its internal affairs,[123] while it failed to stop heroin smuggling at home.[124] Turkey could hardly be blamed for drug addiction of U.S. citizens while the same U.S. addicts even brought their disease to Turkey. In the 1960s and the 1970s, a little restaurant near the Blue Mosque in İstanbul, the Pudding Shop, had become a major stop for U.S. hippies who consumed cheap opium from the underground world. "U.S. citizens were on the one hand threatening to cut off the livelihood of Turkish peasants and on the other pouring into İstanbul to disrupt and corrupt local society."[125]

One of Turkish officials' arguments for not banning opium cultivation completely was the importance of opium for Turkey. In 1971, some 100,000 Turkish farmers in Afyon and

---

[117] Harris, *Troubled Alliance*, pp. 195-196, Turner , *The International Politics of Narcotics*, pp. 143, 204-205, Feroz Ahmad, *The Turkish Experiment in Democracy*, London: C. Hurst and Company, 1977, p. 418.

[118] Ahmad, *The Turkish Experiment in Democracy*, p. 418.

[119] Cem, *Tarih Açısından 12 Mart*, pp. 292-293.

[120] Cağlayangil's interview with Cem in Cem, *Tarih Açısından 12 Mart*, p. 312, Arcayürek, *Çankaya'ya Giden Yol 1971-1973*, p. 147, Köknel, "Haşhaş Ekimi ve ABD".

[121] Köknel, "Haşhaş Ekimi ve ABD," Çağlayangil's interview in Cem *Tarih Açısından 12 Mart*, p. 311.

[122] İlhami Ertem, *MMTD*, 20 and 24 July 1970, op. cit., pp. 566, 630-632.

[123] Turner , *The International Politics of Narcotics*, pp. 122, 139.

[124] Turhan Bilgin, "12 Mart", *Milliyet*, 24 March 1976, quoted by Cem, *Tarih Açısından 12 Mart*, p. 294.

[125] James W. Spain, *American Diplomacy in Turkey*, New York: Praeger, 1984, p. 136.

the surrounding provinces relied on the poppy crop for their survival. The poppy was an integral part of the way of life in the area.[126] In Spain's words,

> it provided the main cash crop. Opium gum, which lasts almost indefinitely, was stored from year to year toward a daughter's dowry or other anticipated essential expenditure. Apart from the profits to be had from the narcotic gum, the young leaves were a favorite salad ingredient. The seeds flavored the local bread. When pressed they made the oil in which food was cooked. The stalks of the plant provided cattle fodder and fuel for the household [and the roofing material]. During the brief harvest period for the gum, otherwise excess skilled labor, much of it female, was utilized profitably in incising and scrapping the poppy pods. In some remote and impoverished mountain villages, the poppy was the only crop that made a subsistence existence possible. To Afyon (the very name means opium in Turkish) and the other hardcore provinces, the poppy meant at least as much as tobacco to Kentucky.[127]

c) Turkish Public's Reaction to U.S. Pressures on Opium

The United States was subjected to heavy criticism by Turkish public opinion for pressing Turkey to abandon poppy cultivation. In the parliament, MPs such as Süleyman Mutlu and Celal Kargılı and senator and former prime minister Suat Hayri Ürgüplü criticized the United States for its unfair pressure tactics and accused the Turkish government of yielding to U.S. pressures. Pressure groups such as university students,[128] the leftist Dev-Genç organization,[129] the union of agriculture engineers,[130] and the union of agriculture chambers[131] issued statements condemning the Turkish government's actions to restrict opium production under U.S. influence. Leftist groups and peasants arranged demonstrations[132] and newspaper columnists continuously wrote articles for the same purpose.

Some points voiced by Turkish critics were as follows:[133] The United States was right in wishing to find a solution to the serious drug addiction problem among its citizens. However, the U.S. pressure tactics aimed at forcing Turkey to ban its opium cultivation were not the right way to deal with the problem. U.S.-Turkish cooperation on the opium issue was reminiscent of the organization of Duyunu Umumiyye during the Ottoman Empire period, which made Turkish gendarmes shoot their own people who produced and used tobacco outside the permission of this organization. The drug addiction was a disease of the American society, which was caused by sociological and psychological problems of the American people. It was unfair to impose the price of the American people's disease on Turkish farmers who had nothing to do with it. The United States itself was subsidizing, advertising and

---

[126] Spain, "The United States, Turkey and the Poppy", p. 305, Turner , *The International Politics of Narcotics,* p. 32.

[127] Spain, "The United States, Turkey and the Poppy", p. 305, see also *Facts on Turkish Poppy,* p. 7.

[128] *Cumhuriyet,* 4 July 1970, p. 1.

[129] Ibid., 25 July 1970, p. 7.

[130] Ibid., 31 July 1970, p. 1.

[131] Acar, "Afyon Raporu", 20 July 1970.

[132] *Cumhuriyet,* 11 August 1970, p. 7, Turner , *The International Politics of Narcotics,* p. 142.

[133] Süleyman Mutlu (20 July 1970) and Celal Kargılı (24 July 1970), *MMTD,* term 3, sess. 1, vol. 8, pp. 564-565, 626-629; in *Cumhuriyet:* Suat Hayri Ürgüplü's speeches, 3 and 10 July 1970, p. 1, Ö. Acar, "Afyon Raporu", 5-20 July 1970, Oktay Akbal, "Amerikasız da Yaşanır", 24 July 1970, Cihat Baban, "Demirel Haklı", 28 July 1970, Ragıp Üner, "Afyon Sorunu ve Amerika", 18 March 1971; in *Milliyet:* Abdi İpekçi, "Türkiye

selling harmful goods such as tobacco and destructive war weapons. Illegal American goods were sold in Turkish markets, but nobody was complaining about it. Automobile accidents were the leading cause of deaths in Turkey and most automobiles in Turkey were American-made, but no Turks were demanding that the United States shut down its automobile factories.[134] It was strange that while demanding an end to opium cultivation in Turkey, American officials and journalists were constantly pressing for a reduction in the stiff sentences, which were applied, to American narcotics offenders convicted in Turkey.

4. THE OPIUM ISSUE IN THE 1971-1974 PERIOD

a) The Erim Government's Decision to Ban Opium Cultivation

After the Demirel government was forced out of office by the Turkish military on 12 March 1971, a non-party government under Nihat Erim's premiership came to power. The new government made the opium issue one of its first priorities.[135] A licensing decree, which was prepared by the Demirel government on the basis of existing legislation, was issued on 19 March 1971.[136] However, the long-awaited bill providing strict licensing procedures with severe penalties for those who violated the terms of act would be passed by the Turkish parliament as late as 18 August 1971.[137] In his statement on the government's program before the Turkish Parliament, Nihat Erim declared: "Believing that contraband trade in opium - which has assumed the aspect of an overwhelming blight for the youth of the whole world - is offensive on humanitarian grounds in the first place, the government will pay serious attention to this problem. Turkish opium growers will be shown a way to earn a better-living."[138]

Immediately after the Erim government won the vote of confidence in the parliament, U.S. officials started an intensive campaign to achieve the prohibition of Turkish opium cultivation. In Spain's words, "every American official in Turkey became a walking encyclopaedia on the subject and both socially and professionally their Turkish contacts heard about little else."[139] After U.S. Secretary of State William P. Rogers visited Ankara in April 1971 to discuss the opium question, U.S. and Turkish officials began discussions on the technical aspects of the problem.[140] In May 1971, the Erim government announced that it was going to move against the illicit opium production by purchasing the entire 1971 crop, licensing poppy growers, and encouraging the cultivation of other crops by poppy farmers.[141] On 16 May, the government's purchasing price of opium was raised by two-thirds in order to increase sales to the authorities.[142]

Cezalandırılacakmış", 22 July 1970, İsamil Cem "Afyon mu Silah mı?", 23 and 24 July 1970; Spain, "The United States, Turkey and the Poppy", pp. 305-306.

[134] *International Aspects of the Narcotics Problem*, p. 22.

[135] Spain, "The United States, Turkey and the Poppy", p. 298.

[136] Harris, *Troubled Alliance*, p. 196.

[137] Ibid., p. 197, for detailed information see *Facts on Turkish Poppy*, pp. 13-14.

[138] Ahmad, *The Turkish Experiment in Democracy*, p. 417.

[139] Spain, "The United States, Turkey and the Poppy", p. 299.

[140] Harris, *Troubled Alliance*, p. 196, Turner , *The International Politics of Narcotics*, p. 135, Arcayürek, *Çankaya'ya Giden Yol 1971-1973*, pp. 153-154.

[141] Roy, *Drugs, Society and Human Behaviour*, p. 193.

[142] *Cumhuriyet*, 17 May 1971, p. 1.

In their meeting on 17 May, U.S. Ambassador Handley presented to Erim a document stating the U.S. aid to the Turkish government and poppy farmers in the case of the prohibition of opium cultivation.[143] On 11 June, Handley informed Erim that President Nixon was waiting for the Turkish government's reply to the American proposals. Erim said to Handley that his government could ban opium cultivation in the three provinces immediately instead of the next year.[144]

On 14 June 1971, President Nixon summoned the American ambassadors in France, Mexico, Thailand, Turkey, Vietnam and the United Nations to a White House conference. Reportedly, Nixon told the ambassadors that "the interdiction of narcotics was to be a first order priority of U.S. foreign policy" and he instructed them "to make clear to their host governments that their actions to suppress narcotics trafficking would have a definite bearing on U.S. economic and military support."[145] In the meeting, William Handley explained the peculiar nature of the Turkish opium problem and came away with a presidential commitment to provide assistance in establishing alternative sources of income if the Turks would stop opium cultivation immediately. He was given a maximum of 35 million dollars to offer the Turks for their cooperation.[146]

Eventually, the Turkish government's opium decree on 30 June 1971 announced that the planting and production of poppies within the borders of Turkey was forbidden beginning from the autumn of 1972.[147] On the same day, Erim and U.S. President Nixon explained the Turkish government's decision to their people.[148]

Some points mentioned by Erim in his speech are as follows:

> Smuggling from our country in recent years has become very distressing for us... Now planting has been decreased to four provinces. In this way, it was hoped to prevent smuggling. However, unfortunately, this system did not give results... It is certain that a smugglers' gang organized on an international scale, constitutes an economic and political problem for Turkey... In countries where health is endangered through this opium, because smuggling cannot be prevented in Turkey, anti-Turkish opinions are created. The measures to be applied to control smuggling are extremely expensive... Our nation, which is known for its honesty and integrity, is now under grave accusation. The time when we must end the placing of blame for deaths in other countries on Turkey is so long overdue. We cannot allow Turkey's supreme interests and the prestige of our nation to be further shaken... Our government forbids completely the planting of poppies... The agreement ratified in 1966 [the Single Convention] also stipulates this arrangement.. In order to make up for the income farmers who are planting in seven provinces at present will lose, they will be given compensation beginning from the coming year... In the long term, investments will be made in the region to compensate the lost income of farmers through other ways and to provide new income sources for them...[149]

---

[143] Arcayürek, *Çankaya'ya Giden Yol 1971-1973*, p. 154.

[144] Ibid., p. 154.

[145] Turner , *The International Politics of Narcotics*, p. 131.

[146] Spain, "The United States, Turkey and the Poppy", p. 299.

[147] *Cumhuriyet*, 30 June 1971, p. 1, Zentner, "The 1972 Turkish Opium Ban", p. 39, *Keesing's Contemporary Archives*, vol. 18, p. 24717.

[148] For the statements of the two premiers in Turkish see *Dışişleri Bakanlığı Belleteni*, June 1971, pp. 137-142.

[149] Turner , *The International Politics of Narcotics*, pp. 311-315. For Erim's ideas on the opium ban see also *Resmi Temaslar: Sayın Başbakan ve Bn. Erim'in Birleşik Amerika'yı Ziyareti*, 18-23 March 1972, no date, publisher and place, pp. 37, 50-51, 63. Erim stated that he was happy for doing something for the USA in return for U.S. economic and military aid to Turkey.

President Nixon's speech contained the following points:

> ... Today, Erim declared that the Republic of Turkey, our friend and staunch ally within NATO, would abandon a traditional agricultural practice in order to make a significant contribution to the well-being of the world... This farsighted step will provide an example, which we trust, will soon be followed by other nations... We know well the importance of the agricultural sector of Turkey's economy and we are prepared to put at the disposal of the Turkish government our best technical brains to assist Turkey's program to bring about a better life for the Turkish farmer. We are proud to assist in a program from which we will all benefit... We in the United States are obligated to a friend and ally whose firm military and political commitment to the welfare and defense of the Atlantic Community is well known... I pledge continued cooperation with Turkey in its efforts to increase the well-being of its people and to maintain its independence and security.[150]

On the same day, President Nixon also joined a press conference together with the U.S. Secretary of State and the Turkish Ambassador to Washington. He told journalists that the Turkish government's decision was the most important initiative in the struggle to eradicate the source of heroin. Nixon explained that the Turkish decision was a result of negotiations between U.S. and Turkish officials.[151]

b) Motivations of the Turkish Government in Banning Opium

Turkish officials always claimed that they decided to stop poppy cultivation for two reasons: (a) to serve humanity and (b) to save the prestige of Turkey in the eyes of international community.[152] In their opinion, Turkey, as a country, which wanted to be a part of the Western civilization, could not be indifferent to a matter threatening the Western societies and other nations. Turkey also could not afford being seen as a country, which poisoned other nations with its opium. According to Haluk Bayülken, who served as foreign minister for some time during the military-supported governments, the elected governments before 12 March 1971 were responsible for Turkey's bad reputation on the opium issue because they ignored the criticism by other countries and did not take effective measures because of electoral concerns.[153]

It seems that the most important reason, which pushed the Erim government to ban poppy cultivation, was the desire of Turkish rulers to strengthen relations with the United States.[154] The U.S. was really taking the opium issue very seriously. The Erim regime, which did not enjoy parliamentary and popular support at home, did not want to lose the American support as well. Turkish authorities and "their bosses", Turkish generals, were determined to prevent deterioration of U.S.-Turkish relations because they needed U.S. economic and military aid and political support. In Mango's opinion, the total ban on opium cultivation "symbolized the

---

[150] Turner , *The International Politics of Narcotics*, pp. 316-317.

[151] *Dışişleri Bakanlığı Belleteni*, June 1971, pp. 141-142.

[152] See Nihat Erim's speech, Turner , *The International Politics of Narcotics*, p. 311-315.

[153] Bayülken told the author that these governments either should have proved that Turkey was not the source of the world's narcotic problem or should have taken really effective measures.

[154] Osman Olcay, who served as foreign minister for some time during the Erim government, told the author that Turkish authorities had to consider the fact that the United States was the main military and economic aid supplier of Turkey.

desire of Turkish generals and their proteges to do business with the United States."[155] Mango also claims: "With a Marxist insurgency on their hands, the authorities took care not to antagonize the United States. The cultivation of opium was thus banned; and in economic policy, military-backed governments became noticeably more accommodating after the resignation of eleven radical ministers."[156]

It is clear that constant U.S. pressures played a role in the Turkish decision. The presentation of the decision to American public by U.S. rulers as their success strengthens this point. However, U.S. officials publicly claimed that it was persuasion and not coercion, which brought about the Turkish opium ban and that if they had threatened to cut off aid, Turkey would not have complied with their demand.[157] On the other hand, many congressmen were of the opinion that Congress's threats to cut off aid played a role in the Turkish decision and that if the United Stated had pressurized Turkey previously, the opium ban would have been achieved much earlier.[158]

Another reason for the Turkish poppy prohibition was to prevent leftist radicals from getting weapons from abroad.[159] Turkish political and military authorities believed that leftist terrorists were obtaining large amounts of weapons illegally from opium smugglers. When opium production was halted, drug traffickers would not be able to smuggle weapons into the country.

c) The Implementation of the Opium Prohibition

In return for the prohibition of opium cultivation, the United States undertook to provide Turkey with 35 million dollars in loans over a three-year period. Of this amount, 20 million dollars would be devoted to development programs and projects which could provide alternative sources of income and employment opportunities for poppy farmers. 15 million dollars would be for compensation to the Turkish government for its loss of foreign exchange earnings from legal export of opium and would be used to compensate the losses of opium growers.[160] The United States also promised to provide 300,000 dollars for controlling the 1972 crop and 400,000 dollars for covering miscellaneous expenses.[161]

Arrangements to determine an U.S. loan to Turkey on the opium issue were made secretly between Turkish and U.S. officials. As Spain stated, "due to Turkish political sensitivities, these arrangements were never welded into a single formal document but were incorporated into various exchanges of letters."[162] Later Prime Minister Erim and other Turkish officials claimed that they banned opium cultivation unilaterally for humanitarian concerns without an agreement between the United States and Turkey on the matter. If the Turkish government felt that the ban was harming interests of poppy farmers, then it could resume poppy production. In their opinion, after Turkey took the decision, the United States

[155] Andrew Mango, *Turkey: A Delicately Poised Ally*, Beverly Hills, Calif.: Sage, 1976, p. 37.
[156] Ibid., p. 42.
[157] *International Aspects of the Narcotics Problem*, pp. 17, 22, 28, 75, 76, 163, 164.
[158] Ibid., pp. 21, 48.
[159] Turner, *The International Politics of Narcotics*, pp. 152, 156, 159-160, 278.
[160] Zentner, "The 1972 Turkish Opium Ban", p. 40, Spain, "The United States, Turkey and the Poppy", p. 299, Harris, *Troubled Alliance*, p. 197, Nihat Erim's statements, *Cumhuriyet*, 25 February 1972, 23 March 1972.
[161] Turner, *The International Politics of Narcotics*, pp. 149-150.
[162] Spain, "The United States, Turkey and the Poppy", p. 299.

offered aid to help them.[163] However, American officials expressed the view that the Turkish action was primarily the result of an agreement between the two countries. They pointed out that the 35 million-dollar U.S. loan was an integral part of the negotiations and the agreement between U.S. and Turkish officials.[164]

The United States transferred 20 million dollars of 35 millions by July 1974.[165] In mid-1972 the United States gave 300,000 dollars to the Turkish Soil Products Office to assist its campaign to control and collect the opium harvest during the final growing season.[166]

Turkish officials and public opinion argued that the U.S. aid was not enough to compensate losses of Turkish farmers and Turkey generally.[167] They maintained that the amount envisaged would cover only one-twelfth of the total loss which was estimated as more than 6 billion Turkish liras or 400 million U.S. dollars.[168] The Turkish government had declared that it would pay compensation to farmers who chose not to grow the poppy in 1971-1972 and to all who had formerly grown it in the four provinces but were forbidden to do so in 1972-1973 and the succeeding years. The basis for payment under the government's formula would be the value on the international market of the whole produce, such as opium, seeds and stems that the growers would sell to the Soil Products Office in 1972.[169] But the compensation envisaged did not include all losses of growers.[170] For example, for the relatively high illegal revenue the farmers were earning before, there would be no compensation.[171] The individual farmer also had other indirect benefits that were harder to compensate.[172] Moreover, former poppy farmers and small businessmen involved indirectly with opium production were kept outside the compensation.[173] Allegedly, the Turkish government transferred only 2 million dollars of the 10 million dollars, which it received, from the U.S. to Turkish farmers. The rest of it went either into planning at the top levels of the government or was reserved for other purposes.[174]

When Turkey announced the prohibition of poppy cultivation, U.S. President Nixon had promised to send American technical experts to Turkey to assist the Turkish government's projects of helping poppy farmers to survive in the face of economic hardship.[175] As a part of this promise, the U.S. Secretary of Agriculture, Clifford Hardin, and a team of American agricultural experts visited Turkey in November 1971.[176] The Turks generally thought that Hardin had brought offers of substantial aid. During his visit, the Turkish press carried

---

[163] Erim's statements, *Cumhuriyet*, 25 February 1972, 21 March 1972, *Resmi Temaslar*, p. 50.

[164] Turner , *The International Politics of Narcotics*, pp. 146-147, 148, 150, 217. U.S. Congressman Lester L. Wolff told a House committee that he had "a statement from the U.S. State Department, which puts on paper the exact agreement that was made with" Turkey. *Turkish Opium Ban Negotiations*, p. 2.

[165] Turner , *The International Politics of Narcotics*, pp. 215-216, 241.

[166] Zentner, "The 1972 Turkish Opium Ban", p. 41.

[167] Aytunç Altındal, "Haşhaş Politikası", *Cumhuriyet*, 11 September 1973, K. Cemal Güven, "Haşhaş Sorunu", *Cumhuriyet*, 23 March 1974.

[168] Geoffrey Lewis, *Modern Turkey*, New York: Praeger, 1974, p. 218, Zentner, "The 1972 Turkish Opium Ban", p. 47n, *The Heroin Trail*, p. 3.

[169] Agriculture Minister Orhan Dikmen, *MMTD*, 24 February 1972, term 3, sess. 3, vol. 22, p. 137.

[170] See the report of some U.S. congressmen, expressing doubts about the compensation formula, in *Turkish Opium Ban Negotiations*, p. 67.

[171] *The Heroin Trail*, p. 4.

[172] Spain, "The United States, Turkey and the Poppy", p. 305, Zentner, "The 1972 Turkish Opium Ban", p. 41.

[173] Turner , *The International Politics of Narcotics*, p. 217.

[174] Ibid., pp. 217, 220. See also statements of U.S. congressmen in *Turkish Opium Ban Negotiations*, pp. 2-3, 18, 55, 61, 62.

[175] See also U.S.-Turkish joint statement at the end of Erim's visit to the USA, *Resmi Temaslar*, p. 63.

[176] *Cumhuriyet*, 3,7 November 1971, pp. 1 and 7.

estimates evaluating Turkey's real losses caused by the poppy prohibition. At one point, Turkish Agriculture Minister Orhan Dikmen found it necessary to issue a formal statement denying a widely circulated report that the Turkish government would resume opium production if the United States failed to provide sufficient compensation.[177] In fact, Hardin had come to Turkey to explore with Turkish experts agricultural plans for substitute crops and sources of income and to provide technical advice on the transition from poppy cultivation.[178]

As a result of the Hardin mission, a task force was established "to study the agricultural situation in the seven-province region, to assess the potential for improved agricultural output and associated agri-industries and to provide specific programs and policy recommendations for consideration by the Turkish government." In February 1972, the task force issued a report, titled as "Improving Farm Income in the Poppy Region -A Program for Action, Recommendations of the Joint Turkish-American Agricultural Team."[179] The U.S.-Turkish joint declaration on 15 February 1972 stated that research and experiments would be given a start to find substitute crops for opium and specified the actions which would be implemented immediately: irrigation; animal feeding; cultivation of sunflower, various fruits, and wheat; marketing; and the establishment of a sugar factory.[180]

Turkish officials continuously reiterated their commitment to developing the poppy region and explained that they took necessary measures and prepared plans and projects for this purpose.[181] On 29 February 1972, the Turkish government issued a decree stating long-term projects for the economic and social development of the poppy region.[182] In March, the Poppy Region Development Organization was established.[183]

In spite of all these initiatives, the program of crop substitution never brought any positive results. It was realized that there was simply no single substitute crop, which could replace poppy and yield as high a return per unit of land as does opium.[184] The poppy was the only autumn-sown crop. It was not easily replaceable by spring crops such as cotton, maize, sugar beets or tobacco. It was harvested before the grain and thereby provided expense money for the main harvest. Some of the areas where opium had been grown had extremely limited soil and water resources, and therefore were not suitable for a viable alternative agriculture.[185]

Meanwhile, the United States decided that it did not want to get deeply and directly involved in the development program for the poppy region.[186] It "made it clear to Turkey that it expected the Turks themselves to devise and implement it with only limited numbers of U.S. Department of Agriculture personnel being available under contract to advise."[187] Both the Turkish and the American sides grew pessimistic. The Turkish press was criticizing the

---

[177] Harris, *Troubled Alliance*, p. 198.
[178] Ibid., p. 198, Spain, "The United States, Turkey and the Poppy", pp. 299-300.
[179] Zentner, "The 1972 Turkish Opium Ban", pp. 40, 47n.
[180] *Cumhuriyet*, 16 February 1972.
[181] Agriculture Minister Orhan Dikmen, *MMTD*, 24 February 1972, term 3, sess. 3, vol. 22, p. 137, P.M. Nihat Erim's statements, *Cumhuriyet*, 25 February and 23 March 1972, P.M. Ferit Melen's statement, *Cumhuriyet*, 18 September 1972.
[182] Melen's statement, op. cit.
[183] Spain, "The United States, Turkey and the Poppy", p. 300.
[184] Turner, *The International Politics of Narcotics*, p. 237, Ahmet Kerse, "Afyon Savaşı", *Cumhuriyet*, 5 January 1972, Spain, "The United States, Turkey and the Poppy", p. 300. See also the report of U.S. congressmen in *Turkish Opium Ban Negotiations*, pp. 62, 67.
[185] Zentner, "The 1972 Turkish Opium Ban", p. 41, *The Heroin Trail*, pp. 16-17.
[186] During a committee discussion, some U.S. congressmen admitted that the USA did not do enough to help the Turks in the development program. *Turkish Opium Ban Negotiations*, pp. 33, 39, 40.
[187] Spain, "The United States, Turkey and the Poppy", p. 301.

opium ban and interviewing discontented farmers and pointing to mistakes. Villagers did not see substantial progress in their situation and were becoming impatient to resume poppy growing.[188] Seeing development projects as unbearable burdens Turkish officials were thinking that U.S. funds would not be sufficient to implement them.[189] American journalists who visited Turkey were emphasizing the tremendous financial losses to those in the illegal trade and warning that total suppression would not work under any circumstances. U.S. diplomats and officials who played a part in bringing about the ban had the feeling that the 1971 arrangement could not last forever.[190]

During the poppy prohibition period, Turkish narcotics officers were trained and helped by U.S. narcotic agents in capturing illegal opium and smugglers.[191] Turkish authorities established a Central Police Drugs Bureau to direct and coordinate the activities of thirty-three provincial narcotics offices. The Turks also arranged commissions to conduct regular inspection missions in the provinces where poppy cultivation was forbidden.[192]

d) Turkish Public's Reaction to the Opium Ban

The opium prohibition really hurt the pride and honor of the Turkish nation. In their eyes, the interests of Turkish people had been bargained with a foreign country. The government had accepted that Turkish farmers had been poisoning the American people.[193] The opium prohibition also symbolized the Turkish subservience to U.S. interests and showed the humiliating dependence of Turkey on the United States.

However, the opium prohibition did not attract public criticism at that time because the military-backed regime did not allow free expression of ideas. Only some MPs dared to express opposition to the ban[194] and, in December 1971, 21 deputies and in September 1972 111 deputies introduced bills to authorize resumption of opium production under strict control.[195]

e) The U.S. Attitude toward the Opium Ban

The Americans praised the Turkish decision to prohibit opium cultivation as a major step in fighting against the drug abuse problem of the USA.[196] However, some Americans expressed the following doubts: It was highly likely that the Turkish ban would increase the cost of heroin in the American street market by causing a temporary shortage. This would

---

[188] *The Heroin Trail*, pp. 7, 17.

[189] *Facts on Turkish Poppy*, p. 7.

[190] Spain, "The United States, Turkey and the Poppy", pp. 301, 303.

[191] Ibid., p. 300.

[192] Zentner, "The 1972 Turkish Opium Ban", p. 42.

[193] Arcayürek, *Çankaya'ya Giden Yol 1971-1973*, pp. 139, 144, 149, Özer Ölçmen and Süleyman Mutlu, *MMTD*, 24.2.1972, term 3, sess. 3, vol. 22, pp. 133-135.

[194] See speeches of Özer Ölçmen and Süleyman Mutlu, op. cit..

[195] Harris, *Troubled Alliance*, p. 198, *Cumhuriyet*, 18.9.1972, p. 1, *Keesing's Contemporary Archives*, 1974, vol. 20, p. 26722.

[196] President Nixon's statements, *Dışişleri Bakanlığı Belleteni*, June 1971, pp. 140-142, the State Department's statement quoted by Turner, *The International Politics of Narcotics*, p. 148, Congressman Benjamin S. Rosenthal's statement to Turkish journalists, *Cumhuriyet*, 14 January 1972, p. 7, Secretary of State Roger's report to Congress mentioned by *Cumhuriyet*, 21 April 1973, p. 3.

result in more crime being committed and would only make the social consequences of addiction even greater.[197] Even the eradication of Turkish opium was not certain. The Turkish police and gendarmes were vulnerable to corruption and bribery by heroin smugglers because they had very low salaries. The Turks also lacked the logistical equipment and sophisticated enforcement capability that was necessary to enforce the opium ban adequately.[198] As a tradition, Turkish farmers would hide and had already hidden the opium crop from the past harvest, which would continue to reach the American market for several years.[199]

American critics also pointed out that when the Turkish opium ceased to be a supply source, drug traffickers would shift their operations to somewhere else.[200] It was estimated at that time that Turkey produced only 5 to 8 percent of the illicit opium available throughout the world.[201] Some countries were already replacing Turkey as supply source. According to one estimate in 1972, Mexico supplied 15 percent of American heroin.[202] Burma, Thailand and Laos, which were called the Golden Triangle countries, produced more than half of the world's opium supply. In Afghanistan, Pakistan and India, illegal opium production was increasing rapidly.[203] It was stated in the House Select Committee of the U.S. Congress on 2 January 1971: "Our hope for international control and, or eradication of the opium poppy becomes increasingly more difficult when we are dealing with opium-producing countries that do not have control over the areas within their borders where substantial quantities of opium poppies are cultivated and ultimately processed into morphine base. Several Southeast Asian countries fall clearly within this category."[204] Allegedly the United States did not press high-level officials in some Southeast Asian countries, who directed opium smuggling, because they protected U.S. interests in the region.[205]

Zentner reached the following conclusion, which was written in italics, in his article in 1973: "It seems probable that attempts to control or abolish opium production in Turkey will have little long-range effect on the American opiate problem as illicit marketers turn to new and readily available sources of supply. This is the key element in understanding the futility of the present Turkish endeavor."[206] On 27 June 1972, the U.S. Undersecretary of the Treasury Department, Eugene T. Rossides, went so far to say: "Stopping the source, the idea of putting in the amount of money that would be required for crop substitution is ludicrous. It was a misguided thought in the past and has led us to most of the problems we have today because less than 2 percent of the total production of opium would easily supply all the U.S. markets."[207]

Unfortunately, after achieving the Turkish opium ban, U.S. authorities ignored internal aspects of the drug trafficking and paid little attention to the availability of other sources.

---

[197] Roy, *Drugs, Society and Human Behaviour*, p 194, Zentner, "The 1972 Turkish Opium Ban", p. 44.

[198] Zentner, "The 1972 Turkish Opium Ban", p. 43, *Turkish Opium Ban Negotiations*, pp. 66, 67.

[199] Zentner, "The 1972 Turkish Opium Ban", p. 44, *The Heroin Trail*, pp. 8-9, *Turkish Opium Ban Negotiations*, pp. 66, 67.

[200] See comments of U.S. congressmen in *International Aspects of the Narcotics Problem*, pp. 3, 25, 34, 49, 54, 61, 148, 149.

[201] Zentner, "The 1972 Turkish Opium Ban", p. 45, *Facts on Turkish Poppy*, p. 21.

[202] Roy, *Drugs, Society and Human Behaviour*, p. 194, *International Aspects of the Narcotics Problem*, p. 25.

[203] Roy, *Drugs, Society and Human Behaviour*, pp. 194, 196, Zentner, "The 1972 Turkish Opium Ban", pp. 45-46.

[204] Zentner, "The 1972 Turkish Opium Ban", p. 47n. See also *International Aspects of the Narcotics Problem*, pp. 54, 119, 148.

[205] "Afyon, CIA ve Türkiye", *Le Monde*'s article translated by *Cumhuriyet*, 26 August 1972.

[206] Zentner, "The 1972 Turkish Opium Ban", p. 46.

[207] Ibid., p. 47n.

They did not even show enough determination to ensure the success of the Turkish ban. They failed to give enough help to the Turks and while high-level U.S. officials visited the neighboring Arab countries for other reasons they did not stop in Turkey to talk to Turkish authorities on the opium problem.

f) The Effect of the Opium Ban

American officials generally claimed that the prohibition of poppy cultivation in Turkey had the desired effect in the United States. According to them, the international illegal drug network was disrupted. Big drug traffickers needed new sources and when they got to Afghanistan, Pakistan and India, they found American agents and local enforcement officials already organized to make life difficult for them. In the United States, the rate of new drug addiction decreased and more and more addicts turned them in for treatment since they could not find the drug and could not afford to buy it.[208]

According to the investigation of *Newsday* reporters, law enforcement officials first reported a heroin shortage in New York during the presidential campaign in August 1972. However, in the following years the availability of drugs was a disputed issue between U.S. officials. Some claimed that the shortage continued, others argued that the supply was still as plentiful as ever though perhaps more adulterated than in the past. The survey which was released by the federal government's Cabinet Committee on International Narcotics Control in the summer of 1972 acknowledged increased seizures of illegal heroin, but it said that "the rising level of seizures still represents only a small fraction of the illicit flow... The international heroin market almost certainly continues to have adequate supplies to meet the demand in the consuming countries."[209]

During the meeting of the UN narcotics and dangerous drugs committee in 1974, U.S. official Robert Dupent said that for the first time deaths and crimes in the U.S., which were caused by drug addiction, decreased. He stated that the amount and quality of U.S. heroin decreased whereas its price increased and that the number of U.S. drug addicts reduced from 700,000 to 200,000. Another high level U.S. official, John R. Bartels, pointed that the heroin trafficking in North and South America fell considerably because of the Turkish opium prohibition. The chief of the French narcotics police, Francois Le Moel, claimed that the Turkish ban caused shortage of morphine base in Europe and this cut the amount of heroin smuggled into the U.S.[210]

The Turks generally believed that the American drug addiction problem did not ease because of their opium ban. In their opinion, the apparent shortage of heroin and the increase in heroin prices was a result of the intensive U.S. and French police campaign against drug traffickers.[211] In fact, it seems that both the ban and the increased police activities contributed to the heroin shortage and hence to the increased heroin prices, but the Turkish ban on its own proved an inadequate solution to the American drug abuse problem.

---

[208] Spain, "The United States, Turkey and the Poppy", p. 304, *Turkish Opium Ban Negotiations*, pp. 10, 20, 31, 49, 59, 62, 71, 76, 77.

[209] *The Heroin Trail,* p. xiii.

[210] *Milliyet*, 14 March 1974.

[211] Özcan Köknel, "Haşhaş Ekimi ve ABD", *Milliyet*, 4 November 1975.

5. THE TURKISH DECISION TO RESUME OPIUM CULTIVATION

a) The Period before the Decision

When normal party politics returned in Turkey with the 1973 elections, the opium issue became one of the most important subjects of the election campaign. Since the people of the poppy region strongly demanded restoration of opium cultivation, almost all the parties competed with each other in trying to increase their votes by condemning the 1971 poppy ban and promising to resume opium production under strict controls if they came to power. The election manifestos of all parties made the withdrawal of the ban a primary target.[212]

During the elections and after Bülent Ecevit assumed the premiership in January 1974 by establishing a coalition with the National Salvation Party, Turkish public opinion, especially the press, continuously encouraged the authorities to fulfil their promises by legalizing opium production.[213] The resumption of poppy cultivation had become a matter of national honor and prestige. The Turks urged their prime minister to resist all kinds of U.S. pressures and to restore their honor sullied by the Erim regime. In their opinion, objective facts supported the Turkish government's stance for resumption of opium production. Turkey had been the world's largest legal exporter of opium and its opium had been the most valuable of all from a medicinal standpoint. Now, since Turkey stopped its production, a world shortage of medicinal opium was developing rapidly. Turkey itself was finding it increasingly difficult and expensive to acquire its own requirements of opium for medical use.[214] International and American pharmaceutical companies were complaining of opium shortages and were pressurizing the Congress and the administration to meet their demands.[215] The United States itself announced plans to go into poppy cultivation in the areas selected in the Far West, Walla Walla and Phoenix.[216] It was also allowing the production of synthetic drugs, which were available to drug addicts. Moreover, the United States encouraged India to increase its opium production and decided to meet needs of the medical sector from strategic stockpiles.[217]

b) The Ecevit Government's Actions on Opium

The Ecevit government had come to office by promising dynamic policies in every area, which would protect Turkish interests more effectively. Its program proclaimed the

---

[212] Nuri Eren, *Turkey, NATO and Europe*, Paris: Atlantic Institute for International Affairs, 1977, p. 24, Turner, *The International Politics of Narcotics*, p. 251, Ahmad, *The Turkish Experiment in Democracy*, pp. 419, 429n, Spain, "The United States, Turkey and the Poppy", pp. 301-302, *Cumhuriyet*, 9 October 1973.

[213] In *Cumhuriyet*: Aytunç Altındal, "Haşhaş Politikası", 11.9.1973, İlhan Selçuk, "Haşhaş", 21 February 1974, Hasan Sever, "Haşhaş Sorunu ve Çözümü", 15 March 1974, Oktay Akbal, "Afyon Savaşı", 16 March 1974, İ. Selçuk, "Onurumuzu Koruyalım", 16 March 1974, İlhan Selçuk, "Afyonu Afyon Söker", 17 March 1974, K. Cemal Güven, "Haşhaş Sorunu", 23 March 1974.

[214] Spain, "The United States, Turkey and the Poppy", p. 307.

[215] *Cumhuriyet* 14.6.1973, the article of *New England Journal of Medicine* quoted by *Cumhuriyet*, 27 January 1975, Turner , *The International Politics of Narcotics*, pp. 203-204, 229, *Cumhuriyet*, 14 March 1974, *Facts on Turkish Poppy*, pp. 7-8, 11.

[216] Spain, "The United States, Turkey and the Poppy", p. 307, Eren, *Turkey, NATO and Europe*, p. 24.

[217] *Cumhuriyet*, 14 and 20 March 1974, Spain, "The United States, Turkey and the Poppy", p. 307, Turner, *The International Politics of Narcotics*, p. 228.

independence of Turkey as the aim of foreign policy.[218] It soon became clear that Ecevit and his ministers had every intention of canceling the opium ban and were not after more money from the United States as compensation. They continuously made public statements for this end.[219] In March, the Turkish government officially informed Washington that it would resume poppy production soon and asked U.S. authorities to join in re-examination of the opium ban.[220] In the same month, the Ecevit regime allowed opium production in state farms and agricultural institutions to protect the opium crop's genetic value[221] and the Ministry of Agriculture started work on cultivation plans for 1974-75. Farmers were authorized to germinate poppy seeds in state farms for the next year's cultivation.[222] Meanwhile, repeated strong approaches by U.S. Ambassador Macomber and other American officials received a negative response from Turkish authorities. Visiting U.S. congressmen and journalists were told that the opium ban would come to an end soon.[223]

Eventually, on 1 July 1974, the Turkish government announced that poppy cultivation would resume in the autumn of 1974 in seven provinces; Afyon, Burdur, Denizli, Isparta, Kütahya, Uşak and four towns of Konya. Prime Minister Bülent Ecevit explained the government's decision in his speech to the Turkish National Assembly on 2 July 1974:[224] The prohibition of poppy cultivation by an unelected government had been a mistake because it created an unfillable gap in the poppy farmers' life in the absence of a viable alternative. The previous governments took some measures to compensate the losses of growers, but these measures were insufficient and met with the understandable resistance of people. The eradication of Turkish opium production caused a serious opium shortage in the world pharmaceutical industry and did not help the drug abuse problem in other countries. In the light of these facts, the Turkish government decided to resume limited poppy cultivation under strict state control. It would take every kind of measure to prevent Turkish opium from harming other nations and would be willing to listen to the advice of any interested international organizations and friendly countries for this purpose. If the envisaged measures proved ineffective, the government would seek authority from the parliament to implement more forceful methods. It would also continue to explore substitute crops and new sources of income in the poppy region. The Turkish government believed that it followed the will of the people by allowing opium cultivation. No democratic regime could tell its people to change their way of life and to give up a traditional way of earning which had been practiced for centuries.

As elected rulers, the Ecevit government's officials could justify resumption of opium cultivation in response to the will of people. But publication of the matter, its presentation as an act of independence against the USA and ignoring protests of the Americans were mistakes made by Turkish authorities. U.S. rulers, too, failed in the matter by not responding to Turkish suggestions to review the opium ban.

---

[218] Mango, *Turkey: A Delicately Poised Ally*, pp. 42-43.

[219] *Cumhuriyet*, 16,17 February 1974, 14, 16, 17, 20 March 1974.

[220] Turner , *The International Politics of Narcotics,* pp. 252-253, *Keesing's Contemporary Archives,* vol. 20, p. 26722.

[221] Ecevit's statement, *Cumhuriyet*, 17 March 1974, Bülent Ecevit, *MMTD*, 2 July 1974, term 4, sess. 1, vol. 6, p. 347, *Keesing's Contemporary Archives*, vol. 20, p. 26722.

[222] Turner , *The International Politics of Narcotics*, p. 252.

[223] Spain, "The United States, Turkey and the Poppy", p. 302.

[224] *MMTD*, term 4, sess. 1, vol. 6, pp. 347-349. For reasons for the decision from Turkish point of view see also *Facts on Turkish Poppy*, pp. 8,10.

c) Turkish Public's Reaction to the Lifting of the Opium Ban

The Ecevit government's decision to resume poppy cultivation received popular and political support at home.[225] Some saw it as restoring Turkey's dignity and independence and some supported it in principle, but expressed doubts about its long-term consequences. In his speech to the Turkish Parliament on 3 July 1974, Reliance Party leader Turhan Feyzioğlu expressed support for the decision as an act fulfilling people's demands, but warned that the opium issue should not be exploited by the government for political purposes in a manner which would harm Turkey's alliance relations with the USA and the West.[226] Justice Party leader Demirel saw the lifting of the opium ban as an act of an independent country but stated that the government should consider advantages and disadvantages of its decision carefully.[227] Nationalist Movement Party leader Alparslan Türkeş later claimed that the Ecevit government acted on the matter in pursuit of gaining political gains rather than protecting interests of poppy farmers and thus caused the isolation of Turkey in the Western camp and damaged its interests in the Cyprus question.[228] Faruk Sükan, the secretary general of the Democrat Party, argued that the government's opium policy harmed Turkey's friendly relations with the United States and Europe.[229]

The opinions expressed by İsmet Giritli and Metin Toker constitute good examples of the criticism directed against the resumption of poppy cultivation:[230] The lifting of the opium ban was not related to Turkey's interests, pride and independence. The Ecevit government made a grave mistake by not demanding funds from the United States but allowing opium production without consulting with the Americans. As a response to Turkey's hostile decision, the United States would not care any more about Turkey's security and economic interests. Turkey would face the danger of being isolated against its enemies such as Greece and the Soviet Union. The decision would please only three groups: anti-Americans, opium and arms smugglers. The best solution might be the implementation of the development projects, which were considered by the previous governments with the help of the Americans.

6. THE U.S. REACTION TO THE RESUMPTION OF TURKISH OPIUM PRODUCTION

a) The Reaction of the Congress

When the Ecevit government made clear its intention to resume poppy production, U.S. congressmen threatened Turkey with cutting off aid. During their visit to Turkey on 15 and 16 March, U.S. congressmen Wolff and Rangel warned Turkish officials and journalists that the cancellation of the opium ban would cause a severe reaction among American congressmen

---

[225] In *Tercüman*: Ahmet Kabaklı, "Haşhaş Mutluluğu", 6 July 1974, Hayrettin Erkmen, "Ambargo ve Ötesi", 1 August 1975; in *Cumhuriyet*: A. Sirmen, "Amerikan Bombaları", 11 July 1974, A. Sirmen, "Alavere Dalavere", 15 July 1974; "Durum: Haşhaş Kararı ve Amerika", *Milliyet*, 3 July 1974.
[226] *MMTD*, term 4, sess. 1, vol. 6, p. 398.
[227] *Cumhuriyet*, 19 March 1974, p. 7, Altan Öymen, "Ecevit Başbakanlık Dönemini Anlatıyor", op. cit..
[228] Öymen, "Ecevit Başbakanlık Dönemini Anlatıyor".
[229] *Cumhuriyet*, 14 July 1974, p. 1.
[230] İsmet Giritli, "Haşhaş ve Türk-Amerikan İlişkileri", *Tercüman*, 15 July 1975; Metin Toker, "Haşhaş Ötesi ve Berisi", 24 March 1974, "Haşhaşın Sonrası", 14 July 1974, *Milliyet*.

and people.[231] As reported by Turner, in the wake of the Turkish decision on 1 July 1974, more than 250 bills suggesting cutting off aid to Turkey were pending in Congress.[232] On 12 July, the Senate passed a resolution by 81 to 8, which required stopping economic and military aid to Turkey if it did not take effective measures on the opium issue.[233]

Discussions of U.S. congressmen during a committee meeting on 16 July 1974 give their ideas on the Turkish decision to resume poppy production:[234] The Turkish decision was taken because of political concerns rather than economic ones. The Turkish government failed to use the U.S.-supplied funds to ease difficulties of poppy farmers. Poppy production contributed very little to the Turkish economy and provided income for a very small percentage of the Turkish population. The Turkish opium ban between 1971 and 1974 did not cause great economic and social hardship in Turkey. Ignoring economic aspects of the problem, some "demagogic" Turkish politicians used the issue as a symbol of Turkish nationalism to gain political support. Organized crime in Turkey, too, inspired the opium campaign. Turkish authorities decided to resume poppy cultivation unilaterally without consulting with U.S. officials in spite of the existence of an agreement on the matter between the two countries. As the past experiences had shown, Turkey could not prevent the diversion of opium into illicit channels because of the ineffectiveness of its bureaucracy. The Turkish government recently released from jail charged narcotic traffickers who would go back to business.

U.S. congressmen further argued: The Turkish opium ban had substantially contributed to the reduction of the number of heroin addicts and heroin-related problems in the USA. With the new Turkish decision, there would be a big increase in heroin supply in America and all the success achieved in the drug abuse problem would be reversed. Therefore, this decision constituted a direct attack upon the people of the USA. As *Washington Post*'s article stated, "if the Turkish government had announced that it intended to land secret agents at night on American shores to poison and kill thousands of Americans, and to subvert the foundations of American society - which is, of course, exactly what heroin does - then that would be regarded as an act of war and handled accordingly." The threat of Turkish opium to the American nation was much greater than the Turkish contribution to NATO. In fact, U.S. facilities in Turkey and Turkey's cooperation in the defense field was no longer important for the USA. In any case, congressmen had the commitment to their constituents rather than to Turkey. The Congress should authorize the President to cut off aid to Turkey, showing its seriousness on the matter. This could exert pressure upon Turkey and change its decision.

There were also some congressmen who claimed that such a decision would not force the Turks to change their policies. They also argued: As other states could do, Turkey, too, could develop a strict control program on opium production. It was a fact that the U.S. administration, too, failed in this matter. It did not give enough help to the Turks in their development projects in the poppy region and did not take action to persuade Turkish rulers to change their decision after they expressed their intention. The United States itself should take effective measures at home rather than expecting the others to solve its problem.

---

[231] *Cumhuriyet*, 16 and 17 March 1974.
[232] Turner , *The International Politics of Narcotics*, p. 201.
[233] *Cumhuriyet*, 13 July 1974, pp. 1, 7, *Keesing's Contemporary Archives*, vol. 20, p. 26722.
[234] *Turkish Opium Ban Negotiations*, pp. 1-77.

At the end of July, the Congress forbade the Export-Import Bank to grant further credit to Turkey because of its resumed poppy cultivation.[235] On 6 August 1974, House Concurrent Resolution 507, sponsored by 239 Congressmen, was passed by the House. The resolution urged the president to "1- immediately initiate negotiations at the highest level of the Turkish government to prevent the resumption of opium production; and 2- if such negotiations prove unfruitful, exercise the authority provided by the Congress under the Foreign Assistance Act [of 1971], to terminate all assistance to the Government of Turkey."[236] The Senate passed an amendment to the Comprehensive Drug Abuse and Control Act of 1970, which required the president to terminate all aid by 1 January 1975 to any government that failed to ban opium production.[237] After the second Turkish military intervention in Cyprus on 14 August 1974, an initiative was launched by the U.S. Congress to impose an arms embargo on Turkey because of its actions in Cyprus. Thus opium became a secondary issue. Opponents of the Turkish opium cultivation supported the arms embargo and supporters of the embargo exploited the opium issue for their purposes.[238]

b) The U.S. Administration's Reaction

The U.S. administration was not happy with the Ecevit government's intention to resume poppy production. In their opinion, the ban should not be lifted because it had proved a success. On 6 May 1974, U.S. officials privately warned that U.S.-Turkish relations would deteriorate if poppy cultivation were resumed.[239] On 8 May 1974, U.S. narcotics official Sheldon B. Vance told the Senate that 20 million dollars of aid intended for Turkey had been held because Turkey's decision on the opium issue was not clear yet.[240]

When Turkey decided to resume opium production, the U.S. administration attacked the Turkish action as a breach of an agreement.[241] The State Department commented that "we deeply regret the decision of the Turkish government... It was taken without any official Turkish notification to U.S. Ambassador William B. Macomber."[242] State Department spokesman John King expressed the American worry about the Turkish action but he said that economic and military aid to Turkey would not be stopped though the 20 million-dollar promised loan would not be paid.[243] As a means of displaying its displeasure, on 7 July 1974, the U.S. administration recalled its ambassador to Turkey for consultations and to review the situation arising from the Turkish government's decision.[244]

---

[235] Turner, *The International Politics of Narcotics*, p. 261, *Cumhuriyet*, 2 August 1974, p. 1.

[236] *Turkish Opium Ban Negotiations*, p. 1, Bölükbaşı, *Super Powers and the Third World*, pp. 180-181, *Cumhuriyet*, 7 August 1974, p. 1, K. R. Legg, "Congress as Trojan Horse?" in John Spanier and Joseph Nogee (eds.), *Congress, the Presidency and American Foreign Policy*, New York: Pergamon Press, 1981, pp. 118-119, Turner, *The International Politics of Narcotics*, p. 257.

[237] Turner, *The International Politics of Narcotics*, p. 258.

[238] Bülent Ecevit claimed in Kurtul Altuğ's program on Turkish TV, Bunalımlı Yıllar, 1993, that contrary to the general belief the arms embargo was imposed on Turkey because of its decision to lift the opium ban, not its intervention in Cyprus.

[239] Richard C. Campany, *Turkey and the United States*, New York: Praeger, 1986, p. 26.

[240] *Cumhuriyet*, 9 May 1974, p. 1.

[241] *Keesing's Contemporary Archives*, vol. 20, p. 26722.

[242] Turner, *The International Politics of Narcotics*, p. 256.

[243] *Cumhuriyet*, 4 July 1974, p. 1.

[244] Ibid., 6 July 1974, p. 1, Campany, *Turkey and the United States*, p. 26, Bölükbaşı, *Super Powers and the Third World*, p. 180, Turner, *The International Politics of Narcotics*, p. 256.

In the aftermath of the Turkish decision, U.S. officials reportedly opposed the actions of Congress to cut off aid to Turkey because they believed that these kinds of threats would not reverse the Turkish action but would harm strategic interests of the United States.[245] Before the Cyprus issue overtook the opium question, the administration managed to fight off a flat cut-off of aid and to introduce consideration of control into the handling of the matter.[246]

American public opinion showed great anger toward the Turkish decision to resume poppy cultivation. Parents, doctors, law enforcement officials believed that Turkish opium would resume poisoning the youth of American at a high rate. American newspapers carried articles severely criticizing the Turkish decision. The most extreme of these was Pete Hamill's article in *New York Post* on 8 July 1974, "Act of War".[247] Seeing the Turkish action as an act of war against American people, Hamill suggested the bombing of Turkish poppy fields by the U.S. Air Force.

7. THE AFTERMATH OF THE OPIUM ISSUE

While allowing the opium production in seven provinces under state licensing, the Ecevit government took the strictest measures to prevent illicit drug traffic.[248] The most important of them was the introduction of a new method of harvesting poppies, the "poppy straw process". Formerly, raw opium had been scraped by poppy farmers from the incised poppy pod, and therefore, given high prices for illicit sales, it had been impossible to control opium supply in thousands of hands. The straw process method completely bypassed the production of gum opium by farmers through incision. The government forbade farmers to incise poppy pods. The entire plant would be cut in the field and taken to a government factory employing the straw process, which would use a sophisticated technique to extract maximum narcotic from the plant. Thus the government monopoly would purchase the whole product and process it into morphine, which would be marketed to meet legitimate world medical needs for codeine and other opium derivatives. For a few years, until Turkey built such an opium factory, the harvested, unincised poppies would be exported to Western Europe.[249]

These Turkish actions were generally praised by the international community. On 19 September 1974, the United Nations issued an official statement welcoming Turkey's decision to implement a new method as an act of strict compliance with international obligations.[250] In another statement on 16 October, the United Nations presented the Turkish action to other states as an example to be carried out in opium production and stated that the new method would prevent illegal opium traffic and increase earnings of poppy farmers.[251] A UN narcotics mission that visited Turkey in July 1975 reported that it was greatly impressed

---

[245] *Cumhuriyet*, 13 July 1974, p. 7.

[246] Spain, "The United States, Turkey and the Poppy", p. 304.

[247] Quoted by *Turkish Opium Ban Negotiations*, pp. 73-75. See also Spain, "The United States, Turkey and the Poppy", p. 302, Bölükbaşı, *Super Powers and the Third World*, p. 181; in *Cumhuriyet*, Oktay Akbal, "Haşhaş Soğuk Savaşı", 15 July 1974, A. Sirmen, "Amerikan Bombaları", 11 July 1974.

[248] For detailed information see *Facts on Turkish Poppy*, pp. 12-13.

[249] Spain, "The United States, Turkey and the Poppy", p. 308, Spain, *American Diplomacy in Turkey*, p. 83, Harris, "Turkey and the United States" in Karpat (ed.), *Turkey's Foreign Policy in Transition*, p. 70, Turner , *The International Politics of Narcotics*, p. 253, *Facts on Turkish Poppy*, pp. 15,17.

[250] Ümit Gürtuna, "Diplomaside Kulis", *Cumhuriyet*, 23 September 1974, Altan Öymen, "Ecevit Başbakanlık Dönemini Anlatıyor".

[251] Altan Öymen, "Ecevit Başbakanlık Dönemini Anlatıyor".

by the success of the Turkish control system.[252] The investigation of the International Narcotics Control Board and the UN Secretariat, which was completed on 13 July 1976, indicated that Turkish controls were fully effective and that there had not been any diversion or leakage to the illicit market.[253] After receiving complaints of illegal opium trafficking another UN mission went to Turkey in early 1977, but found "no evidence that there have been any leaks since poppy cultivation was resumed in 1975."[254]

The United States, too, praised the Turkish actions as effective ways of preventing opium smuggling. On 20 September 1974, the State Department expressed the American pleasure with the Turkish decision to apply the straw process.[255] In a message to Congress, President Ford praised the effectiveness of the Turkish controls.[256] In fact, the U.S. government financed the straw process plant built by Turkey.[257]

In the mid and late 1970s, the most important problem for Turkey on the opium issue was narcotics originating outside the country and passing through it on the way to Western Europe.[258] Developments concerning opium in the 1980s were mentioned by former U.S. ambassador to Turkey, James W. Spain, in his book: At the beginning of the 1980s, "there was an enormous stock [in Turkey] from the poppy fields waiting for completion of the straw process plant so that processing could be taken. The key to the success of the whole venture was the U.S. medical market for which the major pharmaceutical companies made large purchases. In July 1981 a team of company representatives and officials from the U.S. Drug Enforcement Administration arrived in Turkey to try to put the whole operation together." After the plant started working in good condition, another question emerged: whether the United States would buy the Turkish opium. "The General Services Administration, which is responsible for maintaining U.S. strategic stockpiles, was contemplating a large replenishment of its holdings, which could sop up all the backlog of the Turkish plant. However, no one was eager to assign Turkey a specific quota - which would limit freedom in the market. After much haggling it was agreed not to set individual country quotas, but to allocate 80 percent of the market to Turkey and India together and 20 percent to all other producers."[259]

Another problem that concerned the U.S. and Turkey on opium was a number of U.S. travelers serving long-term sentences in Turkish prisons for narcotic offences. There was an antipathy among the American people toward Turkey on this issue, which stemmed from a famous film, "Midnight Express". U.S. ambassadors "Spiers and Macomber had negotiated a U.S.-Turkey treaty on the Enforcement of Judicial Judgements, which provided the long-term prisoners in each country of the opposite nationality could opt to serve their remaining sentences in their country." When Ambassador Spain left Turkey in August 1981, "the prisoners had gone home and they were released soon on parole since the parole system is

---

[252] Eren, *Turkey, NATO and Europe*, p. 25, *Facts on Turkish Poppy*, pp. 15-16.
[253] Stanford J. Shaw and Ezel Kural Shaw, *History of The Ottoman Empire and Modern Turkey*, vol. II, Cambridge: Cambridge University Press, 1977, p. 432.
[254] Eren, *Turkey, NATO and Europe*, p. 25.
[255] Öymen, "Ecevit Başbakanlık Dönemini Anlatıyor".
[256] Eren, *Turkey, NATO and Europe*, p. 25, *Facts on Turkish Poppy*, p. 18.
[257] Spain, *American Diplomacy in Turkey*, p. 83.
[258] Richard F. Nyrop (ed.), *Turkey: A Country Study*, p. 295.
[259] Spain, *American Diplomacy in Turkey*, pp. 83-84.

provided for in the U.S. legal structure and not in the Turkish. At my departure, we did not have a single U.S. long-term prisoner in Turkey."[260]

8. CONCLUSION

Up to 1971 U.S. pressures led Turkish rulers to take some measures to control illegal opium production and trafficking, but failed to force Turkish authorities to ban opium cultivation completely. Internal concerns prevented the Turkish government from falling under the influence of the USA in this regard. The non-party Erim government, not bound by electoral considerations, easily gave in to U.S. pressures, but also maintained that the ban was in Turkey's interests. The Ecevit government in 1974 resumed poppy cultivation as a proof of its independence from the USA, but faced threats from the Congress. It would have certainly been subjected to heavy U.S. pressures if the Cyprus crisis had not forestalled the issue.

Like the Cyprus question, the opium issue was a matter which did not concern the basis of the Turkish-American alliance, i.e. maintaining security in the context of the East-West confrontation. Although it was not originally serious or fundamental enough to strain relations between the two countries, the opium question would have shaken the alliance dramatically if the Cyprus issue had not emerged. If the two governments tried, they could have found a mutually satisfactory solution because the essence of the problem was not the production of opium, but the leaking of the product into illicit channels. Other producer countries had been able to establish effective controls, and Turkey could have easily followed their example. However, the two states mainly tried to appeal to their domestic opinion with their policies. By propagating that halting the flow of Turkish opium at the source would ease the drug abuse problem, the Americans disregarded the importance of relations with Turkey, misjudged the true nature of Turkey's domestic politics and ignored the realities of heroin supply and demand. While using forceful tactics against Turkey with heavy Congressional and press involvement, they neglected the possible damage to the reputation of the Turkish government in the eyes of international community and Turkish people. Turkish authorities first did not take effective measures to prevent illegal production and trade of opium and allowed their country to gain a bad reputation on the matter. Then, they saw the resumption of poppy cultivation as a gesture against the United States and more specifically as a challenge to the U.S. Congress. Presenting the action as an act of independence, they aimed to increase their popular support, but ignored the possible alienation of the American people from the presentation of the decision.

---

[260] Ibid., pp. 137-138.

Chapter 10

TURKISH-AMERICAN RELATIONS IN THE 1980S: COOPERATION AND PROBLEMS

1. INTRODUCTION

The uneasy relationship between Turkey and the United States was further exacerbated by the resumption of poppy cultivation by the Turkish government in June 1974. The Americans, who believed that the main cause of the American drug addiction problem was the smuggling of Turkish opium into the United States, perceived this Turkish initiative as an anti-American act. While Congress was busy with trying to cut off aid to Turkey as retaliation, a coup occurred in Cyprus on 15 July 1974, bringing about the Turkish intervention in the island. In both cases, the American government inclined toward accepting the new situations and avoided showing strong responses, which would alienate both the Greeks and the Turks. Imposing of an arms embargo on Turkey by the U.S. Congress, starting on 5 February 1975, was mainly a result of a power competition between the U.S. administration and the Congress, which was determined to make the arrogant rulers respect the rule of law and to regain its power in foreign policy-making. The unhappiness of congressmen on the Turkish poppy decision and propaganda activities of the Greek lobby, too, played role in the embargo decision.

The American administration was opposed to the embargo on the ground that it would harm America's military cooperation with Turkey, which was vital for U.S. global security interests. However, American rulers also used the matter to force Turkish leaders to make concessions in the Cyprus question. In the Turkish eyes, Cyprus and U.S.-Turkish military relations were separate issues and should not be linked to each other. In this context, they saw the embargo as a hostile act of the United States, which undermined the capability, preparedness and effectiveness of the Turkish armed forces. On 25 July 1975, the Turkish government declared that the Defence Cooperation Agreement of 1969 and all other related agreements between the two countries lost their legal validity and that all U.S. military installations in Turkey passed under the full control and custody of the Turkish authorities.[1] Thus, relations between Turkey and the United States hit their lowest level though their alliance continued within the NATO framework. After long intensive efforts of the U.S.

---

[1] *Cumhuriyet*, 26 July 1975.

administration, the Senate voted to repeal the embargo on 26 July 1978 and the House followed through on August 1. In return, on 9 October the Turkish government terminated the suspension measures implemented in U.S. bases and facilities. Whether the two states would manage in the 1980s to return to cordial relations had gained importance at that point.

2. MILITARY RELATIONS

The reasons for formation and continuity of the Turkish-American military alliance were also valid in the 1980s. Turkish leaders remained keen to continue the alliance because they saw it as a warranty of Turkish security against the Soviet Union and other possible threats, as a source of military and economic assistance and as a guarantee for westernizing Turkey and making her a part of the Western world. Turkey's strategic importance for U.S. interests in the Middle East and the Eastern Mediterranean, Turkey's contribution to NATO and the desire to keep Turkey within the Western camp so as not to lose prestige vis-a-vis the Soviet bloc were the main reasons for the Americans to maintain their alliance with Turkey.

The framework of Turkish-American military relations was drawn with a Defence and Economic Cooperation Agreement (DECA), signed on 29 March 1980.[2] It was a five-year executive agreement, renewable annually, which would implement the NATO treaty. The United States undertook to provide defense equipment, services, and training to Turkish forces; Turkey, in return, authorized the USA to maintain forces and carry out military activities at specified installations. An U.S.-Turkish Joint Commission was created as a mechanism for discussing how to use Turkey's resources for its security objectives. The agreement had been negotiated by the successive leftist and rightist governments under Bülent Ecevit and Süleyman Demirel and it was to be implemented by the military regime headed by General Kenan Evren. This demonstrated 'once again the non-partisan character of Turkey's foreign policy and of its commitment to the special relationship with the United States.'[3] Turkey's military rulers further proved their goodwill by accepting NATO's American commander General Rogers' proposal of allowing the return of Greece to NATO's military structure in return for the abolition of Greece's single-handed control over air traffic in the Aegean. Nevertheless, Greek Prime Minister Papandreou did not implement this plan and General Rogers did not make serious efforts to force the Greeks in this direction.

The Americans showed their friendship by not criticizing the Turkish military coup on 12 September 1980 unlike the other Western powers. The statement of the U.S. State Department on the same day expressed worry on the fall of an elected government by military commanders, but it stated that Turkey had been facing terrorism and economic difficulties for a number of years and that Turkish military commanders promised to return to party politics. The statement also announced that American military and economic aid to Turkey would continue.[4]

The Özal government, which came to power in November 1983, did its best to continue the DECA though it had some reservations on the implementation and content of the

---

[2] Richard C. Campany, *Turkey and the United States: the Arms Embargo Period*, New York: Praeger, 1986, pp. 103-123.

[3] Dankwart A. Rustow, *Turkey: America's Forgotten Ally*, New York: Council on Foreign Relations, 1987, pp. 104-105.

[4] Fahir Armaoğlu, *20. Yüzyıl Siyasi Tarihi*, vol. II, Ankara: Türkiye İş Bankası, 1994, p. 297.

agreement. Its main complaints were as follows: a- The United States had unfairly observed a 7:10 ratio in determining aid to Greece and Turkey. b- American aid to Turkey had been linked to the Cyprus question, human rights and the claim that the Ottoman Empire massacred the Armenians at the beginning of this century. c- The discussion of these matters by Congress during aid bill negotiations was alienating Turkish public opinion. d- Though the DECA included economic cooperation, the United States had not provided suitable trade conditions especially to Turkish textiles.[5]

Three months before the first five-year period of the DECA ended (17 September 1985), the Özal government called the Americans to negotiate changes in the agreement. It was interesting that though Turkish leaders were not happy with the DECA and were demanding radical changes in it, they allowed it to be extended on an annual basis 'so as to allow for broader negotiations.'[6] At the end, what Turkey got was not a new agreement, but supplementary letters which extended the DECA, including U.S. base rights, to 1990. The letters were initialed on 12 December 1986 and exchanged on 16 March 1987. They included almost the same terms in the DECA and did not bring any radical changes or any new commitments for the United States. Congress' cutting of military aid to Turkey from 913 million dollars to 525 million dollars led the Turkish government to suspend the ratification of the letters. President Evren's planned visit to Washington, which would have been the first by a Turkish president in twenty-five years, was also postponed.[7] The letters were finally ratified by the Turkish government on 28 February 1988, on the eve of President Evren's visit to the USA.

The DECA would expire at the end of December 1990 and Turkey should inform the United States of its demands and complaints before 17 September. However, Turkey was having a close relationship with the United States in the aftermath of the Iraqi occupation of Kuwait and Turkish leaders did not want to spoil this cooperation by making nuisance on the DECA. Thus, the agreement was extended for five years automatically and quietly. Although Turkish rulers had always felt resentment toward the American indifference to Turkish worries and complaints on the DECA, they provided the continuity of the agreement under all conditions. This could be explained with the Turkish determination to have the alliance, support and assistance of the United States.

3. MILITARY ASSISTANCE

One of the major problems between Turkey and the USA was that the U.S. Congress had a pattern of conditioning aid on good Turkish behavior on the Cyprus and Armenian questions and limiting it to a ratio (7:10) between the assistance given to Greece and Turkey. The 1978 amendment to the Foreign Assistance Act of 1961, which lifted the arms embargo, required that U.S. aid to Greece and Turkey should be designed to maintain the present balance of military strength in the Aegean region. A Congressional majority, who accepted the views of the Greek government in its problems with Turkey and who had significant

---

[5] Ibid., pp. 304-305.
[6] Rustow, *Turkey*, p. 106.
[7] Paul B. Henze, "Out of Kilter: Greeks, Turks and U.S. Policy", *National Interest*, vol. 8, 1987, p. 82, Monteagle Stearns, *Entangled Allies: US Policy Toward Greece, Turkey and Cyprus*, New York: Council on Foreign Relations, 1992, pp. 43,167n.

Greek-American constituencies, decided that the Aegean status quo could be protected if Greece received 7 dollars in aid every 10 dollars going to Turkey.[8]

Although the 7:10 ratio was not spelled out in any legislation, Congress maintained it in all American aid bills concerning Turkey and Greece in the 1980s in spite of the administration's aid requests diverging from the ratio. The official views of the Turkish and American administrations were that assistance should be provided to both Greece and Turkey in accordance with their own particular NATO-related requirements without regard to any mechanical ratio. To determine the balance of military forces in the Aegean, stipulated by the law, a whole range of factors from geography and existing inventories to troop quality and tactics would have to be identified and weighed. However, while the American rulers chose the easy way by blaming Congress on the non-realization of the projected amounts of aid for Turkey, Turkish leaders used this fact to justify tight control of U.S. military activities on the Turkish territory.[9]

Since the American policy-makers saw a strong and stable Turkey in the national interest of the United States, it was essential for them to continue a strong program of economic and security assistance to Turkey. The Turkish armed forces, the second largest standing army in NATO and an important factor in its region for the Western security, should be modernized and Turkey should be compensated for the indignities and material losses suffered during the arms embargo.[10] Particularly the Reagan administration placed Turkey high on the priority list for increased security assistance, calling its needs 'urgent', 'pressing', and 'most demanding'. In 1983, the Pentagon estimated that bringing Turkish forces up to minimum NATO standards would take $ 18 billion over 13 years. Doubling of U.S. security assistance to Turkey during the Reagan administration showed the seriousness of American rulers on their security relationship with Turkey.[11] The modernization of the Turkish army had been a prime objective for the following administrations, too.

The difficulty of reconciling the U.S. dependence on Turkish military forces and bases with the continuing Turkish need for U.S. economic and military assistance was one negative element causing irritations and conflict in U.S.-Turkish relations. Turkish leaders naturally wanted to maximize the aid received from the United States and to make the conditions attached to it as favorable as possible. Although the U.S. aid to Turkey was substantial by any standard and Turkey became the third largest recipient of U.S. aid at one point, the aid levels appropriated by Congress were still far short of Turkish needs and did not fill the gap between Turkey's current capabilities and NATO responsibilities. As the Americans resisted the excessive Turkish aid demands and the Turks were careful about the conditions of the aid, this resulted in difficult and bitter negotiations, which often ended in disappointment and resentment in both sides.[12]

---

[8] Stearns, *Entangled Allies*, pp. 40-41, R. N. Haass, "Managing NATO's Weakest Flank: the United States, Greece and Turkey", *ORBIS*, vol. 30 (3), 1986, p. 467n.

[9] Stearns, *Entangled Allies*, pp. 42-44, Haass, "Managing NATO's Weakest Flank: the United States, Greece and Turkey", p. 467n.

[10] Stearns, *Entangled Allies*, p. 40, Richard Burt, "Turkey and Reagen Administration" in George S. Harris (ed.), *The Middle East in Turkish-American Relations*, Washington: The Heritage Foundation, 1985, p. 20, Barry Rubin, "U.S. Middle East Policy in the Turkish Context" in ibid., p. 78.

[11] Bruce R. Kuniholm, "Turkey in the World" in ibid., p. 11, Richard Perle, "Turkey and U.S. Military Assistance" in ibid., p. 23, Ellen B. Laipson, "U.S.-Turkish Friendly Friction", *Journal of Defense and Diplomacy*, vol. 3 (9), 1985, p. 22.

[12] George McGhee, *The US-Turkish-NATO-Middle East Connection*, London: Macmillan, 1990, pp. 168-169.

The conditioning of U.S. aid to the Cyprus and Armenian issues particularly undermined the Turkish confidence in the U.S. capacity to provide a powerful program for Turkish needs that was not hostage to Congress's arbitrary use of power of the purse. At the end, a political process, which hurt their national pride, led the Turks to feel little satisfaction over the substantial aid, but instead they filled them with resentment.[13] As the Congress debates on aid bills made Greece and Turkey professional lobbyists, the U.S. executive and legislative branches, too, were drawn into the Greek-Turkish contest, hampering the American ability to establish realistic alliance relations with the two states.[14]

From the start of the DECA, the United States allocated to Turkey annually about $ 700 million through its Military Assistance Program, Economic Support Fund and International Educational Training Program. Meanwhile, some methods were used to reduce the impact of the 7:10 formula: increased economic aid, better financial terms, use of NATO infrastructure funds and grants of excess equipment.[15] Early in 1983, the American government asked for a total package of $ 930 million for Turkey for the fiscal year 1984. It was an open challenge to Congress' 7:10 ratio. But within one month the initial request of $ 280 million for Greece was amended to $ 500 million and $ 930 million for Turkey was reduced to $ 715 million to restore the ratio.[16] The U.S. aid for Turkey reached its peak in 1985 by totaling $ 878 million in comparison with $ 200 million in 1979, but in the following years it materialized around $ 500 million. The reduction of the total aid from an administration request for $ 913.5 million to $ 525.3 million for the fiscal year 1988 led the Turkish government to suspend temporarily ratification of the letters on extending the DECA, causing an impasse in U.S.-Turkish relations.[17] Even the reinforcement of Turkey's importance for the United States during the Gulf crisis of 1990-1991 were not powerful enough to increase the aid substantially. The last aid request of the Bush administration was reduced from $ 543 million to $ 450 million as credits by Congress.[18]

4. TURKEY'S STRATEGIC IMPORTANCE

Turkey continued to have a great strategic importance for the United States throughout the 1980s. Although American policy analysts tended to class Turkey along with Spain and Portugal in NATO's southern flank, Turkey's central importance for the USA stemmed from the fact that it was an indispensable strategic factor linking the Western world with the turbulent Middle East and was a stepping stone or a barrier to gaining access to the region. The American policy-makers frequently cited this connection in U.S. public statements and in congressional testimonies as one of the main justification for large military aid programs for

---

[13] Kuniholm, "Turkey in the World", p. 12, Perle, "Turkey and U.S. Military Assistance", p. 23, Henze, "Out of Kilter", p. 82, Haass, "Managing NATO's Weakest Flank: the United States, Greece and Turkey", pp. 466-467.

[14] Stearns, *Entangled Allies*, pp. 49-50.

[15] Henze, "Out of Kilter", p. 82, McGhee, *The US-Turkish-NATO-Middle East Connection*, p. 173.

[16] Ellen B. Laipson, "Turkey and the US Congress" in Harris (ed.), *The Middle East in Turkish-American Relations*, pp. 29-30, Bruce R. Kuniholm, "Turkey and NATO: Past, Present and Future", *ORBIS*, Summer 1983, p. 442, L. H. Bruce, "Cyprus: A Last Chance", *Foreign Policy*, No. 58, 1985, p. 118.

[17] Stearns, *Entangled Allies*, pp. 43,167n.

[18] S. C. Pelletiere, "Ortadoğu'da Türkiye ve Amerika: Kürt Bağlantısı", *Avrasya Dosyası*, vol. 1(3), 1994, p. 176.

Turkey.[19] As a strategic barrier between the Soviet Union and the Middle Eastern countries, Turkey played a crucial role in preserving stability in the region and neutralizing the potential risks of the area for world peace and U.S. global strategy in the context of the East-West conflict. American Assistant Secretary of Defence Richard Perle's speech to a Senate committee is illuminating in this context: "If the United States is unable to keep the Soviet Union's massive maritime capability bottled up in the Black Sea, the balance of power in the Eastern Mediterranean in a conventional war could and almost certainly would shift against the United States."[20]

The new developments such as the high increases in oil prices, the Iranian revolution and the invasion of Afghanistan by the Soviet Union led American officials to appreciate better Turkey's role in deterring the Soviet adventurism, preventing a decrease in the American influence in the region and protecting the West's access to oil in the Gulf.[21] Former American ambassador George McGhee supports this view: 'The fluid situation in Afghanistan since the Soviet withdrawal, the withdrawal of Iran from cooperation with the West, and the uncertainty regarding the Greek NATO commitment leave Turkey as the only reliable element in the northern tier of the Middle East.'[22] In the light of these facts, it was natural to conclude that the United States had as much to lose as Turkey from breakdown in the bilateral relationship and that since Washington's leverage with Turkey was limited, any heavy-handed pressure of the Americans on the Turks could backfire.

When the Cold War came to an end with the collapse of the Eastern bloc and the Soviet Union, some doubts began to emerge on the strategic importance of Turkey for the West. Particularly Turkish officials seemed to concern that international developments could weaken Turkey's diplomatic leverage in Washington and that this could bring about a sharp reduction in U.S. military and economic assistance allocations for Turkey and a greater Greek influence over U.S. policy-makers on the issues relating to Turkish interests. These concerns led Turkish officials to emphasize repeatedly Turkey's role as NATO's only Muslim member in promoting stability in the Middle East and improving mutually beneficial economic relations between the West and the Muslim World.

In the eyes of Turkish leaders, instabilities and conflicts in the Caucasus as well as the Middle East, uncertainties in the former Soviet republics and competitions for oil and gas reserves of the Central Asia had reinforced the importance of Turkey as a stable, democratic, secular and Western oriented state located in the region. The Americans had to reassure "the Turks that as long as the geography of the region remained unchanged, so would Turkey's strategic importance."[23] The Gulf Crisis of 1990-1991 proved that the end of the Cold War had not changed the crucial position of Turkey in the global strategic interests and initiatives of the big powers. The United States needed reliable access routes to the Middle East and Turkey's land, sea and air spaces commanded the best Western approaches to the region.[24]

---

[19] Rustow, *Turkey*, pp. 108-111, Stearns, *Entangled Allies*, pp. 52,150, McGhee, *The US-Turkish-NATO-Middle East Connection*, p. 176, *The Economist*, "Star of Islam", 14 December 1991, p. 4.

[20] Bruce, "Cyprus: A Last Chance", p. 117.

[21] Kuniholm, "Turkey in the World", p. 14, Rubin, "U.S. Middle East Policy in the Turkish Context", p. 79, Haass, "Managing NATO's Weakest Flank: the United States, Greece and Turkey", p. 465, Bruce, "Cyprus: A Last Chance", p. 116.

[22] McGhee, *The US-Turkish-NATO-Middle East Connection*, p. 177.

[23] Stearns, *Entangled Allies*, p. 130, İrfan C. Acar, *Dış Politika*, Ankara, 1993, pp. 92-93.

[24] Stearns, *Entangled Allies*, pp. 51,149, Bruce R. Kuniholm, "Turkey and the West", *Foreign Affairs*, vol. 70(2), 1991, p. 36.

The U.S. bases in Turkey, too, continued to be valuable assets for the U.S. defense with their key roles in supporting America's Middle East policy and in monitoring abnormal military activities around that region.

5. MILITARY COOPERATION

The changes in the 1980s such as the Iranian revolution and the Soviet invasion of Afghanistan and the uncertainty prevailing in nearby Iran, Iraq, Syria, Lebanon and even in Greece strengthened the Turkish-American cooperation in the security area.[25] As Richard Perle states, there were eighteen to twenty matters that were being worked on in harmonious fashion between the two states at the end of 1984 and it had been possible to resolve such delicate matters as the strengthening of the structure of NATO facilities in Turkey and Turkey's role in assisting the Multi-National Force in Lebanon.[26] Training programs and joint ventures in military production carried out by Turkey with Saudi Arabia and Egypt were serving U.S. interests by contributing the Gulf stability. A major step in the cooperation of the two countries was the projected Turkish-American coproduction of F-16s in Turkey. In a ten-year period, 160 F-16s worth $ 4.2 billion were to be produced.[27]

In October 1982, the Turkish and U.S. officials signed a co-locator operating base agreement, which would provide for the modernization of ten Turkish airfields and the building of two new ones at Muş and Batman, in eastern Turkey. These airfields were to be large enough to accommodate long-range bombers and cargo planes and would place American and NATO aircraft within 700 miles of the Gulf and within striking distance of the Transcaucasus, thus enhancing Turkey's role in deterring aggressive Soviet intentions against the region. The agreement would make Turkey more valuable not only as a part of NATO's southern flank, but also as a possible base for rapid deployment in the case of a Middle Eastern crisis.

American officials would like a clearer commitment on the use of the bases by the Western forces in contingencies involving the Gulf. But the Turks were understandably reluctant to permit the use of the airfields for one-sided Western interventions in regional matters. Although pleased with the improved bilateral relations, the Turkish authorities were skeptical about the idea that the United States saw a potential role for Turkey in the Gulf and they feared that a U.S. move from the bases against the region could involve Turkey in some military conflicts and attract hostilities of the regional powers, with which Turkey had growing trade relations. Turkish officials repeatedly declared that the 1982 agreement had no connection with the Rapid Deployment Force and that the use of the airfields would be limited strictly to NATO missions. It seems that the Turks wanted to reserve the right to join or stand back from any possible Western intervention in the region, but they had no reservations on protection of the Middle East against a Soviet military push across Iran toward the Gulf.[28]

---

[25] Laipson, "U.S.-Turkish Friendly Friction", p. 21, Rubin, "U.S. Middle East Policy in the Turkish Context", p. 78.
[26] Perle, "Turkey and U.S. Military Assistance", p. 23.
[27] Rubin, "U.S. Middle East Policy in the Turkish Context", p. 79, Acar, *Dış Politika*, p. 92.
[28] Kuniholm, "Turkey and NATO: Past, Present and Future", pp. 438-439, Kuniholm, "Turkey in the World", pp. 14-15, William Hale, "Turkey, NATO and the Middle East" in Richard Lawless (ed.), *Foreign Policy Issues in the Middle East*, Durham: University of Durham, 1985, p. 57, Kuniholm, "Turkey and NATO: Past, Present and Future", pp. 113-114, Perle, "Turkey and U.S. Military Assistance", p. 26, Rubin, "U.S. Middle East

In the following years, the U.S. preoccupation with preventing local uprisings and conflicts in the region which could harm U.S. interests underlined Turkey's vital place in American defense strategies as a possible base for rapid deployment of American forces. *The Economist* stated in December 1991: "It is useful that the United States is strengthening the force of bomber aircraft it keeps in south-eastern Turkey, to discourage present and future Saddam Husseins".[29]

There were some other matters, which affected the U.S.-Turkish military cooperation negatively. The competition and deadlock between Greece and Turkey within NATO hampered their cooperation with the United States. After 1984, the two states vetoed each other's 'national chapters', the yearly inventory of forces assigned to NATO, which served as a basis for NATO planning and for the alliance's annual 'Comparison of NATO and Warsaw Pact Forces', a document that was not published after 1984 for this reason. In 1987 and 1988, objections of Turkey and Greece to specific projects proposed for infrastructure funding on each other's territory ended with failure to approve about half of the projects.

Since Turkish leaders believed that security policies of the United States were influenced by domestic political considerations which were under strong pressures of the anti-Turkish forces, they came to the conclusion that doing business with the U.S. government was full of uncertainties and that therefore Turkey should try to use NATO as a safeguard against over-reliance on the United States.[30] In the Turkish eyes, although the United States was the strongest guarantee for Turkey's security, Turkey should have alternative sources of security and military equipment in the case of having serious problems with the USA.

The Turkish worries on the excessive American tilt toward Iraq in the 1980s, which was thought to have a potential to push Iran toward the Soviet Union or causing instabilities in the region and the tough Turkish bargaining on the kind of access to Turkish facilities the United States would enjoy, too, showed how the U.S.-Turkish cooperation was far from smoothly operating. The criticism of the security partnership of Turkey with NATO and the United States by the Turkish opposition was another negative factor. It was claimed that although Turkey undertook a heavy burden for Western security by keeping a large army which required allocating large amounts of economic sources, it did not get any reasonable advantages in return and it did not have any voice or influence on the decisions taken within NATO. The Americans had the last word in Turkey's security matters and they had not allowed Turkey to use its armed forces for its own national interests.[31]

From their alliance with the United States, Turkish authorities expected that they would be given adequate assistance in arms and training and hoped that the Americans would provide supplies and reinforcements in the event of war. In their eyes, there should be no doubt whatsoever of America's commitment to fulfil its solemn obligations to Turkey if its security were threatened. The Turks also expected that their views would be considered in NATO councils before important decisions were taken. On the other hand, Turkish authorities appreciated the American support during their domestic difficulties in contrast with the European criticism, which led the Turkish government to withdraw from the Council of Europe's Parliamentary Assembly in 1982. Meanwhile, American officials were of the

---

Policy in the Turkish Context", pp. 77-79, Haass, "Managing NATO's Weakest Flank: the United States, Greece and Turkey", pp. 465-468.

[29] *The Economist*, "Star of Islam", p. 4.

[30] Stearns, *Entangled Allies*, pp. 68-69, 81.

[31] Necmettin Erbakan, *Türkiye'nin Temel Meseleleri*, Ankara: Rehber, 1991, pp. 53-54.

opinion that the special relationship between Turkey and the United States was on the solid ground and would continue in a foreseeable future though it was inevitable to have ups and downs on the Cyprus and Armenian issues.[32]

6. THE ISRAELI DIMENSION

The closeness of Turkey's relations with Israel was a factor, which strengthened the U.S.-Turkish cooperation. Turkey and Israel were the closest allies of the United States in the Middle East and their enemies coincided with those of the USA. The Americans saw these states as the most important partners, which would help the establishment and maintenance of a future Middle Eastern peace, and the protection of the American interests in the region. The Americans would like to see that Ankara adopt policies, which would improve its relations with Israel.[33] For the American Congress, Turkey's relations with Israel were an important matter, which needed special attention. Congressmen became concerned about occasional reports that Turkey might reduce its relations with Israel.[34]

Since Israel was an indispensable partner of the West in the Middle East, Turkey could not completely contradict the Western positions on Israel as long as it remained active in Western institutions and received economic and military aid from the United States.[35] Although Turkey kept its relations with Israel cool in the 1980-1982 period to gain Arab support in the Cyprus conflict and to be in a better position in getting oil, the concern of both states on Syria's Soviet-backed policies attracted them to each other. In the early 1980s, Israeli and Turkish experts had began to secretly exchange information in their common fight against terrorism. The full cooperation of Turkish law enforcement authorities with their Israeli and American counterparts during the terrorist bombing of the İstanbul synagogue in December 1986 pleased both the Americans and Israelis.[36] Before the Gulf Crisis erupted, Turkey had gone a good way in improving its relations with Israel in trade and intelligence. It seems that the first signal for the new momentum of the Turkish-Israeli relationship came from Washington. The American Jewish lobby followed Israeli instructions on supporting Turkey against the campaigns of the Armenian and Greek lobbies in Congress.[37] The growing defense dimension of the Turkish-Israeli cooperation in the following years seemed to have the potential to be one of the most important bases of U.S.-Turkish relations.

7. THE ECONOMIC ASPECT

The United States naturally wants Turkey to shape its economy under a free enterprise market system, together with a liberal international economic policy. Therefore Turgut Özal's market-oriented economic reforms were bound to be welcomed in Washington. Özal's liberal

---

[32] Kuniholm, "Turkey in the World", p. 12, Kuniholm, "Turkey and NATO: Past, Present and Future", p. 444.

[33] Kuniholm, "Turkey and NATO: Past, Present and Future", pp. 114-115, Hasan Köni, "Yeni Uluslararası Düzende Türk-Amerikan İlişkileri", *Yeni Türkiye*, No. 3, 1995, p. 434.

[34] Laipson, "Turkey and the US Congress", p. 32.

[35] M. Hakan Yavuz and M. R. Khan, "Turkish Foreign Policy Toward the Arab-Israeli Conflict: Duality and the Development (1950-1991)", *Arab Studies Quarterly*, vol. 14 (4), 1992, p. 81.

[36] Rustow, *Turkey*, pp. 115,133n.

[37] Yavuz and Khan, "Turkish Foreign Policy Toward the Arab-Israeli Conflict", pp. 81-82.

revolution had the characteristic of being an American answer to Turkish problems: "privatization of state enterprise; economic mobility of capital and labor across frontiers; televised contests among political leaders and bids for the second Bosporus bridge thrown wide open to international competition."[38] These reforms made Turkey in the 1980s particularly attractive for American and European investments in agribusiness, processed foods, textiles, electronics manufacturing and regional banking.

Meanwhile, Turkey's rapid economic development progressed to the point where Turkish leaders preferred more trade to aid in their dealings with the United States. Since he saw a strong economy as the most important condition for maintaining national security, Özal tried to encourage foreign and domestic investment in Turkish economy and to build a national military industry. In these efforts, opening the U.S. market to Turkish goods, especially textile, and having advantageous partnership arrangements with the U.S. industry had a great importance.[39]

One problem in this context was the quota established by the American authorities for the Turkish textile imports to the United States. During his visit to Turkey in March 1986, American Secretary of State Shultz was informed of the Turkish demand that the new DECA be linked to a substantial increase in this quota.[40] The imbalance in the U.S.-Turkish trade, proved by the Turkish export to the USA worth $ 534 million in contrast with $ 1.7 billion U.S. export to Turkey in 1991, caused the demands on the Turkish side in the direction of abolishing this inequality.[41] While not getting any positive results on the textile quota and trade imbalance issues, the U.S. support for Turkey's future membership in the European Community was one valuable development for Turkish leaders. Turgut Özal had made Turkey's EC membership one of the main objectives of Turkish foreign policy and now the United States could show its friendship by assisting Turkey in this matter even if this could be materialized at the expense of U.S. bilateral trade with Turkey.[42] The Bush administration particularly put emphasis on this matter to gain the Turkish support during the Gulf crisis of 1990-1991.

8. THE IDEOLOGICAL AND CULTURAL ASPECT

The United States generally would prefer that Turkey adopts a true parliamentary democracy and try to protect and improve it. Turkey's chief value for the West was to be an example to the region around it. Turkey would demonstrate that a Muslim country could become a prosperous democracy and a full member of the modern world.[43] During the 1980s Turgut Özal symbolized the revival of democracy in Turkey. But there were still doubts in the minds of the Americans on Turkey's future: "Might Turkey's still somewhat precarious

[38] Rustow, *Turkey*, p. 124.
[39] Ibid., p. 106, Yavuz and Khan, "Turkish Foreign Policy Toward the Arab-Israeli Conflict", p. 83, Acar, *Dış Politika*, p. 92, Köni, "Yeni Uluslararası Düzende Türk-Amerikan İlişkileri", p. 435, Henze, "Out of Kilter", p. 82.
[40] Rustow, *Turkey*, p. 106, Acar, *Dış Politika*, p. 92, Haass, "Managing NATO's Weakest Flank: the United States, Greece and Turkey", p. 466.
[41] Acar, *Dış Politika*, p. 92.
[42] McGhee, *The US-Turkish-NATO-Middle East Connection*, p. 180, Pelletiere, "Ortadoğu'da Türkiye ve Amerika: Kürt Bağlantısı", p. 180.
[43] McGhee, *The US-Turkish-NATO-Middle East Connection*, p. 176, *The Economist*, "Star of Islam", p. 4.

balance between military and democratic politics be upset by future waves of terrorism and by a renewed combination of economic crisis and parliamentary deadlock"; and thus might Turkey come under the military control again? More importantly, "might future Turkish citizens become more susceptible than were their parents to the appeals of Islamic fundamentalism?"[44]

While improving its democracy and protecting itself against Islamic movements, Turkey should exert its leadership abilities over the regional states which experienced conflict with the West in recent years and should take advantage of its membership in the Islamic Conference Organization to help disrupt "the efforts being made by Iran's Ayatollah Khomeini to desecularise the Islamic world and make it a base for a modern-day religious war against the West."[45] As the American authorities hoped to replace Turkey's role as a guardian of the southern flank of NATO with "the mission of serving as a secular pro-Western alternative to Iran's Islamic assertiveness in the region",[46] as *Newsweek* stated, Washington had been "actively courting Turkey as its chief secular ally in a region threatened by the rise of Islamic fundamentalism."[47]

Özal's efforts in the final months of his presidency to link Turkey with ethnically Turkic republics of the former Soviet Union in a union loosely modeled on the British Commonwealth[48] brought about the possibility of Turkey's initiating campaigns in the Central Asia on behalf of the West against the moves of the 'fundamentalist' Saudi Arabia and Iran. The American think-tank institutions were suggesting that the United States should support the Turkish initiatives because Turkey was a secular state which had Western-oriented policies, a free-market economic regime and close cultural and ethnic ties with the Central Asian nations. Turkey's bold initiatives in the region in the early 1990s in spite of its scarce resources shows that Turkish authorities had strongly expected American aid and support.[49] In the following years, the apparent convergence of American and Turkish interests in Central Asia became a constant factor of the general U.S.-Turkish cooperation.

One issue, which caused complaints against the Turkish government, was Turkey's drastic actions in facing the Kurdish rebellion and terrorism. As the European states directed more human rights accusations against Turkey on the Kurdish question, the American authorities seemed to appreciate Turkey's quite extraordinary success in coping with anarchy and terrorism. Nevertheless, the Americans, especially Congress, joined the others in urging Turkish rulers to take impressive steps in restoring democracy and parliamentary government and respecting human rights.[50] It seemed that Turkey's alleged occasional departures from the democracy and human rights standards advocated in the United States would have an impact on relations between the two states. In spite of their common interests and similar democratic institutions, it was a fact that the Turkish and American nations differed in ethnic, religious, political, geographic and historical background. However, apart form minor disagreements, it was hard to attribute the major issues between the two states to these mainly ideological and

---

[44] Rustow, *Turkey*, p. 116.
[45] McGhee, *The US-Turkish-NATO-Middle East Connection,* p. 176.
[46] Yavuz and Khan, "Turkish Foreign Policy Toward the Arab-Israeli Conflict", p. 86.
[47] *Newsweek*, 06 April 1992, p. 15.
[48] *Newsweek*, 26 April 1993, p. 13.
[49] Köni, "Yeni Uluslararası Düzende Türk-Amerikan İlişkileri", p. 429.
[50] Perle, "Turkey and U.S. Military Assistance", p. 25, McGhee, *The US-Turkish-NATO-Middle East Connection,* p. 167, Laipson, "Turkey and the US Congress", p. 31.

cultural factors.[51] It could be fair to state that these factors affected the degree of the U.S. Congress' reactions on some issues or they were used as a pretext for making life difficult for Turkey.

Turkey's Islamic connection, too, had the potential to be a straining force in its relations with the United States. Turkish leaders had to emphasize Turkey's Islamic identity to gain support of the Muslim world for Turkey's economic growth and some important objectives of its foreign policy. In the late 1970s, the Turkish government had refused to join the American-led economic and diplomatic sanctions against Iran following the Islamic revolution and the captivity of American diplomats in Iran.[52] Turkey's increased political and economic interactions with the Muslim countries in the 1980s were initiated by the military regime. Turkish efforts to become more deeply involved in the Middle East, which required altering its image as an American proxy, caused a slight coolness in the U.S. Turkish relations even during the Reagen administration period in comparison to earlier periods.[53]

9. GREEK-TURKISH DIFFERENCES

The Greek-Turkish disagreements over such issues as the boundaries of territorial waters and continental shelf, the control of airspace, surface navigation and oil rights in the Aegean, where many Greek islands lie within sight of the Turkish coast, inevitably affected the Turkish-American cooperation, too. American authorities tried to avoid involvement in these disputes, but their actions or failure to take actions were often criticized by both sides.[54] In March 1987, the indications that Greece might be planning to explore oil in the parts of the Aegean which were considered as international waters by Turkey led Turkish leaders to send a research vessel of their own into the same area. The United States and NATO were then obliged to intervene in the matter to prevent an armed conflict between the two sides by persuading them staying outside the disputed area.[55] It seemed that these kinds of crises would irritate the Americans in the future as well, by putting them in a difficult position to prevent a conflict between their two allies not to cause instability in a strategic region.

The Cyprus question was another negative factor affecting U.S.-Turkish relations. As the American side tried not to lose its influence on Cyprus, located in a strategic place, by adding the Cyprus-related conditions to U.S. military interactions with Turkey, this shook the Turkish confidence in the USA. After the Turkish arms embargo was lifted in 1978, the American administrations had to submit bimonthly reports to Congress certifying that progress was being made toward a Cyprus settlement.[56] When the Turkish side declared statehood on northern Cyprus, both chambers of the American Congress condemned the declaration and called on the Administration to try to reverse that was viewed as a dangerous move by the Turkish Cypriots. The American aid bill in 1984 tied the U.S. aid to Turkey to the presidential certification that (a) the U.S. government was acting to prevent moves to partition Cyprus and was calling on Turkey to take steps to reverse the independence of

---

[51] McGhee, *The US-Turkish-NATO-Middle East Connection*, p. 161.
[52] Yavuz and Khan, "Turkish Foreign Policy Toward the Arab-Israeli Conflict", pp. 76,78.
[53] Bruce, "Cyprus: A Last Chance", p. 131.
[54] McGhee, *The US-Turkish-NATO-Middle East Connection*, p. 161.
[55] Stearns, *Entangled Allies*, p. 126.
[56] Ibid., p. 125.

Northern Cyprus and (b) Turkey was making efforts to insure that the Turkish Cypriots took no action in Varosha that would impede negotiations on the future of Cyprus.[57] These were unacceptable conditions to the Turks.

Since Cyprus-related tensions kept alive the possibility of a disastrous war between two NATO allies, led these countries to spend enormous amount of money and energy and thus threatened the stability of the region, the Americans put pressures on both sides to find a permanent solution to the problem. American President Reagan's letter to Turkish President Kenan Evren on 22 November 1984 warned that the U.S. administration might not be able to overcome congressional opposition in the future. The letter persuaded Turkish officials to reduce their demands for territory from 37 percent to 29 percent, drop the idea of a rotating presidency and soften their insistence on absolute veto rights in all institutions of government.[58] The American insistence on the solution of the Cyprus question and the Turkish failure to fulfil this demand because of the complexity of the problem and the sensitivity of the Turkish people toward Cyprus always cast a shadow on U.S.-Turkish relations. It seemed that the problem would not disappear in a near future.

10. THE ARMENIAN ISSUE

Another problem that affected the U.S.-Turkish relationship was the continuing effort of the Americans of Armenian descent to persuade some Congressmen to introduce resolutions which sought to establish a day of remembrance to commemorate 'man's inhumanity to man', calling particular attention to the alleged genocide of Armenians at the hands of the Ottoman Turks early in the twentieth century and somehow associating the present-day Turkish Republic with those events. While the Armenians launched propaganda campaigns and lobbying for Congressional actions censuring Turkey, more then 50 Turkish diplomats in a number of countries were assassinated by the Armenian Secret Army. The Turkish government reasoned that many people along with the Armenians died amid the breakdown of order during the World War I especially because of the encouragement of the Armenians by the Soviets and later by the Western powers to set up an independent state, but no genocide-type killings occurred.[59] Turkish officials alleged that Armenians were using the issue just an excuse to justify their terrorist campaigns against Turkey and the U.S. Congress was encouraging them with its resolutions on the issue.

To scale down the Turkish anger, the Americans stressed that non-binding resolutions passed by Congress did not constitute major U.S. foreign policy pronouncements and that they were not connected directly to the foreign aid legislation or to the general tone of U.S.-Turkish cooperation in security and defense matters.[60] There were Americans who suggested that the Turkish government might reemphasize Atatürk's repudiation of the Ottoman mass killings of Armenians or who criticized the Turkish press on the ground that its behavior blew the issue out of proportion and "made as though a good and faithful ally -the USA- was any

---

[57] Laipson, "Turkey and the US Congress", pp. 29-30.
[58] Bruce, "Cyprus: A Last Chance", pp. 115-116,119,129,133.
[59] Rustow, *Turkey*, pp. 101-102, McGhee, *The US-Turkish-NATO-Middle East Connection*, pp. 167-168, Haass, "Managing NATO's Weakest Flank: the United States, Greece and Turkey", p. 466.
[60] Laipson, "Turkey and the US Congress", p. 33, Perle, "Turkey and U.S. Military Assistance", p. 24, Rustow, *Turkey*, p. 103.

way departing from a desire for close and continuing constructive relations with Turkey."[61] However, there was no doubt that mere introduction and consideration of Armenian resolutions had become a major sore point in the U.S.-Turkish relationship and that, as one American author admits, "to dwell on a one-sided picture of the past" would not help improve America's relations with its key Atlantic-Middle Eastern ally and Armenian terrorism was "one of the prime means by which Moscow and Damascus" hoped "to drive a wedge between Turkey and the West."[62]

11. CONCLUSION

As it has always been the case, the military and security aspect constituted to be the most important part of U.S.-Turkish relations in the 1980s as well. Located in a strategic and unstable region, which always attracted the attention of big powers, Turkey found a great advantage in having alliance relations with the leader of the West, in spite of its unhappiness on some important issues. The conditioning of the U.S. aid by Congress to the Cyprus and Armenian issues, the Turkish-Greek differences and human rights was particularly hurtful for Turkish leaders and led them even to think about alternative security partners. In spite of their failure in getting positive results from negotiating the extension of the DECA, in changing the negative attitude of the U.S. Congress, in overcoming the 7:10 ratio and in abolishing the U.S. textile quotas and the imbalance in the U.S.-Turkish trade, Turkish leaders' cooperation in providing the legal basis of U.S.-Turkish security relations proved their appreciation of America's alliance, but it gave signals for the possibility that they could play it hard against the Americans when they felt it necessary.

Turkey's strategic location at the crossroads of important and unstable regions such as the Middle East, the Central Asia and the Balkans always made her an indispensable element for the Americans. As Turkey had served as a barrier against foreign interventions in the Middle East in the past, with new developments, it could play an important role in providing the Western access to the Gulf oil and could serve as a base for rapid deployment of Western forces in the case of regional crises affecting Western interests. Being an example for regional states against fundamentalist Islamic movements and establishing close ties with Israel were new roles of Turkey, which gained importance for the Americans. Turkey's unwillingness to involve itself in one-sided Western initiatives in the Middle East, the possibility of a Greek-Turkish war on the Cyprus and Aegean issues, excessive Turkish demands on the military area, and Turkey's different historical background together with the possibility of Turkey's inclination to the Muslim world with the development of conservative movements were main sore points of America's relations with Turkey. In spite of all negative elements, the U.S.-Turkish cooperation was much stronger than that of the 1970s.

---

[61] Perle, "Turkey and U.S. Military Assistance", p. 26, Rustow, *Turkey*, p. 103.
[62] Rustow, *Turkey*, p. 103.

Chapter 11

TURKISH-AMERICAN RELATIONS IN THE POST-COLD WAR PERIOD

The end of the Cold War marked a radical change in the world order. In the new era, the globalization became the main force affecting policies and actions of the world states. The domination of the West (especially the United States) over the world politics was much more evident. The other states of the world were prone to the intervention of the major powers. While the world went through a radical change, Turkish leaders chose to be on the side of the founders of the new order, mainly America, as they exactly had done in the aftermath of the Second World War. There was no one single distinct common threat now facing the alliance in which Turkey was a member, but Turkish rulers felt surrounded by more threats. The Turkish economy was much stronger compared with its situation in the Cold War period, but entering into a balanced economic cooperation with the United States and the European Union had a great importance for Turkey in order to be able to compete with the other powers in an era in which the globalization was the dominant force. The West was still the most important source for Turkey in getting high-tech military equipment, but it seemed that the conditions of obtaining them would not be as suitable as it was in the past. Turkey also needed to make some changes in its domestic system in accordance with global values in order not to stay outside the West. In short, Turkey was going through the process of participating in the new world system as a more active world power. Its relationship with the United States, which constituted the most important aspect of its foreign policy, was affected by this process as much as it influenced it. This chapter will try to analyze the factors behind this interaction in the post-Cold War period.

1. TURKEY'S NEW ENVIRONMENT

Turkish-American relations would be inevitably influenced by the new environment surrounding Turkey. Turkey's proximity to the trouble spots of the new world order made it the frontline country of NATO in compared to its position as a flank state of the West during the Cold War and put it in a very epicenter of the new international environment.[1] With the

---

[1] Şükrü Gürel, "A General Appraisal of Current Turkish Foreign Policy" in Mustafa Aydın (ed.), *Turkey at the Threshold of the 21st Century*, Ankara: International Relations Foundation, 1998, p. 11, *Beyaz Kitap, Savunma*

outbreak of regional conflicts, Turkey's position as an island of stability in the center of volatile region, as a barrier against the outbreak and spread of these local wars and as a promoter of regional cooperation gained more importance.[2] The new developments also helped Turkey to gain a weight in regional and world politics with its increased physical and strategic strength. The disintegration of the Soviet Union terminated the major security threat for Turkey and weakened her regional enemies such as Syria, Iran and Iraq and thus its foreign and security policies were relieved of certain constraints. Moreover, the factors such as the revival of Turkey's cultural, linguistic and historical ties with "the vast land mass of Eurasia" extending from the Balkans to the Caucasus broadened the scope of Turkish foreign policies and opened up new areas for Turkish economic and political activities.[3]

Turkey was now in a unique period which forced Turkish rulers to observe "simultaneously developments on several fronts, ranging from the process of European integration to the emergence of a belt of countries of Turkic language in the Caucasus and Central Asia, from tragic developments in the Balkans to the instability and conflict in the Middle East and the Caucasus."[4] Turkey was surrounded by the most unstable, uncertain and unpredictable regions and it was the most exposed to dangers of the new security environment.[5] Although Turkey still remained wary of the developments on its borders with the former Soviet Union, its strategic priorities shifted toward the new dangers in the south, including those originated from the activities of Iran, Iraq, Syria and Kurdish separatists.[6]

Among the potential threats perceived by Turkish rulers were there the religious radicalism; the spread of terrorism; the ethnic nationalism; the proliferation of nuclear weapons and other weapons of mass destruction in the region; regional rivalries and hegemonic aspirations and moves; instabilities emanating from mass migration, civil breakdowns, etc.; the loss of prestige and credibility of international institutions; and the possibility of disruption of Middle Eastern oil flows.[7] Apart from staying outside the Western security structures, Turkish rulers also feared from the establishment of defense cooperation and alliance relations between Turkey's regional rivals and enemies. Especially Greek rulers' attempts to encircle Turkey with bilateral and multilateral relationships alarmed Turkish

1998, Ankara: Milli Savunma Bakanlığı, 1998, p. 6, Mahmut Bali Aykan, "Turkish Perspectives on Turkish-US Relations Concerning Persian Gulf Security in the Post-Cold War Era: 1989-1995", *Middle East Journal,* vol. 50, No. 3, Summer 1996, p. 346, Şadi Ergüvenç, "Turkey: Strategic Partner of the European Union", *Foreign Policy* (Ankara), vol. 20, No. 1-2, 1996, p. 9, Süleyman Demirel, "Turkey and NATO at the Threshold of a New Century", *Perception,* vol. 4, No. 1, March-May 1999, p. 7, Javier Solana, "NATO in the Twenty-First Century", *Perception,* vol. 4, No. 1, March-May 1999, p. 21.

[2] Meltem Müftüler-Bac, "Turkey's Predicament in the Post-cold War Era", *Futures,* vol. 28, No. 3, April 1996, p. 256 quotes Marc Grossman.

[3] Gürel, "A General Appraisal...", p. 11, William Hale, "Turkish Foreign Policy After the Cold War", *Turkish Review of Balkan Studies,* No. 1, 1993, p. 234, Shireen Hunter, "Bridge or Frontier? Turkey's Post-Cold War Geopolitical Posture", *The International Spectator,* vol. 34, No. 1, January-March 1999, p. 66.

[4] Gürel, "A General Appraisal...", p. 12.

[5] Demirel, "Turkey...", p. 9, Malik Mufti, "Daring and Caution in Turkish Foreign Policy", *Middle East Journal,* vol. 52, No. 1, Winter 1998, p. 33 quotes Hikmet Çetin.

[6] Ian O. Lesser, *Bridge or Barrier: Turkey and the West After the Cold War,* Santa Monica: Rand, 1992, pp. 24, 27, James Brown, *Delicately Poised Allies: Greece and Turkey: Problems, Policy Choices and Mediterranean Security,* London: Brassey's, 1991, pp. 98, 114.

[7] *Beyaz Kitap,* pp. 3, 6, 60, Nur-Bilge Criss, "International Institutions and European Security: A Turkish Perspective" in M. Carnovale (ed.), *European Security and International Institutions After the Cold War,* London: Macmillan, 1995, pp. 204, 211, Duygu B. Sezer, "Turkey's New Security Environment, Nuclear Weapons and Proliferation", *Comparative Strategy,* vol. 14, No. 2, 1995, p. 169, John Roper, "The West and Turkey: Varying Roles, Common Interests", *The International Spectator,* vol. 34, No. 1, January-March 1999, p. 99, Demirel, "Turkey...", p. 12.

rulers and led them to seek balancing alternatives.[8] Each of Turkey's hostile neighbors had no power to threaten it with general aggression, but they might cause problems for Turkey when they acted together.[9] Turkish leaders, at least, have to consider the possibility of conducting military operations in more than one front in case of a regional conflict and to direct their sources in conformity of this possibility.

2. TURKEY'S PROBLEMS AND THE USA

a) The Decrease in Turkey's Strategic Importance

The warming of East-West relations with the end of the Cod War brought about the possibility of Turkey's becoming "a leading casualty of strategic neglect" in the new era. This would be a serious setback for Turkish rulers because a decrease in Turkey's strategic importance was likely to result in less Western economic and military assistance and a harsher Western attitude toward Turkey in its national causes. Staying outside the Western political economic, cultural and security structures would mean the failure of Turkish traditional foreign policy and its Western-type political system. With the outbreak of the Gulf War, which was the first occurrence of use of force outside the NATO area in the post-cold War era, it was believed that Turkey returned to the strategic forefront. However, some factors such as the Western conciliatory attitude toward Russia and the European intention of leaving Turkey outside the European Community (EC) and the Western European Union (WEU) still kept Turkish rulers vigilant.[10] The fact that America was the most insistent on Turkey's strategic importance for the West maintained Turkish-American relations on a sound track and led Turkish rulers to be more inclined toward the USA rather than the Western Europe.

b) Doubts about NATO

The best option among the available alternatives for guaranteeing Turkey's security was to remain a full member of NATO with an emphasis on the Atlantic link within this alliance. Turkey's membership of NATO was a symbol of its participation in the Western democratic club, enhancing Western interest in Turkey and giving it a greater voice in international affairs and a seat in the highest councils of the West.[11] NATO also provided Turkey multilateral Euro-Atlantic framework for its defense cooperation with the West and thus reduced its over-reliance on the United States. Turkey also seemed to share with Europe the concerns about the US patronage in international events, the ambiguity of US commitments and unilateral US initiatives launched without consultations with other members.[12] However,

---

[8] Mufti, "Daring...", pp. 35-36, 37, 40.

[9] Şadi Ergüvenç, "Turkey's Strategic Importance in Military Dimension: A Regional Balance Holder" in Aydın, *Turkey...*, pp. 63, 67.

[10] Lesser, *Bridge or Barrier*, p. 1, Criss, "International Institutions...", p. 204, Hunter, "Bridge or Frontier?...", p. 67.

[11] Criss, "International Institutions...", p. 201, Sezer, "Turkey's...", p. 167, M. Stearns, *Entangled Allies: U.S. Policy Toward Greece, Turkey and Cyprus,* New York: Council on Foreign Relations Press, 1992, p. 29, Hale, "Turkish Foreign Policy...", p. 234, Ömür Orhun, "The Uncertainties and Challenges Ahead: A Southern Perspective", *Perceptions,* vol. 4, No. 1, 1999, p. 30.

[12] Lesser, *Bridge or Barrier*, p. 24, Brown, *Delicately Poised Allies,* p. 5, Hunter, "Bridge or Frontier?...", p. 66.

the European states could not replace America as the main security partner of Turkey because they lacked resources and the intention to help Turkish defense efforts and they could not solve regional conflicts without the help of the United States by establishing a consensus among themselves.

Turkish rulers expected that under the new NATO, "collective defense should stay, for it not only underpins... [Turkey's] fundamental security but it is also the basis, on which... [Turkey's] commitment rests."[13] The United States and NATO should deter Russia and other potential enemies in a real sense and should avoid to act in the way which would lead Russia and other potential enemies in the region to think that NATO's commitment to Turkey's security is not so genuine.[14] However, doubts about the solidity of the NATO commitment to Turkish security could not be removed from the minds of Turkish rulers easily. As NATO went through an adaptation process, the possibility of NATO's neglecting Article 5 commitments to the defense of its members, especially in the case of an outside-area issue seemed more likely. Turkish rulers are certainly alarmed when they heard the debates about the "gray area" threats that might require more conditional guarantees.

Turkish anxieties were reinforced during the Gulf War when some NATO allies responded to the Turkish request for assistance and reinforcement reluctantly and tardily.[15] Lesser points out that one important way of dispelling Turkish doubts about the solidity of the NATO guarantee and the emergence of a "gray area" debate was the maintenance of a permanent land-based U.S. tactical air presence (the 401st Tactical Fighter Wing) in the Southern Region of NATO. Turkish rulers saw this force as the evidence of a continued Alliance commitment to the security of Turkey.[16] In fact, NATO established the AMF (ACE Mobile Force) in 1960 in order to come rapidly to the aid of NATO states in the flanks. This force had been carrying out field training exercises in eastern Turkey and in Turkish Thrace.[17]

Some criticisms that had been made in the past on Turkey's role in shaping the defense strategies of NATO might still be valid. According to these critics, the United States determined and directed general policies of the alliance by ignoring special priorities of other members. Turkey's security needs required taking extra measures in addition to the policies determined by the Americans. Turkey's capability of action was limited with the goals of NATO to the extent that it could not make even tactical changes in its security strategies decided by NATO's main powers. The United States felt free to consider intervening in Turkey's surrounding region for its national interests, harming Turkey's geo-strategic relations with the regional countries. Western powers did not show sensitivity toward Turkey's improving its defense structure, widening its security resources and options and adopting itself to the region's realities.[18] Turkey had contributed to the Western security beyond its capacity by remaining always faithful to its alliance responsibilities in contrast to the attitude of some members. It had played a vital role in the creation of the perfect conditions prevailed throughout the central region by making great sacrifices such as

---

[13] Demirel, "Turkey...", p. 9.
[14] Sezer, "Turkey's...", p. 168.
[15] Lesser, *Bridge or Barrier*, pp. 14, 26, 35, Ian O. Lesser, "Turkey's Strategic Options", *The International Spectator*, vol. 34, No. 1, January-March 1999, pp. 83, Brown, *Delicately Poised Allies*, p. 107.
[16] Lesser, *Bridge or Barrier*, pp. 35-36, 43.
[17] Brown, *Delicately Poised Allies*, pp. 87, 93.
[18] Muzaffer Özsoy, "Dünü ve Bugünüyle Türk Savunma Stratejisi" in *Türkiye'nin Savunması*, Ankara: Dış Politika Enstitüsü, 1987, pp. 80-81.

alienating itself from its neighbors.[19] Turkish rulers now expected understanding for their efforts of diversifying Turkey's security resources, getting more aid and not provoking their neighbors.[20] If their doubts on the uncertainty of the future role of NATO could not be eradicated, they would naturally have more interest in the emerging European defense arrangements and would seek different alternatives to strengthen their position vis-à-vis the West.[21]

c) The Future of NATO

NATO officials frequently emphasized that they committed themselves to a robust "open door" policy concerning further accessions.[22] At the Madrid Summit, NATO powers decided to invite Czech Republic, Hungary and Poland to take up accession talks. Turkish authorities were interested in this development because it was closely related to their wishes of occupying a central position in new defense and political structures of the West. They had some reservations in supporting the enlargement of NATO. The internal and external adaptation process should not impair the effectiveness and essential defensive role of NATO and the alliance should continue to be the main defense structure and political consultation forum of the West.[23] The enlargement should be a gradual process and should be carried out in conjunction with the Partnership for Peace project not to alienate but to attract Russia to the Western defense system.[24] If Moscow was left outside and was led to adopt a heavy-handed approach towards Eastern European countries that expressed a desire to join NATO, then it was inevitable to turn to power politics for spheres of influence, especially in the region surrounding Turkey.[25]

The ultimate goal of NATO was to preserve the collective defense and the stability of its members and to establish an Euro-Atlantic region where peace was the central feature and resort to military force is banished.[26] However, there seemed to be some differences between Europe and the United States in establishing defense structures concerning Europe and the surrounding regions. Some Europeans believed that NATO was outdated and it should be put aside by giving more roles to other organizations such as the Organization of Security Cooperation in Europe (OSCE) and the European Union (EU). In their views, NATO could be maintained to be called for help in the case of an outside aggression, but it should be transformed away from being a vehicle for US involvement and domination in European security affairs.[27] The Bosnian conflict embarrassingly showed that the United States and

---

[19] *Beyaz Kitap*, p. 25, Tuğrul Çubukçu, "Savunma Harcamaları: İç ve Dış Kaynaklar" in *Türkiye'nin Savunması*, Ankara: Dış Politika Enstitüsü, 1987, 132.

[20] Ali Karaosmanoğlu, "Turkey and the Southern Flank: Domestic and External Contexts" in John Chipman (ed.), *NATO's Southern Allies: Internal and External Challenges*, London: Routledge, 1988, p. 300, John Chipman, "Allies in the Mediterranean: Legacy of Fragmentation" in Chipman (ed.), *NATO's...*, p. 79.

[21] Lesser, *Bridge or Barrier*, p. 12.

[22] John Barrett, "Current Political Agenda of the Atlantic Alliance and Turkey" in Aydın, *Turkey...*, p. 25.

[23] *Beyaz Kitap*, pp. 25-26.

[24] Ömür Orhun, "Turkey, Norway and the US in the New European Security Context, *Foreign Policy* (Ankara), Nos. 1-2, 1997, pp. 10-11.

[25] Criss, "International Institutions...", pp. 207-208.

[26] Barrett, "Current...", p. 7.

[27] Ibid., p. 57.

Europe shared very little sense of values, vision and political will.[28] While Europe wanted to keep NATO by diminishing its financial burdens and seemed to be unwilling to accept the burden of a direct exposure in regions such as the Middle East, the United States preferred to keep NATO strong and asked the Europeans to shoulder more burden for the Western defense.[29] The United States was insistent on seeing the Western security in the trans-regional basis and it was joined by Turkey in this.[30]

Western statesmen think that the instabilities and conflicts originated outside the NATO area threatened Western security, requiring NATO respond to them effectively by undertaking new responsibilities and missions such as peacemaking, peacekeeping and crisis management.[31] Especially the United States believed that the area, which NATO needed to reach, passed beyond its borders. For example, it considered NATO's southern flank extending until the Gulf region beyond Turkey's borders. However, the European states and Turkey did not see the link as clearly as the Americans did. They hesitated in accepting the extension of NATO's responsibility automatically to the regions outside the NATO area. While Turkey considered the defense of its eastern and southern borders totally inside the NATO responsibility, it approached to the expansion of the NATO area cautiously.[32] Although it was ready to discuss the out-of-area issues within NATO, Turkey did not want to undertake automatic responsibility to provide military force and to allow the use of its territory in developments outside the NATO area. Turkish rulers would not join the out-of-area operations unless all NATO allies agreed to do so or unless they saw joining the operation as vitally important for Turkish interests.[33]

d) The Future of the European Security

The Europeans' intention of having more voice in their defense and saving themselves from the American domination was proved by their efforts of strengthening the Western European Union as the defense organ of the European Union. The Maastrich Treaty in 1991 considered the WEU also a means to strengthen the European pillar of the Atlantic Alliance to overcome the objections.[34] Meanwhile, in order not to alienate the Europeans from NATO, a European Security and Defence Identity (ESDI) was created as having relation with the Atlantic Alliance.[35] The American administration genuinely supported making NATO a two-pillar alliance by welcoming the emergence of Europe as a more autonomous and responsible actor.[36] But it also shared the concern of NATO's flank countries such as Turkey, Denmark and Norway that the small group of the WEU countries might contribute to instabilities in a wider region by concentrating only on their geo-strategically narrow, selfish defense look.[37]

---

[28] Ibid., p. 33, Ronald D. Asmus, "The Rise or Fall? Of Multilateralism: America's New Foreign Policy and What it Means for Europe" in Carnovale (ed.), *European Security...*, p. 167.
[29] Çiğdem Nas, "Batı Avrupa Birliği Oluşumu Karşısında Türkiye'nin Durumu" in Faruk Sönmezoğlu (ed.), *Değişen Dünya ve Türkiye*, Ankara: Bağlam Yay., 1996, pp. 74, 75.
[30] Roper, "The West and Turkey...", p. 90.
[31] Barrett, "Current...", p. 25, Roper, "The West and Turkey...", p. 102.
[32] Chipman, "Allies in the Mediterranean...", p. 63, Lesser, *Bridge or Barrier*, p. 26.
[33] Karaosmanoğlu, "Turkey and the Southern Flank", p. 331.
[34] Nas, "Batı Avrupa Birliği...", pp. 68-69, 79, Ergüvenç, "Turkey: Strategic Partner...", pp. 5, 8.
[35] *Beyaz Kitap*, p. 1.
[36] Asmus, "The Rise or Fall?...", pp. 165-166.
[37] Nas, "Batı Avrupa Birliği...", p. 78.

These states asserted that American political, economic and security interests were too closely intertwined with those of Europe and the problems involving a wide region were too complex to permit the Americans to leave the Europeans struggling to cope with wide range issues.[38]

Especially Turkish rulers shared with the Americans the concern about the possibility of Europe's competing with the USA on the defense area. In the view of both sides, "NATO must remain the main forum for consultations among the Allies on issues concerning the security and defense of Europe. This was required not only because the transatlantic link was vital for the European security, but also since NATO was the only forum where all European allies enjoyed equal opportunities and rights on matters of common concern."[39] The fact that "the ally furthest to the East geographically [Turkey] is the one quite often most worried and most concerned about preserving the connections with the allies to the West [the USA, Canada] attracts attention."[40]

However, Turkish officials also stated that they supported the Europeans' taking more responsibility for their own defense, the improvement of the ESDI and WEU's bridge role between the EU and NATO. Their condition was that Turkey should be acceded to the security dimension of the EU, saving it from associating itself with decisions taken elsewhere. They asserted that "in order to make a meaningful contribution to ESDI, Turkey has to be included in the policy formulation phase within the EU's common Foreign and Security Policy."[41] Turkish leaders expected the Americans help them in this issue by using their leverage with the European powers.

Turkey also needed the American help in its problems with the Europeans. The European powers tended to consider Turkey as a peripheral strategic partner and as a strategic and political liability because of its complex and immediate problems. They believed that they could get the help of Turkey in the event of a Middle Eastern crisis without giving it a full membership and they did not want to accept the burden of a direct exposure in the Middle East. The Europeans were more likely to see Turkey as a barrier to turmoil and military threats outside Europe rather than as an agent for dialogue in relation to security problems in the Middle East.[42]

The diversification of interest areas and security priorities reduced the possibility of defense cooperation between Turkey and the European Union.[43] The European refusal of integrating Turkey into WEU was rightly seen by Turkish rulers as Europe's unwillingness to grant Turkey a legitimate security role on the continent.[44] The inclusion of Greece in and the exclusion of Turkey from the European security umbrella had important repercussions for Turkey's defense and security. Turkish rulers concerned that Greece would have great advantages with its full membership in WEU over Turkey and the stability and balance in the Aegean would be harmed seriously.

---

[38] Ergüvenç, "Turkey: Strategic Partner...", pp. 6-7, Orhun, "The Uncertainties...", p. 28, Stearns, *Entangled Allies*, p. 23.

[39] Demirel, "Turkey...", p. 21, Orhun, "The Uncertainties...", pp. 27-28, Şadi Ergüvenç, "Turkey in the New European Security Context, Turkey's Role and Expectations in the Transatlantic Partnership", *Foreign Policy* (Ankara), Nos. 1-2, 1997, pp. 30, 33.

[40] Barrett, "Current...", p. 35.

[41] Orhun, "Turkey, Norway...", p. 10, *Beyaz Kitap*, p. 28.

[42] Lesser, *Bridge or Barrier*, p. 4, Seyfi Taşhan, "The Peripheries: Adjusting to Change", *Foreign Policy* (Ankara), Nos. 1-2, 1997, p. 58.

[43] Brown, *Delicately Poised Allies*, p. 66, Lesser, *Bridge or Barrier*, p. 24, Özlem Eraydın, "Avrupa'nın Yeni Güvenlik Düzeni ve Türkiye" in Sönmezoğlu (ed.), *Değişen...*, pp. 35-36.

[44] Lesser, *Bridge or Barrier*, pp. v, 12, Criss, "International Institutions...", pp. 204-205.

In order to overcome the Turkish worries on the WEU guarantee for Greece against Turkey, it was declared that the automatic guarantee in the Article five of WEU would be applied only against aggression by non-members of NATO and not to internal disputes within the alliance.[45] But Greece still had the upper hand by at least feeling the support of the Europeans in its behind. The Document on Associate Membership of the WEU of Turkey clearly stated that the association of this country "represents a significant step in the strengthening of the European pillar of the Atlantic Alliance."[46] The WEU Erfurt Ministerial Declarations of November 1997 made it clear that Turkey would have the right to a full role of participation and decision-making in any WEU-led operations using NATO assets and capabilities. However, all these reassurances stayed short of Turkey's objective of the full integration into the mainstream of European security planning.[47]

Turkish leaders were insistent on that Turkey's long-standing European vocation should have a security and defense aspect as well. They demanded the rigid principle that full membership in WEU required full membership in the EU should be reconsidered. They were of the opinion that a broad congruence should be achieved between NATO and the other European institutions such as the EU and WEU.[48] In order to prove Turkey's importance for the European defense, Turkish authorities asserted that Turkey had a weight in the determination of transatlantic balances. They stated that Turkey was the only country which could defend and represent the interests of Europe in the Middle East[49] and which could help the Europeans in facing new threats. In their view, Turkey's steady efforts in being active in all of the three main foundations of the European security (EU-WEU, NATO and OSCE) and its support for the Mediterranean dialogue within NATO and the Europe-Mediterranean process within the EU[50] showed Turkey's sincerity in contributing to the European security.

In spite of all negative attitudes of the Europeans, Turkish leaders felt that Turkey could not afford severing its ties with the Western Europe, knowing that Turkey had a great interest in being a serious actor in the evolving European scene.[51] However, they preferred to pursue their security interests in a multidimensional way, being the members of both WEU and NATO. This would promote Turkey's importance in Europe, reduce political challenges at home, balance burden sharing within the Western alliance and help Turkish rulers to feel more comfortable on Turkey's security and strategic positions. The United States was in the best position to press the Europeans for Turkey's involvement in the emerging European security arrangements. If the Americans focused solely on Turkey's position in the context of Middle Eastern and Central Asian security, they might alienate Turkish rulers.[52]

---

[45] Jamie Shea, "Should NATO be Enlarged to the East" in Carnovale (ed.), *European Security...*, p. 89.
[46] Criss, "International Institutions...", p. 203.
[47] Roper, "The West and Turkey...", p. 92.
[48] Orhun, "Turkey, Norway...", pp. 9-10.
[49] Müftüler-Bac, "Turkey's Predicament...", pp. 256, 260, 265.
[50] *Beyaz Kitap*, p. 38.
[51] Ergüvenç, "Turkey: Strategic Partner...", p. 9, Stearns, *Entangled Allies*, p. 29, Solana, "NATO...", p. 21, Lesser, "Turkey's Strategic Options", pp. 85, 88, M. Evert, "Turkey's Strategic Goals: Possibilities and Weaknesses", *Mediterranean Quarterly*, vol. 4, No. 4, Fall 1993, p. 31, Bruce Kuniholm, "East or West? Geopolitics of Turkey and its NATO Alliance" in A. L. Karaosmanoğlu and Seyfi Taşhan (eds.), *Middle East, Turkey and the Atlantic Alliance*, Ankara: Foreign Policy Institute, 1987, p. 145.
[52] Lesser, *Bridge or Barrier*, pp. 39, 43.

e) The Enlargement of the EU

It was clear that the proposed enlargement of the European Union would include Central and Eastern European countries, but exclude Turkey. Thinking their institution as a stable and promising world actor, the Europeans did not want to share borders with Iran, Iraq and Syria, which produced instabilities continuously.[53] Unlike the United States, European states seemed to give priority to the democratization before the stability. The role of the Turkish army, which had been the strongest point of contact for NATO and the USA with Turkey, could not be denied, but Western Europeans "find the role of the Turkish armed forces in the Turkish state system... quite out of keeping with Western practice".[54] On the other hand, Turkish authorities sometimes did not hesitate to say that the exclusion of Turkey from the EU "would not be as vital for Turkey as some people think it would be, because Turkey has other options."

Turkish rulers believed that the Turkish candidacy for full membership in the EU was not judged by the same objective criteria applied to other candidates.[55] They also complained that Europeans did not understand Turkey's domestic difficulties and special problems.[56] Turkish rulers were especially worried that Europeans would continue to be biased toward Greece on the Turkish-Greek problems and the Cyprus issue and that thus Turkish-EU relations would become captive to Greek initiatives. In their opinion, the enlargement of the EU without Turkey would decrease the possibility of a solution of Turkish-Greek problems.[57] The fact that the Turkish economy was essentially tied to Europe was formalized with the customs union between Turkey and the EU. Turkey needed the EU membership not to be marginalized, not to weaken its position against Greece, to be less dependent on the United States and to have a greater freedom of action in regional and global affairs.[58] It was very important for Turkey that the United States would not try to detach it from the EU, but it would support genuinely its initiatives of being a part of Europe.

f) Relations with Russia

In order to keep their traditional enemy (Russia) under the control of the multilateral Western security structures in the post-Cold War era, Turkish authorities paid a special attention to NATO's Partnership for Peace (PfP) project, which would serve this purpose.[59] In their view, the enhanced PfP was not a consolation prize, but it was a means through which "a sense of security and a sense of belonging are projected" to NATO's partners and which would facilitate the involvement of these partners in NATO's decision-making processes. Turkish officials further suggested that relations between NATO, Russia and Ukraine should be formalized in politically binding documents and that these partners should not have the

---

[53] Hüseyin Bağcı, "Changing Security of Turkey" in Aydın, *Turkey...*, p. 81.
[54] Roper, "The West and Turkey...", pp. 96, 100.
[55] Gürel, "A General Appraisal...", pp. 12, 21.
[56] Kuniholm, "East or West?...", p. 141.
[57] Ergüvenç, "Turkey's Strategic...", pp. 67-68.
[58] A. L. Karaosmanoğlu, "Turkey's Discreet Foreign Policy Between Western Europe and the Middle East" in Karaosmanoğlu and Seyfi Taşhan (eds.), *Middle East...*, p. 94.
[59] *Beyaz Kitap*, pp. 1, 33.

right to veto the decisions of NATO.[60] To prove the sincerity of their support for the PfP, they suggested expanding it through joint military exercises and training opportunities between Turkey and the Russian federation.[61] They established a PfP Training Center in Ankara, finalized the project of establishing a multinational peace force in south-eastern Europe with the participation of all regional NATO and PfP nations[62] and welcomed the American suggestion of establishing new forms of cooperation with the partner countries, namely the Atlantic Partnership Council.[63]

With the collapse of the Soviet Union, Turkey had no common border with Russia and it did not have to fear direct exposure to the political and military power of its giant neighbor.[64] Nevertheless, it seemed that the two states were engaged in a stiff competition. Russia was the strongest force in the region and through its heavy-handed approach toward the regional countries, it gave the impression that it still pursued the power politics to expand its spheres of influence. Russia's effort of controlling developments in the region would clash with Turkey's seeing itself as the principal link between Asia and Europe.[65] It was speculated that Turkey might be among the primary targets of Russian nuclear weapons, which had been de-targeted from civilian and military centers in the United States. The extension of Russian nuclear umbrella to all the member countries of the Collective Security Treaty could be interpreted as a veiled warning to Turkey on its efforts of establishing close economic and political links with the former republics of the Soviet Union.[66]

Russia also refused to reduce the military concentrations on its southern flank as required by the CFE Treaty of 1990 and signed treaties with some rivals of Turkey such as Armenia and Greece. It remained Syria's main military supplier and diplomatic ally and saw Iran as its strategic partner. The Russian attempt of selling sophisticated arms and missiles to Greek Cypriots might be interpreted as a direct threat against the Turkish security. The establishment of Confederation of Kurdish Organization of the CIS in Moscow on 1 November 1994 and the meeting of the third session of the Kurdish parliament-in-exile on 19 October 1995 in a building attached to the Russian Duma were also irritating for Turkish leaders.[67]

The more alarming for Turkey was that the Europeans and Americans were inclined to be optimistic about developments in Russia and they did not see Russia as much threat as Turkey saw. It seemed possible that the West might give a relatively free hand to Russia in the Caucasus and Central Asia and might tolerate its violating the CFE Treaty limits in exchange for Russia's leaving the Baltic states to the West and not causing any problems in the enlargement of NATO.[68] Turkish authorities really had feared at the beginning that the United States might build a partnership with Russia's new imperial designs. Some Turkish politicians believed that the United States had contributed to the consolidation of the Russian influence

---

[60] Orhun, "Turkey, Norway...", pp. 10, 11-12, Orhun, "The Uncertainties...", p. 28.
[61] *Beyaz Kitap*, pp. 7, 27.
[62] Demirel, "Turkey...", p. 10.
[63] Orhun, "Turkey, Norway...", p. 11.
[64] Sezer, "Turkey's...", p. 149, 150, 158.
[65] Criss, "International Institutions...", p. 208, Eraydın, "Avrupa'nın Yeni...", p. 33, Hunter, "Bridge or Frontier?...", p. 74.
[66] Sezer, "Turkey's...", pp. 153, 154, 155.
[67] Mufti, "Daring...", pp. 37, 38, 40.
[68] Criss, "International Institutions...", p. 208, Roper, "The West and Turkey...", p. 91.

in the region by ignoring the new Russian imperialism.[69] The US administration seemed to support Russian leaders in spite of their bold actions because of their fears that more hawkish leaders might come to power in Russia.[70]

Later, it seemed that the United States shared increasingly more concerns with Turkey on the assertion of the Russian influence in the Central Asia and the Caucasus with the possibility of gaining control of the energy resources in the region and on Russia's cooperation with anti-Western states such as Iran.[71] The agreement on maintaining Ukraine's independence to check the Russian expansionism was one example of the convergence of US and Turkish interests. Turkey's position increasingly became more secure in the region. The United States gave increasingly more support to Turkish initiatives and the Russian influence became less effective. Russia's heavy-handed approach toward some former Soviet republics led these states to try to balance the Russian force by expanding their ties with other countries including Turkey and the USA.[72]

g) The Implementation of the CFE Treaty

The CFE Treaty, signed in 1990 and came to effect in 1992, had stemmed originally from the view that a stable and secure balance of conventional forces should be established in Europe, where the former Warsaw Pact had superiority in numbers of ground forces. The CFE Treaty was considered in the following period as a cornerstone of the stability and security of Europe.[73] Turkey attributed importance especially to the flank regime of the CFE Treaty, according to which the signatories would not be able to concentrate military equipment and weapons on the flank of Europe and would not be able to exceed the sub-regional ceilings determined by the Treaty.[74]

Turkey became a party to the CFE Treaty, but it managed to keep its southeastern region, bordering Syria, Iraq and Iran, outside it. The large conventional arsenals in these countries, facing Turkey in the Middle East, fell outside the current arms control initiatives and Turkey needed to balance these forces.[75] However, Turkish rulers worried that the CFE talks might gain more importance than other security structures such as NATO and that his might result in the lose of its strategic importance for the West.[76] Moreover, the withdrawal of former Soviet forces from the central Europe to behind the Urals in accordance with the CFE Treaty was expected to leave Turkey in an unfavorable position both within NATO and against Russia.[77] Turkish rulers were also concerned on the Russian refusal of reducing military

---

[69] Obrad Kesic, "American-Turkish Relations at a Crossroads", *Mediterranean Quarterly*, vol. 6, No. 1, 1995, pp. 101, 106.
[70] Ali Faik Demir, "SSCB'nin Dağılmasından Sonra Türkiye-Azerbeycan İlişkileri" in Sönmezoğlu (ed.), *Değişen...*, p. 243.
[71] Aykan, "Turkish Perspectives...", p. 356.
[72] Hunter, "Bridge or Frontier?...", p. 77.
[73] Barrett, "Current...", p. 34.
[74] *Beyaz Kitap*, p. 30.
[75] Lesser, *Bridge or Barrier*, p. 26, Brown, *Delicately Poised Allies*, pp. 114, 134, Sezer, "Turkey's...", p. 166.
[76] Brown, *Delicately Poised Allies*, pp. 138, 141.
[77] Lesser, *Bridge or Barrier*, pp. 26, 27.

concentrations on its southern flank[78] and on the seemingly sympathetic attitude of the West toward Russia in this issue.[79]

Russia informed Turkey and other Western powers that the force ceilings established by the CFE Treaty fell short of meeting its security needs and it demonstrated its willingness to violate these ceilings. Western powers including the United States generally reiterated their insistence on the fulfillment of the CFE Treaty's requirements,[80] but their attitude was far from carrying a full force. Turkey made it clear that it did not want the CFE Treaty changed in favor of Russia, asserting that it would cause a great disequilibrium in favor of Russian forces in the Caucasus and the Central Asia, resulting in returning the Cold War conditions.[81] This thinking was proved by the Russian activism such as the stationing its troops in Armenia and Georgia, which contributed to the fall of Elçi Bey, Turkey's friend in Azerbaijan and the occupation of the Azeri territory by the Armenians.[82] Turkey could not exert its influence in these events because of its concern on the reaction of its allies such as the United States and France, sympathetic toward Armenia, and on the possibility of a confrontation with Russia.[83] The US pressures on Turkey on allowing its territory to be used in providing aid to Armenia were bound to irritate Turkish leaders as a double standard because the US embargo on another state, Iraq, hurt mostly Turkish interests.

h) The Iraqi Problem

The general Turkish view on Iraq was that Iraq's independence, sovereignty and territorial integrity should be preserved and Iraq should comply fully with the relevant UN Security Council resolutions.[84] While the United States remained focused on removing Saddam from power and challenged Iraq's territorial integrity with its policies, Turkey did not want to see Iraq destroyed and divided, fearing that it would destabilize the balance of power in the region and contribute to the expansion of the Iranian influence.[85] Occasional Turkish attempts aimed at easing Baghdad's political and economic isolation and strengthening its territorial integrity (such as holding tripartite meetings with Iran and Syria) were bound to create uneasiness in Washington.[86]

Apart from their unhappiness on the use of the İncirlik airbase for the protection of the Kurdish zone in northern Iraq, Turkish authorities thought that the emergence of a *de facto* Kurdish state in the northern Iraq with the America help might not only affect the boundaries of the regional states, but it might also have a domino effect on Turkey's territorial integrity.[87] In the view of Bülent Ecevit, the United States was the most responsible state for the division

---

[78] Brown, *Delicately Poised Allies*, p. 142, Mufti, "Daring...", p. 37.
[79] Criss, "International Institutions...", p. 208, Taşhan, "The Peripheries...", p. 62, Roper, "The West and Turkey...", p. 91.
[80] Sezer, "Turkey's...", p. 152.
[81] Criss, "International Institutions...", p. 210.
[82] Hunter, "Bridge or Frontier?...", p. 75.
[83] Mufti, "Daring...", pp. 37, 47, Hale, "Turkish Foreign Policy...", pp. 242, 245.
[84] Gürel, "A General Appraisal...", p. 15, *Beyaz Kitap*, p. 36.
[85] Alain Gresh, "Turkish-Israeli-Syrian Relations and Their Impact on the Middle East", *Middle East Journal,* vol. 52, No. 2, 1998, p. 194, Kesic, "American-Turkish Relations...", pp. 99-100, Mufti, "Daring...", p. 48.
[86] Aykan, "Turkish Perspectives...", p. 354, Turan Yavuz, *ABD'nin Kürt Kartı*, İstanbul: Milliyet Yayınları, 1993, pp. 268-269.
[87] Aykan, "Turkish Perspectives...", p. 353.

of Iraq because it deliberately prevented the democratization and territorial integrity of Iraq[88] in order to establish an Iraqi rule friendly with the USA or to weaken Iraq in the region for US and Israeli interests.

The American-led embargo against Iraq and the closure of the Yumurtalık-Kirkuk oil pipeline were other sore points in Turkey's relations with the USA, causing the loss of billions of dollars to Turkey from trade with Iraq, and tourism and war-related expenditures. It was not only considered a loss of fairly high income, but it was also seen as a threat to Turkey's national interests.[89] It had been discussed previously that if the flow oil through this pipeline could not be secured, Turkey might make changes in its border with Iraq to include Mosul and Kirkuk.[90] The United States worked to raise international support to compensate Turkey's economic losses caused by the Gulf Crisis. The UN Security Council resolution 986 reopened the Kirkuk-Yumurtalık pipeline partially, providing Iraq with the limited opportunity to export oil in return for purchasing food, medicine and fundamental humanitarian goods. However, Turkish rulers still felt that these limited relieves were too minor to compensate Turkey's losses.[91]

The security consequences of the Gulf crisis (solved mostly to the American advantage) for Turkey were much more difficult to compensate. The insurgency in the south-eastern Turkey was deepened. Turkey had to spend more resources to contain the increasing terrorist activities and had to intervene in the Iraqi territory, which resulted in its isolation in Western forums. It also needed to consider reactions of the Western powers, especially the USA, not to damage the basic links on which the overall Turkish foreign and security policy strategy depended.[92] When Turkey left contingents in northern Iraq after its operations, it was interpreted as that it intended to create a buffer zone in the area, desiring in the long-term to control the oil-rich Iraqi provinces of Mosul and Kirkuk. The interventions also had the effect of dragging Turkey into the Iraqi quagmire and unresolved conflicts of the region.[93]

While Turkey shared a more common approach with Western European countries on the overthrow of Saddam Hussein and the division of Iraq, it was ironic that it was the Western Europeans, who expressed the most severe criticism toward the Turkish interventions, which were necessitated by mainly US initiatives.[94] On the other hand, Turkey needed the American support for its operations as demonstrated by the following American attitude: they were "conducted by a legitimate, democratic government and a close ally of the West against a brutal terrorist organization... Turkey remains our friend in a troubled region and deserves our support."[95] Turkey needed to cooperate with the USA in the future of the region.

i) The Kurdish Question

The Kurdish question seemed at one point the biggest problem of Turkey, having negative effects on its other problems as well. Turkish rulers found it difficult to understand

---

[88] M. Hüseyin Buzoğlu, *Körfez Krizi ve PKK*, Ankara: Strateji, p. 139.

[89] Sezer, "Turkey's...", p. 162.

[90] Taşhan, "The Peripheries...", p. 63.

[91] Gürel, "A General Appraisal...", p. 15, Lesser, *Bridge or Barrier*, p. 36.

[92] Hale, "Turkish Foreign Policy...", p. 245.

[93] Gresh, "Turkish-Israeli...", p. 195, Müftüler-Bac, "Turkey's Predicament...", p. 261, Mufti, "Daring...", p. 39.

[94] Roper, "The West and Turkey...", pp. 97, 98.

[95] Müftüler-Bac, "Turkey's Predicament...", p. 262.

the apparent support given by the European states to the separatist Kurdish organization (PKK) under the auspices of human rights and political solution.[96] As the Kurdish uprising and the oppression of the Kurds by the Iraqi regime in the aftermath of the Gulf War attracted the attention of international public opinion to the plight of the Kurds in Turkey as well, Turkey's neighbors had a clear opportunity to exploit Turkey's problems with the PKK. The creation of the Kurdish autonomy in northern Iraq, protected by the Western air forces in the İncirlik airbase, had the potential to upset the integrity of Turkey and the regional balance of power. PKK terrorists, who got courage from the autonomous Kurdish entity, increased their attacks against Turkey and Turkey's retaliatory interventions spoiled its relations with its neighbors and Western allies.[97]

Some American actions were particularly hurting for Turkish rulers. The American human rights reports mentioned the Turkish Kurds as a minority and American officials occasionally warned their Turkish counterparts on not forgetting their responsibilities and promises concerning basic human rights. American Congressmen questioned the seemingly tolerant attitude of the administration toward Turkish actions against the Kurds.[98] Steny H. Hayer had told the American Congress: "Passage of this bill sends an unequivocal message to the government of Turkey that this Congress will conduct business as usual when US-supplied equipment is used against civilians."[99] In spite of their generally tolerant attitude toward Turkish military operations in northern Iraq, the Americans did not give totally a free hand to Turkish authorities and expressed their worries on the establishment of a buffer zone by Turkey.[100]

One important consequence of the Gulf War was the establishment of an international force to protect the Kurdish region in northern Iraq. When Turkish President Turgut Özal proposed the establishment of a safe heaven in the northern Iraq to prevent the exodus of the Iraqi Kurds to Turkey,[101] this proposal became a golden opportunity for the American rulers to initiate their long-pursued rapid deployment force project in a different form. The process was started with a note sent from Washington to Ankara in the first half of May 1991, asking permission for bringing to Turkey a special force constituted of 600 soldiers, which would pass to the northern Iraq.[102] Once the force was positioned on Turkish and Iraqi territories, Turkish authorities extended its term each time in spite of the fact that it caused a lot of problems for Turkey's security and foreign policies. Turkish rulers also cooperated with their American counterparts in bringing Kurdish groups together and in helping the establishment of the American control in the region though these actions attracted the enmity of the regional powers such as Iraq, Syria and Iran.[103]

It was widely believed in Turkey that if the safe heaven project were not implemented, Turkey would have managed to stop the activities of PKK much earlier. The project allegedly

---

[96] Kesiç, "American-Turkish Relations...", pp. 99-100, *Beyaz Kitap*, p. 44, Roper, "The West and Turkey...", p. 97.
[97] Sezer, "Turkey's...", p. 163, Müftüler-Bac, "Turkey's Predicament...", p. 261, İhsan D. Dağı, "Turkey in the 1990s: Foreign Policy, Human Rights and the Search for a New Identity", *Mediterranean Quarterly*, vol. 4, No. 4, Fall 1993, pp. 66, 70, Hale, "Turkish Foreign Policy...", p. 245, Criss, "International Institutions...", p. 211, Aykan, "Turkish Perspectives...", p. 352.
[98] Kesiç, "American-Turkish Relations...", p. 97, Yavuz, *ABD'nin Kürt Kartı*, pp. 103, 231-234, 235, Buzoğlu, *Körfez Krizi ve PKK*, p. 136.
[99] Kesiç, "American-Turkish Relations...", p. 107.
[100] Yavuz, *ABD'nin Kürt Kartı*, pp. 266-267, Buzoğlu, *Körfez Krizi ve PKK*, p. 137.
[101] Yavuz, *ABD'nin Kürt Kartı*, p. 197.
[102] Ibid., p. 200.
[103] Aykan, "Turkish Perspectives...", p. 356.

allowed the PKK guerrillas to improve their activities to the extent that in the seven-month time they reached the point that they could reach in 30 years otherwise.[104] Benefiting from the presentation of the Kurdish question by the world press, PKK activists increased their influence vis-à-vis the Western powers and strengthened their prestige in the eyes of Kurdish people.

Meanwhile, Turkish public opinion gradually came to the belief that the United States tried to use the international force only for its own interests, namely giving a severe lesson to Iraq's dictator, Saddam Hussein. The Americans had obtained a good opportunity to control and irritate the Iraqi administration; they would not easily give up this tool even after they reached the original aim (the protection of the Iraqi Kurds). In this thinking, the use of the İncirlik airbase by the Americans stayed no longer inside the original purposes.[105] Bülent Ecevit went even further in criticizing the international force by claiming that Western powers would use the military force, stationed on the Turkish territory, against Turkey rather than Iraq.[106] In the view of some Turkish observers, the international force became a symbol of the fact that Turkey could not take decisions on its own because it had no genuine economic and political independence.[107]

There was a great concern in Turkey on harmful effects of the international force. Allegedly, the increase in the number of civilian American and British personnel in the region meant the increase in the intelligence operations of these states. Intensive activities of Western humanitarian organizations and NGOs strengthened this worry.[108] As a result, Turkish Foreign Minister Mümtaz Soysal declared that the Turkish government put strict controls on the travel by members of these organizations to and from northern Iraq.[109] Turkish military authorities, too, were not happy on the free movement of thousands of military and civilian personnel on the Iraqi-Turkish border. They also complained that American officials did not share the intelligence they obtained with their Turkish counterparts, such as the military preparations of PKK guerrillas. Allegedly, a helicopter belonging to the international force picked up injured PKK terrorists and took them to an unknown place. According to Turkish journalist M. Yaşar Bostancı, the Americans dropped heavy weaponry to the Kurdish region in the disguise of humanitarian aid. Uğur Mumcu claimed that the main duty of the international force was to give the air support to the Kurdish Federated State. DSP Leader Ecevit had worries on that the arrangements concerning Kurdish people could turn into permanent structures such as the Palestinian camps. In his view, the American administration did not want Kurdish leaders reach an agreement with the Iraqi government, thus preventing the Iraqis from establishing a stable regime and protecting their territorial integrity.[110] Turkish authorities demonstrated their unhappiness by calling the Kurdish leaders of northern Iraq to Ankara without informing the Americans. American Ambassador Morton Abramovitz was really furious on the incident.[111]

---

[104] Hasan Köni, "Gulf Savaşı Sonrasında Orta Doğunun Durumu", in *Değişen Dünyada Türkiye ve Türk Dünyası Sempozyumu*, Ankara: Hacettepe Üniversitesi Atatürk İlkeleri ve İnkılap Tarihi Enstitüsü, 1993, p. 48.
[105] Yavuz, *ABD'nin Kürt Kartı*, p. 276.
[106] Buzoğlu, *Körfez Krizi ve PKK*, p. 138.
[107] Ibid., p. 205.
[108] Ibid., pp. 136-137, Yavuz, *ABD'nin Kürt Kartı*, p. 204.
[109] Aykan, "Turkish Perspectives...", p. 354.
[110] *TBMM Tutanak Dergisi*, Term 19, Year 1, vol. 4, 26.6.1992, p. 213.
[111] Yavuz, *ABD'nin Kürt Kartı*, pp. 163, 205-206, 207, 223, 273-274, 277.

Since it needed the American support on the Kurdish question, Turkey did not raise views and did not carry out activities, which might clash with the American interests. The approval of Turkish military operations in northern Iraq by the American government was a vital necessity for Turkish rulers. However, American proposals for solving the problem were not totally to the liking of the Turkish administration. In contrast, Turkish rulers thought that American proposals would cause the collapse of the Iraqi regime and harm Turkey's security. The political solution in the minds of the Americans might result in giving more autonomy to Kurds inside Turkish borders, which was totally an unacceptable alternative from Turkish point of view.[112] It seemed that developments around the Kurdish issue would continue to be a sore point in Turkish-American relations.

j) Turkey's Problems with Greece

Turkey sees Greece as one of the most important dangers to its security and prepares its defense doctrines accordingly as proved by the existence of its Aegean army.[113] The main concern of Turkish authorities regarding Greece is to prevent it from destroying the balance in the Aegean established by the Treaty of Lausanne.[114] Greece's various agreements with Bulgaria, Iran, Syria and Russia in the 1990s might shook this balance by isolating Turkey. Greek Foreign Minister Theodore Pangalos suggested the formation of a regional cooperation system among Armenia, Iran and Greece, which would be open to other regional states.[115]

Turkish-Greek disagreements on the Aegean, the Cyprus question and the Turkish minority in the Western Thrace did not only cause headaches for Turkish rulers but also concerned the Western powers. The eruption of a serious fight between the two members of NATO might harm the cohesion of the Western alliance and might open the way to further conflicts inside the boundaries of the West. Turkish rulers argued in this matter that if Turkey was left outside the Western integration process, the possibility of solving Turkish-Greek problems might decrease with serious repercussions for the Western security. They also worried that their problems with Greece might hurt their relations with Western powers. Protecting their interests in the Aegean and Cyprus and not alienating their Western allies at the same was a difficult goal, which they needed to reach.[116]

The Americans, for example, were not happy on the present situation. NATO's two members, which were supposed to cooperate for the joint defense, weakened the Western alliance with their disagreements. The two states looked at the United States to get political and diplomatic support against each other and accused the USA of giving more support to the other side.[117] Turkish leaders particularly complained that coming under the influence of the Greek lobby, the American Congress inserted outsider elements such as the Cyprus question to Turkish-American relations. There were even Turkish critics who claimed that the United

---

[112] Aykan, "Turkish Perspectives...", p. 350.
[113] Brown, *Delicately Poised Allies*, p. 97.
[114] *Beyaz Kitap*, p. 45, Taşhan, "Türkiye'nin Tehdit Algılamaları", p. 35.
[115] Mufti, "Daring...", p. 40.
[116] Lesser, *Bridge or Barrier*, p. 22, Lesser, "Turkey's Strategic Options", p. 83, Karaosmanoğlu, "Turkey and the Southern Flank", p. 288.
[117] Campbell, "The Superpowers...", p. 67.

States tolerated the continuation of the Turkish-Greek enmity in order to keep Turkey under control.[118]

American pressures on Turkey to solve the Cyprus question and the sympathetic attitude of the European powers toward the application of Greek Cypriots to the EU constituted problems for Turkey. The Turkish side insisted that the political and legal equality should be established between the Greek and Turkish Cypriots before a start was given to the solution process.[119] The hopes were renewed with the acceptance of Turkey's candidacy for the EU. However, it was not clear whether Turkey would be accepted as the full member. Therefore, it could be said that Turkey's problems with Greece in the Aegean and Cyprus would continue to irritate Turkish-American relations in the near future.

3. THE EXPECTATIONS ON THE FUTURE OF TURKISH FOREIGN POLICY AND TURKISH-AMERICAN RELATIONS

a) Turkey's Strategic Importance

Turkish rulers are certainly eager to make Turkey an integral part of the West. Staying outside the Western camp is not an option for them. In order to strengthen the Western interest in Turkey, they emphasize its strategic importance for the West. Turkey is the only democratic and secular Muslim country in the Middle East, maintaining its basic goal of the full integration with the West. It might play a bridge-building role in a region of considerable geopolitical complexity and serve as a democratic, secular and free enterprising role model for the regional states.[120] In Demirel's words, "by her very existence, Turkey could be a model for her neighbors to plant the seeds of secular democracy."[121] It also constitutes the most important barrier preventing the export of radical religious movements to the West and neutralizing the effect of Iran's theocratic government model.[122]

Some European observers consider the Turkish democracy defective and identify some Middle Eastern elements in Turkish politics. It is also argued that the Kemalist secular model for Muslim countries as a form of governance is less effective and attractive, considering the traditional hatred of the Arabs toward Turkey.[123] However, particularly the American administration continues to stress Turkey's model role. Meanwhile, Turkey's effort of improving its democracy and human rights records will increase its prestige in the eyes of the Europeans and the Americans and will place its relations with the West on a more stable ground.

With its geographic location, Turkey is able to serve both as a bridge and barrier on critical sea, land and air routes, reaching the world's vital natural resources, and affect developments and crises in the strategic regions such as the Balkans, the Black Sea, the

---

[118] Lesser, *Bridge or Barrier*, p. 23.

[119] Gürel, "A General Appraisal...", p. 13.

[120] Celal Göle, "Welcome Address" in Aydın (ed.), *Turkey...*, p. 3, Gürel, "A General Appraisal...", pp. 12, 14, "Turkey-European Union Relations...", p. 151, Demirel, "Turkey...", pp. 8-9, Solana, "NATO...", p. 21.

[121] Demirel, "Turkey...", p. 9.

[122] *Beyaz Kitap*, p. 3, Kesic, "American-Turkish Relations...", p. 98, Hunter, "Bridge or Frontier?...", p. 71.

[123] Lesser, *Bridge or Barrier*, pp. 4-5, Roper, "The West and Turkey...", p. 96.

Caucasus, the Middle East and the Eastern Mediterranean.[124] With its wide massive land, Turkey might resist the military attacks launched against the West in its strategic depth. It can mobilize a considerable number of soldiers and keep them ready to fight for a long time. Turkey is eager to help the West in facing many dangers such as regional wars, terrorism, drug smuggling, and organized crime.[125] In Demirel's words, "through her actions, fostering economic and political interdependence and cooperation, Turkey will not only remain central to the security and prosperity of the West, but will also be the key state in the containment and resolution of a host of problems of our era."[126] In Orhun's view, "Turkey has been on of the major providers of security and stability in the Euro-Atlantic era, rather than being a net consumer."[127]

By maintaining its alliance with Turkey, the West ensures that the balance in a strategic region is formed to its advantage and the stability is maintained in its flanks.[128] The West, especially the USA might intervene in events in the Middle East in the fastest, the easiest and the most suitable way by using the Turkish territory. Turkey particularly wants to give the image that "it influences directly and decisively all developments in the Persian Gulf... by making available to the West military bases during critical... instances... and by controlling the freshwater resources."[129] Turkey's ability to control the sea traffic from the Black Sea to the Mediterranean through its Straits is another important factor, which has the potential of affecting the balances in the region.[130] Turkey's strategic importance will continue to be the most important base of Turkish-American relations.

b) Turkey's New More Assertive Attitude and Turkish-American Relations

aa- Turkey and the Balkans

Turkey is more concerned in developments in the Balkans and ready to insert itself as the protector of the Muslims in the region. During the Balkan crises, staying under the influence of public opinion, the Turkish governments demanded more forceful actions against Serbia. However, Turkish rulers also had to consider the possibility of outbreak of a general war encompassing the whole Balkans and had to balance their policies not to annoy the Western powers, which might accuse them of claiming rights in the former territories of the Ottoman Empire.[131] The American administration was particularly disturbed by the criticism of the non-intervention of the West in Bosnia by the Turkish people, giving the signal that an assertive Turkish attitude might clash with the American interests in the region.

---

[124] Ergüvenç, "Turkey's Strategic...", pp. 62-63, Karl-Heinz Kamp, "European Security Outside of Europe" in Carnovale (ed.), *European Security...*, p. 99.

[125] Ergüvenç, "Turkey's Strategic...", pp. 63, 65.

[126] Demirel, "Turkey...", p. 9.

[127] Orhun, "The Uncertainties...", p. 30.

[128] Ergüvenç, "Turkey's Strategic...", pp. 65, 66, 67.

[129] Evert, "Turkey's Strategic Goals...", p. 32, Jed C. Snyder, *Defending the Fringe: NATO, the Mediterranean and the Persian Gulf,* London: Westview Press, 1987, pp. 77, 122-123.

[130] Brown, *Delicately Poised Allies,* pp. 77, 112, 159.

[131] Evert, "Turkey's Strategic Goals...", p. 31, Hale, "Turkish Foreign Policy...", p. 241, Sezer, "Turkey's...", p. 161, Hunter, "Bridge or Frontier?...", p. 73.

Consequently, Turkey chose to try to affect developments in the Balkans in the context of multilateral structures such as NATO without taking bold actions.[132]

As a sign of the importance that it gave to the security cooperation in the Balkans, Turkey made mutual arrangements with its neighbors based on the Security Building and Increasing Measures.[133] It seemed that the possibility of the convergence of Turkish interests with those of the Americans in the Balkans was higher than the convergence of Turkish and European ones. The Europeans did not like the idea of the armament and training of the Bosnian Federation Army by the West. However, Turkey and the United States played an important role in this program and Turkey's contribution was appreciated by the Americans as an alternative neutralizing the Iranian influence in the region. In the Kosova crisis, Turkish rulers had similar worries with the Americans and they gave support to the initiatives led by the USA.[134]

bb- *Turkey and the Middle Eastern Countries*

Turkey traditionally is in favor of having close relations with the Arab and Muslim world and wants to solve its problems with the Middle Eastern states to strengthen its security.[135] Apart from having mutually beneficial trade relations with the regional states,[136] Turkey attributes importance to the establishment of security and stability in the Persian Gulf together with preventing the domination of one power in the region.[137] It avoids taking any side in Middle Eastern conflicts and tries not to antagonize regional countries while cooperating with the West in the security area.[138] Even if it is attracted to some regional issues and interactions, Turkey never deeply institutionalizes its ties with the region because of the fear that it will not be seen as a Western country. President Özal's efforts of having excessive roles during and after the Gulf Crisis attracted criticism and did not bring for Turkey benefits, which were expected.[139]

While the United States points to the global character of Middle Eastern crises and expects from its all Western allies respond in the same way, Turkish rulers do not want to pursue active policies on behalf of the West and to involve in US-led Western interventions in the region. They fear that Western interventions will draw Turkey to military conflicts outside its will and damage its relations with the regional states.[140] Turkish authorities do not want to undertake a general responsibility toward the United States in the Middle East, but they prefer to analyze the situation in each case to decide whether they join the American initiative.[141] They are also not sure that the increase in the existence of the United States in the region will promote the peace cause. The support given by the United States to some authoritarian regimes of the region might harm sensitive balances and cause conflicts. Moreover, the

---

[132] Kesic, "American-Turkish Relations...", p. 102, Lesser, *Bridge or Barrier*, s.. 40, Hale, "Turkish Foreign Policy...", p. 245.

[133] *Beyaz Kitap*, p. 30.

[134] Roper, "The West and Turkey...", p. 95.

[135] *Beyaz Kitap*, p. 35, Karaosmanoğlu, "Turkey and the Southern Flank", p. 300.

[136] Kuniholm, "East or West?...", p. 141, Lesser, "Turkey's Strategic Options", p. 86.

[137] Sezer, "Turkey's...", p. 162.

[138] Aykan, "Turkish Perspectives...", p. 348, Karaosmanoğlu, "Turkey and the Southern Flank", p. 334.

[139] Hunter, "Bridge or Frontier?...", p. 70.

[140] Helmut Hubel, "Turkey and the Crisis in the Middle East" in Karaosmanoğlu ve Taşhan (ed.), *Middle East...*, pp. 117-118, Lesser, *Bridge or Barrier*, p. 26, Taşhan, "Türkiye'nin Tehdit Algılamaları", p. 38, Karaosmanoğlu, "Turkey and the Southern Flank", p. 334.

[141] Aykan, "Turkish Perspectives...", p. 349.

American efforts of trying to contain Iran and Iraq and using pressure tactics against Syria might bring about clashes between Turkey and these states.[142]

Turkish officials have similar ideas in many political and economic issues of the Middle East with the Europeans rather than the Americans. Nevertheless, they need to cooperate with the USA because of common security and strategic concerns.[143] They want to keep developments under control by pursuing the policy of peaceful coexistence whereas the Americans do not hesitate to resort to forceful measures. In spite of American calls for implementing embargo against Iran, Turkey made a natural gas agreement with this state for a 23-year period. However, Turkish authorities did not join the project, which would carry the Turkmenistan gas to world markets through Iran, since they did not want to alienate the Americans totally.[144] The American administration's mild attitude toward Syria, aimed at drawing this state to the Middle Eastern peace process, did not please Turkey. There were rumors that the Americans considered the use of Turkish water resources by Syria in return for leaving the water resources in the Golan Heights to Israel.[145]

On the other hand, unlike the Europeans, the American administration assures Turkish rulers on Turkey's vital strategic importance for the West in the Middle Eastern context. On the Palestinian problem, Turkey sees the United States as the only country, which will encourage and guide the sides for a solution and supports US-led peace process for the sake of regional security. Turkish rulers put emphasis on granting the self-determination right to the Palestinians and on the withdrawal of Israel from the occupied territories, promise to provide financial aid to the Palestinian administration, but they do not want involving in the process closely. [146]

cc- *Turkey and the Central Asian Countries*

Some prominent Turkish politicians spoke of a large unified Turkic world, stretching from the Chinese Wall to the Adriatic. They thought at the beginning that a political and economic unity could be established among Turkic states under the leadership of Turkey even if a tight political organization could not be formed. This gave the impression that Turkey might pursue a brave and comprehensive foreign policy, departing from its traditional line.[147] However, Turkish efforts of inserting their models in the region implied a big brother attitude that was hurting for the regional states. Turkish rulers realized soon that the idea of establishing a strong Turkic union was not a viable alternative.

The Central Asian states were unstable and demanded much more military and economic aid than that Turkey could give. Although they seemed very close to Ankara, it was proved that they could turn to Moscow easily in vital economic, political and security issues. What they preferred was a loose grouping, which held summit meetings occasionally. Turkey might help them mostly by serving as an agent in getting the capital, technology and friendship of

---

[142] Buzoğlu, *Körfez Krizi ve PKK*, pp. 33, 34, 139.
[143] Hubel, "Turkey and the Crisis...", p. 118.
[144] Aykan, "Turkish Perspectives...", pp. 352, 354, Roper, "The West and Turkey...", p. 98.
[145] Gresh, "Turkish-Israeli...", pp. 197, 198.
[146] *Beyaz Kitap*, p. 35, Gürel, "A General Appraisal...", p. 16.
[147] Mufti, "Daring...", pp. 38, 46, Criss, "International Institutions...", p. 208, Hunter, "Bridge or Frontier?...", pp. 69, 71.

the West. [148] Meanwhile, irritated by Turkey's activities, Russia tried to reinsert its influence in the Central Asia, made special arrangements with the regional states, and even resorted to the military force.[149] The Americans seemed at that time to consider the region in the realm of the Russians. Only after Russia faced with great difficulties in establishing its influence, American leaders began to think that helping Turkey in increasing its influence in the region might be to the advantage of the United States.[150]

In the eyes of the Americans, Turkey might affect the regional states in shaping their system in accordance with democratic and secular models. With the help of having the same language and religion, Turkey could prevent or at least limit the expansion of the Russian and Iranian influence in the Central Asia.[151] Turkish rulers emphasized that they could help Western initiatives in the region and undertake the leadership role in tying the Central Asia to the West through technical, economic and financial aids.[152] As the United States showed more interest in the region and the regional countries expected US help, Turkey maintained close contact with both sides to help their relations and attributed special importance to the participation of the Central Asian and Caucasian states to the Partnership for Peace project of NATO in this context. It took the lead in the summit meetings of the Turkic states and joined economic projects and encouraged its private companies' activities in these countries. Helping the regional states in this way to reduce their dependence on Russia would be helpful for both Turkey and the USA.[153]

In the last analysis, Turkey's relations with the Central Asian countries are not alternatives to Turkey's ties with the West, but they could be seen as the means for strengthening these ties with their original aim of attracting attention to the fact that Turkey is an indispensable ally of the West.[154]

Another important issue for Turkey in the Central Asian context is to ensure that the region's oil and gas will reach to the Western markets through the Turkish territories. At the beginning, Turkey wanted all oil pipelines pass through its territories because in this way it could become an energy terminal on which the West is dependent. [155] However, with the intervention of the United States, which did not want to alienate the Russians totally, Turkey accepted that oil could be transferred through multiple pipelines, meaning that some other states such as Russia, too, could get benefit from the transportation of oil.[156] In the eyes of Turkish rulers, "the project tabled by Turkey to transport oil from the vast reserves of the Caspian basin through a main pipeline from Baku to Ceyhan will have significant consequences for the prosperity of the entire region... Turkey offers a viable, reliable, rantable, technologically and environmentally most feasible and safe option."[157]

---

[148] Kesic, "American-Turkish Relations...", p. 101, Jesus N. Villaverde, "Turkey-European Union Relations in the Framework of the Euro-Mediterranean Partnership" in Aydın, *Turkey...*, p. 151, Hunter, "Bridge or Frontier?...", p. 75, Hale, "Turkish Foreign Policy...", pp. 239, 247.

[149] Sezer, "Turkey's...", p. 155, Hale, "Turkish Foreign Policy...", pp. 247-248.

[150] Demir, "SSCB'nin Dağılmasından...", p. 243.

[151] Kesic, "American-Turkish Relations...", p. 98.

[152] Lesser, *Bridge or Barrier*, pp. vii-viii, 7, Müftüler-Bac, "Turkey's Predicament...", s 265.

[153] Hale, "Turkish Foreign Policy...", p. 243, *Beyaz Kitap*, p. 33.

[154] Evert, "Turkey's Strategic Goals...", p. 32, Lesser, "Turkey's Strategic Options", p. 86, Hunter, "Bridge or Frontier?...", p. 78.

[155] Aykan, "Turkish Perspectives...", p. 355, *Beyaz Kitap*, p. 7.

[156] Duygu Sezer, "The Black Sea Politics and Turkey" in Aydın (ed.), *Turkey...*, pp. 75-76.

[157] Gürel, "A General Appraisal...", p. 16.

The transportation of oil through Russia meant that the tanker traffic in the Turkish Straits would increase greatly, causing environmental problems for Turkey. Turkish rulers obtained the support of some regional states such as Azerbaijan for the Baku-Ceyhan project. However, the major powers of the world, including oil companies, had more voice in taking the final decision. Therefore, Turkish leaders attributed great importance to the support of the United States in this matter.[158] The United States and Turkey agreed on that the Azeri oil should be saved from the monopoly of Russia and that Iran and Russia should not be allowed to have an influential voice in the transportation of oil. The American administration decided that the Baku-Ceyhan pipeline would be most beneficial for American interests.[159]

dd- Turkish-Israeli Relations

The improvements in Turkish-Israeli relations in the post-Cold War period strengthened Turkey's relations with the United States and increased its importance in the eyes of the Americans. The Turkish-Israeli defense cooperation agreements in February and August 1996 symbolized the introduction of the security aspect to the relations between the two states. According to the agreements, the air forces and the navy of the two states would carry out joint military exercises, the Israeli navy would use the Turkish ports, and the Israeli air forces would perform training flights upon the wide Anatolian plateau. With the help of America, a border control system, which included sensitive cameras, receivers and satellites, would be put into operation.

Demirel's official visit to Jerusalem in December 1996 was the first visit of a Turkish president to Israel. During the visit, it was declared that Turkish forces would carry out joint military exercises with the Israeli and American forces in the Eastern Mediterranean.[160] Turkish Defence Minister Turhan Tayan's visit to the Golan Heights in May 1997 was a brave action. In return, Israeli Prime Minister Netenyahu criticized the idea of the establishment of a Kurdish state and condemned the separatist PKK organization for the first time in his interview with a Turkish television. In spite of the intensive protests of the regional states, Turkish, American and Israeli navies performed the planned joint military exercise in January 1998.

As stated by Israeli Minister Moshe Arens, the Turkish-Israeli military axis was the most important development of the recent Middle Eastern history, having the potential to change the regional balance of power. The fear of the Arabs that the Western powers and their regional allies might establish an anti-Arab coalition was renewed. Syria activated the Arab world against the new development and obtained the political support of the Arab states to break its isolation. Saudi Arabia, Egypt and Syria formed a strategic partnership and Iran won important successes in getting recognition of the Middle Eastern countries.[161] Responding to reactions, Turkish authorities asserted that the Turkish-Israel cooperation was not against any regional state, but it contributed to the establishment of peace, stability and order in the region.[162]

Turkish leaders see their cooperation with Israel as an alternative to be used in the case the Western powers cause problems. While the European countries and the United States

---

[158] Sezer, "The Black Sea Politics and Turkey", pp. 74-75.
[159] Demir, "SSCB'nin Dağılmasından...", pp. 238, 244.
[160] Mufti, "Daring...", pp. 35-36, 47-48,
[161] Gresh, "Turkish-Israeli...", pp. 189-190, 193-194, 203.
[162] Gürel, "A General Appraisal...", pp. 20-21, Beyaz Kitap, p. 35.

seem unreliable in providing weapons because of their heavy conditions, Israel has become an alternative for Turkey, diminishing its dependence on the West and diversifying its defense sources. Turkey might get from Israel weapons and military technology that will never be able to get from the United States and the European countries. In 1996 the Israeli companies undertook half a billion-dollar project of the modernization of Turkey's 54 F-14 warplanes. In December 1997, the modernization of Turkey's 48 F-5 warplanes was given to Israel. Turkey and Israel also agreed on the joint manufacture of Arrow missiles.[163]

In the light of the serious increase in the military armament in the region, Israel seems a valuable partner, helping Turkey to defend itself against ballistic missiles. The cooperation with Israel has also provided important opportunities to Turkey in limiting the power of Syria, Iraq and Iran.[164] However, the most important motive of Turkish rulers in improving their relations with Israel is to strengthen their alliance relations with the United States. They expect that the mighty Israeli lobby in America will affect the Congress in taking more pro-Turkish decisions in important issues such as the military sales, the Cyprus question and the allegations of Armenian massacres at the hands of the Turkish Ottomans.[165]

The American administration clearly supports the Turkish-Israeli rapprochement. When Turkey and Israel decided to carry out joint military exercises, America expressed its worries only on its timing. After persuading the sides in changing its time, the United States itself joined the exercise. The Americans suggested calling a Jordanian commander to the exercise seemingly to appease the Arab opposition or to expand the Turkish-Israeli cooperation to a Middle Eastern grouping. In the last analysis, Turkey needs to pursue a flexible policy by taking into consideration the possibilities that Israel might solve its problems with the Arabs and Turkish-Israeli relations might deteriorate. Such a development might decrease the importance of Turkey for the Americans in the Israeli context and might leave Turkey alone in facing the Middle Eastern powers alienated by the Turkish-Israel cooperation.[166]

c) The Future of Turkish Foreign Policy

Turkish disappointment toward the Western powers in some issues in the 1990s underlined the possibility that Turkey might seek a new identity outside the West and new roles in the Balkans and Turkic republics. In the view of Süleyman Demirel (prime minister, later president), the effectiveness and reliability of the Western organizations failed in the recent international crises. The prestige of Western values and ideas were sharply decreased in the eyes of Turkish people because they believed that the West showed a biased attitude toward the oppressed Muslims of Bosnia, Chechnya and Kosova.[167] Turkish people also thought that Turkey was not accepted to the EU because of its Muslim identity. With the new developments, they felt that Turkey could not trust any more in the West in getting benefits in economic, political and security areas. That strengthened the hand of the conservative and nationalist elements in Turkish politics, demanding closer relations with the Muslim and Turkic world respectively.[168]

---

[163] Gresh, "Turkish-Israeli...", pp. 190, 191.
[164] Lesser, "Turkey's Strategic Options", p. 84.
[165] Gresh, "Turkish-Israeli...", p. 191, Roper, "The West and Turkey...", p. 98,
[166] Hunter, "Bridge or Frontier?...", p. 72.
[167] Dağı, "Turkey in the 1990s...", pp. 71, 72, 77, Lesser, "Turkey's Strategic Options", pp. 82, 88.
[168] Hale, "Turkish Foreign Policy...", p. 238.

Islamic-oriented Welfare Party became successful in the local and general elections by playing off "Turkey's economic, political and security turmoil with a nationalistic message of contempt for the West." Its message found fertile ground among average Turks, who believed that the West let them down on a number of vital issues central to Turkey's future.[169] While the centrist parties could not satisfy demands of the average person, the dynamic character of conservatives and nationalists hinted a radical shake up in the Turkish political life with its repercussions on Turkey's foreign policy.[170] The process was interrupted by a series of initiatives launched by the Turkish military, starting on 28 February 1997 and radical elements themselves became pro-integration with the West. However, anti-Western feeling might also overcome Turkey's traditional elite as shown by Şükrü Gürel's statement that Turkey was not doomed to wait for an ambiguous time or outcome and had no intention to turn EU membership into an obsession.[171]

Turkey's close relationship with the West, including the United States cannot be taken granted. The West has to be careful on not antagonizing Turkey if it wants to protect its own interests. Turkish estrangement from the West is likely to make the process of political and economic change in Turkey more difficult and crisis-prone.[172] Turkish rulers warn that the fall of Turkey to the hands of radical groups will affect Western security directly. Particularly the Turkish military has sought to attract the US support for Turkey's traditional line. "By designating Islamic fundamentalism as the enemy within, [it] made itself part of the anti-Iranian strategy... By allying itself to Israel, it could be sure of strong support from the USA and the Congress."[173] Nevertheless, Turkish people's lack of confidence in the West continues and the centrist parties still face heavy defeats in Turkish elections. Therefore, there are still valid reasons for the Americans to worry on a possible change in the structure of Turkey's traditional ruling elite and its Western-oriented foreign policy line. Relying on the military in maintaining the traditional structure is both unreliable and contrary to democratic principles.

In the new atmosphere created after the end of the Cold War, Turkey's foreign policy alternatives were discussed by public opinion, politicians and officials in the way which could not be compared with the past and new proposals were put forward. The changes in Turkish domestic politics and the affinity of the Turkish nation to the people in the crisis regions put pressures on the Turkish administrations to pursue more active foreign policies. As a result, the horizon of Turkey's foreign and security policies broadened both regionally and functionally. Turkey was more active in the international crises, it tried to protect its interests more assertively (such as its actions against Syria and its operations in northern Iraq) and the sensitivity of Turkish officials on Turkey's sovereignty was more prominent with the increasing Turkish nationalism.[174] Turkish rulers tried to protect their interests through the organizations such as the UN, NATO and OSCE, rather than emphasizing bilateral relations with the countries such as the United States. In Demirel's words, Turkey sought "to explore opportunities for political, economic, commercial, social and cultural joint initiatives in meeting daunting challenged by pursuing a multi-dimensional foreign policy." "Turkey's

---

[169] Kesic, "American-Turkish Relations...", pp. 105, 106.
[170] Kuniholm, "East or West?...", p. 141, Dağı, "Turkey in the 1990s...", p. 76.
[171] Gürel, "A General Appraisal...", pp. 13, 21.
[172] Lesser, "Turkey's Strategic Options", p. 88.
[173] Gresh, "Turkish-Israeli...", p. 191.
[174] Lesser, "Turkey's Strategic Options", pp. 80, 87, 88, Roper, "The West and Turkey...", p. 90.

strategic relevance in the post-Cold War era lies in her very ability to look both to the West and the East; to remain firmly committed to her Western orientation while simultaneously recognizing the complexities of her geography as well as the harsh realities of her immediate neighborhood."[175]

The establishment of the D-8 group among the Muslim states during the brief period of Erbakan's government symbolized an important change in Turkish foreign policy. But Erbakan had to leave the power because of the severe opposition to his government. In fact, Erbakan himself could not take any contrary actions to the traditional policies concerning the membership in NATO, the relations with Israel and the custom union with the European Union. Finally the economic crises in Asia reiterated the notion that the integration with the Muslim world could not be an alternative to relations with the West.[176] Nevertheless, Erbakan's successors chose to keep the D-8 in case they need it. Turkey's leading role in the Organization of Black Sea Economic Cooperation (BSEC), too, was aimed at pursuing more active foreign policy and increasing its importance for the West. It enhanced Turkey's influence in the region and contributed to its security by strengthening the peace in the surrounding region. But Turkish authorities frequently emphasized that their leadership role in the BSEC project was not an alternative to future membership in the European Union. They stated that their activities would serve the Western interests and would deepen Turkey's integration with the West. The support given by the USA to this project, therefore, was valuable for Turkish rulers[177]

As a part of pursuing more independent foreign policy, Turkish rulers tried to be self-sufficient in defense. The impact of the American arms embargo and occasional sanctions imposed by the Western powers on Turkish arms purchases were always in their minds. The formulation of a new defense concept and the creation of the Defence Industrial Development and Support Administration and other organs, including a fund were some of the initiatives launched in this direction.[178] Meeting the modernization needs of the Turkish armed forces by establishing a national defense industry infrastructure was continuously in the agenda of Turkish authorities.[179] Strengthening the air defense through the Patriot missiles and more F-16 warplanes was an urgent priority for Turkey. The lack of these systems would make Turkey defenseless against air attacks, leading Turkish authorities to be more reluctant in allowing the use of the Turkish territory by the Western states in the future military clashes outside the NATO area.[180] Turkish rulers also opened the defense sector to Western and Turkish private companies to benefit from their technological, financial and management capabilities.[181]

The Turkish defense industry has developed greatly with recent efforts. However, Turkey still has to import military equipment and technology to meet military needs. The Turkish

---

[175] Demirel, "Turkey...", p. 8.

[176] Hunter, "Bridge or Frontier?...", p. 76, Lesser, "Turkey's Strategic Options", p. 87.

[177] Hale, "Turkish Foreign Policy...", p. 244.

[178] *Beyaz Kitap*, pp. 54-55.

[179] Lesser, *Bridge or Barrier*, pp. 27-28, 30, Cengiz Okman, "NATO Stratejileri ve Türkiye Bakımından Sonuçları" in *Türkiye'nin Savunması*, p. 97, Mufti, "Daring...", p. 47, *Beyaz Kitap*, p. II.

[180] Lesser, *Bridge or Barrier*, p. 31.

[181] Brown, *Delicately Poised Allies*, pp. 152, 153, Karaosmanoğlu, "Turkey and the Southern Flank", p. 327-328, Safa Atalay, "ABD Güvenlik Yardımı ABD Türkiye İlişkileri", *Avrasya Dosyası*, vol. 1, No. 3, Fall 1994, p. 237, Lesser, *Bridge or Barrier*, pp. 38-39, Erol Manisalı, "Savunma Sanayii ve Türkiye'deki Savunma Sanayiinin Gelişimi" in *Türkiye'nin Savunması*, p. 114, *Beyaz Kitap*, p. 129.

army is tied to the United States functionally and its weapons systems have been established according to American standards. Therefore, Turkey will continue to need American military assistance and equipment in suitable conditions. Getting certain equipment (such as Black Hawk and Skorsky helicopters), spare parts and military training from the USA will always be vitally important for Turkey since its army will be mutilated otherwise.[182] The statement of the Turkish Defence Industry is meaningful in this regard: "The Turkish armed forces are national forces. It is essential that its critical equipment should be produced in the national industrial complexes."[183]

d) Military Assistance

With the outbreak of the Gulf Crisis, it became clear that Turkey's importance for the United States would not decrease, but it was also realized that American aid to Turkey would not continue in the same level and way. The failure in getting more financial and military assistance from the United States in spite of its faithfulness and cooperation inside NATO displeased Turkish rulers.[184] After the Gulf War, American aid to Turkey was increased from 553.4 million dollars to 635.4 million dollars and the most of this aid was in the form of outright grants. With the inclusion of CFE-related equipment, Turkey would be recipient of US and German military equipment worth of 8 billion dollars. But this extraordinary increase resulted from the CFE treaty and special conditions of the Gulf War. The normal tendency was that the American Congress would be less enthusiastic in providing security assistance. Turkish rulers were also aware that the Cyprus and Kurdish issues, the human rights violations and the Balkan conflicts would be debated during the foreign aid bill discussions.[185] When the American Congress suspended 10 % of the 453 million-dollar aid on 29 July 1994 because of Turkey's failure in making improvements in its human rights records and the Cyprus issue, the Turkish government responded by refusing the part of the aid, which was made conditional. This caused a serious cutback in the US supplementary weapons and equipment program, on which Turkey relied heavily especially in its fighting against the separatist PKK.[186]

Turkey's traditional ways of receiving aid from the United States gradually disappeared and the aid, which was turned to a commercial arms sale, were filled by the Congress with outsider elements harming Turkish interests. Turkey bought weapons from private American companies and received military equipment from the US administration in the form of credits or grants (Foreign Military Sales, FMS). In the aftermath of the Gulf War, the USA provided aid to Turkey as FMS credits, southern-region aid (SRA) and CFE-surplus weapons to Turkey, trying to reduce the effect of the Congress' limitations. By pointing to the SRA, American authorities cancelled the grant aid totally and turned it to interest-bearing FMS credits. The 450 million-dollar aid in 1993 was totally this kind. Owing to high interest rates, Turkey's debt payments exceeded in some years the actual amount of the so-called American aid and even reached the 10 % of Turkey's total expenditures. There was no difference

---

[182] Aykan, "Turkish Perspectives...", p. 355.
[183] *Beyaz Kitap,* pp. 63, 125-126, 129.
[184] Brown, *Delicately Poised Allies,* pp. 159-160.
[185] Lesser, *Bridge or Barrier,* p. 36.
[186] Aykan, "Turkish Perspectives...", p. 351.

between taking credits from a commercial bank and receiving military aid from the United States any longer.

The reduction of the FMS credits to 400 million dollars for 1995 with the 7 % interest rate and its conditioning in the way that it meant intervention in Turkish domestic politics resulted in the loss of the attractiveness of the American security aid for Turkey. Meanwhile, with the limitation of the commercial purchase with 10 million dollars, Turkey could not benefit from bargaining opportunities with private companies. Moreover, political disputes prevented the transfer of some US military equipment that was appropriated for Turkey. Consequently, it can be said that the limitations in the American aid negatively affected Turkey's security principles and priorities. Turkey's dependence on the USA on logistics, maintenance and training limited Turkey's security alternatives. The American' allowing only limited technology transfer in military sales and joint projects sanctioned Turkey's efforts to establish a strong defense infrastructure.[187]

e) The Turkish-American Strategic Partnership

Turkish authorities were not happy in the content and implementation of the Defence and Economic Cooperation Agreement (DECA) signed between Turkey and the USA in 1980. They were of the opinion that the Americans did not fulfil their responsibilities concerning the modernization of the Turkish armed forces. Turkish leaders particularly demanded that the security relationship between the two countries should be saved from the outsider elements such as the Cyprus question and that the economic aspects of the DECA should be implemented satisfactorily. When their demands were not met, they became reluctant in the expansion of the defense cooperation with America though they allowed the extension of the DECA annually.

However, the Gulf Crisis provided a good opportunity for Turkey in proving its strategic importance for the West by cooperating with Washington closely. The Turkish government closed the Kirkuk-Yumurtalık pipeline immediately and allowed the use of its territory by the coalition forces. The alleged intention of President Özal of opening a second front against Iraq on the Turkish border to annex Mosul and Kirkuk was not materialized because of severe domestic opposition. Nevertheless, the unhesitant help provided by Turkey for America in its hour of need during the war had vital importance. In this way, Turkey guaranteed its place within the Western camp in the post-Cold War period. Ankara never received compensation for its war losses in the amount, which it expected,[188] but it became one of major strategic partners of the United States by deepening its security relationship with it.

After the Gulf War, by extending the DECA in December 1991, Turkish authorities pre-empted in a sense the Americans' putting forward new demands concerning the use of the bases.[189] In March 1993, the Turkish administration conveyed its demands again to the Americans on making changes in the DECA. In this way, the two sides returned to the period of endless negotiations in the 1980s with the extension of the agreement annually. Meanwhile, the American decision of withdrawing military personnel and nuclear weapons in the Erhac and Eskişehir air bases without consulting the Turkish side displeased Ankara. By

---

[187] Atalay, "ABD Güvenlik Yardımı...", pp. 241, 246-250.
[188] Köni, "Gulf Savaşı..." pp. 48-49.
[189] Lesser, *Bridge or Barrier*, p. 35.

the middle of 1994, ten out of twelve NATO bases in Turkey had been closed. The dissatisfaction of Turkish rulers on the DECA continued in the following years. They mainly wanted America provide more help and transfer high military technology in developing Turkey's defense industry.[190]

It was expected that the Turkish-American defense cooperation would not expand any longer in the 1990s. The Americans should have appreciated the cautious attitude of Turkish authorities on the use of Turkish airfield and military bases. Turkey would demand a more mature and diversified relationship in which traditional security contacts were supported by more emphasized political and economic cooperation, benefiting both states. The new security initiatives concerning Turkey should have been materialized in a multilateral context and in the way that they would increase Turkey's importance for the West, they would be accepted by Ankara and they would encourage to share the Transatlantic responsibilities.[191] However, Turkish authorities launched brave initiatives on the strategic partnership with the United States. The daily use of the İncirlik airbase by America, the consideration of use of the Turkish territory for the NATO attacks against Yugoslavia and the active participation of Turkish authorities in many US-led operations were some examples in this regard. Turkey might benefit in many issues from its strategic partnership with the most powerful state of the world.

However, it is still in the minds of Turkish authorities how the close relationship between the two states in the 1950s caused big problems for Turkey in the 1960s and the 1970s. By taking to the consideration the possibilities that Turkish-American relations might deteriorate and the American administration might apply pressure tactics against Turkey, Turkish rulers need to be cautious in their attitude on improving the partnership with the USA. Not showing the old sensitivities on the use of the İncirlik airbase, for example, seems a departure for them from their traditional policies. They are supposed to be reluctant in undertaking wide responsibilities on the use of the Turkish territory by the Americans and in involving in American interventions in the region.[192] As Uğur Mumcu warns, the main agreement on the use of the İncirlik airbase is the DECA. However, after Turkey accepted the international force to its territory for the protection of the Iraqi Kurds, the DECA has been forgotten. The possibility that the United States might involve Turkey in a military conflict with Iraq through its in İncirlik is taken lightly.[193]

4. Conclusion

For America, Turkey is an indispensable country which has contributed to its security and political and economic stability by remaining faithful to its responsibilities toward the Western alliance. Turkey occupies a vital place for the main American goals in the new era such as "a) elevating global economic growth as a primary foreign policy goal; b) promoting the spread of democracy and free markets; c) updating American-led alliances created during the Cold War as well as working to revitalize and reform the United Nations; and d) updating

[190] Aykan, "Turkish Perspectives...", pp. 345-346, 347.

[191] Lesser, *Bridge or Barrier*, pp. vi-vii, 24, 34, 38, 43-44.

[192] Snyder, *Defending the Fringe*, p. 122, Lesser, *Bridge or Barrier*, pp. 36, 37, Brown, *Delicately Poised Allies*, pp. 60-61.

[193] Yavuz, *ABD'nin Kürt Kartı*, p. 278.

America's security arrangements and armed forces to meet new threats and challenges, including a higher emphasis on peace-support operations."[194] The new tendencies in the American security thinking ("the rediscovery of geopolitics on Europe's periphery especially in the Caspian and growing emphasis on the challenges of weapons of mass destruction and missile proliferation and regional power projection") have resulted in America's showing more interest in Turkey as a strategic partner. High-level American officials consider Turkey as the new frontline country of NATO and one of the major actors which might affect developments in the Balkans, the Middle East, the Central Asia and Europe.[195]

For Turkey, the United States is the most suitable partner, which can provide security guarantees in facing new threats. Turkish rulers aim at improving Turkish-American relations in the way that they will serve the mutual interests. They think that furthering the bilateral relationship, which is called as the Improved Partnership in the areas of politics, defense cooperation, economy and energy will serve the regional and global peace and stability.[196] Finally, it has to be known that being strategic partners and making strategic cooperation do not mean that Turkey and the United States will have the same views in every matter in a wide region stretching from the Aegean to the Gulf region.

---

[194] Asmus, "The Rise or Fall?...", p. 162.
[195] Lesser, "Turkey's Strategic Options", pp. 83-84.
[196] *Beyaz Kitap,* p. 27.

Chapter 12

CONCLUSION

1. GENERAL EVALUATION OF U.S.-TURKISH RELATIONS

The only shadow over close relations between Turkey and the United States in the 1950s had been U.S. unwillingness to supply a stabilization fund to Turkey to help its balance of payments problems. After a four-year debate, the Turkish government had to accept strict U.S. conditions in 1958 to be able to obtain the fund.[1] After the withdrawal of Iraq from the Baghdad Pact as a result of a military coup, the United States assured Turkish rulers of U.S. commitment to Turkish security by signing a bilateral agreement in 1959. In the eyes of opposition Republican People's Party's members, this American act was aimed at saving the rightist Democrat Party government. While RPP leaders warmly welcomed the overthrow of the DP regime by the military coup of 27 May 1960, which could be seen by them as an anti-American act in those circumstances, DP supporters believed that the Americans abandoned them and cite as proof growing U.S. displeasure with their government toward the end of the 1950s.

Hence both the U.S. attitude toward the coup and the military junta's actions in Turkey's alliance relations with the United States and NATO became particularly sensitive matters. In fact, in their first public announcement, Turkish officers expressed their loyalty to their existing alliances and NATO, showing their intention not to make any changes in the traditional direction of Turkish foreign policy. The quick recognition of the new regime and the promise of economic and military aid to it by the United States proved that there would be no changes in U.S.-Turkish relations. In fact, the Turkish military junta soon became more dependent on the USA because of its need for U.S. financial assistance to achieve economic development and to improve the welfare of Turkish military officers. Therefore, it did not hesitate to sign bilateral agreements with the United States, to station the U.S.-supplied Jupiter missiles on Turkish territory and even to facilitate the legislation of bilateral agreements with the USA by introducing a new constitutional procedure. Military rulers wanted to make some changes in rules applied to U.S. personnel in Turkey, but, when the Americans seemed unwilling to give up their existing privileges, they did not pursue the matter.

---

[1] George S. Harris, *Troubled Alliance*, Washington: American Enterprise Institute, 1972, pp. 74-75, Theodore A. Couloumbis, *The United States, Greece and Turkey*, New York: Praeger, 1983, p. 19.

When the Cuban missile crisis broke in October 1962, the Turks still had warm feelings toward the United States. Turkish rulers and MPs proudly supported the U.S. stance to expel the Soviet missiles from the Caribbean. There was no criticism in the Turkish press directed toward the firm U.S. stance against the Soviet Union, which could cause a global nuclear war. When the possibility of trading Soviet missiles in Cuba with the Jupiters in Turkey was discussed in Western states and when it was proposed by Soviet Premier Khrushchev, the Turks did not make any comment about it and sincerely believed that their close ally America would not bargain the interests of a NATO member with the enemy camp.

Meanwhile, the pluralist 1960 constitution began to have its effects in Turkish politics. Using means provided by the constitution, marginal groups were able to voice their opinions and criticize basic tenets of the regime, including the traditional foreign policy line, which was considered a taboo. Newspaper columns became the main platform of such discussions and criticism. As a start, the withdrawal of the Jupiter missiles was criticized on the ground that it decreased Turkey's strategic importance for the West and created a security gap for Turkish defense. During parliamentary discussions in 1963, the inadequacy of U.S. military aid was subjected to criticism.

The most important thing which triggered the widespread anti-Americanism in Turkey was the Turkish belief that the United States did not work enough to stop atrocities against Turkish Cypriots, which began at the end of December 1963, but continuously prevented the Turkish government from intervening in Cyprus to protect lives and rights of Turkish people on the island. President Johnson's letter to Turkish P.M. İnönü in June 1964 further fuelled the anti-Americanism among Turkish people and brought radical changes in the thinking of Turkish rulers. Johnson had threatened that NATO might not come to Turkey's help if the Soviet Union attacked Turkey because of its intervention in Cyprus and he had reminded the Turks that they could not use U.S.-supplied weapons in their actions in Cyprus. While mainly leftist groups and university students arranged mass demonstrations against the USA and attacked American buildings in major Turkish cities, Turkish authorities showed their disappointment over the U.S. attitude with their statements. In one point Turkish Prime Minister İnönü hinted that Turkey could leave the Western camp. Nevertheless, frictions between the USA and Turkey on the official level did not last long. To change the unpleasant image of the United States among Turkish people, U.S. leaders reiterated their commitment to Turkish security, offered more financial assistance and voted against the UN decision in December 1965, which supported the Greek cause. Turkish rulers announced that it was not their intention to change their foreign policy line and leave the Western camp.

After the rightist Justice Party came to power at the end of 1965, Turkish leftist groups increased their attacks against the United States and Turkey's alliance with this state and NATO. Columnists of Turkish newspapers except rightist ones joined leftists in criticizing all aspects of Turkish-American relations, especially military contacts. Under public pressure and to prove their independence, Turkish rulers took the following major actions which could be interpreted as anti-American: the withdrawal from the Multilateral Force, banning U-2 flights using Turkish territory, changing the duty status formula applied to U.S. personnel, not allowing the use of the İncirlik base for non-NATO purposes, reviewing all bilateral military agreements with the USA and forcing this state to sign a new general military agreement. Turkish leaders also tried to improve relations with Eastern bloc countries through intensive state visits and economic agreements and to gain the sympathy of Third World and Arab countries by supporting their causes in the United Nations.

The Americans were not happy about the Turkish actions, but they did not show resentment because these actions did not harm their fundamental interests, which were fulfilled by the strong Turkish commitment to NATO and the U.S. use of military facilities and bases on Turkish territory. The apparent pro-Turkish attitude of the United States during the November 1967 Cyprus crisis also ensured the closeness of U.S.-Turkish relations on the official level until 1969.

After 1969, Turkish rulers were subjected to U.S. pressure on their opium production. The Americans had believed that Turkish opium provided 80 percent of heroin at U.S. streets and thus made great contribution to the harrowing drug addiction problem among the youth of the USA. Turkish authorities did not fulfil the U.S. demand to prohibit opium cultivation because they did not want to lose the votes of poppy growers. Meanwhile, increasing terrorist actions against U.S. personnel by Turkish leftists, who lost representation in the parliament to voice their opinion, posed another problem for the Americans.

The removal of the Turkish government from power by the military on 12 March 1971 and the subsequent rule by non-party, technocrat governments served mostly U.S. interests. Under the martial law, extreme leftist groups were suppressed and thus anti-American criticism in newspaper columns and terrorist acts against U.S. personnel were terminated. More importantly, opium cultivation in Turkey was completely prohibited. However, the return of normal party politics at the end of 1973 brought problems for U.S.-Turkish relations again. After an election period in which heavy criticism was directed against the opium ban, the coalition government of leftist Republicans and Islamist Salvationists decided to resume poppy production in June 1974 as an act of independence in spite of American protests. While the U.S. Congress was busy with trying to cut off economic and military assistance to Turkey because of the new Turkish decision, the military coup in Cyprus and the subsequent Turkish intervention in Cyprus forestalled them.

The Turkish government was not unhappy with the U.S. attitude toward its action, which resulted in capturing 36 percent of Cyprus because the United States had not taken direct action to prevent or later to reverse the Turkish action. In fact, Turkish rulers were of the opinion that they had proved that their government was not under the U.S. influence and was able to pursue Turkey's national interests effectively. However, the U.S. Congress's action to impose an arms embargo on Turkey because of its intervention in Cyprus, starting from 5 February 1975, caused a new wave of anti-Americanism in Turkey. Turkish authorities were angry because they believed that the Congress action unilaterally violated principles of the U.S.-Turkish alliance and undermined its basis. As a response, in July 1975 the coalition government of rightist parties, "the nationalist front", announced invalidity of U.S.-Turkish bilateral agreements and closed down U.S. facilities and bases in Turkey. Thus, relations between Turkey and the United States hit their lowest level though the alliance of the two states continued within the NATO framework.

2. EVALUATION OF VALIDITY OF THEORIES

Alliance theories studied in Chapter II proved to be a great help to explain Turkish-American relations between 1960 and 1975. It became clear in the course of the study that reasons adumbrated in those theories for alliance formation and continuation were also valid for the U.S.-Turkish relationship. Although they had serious disputes with the USA on some matters, the Turks remained very keen to continue their alliance with America because they saw it as a warranty of Turkish security against the Soviet threat and other possible threats, as a source of considerable military and economic assistance and as a guarantee for westernizing Turkey and making her a part of the Western world. Turkey's strategic importance for U.S. interests, which were explained in Chapter IV, and the desire to keep Turkey within the Western camp so as not to lose prestige vis-a-vis the Soviet bloc were the main reasons for the USA continuing the alliance with Turkey.

Both sides clearly believed that the alliance brought far more benefits than costs for their national interests.[2] However, the implications of the Cuban missile crisis and the Johnson letter caused doubts in the Turkish side on the security provided by the alliance and thus decreased the value of the alliance for Turkey. Technological developments in intelligence collecting and nuclear missiles, withdrawal of the Jupiters from Turkey and unavailability of Turkish bases for operations in the Middle East led American leaders to attribute less importance to their alliance with Turkey.

In the 1960s and the 1970s, the goals and expectations of Turkey and the United States from their alliance were not so similar as they had been during the 1950s. Turkey wanted the alliance help its Cyprus cause whereas the United States expected that the close alliance relationship would induce the Turks to do a favor for America by prohibiting opium cultivation. This situation caused problems in the two states' relations.

In the 1960-1975 period, the U.S.-Turkish alliance was considerably affected by developments in the international arena. The decrease of tension and conflict between the Eastern and Western blocs (détente) allowed both states to act more independently from restrictions of their alliance. The apparent decrease in the Soviet threat particularly let Turkish rulers improve their relations with Eastern bloc and Third World countries and put more emphasis on their national causes, especially the Cyprus problem. The Americans became less anxious about providing military and economic assistance to Turkey and went so far as to threaten Turkey with not protecting it against the Soviet camp.

The study has showed that U.S.-Turkish contacts between 1960 and 1975 did not amount to a patron-client relationship though some individual events implied the opposite result. Generally, until 1964 Turkey acted as if it was under close and strong American influence. The Cuban missile crisis of October 1962 supported this conclusion. Turkish rulers proudly announced their support for the U.S. stance during the crisis without thinking that Turkey's interests and even its survival could be put under threat because of their attitude and they expected only U.S. praise in return, nothing else. On the other side, the Americans bargained the Jupiter missiles belonging to Turkey with the Soviet Union without informing the Turks and they did not tell the Turks how Turkey's survival was under threat. Before 1964, Turkey's voting patterns in the United Nations very largely coincided with those of the United States.

In 1964, heavy U.S. pressures on Turkish rulers prevented them from taking a major action in Cyprus, including military intervention. The Johnson letter in June 1964 in particular resembled an ultimatum sent by a colonial power to its vassal. However, the severe reaction of Turkish rulers and people induced the Americans to be more careful in their

---

[2] Turkish rulers' opinions in this regard were mentioned in the section of NATO discussion in Chapter IV and U.S. officials' opinions in the section of Turkey's strategic importance in the same chapter and in the section of the arms embargo in Chapter IX.

dealings with the Turks and avoid alienating them because they certainly did not want to lose benefits of their alliance with Turkey. Turkish actions after 1964 implied more independence from U.S. influence. Turkey improved relations with the states outside the Western camp, took some actions in military relations with the USA and supported causes of the Arab and Third World countries in UN votings. However, it also remained strictly loyal to its commitment toward NATO, allowed the use of military bases on its territory by the United States and followed the U.S. lead in UN votings on cold-war matters.

Before 1971 Turkish rulers complied with most of the U.S. demands on the opium question and showed sincere efforts to help the United States in this issue. However, in order not to lose electoral support and not to be seen as acting under the U.S. influence, they did not fulfil the main American demand, prohibiting opium cultivation completely. The military-backed governments after March 1971 proved to be more receptive to U.S. influences. They banned opium cultivation to prevent deterioration of relations with the United States.

The Ecevit government of 1974 was seen by many as the most independent of Turkish governments, pursuing Turkish interests without staying under U.S. influence. In fact, it resumed poppy production and intervened in Cyprus militarily in spite of U.S. opposition. But at the same time it was anxious not to destroy the alliance with the USA nor to allow a serious deterioration of U.S.-Turkish relations. Therefore, the Ecevit government was very careful in taking these decisions not to alienate the Americans. Moreover, the U.S. administration was not altogether determined to prevent the Turkish intervention in Cyprus and on the opium question the Congress was doing enough to punish Turkey. The U.S. arms embargo in February 1975 and the closure of bases by Turkey in July 1975 clearly showed that the Turkish-American alliance was not a patron-client relationship. However, Turkey's economic and military dependence on the USA was always a continuing fact in relations.

3. THE OTHER RESULTS OF THE STUDY

It will now be appropriate to answer the questions, which are raised in the Introduction though they are dealt with partially in different parts of the study. It has become clear from the study that a superpower inevitably gets involved in a matter which mainly concerns its small ally if this issue seems to have the potential to affect the alliance established by the superpower and the balance of power in a strategic region. As the leader of the Western camp, which had global interests, the United States got involved in the Cyprus question, which mainly concerned Turkey and Greece, and tried to influence its development to prevent any possible damage to NATO and its interests in the eastern Mediterranean.

Superpowers certainly have the potential to influence decisions and actions of their small allies and even to force them to act in a certain way through threats of punishment. But they are restricted by certain factors such as their own interests while acting in this way. While they tried to prevent a proposed Turkish intervention in Cyprus, the Americans did not want to alienate the Turks totally and lose their alliance, which brought considerable benefits for U.S. interests. Moreover, Turkey was an independent state, which could resist American demands especially on its vital national causes. Turkey's membership of NATO also diminished the possibility of any U.S. armed action against Turkey.

Open threats generally fail to force a small state to act in a certain way because they arouse public emotions. Public consensus on a matter, which touches national feelings, plays a great role in the determination of the small state's government in not yielding to pressures of its big ally. Turkey's adamant position on the Cyprus question and its military intervention in Cyprus could be explained by the tremendous support given by all segments of the Turkish population including the military.

Pressures from a superpower may lead its small ally to seek alternative sources of support for its security and national interests, but the decision of this small ally to change sides or to opt for neutrality depends on its military and economic capabilities and the character of the international system. The small state may improve its relations with members of other blocs with the help of détente, but it does not enter into defense contacts with these states if it does not want to lose its existing alliance. Turkish authorities had economic and cultural contacts with the Eastern bloc and the Third World and supported some of their causes in international forms, but they did not buy a single weapon from these states in order not to loosen their defense cooperation with the West. In their eyes, the Western alliance provided the vital guarantee for Turkey's security.

Having alliance relations with a superpower may always bring difficulties for a small state. It may attract the threat of another superpower and may cause the involvement of the small state in superpower conflicts. The big ally's interference in internal affairs and its influence on domestic and foreign policy decisions are also possibilities. If the small power's elite are not careful in their dealings with the superpower and follow its lead with full trust, dangers for the small state increase. The Cuban crisis demonstrated all these dangers for Turkey, as was explained in Chapter VI. Turkey had to stop its opium production because of its alliance relationship with the USA. This incident also proved that military regimes, which are militarily dependent on a superpower, are more responsive to demands of the superpower.

One important conclusion of the study is that internal conditions and public opinion on both sides played an important role in relations between the United States and Turkey. Turkish policies on the opium and Cyprus questions and the U.S. attitude on the opium and arms embargo issues were strongly influenced by internal public opinion. The sensitiveness of Turkish rulers to foreign influence and intervention, their long-pursued aim of integrating Turkey into the Western world, their evaluation of Turkey's strategic importance, their seeing the Cyprus issue as a vital national cause and the continuity of Turkey's traditional foreign policy line, too, had effects on U.S.-Turkish relations. On the American side, anti-communism, the world leadership concept, realism during the Nixon administration, the Vietnam issue, the president's wide powers in formulating foreign policy, and the Congress's actions to curb the presidential power and to have a voice in foreign policy decisions were general elements of U.S. foreign policy which also had repercussions on the U.S.-Turkish alliance.

Chapter IV showed that the following factors played role in Turkish actions in the military field, which appeared as anti-American: intensive public criticism of Turkey's military relations with the USA, misconduct in signing of bilateral military agreements, untidiness of these agreements, U.S. personnel's actions antagonizing the Turkish public, and the humiliation of Turkey by U-2 flights which took place without its knowledge. The Turks succeeded in banning U-2 flights, rearranging bilateral agreements under a new general treaty, in changing the duty status formula and in not allowing the use of the İncirlik base by the Americans for their operations in the Middle East. However, other facts show that these Turkish actions were not so successful as they appeared. Turkish withdrawal from the MLF would not achieve a radical result because most NATO members were opposed to it. The use of the İncirlik base for Middle East operations was not required by the NATO alliance. In the duty status issue, the Americans kept their right to have the last word. Turkey had to accept NATO's flexible response strategy though it did not like it entirely. Its efforts to gain a voice in the control of nuclear weapons on its territory did not bring any positive result. Bilateral agreements with the USA remained secret and the public did not know their contents. The amount and allocation of U.S. military aid, too, did not make the Turks happy. Chapter IV also showed that considerable U.S. economic and military assistance to Turkey and Turkey's importance for U.S. strategic interests constituted the most important factor in the continuity of the two states' alliance.

Chapter VI has demonstrated that the stationing of the Jupiter missiles on Turkish territory inspired the Soviet decision to deploy nuclear missiles to Cuba and made Turkey a part of the Cuban crisis. The chapter has also showed that a trade off between Turkish and Cuban missiles was considered by U.S. officials and that the Americans at the end made a secret deal with the Russians in this direction. Another result was that because of its alliance relations with America Turkey came close to being one of first targets of a nuclear war which could have broken out between the United States and the Soviet Union.

Some conclusions of the chapters on the Cyprus question may be summarized as follows: the United States reluctantly became involved in the matter and reluctantly supported the scheme to station NATO soldiers in Cyprus. U.S. officials believed that unification of Cyprus with Greece (enosis) or enosis with some concessions to Turkey would be the best solution of the Cyprus problem and worked for such schemes. While threatening to intervene in Cyprus militarily, Turkish rulers, especially Prime Minister İnönü, were not altogether determined to initiate such an action because of unpreparedness of the Turkish army. In any case, in 1964, American authorities were determined to stop a Turkish intervention in Cyprus. In the same period, Turkish authorities' hints on making changes in Turkey's traditional Western-oriented foreign policy were not genuine, but were aimed at showing their disappointment over the Western attitude toward the Cyprus question.

During the Cyprus crisis of November 1967, U.S. rulers did not show the same harsh attitude toward Turkish intervention threats, but seemed to give more support to the Turkish position by working for the acceptance of Turkish demands. U.S. officials ignored assassination and coup attempts against Greek Cypriot President Makarios between 1967 and 1974, but failed to predict the Cyprus coup on 15 July 1974. The U.S. attitude after the coup showed that it was willing to accept the new situation and this forced and also gave a green light to Turks to intervene in Cyprus. U.S. efforts to stop the Turkish action were not adequate and effective, but the Turks were also unstoppable at that stage. The U.S. attitude after the Turkish intervention tended to accept the new situation. The U.S. arms embargo against Turkey in 1975 was mainly as a result of power competition between the Congress and the administration. But efforts of Greek-American lobbies and the Congress dislike for the Turkish decision to resume poppy production also played a role in the embargo.

Chapter IX has showed that U.S. officials and especially the U.S. Congress used pressure tactics against Turkey on the opium issue and that they were considerably influenced in their efforts by the desire to placate American voters. Before 1971, Turkish rulers were willing to comply with U.S. demands on the matter, but they did not prohibit opium production in order not to lose their thin majority in the parliament. The chapter has also proved that the Turkish government's opium ban decision, which was reached as a result of negotiations with the Americans to please them, was not an adequate arrangement to provide a permanent solution to the problem and that both the United States and Turkey made mistakes in its implementation. It further became clear from the chapter that public emotions considerably motivated the Turkish decision to resume poppy production and the reaction of the U.S. Congress to it. Finally, the chapter showed that, contrary to U.S. predictions, the Turkish control over opium production proved a success.

4. THE PRESENT SITUATION OF TURKISH-AMERICAN RELATIONS

a) The U.S. Approach to Turkey

American authorities consider Turkey as "an influential and active pivotal state because of its strategic location, its physical size and large population, its economic potential and its capacity to affect regional and international stability."[3] In fact, there are few countries, which the Americans hold in higher regard than they do Turkey. The present Bush administration has considerable number of "senior officials intimately familiar with and sympathetic to Turkey and strongly supportive of US-Turkish relations."[4] The post-Cold War period has witnessed an extraordinary increase in Turkey's importance in the eyes of American politicians and strategists.

Turkey is now at the center of a new phenomenon, which has important meanings for the United States: the emergence of new security areas or new alliances in critical regions.[5] Apart from receiving Turkey's co-operation in protecting American interests in these regions, the American administration also needs the Turkish help in continuing and diversifying the functions of NATO for the sake of the American global hegemony. The expansion of NATO's functions with interventions in regions outside the NATO area necessitates obtaining the support of Turkey, which is located in the central place of geo-strategic knots and which has a large and effective army to provide for US interventions.[6] Turkey's role in NATO, its growing potential in regional cooperation movements and its approach of coalition (acting together with Western countries) in critical regions such as the Balkans affect inevitably the security and political perceptions of American leaders.

The United States also needs Turkey in order to be able to establish its control over the strategic Eurasian region and to counter the Russian power, which may extend its domination to the former Soviet territory and may gain control huge energy resources. Turkey is a unique partner for the USA in relation to developments concerning the future of Europe, the Middle East and Eurasia. American rulers also hold Turkey' value highly for the success of the Middle Eastern peace process. The Turkish cooperation with and support for Israel, America's crucial ally in the region, is indispensable from the American point of view. Moreover, the use of Turkish bases by American forces in operations and interventions in the

---

[3] Gareth M. Winrow, *Turkey and the Caucasus: Domestic Interests and Security Concerns,* London: the Royal Institute of International Affairs, 2000, p. 2.

[4] Alan Makovsky, "Turkey's Unfinished Role in the War on Terrorism", *Insight Turkey,* vol. 4, No. 1, January-March 2002, p. 43.

[5] Ian O. Lesser, "Değişmekte Olan Bir Türkiye'de Batının Çıkarları" in Zalmay Khalilzad, Ian O. Lesser and F. Stephen Larrabee, *Türk-Batı İlişkilerinin Geleceği: Stratejik Bir Plana Doğru",* translated by Işık Kuşçu, Ankara: ASAM, 2001, p. 59.

[6] Baskın Oran, "Dönemin Bilançosu (1990-2001)" in Baskın Oran (ed.), *Türk Dış Politikası: Kurtuluş Savaşından Bugüne Olgular, Belgeler, Yorumlar,* vol. 2, İstanbul: İletişim, 2001, p. 231.

Middle East has paramount importance for American interests in the region. In this context, Turkey's active support for the American intention of expanding NATO's functions to turn it to a more global organization effective in different parts of the world serve American interests.

The most important issue in the recent history, which dominated and directed Turkish-American relations, was the American determination of overthrowing the Saddam regime in Iraq and the American need for Turkish support and cooperation for this important goal. In the aftermath of the Saddam's overthrow, Turkey will still be crucial to the success of any US strategy on the Iraqi issue from containment to outright invasion.[7] In fact, "vast improvement in US-Turkish relations in recent years is rooted mainly in Turkey's role in containment of Iraq" in addition to American support for Turkey's three main issues (namely opposition to the Kurdish separatist organization, and the support for Turkey's candidacy for EU membership and the Baku-Ceyhan pipeline project).[8] Turkey's strategic importance in the eyes of the Americans is mainly because of its place in America's projects regarding Iraq.

The American approaches to Islamist parties and groups in Turkey also have repercussions for Turkey's domestic and foreign policies. From the late 1980s, there were rumors that Washington was in favor of a moderate Islamic administration in Turkey, which it would be able to control. Some statements by American experts close to the American government to the effect that such concepts and practices as Kemalism and secularism became outdated caused the feeling that Washington was not happy with the existent regime in Turkey. Some movements, which appeared in Turkey at the end of the 1980s, such as Neo-Ottomanism and Second Republicanism further strengthened these doubts. In the 1990s, the United States approached to the rise of Islamic groups in Turkish politics by choosing to have contacts with them and to treat this development as an issue of human rights. Although the Americans had reasons for not being happy with the Refah-Yol coalition government of Turkey in 1996-1997, whose bigger partner was the Islamist Refah Party, they expressed their opposition to the overthrow of this government through a military coup.[9] American officials also did not approve officially the dissolution of the Refah Party and its successor, the Fazilet Party, by the Turkish Constitutional Court.

The bomb attacks against the United States on 11 September 2001, which have been attributed to Islamic radicals, have created a new stimulus for the American authorities in their approaches to Islamic movements. Now, Washington is more intolerant toward Islamic groups as proved by the treatment of suspected Muslim people in the United States, going beyond practices of human rights. Nevertheless, the American administration needs to make a distinction between the radical groups adopting terrorist tactics and ordinary Muslim people, who have no serious problems with the West apart from being angry about their treatment by this world. Failing in this will bring America face to face with the whole Muslim world, which will not be in conformity with the American interests and which will impair the protection of American internal and external security. Being aware of this fact, the American administration has constantly declared that their war is not against the Muslims, but it is

---

[7] Mark Parris, "Ecevit to Washington: Opportunities for US-Turkish Relations", *Policywatch*, No. 592, 10 January 2002, http//.www.washingtoninstitute.org/watch/Policywatch/policywatch2002/592.htm.

[8] Alan Makovsky, "Turkey: the Armenian Genocide Resolution and Iraq Policy", *Policywatch*, No. 495, 16 October 2000, http//.www.washingtoninstitute.org/watch/Policywatch/policywatch2000/495.htm.

[9] İlhan Uzgel, "ABD ve NATO'yla İlişkiler (1999-2001)" in Oran (ed.), *Türk Dış Politikası*, pp. 303-304.

directed to the terrorists as it has been proved by the American war against the Taliban regime in Afghanistan.

The finalization of American policies in this issue is particularly important for Turkey's domestic and foreign policies. Islamic-oriented political circles, which have gained wide popular support, have come to power in Turkey. These circles declare that they will not pursue Islamist policies and will have normal, friendly relations with the West. If they are sincere and if they succeed in proving that liberal democracy can be reconciled with Islam and its values, this can be a unique model for other Muslim countries from the American point of view, constituting a cure to many of its problems and fears.[10] The American support for such a regime will bring about a new kind of relationship between Turkey and the USA, constituting a sharp contrast to the American approach to the Iranian regime. On the other hand, the failure of the Turks in this process or the American negative approach to it will cause great difficulties and instabilities in Turkey's domestic and foreign relations, bringing the tensions of the past back.

The United State gives precious support to Turkey in many crucial issues, constituting a constant backing for Turkish foreign policies, but it also creates difficulties for Turkish interests. Washington continues to support the Baku-Ceyhan pipeline project, which has vital importance for Turkey, provides valuable help in the process of Turkey's accession to the EU and appreciates Turkey's concerns on developments regarding the European security and defense initiatives, especially the ESDI. The American administration also sees its partnership with Turkey as a special one, constantly increasing its level. It has announced that the strategic cooperation between the two countries has become a reinforced partnership. Moreover, American officials have always seemed to demonstrate more understanding than the Europeans do on the realities of the Turkish domestic political system and Turkey's special internal and external security concerns. Washington has not pressurized Ankara on issues of human rights as much as the Europeans have done. It has offered Turkish officials a full cooperation in the removal of the influence of the separatist PKK. The Americans also supplied crucial military equipment such as the Cobra helicopters vital for the struggle against terrorists. They persuaded Syria in terminating its support to terrorists in the process, which resulted in the ousting of PKK leader Öcalan from Syria. The American role in capturing and bringing Öcalan to Turkey, too, was precious for Turkey.

However, Turkey is not so comfortable in its relationship with the USA. Turkey's heavy dependence on America in the fields of economy and security restrict its policy options and foreign policy initiatives. Turkey always has to take it seriously requests coming from Washington. It cannot easily reject American demands and cannot defy Washington especially in matters concerning American interests seriously. The situation of the Turkish economy, whose future is heavily determined by the IMF policies under the US control, is one of the most sensitive weaknesses of Turkey's domestic and foreign policies. The fact that Turkey's diplomatic efforts with the United States in recent times have focused almost exclusively on financial support underlines this weakness.

Moreover, the American constant pressures on the Cyprus question, one of the most important national causes of Turkish foreign policy, too, constitute irritating headaches for Turkish policy makers. The American firm commitment to finding a solution to the Cyprus

---

[10] Micheal Reynolds, "Demokrasinin Türkiye Sınavı", *Radikal*, 4 September 2002 (the translation of the article appeared in *Los Angeles Times*).

problem has not lost any momentum in the wake of the 11 September attacks against the USA. Washington also has not demonstrated any firm opposition to the Cypriot accession to the EU,[11] which is likely to bring great instabilities and conflicts in the Mediterranean. In addition, there is a possibility that the United States may take Turkey away from Europe, by enforcing Ankara to choose one of the two camps as its main ally. It is reported that some influential American policy analysts have advised the Turks to forget about Europe.[12] Finally, as it has been admitted by American strategists, there has always been a great gap between the rhetoric of Washington emphasizing strategic importance of Turkey and the actual situation of bilateral relations between the two countries. Close, intimate and intensive relations between the United States and some countries have not been observed between Turkey and the United States.

b) The Turkish Approach to the USA

The way of Turkish authorities' perceiving American policies, strategic evaluations and the cooperation offered by the USA, have, of course, important influences on Turkish foreign-policy making and on determination of foreign policy priorities of Turkey. Turkish rulers are aware that they need to obtain the American cooperation in promoting Turkey's interests and in protecting Turkish security against internal and external threats. For example, Turkey cannot deal with the threat of proliferation of weapons of mass destruction and ballistic missiles in its surrounding region on its own without the help of a powerful global actor such as the USA. Moreover, Turkey needs to have a strong cooperation with the United States in the security area since its place in the new European security arrangements have not been secured. It is also a necessity for Turkey to join American defense systems and to have a close contact with the American military to obtain sufficient support for its comprehensive defense and military modernization projects.[13]

It is an undeniable fact that Turkey has close diplomatic and security ties with the United States and this fact constitutes a restrictive factor in Turkish foreign and security policies. "Turkey probably cannot take any action severely damaging to US interests without harming its own interests."[14] It will take a great care not to disappoint the American administration in critical regions concerning American interests closely. Another cost of close relationship with Washington for Turkey is to be compelled to show more tolerance toward the use of Turkish bases by American forces, which sometimes create difficulties. In order to ensure the continuity of the US support for Turkish interests, Turkish rulers also feel it necessary to give widespread support to American initiatives and actions in the international arena. For example, they supported the American attempts of expanding NATO's functions and activity area and joined NATO's out-of-area operations launched by the initiative of the Americans though they had deep doubts about them in the context of Turkish interests. Moreover, Ankara gave the impression that it favored the American Strategic Defence Initiative project

---

[11] Makovsky, "Turkey's Unfinished Role in the War on Terrorism", p. 43.
[12] Helena Kane Finn, "Turkish Political Disarray: Why Now? What Next?", *Policywatch*, No. 633, 10 July 2002, http//.www.washingtoninstitute.org/watch/Policywatch/policywatch2002/633.htm.
[13] Lesser, "Değişmekte Olan Bir Türkiye'de Batının Çıkarları", pp. 77-78.
[14] Makovsky, "Turkey: the Armenian Genocide Resolution and Iraq Policy".

while Russia and China strongly opposed it and the other NATO members showed reluctance in supporting the Americans.

In this point, Oran's warnings may be considered as relevant. For the moment, Turkish foreign policy seems successful since it participates in initiatives and operations along with the United States. However, the USA is a superpower, trying to establish a law of intervention throughout the world to continue its hegemony whereas Turkey is a medium power, whose policies are based on being pro-status quo and on playing global powers against each other. If NATO's series of institutionalized interventions for humanly purposes become a model, Turkey cannot distance itself from such operations (even if it desires to do so) and faces the position of indexing its foreign and security policies to those of the United States. This also brings about the possibility of becoming a puppet (client state) of global powers. Given the extraordinary dependence of the Turkish economy on foreign powers, Turkey may face a deadlock and a dead-end in its foreign policy and may be forced to take actions, which it will never want to take.[15] America's apparent benign neglect vis-à-vis a more active role of the Europeans in security and defense issues, including within NATO, gives signal that Turkey may be isolated even in defense issues. Therefore, Turkey needs to conduct its relations with the United States in the multilateral basis and in accordance with mutual respect and protection of mutual interests. In this sense, the establishment of the US-Turkey Economic Partnership Council, which is "charged with seeking ways to bring US-Turkish economic ties to the same level as the two nations' close strategic partnership,"[16] during Turkish Prime Minister Ecevit's visit to Washington in mid-January 2002 is a good start.

c) The Iraqi Problem

After the Gulf War, Turkey allowed the United States to use the bases in the Turkish territory for non-NATO purposes under the Provide Comfort I and II operations, which ended the Iraqi rule in the northern Iraq and thus divided the country. Turkey's co-operation at the beginning was resulted from the necessity rather than Turkey's choice. It became later apparent that Turkish interests were greatly harmed in this process. Turkish officials feared that Iraq's disintegration and the emergence of a de facto Kurdish state in the northern Iraq might harm the stability of the region and the boundaries of the regional states and it might have a domino effect on Turkey's territorial integrity.[17] Moreover, Turkey lost billions of dollars from trade with Iraq, and tourism and war-related expenditures as a result of the economic sanctions applied against Iraq.[18] The United States worked to raise international support to compensate Turkey for the economic costs of the Gulf War. The UN Security Council resolution 986 provided Iraq with the limited opportunity to export oil the Kirkuk-

---

[15] Oran, "Dönemin Bilançosu (1990-2001)", p. 242.

[16] Makovsky, "Turkey's Unfinished Role in the War on Terrorism", p. 43.

[17] Mahmut Bali Aykan, "Turkish Perspectives on Turkish-US Relations Concerning Persian Gulf Security in the Post-Cold War Era: 1989-1995", *Middle East Journal*, vol. 50, No. 3, Summer 1996, p. 353.

[18] Duygu B. Sezer, "Turkey's New Security Environment, Nuclear Weapons and Proliferation", *Comparative Strategy*, vol. 14, No. 2, 1995, p. 162.

Yumurtalık pipeline. However, Turkish rulers stated that these limited relieves were too minor to compensate Turkey's losses.[19]

Meanwhile, the deepening of the insurgency in the south-east of Turkey as a result of the Gulf Crisis, compelled Turkey to launch military operations in the Iraqi territory and to appropriate more resources to contain terrorist activities. The Turkish operations attracted the harsh reaction of the regional states and the European powers and caused the accusations on the alleged Turkish intention of controlling the oil-rich Iraqi provinces of Mosul and Kirkuk. The interventions were dragging Turkey into the Iraqi quagmire and unresolved conflicts of the region, which was totally against the traditional Turkish policy of keeping itself distant from Middle Eastern politics and were attracting the enmity of regional powers such as Iraq, Iran and Syria.[20]

Recently, Turkey joined the parade of states flying aircraft into Baghdad on humanitarian missions accompanied by businessmen hungry for bilateral trade.[21] Turkish Foreign Minister Cem suggested in April 2001 that sanctions against Iraq should be eased to accommodate the needs of the Iraqi people.[22] Turkey had some reservations about the Operation Northern Watch flights, supervising the safe heaven in Northern Iraq. Turkish authorities were opposed to the US bombardment of Iraq unless the US planes acted in self-defense when they were targeted by Iraqi radar and anti-craft artillery. They also did not feel any urgency about Iraq's capacity of weapons of mass destruction or about the removal of Iraqi leader Saddam and his regime from power. On the contrary, they were wary of the American plans of overthrowing the Saddam regime because they considered these plans as lacking a concise strategy concerning post-Saddam Iraq and they feared that the change of the Iraqi regime could lead to chaos and instabilities in the region together with the disintegration of the Iraq's territorial integrity.[23]

Ankara's fears are mainly focused on the possibility of the emergence of a Kurdish state in northern Iraq with the break-up of Iraq as a result of an US-led war against this country. Even the emergence of a federated Iraq will be a negative development from the Turkish point of view because this will offer the Kurds a robust form of autonomy. Both results (Kurdish state or Kurdish autonomy) will "fan the flames of Kurdish separatism in Turkey itself."[24] The Turkish public, too, has a high degree of skepticism toward the plans in Iraq with its possible negative consequences for Turkey, such as the Turkish involvement in regional chaos and the heavy blow to the Turkish economy. Turkish people and "the inner circles of the Turkish government and military are also worried about the fate of oil-rich

---

[19] Şükrü Gürel, "A General Appraisal of Current Turkish Foreign Policy" in Mustafa Aydın (ed.), *Turkey at the Threshold of the 21st Century*, Ankara: International Relations Foundation, 1998, p. 15, Ian O. Lesser, *Bridge or Barrier: Turkey and the West After the Cold War*, Santa Monica: Rand, 1992, p. 36.

[20] Alain Gresh, "Turkish-Israeli-Syrian Relations and Their Impact on the Middle East", *Middle East Journal*, vol. 52, No. 2, 1998, p. 195, Meltem Müftüler-Bac, "Turkey's Predicament in the Post-cold War Era", *Futures*, vol. 28, No. 3, April 1996, p. 261, Malik Mufti, "Daring and Caution in Turkish Foreign Policy", *Middle East Journal*, vol. 52, No. 1, Winter 1998, p. 39.

[21] Makovsky, "Turkey: the Armenian Genocide Resolution and Iraq Policy".

[22] Cem, İsmail, "Turkey in the Twenty First Century", *Special Policy Forum Report*, No. 529, 3 April 2001, http//.www.washingtoninstitute.org/watch/Policywatch/policywatch2001/529.htm.

[23] Ö. Zeynep Oktav Alantar, "A Thorny Issue Between Turkey and the United States: Northern Iraq (1996-2001)", *Turkish Review of Middle East Studies*, Annual 2001, No. 12, pp. 29, 31-32.

[24] Makovsky, "Turkey's Unfinished Role in the War on Terrorism", p. 45.

Mosul and Kirkuk",[25] which were included in the territorial boundaries of Turkey by the Turkish nationalist movement in the early 1920s.

In order to remove the Turkish doubts, American authorities assure that they support Iraq's territorial integrity and oppose the creation of a Kurdish state. However, they do not seem to oppose the Kurdish autonomy in northern Iraq and they do not insist that the Iraqi government, which will be established after the overthrow of the Saddam regime, should be a strong central one. In this context, it is possible that the US plans on Iraq might go out of control and cause undesired events.[26] Moreover, US initiatives in Iraq might bring about some comprehensive results for Turkey such as Turkish intervention in northern Iraq, the consequent Turkish conflict with Syria and other regional powers and the greater possibility of Turkish cooperation with Israel and Jordan.[27]

However, there were also opinions favoring the Turkish cooperation with the Americans in a military campaign against Iraq on the basis of its potential benefits for Turkey. It was asserted that Turkish participation to the operation would increase considerably Turkey's ability to project power as a player in Gulf politics. In this scenario, Turkey's increased presence in Iraq, which would be one of the consequences of the operation, would enable Turkey to play a more influential role in Gulf developments. As a proof of this it was pointed out that "Turkey's relations with the Kurdish Regional Government in northern Iraq have brought Turkey's geopolitical security perimeter some 200-250 kilometers southward."[28] Some asserted that "refusal to support the US effort would be out of character for Turkey, which has long been a loyal US ally and for years has fashioned itself as strategic partner of the US." In the opinion of Makovsky, the Turkish failure to support the American initiative would impair Turkey's bilateral ties with the USA, which were a crucial source of international political and economic support for Ankara, and would undermine Turkey's ability to influence the course of events in post-Saddam Iraq. Makovsky also stated: "Turkey's hopes to limit the degree of Kurdish autonomy, to restrict the PKK's ability to use northern Iraq, and to assure influence for the Turcomans... will largely depend on its influence with the United States. Turkey may also seek to create a buffer zone on the Iraqi side of the border... Here, the US understanding will be important."[29]

Indeed, the American war against Iraq in March-April 2003 became a great test for Turkish-American relations. The Turkish government seemed to support the American demands from Turkey on war, especially the American request of transferring the American troops to Iraq through the Turkish territory, but the Turkish Parliament rejected the government's request in this issue with a thin margin. This was an unexpected development creating a deep crisis in Turkish-American relations. Nevertheless, both sides state that this dark period has been left behind and that they look at the future cooperation as close allies, which have stayed loyal to each other in a considerably long period though they sometimes faced great hardships and difficulties.

---

[25] Finn, "Turkish Political Disarray: Why Now? What Next?".

[26] Makovsky, "Turkey's Unfinished Role in the War on Terrorism", pp. 45-46.

[27] Mufti, Malik, "Turkish-Syrian Rapprochement: Causes and Consequences", *Policywatch*, No. 630, 21 June 2002, http//.www.washingtoninstitute.org/watch/Policywatch/policywatch2002/630.htm.

[28] Robert Olson, "Turkey-Iran Relations, 2000-2001: The Caspian, Azerbaijan and the Kurds", *Middle East Policy*, vol. 9, No. 2, June 2002, pp. 111, 116.

[29] Makovsky, "Turkey's Unfinished Role in the War on Terrorism", p. 47.

d) The Impact of the September 11 Attacks

Turkey's reaction to the September 11 attacks on the United States was important because the attacks were made on its closest ally, on which most of its foreign policy was based, and because its reaction would have great impact on Turkey's place in the new world order. The first reaction of Turkey to the attacks was one of a strong condemnation. "As a country, which has suffered for long from terrorism..., Turkey has condemned in the strongest terms the culprits and instigators of those attacks and called for intensified international cooperation for the prevention of this scourge."[30] Turkey expressed its unequivocal solidarity with the United States and became an early and firm advocate of invoking Article V at NATO to perform retaliation. The Turkish Parliament quickly passed a resolution authorizing the government to deploy troops abroad and to station additional foreign troops on Turkish soil. Then, Turkey's contribution to Operation Enduring Freedom (OEF) launched against Afghanistan became a significant one. Turkey opened its airspace to US military transport aircraft participating in the operation and "offered the OEF aircraft use of İncirlik, Yenişehir and Afyon air bases; blanket over-flight and landing clearance; and blanket permission to refuel in Turkish airspace. Turkey also facilitated US use of Turkish ports and highways for transport and provided US troops with intelligence support."[31] In the aftermath of the operation, Turkey offered the peacekeeping mission in Afghanistan its troops, accepted to train Afghan police and military and even undertook the leadership of the International Security Assistance Force (ISAF) in Afghanistan.

The view of Turkish authorities were that the Western powers came to recognize the gravity of a problem, which Turkey had been emphasizing for decades, only through the September 11 attacks against the USA. Taking this opportunity, Turkey consistently suggested that terrorism should be accepted as a new threat to the NATO Alliance within the new strategic concept.[32] By benefiting from its European and Islamic identities, Turkey also hosted a historic meeting, which was held in Istanbul on 13 February 2002 and which was attended by foreign ministers of the countries that are members of the EU and the Organization of Islamic Conference to discuss the impact of September 11 on their relations.[33] Turkey's leading role in this meeting was welcomed both by European and Islamic leaders and scholars. Turkey found opportunity in this meeting and other forums to emphasize the gravity of the problem of terrorism, which brought for its security and foreign policy great difficulties in the form of loss of material resources, human life and diplomatic prestige.

Meanwhile, Turkish authorities hoped to obtain important gains from the September 11 attacks by increasing Turkey's strategic importance in the Western eyes. Particularly, they wanted to create a larger strategic role for Turkish foreign policy in the energy corridors of Central Asia and the Caucasus. In fact, as hoped by Turkish rulers, the September 11 events brought about even closer relations with the United States. By the end of 2001, Turkey had assumed a stronger position in developments concerning oil and gas pipelines, the Caspian

---

[30] "Measures Taken by the Republic of Turkey Against Terrorism", Report to the Security Council Committee established pursuant to resolution 1373, December 2001, http://www.mfa. gov.tr/grupa/ac/acf/terrorism.

[31] Makovsky, "Turkey's Unfinished Role in the War on Terrorism", p. 42.

[32] "Measures Taken by the Republic of Turkey Against Terrorism".

[33] Hasan Kösebalan, "Turkey's EU Membership: A Clash of Security Cultures", *Middle East Policy,* vol. 9, No. 2, June 2002, p. 144.

Sea resources, the problems of Azerbaijan and the Kurdish question. It seemed likely that Turkey's influence in the region would increase as a result of America's war against terrorism.

It can be asserted now that Turkey is clearly among the winners of the US-led war against terrorism. "With its focus on Central Asia and the Middle East, the war has enhanced US appreciation for Turkey's strategic importance and for its standing as a secular, democratic state." The two prominent and chronic problems of Turkish foreign policy (namely terrorism and Islamic extremism) have now been considered as number one threats by the most powerful state of the world. By sharing the same concerns with the Americans, Turkish authorities are able to act more comfortably in international forums while defending their causes. They have been extremely happy about "the fact that NATO's first-ever invocation of Article V was for the purpose of an out-of-area action against the twin fundamentalist-terrorist scourge. It marked an important precept to which Turkey itself could some day appeal."[34]

As hoped by Turkish authorities, Turkey's importance has been increased for the Western countries, especially for the United States. The September 11 events and their aftermath have validated Turkey's importance to Washington and have underlined that Turkey remains on the frontlines of the war on terrorism. For American policy-makers, Turkey is a perfect ally for their war on terrorism, both strategically and politically. Among the NATO allies, Turkey is the closest country to trouble points, considered as the originator of terrorism. Moreover, Turkey's Muslim identity provides a great contribution to Washington's war. The early Turkish announcements of support for the American cause prevented the portrayal of the American response to September 11 as a clash between Islam and Christian West and provided cover for other Muslim states to support US efforts.[35] Turkey's role as a coalition partner, having a Muslim majority, has provided a living proof of American President Bush's claim that the war against terrorism is not a war against Muslims or Islam. In the new period, the United States can present Turkey as a model for the people in the Muslim World, who have aspirations for democratic progress and prosperity, and as an example of the reconciliation of religious belief with modern secular democratic institutions.[36] A successful, modern Turkey illustrates that there is no intrinsic contradiction between Islam and Western values including democracy and secularism.

In the period of suitable atmosphere in Turkish-American relations created by the September 11 events, Turkish Prime Minister Ecevit's visit to Washington in January 2002 would be a test for bilateral cooperation in the future. During the visit, Ecevit did not win concessions on textile and steel, but the creation of the Economic Partnership Commission scheduled to meet in February was "an important step in establishing a forum for the development of more specific plans to enhance the trade relationship." Ecevit obtained assurances to the effect that Turkey would be consulted closely in any American initiative regarding the Iraqi issue and that Turkey's primary concern – the preservation of Iraqi

---

[34] Makovsky, "Turkey's Unfinished Role in the War on Terrorism", p. 41.
[35] Parris, "Ecevit to Washington..."
[36] "Remarks by Deputy Secretary of Defence Paul Wolfowitz," the Washington Institute for Near East Policy, St. Regis Hotel, Washington D.C., March 13, 2002, http://www.defenselink.mil/speeches/2002/s20020313-depsecdef.html

territorial integrity – was shared by the United States.[37] In the Commission's first meeting, American Under-secretary of State Alan Larson brought to Turkey the message that the United States saw the US-Turkish relationship as one of economic partners. Meanwhile, President Bush largely excluded Turkey's steel imports from higher duties.[38] American authorities also decided to boost their support for the troubled Turkish economy in return for the steadfast Turkish support for the American war on terrorism. As Operation Endure Freedom reminded that Turkey was too strategically important to be allowed to fail economically and politically, the Americans favored in injecting new life into Turkey's economy, which was in deep chaos. Consequently, the American administration backed a significant IMF bailout package for Turkey.

5. THE LAST WORD

Turkey goes through the process of participating in the new world system as a more active world power with its repercussions on its relations with the USA. It deeply needs the American guarantee for its security because it feels surrounded by more threats. The US insistence on maintaining NATO as the main security organ of the West fits Turkish interests given negative attitude of the Europeans in accepting Turkey to the European security structures. The USA might provide a precious help for Turkey's candidacy for both the EU and its defense aspect. Turkey expects more pro-Turkish policies from the USA on NATO's security guarantee, the Iraqi and Kurdish questions, the Russian expansion and Turkish-Greek problems. Turkey's strategic importance, Turkish-Israeli relations, and cooperation in the transportation of the Central Asian oil and in shaping regional developments are strong points of the Turkish-American relationship.

The possibility of a radical change in Turkish domestic politics and Turkey's departing from its traditional foreign policy line with its bold actions outside the Western alliance worry the Americans. Turkey's problems in getting American military assistance and equipment, the Congress' seemingly anti-Turkish actions and America's frequent interventions in the Middle East might hurt the cooperation between the two states. Turkey's recent expanding strategic partnership with the USA needs to be balanced with a cautious attitude given the Turkish-American disagreements in the 1960s and the 1970s. For America, Turkey is an indispensable country which has contributed to its security, political and economic stability by remaining faithful to its responsibilities toward the Western alliance. For Turkey, the United States is the most suitable partner, which can provide help in facing new threats and in benefiting from new opportunities. But being strategic partners and making strategic cooperation do not mean that Turkey and the United States will have the same views in every matter in a wide region stretching from the Aegean to the Gulf region.

---

[37] Helena Kane Finn, "After the Ecevit Visit: Can Turks Pull Together to Complete the Necessary Reforms", *Policywatch*, No. 597, 24 January 2002.

[38] "Remarks by Deputy Secretary of Defence Paul Wolfowitz".

APPENDICES

APPENDIX A. AID TO TURKEY AGREEMENT, JULY 12, 1947

Agreement between the United States of America and Turkey (signed at Ankara July 12, 1947; entered into force July 12, 1947)[1]

The Government of Turkey having requested the Government of the United States for assistance which will enable Turkey to strengthen the security forces which Turkey requires for the protection of her freedom and independence and at the same time to continue to maintain the stability of her economy; and

The Congress of the United States, in the Act approved May 22, 1947, having authorized the President of the United States to furnish such assistance to Turkey, on terms consonant wiith the sovereign independenc and security of the two countries; and

The Government of the United States and the Government of Turkey believing that the furnishing of such assistance will help to achieve the basic objectives of the Charter of the United Nations and by inaugurating an auspicious chapter in their relations will further strengthen the ties of friendship between the American and Turkish peoples;

The undersigned, being duly authorized by their respective governments for that purpose, have agreed as follows:

Article I

The Government of the United States will furnish the Government of Turkey such assistance as the President of the United States may authorize to be provided in accordance with the Act of Congress approved May 22, 1947, and any acts amendatory or supplementary thereto. The Government of Turkey will make effective use of any such assistance in accordance with the provisions of this agreement.

Article II

The Chief of Mission to Turkey designated by the President of the United States for the purpose will represent the Government of the United States on matters relating to the assistance furnished under this agreement. The Chief of Mission will determine, in consultation with representatives of the Government of Turkey, the terms and conditions upon which specified assistance shall from time to time be furnished under this agreement, except that the financial terms upon which specified assistance shall be furnished shall be determined from time to time in advance by agreement of the two governments. The Chief of Mission will furnish the Government of Turkey such information and technical assistance as may be appropriate to help in achieving the objectives of the assistance furnished under this agreement.

The Government of Turkey will make use of the assistance furnished for the purposes for which it has been accorded. In order to permit the Chief of Mission to fulfil freely his functions in the exercise of his responsibilities, it will furnish him as well as his representatives every facility and every assistance which he may request in the way of reports, information and observation concerning the utilization and progress of assistance furnished.

---

[1] George S. Harris, *Troubled Alliance*, Washington: American Enterprise Institute, 1972, pp. 213-215, *Richard C. Campany, Turkey and the United States*, New York: Praeger, 1986, pp. 96-99.

Article III

The Government of Turkey and the Government of the United States will cooperate in assuring the peoples of the United States and Turkey full information concerning the assistance furnished pursuant to this agreement. To this end, in so far as may be consistent with the security of the two countries:

1. Representatives of the Press and Radio of the United States will be permitted to observe freely and to report fully regarding the utilisation of such assistance; and
2. The Government of Turkey will give full and continuous publicity within Turkey as to the purpose, source, character, scope, amounts, and progress of such assistance.

Article IV

Determined and equally interested to assure the security of any article, service, or information received by the Government of Turkey pursuant to this agreement, the Governments of the United States and Turkey will respectively take after consultation, such measures as the other government may judge necessary for this purpose. The Government of Turkey will not transfer, without the consent of the Government of the United States, title to or possession of any such article or information nor permit, without such consent, the use of any such article or the use or disclosure of any such information by or to anyone not an officer, employee, or agent of the Government of Turkey or for any purpose other than that for which the article or information is furnished.

Article V

The Government of Turkey will not use anny part of the proceeds of an loan, credit, grant, or other form of aid rendered pursuant to this agreement for the making of any payment on account of the principal or interest on any loan made to it by any other foreign government.

Article VI

Any or all assistance authorised to be provided pursuant to this agreement will be withdrawn:

1. If requested by the Government of Turkey;
2. If the Security Council of the United Nations finds (with respect to which finding the United States waives the exercise of any veto) or the General Assembly of the United Nations finds that action taken or assistance furnished by the United Nations makes the continuance of assistance by the Government of the United States pursuant to this agreement unnecessary or undesirable; and
3. Under any of the other circumstances specified in section 5 of the aforesaid Act of Congress or if the President of the United States determines that such withdrawal is in the interest of the United States.

Article VII

This agreement shall take effect as from this day's date. It shall continue in force until a date to be agreed upon by the two governments.

Article VIII

This agreement shall be registered with the United Nations.

Done in duplicate, in the English and Turkish languages, at Ankara, this 12th day of July, 1947.

Edwin C. Wilson for the Government of the United States

Hasan Saka for the Government of the Republic of Turkey

APPENDIX B. CORRESPONDENCE BETWEEN U.S. PRESIDENT JOHNSON AND TURKISH PRIME MINISTER İNÖNÜ, JUNE 1964

LETTER FROM PRESIDENT JOHNSON TO TURKISH PRIME MINISTER İNÖNÜ JUNE 5, 1964[2]

Dear Mr. Prime Minister,

I am gravely concerned by the information which I have had through Ambassador Hare from you and your Foreign Minister that the Turkish Government is contemplating a decision to intervene by military force to occupy a portion of Cyprus. I wish to emphasize, in the fullest friendship and frankness, that I do not consider that such a course of action by Turkey, fraught with such far reaching consequences, is consistent with the commitment of your government to consult fully in advance with us. Ambassador Hare has indicated that you postponed your decision for a few hours in order to obtain my views. I put to you personally whether you really believe that it is appropriate for your government, in effect, to present an ultimatum to an ally who has demonstrated such staunch support over the years as has the United States for Turkey. I must, therefore, first urge you to accept the responsibility for complete consultation with the United States before any such action is taken.

It is my impression that you believe that such intervention by Turkey is permissible under the provisions of the Treaty of Guarantee of 1960. I must call your attention, however, to our understanding that the proposed intervention by Turkey would be for the purpose of effecting a form of partition of the Island, a solution which is specifically excluded by the Treaty of Guarantee. Further, that treaty requires consultation among the Guarantor Powers. It is the view of the United States that the possibilities of such consultation have by no means been exhausted in this situation and that, therefore, the reservation of the right to take unilateral action is not yet applicable.

I must call to your attention also, Mr. Prime Minister, the obligations of NATO. There can be no question in your mind that a Turkish intervention in Cyprus would lead to a military engagement between Turkish and Greek forces. Secretary of State Rusk declared at a recent meeting of the ministerial council of NATO in The Hague that war between Turkey and Greece must be considered as "literally unthinkable." Adhesion to NATO, in its very essence, means that NATO countries will not wage war on each other. Germany and France have buried centuries of animosity and hostility in becoming NATO allies; nothing less can be expected from Greece and Turkey. Furthermore, a military intervention in Cyprus by Turkey could lead to a direct involvement by the Soviet Union. I hope you will understand that your NATO allies have not had a chance to consider whether they have an obligation to protect Turkey against the Soviet Union if Turkey takes a step which results in Soviet intervention without the full consent and understanding of its NATO allies.

Further, Mr. Prime Minister, I am concerned about the obligations of Turkey as a member of the United Nations. The United Nations has provided forces on the island to keep the peace. Their task has been difficult but, during the past several weeks, they have been progressively successful in reducing the incidents of violence on that island. The United Nations Mediator has not yet completed his work. I have no doubt that the general

---

[2] *The Middle East Journal*, vol. 20, Summer 1966, pp. 386-388, Monteagle Stearns, *Entangled Allies*, New York: Council on Foreign Relations Press, 1992, pp. 156-159.

membership of the United Nations would react in the strongest terms to unilateral action by Turkey which would defy the efforts of the United Nations and destroy any prospect that the United Nations could assist in obtaining a reasonable and peaceful settlement of this difficult problem.

I wish also, Mr. Prime Minister, to call your attention to the bilateral agreement between the United States and Turkey in the field of military assistance. Under Article IV of the agreement with Turkey of July 1947, your Government is required to obtain United States consent for the use of military assistance for purposes other than those for which such assistance was furnished. Your Government has on several occasions acknowledged to the United States that you fully understand this condition. I must tell you in all candor that the United States cannot agree to the use of any United States supplied military equipment for a Turkish intervention in Cyprus under present circumstances.

Moving to the practical results of the contemplated Turkish move, I feel obligated to call to your attention in the most friendly fashion the fact that such a Turkish move could lead to the slaughter of tens of thousands of Turkish Cypriots on the Island of Cyprus. Such an action on your part would unleash the furies and there is no way by which military action on your part could be sufficiently effective to prevent wholesale destruction of many of those whom you are trying to protect. The presence of United Nations forces could not prevent such a catastrophe.

You may consider that what I have said is much too severe and that we are disregardful of Turkish interests in the Cyprus situation. I should like to assure you that this is not the case. We have exerted ourselves both publicly and privately to assure the safety of Turkish Cypriots and to insist that a final solution of the Cyprus problem should rest upon the consent of the parties most directly concerned. It is possible that you feel in Ankara that the United States has not been sufficiently active in your behalf. But surely you know that our policy has caused the liveliest resentment in Athens (where demonstrations have been aimed against us) and has led to a basic alienation between the United States and Archbishop Makarios. As I said to your Foreign Minister in our conversation just a few weeks ago, we value very highly our relations with Turkey. We have considered you as a great ally with fundamental common interests. Your security and prosperity have been a deep concern of the American people and we have expressed that concern in the most practical terms. You and we have fought together to resist the ambitions of the communist world revolution. This solidarity has meant a great deal to us and I would hope that it means a great deal to your government and to your people. We have no intention of lending any support to any solution of Cyprus which endangers the Turkish Cypriot community. We have not been able to find a final solution because this is, admittedly, one of the most complex problems on earth. But I wish to assure you that we have been deeply concerned about the interests of Turkey and of the Turkish Cypriots and will remain so.

Finally, Mr. Prime Minister, I must tell you that you have posed the gravest issues of war and peace. These are issues which go far beyond the bilateral relations between Turkey and the United States. They not only will certainly involve war between Turkey and Greece but could involve wider hostilities because of the unpredictable consequences which a unilateral intervention in Cyprus could produce. You have your responsibilities as chief of the government of Turkey; I also have mine as President of the United States. I must, therefore, inform you in the deepest friendship that unless I can have your assurance that you will not take such action without further and fullest consultation I cannot accept your injunction to

Ambassador Hare of secrecy and must immediately ask for emergency meetings of the NATO Council and of the United Nations Security Council.

I wish it were possible for us to have a personal discussion of this situation. Unfortunately, because of the special circumstances of our present constitutional position, I am not able to leave the United States. If you could come here for a full discussion I would welcome it. I do feel that you and I carry a very heavy responsibility for the general peace and for the possibilities of a sane and peaceful resolution of the Cyprus problem. I ask you, therefore, to delay any decisions which you and your colleagues might have in mind until you and I have had the fullest and frankest consultation.

Sincerely,
LYNDON B. JOHNSON

PRIME MINISTER İNÖNÜ'S LETTER TO PRESIDENT JOHNSON, JUNE 13, 1964[3]

Dear Mr. President,
I have received your message of June 5, 1964 through Ambassador Hare. We have, upon your request, postponed our decision to exercise our right of unilateral action in Cyprus conferred to us by the Treaty of Guarantee. With due regard to the spirit of candour and friendship in which your message is meant to be written, I will, in my reply, try also explain to you in full frankness my views about the situation.

Mr. President,
Your message, both in wording and content, has been disappointing for an ally like Turkey who has always been giving the most serious attention to its relations of alliance with the United States and has brought to the fore substantial divergences of opinion in various fundamental matters pertaining to these relations.

It is my sincere hope that both these divergences and the general tone of your message are due to the haste in which a representation made in good-will was, under pressure of time, based on data hurriedly collected.

In the first place, it is being emphasized in your message that we have failed to consult with the United States when a military intervention in Cyprus was deemed indispensable by virtue of the Treaty of Guarantee. The necessity of a military intervention in Cyprus has been felt four times since the closing days of 1963. From the outset we have taken a special care to consult the United States on this matter. Soon after the outbreak of the crisis, on December 25, 1963, we have immediately informed the United States of our contacts with the other guaranteeing powers only to be answered that the United States was not a party to this issue. We then negotiated with the United Kingdom and Greece for intervention and, as you know, a tri-partite military administration under British command was set-up on December 26, 1963. Upon the failure of the London conference and of the joint Anglo-American proposals, due to the attitude of Makarios and in the face of continuing assaults in the island against the Turkish Cypriots, we lived through very critical days in February and taking advantage of the visit of Mr. George Ball to Ankara, we informed again the United States of the gravity of the situation. We tried to explain to you that the necessity of intervention to restore order in the

---

[3] *The Middle East Journal*, vol. 20, Summer 1966, pp. 388-393.

island might arise in view of the vacuum caused by the rejection of the Anglo-American proposals and we informed you that we might have to intervene at any time. We even requested guarantees from you on specific issues and your answers were in the affirmative. However, you asked us not to intervene and assured us that Makarios would get at the United Nations a severe lesson while all the Turkish rights and interests would be preserved.

We complied with your request without any satisfactory result being secured at the United Nations. Moreover the creation of the United Nations force, decided upon by the Security Council, became a problem. The necessity for intervention was felt for the third time to protect Turkish community against the assaults of the terrorists in Cyprus who were encouraged by the doubts as to whetther the United Nations force would be set up immediately after the adoption of the Security Council resolution of March 4, 1964. But assuring us that the force would be set up very shortly, you insisted again that we refrain from intervening. Thereupon we postponed our intervention once again, awaiting the United Nations forces to assume their duty.

Dear Mr. President,

The era of terror in Cyprus has a particular character which rendered ineffective all measures taken so far. From the very outset, the negotiations held to restore security and the temporary set-ups have all helped only to increase the aggressiveness and the destructiveness of the Makarios administration. The Greek Cypriots have lately started to arm themselves overtly and considered the United Nations as an additional instrument to back up their ruthless and unconstitutional rule. It has become quite obvious that the United Nations have neither the authority nor the intent to intervene for the restoration of constitutional order and to put an end to aggression. You are well aware of the instigative attitude of the Greek Government towards the Greek Cypriots. During the talks held in your office, in the United States, we informed you that under the circumstances we would eventually be compelled to intervene in order to put an end to the atrocities in Cyprus. We also asked your Secretary of State at The Hague whether the United States would support us in such an eventuality and we received no answer. I think, I have thus reminded you how many times and under what circumstances we informed you of the necessity for intervention in Cyprus. I do remember having emphasised to your high level officials our due appreciation of the special responsibilities incumbent upon the United States within the alliance and of the necessity to be particularly careful and helpful to enable her to maintain solidarity within the alliance. As you see, we never had the intention to confront you with a unilateral decision on our part. Our grievance stems from our inability to explain to you a problem which caused us for months utmost distress and from your refusal to take a frank and firm stand on the issue as to which party is on the right side in the dispute between two allies, namely, Turkey and Greece.

Mr. President,

In your message you further emphasize the obligation of Turkey, under the provisions of the Treaty, to consult with the other two guaranteeing powers, before taking any unilateral action. Turkey is fully aware of this obligation. Foor the past six months we hav indeed complied with the requirements of this obligation. But Greece has, not only thwarted all the attempts made by Turkey to seek jointly the ways and means to stop Greek Cypriots from repudiating international treaties, but has also supported their unlawful and inhuman acts and has even encouraged them.

The Greek Government itself has not hesitated to declare publicly that the international agreements it signed with us were no longer in force. Various examples to that effect were, in due course, communicated in detail, orally and in writing, to your State Department.

We have likewise fulfilled our obligation of constant consultation with the Government of the United Kingdom, the other guaranteeing power.

In several instances we have, jointly with the Government of the United Kingdom, made representations to the Greek Cypriots with a view to restoring constitutional order. But unfortunately, these representations were of no avail due to the negative attitude of the Greek Cypriot authorities.

As you see, Turkey has earnestly explored every avenue of consulting continuously and acting jointly with the other two guaranteeing powers. This being the fact, it can not be asserted that Turkey has failed to abide by her obligation of consulting with the other two guaranteeing powers before taking unilateral action.

I put it to you, Mr. President, whether the United States Government which has felt the need to draw the attention of Turkey to her obligation of consultation, yet earnestly and faithfully fulfilled by the latter, should not have reminded Greece, who repudiates treaties signed by herself, of the necessity to abide by the precept "pacta sunt servanda" which is the fundamental rule of international law. This precept which, only a fortnight ago, was most eloquently characterised as "the basis of survival" by your Secretary of State himself in his speech at the "American Law Institute," is now being completely and contemptuously ignored by Greece, our NATO ally and by the Greek Cypriots.

Dear Mr. President,

As implied in your message, by virtue of the provisions of Article 4 of the Treaty of Guarantee, the three guaranteeing powers have, in the event of a breach of the provisions of that Treaty, the right to take concerted action and, if that proves impossible, unilateral action with the sole aim of reestablishing the state of affairs created by the said Treaty. The Treaty of Guarantee was signed with this understanding being shared by all parties thereto. The "Gentleman's Agreement" signed on February 19, 1959 by the Foreign Ministers of Turkey and Greece, is an evidence of that common understanding.

On the other hand, at the time of the admission of the Republic of Cyprus to the United Nations, the members of the organisation were fully acquainted with all the international commitments and obligations of the said Republic and no objections were raised in this respect.

Furthermore, in the course of the discussions on Cyprus leading to the resolution adopted on March 4, 1964 by the Security Council, the United States Delegate, among others, explicitly declared that the United Nations had no power to annul or amend international treaties.

The understanding expressed in your message that the intervention by Turkey in Cyprus would be for the purposes of effecting the partition of the island has caused me great surprise and profound sorrow. My surprise stems from the fact that the data furnished to you about the intentions of Turkey could be so remote from the realities repeatedly proclaimed by us. The reason of my sorrow is that our ally, the Government of the United States, could think that Turkey might lay aside the principle constituting the foundation of her foreign policy, i.e., absolute loyalty to international law, commitments and obligations, as factually evidenced in many circumstances well known to the United States.

I would like to assure you most categorically and most sincerely that if ever Turkey finds herself forced to intervene militarily in Cyprus this will be done in full conformity with the provisions and aims of international agreements.

In this connection, allow me to stress, Mr. President, that the postponement of our decision does naturally, in no way affect the rights conferred to Turkey by Article 4 of the Treaty of Guarantee.

Mr. President,

Referring to NATO obligations, you state in your message that the very essence of NATO requires that allies should not wage war on each other and that a Turkish intervention in Cyprus would lead to a military engagement between Turkish and Greek forces.

I am in full agreement with the first part of your statement, but the obligation for the NATO allies to respect international agreements concluded among themselves as well as their mutual treaty rights and commitments is an equally vital requisite of the alliance. An alliance among states which ignore their mutual contractual obligations and commitments is unthinkable.

As to the concern you expressed over the outbreak of a Turco-Greek war in case of Turkey's intervention in Cyprus in conformity with her rights and obligations stipulated in international agreements, I would like to stress that Turkey would undertake a "military operation" in Cyprus exclusively under the conditions and for the purpose set forth in the agreements. Therefore, a Turco-Greek war so properly described as "literally unthinkable" by the Honorable Dean Rusk could only occur in case of Greece's aggression against Turkey. Our view, in case of such an intervention, is to invite to an effective collaboration, with the aim of restoring the constitutional order in Cyprus, both Greece and the United Kingdom in their capacity as guaranteeing powers. If despite this invitation and its contractual obligations Greece were to attack Turkey, we could in no way be held responsible of the consequences of such an action. I would like to hope that you have already seriously drawn the Greek Government's attention on these matters.

The part of your message expressing doubts as to the obligation of the NATO allies to protect Turkey in case she becomes directly involved with the USSR as a result of an action initiated in Cyprus, gives me the impression that there are as between us wide divergence of views as to the nature and basic principles of the North Atlantic Alliance. I must confess that this has been to us the source of great sorrow and grave concern. Any aggression against a member of NATO will naturally call from the aggressor an effort of justification. If NATO's structure is so weak as to give credit to the aggressor's allegations, then it means that this defect of NATO needs really to be remedied. Our understanding is that the North Atlantic Treaty imposes upon all member states the obligation to come forthwith to the assistance of any member victim of an aggression. The only point left to the discretion of the member states is the nature and the scale of this assistance. If NATO members should start discussing the right and wrong of the situation of their fellow-member victim of a Soviet aggression, whether this aggression was provoked or not and if the decision on whether they have an obligation to assist the member should be made to depend on the issue of such a discussion, the very foundations of the Alliance would be shaken and it would lose its meaning. An obligation of assistance, if it is to carry any weight, should come into being immediately upon the observance of aggression. That is why Article 5 of the North Atlantic Treaty considers an attack against one of the member states as an attack against them all and makes it imperative for them to assist the party so attacked by taking forthwith such action as they deem necessary. In this connection I would like to further point out that the agreements on Cyprus have met with the approval of the North Atlantic Council, as early as the stage of the United Nations debate on the prooblem, i.e., even prior to th establishment of the Republic of Cyprus, hence long before the occurrence of the events of December 1963.

As you will recall, at the meeting of the NATO Ministerial Council held three weeks ago at The Hague, it was acknowledged that the treaties continued to be the basis for legality as regards the situation in the island and the status of Cyprus. The fact that these agreements have been violated as a result of the flagrantly unlawful acts of one of the parties on the island should in no way mean that the said agreements are no longer in force and that the rights and obligations of Turkey by virtue of those agreements should be ignored. Such an understanding would mean that as long as no difficulties arise, the agreements are considered as valid and they are no longer in force when difficulties occur. I am sure you will agree with me that such an understanding of law cannot be accepted. I am equally convinced that there could be no shadow of doubt about the obligation to protect Turkey within the NATO Alliance in a situation that can, by no means, be attributed to an arbitrary act of Turkey. An opposite way of thinking would lead to the repudiation and denial of the concept of law and of Article 51 of the United Nations Charter.

In your message, concern has been expressed about the commitments of Turkey as a member of the United Nations. I am sure, Mr. President you will agree with me if I say that such a concern, which I do not share, is groundless especially for the following reasons: Turkey has distinguished herself as one of the most loyal members of the United Nations ever since its foundation. The Turkish people has spared no effort to safeguard the principles of the United Nations Charter, and has even sacrificed her sons for this cause. Turkey has never failed in supporting this organisation and, in order to secure its proper functioning, has borne great moral and material sacrifices even when she had most pressing financial difficulties. Despite the explicit rights conferred to Turkey by the Treaty of Guarantee, my Government's respect for and adherence to the United Nations have recently been demonstrated once more by its acceptance of the Security Council resolution of March 4, 1964 as well as by the priority it has given to the said resolution.

Should the United Nations have been progressively successful in carrying out their task as pointed out in your message, a situation which is of such grave concern for both you and I, would never have arisen. It is a fact that the United Nations operations in the island have proved unable to put an end to the oppression.

The relative calm which has apparently prevailed in the island for the past few weeks marks the beginning of preparations of the Greek Cypriots for further tyranny. Villages are still under siege. The United Nations forces, assuaging Turkish Cypriots, enable the Greeks to gather their crops; but they do not try to stop the Greeks when the crops of Turks are at stake and they act as mere spectators to Greek assaults. These vitally important details may not well reach you, whereas we live in the atmosphere created by the daily reports of such tragic events.

The report of the Secretary-General will be submitted to the United Nations on June 15, 1964. I am seriously concerned that we may face yet another defeat similar to the one we all suffered on March 4, 1964. The session of March 4th had further convinced Makarios that the Treaty of Guarantee did not exist for him and thereupon he took the liberty of actually placing the United Nations forces under his control and direction. From then on the assassination of hostages and the besieging of villages have considerably increased.

Dear Mr. President,

Our allies who are in a position to arbiter in the Cyprus issue and to orient it in the right direction have so far been unable to disentangle the problem from a substantial error. The Cyprus tragedy has been engendered by the deliberate policy of the Republic of Cyprus aimed at annulling the treaties and abrogating the constitution. Security can be established in the island only through the proper functioning of an authority above the Government of Cyprus. Yet only the measures acceptable to the Cypriot Government are being sought to restore security in Cyprus. The British administration set up following the December events, the Anglo-American proposals and finally the United Nations command have all been founded on this unsound basis and consequently every measure acceptable to Makarios has proved futile and has, in general, encouraged oppression and aggression.

Dear Mr. President,

You put forward in your message the resentment caused in Greece by the policy pursued by your Government. Within the content of the Cyprus issues, the nature of the Greek policy and the course of action undertaken by Greece indicate that she is apt to resort to every means within her power to secure the complete annulment of the existing treaties. We are at pains to make our allies understand the sufferings we bear in our rightful cause and the irretrievable plight in which the Turkish Cypriots are living. On the other hand, it is not the character of our nation to exploit demonstrations of resentment. I assure you that our distress is deeply rooted since we can not make you understand our rightful position and convince you of the necessity of spending every effort and making use of all your authority to avert the perils inherent in the Cyprus problem by attaching to it the importance it well deserves.

That France and Germany have buried their animosity is indeed a good example. However, our nation had already given such an example forty years ago by establishing friendly relations with Greece, right after the ruthless devastation of the whole Anatolia by the armies of that country.

Dear Mr. President,

As a member of the Alliance our nation is fully conscious of her duties and rights. We do not pursue any aim other than the settlement of the Cyprus problem in compliance with the provisions of the existing treaties. Such a settlement is likely to be reached if you lend your support and give effect with your supreme authority to the sense of justice inherent in the character of the American nation.

Mr. President,

I thank you for your statement emphasising the value attached by the United States to the relations of alliance with Turkey and for your kind words about the Turkish nation. I shall be happy to come to the United States to talk the Cyprus problem with you. The United Nations Security Council will meet on June the 17th. In the meantime, Mr. Dirk Stikker, Secretary General of NATO, will have paid a visit to Turkey. Furthermore, the United Nations mediator Mr. Tuomioja will have submitted his report to the Secretary-General. These developments may lead to the emergence of a new situation. It will be possible for me to go abroad to join you, at a date convenient for you, immediately after June 20th.

It will be most helpful for me if you would let me know of any defined views and designs you may have on the Cyprus question so that I may be able to study them thoroughly before my departure for Washington.

Finally, I would like to express my satisfaction for the frank, fruitful and promising talks we had with Mr. G. Ball in Ankara just before forwarding this message to you.

Sincerely,

İSMET İNÖNÜ

Prime Minister of Turkey.

APPENDIX C. U.S.-TURKEY DEFENCE AND ECONOMIC COOPERATION AGREEMENT, MARCH 29, 1980[4]

Agreement for cooperation on defence and economy between the governments of the United States of America and the Republic of Turkey in accordance with Articles II and III of the North Atlantic Treaty.

The Governments of the United States of America and of the Republic of Turkey,

Reaffirming their devotion to the aims and principles of the United Nations Charter,

Recognizing that the relationship and cooperation between them rest on the principles of democracy, human rights, justice and social progress,

Expressing their desire to maintain the security and independence of their respective countries and to increase the standard of living of their peoples,

Recognizing that cooperation in the fields of economy and defence, as in all other fields, is based on full respect for the sovereignty of the Parties,

Expressing their willingness to continue their economic and related scientific and technological cooperation both bilaterally and as members of the North Atlantic Treaty Organization and to enhance their defence cooperation as partners within the framework of the North Atlantic Treaty,

Reaffirming their determination to contribute to the strengthening of world peace,

Taking into account the principle that the maintenance of an adequate defence posture is an important element for the preservation of world peace and stability,

Expressing their faith in the acceleration of disarmament efforts and their mutual desire to contribute to this process,

Acting on the basis of their continuing friendship and in recognition of their obligations to the security and defence of the North Atlantic Treaty area and pursuant to Articles II and III of the North Atlantic Treaty,

Have entered into the following Agreement:

ARTICLE I

On the basis of sovereign equality and mutual interest, the Parties shall maintain cooperation so as to foster their economic and social development.

For this purpose, the Parties shall maintain and develop close cooperation between the comprising economic, defence and related scientific and technical fields.

The Governments of the United States of America and the Republic of Turkey shall continuously review their cooperation in all these fields and identify and implement appropriate measures for developing it.

For these purposes consultations shall be held, the level and date of which shall be as mutually agreed between the two Governments.

ARTICLE II

Recognizing the interrelationship of economic and defence matters and the fact that a sound defence rests on a sound economy and in order to assist each other to fulfil their mutual responsibilities as members of the North Atlantic Treaty Organization, the Parties, as

---

[4] Richard C. Campany, *Turkey and the United States*, New York: Praeger, 1986, pp. 103-107.

envisaged in Article II of the North Atlantic Treaty, will exert maximum efforts to develop economic cooperation, including commercial, economic, industrial, scientific and technological relations, between the two Countries.

For this purpose, the Government of the United States will exert its best efforts to provide mutually agreed financial and technical assistance to Turkey's development efforts.

ARTICLE III

For the purpose of strengthening the mutual security cooperation between the two Governments within the framework of Article III of the North Atlantic Treaty, the Government of the United States shall use its best efforts to provide the Government of the Republic of Turkey with defence equipment, services and training in accordance with programs to be mutually agreed upon. The cooperation in this field shall be carried out in accordance with Supplementary Agreement Number 1 on Defense Support.

ARTICLE IV

In the furtherance of the spirit of Article II of this Agreement and in recognition of the mutual benefits to be achieved by both Parties, the Governments of the United States of America and the Republic of Turkey shall seek opportunities to cooperate in the production and purchasing of appropriate defence material. Both Parties will undertake to encourage joint investment in the above areas of economic and defence cooperation.

For this purpose, the Government of the United States shall assist the Government of the Republic of Turkey in mutually agreed efforts aimed at enhancing the production, maintenance, repair and modernisation of defence material and equipment in Turkey and will encourage new defence production projects and two-way trade in defence material.

This cooperation shall be carried out in accordance with Supplementary Agreement Number 2 on Defense Industrial Cooperation.

ARTICLE V

1. The Government of the Republic of Turkey authorises the Government of the United States to participate in joint defence measures at specified Turkish Armed Forces installations.

2. The activities and technical operations of the installations shall be conducted in accordance with mutually agreed purposes and programs.

3. The "Agreement Between the Parties to the North Atlantic Treaty, Regarding the Status of Their Forces" dated June 19, 1951, shall apply to the force and civilian component of the United States of America and their dependents assigned or stationed in the territory of the Republic of Turkey for the purposes of this Agreement.

4. The extent of the defence cooperation envisaged in this Agreement shall be limited to obligations arising out of the North Atlantic Treaty.

5. This cooperation shall be carried out in accordance with Supplementary Agreement Number 3 on Installations.

ARTICLE VI

Taking into consideration the sovereign equality of the Parties and for the purpose of carrying out the provisions of the Agreement and its Supplementary Agreements on the basis of reciprocity, the Parties agree that:

A. The Government of the Republic of Turkey may maintain a military liaison office within its Embassy in the United States to carry out liaison with appropriate authorities of the Government of the United States on questions regarding the exchange of information, cooperation and other defence matters of mutual concern, including security assistance and other related subjects.

B. Likewise, the Government of the United States may maintain its organization in Turkey to carry out similar functions with appropriate authorities of the Government of the Republic of Turkey.

ARTICLE VII

1. This Agreement and the Supplementary Agreements annexed to it shall be valid for a period of 5 years. Unless one of the Parties notifies the other Party of the termination of this Agreement 3 months in advance of the end of this initial 5-year period, it will continue to be in effect from year to year until terminated by agreement of the Parties or by either Party upon 3 months notice prior to the end of each subsequent year.

2. Should disagreement arise from the interpretation or implementation of this Agreement or of the Supplementary Agreements, the Parties shall begin consultations immediately in order to resolve the matter.

3. Either Party may propose, should it find necessary, in writing, the amendment or revision of this Agreement or any of the Supplementary Agreements. In this case, consultations shall begin immediately. If no result is reached in three months, either Party may terminate the Agreement or the Supplementary Agreement in question upon notice in writing of 30 days.

4. In the event that one of the Parties concludes that the other Party is not complying or is unable to comply with the provisions of this Agreement or its Supplementary Agreements, it may propose, in writing, consultations, which will begin immediately. If no result is reached within 30 days, either Party may terminate upon notice in writing of 30 days this Agreement or any of the Supplementary Agreements without prejudicing the validity of this Agreement.

ARTICLE VIII

This Agreement and the Supplementary Agreements annexed to it shall come into effect on the date of exchange of notes in accordance with respective legal procedures.

ARTICLE IX

Done at Ankara in duplicate, in the English and Turkish languages, each of which shall be equally authentic, on this 29th day of March, 1980.

JAMES W. SPAIN, Ambassador of the United States of America, for the Government of The United States of America

HAYRETTIN ERKMEN, Minister of Foreign Affairs, for the Government of The Republic of Turkey

APPENDIX D. U.S.-TURKISH TRADE RELATIONS

Between 1960 and 1975 Turkey was trying to develop its economy through rapid industrialization under the five-year development plans which were prepared by the State Planning Organization. Therefore, Turkey's industry was heavily dependent on imports of machinery, spare parts and fuel. The first five-year plan (1963-1967) predicted that the export of traditional agricultural products would increase and that investment projects would cause an increase in the import of machinery and other investment products.[5] Even the third five-year plan (1973-1977), which aimed at a considerable increase in the export of manufactured goods and in their share of the total exports, predicted that Turkey still would import manufactured and investment goods in large amounts.[6] These predictions proved correct: major Turkish imports in 1960-75 comprised the following items: 1- Non-electric machinery. 2- Iron and steel products. 3- Means of transport (including motor vehicles). 4- Crude oil and petroleum products. 4- Electrical machinery. 5- Rubber and plastics products. 6- Agriculture-based processed products. 7- Cereal (including wheat). 8- Textiles. Turkey's exports were: 1- Cotton. 2- Tobacco. 3- Hazelnuts. 4- Raisins. 5- Minerals (including chromium). 6- Textiles. 7- Food beverages. 8- Industrial products.[7]

In the period of our study, as an industrialized, developed country, the United States was one of the leading powers in the export of manufactured goods though manufactures also occupied the most important place in her imports. Major U.S. exports were: 1- Machinery. 2- Automobiles and parts. 3- Aircraft and parts. 4- Iron and steel products. 5- Chemicals. 6- Electrical, construction and agricultural machinery. 7- Fuels. 8- Wheat. Major U.S. imports were: 1- Machinery. 2- Transport equipment. 3- Petroleum products. 4- Forest products. 5- Iron and steel products. 6- Chemicals. 7- Coffee. The percentages of categories in U.S. exports and imports respectively were the following: 1- Finished manufactures: 60.2 and 44.6. 2- Semi-manufactures: 15.1 and 22.1. 3- Crude materials: 10.7 and 16.0. 4- Crude foodstuffs: 8.6 and 8.8. 5- Manufactured foodstuffs: 5.5 and 9.7.[8]

Trade relations between the USA and Turkey in the 1960-1975 period fit trade patterns of both countries, which are mentioned above, and demonstrate that the U.S.-Turkish trade was complementary rather than competitive. Tables 4 and 5 show items of the U.S.-Turkish trade. In 1960-75, while Turkey exported to the United States agricultural products (mainly tobacco and various fruits, vegetables and nuts), some raw minerals and metals, animal products, textile and cereals, U.S. exports to Turkey included mainly manufactured goods: machinery (including electrical machinery), road vehicles and other transport equipment, cereals (mainly wheat), chemicals, petroleum and products, metal manufactures, iron and steel, textiles and rubber manufactures. The two countries had no competition in any trade products. Although

---

[5] *Kalkınma Planı: Birinci Beş Yıl 1963-1967*, T.C. Başbakanlık Devlet Planlama Teşkilatı, Ankara: Başbakanlık Matbaası, January 1963, p. 509.

[6] *Yeni Strateji ve Kalkınma Planı: Üçüncü Beş Yıl*, T.C. Başbakanlık Devlet Planlama Teşkilatı, Ankara, 1973, pp. 187, 189-190.

[7] Z. Y. Hershlag, *Turkey: the Challenge of Growth*, Leiden: E. J. Brill, 1968, pp. 370-371, Z. Hatiboğlu, *An Unconventional Analysis of Turkish Economy*, İstanbul: Aktif Büro Basım Organizasyon, 1978, pp. 109-112, *Turkey: Prospects and Problems of an Expanding Economy*, Washington: the World Bank, 1975, pp. 346-348.

[8] R. K. Vedder, *The American Economy in Historical Perspective*, Belmont, Calif.: Wadsworth Co. Inc., 1976, p. 404, W. Woodruff, *America's Impact on the World*, London: Macmillan, 1975, pp. 265-266, W. H. Branson, "Trends in United States International Trade and Investment Since World War II" in M. Feldstein (ed.), *The American Economy in Transition*, Chicago: The University of Chicago Press, 1980, pp. 196, 200-201, 222-225.

Turkey was an agriculture country, its cereal (especially wheat) export was not considerable in 1960-75 and she had to import wheat in bad harvest seasons. As a wheat exporter, the United States met Turkey's need under a special arrangement rather than being a competitor of Turkey in this field. Turkey's textile exports, too, were not great enough in this period to cause problems between the two countries.

Table 4: Turkish Exports to the USA
(monthly averages, 000 dollars)

Item	1960	1961	1962	1963	1964	1965	1966	1967
Tobacco and manufactures	4,284	4,295	3,791	3,838	3,670	4,686	4,964	3,888
Fruits, vegetables, nuts	889	679	648	614	572	628	429	347
Metalliferous ores, scrap	286	262	378	137	174	261	102	234
Base metals, mainly copper	100	12				523	218	136
Wool and other animal hair	216	137	83	143	105	29	34	12
Animal and veg. oils, fats					31	75	10	60
Textile manufactures	10	8						
Cereals and products				2	1			9
Total	6,284	5,719	5,868	5,215	5,038	6,822	6,875	6,553

Item	1968	1969	1970	1971	1972	1973	1974	1975
Tobacco and manufactures	6,355	3,815	3,569	2,846	6,717	5,993	6,701	7,896
Fruits, vegetables, nuts	844	702	643	708	1,449	1,488	1,097	1,221
Metalliferous ores, scrap	258	289	615	874	243	431	448	905
Base metals, mainly copper	66	103	22	34	240	56	69	175
Wool and other animal hair	11	3	2		37	3	1	
Animal and veg. oils, fats	4	3		1		35	144	2
Textile manufactures					85	123	123	253
Cereals and products	18							
Total	8,283	5,631	5,096	7,551	8,836	10,767	11,766	12,064

Table 5: Turkish Imports from the USA
(monthly averages, 000 dollars)

Item	1960	1961	1962	1963	1964	1965	1966	1967
Machinery, non-electric	3,334	1,896	3,134	5,265	2,649	2,985	4,162	3,345
Electric machinery	471	475	672	1,764	604	1,199	1,288	988
Road vehicles	2,783	884	1,213	1,165	900	1,473	2,025	2,071
Other transport equipment			18	72	489	723	60	137
Cereals and products	3,980	4,534	5,012	2,824	768	1,680	2,922	103
Chemicals	371	447	982	796	971	943	918	801
Petroleum and products	489	580	672	657	747	737	615	865
Metal manufactures	156	209	612	569	179	272	212	173
Iron and steel	264	257	572	775	1,139	659	505	147
Textiles	10	10	369	206	727	521	298	241
Rubber manufactures	374	283	350	260	165	93	90	120
Total	13,727	10,604	16,132	17,982	13,389	13,360		

Item	1968	1969	1970	1971	1972	1973	1974	1975
Machinery, non-electric	3,104	2,541	2,677	2,980	4,165	4,386	6,810	16,250
Electric machinery	999	1,288	1,676	1,180	1,478	1,479	1,908	2,810
Road vehicles	1,910	1,786	1,332	639	1,890	2,448	2,818	6,845
Other transport equipment	893	1,053	1,119	1,519	2,267	2,457	4,438	1,585
Cereals and products	148	2,141	2,938	2,598	264	3,089	7,783	5,139
Chemicals	967	789	691	695	631	1,235	1,450	3,195
Petroleum and products	704	510	700	466	549	249	380	523
Metal manufactures	166	186	438	401	211	204	236	924
Iron and steel	172	322	751	843	106	292	860	704
Textiles	105	16	68	38	27	29	31	84
Rubber manufactures	117	66	36	65	53	90	157	368
Total	25,058	24,861	23,228	22,378	25,021	28,920	38,547	50,617

Source: *Quarterly Economic Review, Turkey*, November 1961, No. 40, p. 15, June 1964, No. 50, p. 15, June 1966, No. 2, p. 18, June 1968, No. 2, p. 12, June 1970, No. 2, p. 17, June 1972, No. 2, p. 13, September 1972, No. 3, p. 12, June 1974, No. 2, p. 11, September 1976, No. 3, p. 16.

The total value of the U.S.-Turkish trade in U.S. dollars can be seen in Tables 4 and 5. Table 6 shows the value of this trade in Turkish liras. The trade with the USA held a considerable place in Turkey's total exports and imports. Although the USA's share in Turkey's exports and imports fell constantly in the 1960s and the 1970s (see Table 7), she, as a single trade partner, maintained her importance for Turkey's trade. On the other hand, Turkey was not a significant trade partner of the United States. In 1970 her share was 0.7 percent in U.S. export and 0.1 in U.S. import. (This figures became 0.2 and 0.1 in 1978).[9]

---

[9] J. Agnew, *The United States in the World Economy*, Cambridge: Cambridge University Press, 1987, p. 144.

There was no significant disagreement in the economic field between the United States and Turkey in 1960-75 because there was no fierce competition between them in the trade of any products and Turkey's share in the U.S. was not important. Only the amount of U.S. economic and military aid to Turkey and the use of economic aid by U.S. authorities as a leverage against Turkey brought problems as explained in different parts of the thesis.

Table 6: Turkey's Trade with the USA
(000 TL)

	1960	1961	1962	1963	1964	1965	1966	1967
Import	546342	1260835	1631137	1904630	1403371	1458606	1567188	1114406
Export	292556	586841	674069	448049	656885	740965	722156	836390

	1968	1969	1970	1971	1972	1973	1974	1975
Import	1095208	1152964		1951630	2494341	2545112	4813472	5980942
Export	652798	538962		914646	1374859	1797120	1997626	2104976

Source: *Dış Ticaret Yıllık İstatistik*, T.C. Başbakanlık Devlet İstatistik Enstitüsü, 1961-1962, p. xxv, 1963-1964, p. xxi, 1965-1966, p. xxiii, 1967-1968, p. xxiii, 1969, p. xxv, 1975-1976, p. xxv.

Table 7: US Share in Turkish Trade
(percent of total value)

	1960	1961	1962	1963	1964	1965	1966	1967
Export	17.2	18.8	19.6	13.5	17.8	18	16	18
Import	25.8	27.5	29.1	30.6	28.7	28	24	26

	1968	1969	1970	1971	1972	1973	1974	1975
Export	15	12	12	10	12	10	9	10
Import	16	20	19	14	12	11	7	9

Source: *Quarterly Economic Review Annual Supplement, Turkey*, June 1961, p. 9, June 1963, p. 11, June 1965, p. 15, 1967, p. 16, 1969, p. 19, 1971, p. 23, 1973, p. 23, 1975, p. 24, 1976, p. 24.

BIBLIOGRAPHY

I- PRIMARY SOURCES

1- Documents

Agency for International Development (AID), Statistics and Reports Division, Office of Financial Management, *U.S. Overseas Loans and Grants and Assistance from International Organizations, Obligations and Loan Authorizations, July 1, 1945- June 30, 1973*, May 1974.

Arar, İsmail (ed.), *Hükümet Programları 1920-1965*, İstanbul: Burçak Yayınevi, 1968.

Bilge, Suat et al. (eds.), *Cyprus: Past Present Future*, Ankara, 1964.

Bozbeyli, Ferruh (ed.), *Parti Programları, Türkiye'de Siyasi Partilerin Ekonomik ve Sosyal Görüşleri, Belgeler*, İstanbul: Ak Yayınları, 1970.

"Correspondence Between President Johnson and P.M. İnönü, June 1964, as Released by the White House, January 15, 1966", *Middle East Journal*, vol. 20, Summer 1966, pp. 386-393.

Cumhuriyet Senatosu Tutanak Dergisi, 1960-75, Ankara.

Demirel, Süleyman, *Başbakan Süleyman Demirel'in Onuncu Basın Toplantısı*, Ankara, 1968.

Demirel, Süleyman, "Başbakan Süleyman Demirel'in Onyedinci Basın Toplantısı, February 7, 1970", *Dışişleri Bakanlığı Belleteni*, February 1970, pp. 98-140.

Dışişleri Bakanlığı Belleteni, 1960-1975, Ankara.

Dışişleri Güncesi, Ankara: TC Dışişleri Bakanlığı.

Dış Ticaret Yıllık İstatistik, 1960-1976, Ankara: T.C. Başbakanlık Devlet İstatistik Enstitüsü.

Documents on American Foreign Relations 1956, (ed. by Zinner, Paul E.), Council on Foreign Relations, New York: Harper and Brothers, 1957.

Documents on International Affairs, 1951, 1953, 1954, 1955, 1956, 1957, 1958, 1959, The Royal Institute of International Affairs, Oxford University Press.

Faulds, Andrew (ed.), *Excerpta Cypria for Today: a Source Book on the Cyprus Problem*, Lefkosha, İstanbul, London: K. Rustem and Brother, 1988.

Foreign Relations of the United States, 1952-1954, Vol. IX, the Near and the Middle East (in two parts), Glennon, John P. (Ed. in chief), Washington D.C.: the United States Printing Office, 1986.

The Historical Background of Cyprus and the Turkish Republic of Northern Cyprus, Ankara: The Cyprus Turkish Cultural Association.

Kalkınma Planı, Birinci Beş Yıl, 1963-1967, T.C. Başbakanlık Devlet Planlama Teşkilatı, Ankara: Başbakanlık Matbaası, January 1963.

Keesing's Contemporary Archives 1960-1975, Keesing's Publications Limited of Bristol.

Magnus, Ralph P., *Documents on the Middle East*, Washington D.C.: American Enterprise Institute, 1969.

Millet Meclisi Tutanak Dergisi 1960-1975, Ankara.

Ro'i, Yaacov, *From Encroachment to Involvemnt: a Documentary Study of the Soviet Policy in the Middle East, 1945-1973,* vol. V, United Nations by Hottelet, Richard C., New York: Chelsea House Publishers, 1973.

"Soviet-Turkish Exchange of Notes", *Middle Eastern Affairs*, November 1960, vol. 11, No. 10, pp. 317-320.

Survey of International Affairs, 1951, 1953, 1954, 1955-1956, 1956-58, 1959-1960, The Royal Institute of International Affairs, the Oxford University Press.

"Turkish Government Press Release", *Middle East Journal*, Winter 1970, vol. 24, pp. 72-73.

Türkiye'ye Amerikan İktisadi Yardımları 1949-1968, Ankara: Maliye Bakanlığı, November 1968.

U.S. Congress, Committee on Foreign Affairs, Committee on Foreign Relations, *Legislation on Foreign Relations Through 1979, Current Legislation and Related Executive Orders*, vol. 1, Washington: U.S. Government Printing Office, 1980.

U.S. Congress, House of Representatives, *Turkish Opium Ban Negotiations*, Hearing Before the Committee on Foreign Affairs, 93rd Congress, 2nd Session, July 16, 1974, Washington: U.S. Government Printing Office, 1974.

U.S. Congress, House of Representatives, *International Aspects of the Narcotics Problem*, Hearings Before the Subcommittee on Europe of the Committee on Foreign Affairs, 92nd Congress, 1st Session, July 7,8,9, and 30, 1971, Washington: U.S. Government Printing Office, 1971.

U.S. Congress, Senate, *The Military Aspects of Banning Arms Aid to Turkey*, Hearing Before the Committee on Armed Services, 95th Congress, 2nd Session, June 28, 1978, Washington: U.S. Government Printing Office, 1978.

U.S. Congress, Senate, *United States Security Agreements and Commitments Abroad, Greece and Turkey*, Hearings Before the Subcommittee on United States Security Agreements Abroad of the Committee on Foreign Relations, 91st Congress, 2nd Session, Part 7, June 9 and 11, 1970, Washington: U.S. Government Printing Office, 1970.

The Western Powers and the Middle East; A Documentary Record by the Information Department of the Royal Institute of International Affairs, Oxford University Press, November 1958.

"White House Tapes and Minutes of the Cuban Missile Crisis", *International Security*, vol. 10, No. 1, Summer 1985, pp. 164-203.

Yeni Strateji ve Kalkınma Planı: üçüncü Beş Yıl, T.C. Başbakanlık Devlet Planlama Teşkilatı, Ankara, 1973.

2- Other Primary Materials

ABD Dışişleri Bakanı William Rogers'ın Kongre'ye Sunduğu Rapordan Bölümler, Ankara: Amerikan Basın ve Kültür Merkezi, 1972.

Acheson, Dean, *Present at the Creation: My Years in the State Department*, London: Hamish Hamilton Ltd., 1970.

Amerika'da Onbir Gün, Ankara: Yarın Yayınları, 1967. (The Account of the visit of Turkish President Cevdet Sunay to the United States.)

Aybar, Mehmet Ali, *Bağımsızlık, Demokrasi, Sosyalizm: Seçmeler: 1947-1967*, İstanbul: Gerçek Yayınevi, 1968.

Ball, George, *The Past Has Another Pattern: Memoirs*, New York, London: W.W. Norton, 1982.

Binnendijk, Hans and Friendly, Alfred, *Turkey, Greece and NATO: The Strained Alliance*, A Staff Report to the Committee on Foreign Relations, United States Senate, March 1980, Washington D.C.: U.S. Government Printing Office, 1980.

Bitsios, Dimitri S., *Cyprus: the Vulnerable Republic*, Thessaloniki, Greece: Institute for Balkan Studies, 1975.

Boran, Behice, *Türkiye ve Sosyalizm Sorunları*, İstanbul: Tekin Yayınevi, 1970.

Bryson, Thomas A., *American Diplomatic Relations with the Middle East 1784-1975: A Survey*, Metuchen N.J.: the Scarecrowd Press Inc., 1977.

Carter, Jimmy, *Keeping Faith: Memoirs of a President*, London: Collins, 1982.

Collins, John M., *Greece and Turkey: Some Military Implications Related to NATO and the Middle East*, A Report for Special Committee on Investigations of Committee on Foreign Affairs, 94th Congress, 1st Session, February 28, 1975, Washington: U.S. Government Printing Office, 1975.

"Cypriot Complaint of Turkish Aggression and Interference in Its Internal Affairs", *International Organisation*, vol. 18, 1964, pp. 478-485.

"Cypriot Complaint of Turkish Aggression and Interference in its Internal Affairs", *International Organisation*, vol. 19, 1965, pp. 84-88, 331-335, 981-988.

Çağlayangil, İhsan Sabri, *Anılarım*, İstanbul: Yılmaz Yayınları, August 1990.

Demirel, Süleyman, *1971 Buhranı ve Aydınlığa Doğru*, Ankara: Adalet Partisi, 1973.

Demirel, Süleyman, *Büyük Türkiye*, İstanbul: Dergah Yayınları, 1975.

Ecevit, Bülent, *Ortanın Solu*, İstanbul: Tekin Yayınevi, 1973.

Eden, Sir Anthony, *Full Circle*, London: Cassell, 1960.

Erbakan, Necmettin, *Türkiye'nin Temel Meseleleri*, Ankara: Rehber, 1991.

Erim, Nihat, *Bildiğim ve Gördüğüm ölçüler İçinde Kıbrıs*, Ankara: Ajans-Türk, 1975.

Foss, Christopher F., *Jane's Pocket Book Modern Tanks and Armoured Fighting Vehicles*, London, Sydney: Jane's, 1981.

Foss, Christopher F., *Jane's Pocket Book of Towed Artillery*, London: MacDonald and Jane's, 1977.

Grimmett, Richard F., *Turkish-US Defense Relationship: the Arms Embargo Issue*, the Library of Congress, Congressional Research Service, Washington: U.S. Government Printing Office, 1978.

Grimmett, Richard F. and Laipson, Ellen B., *Turkey's Problems and Prospects: Implications for U.S. Interests*, Report Prepared for the Subcommittee on Foreign Affairs, U.S. House of Representatives by the Foreign Affairs and National Defense Division, Congressional

Research Service, Library of Congress, March 3, 1980, Washington: U.S. Government Printing Office, 1980.

Grimmett, Richard F., *United States Military Installations and Objectives in the Mediterranean*, Report Prepared for Subcommittee on Europe and the Middle East of the Committee on International Relations by Foreign Affairs and National Defense Division, Congressional Research Service, Library of Congress, Washington: U.S. Government Printing Office, 1977.

Kennedy, Robert F., *Thirteen Days: A Memoir of The Cuban Missile Crisis*, New York: W.W. Norton and Company Inc., 1971.

Khrushchev, Nikita, *Khrushchev Remembers*, London: Andre Deutsch, 1971.

Kissinger, Henry, *Years of Upheaval*, London: Weidenfield and Nicolson and Michael Joseph, 1982.

Laipson, Ellen B., *Congressional- Executive Relations and the Turkish Arms Embargo*, Washington: U.S. Government Printing Office, June 1981.

Moore, John E., *Jane's Pocket Book 1 Major Warships*, London: MacDonald and Jane's, 1978.

Papandreou, Andreas, *Democracy at Gunpoint: the Greek Front*, London: Andre Deutsch, 1970.

Pretty, Ronald (ed.), *Jane's Pocket Book of Missiles*, London: MacDonald and Jane's, 1978.

"Question of Cyprus", *International Organisation*, vol. 20, 1966, pp. 306-313.

"Question of Cyprus", *International Organisation*, vol. 22, 1968, pp. 974-977.

Quarterly Economic Review, Turkey, 1960-1976, London: The Economist Intelligence Unit.

Resmi Temaslar: Sayın Başbakan ve Bn. Erim'in Birleşik Amerika'yı Ziyareti, 18-23 March 1972. No place, publisher and date.

Salinger, Pierre, *With Kennedy*, London: Jonathan Cape, 1967.

SIPRI (Stockholm International Peace Research Institute), *Arms Trade Registers: the Arms Trade and the Third World*, Stockholm: Almqvist and Wiksell International, 1975.

Spain, James W., *American Diplomacy in Turkey: Memoirs of an Ambassador-Extraordinary and Plenipotentiary*, New York: Praeger, 1984.

Taylor, John W.R., *Jane's Pocket Book 2 Major Combat Aircraft*, London: MacDonald and Jane's, 1978.

Türkeş, Alparslan, *Temel Görüşler*, İstanbul: Dergah Yayınları, 1975.

Türkeş, Alparslan, *Yeni Ufuklara Doğru*, İstanbul: Kutluğ Yayınları, 1974.

Turkey: Industrialization and Trade Strategy, Washington: The World Bank, 1982.

Turkey: Prospects and Problems of An Expanding Economy, Washington: World Bank, 1975.

Wellman, Harvey R., "Drug Abuse: A Challenge to US-Turkish Cooperation in the Seventies", *Department of State Bulletin*, vol. 64, February 1, 1971, pp. 140-146.

II- SECONDARY SOURCES

1- Newspapers and Magazines

Akis, weekly, Turkey.
Cumhuriyet, daily, Turkey.

Forum, weekly, Turkey.
Hürriyet, daily, Turkey.
Milliyet, daily, Turkey.
Tercüman, daily, Turkey.
Yön, weekly, Turkey.

2- Books and Articles

Abadan, Nermin, *Anayasa Hukuku ve Siyasi Bilimler Açısından 1965 Seçimlerinin Tahlili*, Ankara: A.ü. S.B.F. Yayınları, 1966.

Abel, Elie, *The Missile Crisis*, Philadelphia: Lippincott, 1966.

Acar, İrfan C., *Dış Politika*, Ankara, 1993.

Acar, Özgen, "Afyon Raporu", *Cumhuriyet*, 6-20 July 1970.

Adams, Thomas W., "The First Republic of Cyprus: A Review of an Unworkable Constitution", *Western Political Quarterly*, September 1966, No. 19, pp. 475-490.

Adams, Thomas W. and Cottrell, Alvin J., "American Foreign Policy and the UN Peace-Keeping Force in Cyprus", *ORBIS*, vol. 12, No. 2, Summer 1968, pp. 490-503.

Adams, Thomas W. and Cottrell, Alvin J., *Cyprus Between East and West*, Baltimore: The John Hopkins Press, 1968.

Agnew, John, *The United States in the World Economy: A Regional Geography*, Cambridge: Cambridge University Press, 1987.

Ahmad, Feroz, *The Turkish Experiment in Democracy 1950-1975*, London: The Royal Institute of International Affairs, C. Hurst and Company, 1977.

Aktan, Gündüz, "Farklı Vitesler", *Radikal*, 7 September 2002, p. 8.

Alantar, Ö. Zeynep Oktav, "A Thorny Issue Between Turkey and the United States: Northern Iraq (1996-2001)", *Turkish Review of Middle East Studies*, Annual 2001, No. 12, pp. 21-41.

Alford, Jonathan (ed.), *Greece and Turkey: Adversity in Alliance*, Aldershot: Gower, International Institute for Strategic Studies, 1984.

Allison, Graham T., *Essence of Decision: Explaining the Cuban Missile Crisis*, Boston: Little and Company, 1971.

Allison, Graham T., and Szanton, Peter, *Remaking Foreign Policy, The Organizational Connection*, New York: Basic Books Inc. Publishers, 1976.

Altan, Çetin, *Ben Milletvekili İken*, Ankara: Bilgi Yayınevi, 1971.

Altan, Çetin, *Sömürücülerle Savaş*, İstanbul: Dönem Yayınevi.

Arcayürek, Cüneyt, *Çanykaya'ya Giden Yol 1971-1973*, Ankara: Bilgi Yayınevi, 1985.

Arcayürek, Cüneyt, *Yeni Demokrasi, Yeni Arayışlar*, Ankara: Bilgi Yayınevi, 1984.

Arda, Nihat, "Türkiye'deki Amerikan Üsleri", *Yön*, No. 191, November 25, 1966.

Arda, Nihat, "Türkiye'deki Amerikan Askeri Polisi", *Yön*, No. 194, December 16, 1966, p. 10.

Arı, Önder, *Türkiye-ABD İlişkilerinde Çok Yönlü Etkenler*, İstanbul: İ.Ü. İktisat Yayınları, 1977.

Armaoğlu, Fahir H., "Recent Developments in Turkish Foreign Policy", *Foreign Policy*, March 1971, vol. 1, No. 1, pp. 85-94.

Armaoğlu, Fahir H., "Türk-Amerikan Münasebetleri", *Son Çağ Dergisi*, No. 24, June 1967.

Armaoğlu, Fahir H., "Turkey and the United States: A New Alliance", *The Turkish Yearbook of International Relations*, vol. 6, 1965, pp. 1-15.

Armaoğlu, Fahir, "1974 Cyprus Crisis and the Soviets", *Foreign Policy*, vol. 4, Nos. 2-3, 1974, pp. 177-183.

Armaoğlu, Fahir, *20. Yüzyıl Siyasi Tarihi*, vol.II, Ankara: Türkiye İş Bankası, 1994.

Aron, Raymond, "The Quest for a Philosophy of Foreign Affairs" in Hoffmann, Stanley (ed.), *Contemporary Theory in International Relations*, Englewood Cliffs, New Jersey: Prentice-Hall Inc., 1960.

Asmus, Ronald D., "The Rise or Fall? Of Multilateralism: America's New Foreign Policy and What it Means for Europe" in M. Carnovale (ed.), *European Security and International Institutions After the Cold War,* London: Macmillan, 1995.

Atalay, Safa, "ABD Güvenlik Yardımı ABD Türkiye İlişkileri", *Avrasya Dosyası*, vol. 1, No. 3, Fall 1994, pp. 236-256.

Ataöv, Türkkaya, *Amerika, NATO ve Türkiye*, Ankara: Aydınlık Yayınevi, 1969.

Attalides, Michael A., *Cyprus: Nationalism and International Politics*, Edinburgh: Q Press Ltd., 1979.

Attalides, Michael A. (ed.), *Cyprus Reviewed: A Seminar on the Cyprus Problem*, Nicosia: Jus Cypri Association, 1977.

Ausland, John C. and Richardson, Colonel Hugh F., "Crisis Management: Berlin, Cyprus, Laos", *Foreign Affairs*, vol. 44, No. 2, January 1966, pp. 291-303.

Avcıoğlu, Doğan, "Sam Amcanın Türkiye'deki Hazinesi", *Yön*, 25 April 1965, p. 3.

Avcıoğlu, Doğan, "Türkiye'deki Amerikan Üsleri", *Yön*, 26 November 1966, pp. 8-9.

Aydın, Mustafa, "Kafkasya ve Orta Asya'yla İlişkiler (1999-2001)" in Oran, Baskın (ed.), *Türk Dış Politikası: Kurtuluş Savaşından Bugüne Olgular, Belgeler, Yorumlar*, vol. 2, İstanbul: İletişim, 2001, pp. 366-439.

Aykan, Mahmut Bali, "Turkish Perspectives on Turkish-US Relations Concerning Persian Gulf Security in the Post-Cold War Era: 1989-1995", *Middle East Journal*, vol. 50, No. 3, Summer 1996, pp. 344-358.

Ayres, Ron, "Turkish Foreign Relations", *Khamsin* (Journal of Revolutionary Socialists of the Middle East), Special Issue, *Modern Turkey: Development and Crisis*, London: Ithaca Press, No. 11, pp. 117-127.

Bağcı, Hüseyin, "Changing Security of Turkey" in Aydın, Mustafa (ed.), *Turkey at the Threshold of the 21st Century*, Ankara: International Relations Foundation, 1998.

Bahçeli, Tözün S., *Communal Discord and the Stake of Interested Governments in Cyprus 1955-1970*, Ph.D. Thesis, The University of London, the London School of Economics and Political Science, 1972.

Bal, Halil, "Kırgızistan: Çin Gölgesi ve Rus Desteği Altında" in Yalçınkaya, Alaaddin (ed.) *Türk Cumhuriyetleri ve Petrol Boru Hatları*, İstanbul: Bağlam, November 1998, pp. 97-116.

Barnet, Richard J., *Intervention and Revolution: The United States in the Third World*, London: Paladin, 1972.

Barrett, John, "Current Political Agenda of the Atlantic Alliance and Turkey" in Aydın, Mustafa (ed.), *Turkey at the Threshold of the 21st Century*, Ankara: International Relations Foundation, 1998.

Batu, Hamit, "New Developments in Turkish Foreign Policy", *Foreign Policy*, vol. 5, No. 4, 1976, pp. 5-17.

Baykal, Sanem and Arat, Tuğrul, "AB'yle İlişkiler (1999-2001)" in Oran, Baskın (ed.), *Türk Dış Politikası: Kurtuluş Savaşından Bugüne Olgular, Belgeler, Yorumlar*, vol. 2, İstanbul: İletişim, 2001, pp. 326-365.

Bayülken, Ümit Haluk, "The Cyprus Question and the United Nations", *Foreign Policy*, vol. 4, Nos. 2-3, 1974, pp. 71-142.

Bayülken, Ümit Haluk, "Turkey's Foreign Policy", *Foreign Policy*, vol. 3, No. 1, March 1973, pp. 67-82.

Beggs, Robert, *The Cuban Missile Crisis*, London: Longman, 1971.

Bell, Coral, *The Diplomacy of Detente: the Kissinger Era*, London: Martin Robertson, 1977.

Berberoğlu, Berch, *Turkey in Crisis: From State Capitalism to Neo-colonialism*, London: Zed Press, 1982.

Bernstein, Barton J., "The Cuban Missile Crisis: Trading the Jupiters in Turkey?", *Political Science Quarterly*, vol. 95, No. 1, Spring 1980, pp. 97-126.

Bernstein, Barton J., "Reconsidering the Missile Crisis: Dealing With the Problems of the American Jupiters in Turkey" in Nathan, James (ed.), *The Cuban Missile Crisis Revisited*, New York: St. Martin's Press, 1992.

Beschloss, Michael R., *Kennedy v. Khrushchev: the Crisis Years 1960-1963*, London, Boston: Faber and Faber, 1991.

Beyaz Kitap, Savunma 1998, Ankara: Milli Savunma Bakanlığı, 1998.

Bilge, Suat, "The Cyprus Conflict and Turkey" in Karpat, Kemal H.(ed.), *Turkey's Foreign Policy in Transition 1950-1974*, Leiden, Netherlands: E.J. Brill, 1975.

Birand, Mehmet Ali, *Diyet: Türkiye ve Kıbrıs üzerine Uluslarası Pazarlıklar 1974-1979*, İstanbul: Ağaoğlu Yayınevi, 1979.

Birand, Mehmet Ali, *30 Sıcak Gün*, İstanbul: Milliyet Yayınları, 1976.

Birand, Mehmet Ali; Dündar, Can and Çaplı, Bülent, *12 Mart: İhtilalin Pençesinde Demokrasi*, Ankara: İmge Kitabevi, 1994.

Black, Joseph E. and Thompson, Kenneth W. (eds.), *Foreign Policies in a World of Change*, New York: Harper and Row, 1963.

Blight, James G. and Welch, David A., *On the Brink: Americans and Soviets Reexamine the Cuban Missile Crisis*, New York: Hill and Wang, 1989.

Boll, Michael M., "Turkey's New National Security Concept: What It Means for NATO", *ORBIS*, vol. 23, Fall 1979, pp. 609-631.

Botsas, Eleftherios N., "The US- Cyprus- Turkey- Greece Tetragon: the Economics of an Alliance", *Journal of Political and Military Sociology*, vol. 16, No. 2, Fall 1988, pp. 247-262.

Boyd, James M., "Cyprus: Episode in Peacekeeping", *International Organisation*, vol. 20, 1966, pp. 1-17.

Bölükbaşı, Süha, *Superpowers and the Third World: Turkish-American Relations and Cyprus*, New York: University Press of America, 1988.

Brandon, Henry, *The Retreat of American Power*, London: the Bodley Head, 1973.

Brands, H.W., Jr., "America Enters the Cyprus Tangle 1964", *Middle Eastern Studies*, vol. 23, No. 3, July 1987, pp. 348-362.

Branson, William H., "Trends in United States International Trade and Investment Since World War II" in Feldstein, Martin(ed.), *The American Economy in Transition*, Chicago, London: the University of Chicago Press, 1980.

Brown, James, *Delicately Poised Allies: Greece and Turkey: Problems, Policy Choices and Mediterranean Security*, London: Brassey's, 1991.

Bruce, Leigh H., "Cyprus: A Last Chance", *Foreign Policy*, No. 58, Spring 1985, pp. 115-133.

Burt, Richard, "Turkey and Reagen Administration" in Harris, George S. (ed.), *The Middle East in Turkish-American Relations*, Washington: the Heritage Foundation, 1985.

Buzoğlu, M. Hüseyin, *Körfez Krizi ve PKK*, Ankara: Strateji.

Camp, Glen D., "Cyprus Between the Powers 1980-1989", *Cyprus Review*, vol. 1, No. 2, Fall 1989, pp. 65-90.

Camp, Glen D., "Greek-Turkish Conflict Over Cyprus", *Political Science Quarterly*, vol. 95, No. 1, Spring 1980, pp. 43-70.

Campbell, John C., *Defense of the Middle East: Problems of American Policy,* New York: Harper and Brothers, 1960.

Campbell, John C., "The Mediterranean Crisis", *Foreign Affairs*, July 1975, pp. 605-624.

Campbell, John C., "The United States and the Cyprus Question, 1974-1975" in Coufoudakis, Van (ed.), *Essays on the Cyprus Conflict*, New York: Pella Publishing Company, 1976.

Campany, Richard C., *Turkey and the United States: the Arms Embargo Period*, New York: Praeger, 1986.

Caporaso, James A., "Dependence, Dependency, and Power in the Global System: A Structural and Behavioral Analysis", *International Organization*, vol. 32, No. 1, Winter 1978, pp. 13-44.

Castleberry, H. Paul, "Summary of Proceedings of the Pacific Northwest Political Science Association, Conflict Resolution and the Cyprus Problem", *The Western Political Quarterly*, vol. 17, No. 3, September 1964, pp. 118-130.

Cem, İsmail, *Tarih Açısından 12 Mart*, İstanbul: Cem Yayınevi, 1980.

Cem, İsmail, *Türkiye'de Geri Kalmışlığın Tarihi*, İstanbul: Cem Yayınevi, 1973.

Cem, İsmail, "Turkey in the Twenty First Century", *Special Policy Forum Report*, No. 529, 3 April 2001, http//.www.washingtoninstitute.org/watch/Policywatch/policywatch2001/529.htm.

Cem, İsmail, *Turkey in the New Century: Speeches and Texts Presented at International Fora (1995-2001)*, Lefkoşa: Rustem, 2001, 2nd Edition.

Chang, L., "The View From Washington and the View From Nowhere: Cuban Missile Crisis Historiography" in Nathan, James (ed.), *The Cuban Missile Crisis Revisited*, New York: St. Martin's Press, 1992.

Chayes, Abram, *The Cuban Missile Crisis: the International Crises and the Role of Law*, London: Oxford University Press, 1974.

Childers, Erskine B., *The Road to Suez: A Study of Western-Arab Relations*, London: MacGibbon and Kee, 1962.

Chipman, John, "Allies in the Mediterranean: Legacy of Fragmentation" in Chipman, John (ed.), *NATO's Southern Allies: Internal and External Challenges*, London: Routledge, 1988.

Clogg, Richard and Yannopoulos, George (eds.), *Greece Under Military Rule*, London: Secker and Warburg, 1972.

Cohn, Edwin J., *Turkish Economic, Social and Political Change: The Development of a More Prosperous and Open Society*, New York, 1970.

Cooper, Malcolm, "The Legacy of Atatürk: Turkish Political Structures and Policy Making", *International Affairs,* vol. 78, No. 2002, pp. 115-128.

de Cordier, Bruno, "Ekonomik Yardımlaşma Teşkilatı (ECO): Soğuk Savaşın Kalıntıları Üzerinde Yeni Bir İpek Yolu mu?" in Öke, Mim Kemal (ed.), *Geçiş Sürecinde Orta Asya Türk Cumhuriyetleri,* İstanbul: Alfa, 1999, pp. 211-228.

Coufoudakis, Van (ed.), *Essays on the Cyprus Conflict,* New York: Pella Publishing Company, 1976.

Coufoudakis, Van, "The Dynamics of Political Partition and Division in Multiethnic and Multireligious Societies: the Cyprus Case" in Coufoudakis, Van (ed.), *Essays on the Cyprus Conflict,* New York: Pella Publishing Company, 1976.

Coufoudakis, Van, "United States Foreign Policy and the Cyprus Question" in Attalides, Michael A. (ed.), *Cyprus Reviewed: A Seminar on the Cyprus Problem,* Nicosia: Jus Cypri Association, 1977.

Coufoudakis, Van, "Turkey and the United States: the Problems and Prospects of a Post-War Alliance", *Journal of Political and Military Sociology,* vol. 9, No. 2, Fall 1981, pp. 179-196.

Coufoudakis, Van, "United Nations Peacekeeping and Peacemaking and the Cyprus Question", *The Western Political Quarterly,* vol. 29, No. 3, September 1976, pp. 457-473.

Coufoudakis, Van, "US Foreign Policy and the Cyprus Question: An Interpretation", *Millennium,* vol. 5, No. 3, Winter 1976-77, pp. 245-268.

Couloumbis, Theodore A. *The United States, Greece and Turkey: the Troubled Triangle,* New York: Praeger, 1983.

Couloumbis, Theodore A. and Hicks, Sallie M. (eds.), *US Foreign Policy Toward Greece and Cyprus: the Clash of Principle and Pragmatism,* Washington D.C.: Center for Mediterranean and the American Hellenic Institute Studies, 1975.

Couloumbis, Theodore A. and Hicks, Sallie M., "The Impact of Greek Americans Upon United States Foreign Policy: Illusion or Reality?" in Attalides, Michael A. (ed.), *Cyprus Reviewed: A Seminar on the Cyprus Problem,* Nicosia: Jus Cypri Association, 1977.

Crabb, Cecil V. and Holt, Pat M., *Invitation to Struggle: Congress, the President and Foreign Policy,* Washington D.C.: Congressional Quarterly Inc., 1980.

Crawshaw, Nancy, "The Republic of Cyprus: From the Zurich Agreement to Independence", *The World Today,* vol. 16, No. 12, December 1960, pp. 526-540.

Crawshaw, Nancy, "Cyprus: Collapse of the Zurich Agreement", *The World Today,* vol. 20, January-December 1964, pp. 338-347.

Crawshaw, Nancy, "Cyprus After Kophinou", *The World Today,* October 1968.

Crawshaw, Nancy, *The Cyprus Revolt: An Account of the Struggle for Union With Greece,* London, Boston: G. Allen and Unwin, 1978.

Crawshaw, Nancy, "Subversion in Cyprus", *The World Today,* vol. 27, January-December 1971, pp. 25-32.

Crawshaw, Nancy, "Uncertainties in Cyprus", *The World Today,* vol. 28, August 1972, pp. 330-333.

Criss, Nur-Bilge, "International Institutions and European Security: A Turkish Perspective" in M. Carnovale (ed.), *European Security and International Institutions After the Cold War,* London: Macmillan, 1995.

CSIA European Security Group, "Instability and Change on NATO's Southern Flank", *International Security*, vol. 3, Winter 1978, pp. 150-177.

Çamlı, İbrahim *Dünya, Amerika, Türkiye*, İstanbul, 1966.

Çelik, Edip, *Türkiye'nin Dış Politika Tarihi*, İstanbul, 1969.

Çubukçu, Tuğrul, "Savunma Harcamaları: İç ve Dış Kaynaklar" in *Türkiye'nin Savunması*, Ankara: Dış Politika Enstitüsü, 1987.

Denktash, Rauf R., *The Cyprus Triangle*, London: K. Rustem and Brother, 1988.

Dentash, Rauf R., "The Cyprus Problem, 23rd Year", *Turkish Review Quarterly Digest*, vol. 1, No. 4, Summer 1986, pp. 5-48.

Dağı, İhsan D., "Turkey in the 1990s: Foreign Policy, Human Rights and the Search for a New Identity", *Mediterranean Quarterly*, vol. 4, No. 4, Fall 1993, pp. 60-77.

Demir, Ali Faik, "SSCB'nin Dağılmasından Sonra Türkiye-Azerbeycan İlişkileri" in Sönmezoğlu, Faruk (ed.), *Değişen Dünya ve Türkiye*, Ankara: Bağlam Yay., 1996.

Demirel, Süleyman, "Turkey and NATO at the Threshold of a New Century", *Perception,* vol. 4, No. 1, March-May 1999, pp. 5-12.

Detzer, David, *The Brink: Cuban Missile Crisis 1962*, London: J.M. Dent and Sons Ltd., 1979.

Dinerstein, Herbert S., *The Making of a Missile Crisis: October 1962*, Baltimore, London: The John Hopkins University Press, 1976.

Divine, Robert A., *Since 1945 Politics and Diplomacy in Recent American History*, New York, London: John Wiley and Sons Inc., 1975.

Dobell, W.M., "Division Over Cyprus", *International Journal*, vol. 22, No. 2, Spring 1967, pp. 278-292.

Dodd, Clement H., *The Cyprus Issue: A Current Perspective*, Huntingdon: the Eothen Press, 1994.

Domhoff, G. William, "Who Made American Foreign Policy 1945-1963?" in Fox, Douglas M. (ed.), *The Politics of U.S. Foreign Policy Making*, Pacific Palisades, California: Goodyear Publishing Company Inc., 1971.

Dull, James, *The Politics of American Foreign Policy*, Englewood Cliffs, New Jersey: Prentice-Hall Inc., 1985.

Ecevit, Bülent, "Dış Politika", *Özgür İnsan*, September 1972.

Ecevit, Bülent, *Dış Politika*, Ankara: Yarın Yayınları, 1967.

Ecevit, Bülent, "Turkey's Security Policies" in Alford, Jonathan (ed.), *Greece and Turkey: Adversity in Alliance*, Aldershot: Gower, International Institute for Strategic Studies, 1984.

The Economist, "Talks About Talks", 4 December 1999, vol. 353, No. 8148, p. 49.

Editors and Staff of Newsday, *The Heroin Trail*, New York: New American Library, 1973.

Ehrlich, Thomas, *Cyprus: 1958-1967*, London: Oxford University Press, 1974.

Eraydın, Özlem, "Avrupa'nın Yeni Güvenlik Düzeni ve Türkiye" in Sönmezoğlu, Faruk (ed.), *Değişen Dünya ve Türkiye*, Ankara: Bağlam Yay., 1996.

Erdoğan, Bilgin, "ABD'nin Orta Asya Siyaseti" in Öke, Mim Kemal (ed.), *Geçiş Sürecinde Orta Asya Türk Cumhuriyetleri*, İstanbul: Alfa, 1999, pp. 229-246.

Eren, Nuri, *Turkey, NATO, and Europe: a Deteriorating Relationship*, Paris: Atlantic Institute for International Affairs, 1977.

Ergüvenç, Şadi, "Turkey: Strategic Partner of the European Union", *Foreign Policy* (Ankara), vol. 20, No. 1-2, 1996, pp. 3-22.

Ergüvenç, Şadi, "Turkey in the New European Security Context, Turkey's Role and Expectations in the Transatlantic Partnership", *Foreign Policy* (Ankara), Nos. 1-2, 1997, pp. 22-33.

Ergüvenç, Şadi, "Turkey's Strategic Importance in Military Dimension: A Regional Balance Holder" in Aydın, Mustafa (ed.), *Turkey at the Threshold of the 21st Century*, Ankara: International Relations Foundation, 1998.

Ergüvenç, Şadi, "Türkiye-Avrupa Birliği İlişkilerinin Stratejik Boyutu" *Foreign Policy*, Temmuz-Ağustos 2001, pp. 70-77.

Erhan, Çağrı and Kürkçüoğlu, Ömer, "Arap Olmayan Devletlerle İlişkiler (1999-2001)" in Oran, Baskın (ed.), *Türk Dış Politikası: Kurtuluş Savaşından Bugüne Olgular, Belgeler, Yorumlar*, vol. 2, İstanbul: İletişim, 2001, pp. 568-578.

Erim, Nihat, "Reminiscences on Cyprus", *Foreign Policy*, vol. 4, Nos. 2-3, 1974, pp. 156-163.

Eroğlu, Hamza, *Türkiye ile ABD Arasında İmzalanan 3 Temmuz 1969 Tarihli İkili Temel Anlaşma*, Ankara: Bayar Matbaası, 1970.

Ertegün, Necati M., *The Cyprus Dispute and the Birth of the Turkish Republic of Northern Cyprus*, London: K. Rustem and Brother, 1984.

Ertegün, Necati M., *Inter-Communal Talks and the Cyprus Problem*, Nicosia: Turkish Federated State of Cyprus, 1977.

Ertegün, Necati M., *The Status of the Two Peoples in Cyprus*, Lefkosa: The Public Information Office of the Turkish Republic of Northern Cyprus, 1990.

Evans, Peter, *Dependent Development: the Alliance of Multinational, State and Local Capital in Brazil*, Princeton: Princeton University Press, 1979.

Evert, M., "Turkey's Strategic Goals: Possibilities and Weaknesses", *Mediterranean Quarterly*, vol. 4, No. 4, Fall 1993, pp. 30-37.

Evin, Ahmet, *Modern Turkey: Continuity and Change*, Opladen, Germany: Leske Verlag and Budrich Gmblt, 1984.

Fairlie, Henry, *The Kennedy Promise: the Politics of Expectation*, New York: Doubleday and Company, 1973.

Fatouros, A.A., "How to Resolve Problems by Refusing to Acknowledge They Exist: Some Legal Parameters of Recent U.S. Policy Toward Greece and Cyprus" in Couloumbis, Theodore A. and Hicks, Sallie M. (eds.), *US Foreign Policy Toward Greece and Cyprus: the Clash of Principle and Pragmatism*, Washington D.C.: Center for Mediterranean and the American Hellenic Institute Studies, 1975.

Ferguson, Yale H. and Weiker, Walter F. (eds.), *Continuing Issues in International Politics*, Pacific Palisades, California: Goodyear Publishing Co., 1973.

Fırat, Melek and Kürkçüoğlu, Ömer, "Orta Doğuyla İlişkiler (1999-2001)" in Oran, Baskın (ed.), *Türk Dış Politikası: Kurtuluş Savaşından Bugüne Olgular, Belgeler, Yorumlar*, vol. 2, İstanbul: İletişim, 2001, pp. 551-567.

Finn, Helena Kane, "After the Ecevit Visit: Can Turks Pull Together to Complete the Necessary Reforms", *Policywatch*, No. 597, 24 January 2002, http//.www.washingtoninstitute.org/watch/Policywatch/policywatch2002/597.htm.

Finn, Helena Kane, "Turkish Political Disarray: Why Now? What Next?", *Policywatch*, No. 633, 10 July 2002, http//.www.washingtoninstitute.org/watch/Policywatch/policywatch2002/633.htm.

Fisher, Sydney Nettleton, "The Role of the Military in Society and Government in Turkey" in Fisher, S.N. (ed.), *The Military in the Middle East*, Colombus: Ohio State University Press, 1963.

Foley, Charles, *Island in Revolt*, London: Longmans, 1972.

Fox, Douglas M. (ed.), *The Politics of U.S. Foreign Policy Making*, Pacific Palisades, California: Goodyear Publishing Company Inc., 1971.

Franck, Thomas M. and Weisband, Edward, *Foreign Policy by Congress*, New York, Oxford: Oxford University Press, 1979.

Frey, Frederick W., *The Turkish Political Elite*, Cambridge, Mass.: M.I.T. Press, 1965.

Fulbright, J. William, *The Arrogance of Power*, New York: Random House, 1966.

Galen, Justin, "Turkey As a Self-Inflicted Wound: the Narrowing Options for U.S. Defence Policy", *Armed Forces Journal International*, June 1980, pp. 62-73.

Gallman, Waldemar J., *Iraq Under General Nuri: My Collections of Nuri al Said, 1954-1958*, Baltimore: the John Hopkins Press, 1964.

Garthoff, Raymond L., *Reflections on the Cuban Missile Crisis*, Washington D.C.: the Brookings Institution, 1989.

Geyikdağı, Mehmet Yaşar, *Political Parties in Turkey: the Role of Islam*, New York: Praeger Publishers, 1984.

Giritli, İsmet, *Neden NATO'ya Evet?*, İstanbul: Ak Yayınları, 1968.

Goldbloom, M., "United States Policy in Post-War Greece" in Clogg, Richard and Yannopoulos, George (eds.), *Greece Under Military Rule*, London: Secker and Warburg, 1972.

Göle, Celal, "Welcome Address" in Aydın, Mustafa (ed.), *Turkey at the Threshold of the 21st Century*, Ankara: International Relations Foundation, 1998.

Gönlübol, Mehmet, "NATO and Turkey: An Overall Appraisal", *The Turkish Yearbook of International Relations*, vol. 11, 1971, pp. 1-38.

Gönlübol, Mehmet, "NATO, USA and Turkey" in Karpat, Kemal H.(ed.), *Turkey's Foreign Policy in Transition 1950-1974*, Leiden, Netherlands: E.J. Brill, 1975.

Gönlübol, Mehmet, "Türk-Amerikan İlişkilerinde Genel Bir Değerlendirme", *Foreign Policy*, vol. 1, No. 4, December 1971, pp. 5-18.

Gönlübol, Mehmet et al., *Olaylarla Türk Dış Politikası 1919-1973*, Ankara: SBF Yayınları, No. 407, 1977.

Gönlübol, Mehmet and Ulman, Haluk, "Türk Dış Politikasının Yirmi Yılı 1945-1965", *SBF Dergisi*, vol. 21, No. 1, March 1966.

Grantham, Dewey W., *The United States Since 1945: the Ordeal of Power*, New York, London: McGraw-Hill Inc., 1976.

Greek Cypriot Economic Blockade and Embargo Against the Turkish Cypriot Community, Lefkosa: Turkish Cypriot Human Rights Committee, June 1983.

Gresh, Alain, "Turkish-Israeli-Syrian Relations and Their Impact on the Middle East", *Middle East Journal,* vol. 52, No. 2, 1998, pp. 188-203.

Gruen, George E., "Ambivalence in the Alliance: US Interests in the Middle East and the Evolution of Turkish Foreign Policy", *ORBIS*, vol. 24, No. 2, Summer 1980, pp. 363-378.

Gürel, Şükrü, "A General Appraisal of Current Turkish Foreign Policy" in Aydın, Mustafa (ed.), *Turkey at the Threshold of the 21st Century*, Ankara: International Relations Foundation, 1998.

Gürkan, İhsan, "Security In Eastern Mediterranean", *Foreign Policy*, vol. 6, Nos.3-4, 1977, pp. 41-50.

Gürkan, İhsan, *NATO, Turkey and the Southern Flank: A Mideastern Perspective*, New York: National Strategy Information Center, 1980.

Haas, E.B., *Beyond the Nation State*, Stanford: Stanford University Press, 1964.

Haass, Richard N., "Managing NATO's Weakest Flank: the United States, Greece and Turkey", *ORBIS*, vol. 30, No. 3, Fall 1986, pp. 457-473.

Hackett, C., "Ethnic Politics in Congress: the Turkish Embargo Experience" in Said, Abdul A.(ed.), *Ethnicity in U.S. Foreign Policy*, New York: Praeger, 1977.

Hafner, Donald L., "Bureaucratic Politics and Those Frigging Missiles: JFK, Cuba and U.S. Missiles in Turkey", *ORBIS*, vol. 21, No. 2, Summer 1977, pp. 307-334.

Hale, William M., *The Political and Economic Development of Modern Turkey*, London: Croom Helm, 1981.

Hale, William, "Turkey, NATO and the Middle East" in Lawless, Richard (ed.), *Foreign Policy Issues in the Middle East*, Occassional Papers, No. 28, Durham: University of Durham, 1985.

Hale, William M. and Norton, John D., "Turkey and the Cyprus Crisis", *The World Today*, vol. 30, September 1974, pp. 368-371.

Hale, William, "Turkish Foreign Policy After the Cold War", *Turkish Review of Balkan Studies*, No. 1, 1993, pp. 231-248.

Halil, Ali, *Atatürkçü Dış Politika ve NATO ve Türkiye*, İstanbul, 1968.

Hammond, Paul Y., *Cold War and Detente: the American Foreign Policy Process Since 1945*, New York: Harcourt Brace Jovanovich Inc., 1975.

Handel, Michael, *Weak States in the International System*, London: Frank Cass, 1981.

Harris, George S., *Troubled Alliance: Turkish-American Problems in Historical Perspective 1945-1971*, Washington: American Enterprise Institute, 1972.

Harris, George S., "Cross-Alliance Politics: Turkey and the Soviet Union", *The Turkish Yearbook of International Relations*, vol. 12, 1972, p. 1-32.

Harris, George S.(ed.), *The Middle East in Turkish-American Relations*, Washington: the Heritage Foundation, 1985.

Harris, George S., "Turkey Between Alliance and Alienation", *Foreign Policy*, vol. 8, Nos.3-4, 1980, pp. 117-125.

Harris, George S., *Turkey: Coping with Crisis*, Boulder: Westview, 1985.

Harris, George S., "Turkey and the United States" in Karpat, Kemal H.(ed.), *Turkey's Foreign Policy in Transition 1950-1974*, Leiden, Netherlands: E.J. Brill, 1975.

Hatiboğlu, Zeyyat, *An Unconventional Analysis of Turkish Economy, An Essay on Economic Development*, İstanbul: Aktif Büro Basım Organizasyon, 1978.

Heinze, Christian, *Cyprus Conflict 1964-1985*, London, Nicosia, İstanbul: K. Rustem and Brother, 1986.

Hershlag, Z.Y., *Turkey: the Challenge of the Growth*, Leiden: E.J. Brill, 1968.

Henze, Paul B., "Out of Kilter: Greeks, Turks and US Policy", *National Interest*, vol. 8, Summer 1987, pp. 71-82.

Higgins, Rosalyn, "Basic Facts on the U.N. Force in Cyprus", *The World Today*, vol. 20, January-December 1964, pp. 347-350.

Hilsman, Roger, *The Politics of Policy Making in Defense and Foreign Affairs*, New York: Harper and Row Publishers, 1971.

Hitchens, Christopher, *Cyprus*, London: Quartet Books, 1984.

Hoffmann, Stanley (ed.), *Contemporary Theory in International Relations*, Englewood Cliffs, New Jersey: Prentice-Hall Inc., 1960.

Holbraad, Carsten, *Middle Powers in International Politics*, London: Macmillan Press, 1984.

Holsti, Ole R.; Hopmann, P. Terrence and Sullivan, John D. (eds.), *Unity and Disintegration in International Alliances: Comparative Studies*, New York: John Wiley and Sons, 1973.

Hoskins, Halfrod L., *The Middle East: Problem Area in World Politics*, New York: Macmillan Company, 1956.

Hourani, Albert, "The Middle East and the Crisis of 1956" in *Middle Eastern Affairs*, St. Anthony's Papers, Number 4, London: Chatto and Windus, 1958.

Hubel, Helmut, "Turkey and the Crisis in the Middle East" in Karaosmanoğlu, A. L. and Taşhan, Seyfi (eds.), *Middle East, Turkey and the Atlantic Alliance*, Ankara: Foreign Policy Institute, 1987.

Hunter, Shireen, "Bridge or Frontier? Turkey's Post-Cold War Geopolitical Posture", *The International Spectator*, vol. 334, No. 1, January-March 1999, pp. 63-78.

Hurewitz, J. C., *The Middle East Dilemmas: The Background of United States Policy*, New York: Russell and Russell, 1953.

Howard, Harry N., "The Bicentennial in American-Turkish Relations", *Middle East Journal*, Summer 1976, pp. 291-310.

Inan, Kamran, "Cyprus, 1974 Crisis", *Foreign Policy*, vol. 4, Nos. 2-3, 1974, pp. 66-70.

İnan, Kamran, "Yeni Dünya Düzeni İçinde Türkiye ve Oluşan Yeni Dengeler" in *Değişen Dünyada Türkiye ve Türk Dünyası Sempozyumu,* Ankara: Hacettepe Üniversitesi Atatürk İlkeleri ve İnkılap Tarihi Enstitüsü, 1993.

Ionides, Michael, *Divide and Lose: The Arab Revolt of 1955-1958*, London: Geoffrey Bles, 1960.

Jones, Maldwyn A., *The Limits of Liberty: American History 1607-1980*, Oxford, New York: Oxford University Press, 1983.

Joseph, Joseph S., *Cyprus: Ethnic Conflict and International Concern*, New York: Peter Lang, 1985.

Kamp, Karl-Heinz, "European Security Outside of Europe" in Carnovale, M. (ed.), *European Security and International Institutions After the Cold War,* London: Macmillan, 1995.

Karaosmanoğlu, Ali L., "Cyprus: What Kind of a Federal Solution?", *Journal of South Asian and Middle Eastern Studies*, vol. 3, No. 3, Spring 1980, pp. 33-46.

Karaosmanoğlu, Ali, "Turkey and the Southern Flank: Domestic and External Contexts" in Chipman, John (ed.), *NATO's Southern Allies: Internal and External Challenges*, London: Routledge, 1988.

Karaosmanoğlu, A. L., "Turkey's Discreet Foreign Policy Between Western Europe and the Middle East" in Karaosmanoğlu, A. L. and Taşhan, Seyfi (eds.), *Middle East, Turkey and the Atlantic Alliance*, Ankara: Foreign Policy Institute, 1987.

Karpat, Kemal H.(ed.), *Turkey's Foreign Policy in Transition 1950-1974*, Leiden, Netherlands: E.J. Brill, 1975.

Karpat, Kemal H., "War on Cyprus: the Tragedy of Enosis" in Karpat, Kemal H.(ed.), *Turkey's Foreign Policy in Transition 1950-1974*, Leiden, Netherlands: E.J. Brill, 1975.

Keashly, Loraleigh and Fisher, Ronald J., "Toward a Contingency Approach to Third Party Intervention in Regional Conflict: a Cyprus Illustration", *International Journal*, vol. 45, No. 2, Spring 1990, pp. 424-453.

Keohane, Robert O., "The Study of Political Influence in the General Assembly", *International Organization*, vol. 21, 1967, pp. 221-237.

Kesic, Obrad, "American-Turkish Relations at a Crossroads", *Mediterranean Quarterly*, vol. 6, No. 1, 1995, pp. 97-108.

Khalilzad, Zalmay, "Türk-Batı İlişkileri İçin Stratejik Bir Plan" in Khalilzad, Zalmay; Lesser, Ian O. and Larrabee, F. Stephen, *Türk-Batı İlişkilerinin Geleceği: Stratejik Bir Plana Doğru"*, translated by Işık Kuşçu, Ankara: ASAM, 2001, pp. 83-100.

Kibaroğlu, Mustafa, "Turkey's Triple-Trouble: ESDP, Cyprus and Northern Iraq", *Insight Turkey*, January-March 2002, vol. 4, No. 1, pp. 49-58.

Kili, Suna, *1960-1975 Döneminde Cumhuriyet Halk Partisinde Gelişmeler: Siyaset Bilimi Açısından Bir İnceleme*, İstanbul: Boğaziçi üniversitesi Yayınları, 1976.

Kirk, George E., *Contemporary Arab Politics: A Consice History*, London, 1961.

Kitromilides, P.M., "From Coexistence to Confrontation: the Dynamics of Ethnic Conflict in Cyprus" in Attalides, Michael A. (ed.), *Cyprus Reviewed: A Seminar on the Cyprus Problem*, Nicosia: Jus Cypri Association, 1977.

Kolodziaj, Edward A., "The National Security Council: Innovations and Implications" in Fox, Douglas M. (ed.), *The Politics of U.S. Foreign Policy Making*, Pacific Palisades, California: Goodyear Publishing Company Inc., 1971.

Koumoulides, John T.A.(ed.), *Cyprus in Transition 1960-1985*, London: Trigraph, 1986.

Köni, Hasan, "Yeni Uluslar arası Düzende Türk-Amerikan İlişkileri", *Yeni Türkiye*, No. 3, 1995.

Köni, Hasan, "Gulf Savaşı Sonrasında Orta Doğunun Durumu" in *Değişen Dünyada Türkiye ve Türk Dünyası Sempozyumu*, Ankara: Hacettepe Üniversitesi Atatürk İlkeleri ve İnkılap Tarihi Enstitüsü, 1993.

Kösebalan, Hasan, "Turkey's EU Membership: A Clash of Security Cultures", *Middle East Policy,* vol. 9, No. 2, June 2002, pp. 130-146.

Krahenbuhl, Margaret, *Turkish-American Relations: An Affair to Remember*, Santa Monica, California: Rand Corporation, December 1974.

Krueger, Anne O., *Foreign Trade Regimes and Economic Development: Turkey*, New York, London: Columbia University Press, 1974.

Kuniholm, Bruce R., *The Origins of the Cold War in the Near East: Great Power Conflict and Diplomacy in Iran, Turkey and Greece*, Princeton, New Jersey: Princeton University Press, 1980.

Kuniholm, Bruce R., "Turkey and NATO: Past, Present and Future", *ORBIS*, Summer 1983, pp. 421-445.

Kuniholm, Bruce, "East or West? Geopolitics of Turkey and its NATO Alliance" in Karaosmanoğlu, A. L. and Taşhan, Seyfi (eds.), *Middle East, Turkey and the Atlantic Alliance*, Ankara: Foreign Policy Institute, 1987.

Kuniholm, Bruce R., "Turkey and the West", *Foreign Affairs*, vol. 70, No. 2, Spring 1991, pp. 34-48.

Kuniholm, Bruce R., "U.S. Policy in the Near East: the Triumphs and Tribulations of the Truman Administration" in Lacey, Michael J.(ed.), *The Truman Presidency*, New York: Woodrow Wilson International Center for Scholars, 1989.

Kurat, Yuluğ Tekin, *Elli Yıllık Cumhuriyetin Dış Politikası 1923-1973*, Ankara: Türk Tarih Kurumu, 1975.

Kuru, Ahmet T., "Uluslararası Ortam ve Bölgesel Entegrasyon Teorileri Işığında Türk Birliği Meselesi" in Öke, Mim Kemal (ed.), *Geçiş Sürecinde Orta Asya Türk Cumhuriyetleri*, İstanbul: Alfa, 1999, pp. 152-210.

Kürkçüoğlu, Ömer, *Türkiye'nin Arap Ortadoğusuna Karşı Politikası 1945-1970*, Ankara: SBF Yayını, No. 340, 1972.

Lacey, Michael J.(ed.), *The Truman Presidency*, New York: Cambridge University Press, 1991.

Laipson, Ellen B., "US-Turkey: Friendly Friction", *Journal of Defence and Diplomacy*, vol. 3, No. 9, September 1985, pp. 21-37.

Laipson, Ellen B., "Cyprus: A Quarter Century of U.S. Diplomacy" in Koumoulides, John T. A.(ed.), *Cyprus in Transition 1960-1985*, London: Trigraph, 1986.

Landau, David, *Kissinger: the Uses of Power*, London: Robson Books Ltd., 1974.

Landau, Jacob M., *Radical Politics in Modern Turkey*, Leiden, Netherlands: E.J. Brill, 1974.

Landau, Jacob M., *Johnson's 1964 Letter to İnönü and Greek Lobbying of the White House*, Jerusalem: The Hebrew University, 1979.

Landau, Jacob M., "Johnson's 1964 Letter to İnönü and the Greek Lobbying at the White House", *Turkish Yearbook of International Relations*, vol. 14, 1974, pp. 45-58.

Laqueur, Walter Z., *The Soviet Union and the Middle East*, London: Routledge and Kegan Paul, 1959.

Larrabee, F. Stephen, "Türk Dış Politikası ve Güvenlik Politikası: Yeni Boyutlar, Yeni Güçlükler" in Khalilzad, Zalmay; Lesser, Ian O. and Larrabee, F. Stephen, *Türk-Batı İlişkilerinin Geleceği: Stratejik Bir Plana Doğru"*, translated by Işık Kuşçu, Ankara: ASAM, 2001, 23-54.

Lawless, Richard (ed.), *Foreign Policy Issues in the Middle East*, Occassional Papers, No. 28, Durham: University of Durham, 1985.

Lederer, Ivo J., and Vucinich, Wayne S., *The Soviet Union and the Middle East: the Post-World War II Era*, Stanford, California: Hoverd Institution Press, Stanford University, 1974.

Legg, K.R., "Congress as Trojan Horse, the Turkish Embargo Problem 1974-1978" in Spanier, John and Nogee, Joseph(eds.), *Congress, the Presidency and American Foreign Policy*, New York: Pergamon Press, 1981.

Lenczowski, George, *United States Interests in the Middle East*, Washington D.C.: American Enterprise Institute, 1968.

Lenczowski, George, *Soviet Advances in the Middle East*, Washington D.C.: American Enterprise Institute for Public Policy Research, 1971.

Lenczowski, George, *The Middle East in World Affairs*, London: Cornell University Press, 1980.

Lesser, Ian O., *Bridge or Barrier: Turkey and the West After the Cold War*, Santa Monica: Rand, 1992.

Lesser, Ian O., "Turkey's Strategic Options", *The International Spectator*, vol. 34, No. 1, January-March 1999, pp. 79-88.

Lesser, Ian O., "Türk İç Yapısındaki Değişimler ve Bunların Dış Politikaya Etkileri" in Khalilzad, Zalmay; Lesser, Ian O. and Larrabee, F. Stephen, *Türk-Batı İlişkilerinin Geleceği: Stratejik Bir Plana Doğru"*, translated by Işık Kuşçu, Ankara: ASAM, 2001, pp. 7-22.

Lesser, Ian O., "Değişmekte Olan Bir Türkiye'de Batının Çıkarları" in Khalilzad, Zalmay; Lesser, Ian O. and Larrabee, F. Stephen, *Türk-Batı İlişkilerinin Geleceği: Stratejik Bir Plana Doğru"*, translated by Işık Kuşçu, Ankara: ASAM, 2001, pp. 55-82.

Lewis, Jesse W., Jr., *The Strategic Balance in the Mediterranean*, Washington D.C.: the American Enterprise Institute, 1976.

Lewis, Geoffrey, *Modern Turkey*, New York: Praeger, 1974.

Liska, George, *Nations in Alliance*, Baltimore: John Hopkins University Press, 1968.

Liska, George, *Alliances and the Third World*, Baltimore: The Johns Hopkins Press, 1968.

Mackenzie, Kenneth, *Turkey in Transition: the West's Neglected Ally*, London: Institute for European Defence and Strategic Studies, 1984.

Mackenzie, Kenneth, *Turkey: After the Storm*, London: the Institute for the Study of Conflict, 1974.

Makovsky, Alan, "Turkey: the Armenian Genocide Resolution and Iraq Policy", *Policywatch*, No. 495, 16 October 2000, http//.www.washingtoninstitute.org/watch/Policywatch/policywatch2000/495.htm.

Makovsky, Alan, "Turkey's Unfinished Role in the War on Terrorism", *Insight Turkey*, vol. 4, No. 1, January-March 2002, pp. 41-48.

Mango, Andrew, *Turkey: A Delicately Poised Ally*, Beverley Hills, California: Sage, 1976.

Manisalı, Erol, "Savunma Sanayii ve Türkiye'deki Savunma Sanayiinin Gelişimi" in *Türkiye'nin Savunması*, Ankara: Dış Politika Enstitüsü, 1987.

Markides, Kryriacos C., *The Rise and Fall of the Cyprus Republic*, New Haven, Conn., London: Yale University Press, 1977.

Marlowe, John, *Arab Nationalism and British Imperialism: A Study in Power Politics*, London: The Cresset Press, 1961.

McGhee, George, *The U.S.- Turkish- NATO- Middle East Connection: How the Truman Doctrine and Turkey's NATO Entry Contained the Soviets*, London: Macmillan Press Ltd., 1990.

"Measures Taken by the Republic of Turkey Against Terrorism", Report to the Security Council Committee established pursuant to resolution 1373, December 2001, http://www.mfa.gov.tr/grupa/ac/acf/terrorism.

Miller, Linda B., *Cyprus: the Law and Politics of Civil Conflict*, Cambridge, Mass.: Harvard University Center for International Affairs, 1968.

Miroff, Bruce, *Pragmatic Illusions: the Presidential Politics of John F. Kennedy*, New York: David McKay Company Inc., 1976.

Missiroli, Antonio, "EU-NATO Cooperation in Crisis Management: No Turkish Delight for ESDP", *Security Dialogue,* 2002, vol. 33, No. 1, pp. 9-26.

Monroe, Elizabeth, Britain's Moment in the Middle East 1914-1956, London: Chatto and Windus, 1964.

Moon, Bruce E., "Consensus or Compliance? Foreign Policy Change and External Dependence", *International Organization*, vol. 39, No. 2, Spring 1985, pp. 297-329.

Moritz, Charles (ed.), *Current Biography 1975*, New York: H.W. Wilson, 1976.

Morris, Roger, *Uncertain Greatness: Henry Kissinger and American Foreign Policy*, London: Quartet Books, 1977.

Moustakis, Fotios and Sheehan, Micheal, "Greek Security Policy After the Cold-War", *Contemporary Security Politic*s, vol. 21, No. 3, December 2000.

Mufti, Malik, "Daring and Caution in Turkish Foreign Policy", *Middle East Journal*, vol. 52, No. 1, Winter 1998, pp. 32-50.

Mufti, Malik, "Turkish-Syrian Rapprochement: Causes and Consequences", *Policywatch*, No. 630, 21 June 2002, http//.www.washingtoninstitute.org/watch/Policywatch/policywatch2002/630.htm.

Müftüler-Bac, Meltem, "Turkey's Predicament in the Post-cold War Era", *Futures*, vol. 28, No. 3, April 1996, pp. 255-268.

Mütercimler, Erol, *Kıbrıs Barış Harekatının Bilinmeyen Yönleri*, İstanbul: Yaprak Yayınevi, 1990.

Nas, Çiğdem, "Batı Avrupa Birliği Oluşumu Karşısında Türkiye'nin Durumu" in Sönmezoğlu, Faruk (ed.), *Değişen Dünya ve Türkiye*, Ankara: Bağlam Yay., 1996.

Nathan, James (ed.), *The Cuban Missile Crisis Revisited*, New York: St. Martin's Press, 1992.

Nathan, James, "The Missile Crisis: His Finest Hour Now", *World Politics*, vol. 27, No. 2, January 1975, pp. 256-281.

Nelson, H. D. and Kaplan, I., "National Security" in Nyrop, Richard F., *Turkey: A Country Study*, Washington: The American University, 1980.

Nye, Roger Paul, *The Military in Turkish Politics 1960-1973*, Ph.D. Thesis, Graduate School of Arts and Sciences, Washington University, 1974.

Nye, Roger Paul, "Civil-Military Confrontation in Turkey: the 1973 Presidential Election", *International Journal of Middle East Studies*, vol. 8, April 1977, pp. 209-228.

Nyrop, Richard F., *Handbook for the Republic of Turkey*, Washington: the American University, 1973.

Nyrop, Richard F., *Turkey: A Country Study*, Washington: The American University, 1980.

Oberling, Pierre, *The Road to Bellapais: the Turkish Cypriot Exodus to Northern Cyprus*, New York: Columbia University Press, 1982.

Okman, Cengiz, "NATO Stratejileri ve Türkiye Bakımından Sonuçları" in *Türkiye'nin Savunması*, Ankara: Dış Politika Enstitüsü, 1987.

Olson, Robert, "Turkey-Iran Relations, 2000-2001: The Caspian, Azerbaijan and the Kurds", *Middle East Policy*, vol. 9, No. 2, June 2002, pp. 111-129.

Olson, William C.; McLellon, David S. and Sondermann, Fred A., *The Theory and Practice of International Relations*, Englewood Cliffs, New Jersey: Prentice-Hall Inc., 1983.

Oran, Baskın, "Dönemin Bilançosu (1990-2001)" in Oran, Baskın (ed.), *Türk Dış Politikası: Kurtuluş Savaşından Bugüne Olgular, Belgeler, Yorumlar*, vol. 2, İstanbul: İletişim, 2001, pp. 203-242.

Orhun, Ömür, "Turkey, Norway and the US in the New European Security Context", *Foreign Policy* (Ankara), Nos. 1-2, 1997, pp. 5-12.

Orhun, Ömür, "The Uncertainties and Challenges Ahead: A Southern Perspective", *Perceptions,* vol.. 4, No. 1, 1999, pp. 23-30.

Orkunt, Sezai, *Türkiye-ABD Askeri İlişkileri*, İstanbul: Milliyet Yayınları, 1978.

Özbudun, Ergun, *The Role of the Military in Recent Turkish Politics*, Occasional Papers, No. 14, Center for International Affairs, Harvard University, November 1966.

Özkan, Abdullah, *Türkiye'deki Amerika,* İstanbul: Emre Yayınları, 1993.

Özsoy, Muzaffer, "Dünü ve Bugünüyle Türk Savunma Stratejisi" in *Türkiye'nin Savunması*, Ankara: Dış Politika Enstitüsü, 1987.

Parris, Mark, "Ecevit to Washington: Opportunities for US-Turkish Relations", *Policywatch*, No. 592, 10 January 2002, http//.www.washingtoninstitute.org/watch/Policywatch/policywatch2002/592.htm.

Polk, William R., "A Decade of Discovery; America in the Middle East 1947-1958" in Hourani, Albert (ed.), *The Middle Eastern Affairs,* St. Anthony's Papers, Number 11, London: Chatto and Windus, 1961.

Polyviou, Polyvious G., *Cyprus: Conflict and Negotiation 1960-1980*, London: Duckworth, 1980.

Polyviou, Polyvious G., *Cyprus: The Tragedy and the Challenge*, Washington: American Hellenic Institute, 1975.

Psomiades, H.J., "The United States and the Mediterranean Triangle: Greece, Turkey and Cyprus: A New Phase" in Attalides, Michael A. (ed.), *Cyprus Reviewed: A Seminar on the Cyprus Problem*, Nicosia: Jus Cypri Association, 1977.

Purvis, Hoyt, "Tracing the Congressional Role: U.S. Foreign Policy and Turkey" in Purvis, Hoyt and Baker, Steven J.(eds.), *Legislating Foreign Policy*, London: Westview Press, 1984.

Ramady, M. A., "The Role of Turkey in Greek-Turkish Cypriot Communal Relations" in Coufoudakis, Van (ed.), *Essays on the Cyprus Conflict*, New York: Pella Publishing Company, 1976.

Ramazani, Rouhullah K., *Iran's Foreign Policy 1941-1973: A Study of Foreign Policy in Modernising Nations*, Charlottesvilles: University Press of Virginia, 1975.

Ramazani, Rouhullah K., *The Northern Tier: Afghanistan, Iran and Turkey*, Princeton N.J.: D. van Nostrand Company Inc., 1966.

Rasizade, Alec, "The Mythology of Munificent Caspian Bonanza and its Concomitant Pipeline Geopolitics" *Central Asian Survey*, 2002, vol. 21, No. 1, pp. 37-54.

Raşit, Ahmet, *Orta Asya'nın Dirilişi: İslam mı Milliyetçilik mi?,* (translated by Osman Ç. Deniztekin), İstanbul: Cep Kitapları, September 1996.

Reddaway, John, *Burdened with Cyprus: the British Connection*, London, Nicosia, İstanbul: K. Rustem and Brother and Weidenfield and Nicolson Ltd., 1986.

Reeves, Thomas C., *A Question of Character: A Life of John F. Kennedy*, New York: The Free Press, 1991.

"Remarks by Deputy Secretary of Defence Paul Wolfowitz," the Washington Institute for Near East Policy, St. Regis Hotel, Washington D.C., March 13, 2002, http://www.defenselink.mil/speeches/2002/s20020313-depsecdef.html.

Republic of Turkey: Special Report, Journal of Defense and Diplomacy, vol. 3, No. 9, September 1985, pp. 28-37.

Reynolds, Micheal, "Demokrasinin Türkiye Sınavı", *Radikal*, 4 September 2002 (the translation of the article appeared in *Los Angeles Times*).

Richardson, Neil R., "Political Compliance and U.S. Trade Dominance", *American Political Science Review*, vol. 70, No. 4, December 1976, pp. 1098-1109.

Robinson, Richard D., *The First Turkish Republic: A Case Study in National Development*, Cambridge, Mass.: Harvard University Press, 1963.

Roper, John, "The West and Turkey: Varying Roles, Common Interests", *The International Spectator*, vol. 34, No. 1, January-March 1999, pp. 89-102.

Rothstein, Robert L., *Alliances and Small Powers*, New York: Columbia University Press, 1968.

Rothstein, R. L., " On the Problems of Being Small and Poor" in Olson, William C.; McLellon, David S. and Sondermann, Fred A., *The Theory and Practice of International Relations*, Englewood Cliffs, New Jersey: Prentice-Hall Inc., 1983.

Roy, Oakley S., *Drugs, Society and Human Behaviour*, Saint Louis: the C.V. Mosby Company, 1972.

Rubin, Barry, "Middle East Policy in the Turkish Context" in Harris, George S.(ed.), *The Middle East in Turkish-American Relations*, Washington: the Heritage Foundation, 1985.

Rustow, Dankwart A., *Turkey: America's Forgotten Ally*, New York: Council on Foreign Relations, 1987.

Said, Abdul A.(ed.), *Ethnicity in U.S. Foreign Policy*, New York: Praeger, 1977.

Salih, Halil İbrahim, *Cyprus: The Impact of Diverse Nationalism on a State*, Alabama: University of Alabama Press, 1978.

Sander, Oral, "Turkey: the Staunchest Ally of the United States? Forces of Continuity and Change in the Strategic Relationship", *The Turkish Yearbook of International Relations*, vol. 15, 1977, pp. 10-24.

Sarıca, Murat; Teziç, Erdoğan and Eskiyurt, Özer, *Kıbrıs Sorunu*, İstanbul: İstanbul üniversitesi Yayınları, No. 2071, 1975.

Sayarı, Sabri Mustafa, *Party Politics in Turkey: Dimensions of Competition and Organization*, Ph.D. Thesis, Columbia University, Political Science, 1972.

Schlesinger, Arthur M., Jr., *The Cycles of American History*, Boston: Houghton Mifflin Company, 1986.

Schlesinger, Arthur M., Jr., *The Imperial Presidency*, London: Andre Deutsch, 1973.

Schlesinger, Arthur M., *A Thousand Days*, London: Andre Deutsch, 1965.

Sezer, Duygu, *Kamuoyu ve Dış Politika*, Ankara: SBF Yayını, No. 339, 1972.

Sezer, Duygu, *Turkey's Security Policies* in Alford, Jonathan (ed.), *Greece and Turkey: Adversity in Alliance*, Aldershot: Gower, International Institute for Strategic Studies, 1984.

Sezer, Duygu B., "Turkey's New Security Environment, Nuclear Weapons and Proliferation", *Comparative Strategy*, vol. 14, No. 2, 1995, pp. 149-172.

Sezer, Duygu, "The Black Sea Politics and Turkey" in Aydın, Mustafa (ed.), *Turkey at the Threshold of the 21st Century*, Ankara: International Relations Foundation, 1998.

Shaw, Stanford J. and Shaw, Ezel Kural, *History of the Ottoman Empire and Modern Turkey, Reform, Revolution and Republic: the Rise of Modern Turkey, 1808-1975*, vol. 2, Cambridge: Cambridge University Press, 1977.

Shea, Jamie, "Should NATO be Enlarged to the East" in Carnovale, M. (ed.), *European Security and International Institutions After the Cold War,* London: Macmillan, 1995.

Shinn, Rinn S., "Government and Politics" in Nyrop, Richard F., *Turkey: A Country Study*, Washington: The American University, 1980.

Shoemaker, Christopher C. and Spanier, John, *Patron-Client State Relationships: Multilateral Crises in the Nuclear Age*, New York: Praeger, 1984.

Shorter, Frederic C., "Military Expenditures and the Allocation of Resources" in Shorter, Frederic C. (ed.), *Four Studies on the Economic Development of Turkey*, London: Frank Cass and Co. Ltd., 1967.

Smith, Michael L. et al., *Why People Grow Drugs? Narcotics and Development in the Third World*, London: Panos, 1972.

Snyder, Jed C., *Defending the Fringe: NATO, the Mediterranean and the Persian Gulf,* London: Westview Press, 1987.

Solana, Javier, "NATO in the Twenty-First Century", *Perception,* vol. 4, No. 1, March-May 1999, pp. 13-22.

Sowerwine, James Edward, *Dynamics of Decision Making in Turkish Foreign Policy 1961-1980,* Ph.D. Thesis, University of Wisconsin, Madison, 1987.

Spain, James W., "Middle East Defense: A New Approach", *The Middle East Journal,* vol. 8, Summar 1954, pp. 251-266.

Spain, James W., "The United States, Turkey and the Poppy", *Middle East Journal,* vol. 29, No. 3, Summer 1975, pp. 295-309.

Spanier, John and Nogee, Joseph (eds.), *Congress, the Presidency and American Foreign Policy,* New York: Pergamon Press, 1981.

Stavrinides, Zenon, *The Cyprus Conflict: National Identity and Statehood,* Loris Stavrinides Press, 1976.

Stavrou, Nikolas A., "Kissinger's Tilt on Cyprus, the New Style of Crisis Diplomacy" in Couloumbis, Theodore A. and Hicks, Sallie M. (eds.), *US Foreign Policy Toward Greece and Cyprus: the Clash of Principle and Pragmatism,* Washington D.C.: Center for Mediterranean and the American Hellenic Institute Studies, 1975.

Stearns, Monteagle, *Entangled Allies: U.S. Policy Toward Greece, Turkey and Cyprus,* New York: Council on Foreign Relations Press, 1992.

Stephens, Robert, *Cyprus: a Place of Arms,* London: Pall Mall Press, 1966.

Stern, Laurance, "Bitter Lessons: How We Failed in Cyprus", *Foreign Policy,* vol. 19, Summer 1975, pp. 34-78.

Stern, Laurance, *The Wrong Horse: the Politics of Intervention and the Failure of American Diplomacy,* New York: Times Books, 1977.

Stoessinger, John G., *Crusaders and Pragmatists: Movers of Modern American Foreign Policy,* New York, London: W.W. Norton and Company, 1979.

Strong, Robert J., *Bureaucracy and Statesmanship: Henry Kissinger and the Making of American Foreign Policy,* New York, London: University Press of America, 1986.

Szyliowicz, Joseph S., "The Turkish Elections 1965", *The Middle East Journal,* vol. 20, No. 4, Autumn 1966, pp. 473-494.

Şahin, Haluk, *Gece Gelen Mektup: Türk-Amerikan İlişkilerinde Bir Dönüm Noktası,* İstanbul: Cep Kitapları, 1987.

Tachau, Frank, *Turkey: the Politics of Authority, Democracy and Development,* New York, Preager Publishers, 1984.

Tamkoç, Metin, The *Turkish Cypriot State: The Embodiment of the Right of Self-Determination,* London: K. Rustem and Brother, 1988.

Tamkoç, Metin, *The Warrior Diplomats: Guardians of National Security and Modernization of Turkey,* Salt Lake City: University of Utah Press, 1976.

Tansky, Leo, *US and USSR Aid to Developing Countries: A Comparative Study of India, Turkey and U.A.R.,* New York: Frederick A. Praeger Publishers, 1967.

Taşhan, Seyfi, "Turkey's Relations with the U.S.A. and Possible Future Developments", *Foreign Policy,* vol. 8, Nos.1-2, 1979, pp. 11-32.

Taşhan, Seyfi, "Turkish-US Relations and Cyprus", *Foreign Policy,* vol. 4, Nos. 2-3, 1974, pp. 164-176.

Taşhan, Seyfi, "The Peripheries: Adjusting to Change", *Foreign Policy* (Ankara), Nos. 1-2, 1997.

Theophanous, Andreas, "Cyprus, the European Union and the Search for a New Constitution", *Journal of Southern Europe and the Balkans*, vol. 2, No. 2, 2000.

Thomas, Lewis V. and Frye, Richard N., *The United States and Turkey and Iran*, Cambridge, Mass.: Harvard University Press, 1951.

Toker, Metin, *İsmet Paşayla 10 Yıl 1954-1964*, vol. 1, 2, 3, and 4, Ankara, 1965, 1966, 1967, İstanbul, 1969.

Toker, Metin, "İsmet Paşa ile 4 Buhranlı Yıl", *Milliyet*, 4-11 February 1969.

Toker, Metin, *Solda ve Sağda Vuruşanlar: Türkiye'de İki Yönlü İthilal Ortamının Anatomisi*, Ankara: Akis Yayınları, 1971.

Treverton, Gregory F., "Managing Alliance Politics" in Karaosmanoğlu, A. L. and Taşhan, Seyfi (eds.), *Middle East, Turkey and the Atlantic Alliance*, Ankara: Foreign Policy Institute, 1987.

Tunçkanat, Haydar, *İkili Anlaşmaların İçyüzü: İktisadi, Askeri, Siyasi*, İstanbul: Tekin Yayınevi, 1975.

Turner, Michael Allan, *The International Politics of Narcotics: Turkey and the United States*, Ph.D. Thesis, Kent State University, 1975.

"Turkey's Security Perspectives", http://www.mfa.gov.tr/grupa/af/secure.htm.

Ulman, A. Haluk, "Geneva Conferences, July-August 1974", *Foreign Policy*, vol. 4, Nos. 2-3, 1974, pp. 46-65.

Ulman, A. Haluk, "NATO ve Türkiye", *SBF Dergisi*, vol. 22, December 1967.

Ulman, A. Haluk, "Türk Ulusal Savunması üzerine Düşünceler", *SBF Dergisi*, vol. 21, No. 4, December 1966, pp. 201-225.

Ulman, A. Haluk and Dekmeijian, R. H., "Changing Partners in Turkey's Foreign Policy, 1959-1967", *ORBIS*, vol. 11, Fall 1967, pp. 772-785.

"U.S. Foreign Policy Toward Greece: Panel Discussions" in Couloumbis, Theodore A. and Hicks, Sallie M. (eds.), *US Foreign Policy Toward Greece and Cyprus: the Clash of Principle and Pragmatism*, Washington D.C.: Center for Mediterranean and the American Hellenic Institute Studies, 1975.

Uzgel, İlhan, "ABD ve NATO'yla İlişkiler (1999-2001)" in Oran, Baskın (ed.), *Türk Dış Politikası: Kurtuluş Savaşından Bugüne Olgular, Belgeler, Yorumlar*, vol. 2, İstanbul: İletişim, 2001, pp. 243-325.

Uzgel, İlhan, "Balkanlarla İlişkiler (1999-2001)" in Oran, Baskın (ed.), *Türk Dış Politikası: Kurtuluş Savaşından Bugüne Olgular, Belgeler, Yorumlar*, vol. 2, İstanbul: İletişim, 2001, pp. 481-523.

Üstün, Nevzat, *Türkiye'deki Amerika*, İstanbul: Var Yayınevi, 1967.

Vali, Ferenc A., *Bridge Across the Bosporus: the Foreign Policy of Turkey*, London, Baltimore: John Hopkins Press, 1971.

Vanezis, P. N., *Cyprus: the Unfinished Agony*, London: Abelard-Schuman, 1977.

Vanezis, P. N., *Makarios: Pragmatism v. Idealism*, London: Abelard-Schuman, 1974.

Vatikiotis, P. J., *Conflict in the Middle East*, London: George Allen and Unwin Ltd., 1971.

Vedder, Richard K., *The American Economy in Historical Perspective*, Belmont, California: Wadsworth Publishing Company Inc., 1976.

Villaverde, Jesus N., "Turkey-European Union Relations in the Framework of the Euro-Mediterranean Partnership" in Aydın, Mustafa (ed.), *Turkey at the Threshold of the 21st Century*, Ankara: International Relations Foundation, 1998.

Watanabe, Paul Y., *Ethnic Groups, Congress and American Foreign Policy: the Politics of the Turkish Arms Embargo*, London: Greenwood Press, 1984.

Weiker, Walter F., *The Turkish Revolution 1960-61: Aspects of Military Politics*, Washington: Brookings Institution, 1963.

Weintall, Edward and Bartlett, Charles, *Facing the Brink: A Study of Crisis Diplomacy*, London: Hutchinson and Co. Ltd., 1967.

Wildawsky, Agron, "The Two Presidencies" in Fox, Douglas M. (ed.), *The Politics of U.S. Foreign Policy Making*, Pacific Palisades, California: Goodyear Publishing Company Inc., 1971.

Winrow, Gareth M., *Turkey and the Caucasus: Domestic Interests and Security Concerns*, London: the Royal Institute of International Affairs, 2000.

Winsdor, Philip, *NATO and the Cyprus Crisis*, Adelphi Papers No. 14, London: the Institute for Strategic Studies, November 1964.

Wittkopf, Eugene R. "Foreign Aid and United Nations Votes: A Comparative Study", *The American Political Science Review*, vol. 67, No. 3, September 1973, pp. 868-888.

Wolf, Charlotte, *Garrison Community, A Study of an Overseas American Military Colony* Westport, CT: Greenwood, 1969.

Woodruff, William, *America's Impact on the World: a Study of the Role of the United States in the World Economy*, London: Macmillan, 1975.

Xydis, Stephen G., *Cyprus: Reluctant Republic*, The Hague: Mouton and Co., 1973.

Xydis, Stephen G., "Cyprus: What Kind of Problem" in Attalides, Michael A. (ed.), *Cyprus Reviewed: A Seminar on the Cyprus Problem*, Nicosia: Jus Cypri Association, 1977.

Yavuz, M. Hakan and Khan, M. R., "Turkish Foreign Policy Toward the Arab-Israeli Conflict: Duality and the Development (1950-1991)", *Arab Studies Quarterly*, vol. 14 No. 4, 1992.

Yavuz, Turan, *ABD'nin Kürt Kartı*, İstanbul: Milliyet Yayınları, 1993.

Yeşilada, Birol A., "Turkey's Candidacy for EU Membership", *Middle East Journal*, vol. 56, No. 1, Winter 2002, pp. 94-111.

Zentner, Joseph L., "The 1972 Turkish Opium Ban: Needle in the Haystack Diplomacy", *World Affairs*, vol. 136, Summer 1973, pp. 36-47.

INDEX

A

Acheson, Dean, 68, 176, 179, 180
Afghanistan, 105, 242, 243, 258, 259, 306, 311,
 353
Africa, 105, 115, 188
Agency for International Development (AID), vi,
 9, 71, 98, 335
agricultural products, 5, 24, 99, 331
Aid to Turkey Agreement, 317
alliance relations, 1, 3, 4, 13, 36, 67, 156, 160,
 246, 257, 266, 268, 289, 297, 302, 303
American military, 52, 56, 57, 61, 64, 70, 138,
 205, 254, 292, 307, 313
American policy, 29, 52, 53, 56-58, 62, 116, 117,
 129, 161, 183, 198, 256, 257, 307, 312
American President, 55, 58, 151, 156, 265, 312
Anatolia, 14, 82, 96, 101, 219, 327
Arab-Israeli conflict, 2, 26, 28, 76
arms embargo, x, 2, 4, 8, 10, 16, 26, 65, 70, 92-
 96, 211-216, 219, 248, 253, 255, 256, 264,
 291, 299-303
Army Postal Service (APO), 80
Army Security Agency (ASA), 102
Article III, 70, 318, 329
Atatürk, Kemal, 36, 39, 43, 46, 220
Atatürkism, 36
Azerbaijan, 278, 288, 310, 312, 352

B

Baghdad Pact, 6, 10, 72, 111, 112, 116, 117, 120-
 129, 131-134, 297
Baku-Ceyhan pipeline, 288, 305, 306
Balkans, 1, 101, 266, 268, 283-285, 289, 295,
 304, 356
Ball, George, 8, 10, 138, 143, 148, 150, 164, 165,
 166, 170, 174, 176, 177, 179, 212, 322

bargaining power, 25, 160
Bayar, President Celal, 39, 71, 127
Bays of Pigs, 59
bilateral agreements, 2, 29, 70, 71, 73, 83-85,
 106, 113, 133, 297, 299, 302
Black Sea Economic Cooperation (BSEC), 291
Black Sea, 14, 37, 70, 77, 100, 102, 103, 139,
 258, 283, 284, 287, 288, 291, 354
black-market activities, 80
Bosnia, 284, 289
Britain, 29, 32, 111-117, 120, 121, 124, 126-128,
 132, 135, 139, 140, 161, 162, 164, 165, 183,
 194, 203, 204, 208, 351
Bureau of Narcotics and Dangerous Drugs
 (BNDD), vi, 222, 223, 226, 229
Bush administration, 257, 262, 304
Bush, President, 313

C

Cambodia, 53, 60, 62, 65, 212
capitalism, 46, 49, 50, 55, 56
Carter, President Jimmy, 9, 60, 63, 66, 94, 337
Central Asia, 1, 41, 258, 263, 266, 268, 276-278,
 287, 295, 311, 312
Central Intelligence Agency (CIA), 31, 33, 58,
 59, 64, 137, 145, 166, 193, 200, 221, 228, 242
Central Treaty Organization (CENTO), vi, 23,
 73, 134, 137, 139, 221, 226
CFE Treaty, 276, 277, 278
China, 13, 22, 32, 33, 52, 53, 55, 57, 219, 233,
 308
civil service, 30, 43
Cold War, 7, 22, 28, 31, 41, 52, 53, 55, 68, 73,
 111, 125, 129, 159, 258, 267, 268, 278, 288,
 290, 293, 294, 304, 308, 309, 340, 343, 347,
 348, 349, 350, 354
colonialism, 28, 29, 34, 123, 125, 341